Beyond the Page

EN 101: Composition I

Passaic County Community College

First Edition

Bedford/St. Martin's   BOSTON ◆ NEW YORK

Contents

Race and Culture

This Is America

Gender and Sexuality

Fiction

CONTENTS

PCC ENGLISH DEPARTMENT

Writing Portfolio Philosophy

The Passaic County Community College English Department understands the importance of and is committed to the writing process. Each step—from brainstorming to pre-writing then drafting and revising—is equally important. Classroom activities should carve the time needed to dedicate to each step, while pedagogical strategies that foster a writer's growth should incorporate both peer and instructor feedback. We believe that a student's body of work, a comprehensive portfolio including both formal and informal assignments, will be the measure of such growth.

This "learning" or "process portfolio" will showcase constant revision and multi-drafts which will stress our key mantra: we "revise to learn." Writers will rethink ideas, revise words, tweak, add, cut, replace, and switch until they can articulate what they think, feel, and believe. Most importantly, we want students to know that writing does not have to be a lonely and intimidating experience. Passaic County Community College offers help through our writing center tutors, e-tutoring, and resources found on our Blackboard shell.

Good writing takes time, effort, and a leap of faith. If you trust the process and give it your all, a good writer will emerge from within you, too.

PRINCIPLES OF PORTFOLIO KEEPING

1. Keep all of your work in your portfolio binder and stay as organized as possible. Label each step in your writing process and store every draft. Don't forget to save typed files on your computer and/or flashdrive.

2. Manage your time wisely! Remember that good writing takes time and requires several important steps. Factor in tutoring, peer, and instructor feedback turnover time, as well.

3. Add a variety of writing samples to showcase the full breadth of your abilities. We encourage you to combine the academic writing pieces with the more creative ones.

1

4. Become a "reflective learner." Self-assess your writing and thinking through every step, between or after each assignment. Reflect on how you are growing as a writer.

5. Take stock on how you are performing throughout the semester, and think of ways you can improve as a student and as a writer.

6. Just do it!

Mark Hillringhouse, *Poet's Study.*

The Writing Process

Experts often divide the writing process into three major components: prewriting, drafting, and revision (which includes editing). Bear in mind, though, that the process for most people is not as linear as this suggests, and the three components don't always happen in a straightforward fashion. For instance, you might begin revising a partial draft before completing the drafting process. Or you may find yourself stuck at a fairly late point in the draft and decide to revisit your prewriting. Don't think that these three steps need to be completed one at a time. Different projects will likely call for different strategies, and you'll enjoy the process more if you allow yourself to go back and forth between the steps according to the needs of the particular assignment you're trying to complete.

PREWRITING

Prewriting is everything that you do before beginning an actual draft of your paper. It includes annotating and questioning texts, taking notes and participating in class, and discussing the assignment with your instructor and/or classmates. It also includes specific topics covered in this chapter: choosing a topic, developing an argument and a thesis, gathering support, and proposing an organizational strategy for the paper.

Choosing a Topic

Obviously, your choice of a topic for your paper is of key importance, since everything else follows from that first decision. Your instructor may assign a specific topic, or the choice may be left to you. The most important piece of advice for choosing a topic is to write about something that genuinely interests you. If your instructor gives your class a choice, chances are that he or she really wants to see a variety of topics and approaches and expects you to find a topic that works for *you*.

Janet E. Gardner, "The Writing Process," from *Reading and Writing about Literature: A Portable Guide*, Third Edition, pages 21–50. Copyright © 2013 by Bedford/St. Martin's.

You'll write a better paper if your topic is something of genuine interest to you. A bored or uncertain writer usually writes a boring or unconvincing paper. On the other hand, if you care about your topic, your enthusiasm will show in the writing, and the paper will be far more successful.

Even if your instructor assigns a fairly specific topic, you still need to spend a little time thinking about and working with it. You want your paper to stand out from the rest, and you should do whatever you can to make the assignment your own. When you receive an assignment, give some thought as to how it might relate to your own interests and how you might call upon your background and knowledge to approach the topic in fresh and interesting ways.

Finally, if you've put in some thought and effort but still don't know what to write about, remember that you do not need to go it alone. Seek out guidance and help. Talk with other students in your class and see what they have decided to write about; although of course you don't want simply to copy someone else's topic, hearing what others think can often spark a fresh idea. And don't forget your instructor. Most teachers are more than happy to spend a little time helping you come up with a topic and an approach that will help you write a good paper.

Developing an Argument

With the possible exception of a *summary* (a brief recap of a text's most important points), all writing about literature is to some degree a form of argument. Before proceeding, though, let's dispel some of the negative connotations of the word *argument*. In everyday usage, this term can connote a heated verbal fight, and it suggests two (or more) people growing angry and, often, becoming less articulate and more abusive as time passes. It suggests combat and implies that the other party in the process is an opponent. In this sort of argument, there are winners and losers.

Clearly this is not what we have in mind when we say you will be writing argumentatively about literature. Used in a different, more traditional sense, argument refers to a writer's or speaker's attempt to establish the validity of a given position. In other words, when you write a paper, you work to convince your reader that what you are saying is valid and persuasive. The reader is not the enemy, not someone whose ideas are to be crushed and refuted, but rather a person whose thoughts and feelings you have a chance to affect. You are not arguing *against* your reader; rather, you are using your argumentative abilities to *help* your reader see the logic and value of your position.

5

The Thesis

To begin writing a literary argument, then, you must take a position and have a point to make. This principal point will be the *thesis* of your paper. It is important to distinguish between a topic and a thesis: your topic is the issue or area upon which you will focus your attention, and your thesis is a statement *about* this topic.

Here is an example of a topic for Emily Dickinson's "Because I could not stop for Death" from a student journal:

Topic: I am interested in how Dickinson portrays the character of Death.

Here is an example of a thesis statement for a paper on this topic:

Thesis: "Because I could not stop for Death" challenges preconceptions that Dickinson's contemporaries had about death, and in doing so it makes us challenge ours as well.

It might help to phrase your thesis as a complete sentence in which the topic is the subject, followed by a predicate that makes a firm statement or claim regarding your topic. This is your **thesis statement**, and it will probably appear toward the beginning of your paper. The foremost purpose of a paper, then, is to explain, defend, and ultimately prove the truth of its thesis.

Keep the following guidelines in mind as you think about a tentative thesis for your paper:

- **Your thesis should be both clear and specific.** The purpose of a thesis is to serve as a guide to both the reader and the writer, so it needs to be understandable and to point clearly to the specific aspects of the literature that you will discuss. This does not mean it will stand alone or need no further development or explanation—after all, that's what the rest of the paper is for. But a reader who is familiar with the story, poem, or play you are writing about (and it is fair to assume a basic familiarity) should have a good sense of what your thesis means and how it relates to the literature.
- **Your thesis should be relevant.** The claim you make should not only interest you as a writer but also give your reader a reason to keep reading by sparking his or her interest and desire to know more. Not every paper is going to change lives or minds, of course, but you should at least state your thesis in such a way that your reader won't have the most dreaded of responses: "Who cares?"
- **Your thesis should be debatable.** Since the purpose of an argumentative paper is to convince a reader that your thesis is correct (or at

least that it has merit), it cannot simply be an irrefutable fact. A good thesis will be something that a reasonable person, having read the literature, might disagree with or might not have considered at all. It should give you something to prove.

- **Your thesis should be original.** Again, originality does not imply that every thesis you write must be a brilliant gem that nobody but you could have discovered. But it should be something you have thought about independently, and it should avoid clichés, contain something of you, and do more than parrot back something said in your class or written in your textbook.

- **You should be able to state your thesis as a complete sentence.** This sentence, generally referred to as the *thesis statement*, should first identify your topic and then make a claim about it. (Occasionally, especially for longer papers with more complex ideas behind them, you will need more than one sentence to state your thesis clearly. Even in these cases, though, the complete thesis must both identify the topic and make a claim about it.)

- **Your thesis should be stated in strong, unambiguous language.** Avoid thesis statements that begin, "In this paper, I will prove. . . ." If you have a point to prove, just prove it. Keep the reader's attention on the topic, not on your paper. For similar reasons, avoid phrases like "in my opinion . . ." or "I think. . . ." It is assumed that the paper is made up of your thoughts and opinions, and language like this turns the reader's focus to your thought process rather than the topic at hand.

- **Your thesis should be appropriate to the assignment.** This may seem obvious, but as we work with literature, taking notes, asking questions, and beginning to think about topics and theses, it is possible to lose sight of the assignment as it was presented. After you have come up with a tentative thesis, it's a good idea to go back and review the assignment as your instructor gave it, making sure your paper will fulfill its requirements.

Let us take a look at how two students arrived at strong, workable theses for their papers. Jarrad Nunes knew that he wanted to write about how Emily Dickinson dealt with the theme of death in her poetry. His first attempt at a thesis, however, was far too weak and general:

Emily Dickinson's poems about death are some of the most interesting ever written.

This is not so much a thesis statement as an assertion of personal preference and opinion. All we know from reading it is that Jarrad likes

7

Dickinson's death poems. He needs a thesis that is both more specific and more controversial:

> Dickinson's poems look at death in unconventional ways.

This version is better because it makes an assertion that can be defended, but it is still far too general. Here is the final version of Jarrad's thesis:

> "Because I could not stop for Death" challenges preconceptions that Dickinson's contemporaries had about death, and in doing so it makes us challenge ours as well.

Here we have a much stronger thesis. It limits the paper's scope by focusing on a single poem, it makes an assertion to defend (that Dickinson challenged nineteenth-century preconceptions about death), and it shows why this point is significant to a reader (because we too might have our preconceptions challenged).

Here is one more example of the process of refining and developing a thesis. When she first decided to write about the male characters in two nineteenth-century stories, Melanie Smith came up with the following:

> The husbands in the stories "The Yellow Wallpaper" by Charlotte Perkins Gilman and "The Story of an Hour" by Kate Chopin are very controlling of their wives.

This is not an adequate thesis because it is simply a statement of fact, something that will be immediately obvious to anyone who has read the stories. It left Melanie with nothing to defend, no point to prove, so she gave it a little more thought and refined her tentative thesis:

> Though the husbands in "The Yellow Wallpaper" and "The Story of an Hour" are controlling, they are not really as bad as they first appear.

At this point, the writer is definitely moving in the right direction. This version shows that she has a particular interpretation and a point to make, one that is not necessarily shared by everyone who reads the stories. However, it still doesn't give a reader much guidance about what to expect in the paper. In the end, Melanie needed two sentences to get her thesis right:

> By modern standards, the husbands of the two protagonists, particularly John in "The Yellow Wallpaper," seem almost unbearably controlling of their wives. From the vantage point of the late nineteenth century, however, their behavior looks quite different.

This version is much clearer and more precise. After reading this thesis, we are much more focused and have a good sense of what to expect in the paper as a whole.

You will note that in this discussion the phrase *tentative thesis* has come up several times. The word *tentative* is important. As you start to gather support and to write your paper, your thesis will help you focus clearly on your task and sort out which of your ideas, observations, and questions are relevant to the project at hand. But you should keep an open mind as well, realizing that your thesis is likely to evolve as you write. You are likely to change the focus in subtle or not so subtle ways, and you might even change your mind completely as you write and therefore need to create a new thesis from scratch. If this happens, don't regard it as a failure. On the contrary, it means you have succeeded in learning something genuine from the experience of writing, and that is what a literature class is all about.

Gathering Support for Your Thesis

Once you have crafted a tentative thesis, it is time to think about the evidence or support you will need to convince your reader of the claim's validity. But what exactly counts as support? What can you include in your paper as evidence that your thesis is true? Essentially, all support comes from one of three sources:

- **The text itself is the most obvious source of support.** It is not enough to *say* that a certain piece of literature says or means a certain thing. You will need to *show* this by summarizing, paraphrasing, or quoting the literature itself.
- **Other people's ideas are a good source of support.** Chances are you will find a lot of useful material for your paper if you pay attention to easily available sources of ideas from other readers. These include the notes and biographical information in your textbooks, research conducted online or in the library, lectures and discussions in class, and even informal conversations about the literature with your friends and classmates.
- **Your own thoughts are your most important source of support.** Remember that although you may want to integrate ideas and information from a variety of sources, your paper is yours and as such should reflect *your* thinking. The most indispensable source of material for your paper is your own mind; your own thoughts and words should always carry the heaviest weight in any paper you write.

9

One of the best ways to gather supporting ideas for your paper is **brainstorming**. You can brainstorm—alone or with classmates—even before settling on your topic and thesis, to explore the many possible threads that you could follow in your writing. When brainstorming to gather evidence, the idea is to write down, very quickly, every idea that comes to you, every possible idea that might be included in the draft of your paper. Don't censor yourself during this process. Allow yourself to write down everything that interests, puzzles, or delights you. Later you will have ample opportunity to prune your list of repetitions, tangents, or weaker ideas. For the time being, just let the ideas flow, and get as many as you can down on a piece of paper or a word processing document.

At this stage, use every resource available to you to find support for your thesis. What lines in the poem, short story, or play reinforce your claims? Have you looked up words in the dictionary? Have you checked difficult concepts in a respectable encyclopedia or other reference? Have you asked your teacher for further reading suggestions? Have you read articles or book chapters that are appropriate to your topic, and are you formulating your responses to them? Treat ideas from outside sources much as you would your own brainstorming: don't censor too soon. When the time comes to organize and draft your paper, it's far better to have too many ideas and have to eliminate some than to have too few and have to root around for more.

Organizing Your Paper

Once you've determined what evidence to use, it is time to begin sorting and organizing it. The organizing principle for any paper is the sequence of paragraphs, so at this stage you should be thinking at the level of paragraph content. Remember that each paragraph should contain one main idea and sufficient evidence and explanation to support that idea. When added together, these paragraph-level ideas lead a reader to your paper's ultimate point—your thesis. So the first stage of organizing the content of your essay is to cluster together similar ideas in order to begin shaping the substance of individual paragraphs. The second stage is to determine the order in which these paragraphs will appear.

As you write and revise your paper, you may have different ideas about how to structure it. You may want to put the topic sentence somewhere other than at the beginning of a paragraph, or perhaps the topic is so clear that no specific topic sentence is even needed. You may devise a more interesting way to structure your introduction or conclusion. (Some additional, more specific thoughts for those tricky introductory and concluding paragraphs follow.) Unless your instructor has specified the form in which your paper is to be organized, you should feel free to experiment a bit.

For most writers, creating some version of an outline is the best way to approach the task of organizing evidence into a logical sequence for a paper. In the past, you may have been asked to write a formal outline, complete with Roman numerals and capital letters. If this technique has been helpful in organizing your thoughts, by all means continue to use it. For many writers, however, an informal outline works just as well and is less cumbersome. To construct an informal outline, simply jot down a heading that summarizes the topic of each paragraph you intend to write. Then cluster your gathered evidence—quotations or paraphrases from the literature, ideas for analysis, and so on—into groups under the headings.

The following is an example of an informal outline for a paper on Shakespeare's Sonnet 116. In this outline, the student focuses on the positive and negative language in the poem and how it results in a more interesting definition of love than he had seen in other love poems.

Introduction
    Two kinds of typical love poems: happy and sad
    Sonnet 116 is more complex and interesting
    Tentative thesis: By including both negative and positive images and
        language, this sonnet gives a complex and realistic definition of
        love.

Vivid images in poem
    Positive/expected: "star," "ever-fixèd mark," "rosy lips and cheeks"
    Negative/unexpected: "sickle" (deathlike), "wandering bark" (lost
        boat), "tempests"

Negative language
    Words/phrases: "Let me not," "Love is not," "never," "nor," "no," etc.
    Abstractions: "alteration," "impediments," "error"

Conclusion
    Love never changes
    Shakespeare's definition still works some 400 years later

Obviously, this is not a formal outline. It does, however, group similar items and ideas together, and it gives the writer a basic structure to follow as he moves on to drafting, the next stage of the composing process.

DRAFTING THE PAPER

You have a topic. You have a tentative thesis. You have gathered evidence. You have an outline or tentative structure in mind for this evidence. It is time to begin writing your first draft. Every writer has his or her own slightly different process for getting the words down on paper. Some begin at the beginning of the paper and work straight through to the end in a clear, organized fashion. Others begin with the first body paragraph and save the introduction for later. Still others write bits and pieces of the paper out of order and allow the overall structure to emerge at a later time.

Some writers claim that they work better at the last minute and focus better under the pressure of a looming deadline. This, however, is almost always a justification for sloppy work habits, and procrastination rarely if ever results in a superior paper. When habitual procrastinators change their working methods and give themselves more time on a project, they are frequently surprised to discover that the process is more enjoyable and the final product of their efforts better than what they have produced in the past. Start early and work steadily—it will prove more than worth it.

Try to write your first draft fairly quickly. You don't need to get every sentence just right—that's what the revision phase of writing is for. What you want now is just to get as much good raw material as possible into the mix and see what works. Don't worry too much yet about style, transitions, grammar, and so forth. In fact, you don't even need to start at the beginning or work right through to the end. If you get stuck on one part, move on. You can always come back and fill in the gaps later. Introductions can be especially tricky, particularly since you haven't yet finished the essay and don't really know what it is you're introducing. Some writers find it easier to start with the body of the essay, or to write a short, sloppy introduction as a placeholder. You can go back and work on the real introduction when the draft is complete.

Introductions, Conclusions, and Transitions

Ideally, of course, all of the parts of your paper will be equally compelling and polished, but there are certain points in a paper that most often cause trouble for writers and readers, and these points may require a little additional attention on your part. The most typical trouble spots are introductory and concluding paragraphs and the transitional sentences that connect paragraphs. Although there is no one formula to help you navigate these waters, as each writing situation and each paper are different, we offer some general guidelines that can help you think through the problems that might arise in these areas.

Introductions

Essentially, an introduction accomplishes two things. First, it gives a sense of both your topic and your approach to that topic, which is why it is common to make your thesis statement a part of the introduction. Second, an introduction compels your readers' interest and makes them want to read on and find out what your paper has to say. Some common strategies used in effective introductions are to begin with a probing rhetorical question, a vivid description, or an intriguing quotation. Weak introductions tend to speak in generalities or in philosophical ideas that are only tangentially related to the real topic of your paper. Don't spin your wheels: get specific and get to the point right away.

Consider this introduction from a student essay on Susan Glaspell's *Trifles*:

> What is the relationship between legality and morality? Susan Glaspell's short play *Trifles* asks us to ponder this question, but it provides no clear answers. Part murder mystery, part battle of the sexes, the play makes its readers confront and question many issues about laws, morals, and human relationships. In the person of Mrs. Peters, a sheriff's wife, the play chronicles one woman's moral journey from a certain, unambiguous belief in the law to a more situational view of ethics. Before it is over, this once legally minded woman is even willing to cover up the truth and let someone get away with murder.

The student poses a philosophical question at the very beginning of the paper and then offers a tentative answer.

Conclusions

Your conclusion should give your reader something new to think about, a reason not to forget your essay as soon as the reading is done. Some writers like to use the conclusion to return to an idea, a quotation, or an image first raised in the introduction, creating a satisfying feeling of completeness and self-containment.

In this example from the same student paper, note how the student offers a tentative answer in her conclusion to the question that began the essay:

In the end, Mrs. Peters gives in to what she believes to be emotionally right rather than what is legally permissible. She collaborates with Mrs. Hale to cover up evidence of the motive and hide the dead canary. Though very little time has gone by, she has undergone a major transformation. She may be, as the county attorney says, "married to the law," but she is also divorced from her old ideals. When she tries to cover up the evidence, a stage direction says she "goes to pieces," and Mrs. Hale has to help her. By the time she pulls herself together, the new woman she is will be a very different person from the old one. She, along with the reader, is now in a world where the relationship between legality and morality is far more complex than she had ever suspected.

Some writers use the conclusion to show the implications of their claims or the connections between the literature and real life. This is your chance to make a good final impression, so don't waste it with simple summary and restatement.

Transitions

Each paragraph is built around a different idea, and the job of the transitions is to show how these separate ideas are related to one another, to make the juxtaposition of two paragraphs seem as logical to a reader as it is to the writer. When you think a transition isn't working effectively, the first question you should ask yourself is, *why* does one paragraph follow another in this particular order? Would it make more sense to change the placement of some paragraphs, or is this really the best organizational strategy for this portion of the paper? Once you know why your paper is structured as it is, transitions become much easier to write, simply making apparent to your audience the connections you already know to be there. As you begin each new paragraph, give some consideration to the links between it and the previous paragraph, and try to make those links explicit in the opening sentence.

As with any other aspect of your writing, if you've had trouble in the past with introductions, conclusions, or transitions, one of your best sources of help is to be an attentive reader of others' writing. Pay special attention to these potential trouble spots in the writing you admire, whether by a classmate or a professional author, and see how he or she navigates them. Don't stick with the writing methods that have caused you headaches in the past. Be willing to try out different strategies, seeing which ones work best for you. In time you'll find you have a whole array of ways to approach these trouble spots, and you'll be able to find a successful response to each particular writing situation.

REVISING AND EDITING

Once you have a complete, or near-complete, draft, it's time to begin thinking about revision. Try to avoid the common pitfall of thinking of revision as locating and fixing mistakes. Revision is far more than this. Looking at the parts of the word, you can see that *re-vision* means "seeing again," and indeed the revision stage of the writing process is your chance to see your draft anew and make real and substantial improvements to every facet of it, from its organization to its tone to your word choices. Most successful writers will tell you that it is in the revision stage that the real work gets done, where the writing takes shape and begins to emerge in its final form. Most professional writers spend much more time revising than they do writing the first draft. Don't skimp on this part of the process or try to race through it.

It is a good idea not to start a major revision the minute a draft is complete. Take a break. Exercise, have a meal, do something completely different to clear your mind. If possible, put the draft aside for at least a day, so that when you return to it you'll have a fresh perspective and can begin truly re-seeing it. Print out your draft. Attempting serious revision on-screen is generally a bad idea—we see differently, and we usually see more, when we read off a printed page. Read with a pen in your hand and annotate your text just the way you would a piece of literature, looking for the strengths and weaknesses of your argument. The process laid out here consists of three phases: *global revisions*, or large-scale revisions; *local revisions*, or small-scale revisions; and a final *editing and proofreading*. If you haven't done so before, revising your paper three times may seem like a lot of work, but bear in mind that most professional writers revise their work many more times than that. Revision is the real key to writing the best paper you can.

Global Revision

On a first pass at revision—the large-scale, global part of the process—don't worry too much about details like word choice, punctuation, and so forth. Too many students focus so much on these issues that they miss the big picture. The details are important, but you will deal with them in depth later. You wouldn't want to spend your time getting the wording of a sentence just right only to decide later that the paragraph it is in weakens your argument and needs to be deleted. So at first, look at

15

the overall picture—the argument, organization, and tone of the paper as a whole. While there's nothing wrong with making a few small improvements as you read, nothing smaller than a paragraph should concern you at this point. Here are some possibilities for how you might revise your paper globally.

GLOBAL REVISION CHECKLIST

Further develop your focus and thesis.

☐ Can your reader immediately identify what the topic of the essay will be—that is, which text(s), and which aspect of the text (for example, character development or the use of particular language features), you will analyze?

☐ Have you narrowed the scope of the thesis for your reader? How could it be further narrowed? Remember, it's not enough to say "Women are portrayed differently in *X* and *Y*." What do you mean by "differently"? Get as specific as possible.

☐ Does your thesis clearly identify a claim that is debatable but valid?

☐ Has your thinking about the issues evolved as you have written? If so, how will you change the thesis statement?

☐ Have you answered the larger "So what?" question? Do you get your reader thinking beyond your paper to the question of why this argument is important?

Reorganize your paper, if necessary.

☐ Does the order of the ideas and paragraphs make immediate sense to you, or does some alternate structure suggest itself?

☐ Experiment with different organizing principles, using the cut-and-paste feature of your word processor (or even old-fashioned paper and scissors). You can always put things back if your original organization worked better.

Expand your paper with new paragraphs or with new evidence within existing paragraphs.

☐ What textual evidence have you used? Is it sufficiently provocative and persuasive? Or does it veer off into another direction?

☐ Have you successfully integrated quotations, summaries, or paraphrases into your own writing, while at the same time acknowledging your source?

> ## GLOBAL REVISION CHECKLIST (*continued*)
>
> **Eliminate any unnecessary, contradictory, or distracting passages.**
>
> ☐ Does every piece of evidence, every sentence, and every paragraph contribute to the validity of your argument? If not, eliminate extraneous discussions and save them for another project.
>
> **Clarify difficult passages with more specific explanations or evidence.**
>
> ☐ Have you worked to convey why you are citing a particular passage? What *particular* details in it provide evidence that supports your interpretation? Make sure the reasons for the presence of particular evidence are explicit in your writing. Don't assume a summary or a quotation speaks for itself.

Once you have completed your first, large-scale revision, chances are you will feel more confident about the content and structure of your paper. The thesis and focus are strong, the evidence is lined up, and the major points are clear. Print out the new version, take another break if you can, and prepare to move on to the second phase of revision, the one that takes place at the local level of words, phrases, and sentences.

Local Revision

The focus here is on style and clarity. The types of changes you will make in this stage are, essentially, small-scale versions of the changes you made in the first round of revision: adding, cutting, reorganizing, and clarifying. Are you sure about the meanings of any difficult or unusual words you have used? Is there enough variety in sentence style to keep your writing interesting? Do the same words or phrases appear again and again? Are the images vivid? Are the verbs strong? One way to assess the effectiveness of a paper's style is to read it aloud and hear how it sounds. You may feel a little foolish doing this, but many people find it very helpful.

LOCAL REVISION CHECKLIST

Consider your sentences.

☐ Do you keep the writing interesting by using a variety of sentence types and sentences of different lengths?

☐ Have you perhaps used an occasional rhetorical question to get your readers thinking? (This strategy should be used in moderation. Too many questions in a paper become distracting.)

☐ Does each sentence clearly follow from the last one? Or do you need to reorganize the sentences within a particular paragraph to provide clearer transitions between sentences?

☐ Look at the first and last sentences in each paragraph. Do they provide sufficient transitions from one paragraph to the next?

Consider your word choice.

☐ Do you use the same words and phrases again and again? If so, could you vary your word choice a bit?

☐ If you use any special literary terms or other jargon, are you absolutely certain that you are using these terms correctly?

☐ Take a look at the verbs. Are many of them strong and active, or do most sentences rely on dull linking verbs like *is* or *seems*?

Final Editing and Proofreading

Once you have revised your essay a second time and achieved both content and a style that please you, it's time for final editing. This is where you make it "correct."

FINAL EDITING CHECKLIST

Check your spelling.

☐ Have you spelled everything correctly? (Should it be *their* or *there*? *It's* or *its*?)

☐ Do not rely on your computer's spell-check function. This only tells you if the word you typed is a word, not if it's the correct word. When in doubt, look it up.

Check your punctuation.

☐ Look for things that have caused you trouble in the past. Should you use a comma or a semicolon? Again, when in doubt, look it up.

☐ Pay special attention to quotations. Does the question mark go inside or outside of the quotation marks? Have you used both opening and closing quotation marks for each quotation?

Check your formatting.

☐ Is your manuscript format correct? Unless your instructor has provided other instructions, follow the format described at the end of this section.

☐ Have you italicized or underlined titles of plays and novels (*Othello* or *The Woman Warrior*) and put the titles of short stories and poems in quotation marks ("Love in L.A.," "The Fish")?

☐ Does your works cited list follow MLA format, and do you properly cite your quotations in the body of the text? Nobody expects you to know all the rules on your own, but you should know where to look for them.

☐ If you have questions about citation and formatting, look them up in this book or in a good dictionary, grammar handbook, or other reference. A good online source is Diana Hacker's *Research and Documentation Online*: http://www.dianahacker.com/resdoc/.

19

Here is a paragraph ready for final editing from a student essay on *Hamlet*. Notice the kinds of corrections that the student will have to make before the paragraph is done.

The supernatural relm affects the revenge tragedy in other ways than the appearance and presence of ghosts. In Hamlet, the religious concern with final absolution both inflames Hamlet's desire for revenge and causes him to hesitate in carrying out revenge. Not only has Hamlet's father been murdered, but he was also Cut off even in the blossoms of [his] sin, / Unhousled, disappointed, unanel'd, / No reck'ning made, but sent to [his] account / With all [his] imperfections on [his] head (1.5.77-80). For Hamlet's father, being murdered is doubly disastrous; not only is his life cut short. But he must burn away "the foul crimes done in [his] days of nature" in purgatory before he can be granted access to heaven (1.5.13). A normal death would have afforded him final absolution, and thus a direct route to heaven. The same concern that makes Hamlet's father's death even more terrible also causes Hamlet to pass on a perfect opportunity to exact revenge on his father's murderer. Hamlet finds Claudius praying, alone. To kill a man in prayer means to kill a man who has had all his sins absolved. Hamlet observes Claudius and reasons: "A villain kills my father, and for that, / I, his sole son, do this same villain send / To heaven." (3.3.76-78) Hamlet's concern for the supernatural afterlife affects his carrying out revenge.

Spelling: "realm"

Italicize "Hamlet."

Remember to add quotation marks around the direct quotation.

This should be a comma joining two sentence fragments.

This period belongs outside the parentheses, after the act, scene, and line number.

One final word of advice as you revise your paper: ask for help. Doing so is neither cheating nor an admission of defeat. In fact, professional writers do it all the time. Despite the persistent image of writers toiling in isolation, most successful writers seek advice at various stages. More important, they are willing to listen to that advice and to rethink what they have written if it seems not to be communicating what they had intended.

PEER EDITING AND WORKSHOPS

Some instructors give class time for draft workshops, sometimes called peer editing, in which you work with your fellow students, trying to help one another improve your work-in-progress. Such workshops can benefit you in two ways. First, your classmates can offer you critiques and advice on what you might have missed in your own rereading. Second, reading and discussing papers other than your own will help you grow as a writer, showing you a variety of ways in which a topic can be approached. If you really like something about a peer's paper—say, a vivid introduction or the effective use of humor—make note of how it works within the paper and consider integrating something similar into a future paper of your own. We are not, of course, advocating copying your classmates; rather, we are pointing out that you can learn a lot from other people's writing.

Some students are uncomfortable with such workshops. They may feel they don't know enough about writing to give valid advice to others, or they may doubt whether advice from their peers is particularly valuable. But you don't need to be a great literary critic, much less an expert on style or grammar, to give genuinely useful advice to a fellow writer. Whatever your skills or limitations as a writer, you have something invaluable to give: the thoughts and impressions of a real reader working through a paper. It is only when we see how a reader responds to what we've written that we know if a paper is communicating its intended message. If you are given an opportunity to engage in peer workshops, make the most of them.

Your instructor may give you guidelines regarding what to look for in others' drafts, or you may be left more or less on your own. In either case, keep these general guidelines in mind:

- **Be respectful of one another's work.** You should, of course, treat your peers' work with the same respect and seriousness that you would want for your own. Keep your criticism constructive and avoid personal attacks, even if you disagree strongly with an opinion. You can help your fellow writers by expressing a contrary opinion in a civilized and thoughtful manner.

- **Be honest.** This means giving real, constructive criticism when it is due. Don't try to spare your workshop partner's feelings by saying "That's great" or "It's fine," when it really isn't. When asked what went badly in a peer workshop, students most commonly respond *not* that their peers were too harsh on their work but that they were not harsh enough. Wouldn't you rather hear about a problem with your work from a peer in a draft workshop than from your professor after you have already handed in the final draft? So would your classmates.

- **Look for the good as well as the bad in a draft.** No paper, no matter how rough or problematic, is completely without merit. And no paper, no matter how clever or well written, couldn't be improved. By pointing out both what works and what doesn't, you will help your classmates grow as writers.

- **Keep an eye on the time.** It's easy to get wrapped up in a discussion of an interesting paper and not allow adequate time for another paper. Say you're given half an hour to work with your draft and that of one classmate. When you reach the fifteen-minute mark, move on, no matter how interesting your discussion is. Fair is fair. On the other hand, don't stop short of the allotted time. If you are reading carefully and thinking hard about one another's drafts, it should be impossible to finish early.

- **Take notes on your draft itself or on a separate sheet.** You may be certain that you will remember what was said in a workshop, but you would be amazed how often people forget the good advice they heard and intended to follow. Better safe than sorry—take careful notes.

- **Ask questions.** Asking questions about portions of a draft you don't understand or find problematic can help its writer see what needs to be clarified, expanded, or reworked. Useful questions can range from the large scale (*What is the purpose of this paragraph?*) to the small (*Is this a quote? Who said it?*).

- **Don't assume that explaining yourself to your workshop partner can replace revision.** Sometimes your workshop partners will ask a question, and when you answer it for them, they will say, "Oh, right, that makes sense," leaving you with the impression that everything is clear now. But remember, your classmates didn't understand it from the writing alone, and you won't be there to explain it to your instructor.

- **Be specific in your comments.** Vague comments like "The introduction is good" or "It's sort of confusing here" are not much help. Aim for something more like "The introduction was funny and really made me want to read on" or "This paragraph confused me because it seems to contradict what you said in the previous one." With comments like these, a writer will have a much better sense of where to focus his or her revision energies.

- **Try to focus on the big picture.** When you are reading a draft, it's tempting to zero in on distracting little mistakes in spelling,

22

punctuation, or word choice. While it's generally fine to point out or circle such surface matters as you go along, a draft workshop is not about correcting mistakes. It's about helping one another to re-see and rethink your papers on a global scale.

- **Push your partners to help you more.** If your workshop partners seem shy or reluctant to criticize, prompt them to say more by letting them know that you really want advice and that you are able to take criticism. Point out to them what you perceive as the trouble spots in the essay, and ask if they have any ideas to help you out. It feels good, of course, to hear that someone likes your paper and cannot imagine how to improve it. But in the long run it is even better to get real, useful advice that will lead to a better paper. If your classmates are not helping you enough, it's your responsibility to ask for more criticism.

Even if your class does not include workshop time, you can still use the many resources available to you on campus. Find one or two other members of your class and conduct your own peer workshop, reading and critiquing one another's drafts. Be sure to arrange such a meeting far enough in advance of the due date so that you will have ample time to implement any good revision advice you receive. Many campuses also have writing or tutoring centers, and the workers in these centers, often advanced students who are skilled writers, can offer a good deal of help. Remember, again, that you should make an appointment to see a tutor well in advance of the paper's due date, and you should *not* expect a tutor or mentor to revise or "fix" your paper for you. That is, ultimately, your job. And, of course, you can also approach your instructor at any phase of the writing process and ask for advice and help.

But remember, no matter where you turn for advice, the final responsibility for your paper is yours. Any advice and help you receive from classmates, tutors, friends—or even your instructor—is just that: advice and help. It is *your* paper, and *you* must be the one to make the decisions about which advice to follow and which to ignore, and how to implement changes to improve your paper. The key is to keep an open mind, seek help from all available sources, and give yourself plenty of time to turn your first draft into a final paper that makes you truly proud.

TIPS FOR WRITING ABOUT LITERATURE

Each genre of literature—fiction, poetry, and drama—poses its own, slightly different set of assumptions, opportunities, and problems for writers, which are covered in more detail in the sections that follow.

However, the following general principles can help you as you write about any form of literature:

- **Don't assume that your readers will remember (or consider important) the same ideas or incidents in the literature that you do.** You should assume that your readers have *read* the literature but not necessarily that they have reacted to it the same way you have. Therefore, whenever possible, use specific examples and evidence in the form of quotations and summaries to back up your claims.
- **Do not retell the plot or text at length.** Some writers are tempted to begin with a plot summary or even to include the text of a short poem at the beginning of a paper. However, this strategy can backfire by delaying the real substance of your paper. Be discriminating when you summarize—keep quotations short and get to the point you want to make as quickly as possible.
- **Do not assume that quotations or summaries are self-sufficient and prove your point automatically.** Summaries and quotations are a starting point; you need to analyze them thoroughly in your own words, explaining why they are important. As a general rule, each quotation or summary should be followed by at least several sentences of analysis.
- **It is customary to use the present tense when writing about literature**, even if the events discussed take place in the distant past. Example:
  When she sees that Romeo is dead, Juliet kills herself with his knife.
- **The first time you mention an author, use his or her full name.** For subsequent references, the last name is sufficient. (Do not use first names only; it sounds as if you know an author personally.)
- **Titles of poems, short stories, and essays should be put in quotation marks. Titles of books, plays, and periodicals (magazines, newspapers, etc.) should be italicized or underlined.** In titles and in all quotations, follow spelling, capitalization, and punctuation exactly as it occurs in the work itself.
- **Give your paper a title.** A title doesn't need to be elaborate or super clever, but it should give some clue as to what the paper is about and begin setting up expectations for your reader. Simply restating the assignment, such as "Essay #2" or "Comparison and Contrast Paper," is of little help to a reader and might even suggest intellectual laziness on the part of the writer. For the same reason, avoid giving your paper the same title as the work of literature you are writing

about; unless you're Shakespeare or Hemingway, don't title your paper *Hamlet* or "A Clean, Well-Lighted Place."

• **Above all, use common sense and *be consistent.***

USING QUOTATIONS EFFECTIVELY

At some point, you will want to quote the literature you are writing about, and you might also want to quote some secondary research sources as well. Quotations ground your paper in the literature you are discussing and prevent your argument from being overly abstract. They also allow the author of the literature a chance to shine through in his or her own words, showing that you respect and appreciate the author's work. Quotations bring emphasis, variety, and specificity to your writing. Be selective, though, in your use of quotations so that the dominant voice of the paper is your own, not a patchwork of the words of others. Here is general advice to help you integrate quotations effectively into your essays.

Try to avoid floating quotations. Sometimes writers simply lift a sentence out of the original, put quotation marks around it, and identify the source (if at all) in a subsequent sentence.

> "I met a traveler from an antique land." This is how Shelley's poem "Ozymandias" begins.

Doing so can create confusion for a reader, who is momentarily left to ponder where the quotation comes from and why have you quoted it. In addition to potentially causing confusion, such quoting can read as awkward and choppy, as there is no transition between another writer's words and yours.

Use at least an attributed quotation; that is, one that names the source *within* the sentence containing the quotation, usually in a lead-in phrase.

> Shelley begins his poem "Ozymandias" with the words "I met a traveler from an antique land."

This way the reader knows right away who originally wrote or said the quoted material and knows (or at least expects) that your commentary will follow. It also provides a smoother transition between your words and the quotation.

Whenever possible, use an integrated quotation. To do this, you make the quotation a part of your own sentence.

> When the narrator of "Ozymandias" begins by saying that he "met a traveler from an antique land," we are immediately thrust into a mysterious world.

This is the hardest sort of quoting to do since it requires that you make the quoted material fit in grammatically with your own sentence, but the payoff in clarity and sharp prose is usually well worth the extra time spent on sentence revision.

Adding to or Altering a Quotation

Sometimes, especially when you are using integrated quotations effectively, you will find that you need to slightly alter the words you are quoting. You should, of course, keep quotations exact whenever possible, but occasionally the disparity between the tense, point of view, or grammar of your sentence and that of the quoted material will necessitate some alterations. Other difficulties can arise when you quote a passage that already contains a quotation or when you need to combine quotation marks with other punctuation marks. When any of these situations arise, the following guidelines should prove useful. The examples of quoted text that follow are all drawn from this original passage from *Hamlet*, in which Hamlet and his friend Horatio are watching a gravedigger unearth old skulls in a cemetery:

> HAMLET: That skull had a tongue in it, and could sing once. How the knave jowls it to the ground, as if 'twere Cain's jaw-bone, that did the first murder! This might be the pate of a politician, which this ass now o'erreaches, one that would circumvent God, might it not?
> HORATIO: It might, my lord.
> HAMLET: Or of a courtier, which could say "Good morrow, sweet lord! How dost thou, sweet lord?" This might be my Lord Such-a-one, that prais'd my Lord Such-a-one's horse when 'a meant to beg it, might it not?

If you ever alter anything in a quotation or add words to it in order to make it clear and grammatically consistent with your own writing, you need to signal to your readers what you have added or changed. This is done by enclosing your words within square brackets in order to distinguish them from those in the source. If, for instance, you feel Hamlet's reference to the gravedigger as "this ass" is unclear, you could clarify it either by substituting your own words, as in the first example here, or by adding the identifying phrase to the original quote, as in the second example:

> Hamlet wonders if it is "the pate of a politician, which [the gravedigger] now o'erreaches."

> Hamlet wonders if it is "the pate of a politician, which this ass [the gravedigger] now o'erreaches."

Omitting Words from a Quotation

To keep a quotation focused and to the point, you will sometimes want to omit words, phrases, or even whole sentences that do not contribute to your point. Any omission is signaled by ellipses, or three spaced periods, with square brackets around them. (The brackets are required to distinguish your own ellipses from any that might occur in the original source.)

> Hamlet wonders if the skull "might be the pate of a politician [. . .] that would circumvent God."

It is usually not necessary to use ellipses at the beginning of a quotation, since a reader assumes you are quoting only a relevant portion of text, but MLA style recommends using ellipses at the end of a quotation if words are dropped at the end of the final quoted sentence.

Quotations within Quotations

If you are quoting material that itself contains a quotation, the internal quotation is set off with single quotation marks rather than the standard double quotation marks that will enclose the entire quotation.

> Hamlet wonders if he might be looking at the skull "of a courtier, which could say 'Good morrow, sweet lord! How dost thou, sweet lord?'"

When the text you're quoting contains *only* material already in quotation marks in the original, the standard double quotation marks are all you need.

> Hamlet wonders if the courtier once said "Good morrow, sweet lord! How dost thou, sweet lord?"

Quotation Marks with Other Punctuation

When a period or a comma comes at the end of a quotation, it should always be placed inside the closing quotation marks, whether or not this punctuation was in the original source. In the first example that follows, note that the period following "horse" is within the quotation marks, even though there is no period there in the original. In the second example, the comma following "once" is also within the quotation marks, even though in Shakespeare's original "once" is followed by a period.

> Hamlet muses that the skull might have belonged to "my Lord Such-a-one, that prais'd my Lord Such-a-one's horse."

> "That skull had a tongue in it, and could sing once," muses Hamlet.

Question marks and exclamation points are placed inside quotation marks if they are part of the original quotation and outside of the marks if they are part of your own sentence but not part of the passage you are quoting. In the first example, the question is Hamlet's, and so the question mark must be placed within the quotation marks; in the second example, the question is the essay writer's, and so the question mark is placed outside of the quotation marks.

> Hamlet asks Horatio if the skull "might be my Lord Such-a-one, that prais'd my Lord Such-a-one's horse when 'a meant to beg it, might it not?"

> Why is Hamlet so disturbed that this skull "might be the pate of a politician"?

These sorts of punctuation details are notoriously hard to remember, so you should not feel discouraged if you begin forgetting such highly specialized rules moments after reading them. At least know where you can look them up, and do so when you proofread your paper. A willingness to attend to detail is what distinguishes serious students and gives writing a polished, professional appearance. Also, the more you work with quotations, the easier it will be to remember the rules.

Quoting from Stories

The guidelines that follow should be used not only when you quote from stories but also when you quote from any prose work, be it fiction or nonfiction.

Short Quotations

For short quotations of four lines or fewer, run the quotation in with your own text, using quotation marks to signal the beginning and end of the quotation.

> Young Goodman Brown notices that the branches touched by his companion "became strangely withered and dried up, as with a week's sunshine."

Long Quotations

When a quotation is longer than four lines in your text, set it off from your essay by beginning a new line and indenting it one inch from the left margin only, as shown here. This is called a block quotation.

Young Goodman Brown then notices something strange about his companion:

> As they went, he plucked a branch of maple to serve for a walking stick, and began to strip it of the twigs and little boughs, which were wet with evening dew. The moment his fingers touched them they became strangely withered and dried up, as with a week's sunshine. Thus the pair proceeded, . . . until suddenly, . . . Goodman Brown sat himself down on the stump of a tree and refused to go any further.

Note that no quotation marks are used with block quotations. The indentation is sufficient to signal to your readers that this is a quotation.

Quoting from Poems

Short Quotations

For quotations of up to three lines, run the text right into your own, using quotation marks just as you would with a prose quotation. However, since the placement of line endings can be significant in a poem, you need to indicate where they occur. This is done by including a slash mark, with a single space on each side, where the line breaks occur. (Some students find this awkward-looking at first, but you will quickly get used to it. Your instructor will expect you to honor the poet's choices regarding line breaks.)

In "Sailing to Byzantium," Yeats describes an old man as "a paltry thing, / A tattered coat upon a stick."

Long Quotations

For quotations of four lines or more, "block" the material, setting it off one inch from the left margin, duplicating all line breaks of the original. Do not use quotation marks with block quotations.

In "Sailing to Byzantium," Yeats describes both the ravages of age and the possibility of renewal in the poem's second stanza:

> An aged man is but a paltry thing,
> A tattered coat upon a stick, unless
> Soul clap its hands and sing, and louder sing
> For every tatter in its mortal dress,
> Nor is there singing school but studying
> Monuments of its own magnificence.

Quoting from Plays

Short Single-Speaker Passages

When you quote a short passage of drama with a single speaker, treat the quoted text just as you would prose fiction:

> Nora's first words in *A Doll House* are "Hide the tree well, Helene. The children mustn't get a glimpse of it till this evening, after it's trimmed."

Longer or More Complex Passages

For a longer quotation, or a quotation of any length involving more than one character, you will need to block off the quotation. Begin each separate piece of dialogue indented one inch from the left margin with the character's name, typed in all capital letters, followed by a period. Subsequent lines of the character's speech should be indented an additional one-quarter inch. (Your word processor's "hanging indent" function is useful for achieving this effect without having to indent each separate line.) As with fiction or poetry, do not use quotation marks for block quotations.

> We see the tension between Nora and her husband in their very first confrontation:

> NORA. Oh, but Torvald, this year we really should let ourselves go a bit.
>   It's the first Christmas we haven't had to economize.
> HELMER. But you know we can't go squandering.
> NORA. Oh yes, Torvald, we can squander a little now. Can't we?

Verse Drama

Many older plays, including classical Greek drama and much of the work of Shakespeare and his contemporaries, are written at least partly in poetic verse. When you quote a verse drama, you must respect the line endings, just as you do in quoting poetry. The first example here shows a short quotation with slash marks that indicate line endings; the second shows a longer, block quotation in verse form.

Hamlet's most famous soliloquy begins, "To be, or not to be, that is the question: / Whether 'tis nobler in the mind to suffer / The slings and arrows of outrageous fortune."

Hamlet then begins his most famous soliloquy:
> To be, or not to be, that is the question:
> Whether 'tis nobler in the mind to suffer
> The slings and arrows of outrageous fortune,
> Or to take arms against a sea of troubles,
> And by opposing end them.

Tips for Quoting

- **Double-check the wording, spelling, and punctuation of every quotation you use.** Even if something seems "wrong" in the original source—a nonstandard spelling, a strange mark of punctuation, or even a factual error—resist the urge to correct it. When you put quotation marks around something, you indicate that you are reproducing it exactly as it first appeared. If you feel the need to clarify that an error or inconsistency is not yours, you may follow it by the word *sic* (Latin for *thus*), not italicized, in square brackets. Example: The mother in the anonymous poem "Lord Randal" asks her son "wha [sic] met ye there?"
- **Use the shortest quotation you can while still making your point.** Remember, the focus should always be on your own ideas, and the dominant voice should be yours. Don't quote a paragraph from a source when a single sentence contains the heart of what you need. Don't quote a whole sentence when you can simply integrate a few words into one of your own sentences.
- **Never assume a quotation is self-explanatory.** Each time you include a quotation, analyze it and explain why you have quoted it. Remember that your reader may have a different reaction to the quotation than you did.
- **If you are quoting a *character* in a story, play, or poem, be sure to distinguish that character from the *author*.** Hamlet says "To be or not to be," not Shakespeare, and you should make that distinction clear.

- **Take care not to distort the meaning of a quotation.** It is intellectually dishonest to quote an author or a speaker out of context or to use ellipses or additions in such a way as to change the meaning or integrity of source material. Treat your sources with the same respect you would want if you were to be quoted in a newspaper or magazine.

MANUSCRIPT FORM

If your instructor gives you directions about what your paper should look like, follow them exactly. If not, the following basic guidelines on manuscript form, recommended by the Modern Language Association of America (MLA), will work well in most instances. The most comprehensive guide to MLA style is *MLA Handbook for Writers of Research Papers*, 7th edition (New York: MLA, 2009). For an online guide to MLA style, see Diana Hacker's *Research and Documentation Online*: http://www .dianahacker.com/resdoc/. The guiding principle here is readability—you want the look of your paper to distract as little as possible from the content.

- **Use plain white paper, black ink, and a standard, easy-to-read font.** To make your paper stand out from the masses, it might seem like a nice touch to use visual design elements like colored or decorated paper, fancy fonts, and so forth. However, your instructor has a lot of reading to do, and anything that distracts or slows down that reading is a minus, not a plus, for your paper. For the same reason, avoid illustrations, pictures of authors, and so forth, unless they are needed to clarify a point. Distinguish your paper through content and style, not flashy design.

- **No separate cover page is needed.** Also, don't waste your time and money on report covers or folders unless asked to do so by your instructor. Many instructors, in fact, find covers cumbersome and distracting.

- **Include vital information in the upper left corner of your first page.** This information usually consists of your name, the name of your instructor, the course number of the class, and the date you submit the paper.

- **Center your paper's title.** The title should appear in upper- and lowercase letters, and in the same font as the rest of your paper—not italicized, boldface, or set within quotation marks.

- **Page numbers should appear in the upper right corner of each page.** Do not include the word *page* or the abbreviation *p.* with the page numbers. Use your word processing program's "header" or "running head" feature to include your last name before the page numbers.

See the sample student papers in this book for examples of correct MLA-style formatting. These basic guidelines should carry you through most situations, but if you have any questions regarding format, ask your instructor for his or her preferences.

Writing Processes

You are already a writer with long experience. In school you have taken notes, written book reports and term papers, answered exam questions, perhaps kept a journal. You've recorded minutes in community meetings and composed memos on the job. You've e-mailed friends, made shopping lists, maybe even tried your hand at writing songs or poetry. All this experience is about to pay off.

Unlike parachute jumping, writing in college is something you can go ahead and try without first learning all there is to know. In truth, nothing anyone can tell you will help as much as learning by doing. In this book our purpose is to help you write better, deeper, clearer, and more satisfying papers than you have ever written before. We encourage you to do so by diving into writing—experimenting, practicing, and building confidence as you expand your writing strategies.

WRITING, READING, AND CRITICAL THINKING

In college you will perform challenging tasks that enlarge what you already know about writing. In fact, you can view each writing task as a problem to solve, often through careful reading and objective thinking. You will need to read—and write—actively, engaging with the ideas of others. At the same time, you will need to think critically, analyzing and judging those ideas. To help you assess your own achievement, you will use criteria—models, conventions, principles, standards. As you write and rewrite, you can evaluate what you are doing by asking specific questions:

- Have you considered your audience?
- Have you achieved your purpose?

X. J. Kennedy, Dorothy M. Kennedy, and Marcia F. Muth, *Writing and Revising: A Portable Guide*, pages 1–10. Copyright © 2007 by Bedford/St. Martin's.

- Have you made your point clear by stating it as a thesis or by unmistakably implying it?
- Have you supported your point with enough reliable evidence to persuade your readers?
- Have you arranged your ideas logically so that each follows from, supports, or adds to the one before it?
- Have you made the connections among ideas clear to your readers?
- Have you established an appropriate tone?

In large measure, learning to write well is learning what questions to ask as you write.

A PROCESS OF WRITING

Writing can seem at times an overwhelming drudgery, worse than scrubbing floors; at other moments, it's a sport full of thrills—like whizzing downhill on skis, not knowing what you'll meet around a bend. Surprising and unpredictable as the process may seem, nearly all writers do similar things:

- They generate ideas.
- They plan, draft, and develop their papers.
- They revise and edit.

Although these activities form the basis of most effective writing processes, they aren't lockstep stages: you don't always proceed in a straight line. You can skip around in whatever order you like, work on several parts at a time, or circle back over what's already done. For example, while gathering material, you may feel an urge to play with a sentence until it clicks. Or while writing a draft, you may decide to look for more material. You can leap ahead, cross out, backtrack, adjust, question, test a fresh approach, tinker, polish, and, at the end, spell-check the tricky words.

Generating Ideas

The first activity in writing—finding a topic and something to say about it—is often the most challenging and least predictable.

Finding Something to Write About. Selecting a topic is not always easy, but you may discover an idea while talking with friends, riding your bike, or even staring out the window. Sometimes a topic lies near home, in an everyday event you recall. Often your reading raises questions that call for investigation. When a particular writing assignment doesn't appeal to you, your challenge is to find a slant that does interest you. Find it, and words will flow—words that can engage readers as you accomplish your purpose. (See the graphic below.)

Discovering Material. You'll need information to shape and support your ideas—facts and figures, reports and opinions, examples and illustrations. Luckily you have numerous sources of supporting material to make your slant on a topic clear and convincing to your readers. You can recall your own experience and knowledge, you can observe things around you, you can converse with others who are knowledgeable, you can read materials that draw you to new views, and you can think critically about all the sources around you.

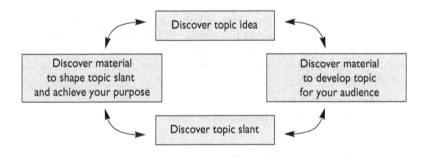

Planning, Drafting, and Developing

After finding a topic and beginning to gather material about it, you will plan your paper, write a draft, and then develop your ideas further. (See the graphic on the following page.)

Planning. Having discovered a burning idea (or at least a smoldering one) to write about, and some supporting material (but maybe not enough yet), you can sort out what matters most. If right away you see one main point, or thesis, for your paper, test various ways of stating it, given your audience and purpose:

MAYBE   Parking in the morning before class is annoying.

OR   Parking on campus is a big problem.

Next arrange your ideas and material in a sensible order that clarifies your point. For example, you might group and label the ideas you have

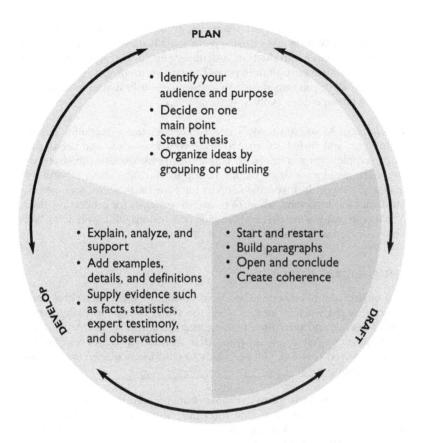

PLAN
- Identify your audience and purpose
- Decide on one main point
- State a thesis
- Organize ideas by grouping or outlining

DRAFT
- Start and restart
- Build paragraphs
- Open and conclude
- Create coherence

DEVELOP
- Explain, analyze, and support
- Add examples, details, and definitions
- Supply evidence such as facts, statistics, expert testimony, and observations

generated, make an outline, or analyze the main point, breaking it down into its parts:

> Parking on campus is a problem for students because of the long lines, inefficient entrances, and poorly marked spaces.

But if no clear thesis emerges quickly, don't worry. You may find one while you draft—that is, while you write an early version of your paper.

Drafting. When your ideas first start to flow, you want to welcome them—lure them forth, not tear them apart, so they don't go back into hiding. Don't be afraid to take risks at this stage: you'll probably be surprised and pleased at what happens, even though your first version will be rough. Writing takes time; a paper usually needs several drafts and may need a clearer introduction, a stronger conclusion, more convincing evidence, or a revised plan. Especially when your subject is unfamiliar or complicated, you may decide to throw out your first attempt and start over as a stronger idea evolves.

Developing. As you draft, you'll weave in explanations, examples, details, definitions, and varied evidence to make your ideas clear and persuasive. For example, you may need to define an at-risk student, illustrate the problems faced by a single parent, or supply statistics about hit-and-run accidents. If you lack specific support for your main point, you can use strategies for developing ideas, or return to strategies for generating ideas. You'll keep gaining insights and drawing conclusions while you draft. Welcome these ideas, and work them in if they fit.

Revising and Editing

You might want to relax once you have a draft, but for most writers revising begins the work in earnest. (See the visual below.) Revising means both reseeing and rewriting, making major changes so that your paper accomplishes what you want it to. After you have a well-developed and well-organized revision, you are ready to edit: to correct errors and improve wording.

Revising. Revision is more than just changing words. In fact, you may revise what you know and what you think while you're writing or when you pause to reread. You can then rework your thesis, reconsider your audience, shift your plans, decide what to put in or leave out, rearrange for clarity, move sentences or paragraphs around, connect points differently, or express ideas better. Perhaps you'll add costs to a paper on parking

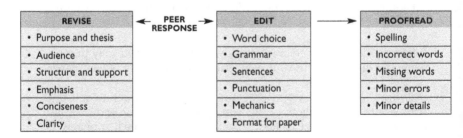

REVISE	PEER RESPONSE	EDIT		PROOFREAD
• Purpose and thesis		• Word choice		• Spelling
• Audience		• Grammar		• Incorrect words
• Structure and support		• Sentences		• Missing words
• Emphasis		• Punctuation		• Minor errors
• Conciseness		• Mechanics		• Minor details
• Clarity		• Format for paper		

38

problems or switch to fathers instead of mothers as you consider teen parenthood.

If you put aside your draft for a few hours or a day, you can reread it with fresh eyes and a clear mind. Other students can also help you—sometimes more than a textbook or an instructor can—by responding to your drafts as engaged readers.

Editing. Editing means refining details and correcting flaws that stand in the way of your readers' understanding and enjoyment. Don't edit too early, though, because you may waste time on some part that you later revise out. In editing, you usually make these repairs:

- Get rid of unnecessary words.
- Choose livelier and more precise words.
- Replace any incorrect or inappropriate wording.
- Rearrange words in a clearer, more emphatic order.
- Combine short, choppy sentences, or break up long, confusing sentences.
- Refine transitions for continuity of thought.
- Check grammar, sentences, punctuation, and mechanics.

Proofreading. Finally you'll proofread your paper, taking a last look, checking correctness, and catching spelling or word-processing errors.

Remembering What Matters Most. Like a hard game of basketball, writing a college paper is strenuous. Without getting in your way, we want to lend you support and guidance throughout the writing process. So, no doubt, does your instructor, someone closer to you than a textbook writer. Still, even the best instructors and textbook writers—like the best coaches—can improve your game only so much. Advice on how to write won't make you a better writer. You'll learn more and have more fun when you take a few sentences to the hoop and make points yourself. After you sink a few baskets, you'll gain confidence in your ability and find the process of writing easier.

■ ACTIVITY: Describing Your Writing Process

Describe your writing process. How do you get started? How do you keep writing? What process do you go through to reach a final draft? Do your steps ever vary depending on the type of writing you're doing? What step or strategy in your writing process would you most like to change?

A SPOTLIGHT ON AUDIENCE AND PURPOSE

At any moment in the writing process, two questions are worth asking:

Who is my audience?   **Why am I writing?**

Writing for Readers

Your audience, or your readers, may or may not be defined in your assignment. Consider the following examples:

ASSIGNMENT 1   Discuss the advantages and disadvantages of home schooling.

ASSIGNMENT 2   In a letter to parents of school-aged children, discuss the advantages and disadvantages of home schooling.

If your assignment defines an audience, as the second example does, you will need to think about how to approach those readers and what to assume about their relationship to your topic. For example, what points would you include in a discussion aimed at parents? How would you organize your ideas? Would you discuss advantages or disadvantages first? On the other hand, how might your approach differ if the assignment read this way?

ASSIGNMENT 3   In a short article for a professional publication for teachers, discuss the advantages and disadvantages of home schooling.

When you analyze what readers know, believe, and value, you can aim your writing toward them with a better chance of hitting your mark. Use these questions to help you write and revise for your audience.

GENERAL AUDIENCE CHECKLIST

☐ Who are your readers? What is their relationship to you?

☐ What do your readers already know about this topic? What do you want them to learn?

☐ How much detail will they want to read about this topic?

(continued)

☐ What objections are they likely to raise as they read? How can you anticipate and overcome their objections?

☐ What's likely to convince them?

☐ What's likely to offend them?

■ **ACTIVITY: Considering Your Audience**

Write a short paragraph describing in detail a "worst" event—your worst date, worst dinner, worst car repair, or some similar catastrophe. Then revise that paragraph so that your audience is a person involved in the event—the person who went on that date with you, cooked or served the dinner, worked on your car. Now revise the paragraph again, this time writing to a person you plan to date soon, a cook at a restaurant you want to try, or a repair person working at another garage. Compare the three paragraphs. How are they similar? How do they differ?

Targeting Academic Readers

Although your future writing is likely to be aimed at a specific audience—the marketing team at work or the other members of an animal rescue group—many of your college assignments will resemble the example labeled Assignment 1 (see the preceding page). Those assignments will assume that you are addressing general academic readers, represented by your instructor and possibly your classmates. General academic readers typically expect clear, logical writing that uses supporting evidence to explain, interpret, or persuade. In addition, the particular expectations of academic audiences may differ by field. For example, biologists might assume you'll supply the findings from your experiment while literature specialists might look for plenty of relevant quotations from the novel you're analyzing. Depending on the field, your readers may expect certain topics, types of evidence, and approaches. Use these questions to help you pinpoint what your college readers expect.

ACADEMIC AUDIENCE CHECKLIST

☐ How has your instructor advised you to write for readers in the field? What criteria will be used for grading your papers?

(continued)

□ What do the assigned readings in your course assume about readers and their expectations? Has your instructor recommended useful models or sample readings?

□ What topics and issues concern readers in the field? What puzzles do they want to solve? How do they want to solve them?

□ How is writing in the field commonly organized? For example, do writers tend to follow a persuasive pattern? That is, do they introduce the issue, state their assertion or claim, explain their reasons, acknowledge other views, and conclude? Do they use a series of conventional headings—for example, Abstract, Introduction to the Problem, Methodology, Findings, and Discussion?

□ What evidence is typically gathered to support ideas or interpretations—facts and statistics, quotations from texts, summaries of research, references to authorities or prior studies, results from experimental research, or field notes from observations or interviews?

□ What style, tone, and level of formality do writers in the field tend to use and readers tend to expect?

■ **ACTIVITY: Considering an Academic Audience**

Working by yourself or with a small group, use the preceding checklist to examine several reading or writing assignments in one of your courses. Try to identify prominent features of writing in the field. Which of these characteristics probably would be expected in student papers? How might you adjust your writing to meet those expectations? How would an academic paper differ from writing on the same topic for a general audience—for example, a letter to the editor, a newspaper article, a consumer brochure, an explanation for middle school students, or a Web page?

Writing for a Reason

Most college writing assignments ask you to write for a definite reason. For example, you might be asked to take a stand on a controversial issue and to persuade your readers to respect your position. Be careful not to confuse the sources and strategies you apply in these assignments with your ultimate purpose for writing. "To compare and contrast two things" is not a very interesting purpose; "to compare and contrast two Web sites *in order to explain their differences*" implies a real reason for writing.

In most college writing, your ultimate purpose will be to explain something to your readers or to convince them of something.

To sharpen your concentration on your purpose, ask yourself from the start, What do I want to do? And, in revising, Did I do what I meant to do? You'll find that these practical questions can help you slice out irrelevant information and remove other barriers to getting your paper where you want it to go.

■ ACTIVITY: Considering Your Purpose

Return to the three paragraphs you wrote for the activity "Considering Your Audience." Write a sentence or two summing up your purpose in writing each paragraph. Given these three purposes, how might you revise the paragraphs?

LORRIE MOORE [b. 1957]

How to Become a Writer

Born in Glens Falls, New York, the daughter of an insurance company executive, **Lorrie Moore** (b. 1957) graduated from St. Lawrence University with a B.A. degree and Cornell University with an M.F.A. She then began teaching at the University of Wisconsin. Since 1976, when she won a *Seventeen* magazine short story contest with a story called "Raspberries," Moore's fiction has appeared regularly in other magazines. Her first collection, *Self-Help* (1985), nine stories including "How to Become a Writer," satirizes self-help books with a subtle blend of humor and seriousness. Her novel *Anagrams* appeared in 1987. Her newest books are *Who Will Run the Frog Hospital?* (1994) and *Birds of America* (1998).

First, try to be something, anything, else. A movie star/astronaut. A movie star/missionary. A movie star/kindergarten teacher. President of the World. Fail miserably. It is best if you fail at an early age—say, fourteen. Early, critical disillusionment is necessary so that at fifteen you can write long haiku sequences about thwarted desire. It is a pond, a cherry blossom, a wind brushing against sparrow wing leaving for mountain. Count the syllables. Show it to your mom. She is tough and practical. She has a son in Vietnam and a husband who may be having an affair. She believes in wearing brown because it hides spots. She'll look briefly at your writing, then back up at you with a face blank as a donut. She'll say: "How about emptying the dishwasher?" Look away. Shove the forks in the fork drawer. Accidentally break one of the freebie gas station glasses. This is the required pain and suffering. This is only for starters.

In your high school English class look only at Mr. Killian's face. Decide faces are important. Write a villanelle about pores. Struggle. Write a sonnet. Count the syllables: nine, ten, eleven, thirteen. Decide to experiment with fiction. Here you don't have to count syllables. Write a short story about an elderly man and woman who accidentally shoot each other in the head, the result of an inexplicable malfunction of a shotgun which appears mysteriously in their living room one night. Give it to Mr. Killian as your final project. When you get it back, he has written on it: "Some of your images are quite nice, but you have no sense of plot." When you are home, in the privacy of your own room, faintly scrawl in pencil beneath his black-inked comments: "Plots are for dead people, pore-face."

Take all the babysitting jobs you can get. You are great with kids. They love you. You tell them stories about old people who die idiot deaths. You sing them songs like "Blue Bells of Scotland," which is their favorite. And when they are in their pajamas and have finally stopped pinching each other, when they are fast asleep, you read every sex manual in the house, and wonder how on earth anyone could ever do those things with someone they truly loved. Fall asleep in a chair reading Mr. McMurphy's *Playboy*. When the McMurphys come home, they will tap you on the shoulder, look at the magazine in your lap, and grin. You will want to die. They will ask you if Tracey took her medicine all right. Explain, yes, she did, that you promised her a story if she would take it like a big girl and that seemed to work out just fine. "Oh, marvelous," they will exclaim.

Try to smile proudly.

Apply to college as a child psychology major.

As a child psychology major, you have some electives. You've always liked birds. Sign up for something called "The Ornithological Field Trip." It meets Tuesdays and Thursdays at two. When you arrive at Room 134 on the first day of class, everyone is sitting around a seminar table talking about metaphors. You've heard of these. After a short, excruciating while, raise your hand and say diffidently, "Excuse me, isn't this Birdwatching One-oh-one?" The class stops and turns to look at you. They seem to all have one face—giant and blank as a vandalized clock. Someone with a beard booms out, "No, this is Creative Writing." Say: "Oh—right," as if perhaps you knew all along. Look down at your schedule. Wonder how the hell you ended up here. The computer, apparently, has made an error. You start to get up to leave and then don't. The lines at the registrar this week are huge. Perhaps you should stick with this mistake. Perhaps your creative writing isn't all that bad. Perhaps it is fate. Perhaps this is what your dad meant when he said, "It's the age of computers, Francie, it's the age of computers."

Decide that you like college life. In your dorm you meet many nice people. Some are smarter than you. And some, you notice, are dumber than you. You will continue, unfortunately, to view the world in exactly these terms for the rest of your life.

*   *   *

The assignment this week in creative writing is to narrate a violent happening. Turn in a story about driving with your Uncle Gordon and another one about two old people who are accidentally electrocuted when they go to turn on a badly wired desk lamp. The teacher will hand them back to you with comments: "Much of your writing is smooth and energetic. You have, however, a ludicrous notion of plot." Write another story about a man and a woman who, in the very first paragraph, have their lower torsos accidentally blitzed away by dynamite. In the second paragraph, with the insurance money, they buy a frozen yogurt stand together. There are six more paragraphs. You read the whole thing out loud in class. No one likes it. They say your sense of plot is outrageous and incompetent. After class someone asks you if you are crazy.

Decide that perhaps you should stick to comedies. Start dating someone who is funny, someone who has what in high school you called a "really great sense of humor" and what now your creative writing class calls "self-contempt giving rise to comic form." Write down all of his jokes, but don't tell him you are doing this. Make up anagrams of his old girlfriend's name and name all of your socially handicapped characters with them. Tell him his old girlfriend is in all of your stories and then watch how funny he can be, see what a really great sense of humor he can have.

Your child psychology advisor tells you you are neglecting courses in your major. What you spend the most time on should be what you're majoring in. Say yes, you understand.

In creative writing seminars over the next two years, everyone continues to smoke cigarettes and ask the same things: "But does it work?" "Why should we care about this character?" "Have you earned this cliché?" These seem like important questions.

On days when it is your turn, you look at the class hopefully as they scour your mimeographs for a plot. They look back up at you, drag deeply, and then smile in a sweet sort of way.

You spend too much time slouched and demoralized. Your boyfriend suggests bicycling. Your roommate suggests a new boyfriend. You are said to be self-mutilating and losing weight, but you continue writing. The only happiness you have is writing something new, in the middle of the night, armpits damp, heart pounding, something no one has yet seen. You have only those brief, fragile, untested moments of exhilaration when you know: you are a genius. Understand what you must do. Switch majors. The kids in your nursery project will be disappointed, but you have a calling, an urge, a delusion, an unfortunate habit. You have, as your mother would say, fallen in with a bad crowd.

Why write? Where does writing come from? These are questions to ask yourself. They are like: Where does dust come from? Or: Why is there war? Or: If there's a God, then why is my brother now a cripple?

These are questions that you keep in your wallet, like calling cards. These are questions, your creative writing teacher says, that are good to address in your journals but rarely in your fiction.

The writing professor this fall is stressing the Power of the Imagination. Which means he doesn't want long descriptive stories about your camping trip last July. He wants you to start in a realistic context but then to alter it. Like recombinant DNA. He wants you to let your imagination sail, to let it grow big-bellied in the wind. This is a quote from Shakespeare.

Tell your roommate your great idea, your great exercise of imaginative power: a transformation of Melville to contemporary life. It will be about monomania and the fish-eat-fish world of life insurance in Rochester, New York. The first line will be "Call me Fishmeal," and it will feature a menopausal suburban husband named Richard, who because he is so depressed all the time is called "Mopey Dick" by his witty wife Elaine. Say to your roommate: "Mopey Dick, get it?" Your roommate looks at you, her face blank as a large Kleenex. She comes up to you, like a buddy, and puts an arm around your burdened shoulders. "Listen, Francie," she says, slow as speech therapy. "Let's go out and get a big beer."

The seminar doesn't like this one either. You suspect they are beginning to feel sorry for you. They say: "You have to think about what is happening. Where is the story here?"

The next semester the writing professor is obsessed with writing from personal experience. You must write from what you know, from what has happened to you. He wants death, he wants camping trips. Think about what has happened to you. In three years there have been three things: you lost your virginity; your parents got divorced; and your brother came home from a forest ten miles from the Cambodian border with only half a thigh, a permanent smirk nestled into one corner of his mouth.

About the first you write: "It created a new space, which hurt and cried in a voice that wasn't mine, 'I'm not the same anymore, but I'll be okay.' "

About the second you write an elaborate story of an old married

47

couple who stumble upon an unknown land mine in their kitchen and accidentally blow themselves up. You call it: "For Better or for Liverwurst."

About the last you write nothing. There are no words for this. Your typewriter hums. You can find no words.

At undergraduate cocktail parties, people say, "Oh, you write? What do you write about?" Your roommate, who has consumed too much wine, too little cheese, and no crackers at all, blurts: "Oh, my god, she always writes about her dumb boyfriend."

Later on in life you will learn that writers are merely open, helpless texts with no real understanding of what they have written and therefore must half-believe anything and everything that is said of them. You, however, have not yet reached this stage of literary criticism. You stiffen and say, "I do not," the same way you said it when someone in the fourth grade accused you of really liking oboe lessons and your parents really weren't just making you take them.

Insist you are not very interested in any one subject at all, that you are interested in the music of language, that you are interested in—in—syllables, because they are the atoms of poetry, the cells of the mind, the breath of the soul. Begin to feel woozy. Stare into your plastic wine cup.

"Syllables?" you will hear someone ask, voice trailing off, as they glide slowly toward the reassuring white of the dip.

Begin to wonder what you do write about. Or if you have anything to say. Or if there even is such a thing as a thing to say. Limit these thoughts to no more than ten minutes a day; like sit-ups, they can make you thin.

You will read somewhere that all writing has to do with one's genitals. Don't dwell on this. It will make you nervous.

Your mother will come visit you. She will look at the circles under your eyes and hand you a brown book with a brown briefcase on the cover. It is entitled: *How to Become a Business Executive.* She has also brought the *Names for Baby* encyclopedia you asked for; one of your characters, the aging clown-schoolteacher, needs a new name. Your mother will shake her head and say: "Francie, Francie, remember when you were going to be a child psychology major?"

Say: "Mom, I like to write."

She'll say: "Sure you like to write. Of course. Sure you like to write."

Write a story about a confused music student and title it: "Schubert Was the One with the Glasses, Right?" It's not a big hit, although your roommate likes the part where the two violinists accidentally blow themselves up in a recital room. "I went out with a violinist once," she says, snapping her gum.

* * *

Thank god you are taking other courses. You can find sanctuary in nineteenth-century ontological snags and invertebrate courting rituals. Certain globular mollusks have what is called "Sex by the Arm." The male octopus, for instance, loses the end of one arm when placing it inside the female body during intercourse. Marine biologists call it "Seven Heaven." Be glad you know these things. Be glad you are not just a writer. Apply to law school.

From here on in, many things can happen. But the main one will be this: you decide not to go to law school after all, and, instead, you spend a good, big chunk of your adult life telling people how you decided not to go to law school after all. Somehow you end up writing again. Perhaps you go to graduate school. Perhaps you work odd jobs and take writing courses at night. Perhaps you are working on a novel and writing down all the clever remarks and intimate personal confessions you hear during the day. Perhaps you are losing your pals, your acquaintances, your balance.

You have broken up with your boyfriend. You now go out with men who, instead of whispering "I love you," shout: "Do it to me, baby." This is good for your writing.

Sooner or later you have a finished manuscript more or less. People look at it in a vaguely troubled sort of way and say, "I'll bet becoming a writer was always a fantasy of yours, wasn't it?" Your lips dry to salt. Say that of all the fantasies possible in the world, you can't imagine being a writer even making the top twenty. Tell them you were going to be a child psychology major. "I bet," they always sigh, "you'd be great with kids." Scowl fiercely. Tell them you're a walking blade.

Quit classes. Quit jobs. Cash in old savings bonds. Now you have time like warts on your hands. Slowly copy all of your friends' addresses into a new address book.

Vacuum. Chew cough drops. Keep a folder full of fragments.

An eyelid darkening sideways.
World as conspiracy.
Possible plot? A woman gets on a bus.
Suppose you threw a love affair and nobody came?

At home drink a lot of coffee. At Howard Johnson's order the cole slaw. Consider how it looks like the soggy confetti of a map: where you've been, where you're going—"You Are Here," says the red star on the back of the menu.

Occasionally a date with a face blank as a sheet of paper asks you whether writers often become discouraged. Say that sometimes they do and sometimes they do. Say it's a lot like having polio.

"Interesting," smiles your date, and then he looks down at his arm hairs and starts to smooth them, all, always, in the same direction.

[1985]

PAUL ROBERTS [1917-1967]

How to Say Nothing in Five Hundred Words

California-born **Paul Roberts** received his B.A. from San Jose State College and his M.A. and Ph.D. from the University of California at Berkeley, where he taught for fourteen years after serving in the merchant marine during World War II. Writing in a down-to-earth, often humorous style, Roberts published several books on English composition, including *Understanding Grammar* (1954), *English Sentences* (1962), and *Modern Grammar* (1954). He died in Rome in 1967.

"How to Say Nothing in Five Hundred Words" is from Roberts's best-known book, *Understanding English* (1958), and is representative of his clarity and wit. Roberts recommends that composition students check their tendency to state the obvious and instead strive for interesting content backed by concrete examples.

NOTHING ABOUT SOMETHING

It's Friday afternoon, and you have almost survived another week of classes. You are just looking forward dreamily to the week end when the English instructor says: "For Monday you will turn in a five-hundred word composition on college football."

Well, that puts a good big hole in the week end. You don't have any strong views on college football one way or the other. You get rather excited during the season and go to all the home games and find it rather more fun than not. On the other hand, the class has been reading Robert Hutchins in the anthology and perhaps Shaw's "Eighty-Yard Run," and from the class discussion you have got the idea that the instructor thinks college football is for the birds. You are no fool, you. You can figure out what side to take.

After dinner you get out the portable typewriter that you got for high school graduation. You might as well get it over with and enjoy Saturday and Sunday. Five hundred words is about two double-spaced pages with normal margins. You put in a sheet of paper, think up a title, and you're off:

WHY COLLEGE FOOTBALL SHOULD BE ABOLISHED

College football should be abolished because it's bad for the school and also bad for the players. The players are so busy practicing that they don't have any time for their studies.

This, you feel, is a mighty good start. The only trouble is that it's only thirty-two words. You still have four hundred and sixty-eight to go, and you've pretty well exhausted the subject. It comes to you that you do your best thinking in the morning, so you put away the typewriter and go to the movies. But the next morning you have to do your washing and some math problems, and in the afternoon you go to the game. The English instructor turns up too, and you wonder if you've taken the right side after all. Saturday night you have a date, and Sunday morning you have to go to church. (You shouldn't let English assignments interfere with your religion.) What with one thing and another, it's ten o'clock Sunday night before you get out the typewriter again. You make a pot of coffee and start to fill out your views on college football. Put a little meat on the bones.

WHY COLLEGE FOOTBALL SHOULD BE ABOLISHED

In my opinion, it seems to me that college football should be abolished. The reason why I think this to be true is because I feel that football is bad for the colleges in nearly every respect. As Robert Hutchins says in his article in our anthology in which he discusses college football, it would be better if the colleges had race horses and had races with one another, because then the horses would not have to attend classes. I firmly agree with Mr. Hutchins on this point, and I am sure that many other students would agree too.

One reason why it seems to me that college football is bad is that it has become too commercial. In the olden times when people played football just for the fun of it, maybe college football was all right, but they do not play football just for the fun of it now as they used to in the old days. Nowadays college football is what you might call a big business. Maybe this is not true at all schools, and I don't think it is especially true here at State, but certainly this is the case at most colleges and universities in America nowadays, as Mr. Hutchins points out in his very interesting article. Actually the coaches and alumni go around to the high schools and offer the high school stars large salaries to come to their colleges and play football for them. There was one case where a high school star was offered a convertible if he would play football for a certain college.

Another reason for abolishing college football is that it is bad for the players. They do not have time to get a college education, because they are so busy playing football. A football player has to practice every afternoon from three to six, and then he is so tired that he can't concentrate on his studies. He just feels like dropping off to sleep after dinner, and then the next day he goes to his classes without having studied and maybe he fails the test.

(Good ripe stuff so far, but you're still a hundred and fifty-one words from home. One more push.)

Also I think college football is bad for the colleges and the universities because not very many students get to participate in it. Out of a college of ten thousand students only seventy-five or a hundred play football, if that many. Football is what you might call a spectator sport. That means that most people go to watch it but do not play it themselves.

(Four hundred and fifteen. Well, you still have the conclusion, and when you retype it, you can make the margins a little wider.)

These are the reasons why I agree with Mr. Hutchins that college football should be abolished in American colleges and universities.

On Monday you turn it in, moderately hopeful, and on Friday it comes 5 back marked "weak in content" and sporting a big "D."

This essay is exaggerated a little, not much. The English instructor will recognize it as reasonably typical of what an assignment on college football will bring in. He knows that nearly half of the class will contrive in five hundred words to say that college football is too commercial and bad for the players. Most of the other half will inform him that college football builds character and prepares one for life and brings prestige to the school. As he reads paper after paper all saying the same thing in almost the same words, all bloodless, five hundred words dripping out of nothing, he wonders how he allowed himself to get trapped into teaching English when he might have had a happy and interesting life as an electrician or a confidence man.

Well, you may ask, what can you do about it? The subject is one on which you have few convictions and little information. Can you be expected to make a dull subject interesting? As a matter of fact, this is precisely what you are expected to do. This is the writer's essential task.

All subjects, except sex, are dull until somebody makes them interesting. The writer's job is to find the argument, the approach, the angle, the wording that will take the reader with him. This is seldom easy, and it is particularly hard in subjects that have been much discussed: College Football, Fraternities, Popular Music, Is Chivalry Dead?, and the like. You will feel that there is nothing you can do with such subjects except repeat the old bromides. But there are some things you can do which will make your papers, if not throbbingly alive, at least less insufferably tedious than they might otherwise be.

AVOID THE OBVIOUS CONTENT

Say the assignment is college football. Say that you've decided to be against it. Begin by putting down the arguments that come to your mind: it is too commercial, it takes the students' minds off their studies, it is hard on the players, it makes the university a kind of circus instead of an intellectual center, for most schools it is financially ruinous. Can you think of any more arguments just off hand? All right. Now when you write your paper, *make sure that you don't use any of the material on this list.* If these are the points that leap to your mind, they will leap to everyone else's too, and whether you get a "C" or a "D" may depend on whether the instructor reads your paper early when he is fresh and tolerant or late, when the sentence "In my opinion, college football has become too commercial," inexorably repeated, has brought him to the brink of lunacy.

Be against college football for some reason or reasons of your own. If they are keen and perceptive ones, that's splendid. But even if they are trivial or foolish or indefensible, you are still ahead so long as they are not everybody else's reasons too. Be against it because the colleges don't spend enough money on it to make it worth while, because it is bad for the characters of the spectators, because the players are forced to attend classes, because the football stars hog all the beautiful women, because it competes with baseball and is therefore un-American and possibly Communist inspired. There are lots of more or less unused reasons for being against college football.

Sometimes it is a good idea to sum up and dispose of the trite and con- 10 ventional points before going on to your own. This has the advantage of indicating to the reader that you are going to be neither trite nor conventional. Something like this:

> We are often told that college football should be abolished because it has become too commercial or because it is bad for the players. These

54

arguments are no doubt very cogent, but they don't really go to the heart of the matter.

Then you go to the heart of the matter.

TAKE THE LESS USUAL SIDE

One rather simple way of getting interest into your paper is to take the side of the argument that most of the citizens will want to avoid. If the assignment is an essay on dogs, you can, if you choose, explain that dogs are faithful and lovable companions, intelligent, useful as guardians of the house and protectors of children, indispensable in police work—in short, when all is said and done, man's best friends. Or you can suggest that those big brown eyes conceal more often than not, a vacuity of mind and an inconstancy of purpose; that the dogs you have known most intimately have been mangy, ill-tempered brutes, incapable of instruction; and that only your nobility of mind and fear of arrest prevent you from kicking the flea-ridden animals when you pass them on the street.

Naturally, personal convictions will sometimes dictate your approach. If the assigned subject is "Is Methodism Rewarding to the Individual?" and you are a pious Methodist, you have really no choice. But few assigned subjects, if any, will fall in this category. Most of them will lie in broad areas of discussion with much to be said on both sides. They are intellectual exercises, and it is legitimate to argue now one way and now another, as debaters do in similar circumstances. Always take the side that looks to you hardest, least defensible. It will almost always turn out to be easier to write interestingly on that side.

This general advice applies where you have a choice of subjects. If you are to choose among "The Value of Fraternities" and "My Favorite High School Teacher" and "What I Think About Beetles," by all means plump for the beetles. By the time the instructor gets to your paper, he will be up to his ears in tedious tales about the French teacher at Bloombury High and assertions about how fraternities build character and prepare one for life. Your views on beetles, whatever they are, are bound to be a refreshing change.

Don't worry too much about figuring out what the instructor thinks about the subject so that you can cuddle up with him. Chances are his views are no stronger than yours. If he does have convictions and you oppose them, his problem is to keep from grading you higher than you deserve in order to show he is not biased. This doesn't mean that you should always cantankerously dissent from what the instructor says;

that gets tiresome too. And if the subject assigned is "My Pet Peeve," do not begin, "My pet peeve is the English instructor who assigns papers on 'my pet peeve.'" This was still funny during the War of 1812, but it has sort of lost its edge since then. It is in general good manners to avoid personalities.

SLIP OUT OF ABSTRACTION

If you will study the essay on college football in [the "Nothing about 15 Something" section], you will perceive that one reason for its appalling dullness is that it never gets down to particulars. It is just a series of not very glittering generalities: "football is bad for the colleges," "it has become too commercial," "football is a big business," "it is bad for the players," and so on. Such round phrases thudding against the reader's brain are unlikely to convince him, though they may well render him unconscious.

If you want the reader to believe that college football is bad for the players, you have to do more than say so. You have to display the evil. Take your roommate, Alfred Simkins, the second-string center. Picture poor old Alfy coming home from football practice every evening, bruised and aching, agonizingly tired, scarcely able to shovel the mashed potatoes into his mouth. Let us see him staggering up to the room, getting out his econ textbook, peering desperately at it with his good eye, falling asleep and failing the test in the morning. Let us share his unbearable tension as Saturday draws near. Will he fail, be demoted, lose his monthly allowance, be forced to return to the coal mines? And if he succeeds, what will be his reward? Perhaps a slight ripple of applause when the third-string center replaces him, a moment of elation in the locker room if the team wins, of despair if it loses. What will he look back on when he graduates from college? Toil and torn ligaments. And what will be his future? He is not good enough for pro football, and he is too obscure and weak in econ to succeed in stocks and bonds. College football is tearing the heart from Alfy Simkins and, when it finishes with him, will callously toss aside the shattered hulk.

This is no doubt a weak enough argument for the abolition of college football, but it is a sight better than saying, in three or four variations, that college football (in your opinion) is bad for the players.

Look at the work of any professional writer and notice how constantly he is moving from the generality, the abstract statement, to the concrete example, the facts and figures, the illustration. If he is writing on juvenile delinquency, he does not just tell you that juveniles are (it seems to him) delinquent and that (in his opinion) something should be done about it. He shows you juveniles being delinquent, tearing up movie theatres in Buffalo, stabbing high school principals in Dallas, smoking marijuana in Palo Alto. And more than likely he is moving toward some specific remedy, not just a general wringing of the hands.

It is no doubt possible to be *too* concrete, too illustrative or anecdotal, but few inexperienced writers err this way. For most the soundest advice is to be seeking always for the picture, to be always turning general remarks into seeable examples. Don't say, "Sororities teach girls the social graces." Say, "Sorority life teaches a girl how to carry on a conversation while pouring tea, without sloshing the tea into the saucer." Don't say, "I like certain kinds of popular music very much." Say, "Whenever I hear Gerber Spinklittle play 'Mississippi Man' on the trombone, my socks creep up my ankles."

GET RID OF OBVIOUS PADDING

The student toiling away at his weekly English theme is too often tormented by a figure: five hundred words. How, he asks himself, is he to achieve this staggering total? Obviously by never using one word when he can somehow work in ten. 20

He is therefore seldom content with a plain statement like "Fast driving is dangerous." This has only four words in it. He takes thought, and the sentence becomes:

In my opinion, fast driving is dangerous.

Better, but he can do better still:

In my opinion, fast driving would seem to be rather dangerous.

If he is really adept, it may come out:

In my humble opinion, though I do not claim to be an expert on this complicated subject, fast driving, in most circumstances, would seem to be rather dangerous in many respects, or at least so it would seem to me.

Thus four words have been turned into forty, and not an iota of content has been added.

Now this is a way to go about reaching five hundred words, and if you are content with a "D" grade, it is as good a way as any. But if you aim higher, you must work differently. Instead of stuffing your sentences with straw, you must try steadily to get rid of the padding, to make your sentences lean and tough. If you are really working at it, your first draft will greatly exceed the required total, and then you will work it down, thus:

> It is thought in some quarters that fraternities do not contribute as much as might be expected to campus life.
> Some people think that fraternities contribute little to campus life.

> The average doctor who practices in small towns or in the country must toil night and day to heal the sick.
> Most country doctors work long hours.

> When I was a little girl, I suffered from shyness and embarrassment in the presence of others.
> I was a shy little girl.

> It is absolutely necessary for the person employed as a marine fireman to give the matter of steam pressure his undivided attention at all times.
> The fireman has to keep his eye on the steam gauge.

You may ask how you can arrive at five hundred words at this rate. Simply. You dig up more real content. Instead of taking a couple of obvious points off the surface of the topic and then circling warily around them for six paragraphs, you work in and explore, figure out the details. You illustrate. You say that fast driving is dangerous, and then you prove it. How long does it take to stop a car at forty and at eighty? How far can you see at night? What happens when a tire blows? What happens in a head-on collision at fifty miles an hour? Pretty soon your paper will be full of broken glass and blood and headless torsos, and reaching five hundred words will not really be a problem.

CALL A FOOL A FOOL

Some of the padding in freshman themes is to be blamed not on anxiety about the word minimum but on excessive timidity. The student writes, "In my opinion, the principal of my high school acted in ways that I believe every unbiased person would have to call foolish." This isn't exactly what he means. What he means is, "My high school principal was a fool." If he was a fool, call him a fool. Hedging the thing about with "in-my-opinion's" and "it-seems-to-me's" and "as-I-see-it's" and "at-least-from-my-point-of-view's" gains you nothing. Delete these phrases whenever they creep into your paper.

The student's tendency to hedge stems from a modesty that in other 25 circumstances would be commendable. He is, he realizes, young and inexperienced, and he half suspects that he is dopey and fuzzy-minded beyond the average. Probably only too true. But it doesn't help to announce your incompetence six times in every paragraph. Decide what you want to say and say it as vigorously as possible, without apology and in plain words.

Linguistic diffidence can take various forms. One is what we call *euphemism*. This is the tendency to call a spade "a certain garden implement" or women's underwear "unmentionables." It is stronger in some eras than others and in some people than others but it always operates more or less in subjects that are touchy or taboo: death, sex, madness, and so on. Thus we shrink from saying "He died last night" but say instead "passed away," "left us," "joined his Maker," "went to his reward." Or we try to take off the tension with a lighter cliché: "kicked the bucket," "cashed in his chips," "handed in his dinner pail." We have found all sorts of ways to avoid saying *mad:* "mentally ill," "touched," "not quite right upstairs," "feeble-minded," "innocent," "simple," "off his trolley," "not in his right mind." Even such a now plain word as *insane* began as a euphemism with the meaning "not healthy."

Modern science, particularly psychology, contributes many polysyllables in which we can wrap our thoughts and blunt their force. To many writers there is no such thing as a bad schoolboy. Schoolboys are maladjusted or unoriented or misunderstood or in need of guidance or lacking in continued success toward satisfactory integration of the personality as a social unit, but they are never bad. Psychology no doubt makes us better men or women, more sympathetic and tolerant, but it doesn't make writing any easier. Had Shakespeare been confronted with psychology, "To be or not to be" might have come out, "To continue as a social unit or not to do so. That is the personality problem. Whether 'tis a better sign of integration at the conscious level to display a psychic tolerance toward the maladjustments and repressions induced by one's lack of orientation in one's environment or—" But Hamlet would never have finished the soliloquy.

Writing in the modern world, you cannot altogether avoid modern jargon. Nor, in an effort to get away from euphemism, should you salt your paper with four-letter words. But you can do much if you will mount guard against those roundabout phrases, those echoing polysyllables that tend to slip into your writing to rob it of its crispness and force.

BEWARE OF THE PAT EXPRESSION

Other things being equal, avoid phrases like "other things being equal." Those sentences that come to you whole, or in two or three doughy lumps, are sure to be bad sentences. They are no creation of yours but pieces of common thought floating in the community soup.

Pat expressions are hard, often impossible, to avoid, because they 30 come too easily to be noticed and seem too necessary to be dispensed with. No writer avoids them altogether, but good writers avoid them more often than poor writers.

By "pat expressions" we mean such tags as "to all practical intents and purposes," "the pure and simple truth," "from where I sit," "the time of his life," "to the ends of the earth," "in the twinkling of an eye," "as sure as you're born," "over my dead body," "under cover of darkness," "took the easy way out," "when all is said and done," "told him time and time again," "parted the best of friends," "stand up and be counted," "gave him the best years of her life," "worked her fingers to the bone." Like other clichés, these expressions were once forceful. Now we should use them only when we can't possibly think of anything else.

Some pat expressions stand like a wall between the writer and thought. Such a one is "the American way of life." Many student writers feel that when they have said that something accords with the American way of life or does not they have exhausted the subject. Actually, they have stopped at the highest level of abstraction. The American way of life is the complicated set of bonds between a hundred and eighty million ways. All of us know this when we think about it, but the tag phrase too often keeps us from thinking about it.

So with many another phrase dear to the politician: "this great land of ours," "the man in the street," "our national heritage." These may prove our patriotism or give a clue to our political beliefs, but otherwise they add nothing to the paper except words.

COLORFUL WORDS

The writer builds with words, and no builder uses a raw material more slippery and elusive and treacherous. A writer's work is a constant struggle to get the right word in the right place, to find that particular word that will convey his meaning exactly, that will persuade the reader or soothe him or startle or amuse him. He never succeeds altogether—sometimes he feels that he scarcely succeeds at all—but such successes as he has are what make die thing worth doing.

There is no book of rules for this game. One progresses through 35 ever-lasting experiment on the basis of ever-widening experience. There are few useful generalizations that one can make about words as words, but there are perhaps a few.

Some words are what we call "colorful." By this we mean that they are calculated to produce a picture or induce an emotion. They are dressy instead of plain, specific instead of general, loud instead of soft. Thus, in place of "Her heart beat," we may write "Her heart *pounded, throbbed, fluttered, danced.*" Instead of "He sat in his chair," we may say, "He *lounged, sprawled, coiled.*" Instead of "It was hot," we may say, "It was *blistering, sultry, muggy, suffocating, steamy, wilting.*"

However, it should not be supposed that the fancy word is always better. Often it is as well to write "Her heart beat" or "It was hot" if that is all it did or all it was. Ages differ in how they like their prose. The nineteenth century liked it rich and smoky. The twentieth has usually preferred it lean and cool. The twentieth century writer, like all writers, is forever seeking the exact word, but he is wary of sounding feverish. He tends to pitch it low, to understate it, to throw it away. He knows that if he gets too colorful, the audience is likely to giggle.

See how this strikes you: "As the rich, golden glow of the sunset died away along the eternal western hills, Angela's limpid blue eyes looked softly and trustingly into Montague's flashing brown ones, and her heart pounded like a drum in time with the joyous song surging in her soul." Some people like that sort of thing, but most modern readers would say, "Good grief," and turn on the television.

COLORED WORDS

Some words we would call not so much colorful as colored—that is, loaded with associations, good or bad. All words—except perhaps structure words—have associations of some sort. We have said that the meaning of a word is the sum of the contexts in which it occurs. When we hear a word, we hear with it an echo of all the situations in which we have heard it before.

In some words, these echoes are obvious and discussable. The word 40 *mother,* for example, has, for most people, agreeable associations. When you hear *mother* you probably think of home, safety, love, food, and various other pleasant things. If one writes, "She was like a mother to me," he gets an effect which he would not get in "She was like an aunt to me." The advertiser makes use of the associations of *mother* by working it in when he talks about his product. The politician works it in when he talks about himself.

61

So also with such words as *home, liberty, fireside, contentment, patriot, tenderness, sacrifice, childlike, manly, bluff, limpid.* All of these words are loaded with favorable associations that would be rather hard to indicate in a straightforward definition. There is more than a literal difference between "They sat around the fireside" and "They sat around the stove." They might have been equally warm and happy around the stove, but *fireside* suggests leisure, grace, quiet tradition, congenial company, and *stove* does not.

Conversely, some words have bad associations. *Mother* suggests pleasant things, but *mother-in-law* does not. Many mothers-in-law are heroically lovable and some mothers drink gin all day and beat their children insensible, but these facts of life are beside the point. The thing is that *mother* sounds good and *mother-in-law* does not.

Or consider the word *intellectual.* This would seem to be a complimentary term, but in point of fact it is not, for it has picked up associations of impracticality and ineffectuality and general dopiness. So also with such words as *liberal, reactionary, Communist, socialist, capitalist, radical, schoolteacher, truck driver, undertaker, operator, salesman, huckster, speculator.* These convey meanings on the literal level, but beyond that — sometimes, in some places — they convey contempt on the part of the speaker.

The question of whether to use loaded words or not depends on what is being written. The scientist, the scholar, try to avoid them; for the poet, the advertising writer, the public speaker, they are standard equipment. But every writer should take care that they do not substitute for thought. If you write, "Anyone who thinks that is nothing but a Socialist (or Communist or capitalist)" you have said nothing except that you don't like people who think that, and such remarks are effective only with the most naïve readers. It is always a bad mistake to think your readers more naïve than they really are.

COLORLESS WORDS

But probably most student writers come to grief not with words that are colorful or those that are colored but with those that have no color at all. A pet example is *nice,* a word we would find it hard to dispense with in casual conversation but which is no longer capable of adding much to a description. Colorless words are those of such general meaning that in a particular sentence they mean nothing. Slang adjectives, like *cool* ("That's real cool") tend to explode all over the language. They are applied to everything, lose their original force, and quickly die.

Beware also of nouns of very general meaning, like *circumstances, cases, instances, aspects, factors, relationships, attitudes, eventualities,* etc. In most circumstances you will find that those cases of writing which contain too many instances of words like these will in this and other aspects have factors leading to unsatisfactory relationships with the reader resulting in unfavorable attitudes on his part and perhaps other eventualities, like a grade of "D." Notice also what "etc." means. It means "I'd like to make this list longer, but I can't think of any more examples."

PETER ELBOW   [b. 1935]

Freewriting

Peter Elbow received his Ph.D. from Brandeis University in 1969. He has taught at several universities, including M.I.T., the University of Massachusetts at Amherst, and SUNY at Stony Brook, where he directed the writing program. Having experienced the inability to write as a graduate student, he has since written widely on the writing process. Often attempting to demystify the process, Elbow offers practical advice on achieving one's writing goals, tackling such issues as writer's block, freewriting, and, for instructors, teaching and evaluating writing. His most well-known books include *Writing With Power: Techniques for Mastering the Writing Process* (1981), *Embracing Contraries: Essays on Learning and Teaching* (1986), *What Is English?* (1990), and, most recently, *Being a Writer* (2002).

The essay "Freewriting" is taken from Elbow's revolutionary work *Writing Without Teachers* (1973) and discusses the rules of freewriting, which amount to not stopping and not editing as you go. Editing is good to do once a piece of writing has been produced, but editing while producing kills the writer's unique voice.

The most effective way I know to improve your writing is to do freewriting exercises regularly. At least three times a week. They are sometimes called "automatic writing," "babbling," or "jabbering" exercises. The idea is simply to write for ten minutes (later on, perhaps fifteen or twenty). Don't stop for anything. Go quickly without rushing. Never stop to look back, to cross something out, to wonder how to spell something, to wonder what word or thought to use, or to think about what you are doing. If you can't think of a word or a spelling, just use a squiggle or else write, "I can't think of it." Just put down something. The easiest thing is just to put down whatever is in your mind. If you get stuck it's fine to write "I can't think what to say, I can't think what to say" as many times as you want; or to repeat the last word you wrote over and over again; or anything else. The only requirement is that you *never* stop.

What happens to a freewriting exercise is important. It must be a piece of writing which, even if someone reads it, doesn't send any ripples back to you. It is like writing something and putting it in a bottle in the sea. The teacherless class helps your writing by providing maximum feedback. Freewritings help you by providing no feedback at all. When I assign one, I invite the writer to let me read it. But I also tell him to keep it if he prefers. I read it quickly and make no comments at all and I do not speak with him about it. The main thing is that a freewriting must never be evaluated in any way; in fact there must be no discussion or comment at all.

Here is an example of a fairly coherent exercise (sometimes they are very incoherent, which is fine):

> I think I'll write what's on my mind, but the only thing on my mind right now is what to write for ten minutes. I've never done this before and I'm not prepared in any way—the sky is cloudy today, how's that? now I'm afraid I won't be able to think of what to write when I get to the end of the sentence—well, here I am at the end of the sentence—here I am again, again, again, at least I'm still writing—Now I ask is there some reason to be happy that I'm still writing—ah yes! Here comes the question again — What am I getting out of this? What point is there in it? It's almost obscene to always ask it but I seem to question everything that way and I was gonna say something else pertaining to that but I got so busy writing down the first part that I forgot what I was leading into. This is kind of fun oh don't stop writing—cars and trucks speeding by somewhere out the window, pens clittering across peoples' papers. The sky is still cloudy—is it symbolic that I should be mentioning it? Huh? I dunno. Maybe I should try colors, blue, red, dirty words—wait a minute—no can't do that, orange, yellow, arm tired, green pink violet magenta lavender red brown black green—now that I can't think of any more colors—just about done—relief? maybe.

Freewriting may seem crazy but actually it makes simple sense. Think of the difference between speaking and writing. Writing has the advantage of permitting more editing. But that's its downfall too. Almost everybody interposes a massive and complicated series of editings between the time words start to be born into consciousness and when they finally come off the end of the pencil or typewriter onto the page. This is partly because schooling makes us obsessed with the "mistakes" we make in writing. Many people are constantly thinking about spelling and grammar as they try to write. I am always thinking about the awkwardness, wordiness, and general mushiness of my natural verbal product as I try to write down words.

But it's not just "mistakes" or "bad writing" we edit as we write. We 5
also edit unacceptable thoughts and feelings, as we do in speaking. In
writing there is more time to do it so the editing is heavier: when speaking, there's someone right there waiting for a reply and he'll get bored or
think we're crazy if we don't come out with *something*. Most of the time
in speaking, we settle for the catch-as-catch-can way in which the words
tumble out. In writing, however, there's a chance to try to get them right.
But the opportunity to get them right is a terrible burden: you can work
for two hours trying to get a paragraph "right" and discover it's not right
at all. And then give up.

Editing, *in itself*, is not the problem. Editing is usually necessary if we
want to end up with something satisfactory. The problem is that editing
goes on *at the same time* as producing. The editor is, as it were, constantly looking over the shoulder of the producer and constantly fiddling
with what he's doing while he's in the middle of trying to do it. No wonder the producer gets nervous, jumpy, inhibited, and finally can't be
coherent. It's an unnecessary burden to try to think of words and also
worry at the same time whether they're the right words.

The main thing about freewriting is that it is *nonediting*. It is an exercise in bringing together the process of producing words and putting
them down on the page. Practiced regularly, it undoes the ingrained
habit of editing at the same time you are trying to produce. It will make
writing less blocked because words will come more easily. You will use
up more paper, but chew up fewer pencils.

Next time you write, notice how often you stop yourself from writing
down something you were going to write down. Or else cross it out after
it's written. "Naturally," you say, "it wasn't any good." But think for a
moment about the occasions when you spoke well. Seldom was it
because you first got the beginning just right. Usually it was a matter of a
halting or even garbled beginning, but you kept going and your speech
finally became coherent and even powerful. There is a lesson here for
writing: trying to get the beginning just right is a formula for failure —
and probably a secret tactic to make yourself give up writing. Make
some words, whatever they are, and then grab hold of that line and reel
in as hard as you can. Afterwards you can throw away lousy beginnings
and make new ones. This is the quickest way to get into good writing.

The habit of compulsive, premature editing doesn't just make writing
hard. It also makes writing dead. Your voice is damped out by all the
interruptions, changes, and hesitations between the consciousness and
the page. In your natural way of producing words there is a sound, a texture, a rhythm — a voice — which is the main source of power in your
writing. I don't know how it works, but this voice is the force that will
make a reader listen to you, the energy that drives the meanings through

his thick skull. Maybe you don't *like* your voice; maybe people have made fun of it. But it's the only voice you've got. It's your only source of power. You better get back into it, no matter what you think of it. If you keep writing in it, it may change into something you like better. But if you abandon it, you'll likely never have a voice and never be heard.

Freewritings are vacuums. Gradually you will begin to carry over into 10 your regular writing some of the voice, force, and connectedness that creep into those vacuums.

ANNE LAMOTT [b. 1954]

Shitty First Drafts

Born in San Francisco in 1954, **Anne Lamott** is the best-selling author of six novels and several works of nonfiction, including *Operating Instructions*, a brutally honest account of motherhood in her son's first year of life, *Bird by Bird: Some Instructions on Writing and Life*, a riotous handbook for aspiring writers, and *Traveling Mercies*, a collection of autobiographical essays on living with faith. The recipient of a Guggenheim fellowship, a one-time food critic for *California* magazine and book reviewer for *Mademoiselle*, Lamott has taught at the University of California, Davis and at numerous writers' conferences. "Word by Word," her biweekly personal reflections contributed to the online *Salon Magazine* from 1996 to 1999, were voted *The Best of the Web* by *Time* magazine. A self-identified recovering alcoholic and born-again Christian, Lamott's writing is frank, candid, and utterly sincere. Her sharp words and strong sense of humor make for a poignantly entertaining read.

"Shitty First Drafts," an excerpt from her book *Bird by Bird: Some Instructions on Writing and Life*, encourages writers to trust in their writing processes. Lamott shares her own writing methods and drolly suggests ways of blocking out even the most annoying distractions.

For me and most of the other writers I know, writing is not rapturous. In fact, the only way I can get anything written at all is to write really, really crummy first drafts.

The first draft is the child's draft, where you let it all pour out and then let it romp all over the place, knowing that no one is going to see it and that you can shape it later. You just let this childlike part of you channel whatever voices and visions come through and onto the page. If one of the characters wants to say "Well, so what, Mr. Poopy Pants?" you let her. No one is going to see it. If the kid wants to get into really sentimental, weepy, emotional territory, you let him. Just get it all down on paper, because there may be something great in those six crazy pages that you would never have gotten to by more rational, grown-up means. There may be something in the very last line of the very last paragraph on page six that you just love, that is so beautiful or wild that you now know what you're supposed to be writing about, more or less, or in what direction you might go — but there was no way to get to this without first getting through the first five and a half pages.

I used to write food reviews for *California* magazine before it folded. (My writing food reviews had nothing to do with the magazine folding, although every single review did cause a couple of canceled subscriptions. Some readers took umbrage at my comparing mounds of vegetable puree with various ex-presidents' brains.) These reviews always took two days to write. First I'd go to a restaurant several times with a few opinionated, articulate friends in tow. I'd sit there writing down everything anyone said that was at all interesting or funny. Then on the following Monday I'd sit down at my desk with my notes, and try to write the review. Even after I'd been doing this for years, panic would set in. I'd try to write a lead, but instead I'd write a couple of dreadful sentences, XX them out, try again, XX everything out, and then feel despair and worry settle on my chest like an x-ray apron. It's over, I'd think, calmly. I'm not going to be able to get the magic to work this time. I'm ruined. I'm through. I'm toast. Maybe, I'd think, I can get my old job back as a clerk-typist. But probably not. I'd get up and study my teeth in the mirror for a while. Then I'd stop, remember to breathe, make a few phone calls, hit the kitchen and chow down. Eventually I'd go back and sit down at my desk, and sigh for the next ten minutes. Finally I would pick up my one-inch picture frame, stare into it as if for the answer, and every time the answer would come: all I had to do was to write a really crummy first draft of, say, the opening paragraph. And no one was going to see it.

So I'd start writing without reining myself in. It was almost just typing, just making my fingers move. And the writing would be *terrible*. I'd write a lead paragraph that was a whole page, even though the entire review could only be three pages long, and then I'd start writing up descriptions of the food, one dish at a time, bird by bird, and the critics would be sitting on my shoulders, commenting like cartoon characters. They'd be pretending to snore, or rolling their eyes at my overwrought descriptions, no matter how hard I tried to tone those descriptions down, no matter how conscious I was of what a friend said to me gently in my early days of restaurant reviewing. "Annie," she said, "it is just a piece of *chicken*. It is just a bit of *cake*."

But because by then I had been writing for so long, I would eventually 5 let myself trust the process — sort of, more or less. I'd write a first draft that was maybe twice as long as it should be, with a self-indulgent and boring beginning, stupefying descriptions of the meal, lots of quotes from my black-humored friends that made them sound more like the

Manson girls° than food lovers, and no ending to speak of. The whole thing would be so long and incoherent and hideous that for the rest of the day I'd obsess about getting creamed by a car before I could write a decent second draft. I'd worry that people would read what I'd written and believe that the accident had really been a suicide, that I had panicked because my talent was waning and my mind was shot.

The next day, though, I'd sit down, go through it all with a colored pen, take out everything I possibly could, find a new lead somewhere on the second page, figure out a kicky place to end it, and then write a second draft. It always turned out fine, sometimes even funny and weird and helpful. I'd go over it one more time and mail it in.

Then, a month later, when it was time for another review, the whole process would start again, complete with the fears that people would find my first draft before I could rewrite it.

Almost all good writing begins with terrible first efforts. You need to start somewhere. Start by getting something—anything—down on paper. A friend of mine says that the first draft is the down draft—you just get it down. The second draft is the up draft—you fix it up. You try to say what you have to say more accurately. And the third draft is the dental draft, where you check every tooth, to see if it's loose or cramped or decayed, or even, God help us, healthy.

What I've learned to do when I sit down to work on a crummy first draft is to quiet the voices in my head. First there's the vinegar-lipped Reader Lady, who says primly, "Well, *that's* not very interesting, is it?" And there's the emaciated German male who writes these Orwellian memos detailing your thought crimes. And there are your parents, agonizing over your lack of loyalty and discretion; and there's William Burroughs, dozing off or shooting up because he finds you as bold and articulate as a houseplant; and so on. And there are also the dogs: let's not forget the dogs, the dogs in their pen who will surely hurtle and snarl their way out if you ever *stop* writing, because writing is, for some of us, the latch that keeps the door of the pen closed, keeps those crazy, ravenous dogs contained. [. . .]

Close your eyes and get quiet for a minute, until the chatter starts up. 10
Then isolate one of the voices and imagine the person speaking as a mouse. Pick it up by the tail and drop it into a mason jar. Then isolate another voice, pick it up by the tail, drop it in the jar. And so on. Drop in any high-maintenance parental units, drop in any contractors, lawyers, colleagues, children, anyone who is whining in your head. Then put the lid on, and watch all these mouse people clawing at the glass, jabbering away, trying to make you feel crummy because you won't do what they

Manson girls: Young, troubled, members of a cult led by Charles Manson (b. 1934). In 1969 Manson and some of his followers were convicted of murder in California.

want—won't give them more money, won't be more successful, won't see them more often. Then imagine that there is a volume-control button on the bottle. Turn it all the way up for a minute, and listen to the stream of angry, neglected, guilt-mongering voices. Then turn it all the way down and watch the frantic mice lunge at the glass, trying to get to you. Leave it down, and get back to your crummy first draft.

A writer friend of mine suggests opening the jar and shooting them all in the head. But I think he's a little angry, and I'm sure nothing like this would ever occur to you.

JONATHAN KOZOL   [b. 1960]

The Human Cost of an
Illiterate Society

Jonathan Kozol is a nonfiction writer, educator, and social activist. In
the mid-sixties, Kozol moved from Harvard Square to teach in a poor
section of Boston. He was fired from his position in the Boston school
system for reading the poetical works of Langston Hughes. As a result,
he became engaged with the politics that permeated the curriculum.
After accepting a job in the more liberal Newton school system, Kozol
devoted more time to issues of racial and social justice and to writing
about the conditions of the schools. His first book, *Death at an Early
Age: The Destruction of the Hearts and Minds of Negro Children in the
Boston Public Schools* (1967), received the National Book Award. His
other works include *The Night Is Dark and I Am Far From Home*
(1975), *Savage Inequalities: Children in America's Schools* (1991), and
Amazing Grace: The Lives of Children and the Conscience of a Nation
(1995). Originally, "The Human Cost of an Illiterate Society" was a
chapter of *Illiterate America* (1985), an analysis of the nature and
causes of illiteracy. The essay proposes a definition of illiteracy as a
condition that degrades the quality of life and makes the illiterate vulnerable, and is as relevant today as when it was written.

> PRECAUTIONS. READ BEFORE USING.
> Poison: Contains sodium hydroxide (caustic soda-lye).
> Corrosive: Causes severe eye and skin damage, may cause
>   blindness.
> Harmful or fatal if swallowed.
> If swallowed, give large quantities of milk or water.
> Do not induce vomiting.
> Important: Keep water out of can at all times to prevent
>   contents from violently erupting . . .
> — WARNING ON A CAN OF DRĀNO

We are speaking here no longer of the dangers faced by passengers on Eastern Airlines or the dollar costs incurred by U.S. corporations and tax-payers. We are speaking now of human suffering and of the ethical dilemmas that are faced by a society that looks upon such suffering with qualified concern but does not take those actions which its wealth and ingenuity would seemingly demand.

Questions of literacy, in Socrates' belief, must at length be judged as matters of morality. Socrates could not have had in mind the moral compromise peculiar to a nation like our own. Some of our Founding Fathers did, however, have this question in their minds. One of the wisest of those Founding Fathers (one who may not have been most compassionate but surely was more prescient than some of his peers) recognized the special dangers that illiteracy would pose to basic equity in the political construction that he helped to shape.

"A people who mean to be their own governors," James Madison wrote, "must arm themselves with the power knowledge gives. A popular government without popular information or the means of acquiring it, is but a prologue to a farce or a tragedy, or perhaps both."

Tragedy looms larger than farce in the United States today. Illiterate citizens seldom vote. Those who do are forced to cast a vote of questionable worth. They cannot make informed decisions based on serious print information. Sometimes they can be alerted to their interests by aggressive voter education. More frequently, they vote for a face, a smile, or a style, not for a mind or character or body of beliefs.

The number of illiterate adults exceeds by 16 million the entire vote cast for the winner in the 1980 presidential contest. If even one third of all illiterates could vote, and read enough and do sufficient math to vote in their self-interest, Ronald Reagan would not likely have been chosen president. There is, of course, no way to know for sure. We do know this: Democracy is a mendacious term when used by those who are prepared to countenance the forced exclusion of one third of our electorate. So long as 60 million people are denied significant participation, the government is neither of, nor for, nor by, the people. It is a government, at best, of those two thirds whose wealth, skin color, or parental privilege allows them opportunity to profit from the provocation and instruction of the written word.

The undermining of democracy in the United States is one "expense" that sensitive Americans can easily deplore because it represents a contradiction that endangers citizens of all political positions. The human price is not so obvious at first.

Since I first immersed myself within this work I have often had the following dream: I find that I am in a railroad station or a large department store within a city that is utterly unknown to me and where I cannot

73

understand the printed words. None of the signs or symbols is familiar. Everything looks strange: like mirror writing of some kind. Gradually I understand that I am in the Soviet Union. All the letters on the walls around me are Cyrillic. I look for my pocket dictionary but I find that it has been mislaid. Where have I left it? Then I recall that I forgot to bring it with me when I packed my bags in Boston. I struggle to remember the name of my hotel. I try to ask somebody for directions. One person stops and looks at me in a peculiar way. I lose the nerve to ask. At last I reach into my wallet for an ID card. The card is missing. Have I lost it? Then I remember that my card was confiscated for some reason, many years before. Around this point, I wake up in a panic.

This panic is not so different from the misery that millions of adult illiterates experience each day within the course of their routine existence in the U.S.A.

Illiterates cannot read the menu in a restaurant.

They cannot read the cost of items on the menu in the *window* of the restaurant before they enter.

Illiterates cannot read the letters that their children bring home from their teachers. They cannot study school department circulars that tell them of the courses that their children must be taking if they hope to pass the SAT exams. They cannot help with homework. They cannot write a letter to the teacher. They are afraid to visit in the classroom. They do not want to humiliate their child or themselves.

Illiterates cannot read instructions on a bottle of prescription medicine. They cannot find out when a medicine is past the year of safe consumption; nor can they read of allergenic risks, warnings to diabetics, or the potential sedative effect of certain kinds of nonprescription pills. They cannot observe preventive health care admonitions. They cannot read about "the seven warning signs of cancer" or the indications of blood-sugar fluctuations or the risks of eating certain foods that aggravate the likelihood of cardiac arrest.

Illiterates live, in more than literal ways, an uninsured existence. They cannot understand the written details on a health insurance form. They cannot read the waivers that they sign preceding surgical procedures. Several women I have known in Boston have entered a slum hospital with the intention of obtaining a tubal ligation and have emerged a few days later after having been subjected to a hysterectomy. Unaware of their rights, incognizant of jargon, intimidated by the unfamiliar air of fear and atmosphere of ether that so many of us find oppressive in the confines even of the most attractive and expensive medical facilities, they have signed their names to documents they could not read and which nobody, in the hectic situation that prevails so often in those overcrowded hospitals that serve the urban poor, had even bothered to explain.

74

Childbirth might seem to be the last inalienable right of any female citizen within a civilized society. Illiterate mothers, as we shall see, already have been cheated of the power to protect their progeny against the likelihood of demolition in deficient public schools and, as a result, against the verbal servitude within which they themselves exist. Surgical denial of the right to bear that child in the first place represents an ultimate denial, an unspeakable metaphor, a final darkness that denies even the twilight gleamings of our own humanity. What greater violation of our biological, our biblical, our spiritual humanity could possibly exist than that which takes place nightly, perhaps hourly these days, within such overburdened and benighted institutions as the Boston City Hospital? Illiteracy has many costs; few are so irreversible as this.

Even the roof above one's head, the gas or other fuel for heating that 15 protects the residents of northern city slums against the threat of illness in the winter months become uncertain guarantees. Illiterates cannot read the lease that they must sign to live in an apartment which, too often, they cannot afford. They cannot manage check accounts and therefore seldom pay for anything by mail. Hours and entire days of difficult travel (and the cost of bus or other public transit) must be added to the real cost of whatever they consume. Loss of interest on the check accounts they do not have, and could not manage if they did, must be regarded as another of the excess costs paid by the citizen who is excluded from the common instruments of commerce in a numerate society.

"I couldn't understand the bills," a woman in Washington, D.C., reports, "and then I couldn't write the checks to pay them. We signed things we didn't know what they were."

Illiterates cannot read the notices that they receive from welfare offices or from the IRS. They must depend on word-of-mouth instruction from the welfare worker—or from other persons whom they have good reason to mistrust. They do not know what rights they have, what deadlines and requirements they face, what options they might choose to exercise. They are half-citizens. Their rights exist in print but not in fact.

Illiterates cannot look up numbers in a telephone directory. Even if they can find the names of friends, few possess the sorting skills to make use of the yellow pages; categories are bewildering and trade names are beyond decoding capabilities for millions of nonreaders. Even the emergency numbers listed on the first page of the phone book—"Ambulance," "Police," and "Fire"—are too frequently beyond the recognition of nonreaders.

Many illiterates cannot read the admonition on a pack of cigarettes. Neither the Surgeon General's warning nor its reproduction on the package can alert them to the risks. Although most people learn by word of mouth that smoking is related to a number of grave physical disorders, they do not get the chance to read the detailed stories which can document this danger with the vividness that turns concern into determination to resist. They can see the handsome cowboy or the slim Virginia lady lighting up a filter cigarette; they cannot heed the words that tell them that this product is (not "may be") dangerous to their health. Sixty million men and women are condemned to be the unalerted, high-risk candidates for cancer.

Illiterates do not buy "no-name" products in the supermarkets. They 20 must depend on photographs or the familiar logos that are printed on the packages of brand-name groceries. The poorest people, therefore, are denied the benefits of the least costly products.

Illiterates depend almost entirely upon label recognition. Many labels, however, are not easy to distinguish. Dozens of different kinds of Campbell's soup appear identical to the nonreader. The purchaser who cannot read and does not dare to ask for help, out of the fear of being stigmatized (a fear which is unfortunately realistic), frequently comes home with something which she never wanted and her family never tasted.

Illiterates cannot read instructions on a pack of frozen food. Packages sometimes provide an illustration to explain the cooking preparations; but illustrations are of little help to someone who must "boil water, drop the food— *within* its plastic wrapper—in the boiling water, wait for it to simmer, instantly remove."

Even when labels are seemingly clear, they may be easily mistaken. A woman in Detroit brought home a gallon of Crisco for her children's dinner. She thought that she had bought the chicken that was pictured on the label. She had enough Crisco now to last a year—but no more money to go back and buy the food for dinner.

Recipes provided on the packages of certain staples sometimes tempt a semiliterate person to prepare a meal her children have not tasted. The longing to vary the uniform and often starchy content of low-budget meals provided to the family that relies on food stamps commonly leads to ruinous results. Scarce funds have been wasted and the food must be thrown out. The same applies to distribution of food-surplus produce in emergency conditions. Government inducements to poor people to "explore the ways" by which to make a tasty meal from tasteless noodles, surplus cheese, and powdered milk are useless to nonreaders. Intended as benevolent advice, such recommendations mock reality and foster deeper feelings of resentment and of inability to cope. (Those, on the other hand, who cautiously refrain from "innovative" recipes in preparation of their children's meals must suffer the opprobrium of "laziness," "lack of imagination . . .")

Illiterates cannot travel freely. When they attempt to do so, they 25 encounter risks that few of us can dream of. They cannot read traffic

76

signs and, while they often learn to recognize and to decipher symbols, they cannot manage street names which they haven't seen before. The same is true for bus and subway stops. While ingenuity can sometimes help a man or woman to discern directions from familiar landmarks, buildings, cemeteries, churches, and the like, most illiterates are virtually immobilized. They seldom wander past the streets and neighborhoods they know. Geographical paralysis becomes a bitter metaphor for their entire existence. They are immobilized in almost every sense we can imagine. They can't move up. They can't move out. They cannot see beyond. Illiterates may take an oral test for drivers' permits in most sections of America. It is a questionable concession. Where will they go? How will they get there? How will they get home? Could it be that some of us might like it better if they stayed where they belong?

Travel is only one of many instances of circumscribed existence. Choice, in almost all of its facets, is diminished in the life of an illiterate adult. Even the printed TV schedule, which provides most people with the luxury of preselection, does not belong within the arsenal of options in illiterate existence. One consequence is that the viewer watches only what appears at moments when he happens to have time to turn the switch. Another consequence, a lot more common, is that the TV set remains in operation night and day. Whatever the program offered at the hour when he walks into the room will be the nutriment that he accepts and swallows. Thus, to passivity, is added frequency—indeed, almost uninterrupted continuity. Freedom to select is no more possible here than in the choice of home or surgery or food.

"You don't choose," said one illiterate woman. "You take your wishes from somebody else." Whether in perusal of a menu, selection of highways, purchase of groceries, or determination of affordable enjoyment, illiterate Americans must trust somebody else: a friend, a relative, a stranger on the street, a grocery clerk, a TV copywriter.

"All of our mail we get, it's hard for her to read. Settin' down and writing a letter, she can't do it. Like if we get a bill . . . we take it over to my sister-in-law . . . My sister-in-law reads it."

Billing agencies harass poor people for the payment of the bills for purchases that might have taken place six months before. Utility companies offer an agreement for a staggered payment schedule on a bill past due. "You have to trust them," one man said. Precisely for this reason, you end up by trusting no one and suspecting everyone of possible deceit. A submerged sense of distrust becomes the corollary to a constant need to trust. "They are cheating me . . . I have been tricked . . . I do not know . . ."

Not knowing: This a familiar theme. Not knowing the right word for 30 the right thing at the right time is one form of subjugation. Not knowing the world that lies concealed behind those words is a more terrifying feeling. The longitude and latitude of one's existence are beyond all easy apprehension. Even the hard, cold stars within the firmament above one's head begin to mock the possibilities for self-location. Where am I? Where did I come from? Where will I go?

"I've lost a lot of jobs," one man explains. "Today, even if you're a janitor, there's still reading and writing . . . They leave a note saying, 'Go to room so-and-so . . .' You can't do it. You can't read it. You don't know."

"The hardest thing about it is that I've been places where I didn't know where I was. You don't know where you are . . . You're lost."

"Like I said: I have two kids. What do I do if one my kids starts choking? I go running to the phone . . . I can't look up the hospital phone number. That's if we're at home. Out on the street, I can't read the sign. I get to a pay phone. 'Okay, tell us where you are. We'll send an ambulance.' I look at the street sign. Right there, I can't tell you what it says. I'd have to spell it out, letter for letter. By that time, one of my kids would be dead . . . These are the kinds of fears you go with, every single day . . ."

"Reading directions, I suffer with. I work with chemicals . . . That's scary to begin with . . ."

"You sit down. They throw the menu in front of you. Where do you go 35 from there? Nine times out of ten you say, 'Go ahead. Pick out something for the both of us.' I've eaten some weird things, let me tell you!"

Menus. Chemicals. A child choking while his mother searches for a word she does not know to find assistance that will come too late. Another mother speaks about the inability to help her kids to read: "I can't read to them. Of course that's leaving them out of something they should have. Oh, it matters. You *believe* it matters! I ordered all these books. The kids belong to a book club. Donny wanted me to read a book to him. I told Donny: 'I can't read.' He said: 'Mommy, you sit down. I'll read it to you.' I tried it one day, reading from the pictures. Donny looked at me. He said, 'Mommy, that's not right.' He's only five. He knew I couldn't read . . ."

A landlord tells a woman that her lease allows him to evict her if her baby cries and causes inconvenience to her neighbors. The consequence of challenging his words conveys a danger which appears, unlikely as it seems, even more alarming than the danger of eviction. Once she admits that she can't read, in the desire to maneuver for the time in which to call a friend, she will have defined herself in terms of an explicit impotence that she cannot endure. Capitulation in this case is preferable to self-humiliation. Resisting the definition of oneself in terms of what one cannot do, what others take for granted, represents a need so great that other imperatives (even one so urgent as the need to keep one's home in winter's cold) evaporate and fall away in face of fear. Even the loss of home and shelter, in this case, is not so terrifying as the loss of self.

"I come out of school. I was sixteen. They had their meetings. The directors meet. They said that I was wasting their school paper. I was wasting pencils . . ."

Another illiterate, looking back, believes she was not worthy of her teacher's time. She believes that it was wrong of her to take up space within her school. She believes that it was right to leave in order that somebody more deserving could receive her place.

Children choke. Their mother chokes another way: on more than 40
chicken bones.

People eat what others order, know what others tell them, struggle not to see themselves as they believe the world perceives them. A man in California speaks about his own loss of identity, of self-location, definition: "I stood at the bottom of the ramp. My car had broke down on the freeway. There was a phone. I asked for the police. They was nice. They said to tell them where I was. I looked up at the signs. There was one that I had seen before. I read it to them: ONE WAY STREET. They thought it was a joke. I told them I couldn't read. There was other signs above the ramp. They told me to try. I looked around for somebody to help. All the cars was going by real fast. I couldn't make them understand that I was lost. The cop was nice. He told me: 'Try once more.' I did my best. I couldn't read. I only knew the sign above my head. The cop was trying to be nice. He knew that I was trapped. 'I can't send out a car to you if you can't tell me where you are.' I felt afraid. I nearly cried. 'I'm forty-eight years old. I only said: 'I'm on a one-way street . . .' "

Perhaps we might slow down a moment here and look at the realities described above. This is the nation that we live in. This is a society that most of us did not create but which our President and other leaders have been willing to sustain by virtue of malign neglect. Do we possess the character and courage to address a problem which so many nations, poorer than our own, have found it natural to correct?

The answers to these questions represent a reasonable test of our belief in the democracy to which we have been asked in public school to swear allegiance.

THOMAS H. BENTON [b. 1968]

The Seven Deadly Sins
of Students

Thomas H. Benton is the pen name of William Pannapacker, an associate professor of English at Hope College in Holland, Michigan. Born in New Jersey, Pannapacker received his Ph.D. in the history of American civilization from Harvard University in 1999 and has published widely on Walt Whitman. His published works include *Revised Lives: Walt Whitman and Nineteenth-Century Authorship* (2004), and he is currently working on a scholarly monograph entitled *Walt Whitman's Cities*, two chapters of which have been published as articles in *Leaves of Grass: The Sesquicentennial Essays* (2007) and *A Companion to Walt Whitman* (2005). Using his pseudonym, Pannapacker also publishes regularly in the *Chronicle of Higher Education* about life and careers in academia.

Using the traditional framework of the "Seven Deadly Sins," Pannapacker analyzes the troubling behavior he has witnessed of undergraduate students in his classes in the following purported sermon. He laments that the consumer mentality many students bring to the classroom is accompanied by a sense of entitlement, particularly in terms of their grades. Per Pannapacker's promise, this article was succeeded by "The Seven Deadly Sins of Professors," published in the *Chronicle of Higher Education* in May 2006.

I've been teaching for about 10 years now, and, of course, I was a student for 20 years before that. So I have some experience observing my students' sins, and perhaps even more experience committing them.

The sins that I see in the everyday life of the typical college student are not great ones. Most of the time, they don't seem like "sins" at all, even if one accepts the religious significance of the term. But they spring from thoughts and behaviors that, over time, become habits.

Enabled by institutions, students repeatedly take the path of least resistance, imagining they are making creative compromises with duty that express their unique talents. So they choose self-indulgence instead of self-denial and self-esteem instead of self-questioning. They do not understand that those choices will eventually cause more unhappiness than the more difficult paths they chose not to walk.

The traditional model of the "Seven Deadly Sins" provides a helpful means of categorizing—and perhaps simplifying—the complicated and cumulative experience I am trying to describe:

Sloth: Students often postpone required readings and assigned prepa- 5 rations, making it hard for them to understand their classes the next day. Gradually, lectures and discussions that were once interesting start to seem boring and irrelevant, and the temptation to skip classes becomes greater and greater, especially when the classes are in the morning. Sometimes students arrive late with—in my opinion—insufficient shame, closing the door behind them with a bang. Slothful students regard themselves as full of potential, and so they make a bargain: "I will be lazy now, but I will work hard later." Like St. Augustine, students say to themselves, "Let me be chaste, but not yet." More on lust later.

Greed: Students often pursue degrees not for the sake of learning itself but with the aim of getting a better-paying job, so they can buy a bigger house and fancier cars than those owned by their parents and their neighbors. That often leads to greed for grades that they have not earned. Some students cheat on exams or plagiarize their papers; others, sometimes the most diligent, harass professors into giving them grades unjustified by their performance. The goal of such cheaters and grade-grubbers is not the reality of achievement but the appearance of it. They will then apply to graduate programs or entry-level jobs that they do not really desire and for which they are not really qualified. They want to be lawyers, but they are bored by law courses. They want to be doctors, but they do not care about healing people. They want to go into business, not to provide useful products and services, but to get rich by any means necessary. And so they come to believe that no one has integrity and that there is no basis—other than the marketplace—by which value can be judged.

Anger: Seemingly more often than in the past, professors encounter students who are angered by challenging assignments, which they label—with bureaucratic self-assurance—"unfair" or even "discrimina-tory." When students do not succeed, they sometimes conclude that their professors are "out to get them" because of some vague prejudice. Students feel entitled to deference by professors who "work for them and should act like it." They do not come to office hours for clarification about an A–; instead, they argue that they are paying a lot of money and, therefore, deserve a high grade, and, if you don't give it to them, they will "complain to management," as if they were sending back food in a restaurant. One hears rumors of cars and homes vandalized by angry students. But, perhaps, the easiest places to find uncensored student rage are the anonymous, libelous evaluations of faculty members found online at Web sites such as RateMyProfessors.com. Often those evaluations say less about the quality of a teacher than they do about the wounded pride of coddled students. More on that topic soon.

Lust: I have seen students come to classes barefoot, with bare midriffs and shoulders, in boxer shorts, bathing suits, and other kinds of clothes that, even by fairly casual standards, are more appropriate for street-walking than higher learning. When did liberation from uniforms transform itself into the social demand that one prepare to be ogled in the classroom? It is hardly a surprise that on RateMyProfessors.com, students are asked to rate their professors' "hotness"—in other words, the teachers' worthiness to be sexually fantasized about by bored students. Even in high-school classes, as an observer of novice teachers, I have overheard lewd remarks about female teachers from denizens of the back row who fear no rebuke because none is forthcoming from the current culture.

Gluttony: It hardly needs saying that most colleges struggle to control alcohol consumption by students and the embarrassing incidents and tragedies that result from it. But there are other manifestations of gluttony these days. For example, when did it become acceptable for students to eat and drink in class as if they were sitting in a cafeteria? Nowadays, I occasionally encounter a student who thinks it's OK to consume a large, messy, and odorous meal in class. I once saw a student eat an entire rotisserie chicken, a tub of mashed potatoes with gravy, several biscuits, and an enormous soft drink during the first 10 minutes of a lecture. I felt like a jester in the court of Henry VIII. It seems hard these days to find a student in class whose mouth is not stuffed with food. Such students will often say that they have no other time to eat, but previous generations—who were no less busy—managed to consume small snacks between classes. That is why colleges have vending machines.

Envy: I think competition is a good thing in education; up to a point, it 10 encourages students to work harder and excel. But the envious student, perhaps daunted by some temporary setback, comes to believe that education is "a rigged game." Envy is the voice of resignation that cringes at the success of one's peers: "Listen to her, trying to impress the teacher, like she's so brilliant. I hate her." Envy is the feeling that no one "earns" anything because there are no objective criteria of accomplishment; and, as a result, success and failure seem to be based on political and personal preferences. But envy is not limited to differences in effort and ability. Even more pervasive is a sense of unjustified economic inequality, but, it seems to me, the fashionable students in their convertibles who jeer the commuters at the bus stop commit a greater sin than those who envy their money and status.

Pride: I once asked a group of 20 students how many thought they were "better than their parents"? All of them raised their hands. I didn't ask, but I assume they all believed they were better than their teachers too. They would rise higher, be more successful, and transcend the limitations of their elders. We read this belief in our students' expressions: "What you know is not worth learning. They're just your opinions anyway. I am young. I have infinite potential. You are old. And you're just a college professor. But I will be rich and famous someday." They have rarely been given a realistic assessment of their abilities and prospects. Out of this pride—nurtured by the purveyors of unearned self-esteem, personal grievance, dumbed-down courses, and inflated grades (often in the guise of liberality)—the opportunity to earn an education is squandered by prideful students who can make a potential heaven seem like hell.

The concept of the "Seven Deadly Sins" comes out of the Christian tradition, but it also has value as an ethical guide or at least as a means of avoiding unhappiness. Increasingly, as a professor who teaches undergraduates, I believe that one of the paramount purposes of a liberal-arts education is to help young people acquire the wisdom to escape those sins, particularly the last one from which the others often spring.

A liberal-arts education, as I see it, is not about acquiring wealth and opportunities to further indulge one's desires. Nor is it about cultivating in students an insular, idolatrous view of their nation, ethnic group, gender, or religion. It is also not about celebrating the so-called "great tradition" of authors, philosophers, and artists.

It is about the recognition, ultimately, of how little one really knows, or can know. A liberal-arts education, most of all, fights unmerited pride by asking students to recognize the smallness of their ambitions in the context of human history, and more. Whether it is grounded in faith or not, a liberal-arts education should help students to combat the Seven Deadly Sins with the "Seven Contrary Virtues" of diligence, generosity, patience, chastity, moderation, contentment and, most important of all, humility.

Of course, moral perfection seldom arrives at graduation, even in 15 the best of cases. I teach the courses, and yet I must present myself, at last, as the "Chief of Sinners." The behaviors I observe in students often reflect the deeper drives—the resentments and weaknesses—of their teachers. Perhaps the impulse to identify the sins of others reflects a corruption more serious than any I have described here. And that is why, next month, I will sermonize on the "Seven Deadly Sins of Professors."

[2006]

HOWARD GARDNER [b. 1943]

A Rounded Version:
The Theory of Multiple
Intelligences

Born in Scranton, Pennsylvania to parents who had fled Nuremberg in 1938, **Howard Gardner** developed ideas about learning that have changed the practice of education in the United States. Educated at Harvard, Gardner graduated with highest honors in 1965. As a graduate student he was influenced by the psychologist Eric Erikson and the cognitive psychologist Jerome Bruner. During his doctoral studies, Gardner became associated with the Project Zero Research Team on arts education, an endeavor that he now codirects. The key point in Gardner's career came in the development of new models for perceiving and measuring intelligence. He outlined his theory in the groundbreaking book *Frames of Mind: The Theory of Multiple Intelligences* (1983). The text asserts that instead of two intelligences, logical and linguistic, human beings possess seven forms, including modes of artistic and personal intelligence. Gardner's influential work led educators and curriculum designers to perceive learning as a multidimensional process that acknowledges variations in human cognition. Gardner has published fifteen books, including *The Unschooled Mind: How Children Learn and How Schools Should Teach* (1991), *Intelligence Reframed* (2000), *The Disciplined Mind* (2000), and *Making Good: How Young People Cope with Moral Dilemmas at Work* (2004).

COAUTHORED BY JOSEPH WALTERS

Two eleven-year-old children are taking a test of "intelligence." They sit at their desks laboring over the meanings of different words, the interpretation of graphs, and the solutions to arithmetic problems. They record their answers by filling in small circles on a single piece of paper.

Later these completed answer sheets are scored objectively: the number of right answers is converted into a standardized score that compares the individual child with a population of children of similar age. The teachers of these children review the different scores. They notice that one of the children has performed at a superior level; on all sections of the test, she answered more questions correctly than did her peers. In fact, her score is similar to that of children three to four years older. The other child's performance is average—his scores reflect those of other children his age.

A subtle change in expectations surrounds the review of these test scores. Teachers begin to expect the first child to do quite well during her formal schooling, whereas the second should have only moderate success. Indeed these predictions come true. In other words, the test taken by the eleven-year-olds serves as a reliable predictor of their later performance in school.

How does this happen? One explanation involves our free use of the word "intelligence": the child with the greater "intelligence" has the ability to solve problems, to find the answers to specific questions, and to learn new material quickly and efficiently. These skills in turn play a central role in school success. In this view, "intelligence" is a singular faculty that is brought to bear in any problem-solving situation. Since schooling deals largely with solving problems of various sorts, predicting this capacity in young children predicts their future success in school.

"Intelligence," from this point of view, is a general ability that is found 5 in varying degrees in all individuals. It is the key to success in solving problems. This ability can be measured reliably with standardized pencil-and-paper tests that, in turn, predict future success in school.

What happens after school is completed? Consider the two individuals in the example. Looking further down the road, we find that the "average" student has become a highly successful mechanical engineer who has risen to a position of prominence in both the professional community of engineers as well as in civic groups in his community. His success is no fluke—he is considered by all to be a talented individual. The "superior" student, on the other hand, has had little success in her chosen career as a writer; after repeated rejections by publishers, she has taken up a middle management position in a bank. While certainly not a "failure," she is considered by her peers to be quite "ordinary" in her adult accomplishments. So what happened?

This fabricated example is based on the facts of intelligence testing. IQ tests predict school performance with considerable accuracy, but they are only an indifferent predictor of performance in a profession after formal schooling.[1] Furthermore, even as IQ tests measure only logical or logical-linguistic capacities, in this society we are nearly "brain-washed" to restrict the notion of intelligence to the capacities used in solving logical and linguistic problems.

To introduce an alternative point of view, undertake the following "thought experiment." Suspend the usual judgment of what constitutes intelligence and let your thoughts run freely over the capabilities of humans—perhaps those that would be picked out by the proverbial Martian visitor. In this exercise, you are drawn to the brilliant chess player, the world-class violinist, and the champion athlete; such outstanding performers deserve special consideration. Under this experiment, a quite different view of *intelligence* emerges. Are the chess player, violinist, and athlete "intelligent" in these pursuits? If they are, then why do our tests of "intelligence" fail to identify them? If they are not "intelligent," what allows them to achieve such astounding feats? In general, why does the contemporary construct "intelligence" fail to explain large areas of human endeavor?

In this chapter we approach these problems through the theory of multiple intelligences (MI). As the name indicates, we believe that human cognitive competence is better described in terms of a set of abilities, talents, or mental skills, which we call "intelligences." All normal individuals possess each of these skills to some extent; individuals differ in the degree of skill and in the nature of their combination. We believe this theory of intelligence may be more humane and more veridical° than alternative views of intelligence and that it more adequately reflects the data of human "intelligent" behavior. Such a theory has important educational implications, including ones for curriculum development.

WHAT CONSTITUTES AN INTELLIGENCE?

The question of the optimal definition of intelligence looms large in   10
our inquiry. Indeed, it is at the level of this definition that the theory of multiple intelligences diverges from traditional points of view. In a traditional view, intelligence is defined operationally as the ability to answer items on tests of intelligence. The inference from the test scores to some underlying ability is supported by statistical techniques that compare responses of subjects at different ages; the apparent correlation of these test scores across ages and across different tests corroborates the notion that the general faculty of intelligence, g, does not change much with age or with training or experience. It is an inborn attribute or faculty of the individual.

veridical: Telling the truth.

Multiple intelligences theory, on the other hand, pluralizes the traditional concept. An intelligence entails the ability to solve problems or fashion products that are of consequence in a particular cultural setting or community. The problem-solving skill allows one to approach a situation in which a goal is to be obtained and to locate the appropriate route to that goal. The creation of a *cultural* product is crucial to such functions as capturing and transmitting knowledge or expressing one's views or feelings. The problems to be solved range from creating an end for a story to anticipating a mating move in chess to repairing a quilt. Products range from scientific theories to musical compositions to successful political campaigns.

MI theory is framed in light of the biological origins of each problem-solving skill. Only those skills that are universal to the human species are treated. Even so, the biological proclivity to participate in a particular form of problem solving must also be coupled with the cultural nurturing of that domain. For example, language, a universal skill, may manifest itself particularly as writing in one culture, as oratory in another culture, and as the secret language of anagrams in a third.

Given the desire of selecting intelligences that are rooted in biology, and that are valued in one or more cultural settings, how does one actually identify an "intelligence"? In coming up with our list, we consulted evidence from several different sources: knowledge about normal development and development in gifted individuals; information about the breakdown of cognitive skills under conditions of brain damage; studies of exceptional populations, including prodigies, idiots savants, and autistic children; data about the evolution of cognition over the millennia; cross-cultural accounts of cognition; psychometric studies, including examinations of correlations among tests; and psychological training studies, particularly measures of transfer and generalization across tasks. Only those candidate intelligences that satisfied all or a majority of the criteria were selected as bona fide intelligences. A more complete discussion of each of these criteria for an "intelligence" and the seven intelligences that have been proposed so far, is found in *Frames of Mind*.[2] This book also considers how the theory might be disproven and compares it to competing theories of intelligence.

In addition to satisfying the aforementioned criteria, each intelligence must have an identifiable core operation or set of operations. As a neutrally based computational system, each intelligence is activated or "triggered" by certain kinds of internally or externally presented information. For example, one core of musical intelligence is the sensitivity to pitch relations, whereas one core of linguistic intelligence is the sensitivity to phonological features.

An intelligence must also be susceptible to encoding in a symbol 15 system — a culturally contrived system of meaning, which captures and conveys important forms of information. Language, picturing, and mathematics are but three nearly worldwide symbol systems that are necessary for human survival and productivity. The relationship of a candidate intelligence to a human symbol system is no accident. In fact, the existence of a core computational capacity anticipates the existence of a symbol system that exploits that capacity. While it may be possible for an intelligence to proceed without an accompanying symbol system, a primary characteristic of human intelligence may well be its gravitation toward such an embodiment.

THE SEVEN INTELLIGENCES

Having sketched the characteristics and criteria of an intelligence, we turn now to a brief consideration of each of the seven intelligences. We begin each sketch with a thumbnail biography of a person who demonstrates an unusual facility with that intelligence. These biographies illustrate some of the abilities that are central to the fluent operation of a given intelligence. Although each biography illustrates a particular intelligence, we do not wish to imply that in adulthood intelligences operate in isolation. Indeed, except for abnormal individuals, intelligences always work in concert, and any sophisticated adult role will involve a melding of several of them. Following each biography we survey the various sources of data that support each candidate as an "intelligence."

Musical Intelligence

When he was three years old, Yehudi Menuhin was smuggled into the San Francisco Orchestra concerts by his parents. The sound of Louis Persinger's violin so entranced the youngster that he insisted on a violin for his birthday and Louis Persinger as his teacher. He got both. By the time he was ten years old, Menuhin was an international performer.[3]

Violinist Yehudi Menuhin's musical intelligence manifested itself even before he had touched a violin or received any musical training. His powerful reaction to that particular sound and his rapid progress on the instrument suggest that he was biologically prepared in some way for that endeavor. In this way evidence from child prodigies supports our claim that there is a biological link to a particular intelligence. Other special populations, such as autistic children who can play a musical instrument beautifully but who cannot speak, underscore the independence of musical intelligence.

A brief consideration of the evidence suggests that musical skill passes the other tests for an intelligence. For example, certain parts of the brain play important roles in perception and production of music. These areas are characteristically located in the right hemisphere, although musical skill is not as clearly "localized," or located in a specifiable area, as language. Although the particular susceptibility of musical ability to brain damage depends on the degree of training and other individual differences, there is clear evidence for "amusia" or loss of musical ability.

Music apparently played an important unifying role in Stone Age (Paleolithic) societies. Birdsong provides a link to other species. Evidence from various cultures supports the notion that music is a universal faculty. Studies of infant development suggest that there is a "raw" computational ability in early childhood. Finally, musical notation provides an accessible and lucid symbol system.

In short, evidence to support the interpretation of musical ability as 20 an "intelligence" comes from many different sources. Even though musical skill is not typically considered an intellectual skill like mathematics, it qualifies under our criteria. By definition it deserves consideration; and in view of the data, its inclusion is empirically justified.

Bodily-Kinesthetic Intelligence

Fifteen-year-old Babe Ruth played third base. During one game his team's pitcher was doing very poorly and Babe loudly criticized him from third base. Brother Mathias, the coach, called out, "Ruth, if you know so much about it, YOU pitch!" Babe was surprised and embarrassed because he had never pitched before, but Brother Mathias insisted. Ruth said later that at the very moment he took the pitcher's mound, he KNEW he was supposed to be a pitcher and that it was "natural" for him to strike people out. Indeed, he went on to become a great major league pitcher (and, of course, attained legendary status as a hitter).[4]

Like Menuhin, Babe Ruth was a child prodigy who recognized his "instrument" immediately upon his first exposure to it. This recognition occurred in advance of formal training.

Control of bodily movement is, of course, localized in the motor cortex, with each hemisphere dominant or controlling bodily movements on the contra-lateral side. In right-handers, the dominance for such movement is ordinarily found in the left hemisphere. The ability to perform movements when directed to do so can be impaired even in individuals who can perform the same movements reflexively or on a nonvoluntary basis. The existence of specific *apraxia* constitutes one line of evidence for a bodily-kinesthetic intelligence.

The evolution of specialized body movements is of obvious advantage to the species, and in humans this adaptation is extended through the use of tools. Body movement undergoes a clearly defined developmental schedule in children. And there is little question of its universality across cultures. Thus it appears that bodily-kinesthetic "knowledge" satisfies many of the criteria for an intelligence.

The consideration of bodily-kinesthetic knowledge as "problem solving" may be less intuitive. Certainly carrying out a mime sequence or hitting a tennis ball is not solving a mathematical equation. And yet, the ability to use one's body to express an emotion (as in a dance), to play a game (as in a sport), or to create a new product (as in devising an invention) is evidence of the cognitive features of body usage. The specific computations required to solve a particular bodily-kinesthetic *problem*, hitting a tennis ball, are summarized by Tim Gallwey:

> At the moment the ball leaves the server's racket, the brain calculates approximately where it will land and where the racket will intercept it. This calculation includes the initial velocity of the ball, combined with an input for the progressive decrease in velocity and the effect of wind and after the bounce of the ball. Simultaneously, muscle orders are given: not just once, but constantly with refined and updated information. The muscles must cooperate. A movement of the feet occurs, the racket is taken back, the face of the racket kept at a constant angle. Contact is made at a precise point that depends on whether the order was given to hit down the line or cross-court, an order not given until after a split-second analysis of the movement and balance of the opponent.
>
> To return an average serve, you have about one second to do this. To hit the ball at all is remarkable and yet not uncommon. The truth is that everyone who inhabits a human body possesses a remarkable creation.[5]

Logical-Mathematical Intelligence

In 1983 Barbara McClintock won the Nobel Prize in medicine or physiology for her work in microbiology. Her intellectual powers of deduction and observation illustrate one form of logical-mathematical intelligence that is often labeled "scientific thinking." One incident is particularly illuminating. While a researcher at Cornell in the 1920s McClintock was faced one day with a problem: while *theory* predicted 50-percent pollen sterility in corn, her research assistant (in the "field") 25 was finding plants that were only 25- to 30-percent sterile. Disturbed by this discrepancy, McClintock left the cornfield and returned to her office, where she sat for half an hour, thinking:

> Suddenly I jumped up and ran back to the (corn) field. At the top of the field (the others were still at the bottom) I shouted "Eureka, I have it! I know what the 30% sterility is!". . . They asked me to prove it. I sat down with a paper bag and a pencil and I started from scratch, which I had not done at all in my laboratory. It had all been done so fast; the answer came and I ran. Now I worked it out step by step — it was an intricate series of steps — and I came out with [the same result]. [They] looked at the material and it was exactly as I'd said it was; it worked out exactly as I had diagrammed it. Now, why did I know, without having done it on paper? Why was I so sure?[6]

This anecdote illustrates two essential facts of the logical-mathematical intelligence. First, in the gifted individual, the process of problem solving is often remarkably rapid — the successful scientist copes with many variables at once and creates numerous hypotheses that are each evaluated and then accepted or rejected in turn.

The anecdote also underscores the *nonverbal* nature of the intelligence. A solution to a problem can be constructed *before* it is articulated. In fact, the solution process may be totally invisible, even to the problem solver. This need not imply, however, that discoveries of this sort — the familiar "Aha!" phenomenon — are mysterious, intuitive, or unpredictable. The fact that it happens more frequently to some people (perhaps Nobel Prize winners) suggests the opposite. We interpret this as the work of the logical-mathematical intelligence.

Along with the companion skill of language, logical-mathematical reasoning provides the principal basis for IQ tests. This form of intelligence has been heavily investigated by traditional psychologists, and it is the archetype of "raw intelligence" or the problem-solving faculty that purportedly cuts across domains. It is perhaps ironic, then, that the actual mechanism by which one arrives at a solution to a logical-mathematical problem is not as yet properly understood.

This intelligence is supported by our empirical criteria as well. Certain areas of the brain are more prominent in mathematical calculation than others. There are idiots savants who perform great feats of calculation even though they remain tragically deficient in most other areas. Child prodigies in mathematics abound. The development of this intelligence in children has been carefully documented by Jean Piaget and other psychologists.

Linguistic Intelligence

At the age of ten, T. S. Eliot created a magazine called "Fireside" to which he was the sole contributor. In a three-day period during his winter vacation, he created eight complete issues. Each one included poems, adventure stories, a gossip column, and humor. Some of this material survives and it displays the talent of the poet.[7]

As with the logical intelligence, calling linguistic skill an "intelligence" is consistent with the stance of traditional psychology. Linguistic intelligence also passes our empirical tests. For instance, a specific area of the brain, called "Broca's Area," is responsible for the production of grammatical sentences. A person with damage to this area can understand words and sentences quite well but has difficulty putting words together in anything other than the simplest of sentences. At the same time, other thought processes may be entirely unaffected.

The gift of language is universal, and its development in children is strikingly constant across cultures. Even in deaf populations where a manual sign language is not explicitly taught, children will often "invent" their own manual language and use it surreptitiously! We thus see how an intelligence may operate independently of a specific input modality or output channel.

Spatial Intelligence

Navigation around the Caroline Islands in the South Seas is accomplished without instruments. The position of the stars, as viewed from various islands, the weather patterns, and water color are the only sign posts. Each journey is broken into a series of segments; and the navigator learns the position of the stars within each of these segments. During the actual trip the navigator must envision mentally a reference island as it passes under a particular star and from that he computes the number of segments completed, the proportion of the trip remaining, and any corrections in heading that are required. The navigator cannot *see* the islands as he sails along; instead he maps their locations in his mental "picture" of the journey.[8]

Spatial problem solving is required for navigation and in the use of the notational system of maps. Other kinds of spatial problem solving are brought to bear in visualizing an object seen from a different angle and in playing chess. The visual arts also employ this intelligence in the use of space.

93

Evidence from brain research is clear and persuasive. Just as the left hemisphere has, over the course of evolution, been selected as the site of linguistic processing in right-handed persons, the right hemisphere proves to be the site most crucial for spatial processing. Damage to the right posterior regions causes impairment of the ability to find one's way around a site, to recognize faces or scenes, or to notice fine details.

Patients with damage specific to regions of the right hemisphere will attempt to compensate for their spacial deficits with linguistic strategies. They will try to reason aloud, to challenge the task, or even make up answers. But such nonspatial strategies are rarely successful.

Blind populations provide an illustration of the distinction between 35 the spatial intelligence and visual perception. A blind person can recognize shapes by an indirect method: running a hand along the object translates into length of time of movement, which in turn is translated into the size of the object. For the blind person, the perceptual system of the tactile modality parallels the visual modality in the seeing person. The analogy between the spatial reasoning of the blind and the linguistic reasoning of the deaf is notable.

There are few child prodigies among visual artists, but there are idiots savants such as Nadia.[9] Despite a condition of severe autism, this preschool child made drawings of the most remarkable representational accuracy and finesse.

Interpersonal Intelligence

With little formal training in special education and nearly blind herself, Anne Sullivan began the intimidating task of instructing a blind and deaf seven-year-old Helen Keller. Sullivan's efforts at communication were complicated by the child's emotional struggle with the world around her. At their first meal together, this scene occurred:

> Annie did not allow Helen to put her hand into Annie's plate and take what she wanted, as she had been accustomed to do with her family. It became a test of wills — hand thrust into plate, hand firmly put aside. The family, much upset, left the dining room. Annie locked the door and proceeded to eat her breakfast while Helen lay on the floor kicking and screaming, pushing and pulling at Annie's chair. [After half an hour] Helen went around the table looking for her family. She discovered no one else was there and that bewildered her. Finally, she sat down and began to eat her breakfast, but with her hands. Annie gave her a spoon. Down on the floor it clattered, and the contest of wills began anew.[10]

Anne Sullivan sensitively responded to the child's behavior. She wrote home: "The greatest problem I shall have to solve is how to discipline and control her without breaking her spirit. I shall go rather slowly at first and try to win her love."

In fact, the first "miracle" occurred two weeks later, well before the famous incident at the pumphouse. Annie had taken Helen to a small cottage near the family's house, where they could live alone. After seven days together, Helen's personality suddenly underwent a profound change—the therapy had worked:

> My heart is singing with joy this morning. A miracle has happened! The wild little creature of two weeks ago has been transformed into a gentle child.[11]

It was just two weeks after this that the first breakthrough in Helen's 40 grasp of language occurred; and from that point on, she progressed with incredible speed. The key to the miracle of language was Anne Sullivan's insight into the *person* of Helen Keller.

Interpersonal intelligence builds on a core capacity to notice distinctions among others; in particular, contrasts in their moods, temperaments, motivations, and intentions. In more advanced forms, this intelligence permits a skilled adult to read the intentions and desires of others, even when these have been hidden. This skill appears in a highly sophisticated form in religious or political leaders, teachers, therapists, and parents. The Helen Keller–Anne Sullivan story suggests that this interpersonal intelligence does not depend on language.

All indices in brain research suggest that the frontal lobes play a prominent role in interpersonal knowledge. Damage in this area can cause profound personality changes while leaving other forms of problem solving unharmed—a person is often "not the same person" after such an injury.

Alzheimer's disease, a form of presenile dementia, appears to attack posterior brain zones with a special ferocity, leaving spatial, logical, and linguistic computations severely impaired. Yet, Alzheimer's patients will often remain well groomed, socially proper, and continually apologetic for their errors. In contrast, Pick's disease, another variety of presenile dementia that is more frontally oriented, entails a rapid loss of social graces.

Biological evidence for interpersonal intelligence encompasses two additional factors often cited as unique to humans. One factor is the prolonged childhood of primates, including the close attachment to the mother. In those cases where the mother is removed from early development, normal interpersonal development is in serious jeopardy. The second factor is the relative importance in humans of social interaction. Skills such as hunting, tracking, and killing in prehistoric societies required participation and cooperation of large numbers of people. The need for group cohesion, leadership, organization, and solidarity follows naturally from this.

Intrapersonal Intelligence

In an essay called "A Sketch of the Past," written almost as a diary entry, 45 Virginia Woolf discusses the "cotton wool of existence" — the various mundane events of life. She contrasts this "cotton wool" with three specific and poignant memories from her childhood: a fight with her brother, seeing a particular flower in the garden, and hearing of the suicide of a past visitor:

> These are three instances of exceptional moments. I often tell them over, or rather they come to the surface unexpectedly. But now for the first time I have written them down, and I realize something that I have never realized before. Two of these moments ended in a state of despair. The other ended, on the contrary, in a state of satisfaction.
> The sense of horror (in hearing of the suicide) held me powerless. But in the case of the flower, I found a reason; and was thus able to deal with the sensation. I was not powerless.
> Though I still have the peculiarity that I receive these sudden shocks, they are now always welcome; after the first surprise, I always feel instantly that they are particularly valuable. And so I go on to suppose that the shock-receiving capacity is what makes me a writer. I hazard the explanation that a shock is at once in my case followed by the desire to explain it. I feel that I have had a blow; but it is not, as I thought as a child, simply a blow from an enemy hidden behind the cotton wool of daily life; it is or will become a revelation of some order; it is a token of some real thing behind appearances; and I make it real by putting it into words.[12]

This quotation vividly illustrates the intrapersonal intelligence — knowledge of the internal aspects of a person: access to one's own feeling life, one's range of emotions, the capacity to effect discriminations among these emotions and eventually to label them and to draw upon them as a means of understanding and guiding one's own behavior. A person with good intrapersonal intelligence has a viable and effective model of himself or herself. Since this intelligence is the most private, it requires evidence from language, music, or some other more expressive form of intelligence if the observer is to detect it at work. In the above quotation, for example, linguistic intelligence is drawn upon to convey intrapersonal knowledge; it embodies the interaction of intelligences, a common phenomenon to which we will return later.

We see the familiar criteria at work in the intrapersonal intelligence. As with the interpersonal intelligence, the frontal lobes play a central role in personality change. Injury to the lower area of the frontal lobes is likely to produce irritability or euphoria; while injury to the higher regions is more likely to produce indifference, listlessness, slowness, and apathy—a kind of depressive personality. In such "frontal-lobe" individuals, the other cognitive functions often remain preserved. In contrast, among aphasics who have recovered sufficiently to describe their experiences, we find consistent testimony: while there may have been a diminution of general alertness and considerable depression about the condition, the individual in no way felt himself to be a different person. He recognized his own needs, wants, and desires and tried as best he could to achieve them.

The autistic child is a prototypical example of an individual with impaired intrapersonal intelligence; indeed, the child may not even be able to refer to himself. At the same time, such children often exhibit remarkable abilities in the musical, computational, spatial, or mechanical realms.

Evolutionary evidence for an intrapersonal faculty is more difficult to come by, but we might speculate that the capacity to transcend the satisfaction of instinctual drives is relevant. This becomes increasingly important in a species not perennially involved in the struggle for survival.

In sum, then, both interpersonal and intrapersonal faculties pass the 50 tests of an intelligence. They both feature problem-solving endeavors with significance for the individual and the species. Interpersonal intelligence allows one to understand and work with others; intrapersonal intelligence allows one to understand and work with oneself. In the individual's sense of self, one encounters a melding of inter- and intrapersonal components. Indeed, the sense of self emerges as one of the most marvelous of human inventions—a symbol that represents all kinds of information about a person and that is at the same time an invention that all individuals construct for themselves.

SUMMARY: THE UNIQUE
CONTRIBUTIONS OF THE THEORY

As human beings, we all have a repertoire of skills for solving different kinds of problems. Our investigation has begun, therefore, with a consideration of these problems, the contexts they are found in, and the culturally significant products that are the outcome. We have not approached "intelligence" as a reified° human faculty that is brought to bear in literally any problem setting; rather, we have begun with the problems that humans *solve* and worked back to the "intelligences" that must be responsible.

Evidence from brain research, human development, evolution, and cross-cultural comparisons was brought to bear in our search for the relevant human intelligences: a candidate was included only if reasonable evidence to support its membership was found across these diverse fields. Again, this tack differs from the traditional one: since no candidate faculty is *necessarily* an intelligence, we could choose on a motivated basis. In the traditional approach to "intelligence," there is no opportunity for this type of empirical decision.

We have also determined that these multiple human faculties, the intelligences, are to a significant extent *independent*. For example, research with brain-damaged adults repeatedly demonstrates that particular faculties can be lost while others are spared. This independence of intelligences implies that a particularly high level of ability in one intelligence, say mathematics, does not require a similarly high level in another intelligence, like language or music. This independence of intelligences contrasts sharply with traditional measures of IQ that find high correlations among test scores. We speculate that the usual correlations among subtests of IQ tests come about because all of these tasks in fact measure the ability to respond rapidly to items of a logical-mathematical or linguistic sort; we believe that these correlations would be substantially reduced if one were to survey in a contextually appropriate way the full range of human problem-solving skills.

Until now, we have supported the fiction that adult roles depend largely on the flowering of a single intelligence. In fact, however, nearly every cultural role of any degree of sophistication requires a combination of intelligences. Thus, even an apparently straightforward role, like playing the violin, transcends a reliance on simple musical intelligence. To become a successful violinist requires bodily-kinesthetic dexterity and the interpersonal skills of relating to an audience and, in a different way, choosing a manager; quite possibly it involves an intrapersonal intelligence as well. Dance requires skills in bodily-kinesthetic, musical, interpersonal, and spatial intelligences in varying degrees. Politics requires an interpersonal skill, a linguistic facility, and perhaps some logical aptitude. Inasmuch as nearly every cultural role requires several intelligences, it becomes important to consider individuals as a collection of aptitudes rather than as having a singular problem-solving faculty that can be measured directly through pencil-and-paper tests. Even

---

reified: Regarding an abstraction (e.g., intelligence) as if it were a concrete thing.

98

given a relatively small number of such intelligences, the diversity of human ability is created through the differences in these profiles. In fact, it may well be that the "total is greater than the sum of the parts." An individual may not be particularly gifted in any intelligence; and yet, because of a particular combination or blend of skills, he or she may be able to fill some niche uniquely well. Thus it is of paramount importance to assess the particular combination of skills that may earmark an individual for a certain vocational or avocational niche.

Notes

1. Jencks, C. (1972). *Inequality*. New York: Basic Books.
2. Gardner, H. (1983). *Frames of Mind: The Theory of Multiple Intelligences*. New York: Basic Books.
3. Menuhin, Y. (1977). *Unfinished Journey*. New York: Knopf.
4. Connor, A. (1982). *Voices from Cooperstown*. New York: Collier. (Based on a quotation taken from *The Babe Ruth Story*, Babe Ruth & Bob Considine. New York: Dutton, 1948.)
5. Gallwey, T. (1976). *Inner Tennis*. New York: Random House.
6. Keller, E. (1983). *A Feeling for the Organism* (p. 104). Salt Lake City: W. H. Freeman.
7. Soldo, J. (1982). Jovial juvenilia: T. S. Eliot's first magazine. *Biography*, 5, 25–37.
8. Gardner, H. (1983). *Frames of Mind: The Theory of Multiple Intelligences*. New York: Basic Books.
9. Selfe, L. (1977). *Nadia: A Case of Extraordinary Drawing in an Autistic Child*. New York: Academic Press.
10. Lash, J. (1980). *Helen and Teacher: The Story of Helen Keller and Anne Sullivan Macy* (p. 52). New York: Delacorte.
11. Lash (p. 54).
12. Woolf, V. (1976). *Moments of Being* (pp. 69–70). Sussex: The University Press.

MARTIN LUTHER KING JR. [1929–1968]

Letter from Birmingham Jail

The foremost leader of the American civil rights movement of the
1950s and 1960s, **Martin Luther King Jr.** was born in Atlanta, Georgia,
in 1929 and assassinated in Memphis, Tennessee, in 1968. He was an
ordained minister with a Ph.D., a deliverer of powerful sermons and
speeches, and a writer of books. A crusader against segregation, an organizer of the Montgomery, Alabama, bus boycott, and head of the
Southern Christian Leadership Conference, King advocated nonviolent
resistance in the face of discrimination and violence. The steadfast
dignity with which he pursued rights for African Americans earned
him worldwide renown and a Nobel Peace Prize.

"Letter from Birmingham Jail" was written while King and hundreds of other protesters were under arrest for demonstrating in
Birmingham, Alabama. It is a response to eight of his fellow clergymen
who questioned his methods of protest even as they supported his ultimate aims. Note, as you read, the combination in his writing of the
cool logic of his argument and his passionate sense of the injustice
African Americans have suffered.

MY DEAR FELLOW CLERGYMEN:

While confined here in the Birmingham city jail, I came across your
recent statement calling my present activities "unwise and untimely."
Seldom do I pause to answer criticism of my work and ideas. If I sought
to answer all the criticisms that cross my desk, my secretaries would
have little time for anything other than such correspondence in the
course of the day, and I would have no time for constructive work. But
since I feel that you are men of genuine good will and that your criticisms are sincerely set forth, I want to try to answer your statement in
what I hope will be patient and reasonable terms.

I think I should indicate why I am here in Birmingham, since you
have been influenced by the view which argues against "outsiders coming in." I have the honor of serving as president of the Southern Christian
Leadership Conference, an organization operating in every southern

state, with headquarters in Atlanta, Georgia. We have some eighty-five affiliated organizations across the South, and one of them is the Alabama Christian Movement for Human Rights. Frequently we share staff, educational, and financial resources with our affiliates. Several months ago the affiliate here in Birmingham asked us to be on call to engage in a nonviolent direct-action program if such were deemed necessary. We readily consented, and when the hour came we lived up to our promise. So I, along with several members of my staff, am here because I was invited here. I am here because I have organizational ties here.

But more basically, I am in Birmingham because injustice is here. Just as the prophets of the eighth century B.C. left their villages and carried their "thus saith the Lord" far beyond the boundaries of their home towns, and just as the Apostle Paul left his village of Tarsus and carried the gospel of Jesus Christ to the far corners of the Greco-Roman world, so am I compelled to carry the gospel of freedom beyond my own home town. Like Paul, I must constantly respond to the Macedonian call for aid.

Moreover, I am cognizant of the interrelatedness of all communities and states. I cannot sit idly by in Atlanta and not be concerned about what happens in Birmingham. Injustice anywhere is a threat to justice everywhere. We are caught in an inescapable network of mutuality, tied in a single garment of destiny. Whatever affects one directly, affects all indirectly. Never again can we afford to live with the narrow, provincial "outside agitator" idea. Anyone who lives inside the United States can never be considered an outsider anywhere within its bounds.

You deplore the demonstrations taking place in Birmingham. But 5 your statement, I am sorry to say, fails to express a similar concern for the conditions that brought about the demonstrations. I am sure that none of you would want to rest content with the superficial kind of social analysis that deals merely with effects and does not grapple with underlying causes. It is unfortunate that demonstrations are taking place in Birmingham, but it is even more unfortunate that the city's white power structure left the Negro community with no alternative.

In any nonviolent campaign there are four basic steps: collection of the facts to determine whether injustices exist; negotiation; self-purification; and direct action. We have gone through all these steps in Birmingham. There can be no gainsaying the fact that racial injustice engulfs this community. Birmingham is probably the most thoroughly segregated city in the United States. Its ugly record of brutality is widely known. Negroes have experienced grossly unjust treatment in the courts. There have been more unsolved bombings of Negro homes and churches in Birmingham than in any other city in the nation. These are the hard, brutal facts of the case. On the basis of these conditions, Negro leaders

101

sought to negotiate with the city fathers. But the latter consistently refused to engage in good-faith negotiation. Then, last September, came the opportunity to talk with leaders of Birmingham's economic community. In the course of the negotiations, certain promises were made by the merchants—for example, to remove the stores' humiliating racial signs. On the basis of these promises, the Reverend Fred Shuttlesworth and the leaders of the Alabama Christian Movement for Human Rights agreed to a moratorium on all demonstrations. As the weeks and months went by, we realized that we were the victims of a broken promise. A few signs, briefly removed, returned; the others remained.

As in so many past experiences, our hopes had been blasted, and the shadow of deep disappointment settled upon us. We had no alternative except to prepare for direct action, whereby we would present our very bodies as a means of laying our case before the conscience of the local and the national community. Mindful of the difficulties involved, we decided to undertake a process of self-purification. We began a series of workshops on nonviolence, and we repeatedly asked ourselves: "Are you able to accept blows without retaliating?" "Are you able to endure the ordeal of jail?" We decided to schedule our direct-action program for the Easter season, realizing that except for Christmas, this is the main shopping period of the year. Knowing that a strong economic withdrawal program would be the by-product of direct action, we felt that this would be the best time to bring pressure to bear on the merchants for the needed change.

Then it occurred to us that Birmingham's mayoral election was coming up in March, and we speedily decided to postpone action until after election day. When we discovered that the Commissioner of Public Safety, Eugene "Bull" Connor, had piled up enough votes to be in the run-off, we decided again to postpone action until the day after the runoff so that the demonstrations could not be used to cloud the issues. Like many others, we wanted to see Mr. Connor defeated, and to this end we endured postponement after postponement. Having aided in this community need, we felt that our direct-action program could be delayed no longer.

You may well ask, "Why direct action? Why sit-ins, marches, and so 10 forth? Isn't negotiation a better path?" You are quite right in calling for negotiation. Indeed, this is the very purpose of direct action. Nonviolent direct action seeks to create such a crisis and foster such a tension that a community which has constantly refused to negotiate is forced to confront the issue. It seeks so to dramatize the issue that it can no longer be ignored. My citing the creation of tension as part of the work of the nonviolent-resister may sound rather shocking. But I must confess that I am not afraid of the word "tension." I have earnestly opposed violent tension, but there is a type of constructive, nonviolent tension which is necessary for growth. Just as Socrates felt that it was necessary to create a tension in the mind so that individuals could rise from the bondage of myths and half-truths to the unfettered realm of creative analysis and objective appraisal, so must we see the need for nonviolent gadflies to create the kind of tension in society that will help men rise from the dark depths of prejudice and racism to the majestic heights of understanding and brotherhood.

The purpose of our direct-action program is to create a situation so crisis-packed that it will inevitably open the door to negotiation. I therefore concur with you in your call for negotiation. Too long has our beloved Southland been bogged down in a tragic effort to live in monologue rather than dialogue.

One of the basic points in your statement is that the action that I and my associates have taken in Birmingham is untimely. Some have asked: "Why didn't you give the new city administration time to act?" The only answer that I can give to this query is that the new Birmingham administration must be prodded about as much as the outgoing one, before it will act. We are sadly mistaken if we feel that the election of Albert Boutwell as mayor will bring the millennium to Birmingham. While Mr. Boutwell is a much more gentle person than Mr. Connor, they are both segregationists, dedicated to maintenance of the status quo. I have hoped that Mr. Boutwell will be reasonable enough to see the futility of massive resistance to desegregation. But he will not see this without pressure from devotees of civil rights. My friends, I must say to you that we have not made a single gain in civil rights without determined legal and nonviolent pressure. Lamentably, it is an historical fact that privileged groups seldom give up their privileges voluntarily. Individuals may see the moral light and voluntarily give up their unjust posture, but, as Reinhold Niebuhr has reminded us, groups tend to be more immoral than individuals.

We know through painful experience that freedom is never voluntarily given by the oppressor; it must be demanded by the oppressed. Frankly, I have yet to engage in a direct-action campaign that was "well timed" in the view of those who have not suffered unduly from the disease of segregation. For years now I have heard the word "Wait!" It rings in the ear of every Negro with piercing familiarity. This "Wait" has almost always meant "Never." We must come to see, with one of our distinguished jurists, that "justice too long delayed is justice denied."

We have waited for more than 340 years for our constitutional and God-given rights. The nations of Asia and Africa are moving with jet-like speed toward gaining political independence, but we still creep at horse-

and-buggy pace toward gaining a cup of coffee at a lunch counter. Perhaps it is easy for those who have never felt the stinging darts of segregation to say, "Wait." But when you have seen vicious mobs lynch your mothers and fathers at will and drown your sisters and brothers at whim; when you have seen hate-filled policemen curse, kick, and even kill your black brothers and sisters; when you see the vast majority of your twenty million Negro brothers smothering in an airtight cage of poverty in the midst of an affluent society; when you suddenly find your tongue twisted and your speech stammering as you seek to explain to your six-year-old daughter why she can't go to the public amusement park that has just been advertised on television, and see tears welling up in her eyes when she is told that Funtown is closed to colored children, and see ominous clouds of inferiority beginning to form in her little mental sky, and see her beginning to distort her personality by developing an unconscious bitterness toward white people; when you have to concoct an answer for a five-year-old son who is asking, "Daddy, why do white people treat colored people so mean?"; when you take a cross-country drive and find it necessary to sleep night after night in the uncomfortable corners of your automobile because no motel will accept you; when you are humiliated day in and day out by nagging signs reading "white" and "colored"; when your first name becomes "nigger," your middle name becomes "boy" (however old you are) and your last name becomes "John," and your wife and mother are never given the respected title "Mrs."; when you are harried by day and haunted by night by the fact that you are a Negro, living constantly at tiptoe stance, never quite knowing what to expect next, and are plagued with inner fears and outer resentments; when you are forever fighting a degenerating sense of "nobodiness"—then you will understand why we find it difficult to wait. There comes a time when the cup of endurance runs over, and men are no longer willing to be plunged into the abyss of despair. I hope, sirs, you can understand our legitimate and unavoidable impatience.

You express a great deal of anxiety over our willingness to break laws. 15 This is certainly a legitimate concern. Since we so diligently urge people to obey the Supreme Court's decision of 1954 outlawing segregation in the public schools, at first glance it may seem rather paradoxical for us consciously to break laws. One may well ask: "How can you advocate breaking some laws and obeying others?" The answer lies in the fact that there are two types of laws: just and unjust. I would be the first to advocate obeying just laws. One has not only a legal but a moral responsibility to obey just laws. Conversely, one has a moral responsibility to disobey unjust laws. I would agree with St. Augustine that "an unjust law is no law at all."

Now, what is the difference between the two? How does one determine whether a law is just or unjust? A just law is a man-made code that squares with the moral law or the law of God. An unjust law is a code that is out of harmony with the moral law. To put it in the terms of St. Thomas Aquinas: An unjust law is a human law that is not rooted in eternal law and natural law. Any law that uplifts human personality is just. Any law that degrades human personality is unjust. All segregation statutes are unjust because segregation distorts the soul and damages the personality. It gives the segregator a false sense of superiority and the segregated a false sense of inferiority. Segregation, to use the terminology of the Jewish philosopher Martin Buber, substitutes an "I-it" relationship for an "I-thou" relationship and ends up relegating persons to the status of things. Hence segregation is not only politically, economically, and sociologically unsound, it is morally wrong and sinful. Paul Tillich has said that sin is separation. Is not segregation an existential expression of man's tragic separation, his awful estrangement, his terrible sinfulness? Thus it is that I can urge men to obey the 1954 decision of the Supreme Court, for it is morally right; and I can urge them to disobey segregation ordinances, for they are morally wrong.

Let us consider a more concrete example of just and unjust laws. An unjust law is a code that a numerical or power majority group compels a minority group to obey but does not make binding on itself. This is *difference* made legal. By the same token, a just law is a code that a majority compels a minority to follow and that it is willing to follow itself. This is *sameness* made legal.

Let me give another explanation. A law is unjust if it is inflicted on a minority that, as a result of being denied the right to vote, had no part in enacting or devising the law. Who can say that the legislature of Alabama which set up that state's segregation laws was democratically elected? Throughout Alabama all sorts of devious methods are used to prevent Negroes from becoming registered voters, and there are some counties in which, even though Negroes constitute a majority of the population, not a single Negro is registered. Can any law enacted under such circumstances be considered democratically structured?

Sometimes a law is just on its face and unjust in its application. For instance, I have been arrested on a charge of parading without a permit. Now, there is nothing wrong in having an ordinance which requires a permit for a parade. But such an ordinance becomes unjust when it is used to maintain segregation and to deny citizens the First-Amendment privilege of peaceful assembly and protest.

I hope you are able to see the distinction I am trying to point out. In 20 no sense do I advocate evading or defying the law, as would the rabid segregationist. That would lead to anarchy. One who breaks an unjust law must do so openly, lovingly, and with a willingness to accept the

105

penalty. I submit that an individual who breaks a law that conscience tells him is unjust, and who willingly accepts the penalty of imprisonment in order to arouse the conscience of the community over its injustice, is in reality expressing the highest respect for law.

Of course, there is nothing new about this kind of civil disobedience. It was evidenced sublimely in the refusal of Shadrach, Meshach, and Abednego to obey the laws of Nebuchadnezzar, on the ground that a higher moral law was at stake. It was practiced superbly by the early Christians, who were willing to face hungry lions and the excruciating pain of chopping blocks rather than submit to certain unjust laws of the Roman Empire. To a degree, academic freedom is a reality today because Socrates practiced civil disobedience. In our own nation, the Boston Tea Party represented a massive act of civil disobedience.

We should never forget that everything Adolf Hitler did in Germany was "legal" and everything the Hungarian freedom fighters did in Hungary was "illegal." It was "illegal" to aid and comfort a Jew in Hitler's Germany. Even so, I am sure that, had I lived in Germany at the time, I would have aided and comforted my Jewish brothers. If today I lived in a Communist country where certain principles dear to the Christian faith are suppressed, I would openly advocate disobeying that country's anti-religious laws.

I must make two honest confessions to you, my Christian and Jewish brothers. First, I must confess that over the past few years I have been gravely disappointed with the white moderate. I have almost reached the regrettable conclusion that the Negro's great stumbling block in his stride toward freedom is not the White Citizen's Counciler or the Ku Klux Klanner, but the white moderate, who is more devoted to "order" than to justice; who prefers a negative peace which is the absence of tension to a positive peace which is the presence of justice; who constantly says, "I agree with you in the goal you seek, but I cannot agree with your methods of direct action"; who paternalistically believes he can set the timetable for another man's freedom; who lives by a mythical concept of time and who constantly advises the Negro to wait for a "more convenient season." Shallow understanding from people of good will is more frustrating than absolute misunderstanding from people of ill will. Lukewarm acceptance is much more bewildering than outright rejection.

I had hoped that the white moderate would understand that law and order exist for the purpose of establishing justice and that when they fail in this purpose they become the dangerously structured dams that block the flow of social progress. I had hoped that the white moderate would understand that the present tension in the South is a necessary phase of the transition from an obnoxious negative peace, in which the Negro passively accepted his unjust plight, to a substantive and positive peace, in which all men will respect the dignity and worth of human personality. Actually, we who engage in nonviolent direct action are not the creators of tension. We merely bring to the surface the hidden tension that is already alive. We bring it out in the open, where it can be seen and dealt with. Like a boil that can never be cured so long as it is covered up but must be opened with all its ugliness to the natural medicines of air and light, injustice must be exposed, with all the tension its exposure creates, to the light of human conscience and the air of national opinion, before it can be cured.

In your statement you assert that our actions, even though peaceful, 25 must be condemned because they precipitate violence. But is this a logical assertion? Isn't this like condemning a robbed man because his possession of money precipitated the evil act of robbery? Isn't this like condemning Socrates because his unswerving commitment to truth and his philosophical inquiries precipitated the act by the misguided populace in which they made him drink hemlock? Isn't this like condemning Jesus because his unique God-consciousness and never-ceasing devotion to God's will precipitated the evil act of crucifixion? We must come to see that, as the federal courts have consistently affirmed, it is wrong to urge an individual to cease his efforts to gain his basic constitutional rights because the quest may precipitate violence. Society must protect the robbed and punish the robber.

I had also hoped that the white moderate would reject the myth concerning time in relation to the struggle for freedom. I have just received a letter from a white brother in Texas. He writes: "All Christians know that the colored people will receive equal rights eventually, but it is possible that you are in too great a religious hurry. It has taken Christianity almost two thousand years to accomplish what it has. The teachings of Christ take time to come to earth." Such an attitude stems from a tragic misconception of time, from the strangely irrational notion that there is something in the very flow of time that will inevitably cure all ills. Actually, time itself is neutral; it can be used either destructively or constructively. More and more I feel that the people of ill will have used time much more effectively than have the people of good will. We will have to repent in this generation not merely for the hateful words and actions of the bad people, but for the appalling silence of the good people. Human progress never rolls in on wheels of inevitability; it comes through the tireless efforts of men willing to be co-workers with God, and without this hard work, time itself becomes an ally of the forces of social stagnation. We must use time creatively, in the knowledge that the time is always ripe to do right. Now is the time to make real the promise of democracy and transform our pending national elegy into a creative psalm of brotherhood. Now is the time to lift our national policy from the quicksand of racial injustice to the solid rock of human dignity.

You speak of our activity in Birmingham as extreme. At first I was rather disappointed that fellow clergymen would see my nonviolent efforts as those of an extremist. I began thinking about the fact that I stand in the middle of two opposing forces in the Negro community. One is a force of complacency, made up in part of Negroes who, as a result of long years of oppression, are so drained of self-respect and a sense of "somebodiness" that they have adjusted to segregation; and in part of a few middle-class Negroes who, because of a degree of academic and economic security and because in some ways they profit by segregation, have become insensitive to the problems of the masses. The other force is one of bitterness and hatred, and it comes perilously close to advocating violence. It is expressed in the various black nationalist groups that are springing up across the nation, the largest and best-known being Elijah Muhammad's Muslim movement. Nourished by the Negro's frustration over the continued existence of racial discrimination, this movement is made up of people who have lost faith in America, who have absolutely repudiated Christianity, and who have concluded that the white man is an incorrigible "devil."

I have tried to stand between these two forces, saying that we need emulate neither the "do-nothingism" of the complacent nor the hatred and despair of the black nationalist. For there is the more excellent way of love and nonviolent protest. I am grateful to God that, through the influence of the Negro church, the way of nonviolence became an integral part of our struggle.

If this philosophy had not emerged, by now many streets of the South would, I am convinced, be flowing with blood. And I am further convinced that if our white brothers dismiss as "rabblerousers" and "outside agitators" those of us who employ nonviolent direct action, and if they refuse to support our nonviolent efforts, millions of Negroes will, out of frustration and despair, seek solace and security in black-nationalist ideologies—a development that would inevitably lead to a frightening racial nightmare.

Oppressed people cannot remain oppressed forever. The yearning for freedom eventually manifests itself, and that is what has happened to the American Negro. Something within has reminded him of his birthright of freedom, and something without has reminded him that it can be gained. Consciously or unconsciously, he has been caught up by the *Zeitgeist*, and with his black brothers of Africa and his brown and yellow brothers of Asia, South America, and the Caribbean, the United States Negro is moving with a sense of great urgency toward the promised land of racial justice. If one recognizes this vital urge that has en-

30

gulfed the Negro community, one should readily understand why public demonstrations are taking place. The Negro has many pent-up resentments and latent frustrations, and he must release them. So let him march; let him make prayer pilgrimages to the city hall; let him go on freedom rides—and try to understand why he must do so. If his repressed emotions are not released in nonviolent ways, they will seek expression through violence; this is not a threat but a fact of history. So I have not said to my people, "Get rid of your discontent." Rather, I have tried to say that this normal and healthy discontent can be channeled into the creative outlet of nonviolent direct action. And now this approach is being termed extremist.

But though I was initially disappointed at being categorized as an extremist, as I continued to think about the matter I gradually gained a measure of satisfaction from the label. Was not Jesus an extremist for love: "Love your enemies, bless them that curse you, do good to them that hate you, and pray for them which despitefully use you, and persecute you." Was not Amos an extremist for justice: "Let justice roll down like waters and righteousness like an ever-flowing stream." Was not Paul an extremist for the Christian gospel: "I bear in my body the marks of the Lord Jesus." Was not Martin Luther an extremist: "Here I stand; I cannot do otherwise, so help me God." And John Bunyan: "I will stay in jail to the end of my days before I make a butchery of my conscience." And Abraham Lincoln: "This nation cannot survive half slave and half free." And Thomas Jefferson: "We hold these truths to be self-evident, that all men are created equal. . . ." So the question is not whether we will be extremists, but what kind of extremists we will be. Will we be extremists for hate or for love? Will we be extremists for the preservation of injustice or for the extension of justice? In that dramatic scene on Calvary's hill three men were crucified. We must never forget that all three were crucified for the same crime—the crime of extremism. Two were extremists for immorality, and thus fell below their environment. The other, Jesus Christ, was an extremist for love, truth, and goodness, and thereby rose above his environment. Perhaps the South, the nation, and the world are in dire need of creative extremists.

I had hoped that the white moderate would see this need. Perhaps I was too optimistic; perhaps I expected too much. I suppose I should have realized that few members of the oppressor race can understand the deep groans and passionate yearnings of the oppressed race, and still fewer have the vision to see that injustice must be rooted out by strong, persistent, and determined action. I am thankful, however, that some of our white brothers in the South have grasped the meaning of this social revolution and committed themselves to it. They are still all too few in quantity, but they are big in quality. Some—such as Ralph McGill,

Lillian Smith, Harry Golden, James McBridge Dabbs, Ann Braden, and Sarah Patton Boyle—have written about our struggle in eloquent and prophetic terms. Others have marched with us down nameless streets of the South. They have languished in filthy, roach-infested jails, suffering the abuse and brutality of policemen who view them as "dirty nigger-lovers." Unlike so many of their moderate brothers and sisters, they have recognized the urgency of the moment and sensed the need for powerful "action" antidotes to combat the disease of segregation.

Let me take note of my other major disappointment. I have been so greatly disappointed with the white church and its leadership. Of course, there are some notable exceptions. I am not unmindful of the fact that each of you has taken some significant stands on this issue. I commend you, Reverend Stallings, for your Christian stand on this past Sunday, in welcoming Negroes to your worship service on a nonsegregated basis. I commend the Catholic leaders of this state for integrating Spring Hill College several years ago.

But despite these notable exceptions, I must honestly reiterate that I have been disappointed with the church. I do not say this as one of those negative critics who can always find something wrong with the church. I say this as a minister of the gospel, who loves the church; who was nurtured in its bosom; who has been sustained by its spiritual blessings and who will remain true to it as long as the cord of life shall lengthen.

When I was suddenly catapulted into the leadership of the bus protest 35 in Montgomery, Alabama, a few years ago, I felt we would be supported by the white church. I felt that the white ministers, priests, and rabbis of the South would be among our strongest allies. Instead, some have been outright opponents, refusing to understand the freedom movement and misrepresenting its leaders; all too many others have been more cautious than courageous and have remained silent behind the anesthetizing security of stained-glass windows.

In spite of my shattered dreams, I came to Birmingham with the hope that the white religious leadership of this community would see the justice of our cause and, with deep moral concern, would serve as the channel through which our just grievances could reach the power structure. I had hoped that each of you would understand. But again I have been disappointed.

I have heard numerous southern religious leaders admonish their worshipers to comply with a desegregation decision because it is the law, but I have longed to hear white ministers declare: "Follow this decree because integration is morally right and because the Negro is your brother." In the midst of blatant injustices inflicted upon the Negro, I have watched white churchmen stand on the sideline and mouth pious irrelevancies and sanctimonious trivialities. In the midst of a mighty struggle to rid our nation of racial and economic injustice, I have heard many ministers say: "Those are social issues, with which the gospel has no real concern." And I have watched many churches commit themselves to a completely otherworldly religion which makes a strange, un-Biblical distinction between body and soul, between the sacred and the secular.

I have traveled the length and breadth of Alabama, Mississippi, and all the other southern states. On sweltering summer days and crisp autumn mornings I have looked at the South's beautiful churches with their lofty spires pointing heavenward. I have beheld the impressive outlines of her massive religious-education buildings. Over and over I have found myself asking: "What kind of people worship here? Who is their God? Where were their voices when the lips of Governor Barnett dripped with words of interposition and nullification? Where were they when Governor Wallace gave a clarion call for defiance and hatred? Where were their voices of support when bruised and weary Negro men and women decided to rise from the dark dungeons of complacency to the bright hills of creative protest?"

Yes, these questions are still in my mind. In deep disappointment I have wept over the laxity of the church. But be assured that my tears have been tears of love. There can be no deep disappointment where there is not deep love. Yes, I love the church. How could I do otherwise? I am in the rather unique position of being the son, the grandson, and the great-grandson of preachers. Yes, I see the church as the body of Christ. But, oh! How we have blemished and scarred that body through social neglect and through fear of being nonconformists.

There was a time when the church was very powerful—in the time 40 when the early Christians rejoiced at being deemed worthy to suffer for what they believed. In those days the church was not merely a thermometer that recorded the ideas and principles of popular opinion; it was a thermostat that transformed the mores of society. Whenever the early Christians entered a town, the people in power became disturbed and immediately sought to convict the Christians for being "disturbers of the peace" and "outside agitators." But the Christians pressed on, in the conviction that they were "a colony of heaven," called to obey God rather than man. Small in number, they were big in commitment. They were too God-intoxicated to be "astronomically intimidated." By their effort and example they brought an end to such ancient evils as infanticide and gladiatorial contests.

Things are different now. So often the contemporary church is a weak, ineffectual voice with an uncertain sound. So often it is an archdefender of the status quo. Far from being disturbed by the presence of the church, the power structure of the average community is consoled by

111

the church's silent—and often even vocal—sanction of things as they are.

But the judgment of God is upon the church as never before. If today's church does not recapture the sacrificial spirit of the early church, it will lose its authenticity, forfeit the loyalty of millions, and be dismissed as an irrelevant social club with no meaning for the twentieth century. Every day I meet young people whose disappointment with the church has turned into outright disgust.

Perhaps I have once again been too optimistic. Is organized religion too inextricably bound to the status quo to save our nation and the world? Perhaps I must turn my faith to the inner spiritual church, the church within the church, as the true *ekklesia* and the hope of the world. But again I am thankful to God that some noble souls from the ranks of organized religion have broken loose from the paralyzing chains of conformity and joined us as active partners in the struggle for freedom. They have left their secure congregations and walked the streets of Albany, Georgia, with us. They have gone down the highways of the South on tortuous rides for freedom. Yes, they have gone to jail with us. Some have been dismissed from their churches, have lost the support of their bishops and fellow ministers. But they have acted in the faith that right defeated is stronger than evil triumphant. Their witness has been the spiritual salt that has preserved the true meaning of the gospel in these troubled times. They have carved a tunnel of hope through the dark mountain of disappointment.

I hope the church as a whole will meet the challenge of this decisive hour. But even if the church does not come to the aid of justice, I have no despair about the future. I have no fear about the outcome of our struggle in Birmingham, even if our motives are at present misunderstood. We will reach the goal of freedom in Birmingham and all over the nation, because the goal of America is freedom. Abused and scorned though we may be, our destiny is tied up with America's destiny. Before the pilgrims landed at Plymouth, we were here. Before the pen of Jefferson etched the majestic words of the Declaration of Independence across the pages of history, we were here. For more than two centuries our forebears labored in this country without wages: they made cotton king; they built the homes of their masters while suffering gross injustice and shameful humiliation—and yet out of a bottomless vitality they continued to thrive and develop. If the inexpressible cruelties of slavery could not stop us, the opposition we now face will surely fail. We will win our freedom because the sacred heritage of our nation and the eternal will of God are embodied in our echoing demands.

Before closing I feel impelled to mention one other point in your state- 45 ment that has troubled me profoundly. You warmly commended the

Birmingham police force for keeping "order" and "preventing violence." I doubt that you would have so warmly commended the police force if you had seen its dogs sinking their teeth into unarmed, nonviolent Negroes. I doubt that you would so quickly commend the policemen if you were to observe their ugly and inhumane treatment of Negroes here in the city jail; if you were to watch them push and curse old Negro women and young Negro girls; if you were to see them slap and kick old Negro men and young boys; if you were to observe them, as they did on two occasions, refuse to give us food because we wanted to sing our grace together. I cannot join you in your praise of the Birmingham police department.

It is true that the police have exercised a degree of discipline in handling the demonstrators. In this sense they have conducted themselves rather "nonviolently" in public. But for what purpose? To preserve the evil system of segregation. Over the past few years I have consistently preached that nonviolence demands that the means we use must be as pure as the ends we seek. I have tried to make clear that it is wrong to use immoral means to attain moral ends. But now I must affirm that it is just as wrong, or perhaps even more so, to use moral means to preserve immoral ends. Perhaps Mr. Connor and his policemen have been rather nonviolent in public, as was Chief Pritchett in Albany, Georgia, but they have used the moral means of nonviolence to maintain the immoral end of racial injustice. As T. S. Eliot has said. "The last temptation is the greatest treason: To do the right deed for the wrong reason."

I wish you had commended the Negro sit-inners and demonstrators of Birmingham for their sublime courage, their willingness to suffer, and their amazing discipline in the midst of great provocation. One day the South will recognize its real heroes. They will be the James Merediths, with the noble sense of purpose that enables them to face jeering and hostile mobs, and with the agonizing loneliness that characterizes the life of the pioneer. They will be old, oppressed, battered Negro women, symbolized in a seventy-two-year-old woman in Montgomery, Alabama, who rose up with a sense of dignity and with her people decided not to ride segregated buses, and who responded with ungrammatical profundity to one who inquired about her weariness: "My feets is tired, but my soul is at rest." They will be the young high school and college students, the young ministers of the gospel and a host of their elders, courageously and nonviolently sitting in at lunch counters and willingly going to jail for conscience' sake. One day the South will know that when these disinherited children of God sat down at lunch counters, they were in reality standing up for what is best in the American dream and for the most sacred values in our Judaeo-Christian heritage, thereby bringing our nation back to those great wells of democracy which were dug deep by the founding fathers in their formulation of the Constitution and the Declaration of Independence.

Never before have I written so long a letter. I'm afraid it is much too long to take your precious time. I can assure you that it would have been much shorter if I had been writing from a comfortable desk, but what else can one do when he is alone in a narrow jail cell, other than write long letters, think long thoughts, and pray long prayers?

If I have said anything in this letter that overstates the truth and indicates an unreasonable impatience, I beg you to forgive me. If I have said anything that understates the truth and indicates my having a patience that allows me to settle for anything less than brotherhood, I beg God to forgive me.

I hope this letter finds you strong in the faith. I also hope that circumstances will soon make it possible for me to meet each of you, not as an integrationist or a civil-rights leader but as a fellow clergyman and a Christian brother. Let us all hope that the dark clouds of racial prejudice will soon pass away and the deep fog of misunderstanding will be lifted from our fear-drenched communities, and in some not too distant tomorrow the radiant stars of love and brotherhood will shine over our great nation with all their scintillating beauty.

> Yours for the cause of Peace and Brotherhood,
> MARTIN LUTHER KING JR.

[1963]

PAUL M. BARRETT

Muslims in America

New Jersey native **Paul M. Barrett** is a journalist, in his father's foot-steps, and a graduate of Harvard Law School. For more than fifteen years, he worked as a reporter and editor at the *Wall Street Journal*, covering topics including legal issues and corporate culture. Barrett is now an assistant managing editor of investigative reporting for *Bloomberg Businessweek*, and his contributions have earned the maga-zine several awards. Barrett also teaches as an adjunct professor at New York University's School of Law. He has authored several books including *The Good Black: A True Story of Race in America*, published in 1999, and *American Islam: The Struggle for the Soul of a Religion*, which was named among the best books of the year in 2007 by the *Washington Post* and *Publishers Weekly*.

In the following excerpt from *American Islam*, Barrett dispels many common stereotypes of and assumptions about Muslims in the United States through an objective presentation of factual data. American Mus-lims are, on average, highly educated and economically prosperous individuals, according to Barrett, and although the exact number of American Muslims is not known, the demographic is growing in num-bers and gaining both cultural and political influence in the process.

Most American Muslims are not Arab, and most Americans of Arab descent are Christian, not Muslim. People of South Asian descent— those with roots in Pakistan, India, Bangladesh, and Afghanistan— make up 34 percent of American Muslims, according to the polling orga-nization Zogby International. Arab-Americans constitute only 26 per-cent, while another 20 percent are native-born American blacks, most of whom are converts. The remaining 20 percent come from Africa, Iran, Turkey, and elsewhere.

Muslims have no equivalent to the Catholic pope and his cardinals. The faith is decentralized in the extreme, and some beliefs and practices vary depending on region and sect. In America, Muslims do not think and act alike any more than Christians do. That said, all observant

Muslims acknowledge Islam's "five pillars": faith in one God, prayer, charity, fasting during Ramadan, and pilgrimage to Mecca. Muslims are also united in the way they pray. The basic choreography of crossing arms, bowing, kneeling, and prostrating oneself is more or less the same in mosques everywhere.

The two major subgroups of Muslims, Sunni and Shiite, are found in the United States in roughly their global proportions: 85 percent Sunni, 15 percent Shiite. Ancient history still animates the rivalry, which began in the struggle for Muslim leadership after the Prophet Muhammad's death in 632. Shiites believe that Muhammad intended for only his blood descendants to succeed him. Muhammad's beloved cousin and son-in-law Ali was the only male relative who qualified. Ali's followers became known as Shiites, a derivation of the Arabic phrase for "partisans of Ali." Things did not go smoothly for them.

The larger body of early Muslims, known as Sunnis, a word related to Sunnah, or way of the Prophet, had a more flexible notion of who should succeed Muhammad. In 661, an extremist assassinated Ali near Najaf in what is now Iraq. Nineteen years later Sunnis killed his son, Hussein, not far away in Karbala. These deaths permanently divided the aggrieved Shiite minority from the Sunni majority.

Sunnis historically have afflicted the weaker Shiites, accusing them of 5 shaping a blasphemous cult around Ali and Hussein. At the Karbalaa Islamic Education Center in Dearborn, Michigan, a large mural depicts mourning women who have encountered the riderless horse of Hussein after his final battle. "You see our history and our situation in this," says Imam Husham al-Husainy, a Shiite Iraqi émigré who leads the center. In Dearborn, Shiite Iraqis initially backed the American invasion to depose Saddam Hussein, who persecuted Iraq's Shiite majority. Most Sunnis in Dearborn condemned the war as an exercise in American imperialism.

Sufism, another important strain of Islam, is also present in the United States. Sufis follow a spiritual, inward-looking path. Only a tiny percentage of American Muslims would identify themselves primarily as Sufis, in part because some more rigid Muslims condemn Sufism as heretical. But Sufi ideas crop up among the beliefs of many Muslims without being labeled as such. Sufism's emphasis on self-purification appeals to New Age seekers and has made it the most common avenue into Islam for white American converts such as Abdul Kabir Krambo of Yuba City, California. Krambo, an electrician who grew up in a conservative German Catholic family, helped build a mosque amidst the fruit arbors of the Sacramento Valley, only to see it burn down in a mysterious arson. Once rebuilt, the Islamic Center of Yuba City was engulfed again, this time by controversy over whether Krambo and his Sufi friends were trying to impose a "cult" on other worshipers.

Although there is a broad consensus that Islam is the fastest-growing religion in the country and the world, no one has provable numbers on just how many American Muslims there are. The Census Bureau doesn't count by religion, and private surveys of the Muslim population offer widely disparate conclusions. A study of four hundred mosques nationwide estimated that there are two million people in the United States "associated with" Islamic houses of worship. The authors of the survey, published in 2001 under the auspices of the Council on American-Islamic Relations (CAIR), a Muslim advocacy group, employed a common assumption that only one in three American Muslims associates with a mosque. In CAIR's view, that suggests there are at least six million Muslims in the country. (Perhaps not coincidentally the American Jewish population is estimated to be slightly below six million.) Other Muslim groups put the number higher, seeking to maximize the size and influence of their constituency.

Surveys conducted by non-Muslims have produced much lower estimates, some in the neighborhood of only two million or three million. These findings elicit anger from Muslim leaders, who claim that many immigrant and poor black Muslims are overlooked. On the basis of all the evidence, a very crude range of three million to six million seems reasonable. Rapid growth of the Muslim population is expected to continue, fueled mainly by immigration and high birthrates and, to a lesser extent, by conversion, overwhelmingly by African-Americans. In the next decade or two there probably will be more Muslims in the United States than Jews. Worldwide, the Muslim head count is estimated at 1.3 billion, second among religions only to the combined membership of Christian denominations.

American Muslims, like Americans generally, live mostly in cities and suburbs. Large concentrations are found in New York, Detroit, Chicago, and Los Angeles. But they also turn up in the Appalachian foothills and rural Idaho—the sites of two of the stories that follow—among other surprising places. Often the presence of several hundred Muslims in an out-of-the-way town can be explained by proximity to a large state university. Many of these schools have recruited foreign graduate students, including Muslims, since the 1960s. In the 1980s Washington doled out scholarships to Arab students as part of a campaign to counter the influence of the 1979 Iranian Revolution. Some of the Muslim beneficiaries have stayed and raised families.

In New York, Muslims are typecast as cab drivers; in Detroit, as owners of grocery stores and gas stations. The overall economic reality is very different. Surveys show that the majority of American Muslims are employed in technical, white-collar, and professional fields. These include information technology, corporate management, medicine, and

117

education. An astounding 59 percent of Muslim adults in the United States have college degrees. That compares with only 27 percent of all American adults. Four out of five Muslim workers earn at least twenty-five thousand dollars a year; more than half earn fifty thousand or more. A 2004 survey by a University of Kentucky researcher found that median family income among Muslims is sixty thousand dollars a year; the national median is fifty thousand. Most Muslims own stock or mutual funds, either directly or through retirement plans. Four out of five are registered to vote.

Relative prosperity, high levels of education, and political participation are indications of a minority population successfully integrating into the larger society. By comparison, immigrant Muslims in countries such as Britain, France, Holland, and Spain have remained poorer, less well educated, and socially marginalized. Western European Muslim populations are much larger in percentage terms. Nearly 10 percent of French residents are Muslim; in the United Kingdom the figure is 3 percent. In the more populous United States the Muslim share is 1 to 2 percent, depending on which Muslim population estimate one assumes. It's unlikely that American cities will see the sort of densely packed, volatile Muslim slums that have cropped up on the outskirts of Paris, for example.

America's social safety net is stingy compared with those of Western Europe, but there is greater opportunity for new arrivals to get ahead in material terms. This may attract to the United States more ambitious immigrants willing to adjust to the customs of their new home and eager to acquire education that leads to better jobs. More generous welfare benefits in Europe allow Muslims and other immigrants to live indefinitely on the periphery of society, without steady jobs or social interaction with the majority. Europeans, who for decades encouraged Muslim immigration as a source of menial labor, have shown overt hostility toward the outsiders and little inclination to embrace them as full-fledged citizens. Partly as a result, violent Islamic extremism has found fertile ground in Western Europe.

[2007]

RICHARD DELGADO

Hate Cannot Be Tolerated

Educated at the University of Washington and the University of California–Berkeley, **Richard Delgado** is a leading commentator on race in the United States. His 1996 book *The Rodrigo Chronicles: Conversations about America and Race* was nominated for the Pulitzer Prize and won the Gustavus Myers Prize for outstanding book on human rights in North America. In addition, he has edited or authored five other books that have won the Gustavus Myers Prize, including the 1995 *The Price We Pay: The Case against Racist Speech, Hate Propaganda, and Pornography*, edited with Laura Lederer, and the 1996 *The Coming Race War? And Other Apocalyptic Tales of America after Affirmative Action and Welfare*, which also won the 1997 American Library Association Choice Outstanding Academic Book Award. Delgado is currently the University Distinguished Professor of Law and Derrick Bell Fellow at the University of Pittsburgh School of Law.

In his essay "Hate Cannot Be Tolerated," Delgado defends hate-speech codes that some colleges have recently enacted. Hate speech, he argues, does not foster conversation and is a veritable "slap in the face" to its victims; thus, rules that govern it should be applauded.

Anonymous vandals scrawl hate-filled graffiti outside a Jewish student center. Black students at a law school find unsigned fliers stuffed inside their lockers screaming that they do not belong there. At a third campus, a group of toughs hurls epithets at a young Latino student walking home late at night.

In response to a rising tide of such incidents, some colleges have enacted hate-speech codes or applied existing rules against individuals whose conduct interferes with the educational opportunities of others. Federal courts have extended "hostile environment" case law to schools that tolerate a climate of hate for women and students of color.

Despite the alarm these measures sometimes elicit, nothing is wrong with them. In each case, the usual and preferred response—"more speech"—is unavailable to the victim. With anonymous hate speech such

119

as the flier or graffiti, the victim cannot talk back, for the hate speaker delivers the message in a cowardly fashion. And talking back to aggressors is rarely an option. Indeed, many hate crimes began just this way: The victim talked back—and paid with his life.

Hate speech is rarely an invitation to a conversation. More like a slap in the face, it reviles and silences. College counselors report that campuses where highly publicized incidents of hate speech have taken place show a decline in minority enrollment as students of color instead choose to attend schools where the environment is healthier.

A few federal courts have declared overly broad hate-speech codes 5 unconstitutional, as well they should. Nothing is gained by a rule so broad it could be construed as forbidding the discussion of controversial subjects such as evolution or affirmative action.

But this is not what most people mean by hate speech, nor are colleges barred from drafting narrow rules that hone in on the conduct they wish to control. And when they do, courts are very likely to find in their favor. Recent Supreme Court rulings striking down laws upholding affirmative action and approving punishment for cross-burning show that the court is not unaware of current trends. Society is becoming more diverse. Reasonable rules aimed at accommodating that diversity and regulating the conduct of bullies and bigots are to be applauded—not feared.

EDWARD SAID [1935–2003]

Clashing Civilizations?

Edward Said (1935–2003), was a world-renowned scholar, literary
critic, and pro-Palestinian activist. Born in Jerusalem to wealthy Christian
Palestinian parents, his father an American citizen, Said spent his
formative years in Cairo and, briefly, Jerusalem. As an adolescent he
continued his education in the United States, eventually earning his
B.A. from Princeton University and his M.A. and Ph.D. from Harvard
University. In 1963 he began teaching English and comparative literature at Columbia University, becoming a University Professor,
Columbia's most-honored academic rank, in 1992. Said also taught at
Harvard, Johns Hopkins, and Yale universities. The recipient of numerous honors and awards, including Columbia's Trilling Award and the
Wellek Prize of the American Comparative Literature Association,
Said's renown comes mostly from his influential albeit controversial
book *Orientalism* (1978), in which he argues that Western scholarship
of Eastern history and peoples is unduly permeated by Eurocentric
prejudices. While academic circles embroiled themselves in the dispu-
tation and endorsement of the validity of his assertions, Said persisted
in his outspoken advocacy of the Palestinian cause, stirring controversy until his death from leukemia in 2003.

Excerpted from Said's essay "We All Swim Together," first published
in *New Statesman* just after the terrorist attacks of September 11,
2001, "Clashing Civilizations?" is Said's refutation of the argument
that Islamic fundamentalists suffer from a sense of cultural inferiority
which has led to a clash of so-called "civilizations." Said takes issue
with both the pejorative relegation of Islamic peoples to the backwater
of history as well as the egotistical and reductive assumption that
there exists a clear line of demarcation separating the "the West" from
"Islam."

Samuel Huntington's article "The Clash of Civilizations?" appeared in
the summer 1993 issue of *Foreign Affairs*, where it immediately attracted
a surprising amount of attention and reaction. Because the article was
intended to supply Americans with an original thesis about "a new
phase" in world politics after the end of the Cold War, Huntington's

terms of argument seemed compellingly large, bold, even visionary. "It is my hypothesis," he wrote,

that . . . the great divisions among humankind and the dominating source of conflict will be cultural. Nation-states will remain the most powerful actors in world affairs, but the principal conflicts of global politics will occur between nations and groups of different civilizations. The clash of civilizations will dominate global politics. The fault lines between civilizations will be the battle lines of the future.

Most of the argument in the pages that followed relied on a vague notion of something Huntington called "civilization identity" and "the interactions among seven or eight [*sic*] major civilizations," of which the conflict between two of them, Islam and the West, gets the lion's share of his attention. In this belligerent kind of thought, he relies heavily on a 1990 article by the veteran orientalist Bernard Lewis, whose ideological colors are manifest in its title, "The Roots of Muslim Rage." In both articles, the personification of enormous entities called "the West" and "Islam" is recklessly affirmed, as if hugely complicated matters such as identity and culture existed in a cartoonlike world where Popeye and Bluto bash each other mercilessly, with one always more virtuous pugilist getting the upper hand over his adversary. Certainly neither Huntington nor Lewis has much time to spare for the internal dynamics and plurality of every civilization; or for considering that the major contest in most modern cultures concerns the definition or interpretation of each culture; or for the unattractive possibility that a great deal of demagogy and downright ignorance is involved in presuming to speak for a whole religion or civilization. No, the West is the West, and Islam is Islam.

The basic model of west versus the rest (the Cold War opposition reformulated) is what has persisted, often insidiously and implicitly, in discussion since the terrible events of September 11. The carefully planned and horrendous, pathologically motivated suicide attack and mass slaughter by a small group of deranged militants has been turned into proof of Huntington's thesis. Instead of seeing it for what it is—the capture of big ideas (I use the word loosely) by a tiny band of crazed fanatics for criminal purposes—international luminaries from the former Pakistani prime minister Benazir Bhutto to the Italian prime minister, Silvio Berlusconi, have pontificated about Islam's troubles and, in the latter's case, have used Huntington's ideas to rant on about the West's superiority, how "we" have Mozart and Michelangelo and they don't.

But why not instead see parallels, admittedly less spectacular in their destructiveness, to Osama Bin Laden and his followers in such cults as the Branch Davidians, or the disciples of the Reverend Jim Jones in Guyana, or the Japanese Aum Shinrikyo? Even *The Economist*, in its issue of September 22–28, 2001, couldn't resist reaching for the vast generalization, praising Huntington extravagantly for his "cruel and sweeping, but nonetheless acute" observations about Islam. "Today," the journal says, Huntington writes that "the world's billion or so Muslims are 'convinced of the superiority of their culture, and obsessed with the inferiority of their power.'" Did he canvass one hundred Indonesians, two hundred Moroccans, five hundred Egyptians and fifty Bosnians? Even if he did, what sort of sample is that?

Uncountable are the editorials in every American and European news- 5 paper and magazine of note adding to this vocabulary of gigantism and apocalypse, each use of which is plainly designed to inflame the reader's indignant passion as a member of the "West," and what we need to do. Churchillian rhetoric° is used inappropriately by self-appointed combatants in the West's, and especially America's, war against its haters, despoilers, destroyers, with scant attention to complex histories that defy such reductiveness and have seeped from one territory into another, overriding the boundaries that are supposed to separate us all into divided armed camps.

This is the problem with unedifying labels such as *Islam* and *the West:* They mislead and confuse the mind, which is trying to make sense of a disorderly reality that won't be pigeonholed. I remember interrupting a man who, after a lecture I had given at a West Bank° university in 1994, rose from the audience and started to attack my ideas as "Western," as opposed to the strict Islamic ones he espoused. "Why are you wearing a suit and tie?" was the first retort that came to mind. "They're Western, too." He sat down with an embarrassed smile on his face, but I recalled the incident when information on the September 11 terrorists started to come in: how they had mastered all the technical details required to inflict their homicidal evil on the World Trade Center, the Pentagon and the aircraft they had commandeered. Where does one draw the line between "Western" technology and, as Berlusconi declared, "Islam's" inability to be a part of "modernity"?

One cannot easily do so. How finally inadequate are the labels, generalizations and cultural assertions. At some level, for instance, primitive passions and sophisticated know-how converge in ways that give

Churchillian rhetoric: A statesman and gifted orator, Winston Churchill (1874–1965) was British prime minister during World War II, when his stirring speeches fortified his embattled nation's resolve to fight the Germans. **West Bank:** Disputed territory adjacent to Israel, controlled partly by Israel and partly by the Palestinian Authority.

the lie to a fortified boundary not only between "West" and "Islam," but also between past and present, us and them, to say nothing of the very concepts of identity and nationality about which there is unending debate. A unilateral decision made to undertake crusades, to oppose their evil with our good, to extirpate terrorism and, in Paul Wolfowitz's° nihilistic vocabulary, to end nations entirely, doesn't make the supposed entities any easier to see; rather, it speaks to how much simpler it is to make bellicose statements for the purpose of mobilizing collective passions than to reflect, examine, sort out what it is we are dealing with in reality, the interconnectedness of innumerable lives, "ours" as well as "theirs."

Paul Wolfowitz: Deputy secretary of defense under President George W. Bush.

CINDY C. COMBS   [b. 1952]

Profile of a Terrorist

Cindy Combs earned her B.A. and M.A. from Appalachian State
University and her Ph.D. in political science from George Washington
University. She has been a political science professor at the University
of North Carolina, Charlotte, since 1989. A nationally recognized
expert on international terrorism, she wrote the book *Terrorism in
the Twenty-First Century* (2002) and was a contributing editor of *The
Encyclopedia of Terrorism* (2003). She has been awarded the Bonnie E.
Cone Professorship teaching award, the 1997 NationsBank Award for
Teaching Excellence, the 1998 UNC Board of Governors Award
for Excellence in Teaching, and the 2000 International Faculty of the
Year Award.

Taken from *Terrorism in the Twenty-First Century*, "Profile of a
Terrorist" uses Frederick Hacker's categorization of those who commit
terrorist acts—as crazies, criminals, or crusaders—to emphasize the
notion that different resistance tactics must be taken by law enforcement officials and hostages themselves depending on the hostage-
takers' motivations.

*Nothing is easier than to denounce the evil doer; nothing is more
difficult than to understand him.*   —FYODOR DOSTOYEVSKY

Why do people become terrorists? Are they crazy? Are they thrill seekers?
Are they religious fanatics? Are they ideologues°? Is there any way to tell
who is likely to become a terrorist?

This final question provides a clue as to why political scientists and government officials are particularly interested in the psychological factors
relating to terrorism. If one could identify the traits most closely related to
a willingness to use terrorist tactics, then one would be in a better position
to predict, and prevent, the emergence of terrorist groups.

ideologues: people who blindly follow a certain set of theories

THREE TYPES OF TERRORISTS

Unfortunately, identifying such traits is not easy. Just as not all violence is terrorism, and not all revolutionaries are terrorists, not all persons who commit acts of terrorism are alike. Frederick Hacker suggested three categories of persons who commit terrorism: *crazies, criminals,* and *crusaders.* He notes that an individual carrying out a terrorist act is seldom "purely" one type or the other but that each type offers some insights into why an individual will resort to terrorism.

Understanding the individual who commits terrorism is vital, not only for humanitarian reasons, but also to decide how best to deal with those individuals *while they are engaged in terrorist acts.* From a law enforcement perspective, for example, it is important to appreciate the difference between a criminal and a crusading terrorist involved in a hostage-taking situation. Successful resolution of such a situation often hinges on understanding the mind of the individual perpetrating the crime.

Let us consider the three categories of terrorists suggested by Hacker: 5 crazies, criminals, and crusaders. For the purposes of this study, we need to establish loose descriptions of these three types. Hacker offers some useful ideas on what is subsumed under each label. **Crazies**, he suggests, are *emotionally disturbed individuals who are driven to commit terrorism "by reasons of their own that often do not make sense to anybody else."*

Criminals, on the other hand, *perform terrorist acts for more easily understood reasons: personal gain.* Such individuals transgress the laws of society knowingly and, one assumes, in full possession of their faculties. Both their motives and their goals are usually clear, if still deplorable, to most of humanity.

This is not the case with the crusaders. These individuals commit terrorism for reasons that are often unclear both to themselves and to those witnessing the acts. Their ultimate goals are frequently even less understandable. Although such individuals are usually idealistically inspired, their idealism tends to be a rather mixed bag of half-understood philosophies. **Crusaders**, according to Hacker, *seek not personal gain, but prestige and power for a collective cause.* They commit terrorist acts in the belief "that they are serving a higher cause," in Hacker's assessment.

The distinction between criminals and crusaders with respect to terrorism needs some clarification. Clearly, when anyone breaks the law, as in the commission of a terrorist act, he or she becomes a criminal, regardless of the reason for the transgression. The distinction between criminal and crusader, though, is useful in understanding the differences in the motives and goals moving the person to commit the act.

A TREND TOWARD CRUSADERS

The majority of the individuals and groups carrying out terrorist acts in the world in the last decade of the twentieth and the beginning of the twenty-first century have been crusaders. This does not mean that there are not occasional instances in which individuals who, reacting to some real or perceived injury, decide to take a machine gun to the target of their anger or kidnap or destroy anyone in sight. Nor does it mean that there are not individual criminals and criminal organizations that engage in terrorist activities.

Nonetheless, the majority of individuals who commit modern terror-　10 ism are, or perceive themselves to be, crusaders. According to Hacker, the typical crusading terrorist appears to be normal, no matter how crazy his or her cause or how criminal the means he or she uses for this cause may seem. He or she is neither an idiot nor a fool, neither a coward nor a weakling. Instead, the crusading terrorist is frequently a professional, well trained, well prepared, and well disciplined in the habit of blind obedience to a cause.

NEGOTIATING WITH TERRORISTS

Table A indicates a few dramatic differences between the types of terrorists Hacker profiles. One is that crusaders are the least likely to negotiate a resolution to a crisis, both because such action can be viewed as a betrayal of a sublime° cause and because there is little that the negotiator can offer, because neither personal gain nor safe passage out of the situation are particularly desired by true crusaders. Belief in the cause makes death not a penalty, but a path to reward and glory; therefore, the threat of death and destruction can have little punitive value. What can a police or military negotiator offer to a crusader to induce the release of hostages or the defusing of a bomb?

In terms of security devices and training, the profiles become even more vital. The events of September 11, 2001, illustrate dramatically the consequences of training and equipping for the wrong type of perpetrators. The pilots of airlines in the United States had been trained to respond to attempts to take over flights as hostage situations and thus were engaged in trying to keep the situation calm and to "talk down" the plane, to initiate a hostage release without violence. But the individuals engaged in the takeover were crusaders, not criminals or crazies, who did

sublime: lofty, highly regarded

127

TABLE A Hacker's Typology of Terrorists

Type of Terrorist	Motive/Goal	Willing to Negotiate?	Expectation of Survival
Crazy	Clear only to perpetrator	Possible, but only if negotiator can understand motive and offer hope/alternatives	Strong, but not based on reality
Criminal	Personal gain/ profit	Usually, in return for profit and/or safe passage	Strong
Crusader	"Higher cause" (usually a blend of religious and political)	Seldom, because to do so could be seen as a betrayal of the cause	Minimal, because death offers reward in an afterlife

not plan to live through the incidents. Only the passengers on the flight that crashed in Pennsylvania were able to offer substantial resistance—perhaps in part because they had not been trained to assume that a peaceful resolution could be negotiated with hostage takers.

This does not suggest that the pilots and crew were not vigilant and did not make every effort to save the lives of the passengers. But because the profile they had been trained to respond to did not match that with which they were confronted, they were unable to respond successfully to the demands of the situation. Thus, inaccurate profiling in pilot training was a serious contributing factor to the sequence of events on that day.

To political scientists, as well as to military, police, and other security and intelligence units assigned the task of coping with terrorism, an understanding of the type of person likely to commit acts of terrorism is invaluable. As our understanding of a phenomenon increases, our ability to predict its behavior with some accuracy also increases. Thus, as we try to understand who terrorists are and what they are like, we should increase our ability to anticipate their behavior patterns, thereby increasing our ability to respond effectively and to prevent more often the launching of successful terrorist attacks.

BEVERLY DANIEL TATUM [b. 1954]

Why Are All the Black Kids Sitting Together in the Cafeteria?

Born in 1954 into a well-educated black family, **Beverly Daniel Tatum** attended marginally integrated schools in Bridgewater, Massachusetts, and then graduated from Wesleyan University in 1975. A clinical psychologist and writer who specializes in the psychology of race and race relations, Tatum served as a professor and dean at Mount Holyoke College before being appointed president of Spelman College, an historically black liberal arts college for women, in 2002. Tatum's book *Why Are All the Black Kids Sitting Together in the Cafeteria? And Other Conversations About Race* was published to wide acclaim in 1999.

This excerpt from *Why Are All the Black Kids Sitting Together in the Cafeteria?* localizes the development of race identity during adolescence. Tatum states that racial groupings occur not in elementary schools but in middle schools, indicating that racial group membership becomes significant during puberty when young people are actively seeking a sense of belonging and a group of peers who readily understand their perspective. Tatum does not condemn racial groupings; instead she sees such self-imposed segregation as a "positive coping strategy" to help people of color deal with racial stress. Her hope is that an increased awareness of the hurt done by cultural stereotypes will decrease both racism and racial exclusivity.

Walk into any racially mixed high school cafeteria at lunch time and you will instantly notice an identifiable group of black students sitting together. Conversely, there are many white students sitting together, though we rarely comment about that. The question is "Why are the black kids sitting together?"

It doesn't start out that way. In racially mixed elementary schools, you often see children of diverse racial boundaries playing with one another,

Beverly Daniel Tatum, "Why Are All the Black Kids Sitting Together in the Cafeteria?" from *The Brown University Child and Adolescent Behavior Letter*, October 1977, v13, #10. Copyright © 1977 by Manisses Communications Group. Reprinted with permission of John Wiley & Sons, Inc.

sitting at the snack table together, crossing racial boundaries with an ease uncommon in adolescence.

Moving from elementary school to middle school means interacting with new children from different neighborhoods than before, and a certain degree of clustering by race might therefore be expected, presuming that children who are familiar with one another would form groups. But even in schools where the same children stay together from kindergarten through eighth grade, racial grouping begins by the sixth or seventh grade. What happens?

One thing that happens is puberty. As children enter adolescence, they begin to explore the question of identity, asking "Who am I? Who can I be?" in ways they have not done before. For black youths, asking "Who am I?" includes thinking about "Who I am ethnically? What does it mean to be black?"

Why do black youths, in particular, think about themselves in terms of 5 race? Because that is how the rest of the world thinks of them. Our self-perceptions are shaped by the messages we receive from those around us, and when young black men and women reach adolescence, the racial content of those messages intensifies.

Here is a case in point. If you were to ask my 10-year-old son, David, to describe himself, he would tell you many things: that he is smart, that he likes to play computer games, that he has an older brother. Near the top of his list, he would likely mention that he is tall for his age. He would probably not mention that he is black, though he certainly knows that he is. Why would he mention his height and not his racial group membership?

When David meets new adults, one of the first questions they ask is "How old are you?" When David states his age, the inevitable reply is, "Gee, you're tall for your age!"

It happens so frequently that I once overheard David say to someone, "Don't say it, I know. I'm tall for my age." Height is salient for David because it's salient for others.

When David meets new adults, they don't say, "Gee, you're black for your age!" Or do they?

Imagine David at 15, six-foot-two, wearing the adolescent attire of the 10 day, passing adults he doesn't know on the sidewalk. Do the women hold their purses a little tighter, maybe even cross the street to avoid him? Does he hear the sound of automatic door locks on cars as he passes by? Is he being followed around by the security guards at the local mall? Do strangers assume he plays basketball? Each of these experiences conveys a racial message.

At 10, race is not yet salient for David, because it's not yet salient for society. But it will be.

UNDERSTANDING RACIAL IDENTITY DEVELOPMENT

Psychologist William Cross, author of *Shades of Black: Diversity in African American Identity*, has offered a theory of racial identity development that I have found to be a very useful framework for understanding what is happening with those black students in the cafeteria. In the first stage of Cross's five-stage model, the black child absorbs many of the beliefs and values of the dominant white culture, including the idea that it's better to be white.

Simply as a function of being socialized in a Eurocentric culture, some black children may begin to value the role models, lifestyles and images of beauty represented by the dominant group more highly than those of their own cultural group. But the personal and social significance of one's racial group membership has not yet been realized, and racial identity is not yet under examination.

THE ENCOUNTER STAGE

Transition to the next stage, the encounter stage, is typically precipitated by an event—or series of events—that forces the young person to acknowledge the personal impact of racism.

For example, in racially mixed schools, black children are much more likely to be in a lower track than in an honors track. Such apparent sorting along racial lines sends a message about what it means to be black. One young honors student said, "It was really a very paradoxical existence, here I am in a school that's 35 percent black, you know, and I'm the only black in my class. That always struck me as odd. I guess I felt that I was different from the other blacks because of that."

There are also changes in the social dynamics outside the school. In racially mixed communities, you begin to see what I call the "birthday party effect." The parties of elementary school children may be segregated by gender, but not by race. At puberty, when the parties become sleepovers or boy–girl events, they become less and less racially diverse.

Black girls who live in predominantly white neighborhoods see their white friends start to date before they do. One young woman from a Philadelphia suburb described herself as "pursuing white guys throughout high school" to no avail. Because there were no black boys in her class, she had little choice. She would feel "really pissed off" that those same white boys would date her white friends.

Another young black woman attending a desegregated school to which she was bussed was encouraged by a teacher to attend the upcoming

131

school dance. Most of the black students did not live in the neighborhood and seldom attended the extracurricular activities. The young woman indicated that she wasn't planning to come. Finally the well-intentioned teacher said, "Oh come on, I know you people love to dance." This young woman got the message.

COPING WITH ENCOUNTER

What do these encounters have to do with the cafeteria? Do experiences with racism inevitably result in so-called self-segregation?

While a desire to protect oneself from further offense is understandable, 20 it's not the only factor at work. Imagine the young eighth-grade girl who experienced the teacher's use of "you people" and the dancing stereotype as a racial affront. Upset and struggling with adolescent embarrassment, she bumps into a white friend who can see that something is wrong. She explains. Her white friend responds—perhaps in an effort to make her feel better—and says, "Oh, Mr. Smith is such a nice guy, I'm sure he didn't mean it like that. Don't be so sensitive."

Perhaps the white friend is right, but imagine your own response when you are upset, and your partner brushes off your complaint, attributing it to your being oversensitive. What happens to your emotional thermostat? It escalates. When feelings, rational or irrational, are invalidated, most people disengage. They not only choose to discontinue the conversation but are more likely to turn to someone who will understand their perspective.

In much the same way that the eighth-grade girl's white friend doesn't get it, the girls at the "black table" do. Not only are black adolescents encountering racism and reflecting on their identity, but their white peers—even if not racist—are unprepared to respond in supportive ways.

The black students turn to each other for the much needed support they are not likely to find anywhere else.

We need to understand that in racially mixed settings, racial grouping is a developmental process in response to an environmental stressor, racism. Joining with one's peers for support in the face of stress is a positive coping strategy. The problem is that our young people are operating with a very limited definition of what it means to be black, based largely on cultural stereotypes.

CURTIS CHANG   [b. 1968]

Streets of Gold: The Myth of the Model Minority

Born in Taiwan, **Curtis Chang** immigrated to the United States with his
family in 1972, settling in Chicago, Illinois. A founding member of the
Minority Student Alliance at Harvard University, he graduated with a
degree in political science in 1991. He then served as director of the
InterVarsity Christian Fellowship for Tufts, MIT, and Harvard. Chang
now serves on the ministry staff of the River Church community in
Sunnyvale, California. His book, *Engaging Unbelief: A Captivating
Strategy from Augustine and Aquinas* (2000), looks at the challenges
facing Christians in a fragmented modern society.

In "Streets of Gold: The Myth of the Model Minority," Chang criticizes
the American media for misrepresenting the economic and social status
of Asian Americans. Chang reports that the latter half of the twentieth
century has seen Asian immigrants labeled as the "Model Minority," the
nonwhite group judged by white America to be most successful, hard-
working, and respectable. The problem for Chang is that the media mis-
construes the economic statistics relating to Asian Americans and
misconceives of a workable definition of "success." Chang asserts that
Asian Americans shouldn't settle for marginalization of any kind;
overlooking discrimination is just as insidious as racism itself.

Over one hundred years ago, an American myth misled many of my
ancestors. Seeking cheap labor, railroad companies convinced numerous Chinese that American streets were paved with gold. Today, the
media portray Asian-Americans as finally mining those golden streets.
Major publications like *Time, Newsweek, U.S. News & World Report, Fortune, The New Republic,* the *Wall Street Journal,* and the New *York Times
Magazine* have all recently published congratulatory "Model Minority"
headline stories with such titles as

America's Super Minority

An American Success Story

A "Model Minority"
Why They Succeed
The Ultimate Assimilation
The Triumph of Asian-Americans.

But the Model Minority is another "Streets of Gold" tale. It distorts Asian-Americans' true status and ignores our racial handicaps. And the Model Minority's ideology is even worse than its mythology. It attempts to justify the existing system of racial inequality by blaming the victims rather than the system itself.

The Model Minority myth introduces us as an ethnic minority that is finally "making it in America," as stated in *Time* (Doerner 42). The media consistently define "making it" as achieving material wealth, wealth that flows from our successes in the workplace and the schoolroom. This economic achievement allegedly proves a minority can, as *Fortune* says, "lay claim to the American dream" (Ramirez 149).

Trying to show how "Asian-Americans present a picture of affluence and economic success," as the New *York Times Magazine* puts it (Oxnam 72), nine out of ten of the major Model Minority stories of the last four years relied heavily on one statistic: the family median income. The median Asian-American family income, according to the U.S. Census Survey of Income and Education data, is $22,713 compared to $20,800 for white Americans. Armed with that figure, national magazines such as *Newsweek* have trumpeted our "remarkable, ever-mounting achievements" (Kasindorf et al. 51).

Such assertions demonstrate the truth of the aphorism "Statistics are 5 like a bikini. What they reveal is suggestive, but what they conceal is vital." The family median income statistic conceals the fact that Asian-American families generally (1) have more children and live-in relatives and thus have more mouths to feed; (2) are often forced by necessity to have everyone in the family work, averaging *more* than two family income earners (whites only have 1.6) (Cabezas 402); and (3) live disproportionately in high cost of living areas (i.e., New York, Chicago, Los Angeles, and Honolulu) which artificially inflate income figures. Dr. Robert S. Mariano, professor of economics at the University of Pennsylvania, has calculated that

when such appropriate adjustments and comparisons are made, a different and rather disturbing picture emerges, showing indeed a clearly disadvantaged group.... Filipino and Chinese men *are no better off than black men with regard to median incomes.* (55)[1]

Along with other racial minorities, Asian-Americans are still scraping for the crumbs of the economic pie.

134

Throughout their distortion of our status, the media propagate two crucial assumptions. First, they lump all Asian-Americans into one monolithic, homogeneous, yellow-skinned mass. Such a view ignores the existence of an incredibly disadvantaged Asian-American underclass. Asians work in low-income and low-status jobs two to three times more than whites (Cabezas 438). Recent Vietnamese refugees in California are living like the Appalachian poor. While going to his Manhattan office, multimillionaire architect I. M. Pei's car passes Chinese restaurants and laundries where 72 percent of all New York Chinese men still work (U.S. Bureau of the Census qtd. in Cabezas 443).

But the media make an even more dangerous assumption. They suggest that (alleged) material success is the same thing as basic racial equality. Citing that venerable family median income figure, magazines claim Asian-Americans are "obviously nondisadvantaged folks," as stated in *Fortune* (Seligman 64). Yet a 1979 United States Equal Employment Opportunity Commission study on Asian-Americans discovered widespread anti-Asian hiring and promotion practices. Asian-Americans "in the professional, technical, and managerial occupations" often face "modern racism — the subtle, sophisticated, systemic patterns and practices...which function to effect and to obscure the discriminatory outcomes" (Nishi 398). One myth simply does not prove another: Neither our "astonishing economic prosperity" (Ramirez 152) nor a racially equal America exist.

An emphasis on material success also pervades the media's stress on Asian-Americans' educational status at "the top of the class" ("Asian Americans" 4). Our "march into the ranks of the educational elite," as *U.S. News & World Report* puts it (McBee et al. 41), is significant, according to *Fortune*, because "all that education is paying off spectacularly" (Ramirez 149). Once again, the same fallacious assumptions plague this "whiz kids" image of Asian-Americans.

The media again ignore the fact that class division accounts for much of the publicized success. Until 1976, the U.S. Immigration Department only admitted Asian immigrants that were termed "skilled" workers. "Skilled" generally meant college educated, usually in the sciences since poor English would not be a handicap. The result was that the vast majority of pre-1976 Asian immigrants came from already well-educated, upper-class backgrounds — the classic "brain drain" syndrome (Hirschman and Wong 507–10).

The post-1976 immigrants, however, come generally from the lower, 10 less educated classes (Kim 24). A study by Professor Elizabeth Ahn Toupin of Tufts University matched similar Asian and non-Asian students *along class lines* and found that Asian-Americans "did not perform at a superior academic level to non-Asian students. Asian-Americans were more likely to be placed on academic probation than their white counterparts.... Twice as many Asian-American students withdrew from the university" (12).

Thus, it is doubtful whether the perceived widespread educational success will continue as the Asian-American population eventually balances out along class lines. When 16.2 percent of all Chinese have less than four years of schooling (*four times* the percentage of whites) (Azores 73), it seems many future Asian-Americans will worry more about being able to read a newspaper rather than a Harvard acceptance letter.

Most important, the media assume once again that achieving a certain level of material or educational success means achieving real equality. People easily forget that to begin with, Asians invest heavily in education since other means of upward mobility are barred to them by race. Until recently, for instance, Asian-Americans were barred from unions and traditional lines of credit (Yun 23–24).[2] Other "white" avenues to success, such as the "old-boy network," are still closed to Asian-Americans.

When *Time* claims "as a result of their academic achievement Asians are climbing the economic ladder with remarkable speed," it glosses over an inescapable fact: There is a white ladder and then there is a yellow one. Almost all of the academic studies on the *actual returns Asians receive* from their education point to prevalent discrimination. A striking example of this was found in a City University of New York research project which constructed résumés with equivalent educational backgrounds. Applications were then sent to employers, one group under an Asian name and a similar group under a Caucasian name. Whites received interviews five times more than Asians (Nishi 399). The media never headline even more shocking data that can be easily found in the U.S. Census. For instance, Chinese and Filipino males only earned respectively 74 percent and 52 percent as much as their *equally educated* white counterparts. Asian females fared even worse. Their salaries were only 44 percent to 54 percent as large as equivalent white males' paychecks (Cabezas 391). Blacks suffer from this same statistical disparity. We Asian-Americans are indeed a Model Minority—a perfect model of racial discrimination in America.

Yet this media myth encourages neglect of our pressing needs. "Clearly, many Asian-Americans and Pacific peoples are invisible to the governmental agencies," reported the California State Advisory Committee to the U.S. Commission on Civil Rights. "Discrimination against Asian-Americans and Pacific peoples is as much the result of omission as commission" (qtd. in Chun 7). In 1979, while the president praised Asian-Americans' "successful integration into American society," his administration revoked Asian-Americans' eligibility for minority small business loans, devastating thousands of struggling, newly arrived small businessmen. Hosts of other minority issues, ranging from reparations for the Japanese-American internment to the ominous rise of anti-Asian violence, are widely ignored by the general public.

The media, in fact, insist to the general populace that we are not a true   15
racial minority. In an attack on affirmative action, the *Boston Globe* pointed out that universities, like many people, "obviously feel that Asian-Americans, especially those of Chinese and Japanese descent, are brilliant, privileged, and wrongly classified as minorities" ("Affirmative Non-actions" 10). Harvard Dean Henry Rosovsky remarked in the same article that "It does not seem to me that as a group, they are disadvantaged.... Asian-Americans appear to be in an odd category among other protected minorities."

The image that we Asians aren't like "other minorities" is fundamental to the Model Minority ideology. Any elementary-school student knows that the teacher designates one student the model, the "teacher's pet," in order to set an example for others to follow. One only sets up a "model minority" in order to communicate to the other "students," the blacks and Hispanics, "Why can't you be like that?" The media, in fact, almost admit to "grading" minorities as they headline Model Minority stories "Asian-Americans: Are They Making the Grade?" (McBee et al.). And Asians have earned the highest grade by fulfilling one important assignment: identifying with the white majority, with its values and wishes.

Unlike blacks, for instance, we Asian-Americans have not vigorously asserted our ethnic identity (a.k.a. Black Power). And the American public has historically demanded assimilation over racial pluralism.[3] Over the years, *Newsweek* has published titles from "Success Story: Out-whiting the Whites" to "The Ultimate Assimilation," which lauded the increasing number of Asian-white marriages as evidence of Asian-Americans' "acceptance into American society" (Kantrowitz et al. 80).

Even more significant is the public's approval of how we have succeeded in the "American tradition" (Ramirez 164). Unlike the blacks and Hispanics, we "Puritan-like" Asians (Oxnam 72) disdain governmental assistance. A New *Republic* piece, "The Triumph of Asian-Americans," similarly applauded how "Asian-Americans pose no problems at all" (Bell 30). The media consistently compare the crime-ridden image of other minorities with the picture of law-abiding Asian parents whose "well-behaved kids" hit books and not the streets ("Asian Americans" 4).

Some insist there is nothing terrible about whites conjuring up our "tremendous" success, divining from it model American traits, then preaching, "Why can't you blacks and Hispanics be like that?" After all, one might argue, aren't those traits desirable?

Such a view, as mentioned, neglects Asian-Americans' true and press-   20
ing needs. Moreover, this view completely misses the Model Minority

image's fundamental ideology, an ideology meant to falsely grant America absolution from its racial barriers.

David O. Sears and Donald R. Kinder, two social scientists, have recently published significant empirical studies on the underpinnings of American racial attitudes. They consistently discovered that Americans' stress on "values, such as 'individualism and self-reliance, the work ethic, obedience, and discipline'...can be invoked, however perversely, to feed racist appetites" (qtd. in Kennedy 88). In other words, the Model Minority image lets Americans' consciences rest easy. They can think: "It's not our fault those blacks and Hispanics can't make it. They're just too lazy. After all, look at the Asians."[4] Consequently, American society never confronts the systemic racial and economic factors underlying such inequality. The victims instead bear the blame.

This ideology behind the Model Minority image is best seen when we examine one of the first Model Minority stories, which suddenly appeared in the mid-1960s. It is important to note that the period was marked by newfound, strident black demands for equality and power.

At a time when it is being proposed that hundreds of billions be spent to uplift Negroes and other minorities, the nation's 300,000 Chinese-Americans are moving ahead on their own—with no help from anyone else....Few Chinese-Americans are getting welfare handouts—or even want them.... They don't sit around moaning. ("Success Story of One Minority Group" 73).

The same article then concludes that the Chinese-American history and accomplishment "would shock those now complaining about the hardships endured by today's Negroes."

Not surprisingly, the dunce-capped blacks and Hispanics resent us apple-polishing, "well-behaved" teacher's pets. Black comedian Richard Pryor performs a revealing routine in which new Asian immigrants learn from whites their first English word, "Nigger." And Asian-Americans themselves succumb to the Model Minority's deceptive mythology and racist ideology.[5] "I made it without help," one often hears among Asian circles; "why can't they?" In a 1986 nationwide poll, only 27% of Asian-American students rated "racial understanding" as "essential." The figure plunged 9 percent in the last year alone (a year marked by a torrent of Model Minority stories) (Hune). We "whitewashed" Asians have simply lost our identity as a fellow, disadvantaged minority.

But we don't even need to look beyond the Model Minority stories themselves to realize that whites see us as "whiter" than blacks—but not quite white enough. For instance, citing that familiar median family income figure, *Fortune* magazine of 17 May 1982 complained that the Asian-American community is in fact "getting *more* than its share of the pie" (Seligman 64). For decades, when white Americans were leading the nation in every single economic measure, editorials arguing that whites were getting more than *their* share of the pie were rather rare.

No matter how "well-behaved" we are, Asian-Americans are still 25 excluded from the real pie, the "positions of institutional power and political power" (Kuo 289). Professor Harry Kitano of UCLA has written extensively on the plight of Asian-Americans as the "middle-man minority," a minority supposedly satisfied materially but forever racially barred from a true, *significant* role in society. Empirical studies indicate that Asian-Americans "have been channeled into lower-echelon white-collar jobs having little or no decision making authority" (Suzuki 38). For example, in *Fortune's* 1,000 largest companies, Asian-American nameplates rest on a mere half of one percent of all officers' and directors' desks (a statistical disparity worsened by the fact that most of the Asians founded their companies) (Ramirez 152). While the education of the upper-class Asians may save them from the bread lines, their race still keeps them from the boardroom.

Our docile acceptance of such exclusion is actually one of our "model" traits. When Asian-Americans in San Francisco showed their first hint of political activism and protested Asian exclusion from city boards, the *Washington Monthly* warned in a long Asian-American article, "Watch out, here comes another group to pander to" ("The Wrong Way" 21). *The New Republic* praised Asian-American political movements because

> Unlike blacks or Hispanics, Asian-American politicians have the luxury of not having to devote the bulk of their time to an "Asian-American agenda," and thus escape becoming prisoners of such an agenda....The most important thing for Asian-Americans...is simply "being part of the process." (Bell 31)

This is strikingly reminiscent of another of the first Model Minority stories:

> As the Black and Brown communities push for changes in the present system, the Oriental is set forth as an example to be followed—a minority group that has achieved success through adaptation rather than confrontation. (*Gidra* qtd. in Chun 7)

But it is precisely this "present system," this system of subtle, persistent racism that we all must confront, not adapt to. For example, we Asians gained our right to vote from the 1964 Civil Rights Act that blacks marched, bled, died, and, in the words of that original Model Minority story, "sat around moaning for." Unless we assert our true identity as a minority and challenge racial misconceptions and inequalities, we will be nothing more than techno-coolies—collecting our wages but silently enduring basic political and economic inequality.

This country perpetuated a myth once. Today, no one can afford to dreamily chase after that gold in the streets, oblivious to the genuine treasure of racial equality. When racism persists, can one really call any minority a "model"?

Notes

1. The picture becomes even more disturbing when one realizes the higher income figures do not necessarily equal higher quality of life. For instance, in New York Chinatown, more than one out of five work more than fifty-seven hours per week, almost one out of ten elderly must labor more than fifty-five hours per week (Nishi 503).

2. For further analysis on the role racism plays in Asian-Americans' stress on education and certain technical and scientific fields, see Suzuki (44).

3. A full discussion of racial pluralism versus assimilation is impossible here. But suffice it to say that pluralism accepts ethnic cultures as equally different; assimilation asks for a "melting" into the majority. An example of the assimilation philosophy is the massive "Americanization" programs of the late 1880s, which successfully erased Eastern European immigrants' customs in favor of Anglo-Saxon ones.

4. This phenomenon of blaming the victim for racial inequality is as old as America itself. For instance, southerners once eased their consciences over slavery by labeling blacks as animals lacking humanity. Today, America does it by labeling them as inferior people lacking "desirable" traits. For an excellent further analysis of this ideology, actually widespread among American intellectuals, see *Iron Cages: Race and Culture in 19th-Century America* by Ronald T. Takaki.

5. America has a long history of playing off one minority against the other. During the early 1900s, for instance, mining companies in the west often hired Asians solely as scabs against striking black miners. Black versus Asian hostility and violence usually followed. This pattern was repeated in numerous industries. In a larger historical sense, almost every immigrant group has assimilated, to some degree, the culture of antiblack racism.

Works Cited

"Affirmative Non-actions." Op-ed. *Boston Globe* 14 Jan. 1985: 10.

"Asian Americans, The Drive to Excel." *Newsweek on Campus* April 1984: 4–13.

Asian American Studies: Contemporary Issues. Proc. from East Coast Asian American Scholars Conf. 1986.

Azores, Fortunata M. "Census Methodology and the Development of Social Indicators for Asian and Pacific Americans." United States Commission on Civil Rights 70–79.

Bell, David A. "The Triumph of Asian-Americans." *New Republic* 15 & 22 July 1985: 24–31.

Cabezas, Armado. "Employment Issues of Asian Americans." United States Commission on Civil Rights.

Chun, Ki-Taek. "The Myth of Asian American Success and Its Educational Ramifications." *IRCD Bulletin* Winter/Spring 1980.

Doerner, William R. "To America with Skills." *Time* 8 July 1985: 42–44.

Dutta, Manoranjan. "Asian/Pacific American Employment Profile: Myth and Reality—Issues and Answers." United States Commission on Civil Rights 445–89.

Hirschman, Charles, and Morrison G. Wong. "Trends in Socioeconomic Achievement Among Immigrants and Native-Born Asian-Americans, 1960-1976." *Sociological Quarterly* 22.4 (1981): 495–513.

Hune, Shirley. Keynote address. East Coast Asian Student Union Conference. Boston University. 14 Feb. 1987.

Kahng, Anthony. "Employment Issues." United States Commission on Civil Rights 1980.

Kantrowitz, Barbara, et al. "The Ultimate Assimilation." *Newsweek* 24 Nov. 1986: 80.

Kasindorf, Martin, et al. "Asian-Americans: A 'Model Minority.'" *Newsweek* 6 Dec. 1982: 39–51.

Kennedy, David M. "The Making of a Classic. Gunnar Myrdal and Black-White Relations: The Use and Abuse of *An American Dilemma*." *Atlantic* May 1987: 86–89.

Kiang, Peter. Personal interview. 1 May 1987.

Kim, Illsoo. "Class Division Among Asian Immigrants: Its Implications for Social Welfare Policy." *Asian American Studies* 24–25.

Kuo, Wen H. "On the Study of Asian-Americans: Its Current State and Agenda." *Sociological Quarterly* 20.2 (1979): 279–90.

Mariano, Robert S. "Census Issues." United States Commission on Civil Rights 54–59.

McBee, Susanna, et al. "Asian-Americans: Are They Making the Grade?" *U.S. News & World Report* 2 Apr. 1984: 41–47.

Nishi, Setsuko Matsunaga. "Asian American Employment Issues: Myths and Realities." United States Commission on Civil Rights 397–99, 495–507.

Oxnam, Robert B. "Why Asians Succeed Here." *New York Times Magazine* 30 Nov. 1986: 72+.

Ramirez, Anthony. "America's Super Minority." *Fortune* 24 Nov. 1986: 148–49.

Seligman, Daniel. "Keeping Up: Working Smarter." *Fortune* 17 May 1982: 64.

"Success Story of One Minority Group in the U.S." *U.S. News & World Report* 26 Dec. 1966: 73–76.

"Success Story: Outwhiting the Whites." *Newsweek* 21 June 1971: 24–25.

Sung, Betty Lee. *A Survey of Chinese American Manpower and Employment.* New York: Praeger, 1976.

Suzuki, Bob H. "Education and the Socialization of Asian Americans: A Revisionist Analysis of the 'Model Minority' Thesis." *Amerasia Journal* 4.2 (1977): 23–51.

Toupin, Elizabeth Ahn. "A Model University for a Model Minority." *Asian American Studies* 10–12.

United States Commission on Civil Rights. *Civil Rights Issues of Asian and Pacific Americans: Myths and Realities.* 1980.

"The Wrong Way to Court Ethnics." *Washington Monthly* May 1986: 21–26.

Yun, Grace. "Notes from Discussions on Asian American Education." *Asian American Studies* 20–24.

BARBARA EHRENREICH   [b. 1941]

Cultural Baggage

A renowned social critic and prolific essayist, **Barbara Ehrenreich** was
born in Butte, Montana, in 1941. In 1963 she graduated with a B.A. in
physics from Reed College and went on to earn a Ph.D. in cell biology
from Rockefeller University. Initially she had no intention of becoming
a writer, but she found herself attracted to a career in social activism
rather than research science and began writing investigative articles for
small newsletters. Her articles have appeared in the *New York Times,
Ms.*, the *Atlantic Monthly, In These Times,* and *The New Republic,* among
others. From 1991 to 1997 Ehrenreich was a regular columnist for *Time*
magazine and is currently a regular columnist for *The Progressive.* Her
national best seller, *Nickel and Dimed* (2001), narrates her efforts to survive on low-income wages and her follow-up book, *Bait and Switch*
(2005), recounts her undercover efforts to find a white-collar job in
corporate America.

In "Cultural Baggage," Ehrenreich appraises her diverse ethnic and
religious heritage and wonders just how much significance she can
allot to any one set of traditions. At first despairing of her rootlessness,
she concludes that living by her parent's greatest tenets — "Think for
yourself" and "Try new things" — are all the cultural roots she needs.

An acquaintance was telling me about the joys of rediscovering her ethnic and religious heritage. "I know exactly what my ancestors were
doing 2,000 years ago," she said, eyes gleaming with enthusiasm, "and *I
can do the same things now.*" Then she leaned forward and inquired
politely, "And what is your ethnic background, if I may ask?"

"None," I said, that being the first word in line to get out of my mouth.
Well, not "none," I backtracked. Scottish, English, Irish—that was something, I supposed. Too much Irish to qualify as a WASP; too much of the
hated English to warrant a "Kiss Me, I'm Irish" button; plus there are a
number of dead ends in the family tree due to adoptions, missing
records, failing memories and the like. I was blushing by this time. Did
"none" mean I was rejecting my heritage out of Anglo-Celtic self-hate? Or
was I revealing a hidden ethnic chauvinism in which the Britannically

derived serve as a kind of neutral standard compared with the ethnic "others"?

Throughout the 60's and 70's, I watched one group after another— African-Americans, Latinos, Native Americans—stand up and proudly reclaim their roots while I just sank back ever deeper into my seat. All this excitement over ethnicity stemmed, I uneasily sensed, from a past in which their ancestors had been trampled upon by *my* ancestors, or at least by people who looked very much like them. In addition, it had begun to seem almost un-American not to have some sort of hyphen at hand, linking one to more venerable times and locales.

But the truth is, I was raised with none. We'd eaten ethnic foods in my childhood home, but these were all borrowed, like the pasties, or Cornish meat pies, my father had picked up from his fellow miners in Butte, Mont. If my mother had one rule, it was militant ecumenism in all matters of food and experience. "Try new things," she would say, meaning anything from sweetbreads to clams, with an emphasis on the "new."

As a child, I briefly nourished a craving for tradition and roots. I 5 immersed myself in the works of Sir Walter Scott. I pretended to believe that the bagpipe was a musical instrument. I was fascinated to learn from a grandmother that we were descended from certain Highland clans and longed for a pleated skirt in one of their distinctive tartans.

But in "Ivanhoe," it was the dark-eyed "Jewess" Rebecca I identified with, not the flaxen-haired bimbo Rowena. As for clans: Why not call them "tribes," those bands of half-clad peasants and warriors whose idea of cuisine was stuffed sheep gut washed down with whisky? And then there was the sting of Disraeli's remark—which I came across in my early teens—to the effect that his ancestors had been leading orderly, literate lives when my ancestors were still rampaging through the Highlands daubing themselves with blue paint.

Motherhood put the screws on me, ethnicity-wise. I had hoped that by marrying a man of Eastern European-Jewish ancestry I would acquire for my descendants the ethnic genes that my own forebears so sadly lacked. At one point, I even subjected the children to a seder of my own design, including a little talk about the flight from Egypt and its relevance to modern social issues. But the kids insisted on buttering their matzohs and snickering through my talk. "Give me a break, Mom," the older one said. "You don't even believe in God."

After the tiny pagans had been put to bed, I sat down to brood over Elijah's wine. What had I been thinking? The kids knew that their Jewish grandparents were secular folks who didn't hold seders themselves. And if ethnicity eluded me, how could I expect it to take root in my children, who are not only Scottish-English-Irish, but Hungarian-Polish-Russian to boot?

But, then, on the fumes of Manischewitz, a great insight took form in my mind. It was true, as the kids said, that I didn't "believe in God." But this could be taken as something very different from an accusation—a reminder of a genuine heritage. My parents had not believed in God either, nor had my grandparents or any other progenitors going back to the great-great level. They had become disillusioned with Christianity generations ago—just as, on the in-law side, my children's other ancestors had shaken their Orthodox Judaism. This insight did not exactly furnish me with an "identity," but it was at least something to work with: we are the kind of people, I realized—whatever our distant ancestors' religions—who do *not* believe, who do not carry on traditions, who do not do things just because someone has done them before.

The epiphany went on: I recalled that my mother never introduced a   10
procedure for cooking or cleaning by telling me, "Grandma did it this way." What did Grandma know, living in the days before vacuum cleaners and disposable toilet mops! In my parents' general view, new things were better than old, and the very fact that some ritual had been performed in the past was a good reason for abandoning it now. Because what was the past, as our forebears knew it? Nothing but poverty, superstition and grief. "Think for yourself," Dad used to say. "Always ask why."

In fact, this may have been the ideal cultural heritage for my particular ethnic strain—bounced as it was from the Highlands of Scotland across the sea, out to the Rockies, down into the mines and finally spewed out into high-tech, suburban America. What better philosophy, for a race of migrants, than "Think for yourself"? What better maxim, for a people whose whole world was rudely inverted every 30 years or so, than "Try new things"?

The more tradition-minded, the newly enthusiastic celebrants of Purim and Kwanzaa and Solstice, may see little point to survival if the survivors carry no cultural freight—religion, for example, or ethnic tradition. To which I would say that skepticism, curiosity and wide-eyed ecumenical tolerance are also worthy elements of the human tradition and are at least as old as such notions as "Serbian" or "Croatian," "Scottish" or "Jewish." I make no claims for my personal line of progenitors except that they remained loyal to the values that may have induced all of our ancestors, long, long ago, to climb down from the trees and make their way into the open plains.

A few weeks ago, I cleared my throat and asked the children, now mostly grown and fearsomely smart, whether they felt any stirrings of ethnic or religious identity, etc., which might have been, ahem, insufficiently nourished at home. "None," they said, adding firmly, "and the world would be a better place if nobody else did, either." My chest swelled with pride, as would my mother's, to know that the race of "none" marches on.

145

JAMES BALDWIN   [1924–1987]

If Black English Isn't a Language, Then Tell Me, What Is?

Born in New York City, the son of a revivalist minister, **James Baldwin** (1924–1987) was raised in poverty in Harlem where, at the age of fourteen, he became a preacher in the Fireside Pentecostal Church. After completing high school he decided to become a writer and, with the help of the black American expatriate writer Richard Wright, won a grant that enabled him to move to Paris, where he lived for most of his remaining years. There he wrote the critically acclaimed *Go Tell It on the Mountain* (1953), a novel about the religious awakening of a fourteen-year-old black youth. Subsequent works, focusing on the intellectual and spiritual trials of black men in a white, racist society, included the novels *Giovanni's Room* (1956), *Another Country* (1962) — both famous at the time for their homosexual themes — *Tell Me How Long the Train's Been Gone* (1968), *If Beale Street Could Talk* (1974), *Just Above My Head* (1979), and *Harlem Quartet* (1987); the play *Blues for Mister Charlie* (1964); and the powerful nonfiction commentaries *Notes of a Native Son* (1955), *Nobody Knows My Name* (1961), and *The Fire Next Time* (1963). Baldwin's short stories are collected in *Going to Meet the Man* (1965).

The argument concerning the use, or the status, or the reality, of black English is rooted in American history and has absolutely nothing to do with the question the argument supposes itself to be posing. The argument has nothing to do with language itself but with the *role* of language. Language, incontestably, reveals the speaker. Language, also, far more dubiously, is meant to define the other — and, in this case, the other is refusing to be defined by a language that has never been able to recognize him.

People evolve a language in order to describe and thus control their circumstances, or in order not to be submerged by a reality that they cannot articulate. (And, if they cannot articulate it, they *are* submerged.) A Frenchman living in Paris speaks a subtly and crucially different language from that of the man living in Marseilles; neither sounds very much like a man living in Quebec; and they would all have great difficulty in apprehending what the man from Guadeloupe, or Martinique, is saying, to say nothing of the man from Senegal—although the "common" language of all these areas is French. But each has paid, and is paying, a different price for this "common" language, in which, as it turns out, they are not saying, and cannot be saying, the same things: they each have very different realities to articulate, or control.

What joins all languages, and all men, is the necessity to confront life, in order, not inconceivably, to outwit death: the price for this is the acceptance, and achievement, of one's temporal identity. So that, for example, though it is not taught in the schools (and this has the potential of becoming a political issue) the south of France still clings to its ancient and musical Provençal, which resists being described as a "dialect." And much of the tension in the Basque countries, and in Wales, is due to the Basque and Welsh determination not to allow their languages to be destroyed. This determination also feeds the flames in Ireland for among the many indignities the Irish have been forced to undergo at English hands is the English contempt for their language.

It goes without saying, then, that language is also a political instrument, means, and proof of power. It is the most vivid and crucial key to identity: it reveals the private identity, and connects one with, or divorces one from, the larger, public, or communal identity. There have been, and are, times, and places, when to speak a certain language could be dangerous, even fatal. Or, one may speak the same language, but in such a way that one's antecedents are revealed, or (one hopes) hidden. This is true in France, and is absolutely true in England: the range (and reign) of accents on that damp little island make England coherent for the English and totally incomprehensible for everyone else. To open your mouth in England is (if I may use black English) to "put your business in the street": You have confessed your parents, your youth, your school, your salary, your self-esteem, and alas, your future.

Now, I do not know what white Americans would sound like if there   5 had never been any black people in the United States, but they would not sound the way they sound. *Jazz*, for example, is a very specific sexual term, as in *jazz me, baby*, but white people purified it into the Jazz Age. *Sock it to me*, which means, roughly, the same thing, has been adopted by Nathaniel Hawthorne's descendants with no qualms or hesitations at all, along with *let it all hang out* and *right on! Beat to his socks*, which was once the black's most total and despairing image of poverty, was transformed into a thing called the Beat Generation, which phenomenon was,

147

largely, composed of *uptight*, middle-class white people, imitating poverty, trying to *get down*, to get *with it*, doing their *thing*, doing their despairing best to be *funky*, which we, the blacks, never dreamed of doing—we *were* funky, baby, like *funk* was going out of style.

Now, no one can eat his cake, and have it, too, and it is late in the day to attempt to penalize black people for having created a language that permits the nation its only glimpse of reality, a language without which the nation would be even more *whipped* than it is.

I say that this present skirmish is rooted in American history, and it is. Black English is the creation of the black diaspora. Blacks came to the United States chained to each other, but from different tribes: neither could speak the other's language. If two black people, at that bitter hour of the world's history, had been able to speak to each other, the institution of chattel slavery could never have lasted as long as it did. Subsequently, the slave was given, under the eye, and the gun, of his master, Congo Square, and the Bible—or, in other words, and under these conditions, the slave began the formation of the black church, and it is within this unprecedented tabernacle that black English began to be formed. This was not, merely, as in the European example, the adoption of a foreign tongue, but an alchemy that transformed ancient elements into a new language: *A language comes into existence by means of brutal necessity, and the rules of the language are dictated by what the language must convey.*

There was a moment, in time, and in this place, when my brother, or my mother, or my father, or my sister, had to convey to me, for example, the danger in which I was standing from the white man standing just behind me, and to convey this with a speed, and in a language, that the white man could not possibly understand, and that, indeed, he cannot understand, until today. He cannot afford to understand it. This understanding would reveal to him too much about himself, and smash that mirror before which he has been frozen for so long.

Now, if this passion, this skill, this (to quote Toni Morrison) "sheer intelligence," this incredible music, the mighty achievement of having brought a people utterly unknown to, or despised by "history"—to have brought this people to their present, troubled, troubling, and unassailable and unanswerable place—if this absolutely unprecedented journey does not indicate that black English is a language, I am curious to know what definition of language is to be trusted.

A people at the center of the Western world, and in the midst of so hostile a population, has not endured and transcended by means of what is patronizingly called a "dialect." We, the blacks, are in trouble, certainly, but we are not doomed, and we are not inarticulate because we are not compelled to defend a morality that we know to be a lie.

148

The brutal truth is that the bulk of the white people in America never had any interest in educating black people, except as this could serve white purposes. It is not the black child's language that is in question, it is not his language that is despised: it is his experience. A child cannot be taught by anyone who despises him, and a child cannot afford to be fooled. A child cannot be taught by anyone whose demand, essentially, is that the child repudiate his experience, and all that gives him sustenance, and enter a limbo in which he will no longer be black, and in which he knows that he can never become white. Black people have lost too many black children that way.

And, after all, finally, in a country with standards so untrustworthy, a country that makes heroes of so many criminal mediocrities, a country unable to face why so many of the nonwhite are in prison, or on the needle, or standing, futureless, in the streets—it may very well be that both the child, and his elder, have concluded that they have nothing whatever to learn from the people of a country that has managed to learn so little.

DAVID SEDARIS [b. 1956]

Me Talk Pretty One Day

Born in 1956 in Johnson City, New York, **David Sedaris** grew up in
Raleigh, North Carolina. He is a playwright (in collaboration with
his sister Amy) and an essayist whose work has been featured regularly
on National Public Radio and in collections such as *Naked* (1997) and
Me Talk Pretty One Day (2000). Sedaris's work tends toward the satiric,
but even the most wickedly pointed of his pieces are marked by an
ironic stance that includes the author among those humans whose
folly must be satirized. This insistence on turning his satiric eye on
himself is evident in "Me Talk Pretty One Day," taken from the collection of the same name, in which he recounts his efforts to learn French,
to the chagrin of his teacher and to his own evident amusement.

At the age of forty-one, I am returning to school and have to think of myself as what my French textbook calls "a true debutant." After paying my
tuition, I was issued a student ID, which allows me a discounted entry
fee at movie theaters, puppet shows, and Festyland, a far-flung amusement park that advertises with billboards picturing a cartoon stego-
saurus sitting in a canoe and eating what appears to be a ham sandwich.

I've moved to Paris with hopes of learning the language. My school is
an easy ten-minute walk from my apartment, and on the first day of
class I arrived early, watching as the returning students greeted one another in the school lobby. Vacations were recounted, and questions were
raised concerning mutual friends with names like Kang and Vlatnya.
Regardless of their nationalities, everyone spoke in what sounded to me
like excellent French. Some accents were better than others, but the students exhibited an ease and confidence I found intimidating. As an
added discomfort, they were all young, attractive, and well dressed,
causing me to feel not unlike Pa Kettle trapped backstage after a fashion show.

The first day of class was nerve-racking because I knew I'd be expected
to perform. That's the way they do it here — it's everybody into the language pool, sink or swim. The teacher marched in, deeply tanned from
a recent vacation, and proceeded to rattle off a series of administrative

announcements. I've spent quite a few summers in Normandy, and I took a monthlong French class before leaving New York. I'm not completely in the dark, yet I understood only half of what this woman was saying.

"If you have not *meimslsxp* or *lgpdmurct* by this time, then you should not be in this room. Has everyone *apzkiubjxow?* Everyone? Good, we shall begin." She spread out her lesson plan and sighed, saying, "All right, then, who knows the alphabet?"

It was startling because (a) I hadn't been asked that question in a   5 while and (b) I realized, while laughing, that I myself did *not* know the alphabet. They're the same letters, but in France they're pronounced differently. I know the shape of the alphabet but had no idea what it actually sounded like.

"Ahh." The teacher went to the board and sketched the letter *a*. "Do we have anyone in the room whose first name commences with an *ahh*?"

Two Polish Annas raised their hands, and the teacher instructed them to present themselves by stating their names, nationalities, occupations, and a brief list of things they liked and disliked in this world. The first Anna hailed from an industrial town outside of Warsaw and had front teeth the size of tombstones. She worked as a seamstress, enjoyed quiet times with friends, and hated the mosquito.

"Oh, really," the teacher said. "How very interesting. I thought that everyone loved the mosquito, but here, in front of all the world, you claim to detest him. How is it that we've been blessed with someone as unique and original as you? Tell us, please."

The seamstress did not understand what was being said but knew that this was an occasion for shame. Her rabbity mouth huffed for breath, and she stared down at her lap as though the appropriate comeback were stitched somewhere alongside the zipper of her slacks.

The second Anna learned from the first and claimed to love sunshine   10 and detest lies. It sounded like a translation of one of those Playmate of the Month data sheets, the answers always written in the same loopy handwriting: "Turn-ons: Mom's famous five-alarm chili! Turnoffs: insecurity and guys who come on too strong!!!!"

The two Polish Annas surely had clear notions of what they loved and hated, but like the rest of us, they were limited in terms of vocabulary, and this made them appear less than sophisticated. The teacher forged on, and we learned that Carlos, the Argentine bandonion player, loved wine, music, and, in his words, "making sex with the womens of the world." Next came a beautiful young Yugoslav who identified herself as an optimist, saying that she loved everything that life had to offer.

The teacher licked her lips, revealing a hint of the sauce-box we would later come to know. She crouched low for her attack, placed her hands on the young woman's desk, and leaned close, saying, "Oh yeah? And do you love your little war?"

While the optimist struggled to defend herself, I scrambled to think of an answer to what had obviously become a trick question. How often is one asked what he loves in this world? More to the point, how often is one asked and then publicly ridiculed for his answer? I recalled my mother, flushed with wine, pounding the tabletop late one night, saying, "Love? I love a good steak cooked rare. I love my cat, and I love . . ." My sisters and I leaned forward, waiting to hear our names. "Tums," our mother said. "I love Tums."

The teacher killed some time accusing the Yugoslavian girl of master-minding a program of genocide, and I jotted frantic notes in the margins of my pad. While I can honestly say that I love leafing through medical textbooks devoted to severe dermatological conditions, the hobby is beyond the reach of my French vocabulary, and acting it out would only have invited controversy.

When called upon, I delivered an effortless list of things that I detest: 15
blood sausage, intestinal pâtés, brain pudding. I'd learned these words the hard way. Having given it some thought, I then declared my love for IBM typewriters, the French word for *bruise,* and my electric floor waxer. It was a short list, but still I managed to mispronounce *IBM* and assign the wrong gender to both the floor waxer and the typewriter. The teacher's reaction led me to believe that these mistakes were capital crimes in the country of France.

"Were you always this *palicmkrexis?*" she asked. "Even a *fiuscrzsa tici-welmun* knows that a typewriter is feminine."

I absorbed as much of her abuse as I could understand, thinking — but not saying — that I find it ridiculous to assign a gender to an inanimate object incapable of disrobing and making an occasional fool of itself. Why refer to crack pipe or Good Sir Dishrag when these things could never live up to all that their sex implied?

The teacher proceeded to belittle everyone from German Eva, who hated laziness, to Japanese Yukari, who loved paintbrushes and soap. Italian, Thai, Dutch, Korean, and Chinese — we all left class foolishly believing that the worst was over. She'd shaken us up a little, but surely that was just an act designed to weed out the deadweight. We didn't know it then, but the coming months would teach us what it was like to spend time in the presence of a wild animal, something completely unpredictable. Her temperament was not based on a series of good and bad days but, rather, good and bad moments. We soon learned to dodge chalk and protect our heads and stomachs whenever she approached us with a question. She hadn't yet punched anyone, but it seemed wise to protect ourselves against the inevitable.

Though we were forbidden to speak anything but French, the teacher would occasionally use us to practice any of her five fluent languages. "I hate you," she said to me one afternoon. Her English was flawless. 20 "I really, really hate you." Call me sensitive, but I couldn't help but take it personally.

After being singled out as a lazy *kfdtinvfm*, I took to spending four hours a night on my homework, putting in even more time whenever we were assigned an essay. I suppose I could have gotten by with less, but I was determined to create some sort of identity for myself: David the hard worker, David the cut-up. We'd have one of those "complete this sentence" exercises, and I'd fool with the thing for hours, invariably settling on something like "A quick run around the lake? I'd love to! Just give me a moment while I strap on my wooden leg." The teacher, through word and action, conveyed the message that if this was my idea of an identity, she wanted nothing to do with it.

My fear and discomfort crept beyond the borders of the classroom and accompanied me out onto the wide boulevards. Stopping for a coffee, asking directions, depositing money in my bank account: these things were out of the question, as they involved having to speak. Before beginning school, there'd been no shutting me up, but now I was convinced that everything I said was wrong. When the phone rang, I ignored it. If someone asked me a question, I pretended to be deaf. I knew my fear was getting the best of me when I started wondering why they don't sell cuts of meat in vending machines.

My only comfort was the knowledge that I was not alone. Huddled in the hallways and making the most of our pathetic French, my fellow students and I engaged in the sort of conversation commonly overheard in refugee camps.

"Sometime me cry alone at night."

"That be common for I, also, but be more strong, you. Much work and 25 someday you talk pretty. People start love you soon. Maybe tomorrow, okay."

Unlike the French class I had taken in New York, here there was no sense of competition. When the teacher poked a shy Korean in the eyelid with a freshly sharpened pencil, we took no comfort in the fact that, unlike Hyeyoon Cho, we all knew the irregular past tense of the verb *to defeat*. In all fairness, the teacher hadn't meant to stab the girl, but neither did she spend much time apologizing, saying only, "Well, you should have been *vkkdyo* more *kdeynfulh*."

Over time it became impossible to believe that any of us would ever improve. Fall arrived and it rained every day, meaning we would now be scolded for the water dripping from our coats and umbrellas. It was mid-October when the teacher singled me out, saying, "Every day spent with you is like having a cesarean section." And it struck me that, for the first time since arriving in France, I could understand every word that someone was saying.

Understanding doesn't mean that you can suddenly speak the language. Far from it. It's a small step, nothing more, yet its rewards are intoxicating and deceptive. The teacher continued her diatribe and I settled back, bathing in the subtle beauty of each new curse and insult.

"You exhaust me with your foolishness and reward my efforts with nothing but pain, do you understand me?"

The world opened up, and it was with great joy that I responded, "I 30 know the thing that you speak exact now. Talk me more, you, plus, please, plus."

[2000]

PETER FARB [1929–1980]

GEORGE ARMELAGOS [b. 1936]

The Patterns of Eating

Naturalist and anthropologist **Peter Farb** was born in New York City. Before his death in 1980, he contributed articles to national magazines such as *Better Homes and Gardens* and *Reader's Digest* and consulted for the Smithsonian and the Museum of Natural History. However, he is best known for his many books for adults and young adults, including *The Face of North America: The Natural History of a Continent* (1963), *Man's Rise to Civilization* (1968), and *Word Play: What Happens When People Talk* (1974). **George Armelagos** is professor and chair of anthropology at Emory University, but has held positions at several institutions, including thirty-two years at the University of Massachusetts–Amherst, during which time he and Farb wrote *Consuming Passions: The Anthropology of Eating* (1980). Farb died of leukemia shortly after their completion of the book. Since then, Armelagos has continued to write on the topic of nutritional anthropology, publishing several books and contributing articles to *Natural History* and *National Geographic*, among others.

In "The Patterns of Eating," which is excerpted from *Consuming Passions*, the authors argue that changes in eating habits reflect changes in human relationships: As society and manners have become more formal and less communal, so have our eating habits, relying less on direct contact with food and more on an array of specialized utensils.

Among the important societal rules that represent one component of cuisine are table manners. As a socially instilled form of conduct, they reveal the attitudes typical of a society. Changes in table manners through time, as they have been documented for western Europe, likewise reflect fundamental changes in human relationships. Medieval courtiers saw their table manners as distinguishing them from crude peasants; but by modern standards, the manners were not exactly refined. Feudal lords used their unwashed hands to scoop food from a common bowl and they passed around a single goblet from which all drank. A finger or two would be extended while eating, so as to be kept free of grease and thus available for the next course, or for dipping into spices and condiments—possibly accounting for today's "polite" custom of extending the little finger while holding a spoon or small fork. Soups and sauces were commonly drunk by lifting the bowl to the mouth; several diners frequently ate from the same bread trencher. Even lords and nobles would toss gnawed bones back into the common dish, wolf down their food, spit onto the table (preferred conduct called for spitting under it), and blew their noses into the tablecloth.

By about the beginning of the sixteenth century, table manners began to move in the direction of today's standards. The importance attached to them is indicated by the phenomenal success of a treatise, *On Civility in Children*, by the philosopher Erasmus, which appeared in 1530; reprinted more than thirty times in the next six years, it also appeared in numerous translations. Erasmus' idea of good table manners was far from modern, but it did represent an advance. He believed, for example, that an upper-class diner was distinguished by putting only three fingers of one hand into the bowl, instead of the entire hand in the manner of the lower class. Wait a few moments after being seated before you dip into it, he advises. Do not poke around in your dish, but take the first piece you touch. Do not put chewed food from the mouth back on your plate; instead, throw it under the table or behind your chair.

By the time of Erasmus, the changing table manners reveal a fundamental shift in society. People no longer ate from the same dish or drank from the same goblet, but were divided from one another by a new wall of constraint. Once the spontaneous, direct, and informal manners of the Middle Ages had been repressed, people began to feel shame. Defecation and urination were now regarded as private activities; handkerchiefs came into use for blowing the nose; nightclothes were now worn, and bedrooms were set apart as private areas. Before the sixteenth century, even nobles ate in their vast kitchens; only then did a special room designated for eating come into use away from the bloody sides of meat, the animals about to be slaughtered, and the bustling servants. These new inhibitions became the essence of "civilized" behavior, distinguishing adults from children, the upper classes from the lower, and Europeans from the "savages" then being discovered around the world. Restraint in eating habits became more marked in the centuries that followed. By about 1800, napkins were in common use, and before long they were placed on the thighs rather than wrapped around the neck; coffee and tea were no longer slurped out of the saucer; bread was genteelly broken into small pieces with the fingers rather than cut into large chunks with a knife.

Numerous paintings that depict meals—with subjects such as the Last Supper, the wedding at Cana, or Herod's feast—show what dining tables looked like before the seventeenth century. Forks were not depicted until about 1600 (when Jacopo Bassano painted one in a Last Supper), and very few spoons were shown. At least one knife is always depicted— an especially large one when it is the only one available for all the guests—but small individual knives were often at each place. Tin disks or oval pieces of wood had already replaced the bread trenchers. This change in eating utensils typified the new table manners in Europe. (In many other parts of the world, no utensils at all were used. In the Near East, for example, it was traditional to bring food to the mouth with the fingers of the right hand, the left being unacceptable because it was reserved for wiping the buttocks.) Utensils were employed in part because of a change in the attitude toward meat. During the Middle Ages, whole sides of meat, or even an entire dead animal, had been brought to the table and then carved in view of the diners. Beginning in the seventeenth century, at first in France but later elsewhere, the practice began to go out of fashion. One reason was that the family was ceasing to be a production unit that did its own slaughtering; as that function was transferred to specialists outside the home, the family became essentially a consumption unit. In addition, the size of the family was decreasing and consequently whole animals, or even large parts of them, were uneconomical. The cuisines of Europe reflected these social and economic changes. The animal origin of meat dishes was concealed by the arts of preparation. Meat itself became distasteful to look upon, and carving was moved out of sight to the kitchen. Comparable changes had already taken place in Chinese cuisine, with meat being cut up beforehand, unobserved by the diners. England was an exception to the change in Europe, and in its former colonies—the United States, Canada, Australia, and South Africa—the custom has persisted of bringing a joint of meat to the table to be carved.

Once carving was no longer considered a necessary skill among the well-bred, changes inevitably took place in the use of the knife, unquestionably the earliest utensil used for manipulating food. (In fact, the earliest English cookbooks were not so much guides to recipes as guides to carving meat.) The attitude of diners toward the knife, going back to the Middle Ages and the Renaissance, had always been ambivalent. The knife served as a utensil, but it offered a potential threat because it was also a weapon. Thus taboos were increasingly placed upon its use: It was to be held by the point with the blunt handle presented; it was not to be placed anywhere near the face; and most important, the uses to which it was put were sharply restricted. It was not to be used for cutting soft foods such as boiled eggs or fish, or round ones such as potatoes, or to be lifted from the table for courses that did not need it. In short, good table manners in Europe gradually removed the threatening aspect of the knife from social occasions. A similar change had taken place much

5

earlier in China when the warrior was supplanted by the scholar as a cultural model. The knife was banished completely from the table in favor of chopsticks, which is why the Chinese came to regard Europeans as barbarians at their table who "eat with swords."

The fork in particular enabled Europeans to separate themselves from the eating process, even avoiding manual contact with their food. When the fork first appeared in Europe, toward the end of the Middle Ages, it was used solely as an instrument for lifting chunks from the common bowl. Beginning in the sixteenth century, the fork was increasingly used by members of the upper classes—first in Italy, then in France, and finally in Germany and England. By then, social relations in western Europe had so changed that a utensil was needed to spare diners from the "uncivilized" and distasteful necessity of picking up food and putting it into the mouth with the fingers. The addition of the fork to the table was once said to be for reasons of hygiene, but this cannot be true. By the sixteenth century people were no longer eating from a common bowl but from their own plates, and since they also washed their hands before meals, their fingers were now every bit as hygienic as a fork would have been. Nor can the reason for the adoption of the fork be connected with the wish not to soil the long ruff that was worn on the sleeve at the time, since the fork was also adopted in various countries where ruffs were not then in fashion.

Along with the appearance of the fork, all table utensils began to change and proliferate from the sixteenth century onward. Soup was no longer eaten directly from the dish, but each diner used an individual spoon for that purpose. When a diner wanted a second helping from the serving dish, a ladle or a fresh spoon was used. More and more special utensils were developed for each kind of food: soup spoons, oyster forks, salad forks, two-tined fondue forks, blunt butter knives, special utensils for various desserts and kinds of fruit, each one differently shaped, of a different size, with differently numbered prongs and with blunt or serrated edges. The present European pattern eventually emerged, in which each person is provided with a table setting of as many as a dozen utensils at a full-course meal. With that, the separation of the human body from the taking of food became virtually complete. Good table manners dictated that even the cobs of maize were to be held by prongs inserted in each end, and the bones of lamb chops covered by ruffled paper pantalettes. Only under special conditions—as when Western people consciously imitate an earlier stage in culture at a picnic, fish fry, cookout, or campfire—do they still tear food apart with their fingers and their teeth, in a nostalgic reenactment of eating behaviors long vanished.

Today's neighborhood barbecue recreates a world of sharing and hospitality that becomes rarer each year. We regard as a curiosity the behavior of hunters in exotic regions. But every year millions of North Americans take to the woods and lakes to kill a wide variety of animals—with a difference, of course: What hunters do for survival we do for sport (and also for proof of masculinity, for male bonding, and for various psychological rewards). Like hunters, too, we stuff ourselves almost whenever food is available. Nibbling on a roasted ear of maize gives us, in addition to nutrients, the satisfaction of participating in culturally simpler ways. A festive meal, however, is still thought of in Victorian terms, with the dominant male officiating over the roast, the dominant female apportioning vegetables, the extended family gathered around the table, with everything in its proper place—a revered picture, as indeed it was so painted by Norman Rockwell, yet one that becomes less accurate with each year that passes.

PHILIP GEFTER

Photographic Icons:
Fact, Fiction, or Metaphor?

Photography critic and writer **Philip Gefter** is a 1973 graduate of the
Pratt Institute. After completing his fine arts degree in painting and
photography, Gefter worked as a picture researcher for the Time-Life
Picture Collection. Since, he has written about photography for publications including the *Daily Beast* and the *New York Times*, and he
has also held the position of picture editor for the *New York Times*,
Aperture, *Forbes*, *Fortune*, and the *San Francisco Examiner*'s Sunday
magazine. In 1991, Gefter was among the founding members of the
National Lesbian and Gay Journalists Association, and in 2008, his
writings on contemporary photography—critical reviews, essays, and
even obituaries—were collected in the book *Photography after Frank*
(2009). Gefter is currently working on a biography of art curator Sam
Wagstaff, as well as producing a feature-length documentary about
photographer Bill Cunningham of the *New York Times*.

In the following essay, originally published in *Aperture*, Gefter
writes, "Truth-telling is the promise of a photograph. . . . A photograph
comes as close as we get to witnessing an authentic moment with our
own eyes while not actually being there." But, as he questions, what is
truth, even in "real" photos that have not been altered or digitally
enhanced? Gefter invites us to reevaluate a collection of famous
images and ask: What is real? Are photographs facts? Fiction? Something in between?

Truth-telling is the promise of a photograph—as if fact itself resides in
the optical precision with which the medium reflects our native perception. A photograph comes as close as we get to witnessing an authentic
moment with our own eyes while not actually being there. Think of all
the famous pictures that serve as both documentation and verification of
historic events: Mathew Brady's photographs of the Civil War; Lewis
Hine's chronicle of industrial growth in America; the birth of the Civil

Philip Gefter, "Photographic Icons: Fact, Fiction, or Metaphor?" From *Photography
after Frank* (Aperture, June 2009) and *Aperture* magazine, Issue 185 (Winter 2006).
Copyright © Philip Gefter. Reprinted by permission.

Rights movement documented in a picture of Rosa Parks on a segregated city bus in Montgomery, Alabama. Aren't they proof of the facts in real time, moments in history brought to the present?

Of course, just because a photograph reflects the world with perceptual accuracy doesn't mean it is proof of what spontaneously transpired. A photographic image might look like actual reality, but gradations of truth are measured in the circumstances that led up to the moment the picture was taken.

The viewer's expectation about a picture's veracity is largely determined by the context in which the image appears. A picture published in a newspaper is believed to be fact; an advertising image is understood to be fiction. If a newspaper image turns out to have been set up, then questions are raised about trust and authenticity. Still, somewhere between fact and fiction—or perhaps hovering slightly above either one—is the province of metaphor, where the truth is approximated in renderings of a more poetic or symbolic nature.

The impulse to define, perfect, or heighten reality is manifest in a roster of iconic photographs that have come to reside in the world as "truth." While Mathew Brady is known for his Civil War pictures, he rarely set foot on a battlefield. He couldn't bear the sight of dead bodies. In fact, most pictures of the battlefield attributed to Brady's studio were taken by his employees Alexander Gardner and Timothy O'Sullivan— both of whom were known to have moved bodies around for the purposes of composition and posterity.

In *Home of a Rebel Sharpshooter, Gettysburg* (1863), a picture by 5 Gardner, the body of a dead soldier lies in perfect repose. His head is tilted in the direction of the camera, his hand on his belly, his rifle propped up vertically against the rocks. There would be no question that this is a scene the photographer happened upon, if it weren't for another picture by Gardner of the same soldier, this time his face turned away from the camera and his rifle lying on the ground.

In the Library of Congress catalog, the photograph *Dead Soldiers at Antietam* (1862) is listed twice, under the names of both Brady and Gardner. In the image, approximately two dozen dead soldiers lie in a very neat row across the field. Could they possibly have fallen in such tidy succession? Knowing what we do about Gardner's picture of the rebel soldier, the possibility lingers that he moved some of these bodies to create a better composition. Or it could be that other soldiers had lined the bodies up before digging a mass grave for burial. But whatever the circumstances that led to this picture, it is verifiable that the battle of Antietam took place on this field. We know that numbers of soldiers were killed. Evidence of the battle remains—the soldiers that died on that date, the battlefield on which they fought, the clothes they wore,

161

Mathew Brady/Alexander Gardner, *Bodies of Confederate Dead Gathered for Burial,* **Battle of Antietam, September, 1862.**
(Library of Congress Prints and Photographs Division, LC# B811-0557C.)

and so on. Just how much of the subject matter does the photographer have to change before fact becomes fiction, or a photograph becomes metaphor?

"Mathew Brady used art to forge a relationship between photography and history, but when the memory of Brady the artist vanished, we came to accept his images as fact," Mary Panzer wrote in her 1997 book *Mathew Brady and the Image of History.* "Acknowledged or not, Brady's careful manipulation of his subjects continues to influence our perception, and still shapes the way in which we see his era, and the story of the nation."

Lewis Hine's 1920 photograph of a powerhouse mechanic symbolizes the work ethic that built America. The simplicity of the photograph long ago turned it into a powerful icon, all the more poignant because of its "authenticity." But in fact, Hine—who was interested in the human labor aspect of an increasingly mechanized world, and once claimed that "there is an urgent need for intelligent interpretation of the world's

Lewis Hine, an early variant of his *Powerhouse Mechanic*.
(Courtesy George Eastman House.)

Lewis Hine, his final, iconic *Powerhouse Mechanic*, 1920.
(Courtesy George Eastman House.)

workers"—posed this man in order to make the portrait. Does that information make the picture any less valid?

We see in the first shot that the worker's zipper is down. Isn't it a sad fact that the flaws in daily life should prevent reality from being the best version of how things really are? In our attempt to perfect reality, we aim for higher standards. A man with his zipper down is undignified, and so the famous icon, posed as he is, presents an idealized version of the American worker—dignity customized, but forever intact. Still, the mechanic did work in that powerhouse and his gesture is true enough to his labor. The reality of what the image depicts is indisputable, and whether Hine maintained a fidelity to what transpired in real time may or may not be relevant to its symbolic import.

Le Baiser de l'Hôtel de Ville (Kiss at the Hôtel de Ville, 1950) by Robert 10 Doisneau, despite its overexposure on posters and postcards, has long served as an example of how photography can capture the spontaneity of life. What a breezy testament to the pleasure of romance! How lovely the couple is, how elegant their gesture and their clothing, how delightful this perspective from a café in Paris! It makes you believe in romantic love: you want to be there, as if you, too, would surely witness love blossoming all around you—or even find it yourself—while sitting at a café in the City of Light.

But despite the story this picture seems to tell—one of a photographer who just happened to look up from his Pernod as the enchanted lovers walked by—there was no serendipity whatsoever in the moment. Doisneau had seen the man and woman days earlier, near the school at which they were studying acting. He was on assignment for *Life* magazine, for a story on romance in Paris, and hired the couple as models for the shot. This information was not brought to light until the early 1990s, when lawsuits demanding compensation were filed by several people who claimed to be the models in the famous picture. Does the lack of authenticity diminish the photograph? It did for me, turning its promise of romance into a beautifully crafted lie.

Ruth Orkin was in Florence, Italy, in the early 1950s when she met Jinx Allen, whom she asked to be the subject of a picture Orkin wanted to submit to the *Herald Tribune. American Girl in Italy* was conceived inadvertently when Orkin noticed the Italian men on their Vespas ogling Ms. Allen as she walked down the street. Orkin asked her to walk down the street again, to be sure she had the shot. Does a second take alter the reality of the phenomenon? How do you parse the difference between Doisneau's staged picture and Orkin's re-creation?

Iwo Jima, Old Glory Goes Up on Mt. Suribachi was taken in 1945 by Joe Rosenthal, an Associated Press photographer. As documentation of a World War II victory, the picture immediately assumed symbolic

Ruth Orkin, *American Girl in Italy,* **Florence, Italy, 1951.**
(Copyright © Ruth Orkin 1951, 1980.)

significance—indeed, it won Rosenthal a Pulitzer Prize, and is one of the most enduring images of the twentieth century. For some time, it was considered a posed picture, but this was due to a misunderstanding. The famous image was the first of three pictures Rosenthal took of the flag being raised. For the last shot, he asked the soldiers to pose in front of the raised flag, thinking that the newspapers back home would expect a picture in which the soldiers' faces were visible. Later, asked if his picture of Iwo Jima was posed, he said yes—referring in his mind to that third frame, not the one that had been published. Still, that the moment captured in the well-known picture occurred just as we see it today surely confirms the truth-telling capability of photography.

The birth of the Civil Rights movement is often dated back to a moment in 1955 when Rosa Parks, a black woman, refused to give up her seat on a crowded city bus to a white man in Montgomery, Alabama. (While she was not the first black bus rider to refuse to give up her seat, her case became the one on which the legal challenge was based.) Many people assume that the famous picture of Parks sitting on a city bus is an actual record of that historic moment. But the picture was taken on December 21, 1956, a year after she refused to give up her seat, and a month after the U.S. Supreme Court ruled Montgomery's segregated bus system illegal. Before she died, Parks told Douglas Brinkley, her biographer, that

Joe Rosenthal, *Flag-Raising on Iwo Jima,* **1945.**
(Courtesy Joe Rosenthal/AP/Wide World Photos.)

she posed for the picture. A reporter and two photographers from *Look* magazine had seated her on the bus in front of a white man. Similar photo opportunities were arranged on the same day for other members of the Civil Rights community, including Martin Luther King. Here is a staged document that has become a historic reference point, and a revealing parable about the relationship of history to myth.

As a witness to events, the photojournalist sets out to chronicle what 15 happens in the world as it actually occurs. A cardinal rule of the profession is that the presence of the camera must not alter the situation being photographed. Four years ago, Edward Keating, among the best staff photographers at the *New York Times*, was fired because of questions raised about one picture he took that ended up in the newspaper. This correction was published in the Times five days later:

A picture in the early editions on September 20, 2002, showed a 6-year-old boy aiming a toy pistol alongside a sign reading "Arabian Foods" outside a store in Lackawanna, N.Y., near Buffalo. The store was near the scene of

167

Rosa Parks, 1956. Rosa Parks sits at the front of a bus on December 21, 1956, the first day that the transportation system in Montgomery, Alabama, was integrated. Parks was arrested on December 1, 1955, for refusing to give up her seat in the front of a bus in Montgomery. The man sitting behind Parks in this photo is Nicholas C. Chriss, a reporter for United Press International out of Atlanta. (Bettmann/Corbis.)

two arrests in a raid described by the authorities as a pre-emptive strike against a cell of Al Qaeda, and the picture appeared with an article recounting the life stories of the detainees. The picture was not relevant to the article and should not have appeared.

The correction went on to say that photographers on the scene from other news organizations had reported that Keating asked the young boy to aim the toy pistol. Upon further inquiry and a full inspection of the

Edward Keating, *Boy with Pistol,* **2002.**
(Edward Keating/The New York Times/Redux.)

images from the entire photo assignment, the "editors concluded, and Mr. Keating acknowledged, that the boy's gesture had not been spontaneous." Altering the reality of the situation is a violation of journalistic policy, and it turned Keating's image from fact to illustration—a potent editorial statement about the Arabic community at a highly sensitive moment.

Paradoxically, looking through the photography archives of the *New York Times,* one is struck by the numbers of prints in which one or more people have been airbrushed out of the picture. The technique has been used at times to highlight an individual relevant to a particular news story, or simply to sharpen a line for better reproduction on newsprint. Other pictures have red-pencil crop marks, with which the art director or picture editor isolated only that part of the image relevant to the news story. To be fair, these changes were made not for the sake of censorship, but rather as part of an editing process simply to filter out unwanted information—perhaps no more egregious than cutting down a subject's spoken quotation to its salient points.

In 1839, the invention of photography provided a revolutionary method of replicating reality in accurate visual terms. What a great tool for artists and painters to construct images with greater perceptual facility.

The history of art is a continuum of constructed images that depict reality as it was truly, or else as it was imagined in ideal terms. Photography did not change that continuum; it only made the difference between perception and reality more difficult to determine.

[2006]

NEIL POSTMAN   [1931–2003]
STEVE POWERS   [b. 1934]

Television News:
The Language of Pictures

Neil Postman was an educator, media theorist, cultural critic, and writer. Born in New York City, Postman received a B.S. from the State University of New York and an M.A. and Ph.D. from Teachers College at Columbia University. He served as Goddard Chair of Media Ecology and chair of the department of culture and communications at New York University. Postman's writings exhibit wit, humor, and intellect, as well as a willingness to challenge prevailing wisdom. Postman wrote over twenty books on topics dealing with language, education, media, technology, and childhood. In one of his most influential works, *Teaching as a Subversive Activity* (1969), cowritten with Charles Weingartner, Postman encourages educators to question curricula that stress rote learning and to replace it with critical thinking and inquiry. Written ten years later, his book *Teaching as a Conserving Activity* (1979) asserts a vision of school as a place of social and ethical stability. Postman's best-known work is *Amusing Ourselves to Death* (1986), which condemns media for its tendency to instill intellectual passivity, and minimize the possibility for reflection. Postman's other books include *The Disappearance of Childhood* (1982), *The End of Education* (1996), and *Building a Bridge to the 18th Century: How the Past Can Improve Our Future* (1999).

With coauthor **Steve Powers,** Postman wrote *How to Watch a Television News Show,* a 1992 work that deconstructs contemporary television news and explains how it makes viewers vulnerable. Powers is a graduate of Bernard M. Baruch College of the City University of New York. Powers's insights originate from his dual career as professional musician and correspondent for FOX Television News and the ABC Radio Network. His interest in media literacy motivated him to collaborate with Postman to produce a lucid, insightful review of news programs.

When a television news show distorts the truth by altering or manufacturing facts (through re-creations), a television viewer is defenseless even if a re-creation is properly labeled. Viewers are still vulnerable to misinformation since they will not know (at least in the case of docudramas) what parts are fiction and what parts are not. But the problems of verisimilitude posed by re-creations pale to insignificance when compared to the problems viewers face when encountering a straight (no-monkey-business) show. All news shows, in a sense, are re-creations in that what we hear and see on them are attempts to represent actual events, and are not the events themselves. Perhaps, to avoid ambiguity, we might call all news shows "re-presentations" instead of "re-creations." These re-presentations come to us in two forms: language and pictures.

. . . It is often said that a picture is worth a thousand words. Maybe so. But it is probably equally true that one word is worth a thousand pictures, at least sometimes—for example, when it comes to understanding the world we live in. Indeed, the whole problem with news on television comes down to this: all the words uttered in an hour of news coverage could be printed on one page of a newspaper. And the world cannot be understood in one page. Of course, there is a compensation: television offers pictures, and the pictures move. Moving pictures are a kind of language in themselves, but the language of pictures differs radically from oral and written language, and the differences are crucial for understanding television news.

To begin with, pictures, especially single pictures, speak only in particularities. Their vocabulary is limited to concrete representation. Unlike words and sentences, a picture does not present to us an idea or concept about the world, except as we use language itself to convert the image to idea. By itself, a picture cannot deal with the unseen, the remote, the internal, the abstract. It does not speak of "man," only of *a* man; not of "tree," only of *a* tree. You cannot produce an image of "nature," any more than an image of "the sea." You can only show a particular fragment of the here-and-now—a cliff of a certain terrain, in a certain condition of light; a wave at a moment in time, from a particular point of view. And just as "nature" and "the sea" cannot be photographed, such larger abstractions as truth, honor, love, and falsehood cannot be talked about in the lexicon of individual pictures. For "showing of" and "talking about" are two very different kinds of processes: individual pictures give us the world as object; language, the world as idea. There is no such thing in nature as "man" or "tree." The universe offers no such categories or simplifications; only flux and infinite variety. The picture documents and celebrates the particularities of the universe's infinite variety Language makes them comprehensible.

172

Of course, moving pictures, video with sound, may bridge the gap by juxtaposing images, symbols, sound, and music. Such images can present emotions and rudimentary ideas. They can suggest the panorama of nature and the joys and miseries of humankind.

Picture—smoke pouring from the window, cut to people coughing, an 5 ambulance racing to a hospital, a tombstone in a cemetery.

Picture—jet planes firing rockets, explosions, lines of foreign soldiers surrendering, the American flag waving in the wind.

Nonetheless, keep in mind that when terrorists want to prove to the world that their kidnap victims are still alive, they photograph them holding a copy of a recent newspaper. The dateline on the newspaper provides the proof that the photograph was taken on or after that date. Without the help of the written word, film and videotape cannot portray temporal dimensions with any precision. Consider a film clip showing an aircraft carrier at sea. One might be able to identify the ship as Soviet or American, but there would be no way of telling where in the world the carrier was, where it was headed, or when the pictures were taken. It is only through language—words spoken over the pictures or reproduced in them—that the image of the aircraft carrier takes on specific meaning.

Still, it is possible to enjoy the image of the carrier for its own sake. One might find the hugeness of the vessel interesting; it signifies military power on the move. There is a certain drama in watching the planes come in at high speeds and skid to a stop on the deck. Suppose the ship were burning: that would be even more interesting. This leads to an important point about the language of pictures. Moving pictures favor images that change. That is why violence and dynamic destruction find their way onto television so often. When something is destroyed violently it is altered in a highly visible way; hence the entrancing power of fire. Fire gives visual form to the ideas of consumption, disappearance, death—the thing that burned is actually taken away by fire. It is at this very basic level that fires make a good subject for television news. Something was here, now it's gone, and the change is recorded on film.

Earthquakes and typhoons have the same power. Before the viewer's eyes the world is taken apart. If a television viewer has relatives in Mexico City and an earthquake occurs there, then he or she may take a special interest in the images of destruction as a report from a specific place and time; that is, one may look at television pictures for information about an important event. But film of an earthquake can be interesting even if the viewer cares nothing about the event itself. Which is only to say, as we noted earlier, that there is another way of participating in the news—as a spectator who desires to be entertained. Actually to see buildings topple is exciting, no matter where the buildings are. The world turns to dust before our eyes.

173

Those who produce television news in America know that their medium 10
favors images that move. That is why they are wary of "talking heads,"
people who simply appear in front of a camera and speak. When talking
heads appear on television, there is nothing to record or document, no
change in process. In the cinema the situation is somewhat different. On a
movie screen, close-ups of a good actor speaking dramatically can sometimes be interesting to watch. When Clint Eastwood narrows his eyes and
challenges his rival to shoot first, the spectator sees the cool rage of the
Eastwood character take visual form, and the narrowing of the eyes is dramatic. But much of the effect of this small movement depends on the size
of the movie screen and the darkness of the theater, which make Eastwood
and his every action "larger than life."

The television screen is smaller than life. It occupies about 15 percent
of the viewer's visual field (compared to about 70 percent for the movie
screen). It is not set in a darkened theater closed off from the world but
in the viewer's ordinary living space. This means that visual changes
must be more extreme and more dramatic to be interesting on television. A narrowing of the eyes will not do. A car crash, an earthquake, a
burning factory are much better.

With these principles in mind, let us examine more closely the structure of a typical newscast, and here we will include in the discussion not
only the pictures but all the nonlinguistic symbols that make up a television news show. For example, in America, almost all news shows begin
with music, the tone of which suggests important events about to unfold.
The music is very important, for it equates the news with various forms
of drama and ritual—the opera, for example, or a wedding procession—
in which musical themes underscore the meaning of the event. Music
takes us immediately into the realm of the symbolic, a world that is not to
be taken literally. After all, when events unfold in the real world, they do
so without musical accompaniment. More symbolism follows. The sound
of teletype machines can be heard in the studio, not because it is impossible to screen this noise out, but because the sound is a kind of music in
itself. It tells us that data are pouring in from all corners of the globe, a
sensation reinforced by the world map in the background (or clocks noting the time on different continents). The fact is that teletype machines
are rarely used in TV news rooms, having been replaced by silent computer terminals. When seen, they have only a symbolic function.

Already, then, before a single news item is introduced, a great deal has
been communicated. We know that we are in the presence of a symbolic
event, a form of theater in which the day's events are to be dramatized.
This theater takes the entire globe as its subject, although it may look at
the world from the perspective of a single nation. A certain tension is
present, like the atmosphere in a theater just before the curtain goes up.

The tension is represented by the music, the staccato beat of the teletype machines, and often the sight of news workers scurrying around typing reports and answering phones. As a technical matter, it would be no problem to build a set in which the newsroom staff remained off camera, invisible to the viewer, but an important theatrical effect would be lost. By being busy on camera, the workers help communicate urgency about the events at hand, which suggests that situations are changing so rapidly that constant revision of the news is necessary.

The staff in the background also helps signal the importance of the person in the center, the anchor, "in command" of both the staff and the news. The anchor plays die role of host. He or she welcomes us to the newscast and welcomes us back from the different locations we visit during the filmed reports.

Many features of the newscast help the anchor to establish the impres- 15 sion of control. These are usually equated with production values in broadcasting. They include such things as graphics that tell the viewer what is being shown, or maps and charts that suddenly appear on the screen and disappear on cue, or the orderly progression from story to story. They also include the absence of gaps, or "dead time," during the broadcast, even the simple fact that the news starts and ends at a certain hour. These common features are thought of as purely technical matters, which a professional crew handles as a matter of course. But they are also symbols of a dominant theme of television news: the imposition of an orderly world — called "the news" — upon the disorderly flow of events.

While the form of a news broadcast emphasizes tidiness and control, its content can best be described as fragmented. Because time is so precious on television, because the nature of the medium favors dynamic visual images, and because the pressures of a commercial structure require the news to hold its audience above all else, there is rarely any attempt to explain issues in depth or place events in their proper context. The news moves nervously from a warehouse fire to a court decision, from a guerrilla war to a World Cup match, the quality of the film most often determining the length of the story. Certain stories show up only because they offer dramatic pictures. Bleachers collapse in South America: hundreds of people are crushed — a perfect television news story, for the cameras can record the face of disaster in all its anguish. Back in Washington, a new budget is approved by Congress. Here there is nothing to photograph because a budget is not a physical event; it is a document full of language and numbers. So the producers of the news will show a photo of the document itself, focusing on the cover where it says "Budget of the United States of America." Or sometimes they will send a camera crew to the government printing plant where copies of the budget are produced. That evening, while the contents of the budget are summarized by a voice-over, the viewer sees stacks of documents being loaded into boxes at the government printing plant. Then a few of the budget's more important provisions will be flashed on the screen in written form, but this is such a time-consuming process—using television as a printed page—that the producers keep it to a minimum. In short, the budget is not televisable, and for that reason its time on the news must be brief. The bleacher collapse will get more time that evening.

While appearing somewhat chaotic, these disparate stories are not just dropped in the news program helter-skelter. The appearance of a scattershot story order is really orchestrated to draw the audience from one story to the next—from one section to the next—through the commercial breaks to the end of the show. The story order is constructed to hold and build the viewership rather than place events in context or explain issues in depth.

Of course, it is a tendency of journalism in general to concentrate on the surface of events rather than underlying conditions; this is as true for the newspaper as it is for the newscast. But several features of television undermine whatever efforts journalists may make to give sense to the world. One is that a television broadcast is a series of events that occur in sequence, and the sequence is the same for all viewers. This is not true for a newspaper page, which displays many items simultaneously, allowing readers to choose the order in which they read them. If newspaper readers want only a summary of the latest tax bill, they can read the headline and the first paragraph of an article, and if they want more, they can keep reading. In a sense, then, everyone reads a different newspaper, for no two readers will read (or ignore) the same items.

But all television viewers see the same broadcast. They have no choices. A report is either in the broadcast or out, which means that anything which is of narrow interest is unlikely to be included. As NBC News executive Reuven Frank once explained:

> A newspaper, for example, can easily afford to print an item of conceivable interest to only a fraction of its readers. A television news program must be put together with the assumption that each item will be of some interest to everyone that watches. Every time a newspaper includes a feature which will attract a specialized group it can assume it is adding at least a little bit to its circulation. To the degree a television news program includes an item of this sort ... it must assume that its audience will diminish.

The need to "include everyone," an identifying feature of commercial 20 television in all its forms, prevents journalists from offering lengthy or complex explanations, or from tracing the sequence of events leading up to today's headlines. One of the ironies of political life in modern democracies is that many problems which concern the "general welfare" are of interest only to specialized groups. Arms control, for example, is an issue that literally concerns everyone in the world, and yet the language of arms control and the complexity of the subject are so daunting that only a minority of people can actually follow the issue from week to week and month to month. If it wants to act responsibly, a newspaper can at least make available more information about arms control than most people want. Commercial television cannot afford to do so.

But even if commercial television could afford to do so, it wouldn't. The fact that television news is principally made up of moving pictures prevents it from offering lengthy, coherent explanations of events. A television news show reveals the world as a series of unrelated, fragmentary moments. It does not—and cannot be expected to—offer a sense of coherence or meaning. What does this suggest to a TV viewer? That the viewer must come with a prepared mind—information, opinions, a sense of proportion, an articulate value system. To the TV viewer lacking such mental equipment, a news program is only a kind of rousing light show. Here a falling building, there a five-alarm fire, everywhere the world as an object, much without meaning, connections, or continuity.

Bruce Chambers, *Edgar Hollingsworth Is Rescued from His Home after Hurricane Katrina*, 2005. An Army veteran is rescued from his home sixteen days after Hurricane Katrina struck New Orleans in 2005. (Copyright © Bruce Chambers.)

Thomas E. Franklin, *Flag-Raising at Ground Zero,* **2001.** Firefighters raise a flag at Ground Zero where the Twin Towers of the World Trade Center stood in New York City before the terrorist attacks on September 11, 2001. (Copyright © 2001 The Record, Bergen County, New Jersey. Photo by AP Photo/Thomas E. Franklin.)

Eddie Adams, *Saigon Execution*, 1968. A Viet Cong suspect is executed by Vietnam's Chief of National Police, General Loan, on February 1, 1968. The photograph taken by Eddie Adams won a Pulitzer Prize in 1969. (AP Photo/Eddie Adams.)

Tommie Smith and John Carlos, gold and bronze medalists in the 200-meter dash, raise their fists in a black power salute on the victory stand at the 1968 Olympics in Mexico City. (AP Photo.)

John Paul Filo, *Kent State Massacre*, 1970. Mary Ann Vecchio kneels over the body of a student killed by National Guardsmen during the Kent State massacre in 1970. Students had been protesting the Vietnam War when the Ohio National Guard arrived to disperse the crowd. The photograph taken by John Paul Filo won a Pulitzer Prize in 1971. (John Paul Filo/Getty Images.)

Rosa Parks sits at the front of a bus on December 21, 1956, the first day that the transportation system in Montgomery, Alabama, was integrated. (Bettmann/Corbis.)

Margaret Bourke-White, *At the Time of the Louisville Flood*, **1937.**
Americans wait in line for food during the Great Depression, under an
advertisement for the "world's highest standard of living." (Copyright ©
Margaret Bourke-White/Time, Inc.)

JIB FOWLES   [b. 1940]

Advertising's Fifteen Basic Appeals

Born in Hartford, Connecticut, **Jib Fowles** was educated at Wesleyan University (B.A.), Columbia University (M.A.), and New York University (Ph.D.). After completing his doctorate, Fowles was a Fulbright scholar in India from 1963 to 1964. His distinguished academic career includes teaching positions at New York University and the University of Houston, where he presently chairs the program in Studies of the Future. As a researcher and writer, Fowles has studied aspects of American popular culture, focusing on the intersections of media, advertising, and celebrity. He has published several books related to his specialization, including *Mass Advertising as Social Forecast* (1976), *Television Viewers and Media Snobs: What TV Does for People* (1989), and *The Case for Television* (1999). Of his work, Fowles states: "My chief preoccupation is with an appreciative analysis of industrial culture—its past, present and future."

In his essay "Advertising's Fifteen Basic Appeals," Fowles examines the human psychology behind the attractive power of elemental advertising strategies.

EMOTIONAL APPEALS

The nature of effective advertisements was recognized full well by the late media philosopher Marshall McLuhan. In his *Understanding Media*, the first sentence of the section on advertising reads, "The continuous pressure is to create ads more and more in the image of audience motives and desires."

By giving form to people's deep-lying desires, and picturing states of being that individuals privately yearn for, advertisers have the best chance of arresting attention and affecting communication. And that is the immediate goal of advertising: to tug at our psychological shirt sleeves and slow us down long enough for a word or two about whatever

Jib Fowles, "Advertising's Fifteen Basic Appeals," from *Etc.* 39, No. 3. Reprinted with permission of the International Society for General Semantics, Concord, California.

is being sold. We glance at a picture of a solitary rancher at work, and "Marlboro" slips into our minds.

Advertisers (I'm using the term as a shorthand for both the products' manufacturers, who bring the ambition and money to the process, and the advertising agencies, who supply the know-how) are ever more compelled to invoke consumers' drives and longings; this is the "continuous pressure" McLuhan refers to. Over the past century, the American marketplace has grown increasingly congested as more and more products have entered into the frenzied competition after the public's dollars. The economies of other nations are quieter than ours since the volume of goods being hawked does not so greatly exceed demand. In some economies, consumer wares are scarce enough that no advertising at all is necessary. But in the United States, we go to the other extreme. In order to stay in business, an advertiser must strive to cut through the considerable commercial hub-bub by any means available—including the emotional appeals that some observers have held to be abhorrent and underhanded.

The use of subconscious appeals is a comment not only on conditions among sellers. As time has gone by, buyers have become stoutly resistant to advertisements. We live in a blizzard of these messages and have learned to turn up our collars and ward off most of them. A study done a few years ago at Harvard University's Graduate School of Business Administration ventured that the average American is exposed to some 500 ads daily from television, newspapers, magazines, radio, billboards, direct mail, and so on. If for no other reason than to preserve one's sanity, a filter must be developed in every mind to lower the number of ads a person is actually aware of—a number this particular study estimated at about seventy-five ads per day. (Of these, only twelve typically produced a reaction—nine positive and three negative, on the average.) To be among the few messages that do manage to gain access to minds, advertisers must be strategic, perhaps even a little underhanded at times.

There are assumptions about personality underlying advertisers' efforts 5 to communicate via emotional appeals, and while these assumptions have stood the test of time, they still deserve to be aired. Human beings, it is presumed, walk around with a variety of unfulfilled urges and motives swirling in the bottom half of their minds. Lusts, ambitions, tendernesses, vulnerabilities—they are constantly bubbling up, seeking resolution. These mental forces energize people, but they are too crude and irregular to be given excessive play in the real world. They must be capped with the competent, sensible behavior that permits individuals to get along well in society. However, this upper layer of mental activity, shot through with caution and rationality, is not receptive to advertising's pitches. Advertisers want to circumvent this shell of consciousness if they can, and latch on to one of the lurching, subconscious drives.

In effect, advertisers over the years have blindly felt their way around the underside of the American psyche, and by trial and error have discovered the softest points of entree, the places where their messages have the greatest likelihood of getting by consumers' defenses. As McLuhan says elsewhere, "Gouging away at the surface of public sales resistance, the ad men are constantly breaking through into the *Alice in Wonderland* territory behind the looking glass, which is the world of subrational impulses and appetites."

An advertisement communicates by making use of a specially selected image (of a supine female, say, or a curly-haired child, or a celebrity) which is designed to stimulate "subrational impulses and desires" even when they are at ebb, even if they are unacknowledged by their possessor. Some few ads have their emotional appeal in the text, but for the greater number by far the appeal is contained in the artwork. This makes sense, since visual communication better suits more primal levels of the brain. If the viewer of an advertisement actually has the importuned motive, and if the appeal is sufficiently well fashioned to call it up, then the person can be hooked. The product in the ad may then appear to take on the semblance of gratification for the summoned motive. Many ads seem to be saying, "If you have this need, then this product will help satisfy it." It is a primitive equation, but not an ineffective one for selling.

Thus, most advertisements appearing in national media can be understood as having two orders of content. The first is the appeal to deep-running drives in the minds of consumers. The second is information regarding the good[s] or service being sold: its name, its manufacturer, its picture, its packaging, its objective attributes, its functions. For example, the reader of a brassiere advertisement sees a partially undraped but blandly unperturbed woman standing in an otherwise commonplace public setting, and may experience certain sensations; the reader also sees the name "Maidenform," a particular brassiere style, and, in tiny print, words about the material, colors, price. Or, the viewer of a television commercial sees a demonstration with four small boxes labelled 650, 650, 650, and 800; something in the viewer's mind catches hold of this, as trivial as thoughtful consideration might reveal it to be. The viewer is also exposed to the name "Anacin," its bottle, and its purpose.

Sometimes there is an apparently logical link between an ad's emotional appeal and its product information. It does not violate common sense that Cadillac automobiles be photographed at country clubs, or that Japan Air Lines be associated with Orientalia. But there is no real need for the linkage to have a bit of reason behind it. Is there anything inherent to the connection between Salem cigarettes and mountains, Coke and a smile, Miller Beer and comradeship? The link being forged in minds between product and appeal is a pre-logical one.

People involved in the advertising industry do not necessarily talk in 10
the terms being used here. They are stationed at the sending end of this
communications channel, and may think they are up to any number of
things—Unique Selling Propositions, explosive copywriting, the optimal use of demographics or psychographics, ideal media buys, high
recall ratings, or whatever. But when attention shifts to the receiving end
of the channel, and focuses on the instant of reception, then commentary becomes much more elemental: an advertising message contains
something primary and primitive, an emotional appeal, that in effect is
the thin end of the wedge, trying to find its way into a mind. Should this
occur, the product information comes along behind.

When enough advertisements are examined in this light, it becomes
clear that the emotional appeals fall into several distinguishable categories, and that every ad is a variation on one of a limited number of
basic appeals. While there may be several ways of classifying these
appeals, one particular list of fifteen has proven to be especially valuable.

Advertisements can appeal to:

1. The need for sex
2. The need for affiliation
3. The need to nurture
4. The need for guidance
5. The need to aggress
6. The need to achieve
7. The need to dominate
8. The need for prominence
9. The need for attention
10. The need for autonomy
11. The need to escape
12. The need to feel safe
13. The need for aesthetic sensations
14. The need to satisfy curiosity
15. Physiological needs: food, drink, sleep, etc.

MURRAY'S LIST

Where does this list of advertising's fifteen basic appeals come from?
Several years ago, I was involved in a research project which was to have
as one segment an objective analysis of the changing appeals made in

post–World War II American advertising. A sample of magazine ads would have their appeals coded into the categories of psychological needs they seemed aimed at. For this content analysis to happen, a complete roster of human motives would have to be found.

The first thing that came to mind was Abraham Maslow's famous four-part hierarchy of needs. But the briefest look at the range of appeals made in advertising was enough to reveal that they are more varied, and more profane, than Maslow had cared to account for. The search led on to the work of psychologist Henry A. Murray, who together with his colleagues at the Harvard Psychological Clinic has constructed a full taxonomy of needs. As described in *Explorations in Personality*, Murray's team had conducted a lengthy series of in-depth interviews with a number of subjects in order to derive from scratch what they felt to be the essential variables of personality. Forty-four variables were distinguished by the Harvard group, of which twenty were motives. The need for achievement ("to overcome obstacles and obtain a high standard") was one, for instance; the need to defer was another; the need to aggress was a third; and so forth.

Murray's list had served as the groundwork for a number of subsequent projects. Perhaps the best-known of these was David C. McClelland's extensive study of the need for achievement, reported in his *The Achieving Society*. In the process of demonstrating that a people's high need for achievement is predictive of later economic growth, McClelland coded achievement imagery and references out of a nation's folklore, songs, legends, and children's tales.

Following McClelland, I too wanted to cull the motivational appeals 15 from a culture's imaginative product—in this case, advertising. To develop categories expressly for this purpose, I took Murray's twenty motives and added to them others he had mentioned in passing in *Explorations in Personality* but not included on the final list. The extended list was tried out on a sample of advertisements, and motives which never seemed to be invoked were dropped. I ended up with eighteen of Murrays' motives, into which 770 print ads were coded. The resulting distribution is included in the 1976 book *Mass Advertising as Social Forecast*.

Since that time, the list of appeals has undergone refinements as a result of using it to analyze television commercials. A few more adjustments stemmed from the efforts of students in my advertising classes to decode appeals; tens of term papers surveying thousands of advertisements have caused some inconsistencies in the list to be hammered out. Fundamentally, though, the list remains the creation of Henry Murray. In developing a comprehensive, parsimonious inventory of human motives, he pinpointed the subsurface mental forces that are the least quiescent and most susceptible to advertising's entreaties.

FIFTEEN APPEALS

1. *Need for sex.* Let's start with sex, because this is the appeal which seems to pop up first whenever the topic of advertising is raised. Whole books have been written about this one alone, to find a large audience of mildly titillated readers. Lately, due to campaigns to sell blue jeans, concern with sex in ads has redoubled.

The fascinating thing is not how much sex there is in advertising, but how little. Contrary to impressions, unambiguous sex is rare in these messages. Some of this surprising observation may be a matter of definition: the Jordache ads with the lithe, blouse-less female astride a similarly clad male is clearly an appeal to the audience's sexual drives, but the same cannot be said about Brooke Shields in the Calvin Klein commercials. Directed at young women and their credit-card carrying mothers, the image of Miss Shields instead invokes the need to be looked at. Buy Calvins and you'll be the center of much attention, just as Brooke is, the ads imply; they do not primarily inveigle their target audience's need for sexual intercourse.

In the content analysis reported in *Mass Advertising as Social Forecast* only two percent of ads were found to pander to this motive. Even *Playboy* ads shy away from sexual appeals: a recent issue contained eighty-three full-page ads, and just four of them (or less than five percent) could be said to have sex on their minds.

The reason this appeal is so little used is that it is too blaring and 20 tends to obliterate the product information. Nudity in advertising has the effect of reducing brand recall. The people who do remember the product may do so because they have been made indignant by the ad; this is not the response most advertisers seek.

To the extent that sexual imagery is used, it conventionally works better on men than women; typically a female figure is offered up to the male reader. A Black Velvet liquor advertisement displays an attractive woman wearing a tight black outfit, recumbent under the legend, "Feel the Velvet." The figure does not have to be horizontal, however, for the appeal to be present as National Airlines revealed in its "Fly me" campaign. Indeed, there does not even have to be a female in the ad; "Flick my Bic" was sufficient to convey the idea to many.

As a rule, though, advertisers have found sex to be a tricky appeal, to be used sparingly. Less controversial and equally fetching are the appeals to our need for affectionate human contact.

2. *Need for affiliation.* American mythology upholds autonomous individuals, and social statistics suggest that people are ever more going it alone in their lives, yet the high frequency of affiliative appeals in ads

belies this. Or maybe it does not: maybe all the images of companionship are compensation for what Americans privately lack. In any case, the need to associate with others is widely invoked in advertising and is probably the most prevalent appeal. All sorts of goods and services are sold by linking them to our unfulfilled desires to be in good company.

According to Henry Murray, the need for affiliation consists of desires "to draw near and enjoyably cooperate or reciprocate with another; to please and win affection of another; to adhere and remain loyal to a friend." The manifestations of this motive can be segmented into several different types of affiliation, beginning with romance.

Courtship may be swifter nowadays, but the desire for pair-bonding is 25 far from satiated. Ads reaching for this need commonly depict a youngish male and female engrossed in each other. The head of the male is usually higher than the female's, even at this late date; she may be sitting or leaning while he is standing. They are not touching in the Smirnoff vodka ads, but obviously there is an intimacy, sometimes frolicsome, between them. The couple does touch for Martell Cognac when "The moment was Martell." For Wind Song perfume they have touched, and "Your Wind Song stays on his mind."

Depending on the audience, the pair does not absolutely have to be young—just together. He gives her a DeBeers diamond, and there is a tear in her laugh lines. She takes Geritol and preserves herself for him. And numbers of consumers, wanting affection too, follow suit.

Warm family feelings are fanned in ads when another generation is added to the pair. Hallmark Cards brings grandparents into the picture, and Johnson and Johnson Baby Powder has Dad, Mom, and baby, all fresh from the bath, encircled in arms and emblazoned with "Share the Feeling." A talc has been fused to familial love.

Friendship is yet another form of affiliation pursued by advertisers. Two women confide and drink Maxwell House coffee together; two men walk through the woods smoking Salem cigarettes. Miller Beer promises that afternoon "Miller Time" will be staffed with three or four good buddies. Drink Dr. Pepper, as Mickey Rooney is coaxed to do, and join in with all the other Peppers. Coca-Cola does not even need to portray the friendliness; it has reduced this appeal to "a Coke and a smile."

The warmth can be toned down and disguised, but it is the same affiliative need that is being fished for. The blonde has a direct gaze and her friends are firm businessmen in appearance, but with a glass of Old Bushmill you can sit down and fit right in. Or, for something more upbeat, sing along with the Pontiac choirboys.

As well as presenting positive images, advertisers can play to the need 30 for affiliation in negative ways, by invoking the fear of rejection. If we don't use Scope, we'll have the "Ugh! Morning Breath" that causes the male and female models to avert their faces. Unless we apply Ultra Brite or Close-Up to our teeth, it's good-bye romance. Our family will be cursed with "House-a-tosis" if we don't take care. Without Dr. Scholl's antiperspirant foot spray, the bowling team will keel over. There go all the guests when the supply of Dorito's nacho cheese chips is exhausted. Still more rejection if our shirts have ring-around-the-collar, if our car needs to be Midasized. But make a few purchases, and we are back in the bosom of human contact.

As self-directed as Americans pretend to be, in the last analysis we remain social animals, hungering for the positive, endorsing feelings that only those around us can supply. Advertisers respond, urging us to "Reach out and touch someone," in the hopes our monthly bills will rise.

3. *Need to nurture.* Akin to affiliative needs is the need to take care of small, defenseless creatures—children and pets, largely. Reciprocity is of less consequence here, though; it is the giving that counts. Murray uses synonyms like "to feed, help, support, console, protect, comfort, nurse, heal." A strong need it is, woven deep into our genetic fabric, for if it did not exist we could not successfully raise up our replacements. When advertisers put forth the image of something diminutive and furry, something that elicits the word "cute" or "precious," then they are trying to trigger this motive. We listen to the childish voice singing the Oscar Mayer weiner song, and our next hot-dog purchase is prescribed. Aren't those darling kittens something, and how did this Meow Mix get into our shopping cart?

This pitch is often directed at women, as Mother Nature's chief nurturers. "Make me some Kraft macaroni and cheese, please," says the elfin preschooler just in from the snowstorm, and mothers' hearts go out, and Kraft's sales go up. "We're cold, wet, and hungry," whine the husband and kids, and the little woman gets the Manwiches ready. A facsimile of this need can be hit without children or pets: the husband is ill and sleepless in the television commercial, and the wife grudgingly fetches the NyQuil.

But it is not women alone who can be touched by this appeal. The father nurses his son Eddie through adolescence while the John Deere lawn tractor survives the years. Another father counts pennies with his young son as the subject of New York Life Insurance comes up. And all over America are businessmen who don't know why they dial Qantas Airlines when they have to take a trans-Pacific trip; the koala bear knows.

4. *Need for guidance.* The opposite of the need to nurture is the need 35 to be nurtured: to be protected, shielded, guided. We may be loath to admit it, but the child lingers on inside every adult—and a good thing it

does, or we would not be instructable in our advancing years. Who wants a nation of nothing but flinty personalities?

Parent-like figures can successfully call up this need. Robert Young recommends Sanka coffee, and since we have experienced him for twenty-five years as television father and doctor, we take his word for it. Florence Henderson as the expert mom knows a lot about the advantages of Wesson oil.

The parent-ness of the spokesperson need not be so salient; sometimes pure authoritativeness is better. When Orson Welles scowls and intones, "Paul Masson will sell no wine before its time," we may not know exactly what he means, but we still take direction from him. There is little maternal about Brenda Vaccaro when she speaks up for Tampax, but there is a certainty to her that many accept.

A celebrity is not a necessity in making a pitch to the need for guidance, since a fantasy figure can serve just as well. People accede to the Green Giant, or Betty Crocker, or Mr. Goodwrench. Some advertisers can get by with no figure at all: "When E.F. Hutton talks, people listen."

Often it is tradition or custom that advertisers point to and consumers take guidance from. Bits and pieces of American history are used to sell whiskeys like Old Crow, Southern Comfort, Jack Daniel's. We conform to traditional male/female roles and age-old social norms when we purchase Barclay cigarettes, which informs us "The pleasure is back."

The product itself, if it has been around for a long time, can constitute 40 a tradition. All those old labels in the ad for Morton salt convince us that we should continue to buy it. Kool-Aid says "You loved it as a kid. You trust it as a mother," hoping to get yet more consumers to go along.

Even when the product has no history at all, our need to conform to tradition and to be guided are strong enough that they can be invoked through bogus nostalgia and older actors. Country-Time lemonade sells because consumers want to believe it has a past they can defer to.

So far the needs and the ways they can be invoked which have been looked at are largely warm and affiliative; they stand in contrast to the next set of needs, which are much more egoistic and assertive.

5. *Need to aggress.* The pressures of the real world create strong retaliatory feelings in every functioning human being. Since these impulses can come forth as bursts of anger and violence, their display is normally tabooed. Existing as harbored energy, aggressive drives present a large, tempting target for advertisers. It is not a target to be aimed at thoughtlessly, though, for few manufacturers want their products associated with destructive motives. There is always the danger that, as in the case of sex, if the appeal is too blatant, public opinion will turn against what is being sold.

Jack-in-the-Box sought to abruptly alter its marketing by going after older customers and forgetting the younger ones. Their television commercials had a seventy-ish lady command, "Waste him," and the Jack-in-the-Box clown exploded before our eyes. So did public reaction until the commercials were toned down. Print ads for Club cocktails carried the faces of octogenarians under the headline, "Hit me with a Club"; response was contrary enough to bring the campaign to a stop.

Better disguised aggressive appeals are less likely to backfire: Triumph 45 cigarettes has models making a lewd gesture with their uplifted cigarettes, but the individuals are often laughing and usually in close company of others. When Exxon said, "There's a Tiger in your tank," the implausibility of it concealed the invocation of aggressive feelings.

Depicted arguments are a common way for advertisers to tap the audience's needs to aggress. Don Rickles and Lynda Carter trade gibes, and consumers take sides as the name of Seven-Up is stitched on minds. The Parkay tub has a difference of opinion with the user; who can forget it, or who (or what) got the last word in?

6. *Need to achieve.* This is the drive that energizes people, causing them to strive in their lives and careers. According to Murray, the need for achievement is signalled by the desires "to accomplish something difficult. To overcome obstacles and attain a high standard. To excel one's self. To rival and surpass others." A prominent American trait, it is one that advertisers like to hook on to because it identifies their product with winning and success.

The Cutty Sark ad does not disclose that Ted Turner failed at his latest attempt at yachting's America Cup; here he is represented as a champion on the water as well as off in his television enterprises. If we drink this whiskey, we will be victorious alongside Turner. We can also succeed with O.J. Simpson by renting Hertz cars, or with Reggie Jackson by bringing home some Panasonic equipment. Cathy Rigby and Stayfree Maxipads will put people out front.

Sports heroes are the most convenient means to snare consumers' needs to achieve, but they are not the only one. Role models can be established, ones which invite emulation, as with the profiles put forth by Dewar's scotch. Successful, tweedy individuals relate they have "graduated to the flavor of Myer's rum." Or the advertiser can establish a prize: two neighbors play one-on-one basketball for a Michelob beer in a television commercial, while in a print ad a bottle of Johnnie Walker Black Label has been gilded like a trophy.

Any product that advertises itself in superlatives—the best, the first, 50 the finest—is trying to make contact with our needs to succeed. For many consumers, sales and bargains belong in this category of appeals, too; the person who manages to buy something at fifty percent off is seizing an opportunity and coming out ahead of others.

7. *Need to dominate.* This fundamental need is the craving to be powerful—perhaps omnipotent, as in the Xerox ad where Brother Dominic exhibits heavenly powers and creates miraculous copies. Most of us will settle for being just a regular potentate, though. We drink Budweiser because it is the King of Beers, and here comes the powerful Clydesdales to prove it. A taste of Wolfschmidt vodka and "The spirit of the Czar lives on."

The need to dominate and control one's environment is often thought of as being masculine, but as close students of human nature advertisers know, it is not so circumscribed. Women's aspirations for control are suggested in the campaign theme, "I like my men in English Leather, or nothing at all." The females in the Chanel No. 19 ads are "outspoken" and wrestle their men around.

Male and female, what we long for is clout; what we get in its place is Mastercard.

8. *Need for prominence.* Here comes the need to be admired and respected, to enjoy prestige and high social status. These times, it appears, are not so egalitarian after all. Many ads picture the trappings of high position; the Oldsmobile stands before a manorial doorway, the Volvo is parked beside a steeplechase. A book-lined study is the setting for Dewar's 12, and Lenox China is displayed in a dining room chock full of antiques.

Beefeater gin represents itself as "The Crown Jewel of England" and 55 uses no illustrations of jewels or things British, for the words are sufficient indicators of distinction. Buy that gin and you will rise up the prestige hierarchy, or achieve the same effect on yourself with Seagram's 7 Crown, which ambiguously describes itself as "classy."

Being respected does not have to entail the usual accoutrements of wealth: "Do you know who I am?" the commercials ask, and we learn that the prominent person is not so prominent without his American Express card.

9. *Need for attention.* The previous need involved being *looked up to,* while this is the need to be *looked at.* The desire to exhibit ourselves in such a way as to make others look at us is a primitive, insuppressible instinct. The clothing and cosmetic industries exist just to serve this need, and this is the way they pitch their wares. Some of this effort is aimed at males, as the ads for Hathaway shirts and Jockey underclothes. But the greater bulk of such appeals is targeted singlemindedly at women.

To come back to Brooke Shields: this is where she fits into American marketing. If I buy Calvin Klein jeans, consumers infer, I'll be the object of fascination. The desire for exhibition has been most strikingly played to in a print campaign of many years' duration, that of Maidenform lingerie. The woman exposes herself, and sales surge. "Gentlemen prefer Hanes" the ads dissemble, and women who want eyes upon them know what they should do. Peggy Fleming flutters her legs for L'eggs, encouraging females who want to be the star in their own lives to purchase this product.

The same appeal works for cosmetics and lotions. For years, the little girl with the exposed backside sold gobs of Coppertone, but now the company has picked up the pace a little: as a female, you are supposed to "Flash 'em a Coppertone tan." Food can be sold the same way, especially to the diet-conscious; Angie Dickinson poses for California avocados and says, "Would this body lie to you?" Our eyes are too fixed on her for us to think to ask if she got that way by eating mounds of guacomole.

10. *Need for autonomy.* There are several ways to sell credit card ser- 60 vices, as has been noted: Mastercard appeals to the need to dominate, and American Express to the need for prominence. When Visa claims, "You can have it the way you want it," yet another primary motive is being beckoned forward—the need to endorse the self. The focus here is upon the independence and integrity of the individual; this need is the antithesis of the need for guidance and is unlike any of the social needs. "If running with the herd isn't your style, try ours," says Rotan-Mosle, and many Americans feel they have finally found the right brokerage firm.

The photo is of a red-coated Mountie on his horse, posed on a snow-covered ledge; the copy reads, "Windsor—One Canadian stands alone." This epitome of the solitary and proud individual may work best with male customers, as may Winston's man in the red cap. But one-figure advertisements also strike the strong need for autonomy among American women. As Shelly Hack strides for Charlie perfume, females respond to her obvious pride and flair; she is her own person. The Virginia Slims tale is of people who have come a long way from subservience to independence. Cachet perfume feels it does not need a solo figure to work this appeal, and uses three different faces in its ads; it insists, though, "It's different on every woman who wears it."

Like many psychological needs, this one can also be appealed to in a negative fashion, by invoking the loss of independence or self-regard. Guilt and regrets can be stimulated: "Gee, I could have had a V-8." Next time, get one and be good to yourself.

11. *Need to escape.* An appeal to the need for autonomy often co-occurs with one for the need to escape, since the desire to duck out of our social obligations, to seek rest or adventure, frequently takes the form of one-person flight. The dashing image of a pilot, in fact, is a standard way of quickening this need to get away from it all.

Freedom is the pitch here, the freedom that every individual yearns for whenever life becomes too oppressive. Many advertisers like appealing to the need for escape because the sensation of pleasure often accompanies escape, and what nicer emotional nimbus could there be for a product? "You deserve a break today," says McDonald's, and Stouffer's frozen foods chime in, "Set yourself free."

For decades men have imaginatively bonded themselves to the 65 Marlboro cowboy who dwells untarnished and unencumbered in Marlboro Country some distance from modern life; smokers' aching needs for autonomy and escape are personified by that cowpoke. Many women can identify with the lady ambling through the woods behind the words, "Benson and Hedges and mornings and me."

But escape does not have to be solitary. Other Benson and Hedges ads, part of the same campaign, contain two strolling figures. In Salem cigarette advertisements, it can be several people who escape together into the mountaintops. A commercial for Levi's pictured a cloudbank above a city through which ran a whole chain of young people.

There are varieties of escape, some wistful like the Boeing "Some day" campaign of dream vacations, some kinetic like the play and parties in soft drink ads. But in every instance, the consumer exposed to the advertisement is invited to momentarily depart his everyday life for a more carefree experience, preferably with the product in hand.

12. *Need to feel safe.* Nobody in their right mind wants to be intimidated, menaced, battered, poisoned. We naturally want to do whatever it takes to stave off threats to our well-being, and to our families'. It is the instinct of self-preservation that makes us responsive to the ad of the St. Bernard with the keg of Chivas Regal. We pay attention to the stern talk of Karl Malden and the plight of the vacationing couples who have lost all their funds in the American Express travelers cheques commercials. We want the omnipresent stag from Hartford Insurance to watch over us too.

In the interest of keeping failure and calamity from our lives, we like to see the durability of products demonstrated. Can we ever forget that Timex takes a licking and keeps on ticking? When the American Tourister suitcase bounces all over the highway and the egg inside doesn't break, the need to feel safe has been adroitly plucked.

We take precautions to diminish future threats. We buy Volkswagen 70 Rabbits for the extraordinary mileage, and MONY insurance policies to avoid the tragedies depicted in their black-and-white ads of widows and orphans.

We are careful about our health. We consume Mazola margarine because it has "corn goodness" backed by the natural food traditions of the American Indians. In the medicine cabinet is Alka-Seltzer, the "home remedy"; having it, we are snug in our little cottage.

We want to be safe and secure; buy these products, advertisers are saying, and you'll be safer than you are without them.

13. *Need for aesthetic sensations.* There is an undeniable aesthetic component to virtually every ad run in the national media: the photography or filming or drawing is near-perfect, the type style is well chosen, the layout could scarcely be improved upon. Advertisers know there is little chance of good communication occurring if an ad is not visually pleasing. Consumers may not be aware of the extent of their own sensitivity to artwork, but it is undeniably large.

Sometimes the aesthetic element is expanded and made into an ad's primary appeal. Charles Jordan shoes may or may not appear in the accompanying avant-grade photographs; Kohler plumbing fixtures catch attention through the high style of their desert settings. Beneath the slightly out of focus photograph, languid and sensuous in tone, General Electric feels called upon to explain, "This is an ad for the hair dryer."

This appeal is not limited to female consumers: J&B scotch says "It 75 whispers" and shows a bucolic scene of lake and castle.

14. *Need to satisfy curiosity.* It may seem odd to list a need for information among basic motives, but this need can be as primal and compelling as any of the others. Human beings are curious by nature, interested in the world around them, and intrigued by tidbits of knowledge and new developments. Trivia, percentages, observations counter to conventional wisdom—these items all help sell products. Any advertisement in a question-and-answer format is strumming this need.

A dog groomer has a question about long distance rates, and Bell Telephone has a chart with all the figures. An ad for Porsche 911 is replete with diagrams and schematics, numbers and arrows. Lo and behold, Anacin pills have 150 more milligrams than its competitors; should we wonder if this is better or worse for us?

15. *Physiological needs.* To the extent that sex is solely a biological need, we are now coming around full circle, back toward the start of the list. In this final category are clustered appeals to sleeping, eating, drinking. The art of photographing food and drink is so advanced, sometimes these temptations are wondrously caught in the camera's lens: the crab meat in the Red Lobster restaurant ads can start us salivating, the Quarterpounder can almost be smelled, the liquor in the glass glows invitingly. Imbibe, these ads scream.

STYLES

Some common ingredients of advertisements were not singled out for separate mention in the list of fifteen because they are not appeals in and of themselves. They are stylistic features, influencing the way a basic appeal is presented. The use of humor is one, and the use of celebrities is another. A third is time imagery, past and future, which goes to several purposes.

For all of its employment in advertising, humor can be treacherous, 80 because it can get out of hand and smother the product information. Supposedly, this is what Alka-Seltzer discovered with its comic commercials of the late sixties; "I can't believe I ate the whole thing," the sad-faced husband lamented, and the audience cackled so much it forgot the antacid. Or, did not take it seriously.

But used carefully, humor can punctuate some of the softer appeals and soften some of the harsher ones. When Emma says to the Fruit-of-the-Loom fruits, "Hi, cuties. Whatcha doing in my laundry basket?" we smile as our curiosity is assuaged along with hers. Bill Cosby gets consumers tickled about the children in his Jell-O commercials, and strokes the need to nurture.

An insurance company wants to invoke the need to feel safe, but does not want to leave readers with an unpleasant aftertaste; cartoonist Rowland Wilson creates an avalanche about to crush a gentleman who is saying to another, "My insurance company? New England Life, of course. Why?" The same tactic of humor undercutting threat is used in the cartoon commercials for Safeco when the Pink Panther wanders from one disaster to another. Often humor masks aggression: comedian Bob Hope in the outfit of a boxer promises to knock out the knock-knocks with Texaco; Rodney Dangerfield, who "can't get no respect," invites aggression as the comic relief in Miller Lite commercials.

Roughly fifteen percent of all advertisements incorporate a celebrity, almost always from the fields of entertainment or sports. The approach can also prove troublesome for advertisers, for celebrities are human beings too, and fully capable of the most remarkable behavior. If anything distasteful about them emerges, it is likely to reflect on the product. The advertisers making use of Anita Bryant and Billy Jean King suffered several anxious moments. An untimely death can also react poorly on a product. But advertisers are willing to take risks because celebrities can be such a good link between producers and consumers, performing the social role of introducer.

There are several psychological needs these middlemen can play upon. Let's take the product class of cameras and see how different celebrities can hit different needs. The need for guidance can be invoked by Michael

199

Landon, who plays such a wonderful dad on "Little House on the Prairie"; when he says to buy Kodak equipment, many people listen. James Garner for Polaroid cameras is put in a similar authoritative role, so defined by a mocking spouse. The need to achieve is summoned up by Tracy Austin and other tennis stars for Canon AE-1; the advertiser first makes sure we see these athletes playing to win. When Cheryl Tiegs speaks up for Olympus cameras, it is the need for attention that is being targeted.

The past and future, being outside our grasp, are exploited by adver- 85
tisers as locales for the projection of needs. History can offer up heroes (and call up the need to achieve) or traditions (need for guidance) as well as art objects (need for aesthetic sensations). Nostalgia is a kindly version of personal history and is deployed by advertisers to rouse needs for affiliation and for guidance; the need to escape can come in here, too. The same need to escape is sometimes the point of futuristic appeals but picturing the avant-garde can also be a way to get at the need to achieve.

ANALYZING ADVERTISEMENTS

When analyzing ads yourself for their emotional appeals, it takes a bit of practice to learn to ignore the product information (as well as one's own experience and feelings about the product). But that skill comes soon enough, as does the ability to quickly sort out from all the non-product aspects of an ad the chief element which is the most striking, the most likely to snag attention first and penetrate brains farthest. The key to the appeal, this element usually presents itself centrally and forwardly to the reader or viewer.

Another clue: the viewing angle which the audience has on the ad's subjects is informative. If the subjects are photographed or filmed from below and thus are looking down at you much as the Green Giant does, then the need to be guided is a good candidate for the ad's emotional appeal. If, on the other hand, the subjects are shot from above and appear deferential, as is often the case with children or female models, then other needs are being appealed to.

To figure out an ad's emotional appeal, it is wise to know (or have a good hunch about) who the targeted consumers are; this can often be inferred from the magazine or television show it appears in. This piece of information is a great help in determining the appeal and in deciding between two different interpretations. For example, if an ad features a partially undressed female, this would typically signal one appeal for readers of *Penthouse* (need for sex) and another for readers of *Cosmopolitan* (need for attention).

It would be convenient if every ad made just one appeal, were aimed at just one need. Unfortunately, things are often not that simple. A cigarette ad with a couple at the edge of a polo field is trying to hit both the need for affiliation and the need for prominence; depending on the attitude of the male, dominance could also be an ingredient in this. An ad for Chimere perfume incorporates two photos: in the top one the lady is being commanding at a business luncheon (need to dominate), but in the lower one she is being bussed (need for affiliation). Better ads, however, seem to avoid being too diffused; in the study of post–World War II advertising described earlier, appeals grew more focused as the decades passed. As a rule of thumb, about sixty percent have two conspicuous appeals; the last twenty percent have three or more. Rather than looking for the greatest number of appeals, decoding ads is most productive when the loudest one or two appeals are discerned, since those are the appeals with the best chance of grabbing people's attention.

Finally, analyzing ads does not have to be a solo activity and probably 90 should not be. The greater number of people there are involved, the better chance there is of transcending individual biases and discerning the essential emotional lure built into an advertisement.

DO THEY OR DON'T THEY?

Do the emotional appeals made in advertisements add up to the sinister manipulation of consumers?

It is clear that these ads work. Attention is caught, communication occurs between producers and consumers, and sales result. It turns out to be difficult to detail the exact relationship between a specific ad and a specific purchase, or even between a campaign and subsequent sales figures, because advertising is only one of a host of influences upon consumption. Yet no one is fooled by this lack of perfect proof; everyone knows that advertising sells. If this were not the case, then tight-fisted American businesses would not spend a total of fifty billion dollars annually on these messages.

But before anyone despairs that advertisers have our number to the extent that they can marshal us at will and march us like automatons to the check-out counters, we should recall the resiliency and obduracy of the American consumer. Advertisers may have uncovered the softest spots in minds, but that does not mean they have found truly gaping apertures. There is no evidence that advertising can get people to do things contrary to their self-interests. Despite all the finesse of advertisements, and all the subtle emotional tugs, the public resists the vast majority of the petitions.

According to the marketing division of the A.C Nielsen Company, a whopping seventy-five percent of all new products die within a year in the marketplace, the victims of consumer disinterest which no amount of advertising could overcome. The appeals in advertising may be the most captivating there are to be had, but they are not enough to entrap the wiley consumer.

The key to understanding the discrepancy between, on the one hand, the fact that advertising truly works, and, on the other, the fact that it hardly works, is to take into account the enormous numbers of people exposed to an ad. Modern-day communications permit an ad to be displayed to millions upon millions of individuals; if the smallest fraction of that audience can be moved to buy the product, then the ad has been successful. When one percent of the people exposed to a television advertising campaign reach for their wallets, that could be one million sales, which may be enough to keep the product in production and the advertisements coming.

In arriving at an evenhanded judgment about advertisements and their emotional appeals, it is good to keep in mind that many of the purchases which might be credited to these ads are experienced as genuinely gratifying to the consumer. We sincerely like the goods or service we have bought, and we may even like some of the emotional drapery that an ad suggests comes with it. It has sometimes been noted that the most avid students of advertisements are the people who have just bought the product; they want to steep themselves in the associated imagery. This may be the reason that Americans, when polled, are not negative about advertising and do not disclose any sense of being misused. The volume of advertising may be an irritant, but the product information as well as the imaginative material in ads are partial compensation.

A productive understanding is that advertising messages involve costs and benefits at both ends of the communications channel. For those few ads which do make contact, the consumer surrenders a moment of time, has the lower brain curried, and receives notice of a product; the advertiser has given up money and has increased the chance of sales. In this sort of communications activity, neither party can be said to be the loser.

95

PATRICK VALA-HAYNES   [b. 1953]

What Does Online Shopping Cost Us?

Born in Oregon, **Patrick Vala-Haynes** studied humanities at New College of California. After college he pursued varied interests, including dance, theater, choreography, and writing. He has been a choreographer of swordfights and hand-to-hand combat for the stage for twenty-five years. As a writer, he is the author of several short stories and essays, and he is currently seeking a home for his screenplays, including *Colette at 15*, *The Tutor*, and *At the Point of a Sword*. Vala-Haynes presently lives in Oregon and divides his time between work in a bicycle shop, his family, a passion for writing, and soccer. His essay "What Does Online Shopping Cost Us?" was originally published in *Newsweek*.

It's NOT about the money. It's never been about the money. As a young couple with degrees in humanities and history, my wife, Robbie, and I didn't buy a bicycle shop 20 years ago near the Oregon Coast Range because we had dreams of great riches. We simply hoped that being self-employed would allow us to pursue our many interests—gardening, horses, theater—and maybe support a family. Robbie chose another career a few years after our daughter and son were born, but I've yet to find a good reason to change my profession.

Four days before Christmas last year, a gentleman walked into my shop near closing time. He wore a fine wool suit and a silk tie.

"How are you tonight?" I asked.

"Good, good," he huffed, his eyes wandering around the store.

"Can I help you find something?"   5

"Yes, yes. I'm looking for a—I'm not sure what you call it—one of those!" He pointed at a bicycle touring trailer and seemed relieved to have found it. "I've been searching for one all week."

"Really? Where have you looked?" I was curious as to why he hadn't bothered to check our store first, since we have the only bicycle shop in town. I wheeled the trailer to the counter.

"All over the Internet," he said. "I've been doing all my Christmas shopping that way. This is the first store I've set foot in all season." He seemed proud.

I offered to give him the name of some Web sites where he could buy the device, but he admitted that it was too late, he'd never get it before Christmas. I told him that I knew the going price of the item on the Net, and had he purchased the trailer online he could have saved $7.50 on his $185 purchase. "Of course, the assembly would have taken you about an hour," I added.

"Longer than that. I don't own a single wrench." He spun around on his feet and held up one hand as though he was hoping to sight land. "You know, I've never been in this store before tonight."

As I collapsed the item, what struck me was the man's genuine sense of unease that he was wasting valuable minutes of his day in a brick-and-mortar store, conversing with a merchant. He could have been at his keyboard, spending money by making even more purchases, more quickly. He tossed his Visa card on the counter, and tapped his thumb against his palm as we waited for the electronic transaction to be completed.

"Must be a lot of people shopping right now, for this to take so long," 10 he said impatiently. He signed the slip and I handed him his receipt. When I offered to carry his purchase to his car, he froze as though in shock. I'd wondered if I'd accidentally hit his OFF switch.

"Really?" he asked.

"No problem," I said. "I might even thank you and tell you to have a good evening," I teased.

He laughed, and we stepped outside into the clear night. The street lights glowed pale yellow on Third Street. A few cars crept by. I loaded the trailer and waved as the man pulled away.

As I closed up my shop I pictured a world where people had no reason to extend the common courtesies of "thank you" and "you're welcome," in which all their transactions were electronic. Such a world wasn't hard to imagine. I've owned my business for 20 years, and, like most merchants, I've worried about the impact of Internet and mail-order shopping on my livelihood. Though I have noticed some effect, moments like the one I experienced a few days before Christmas steel my resolve to survive, and point up the need all communities have for businesses such as mine. Yes, shop owners provide a needed service, but just as important, we provide a forum where people from different circles of society rub elbows with each other.

In the early '70s, an obscure writer from Texas, W.D. Norwood Jr., 15 wrote that progress was a myth. Culture is a seesaw, he contended. Something goes up, something comes down. There is no gain without loss. As Americans communicate faster and faster, exchanging more and more money and words in an electronic world, we have to begin to question the value of all this speed. If we believe that commerce is only about the exchange of money for products in as short a time as possible, then we as a culture have suffered a terrible loss of perspective. The seesaw is tipping.

I think my customer had a pleasant time in my shop. For just one moment, his heart calmed and he laughed. And he found something he wanted. I hope he'll come back. I can't promise I'll always have what he wants, but if I don't, I'll help him find it elsewhere. He won't have wasted his time.

Good retail business is a dialogue, not the punching of a few keys and the exchange of an address and a credit-card number. Those little moments of contact that we brick-and-mortar shops can offer are part of our social contract. Maybe we are meant to slow the world down.

HOLLY BRUBACH   [b. 1953]

Mail-Order America

Holly Brubach was born in 1953 and attended Duke University. She
began her career as a dancer, but shifted to writing after she was side-
lined by an injury. In 1978 she began writing about fashion for *Vogue*,
and later joined the staff of *The Atlantic* and *The New Yorker* as a fashion columnist. Brubach has also written about dance, scripting programs for the PBS "Dance in America" series and collaborating on
Choura: The Memoirs of Alexandra Danilova, a biography of the
famous Russian ballerina. Brubach has published two collections of
essays, *A Dedicated Follower of Fashion* and *Girlfriend: Men, Women
and Drag*, both in 1999. Her works combine insights about fashion,
gender politics, and culture. In "Mail-Order America," Brubach examines mail-order catalogues as indicators of human identity.

Growing up in Pittsburgh, I had an uncle who never obtained a passport
because he had made up his mind that he was never going to need one:
he had no intention of ever leaving the country. For that matter, he had
never left the state of Pennsylvania, except for one brief foray into Ohio,
which, he realized in retrospect, had been a mistake. For a soul so
utterly lacking in wanderlust, however, he was full of curiosity. In the
pages of *National Geographic*, he visited the steppes of Russia and the
Pyramids and the Great Wall, and on those rare occasions when bona
fide travelers happened to cross his path, he could converse with them
about the average rainfall in the month of August or the mathematical
basis of the architecture or the worsening condition of the mortar, as if
he'd not only gone on a tour but guided it. I remember regarding this
knowledge as somehow illegitimate, acquired rather than earned. And
with all the superiority of youth, I viewed him as lazy and complacent
for not having gone out and seen the world for himself.

Now, however, I confess that the older I get, the more I'm inclined to
follow his example, in my way. Late at night, when the stores are closed,
or on a Saturday afternoon, while weary women with swollen feet and
cranky children are competing for an overworked salesman's attention,

I'm at home with a stack of mail-order catalogues, redecorating my apartment and browsing for Christmas presents and planning what I'll wear next season. With time, I find, the best catalogues come to seem familiar: you recognize their tone of voice, their quirks, the faces that appear over and over again in their pages. Leafing through one recent arrival, a friend shook his head at the sight of so many models who for years now have been turning up in his mailbox on a regular basis. "I feel like I know these people better than the people I know," he said.

For those of us who feel that our lives have been inundated with catalogues, there is corroboration in statistics: last year, according to the Direct Marketing Association, more than 10,000 mail-order companies sent out 13.5 billion catalogues and some 55 percent of the adult population bought $51.5 billion worth of goods by mail. These figures have been steadily on the rise, climbing steeply during the '80s, when mail-order businesses grew at triple the rate of most retailers. Industry analysts say that this boom has come about for a variety of reasons, including the introduction of ZIP codes and toll-free telephone numbers, the spread of credit cards, the use of computer networks that cross-check information about individual spending habits and the sizable contingent of women in the work force. Women no longer have the time for recreational shopping, it seems, and men, who never had the time to shop, can no longer expect women to do their shopping for them.

Somehow, over the course of the past fifteen years or so, our collective attitude toward shopping—or at least toward the idea of it—seems to have shifted from delight to loathing. Those who once relished the chase, tracking down the perfect raincoat or duffel bag or fly-fishing rod or coffee maker or scented candle, can no longer be bothered. The audience for the department-store-as-theater has pretty much disappeared. In 1978, shoppers flocked to Bloomingdale's India promotion, buying souvenirs and saving themselves the trip (an idea that would have appealed to my uncle); now they can save themselves the trip across town. Although (or maybe because) we still look on the things with which people surround themselves as indicative of something deeply personal—as a form of self-expression—the act of furnishing our lives now strikes us as a chore. Perhaps it's our conscience, which we misplaced during the '80s, that is telling us not to set foot in the temples of consumerism. Perhaps it's our sense of decorum: we haven't stopped spending our money, but we're more reluctant to spend it in public. Most likely, mail-order catalogues are about sheer convenience: the catalogues have done for stores what videos have done for movie theaters.

Possibly due to the mistaken assumption that people who can afford 5 expensive clothes have more time to shop or that luxury goods would be tainted by the stigma of catalogue shopping, the top of the retail market has yet to be colonized by the mail-order business. Despite the occasional exception . . ., mail order in many people's minds retains the down-market connotations of the "wish books" that peddled dinette sets to the children of immigrants. Within the past few years, however, fashion designers have begun to view the success of catalogues like J. Crew with increasing envy, and some—among them Calvin Klein and Carolyne Roehm—have begun to make inroads into the field.

What industry analysts leave unsaid, but what millions of mail-order customers know firsthand, is that the catalogues are beating not only the stores but also the fashion magazines at their own game. Fashion magazines now find themselves preaching almost exclusively to the converted, reporting designers' runway proclamations as if they mattered (which they do, in a way). Mail-order catalogues, however, insinuate themselves into the homes of the indifferent and the disaffected, who couldn't care less what Karl Lagerfeld has to say. Where magazines have come to look more and more like catalogues, offering a little something for everyone (the advertisers, the designers, the multitudes of readers), catalogues have come to look more and more like magazines, with a distinct editorial point of view. While magazines have waxed prosaic, catalogues have turned poetic, portraying a world that, for all its resemblance to the one in which we live, is of their own creation—a place with its own landscape, its indigenous population, its native customs, its dialect. If our forays into this world are increasingly frequent, perhaps it's because they confirm a number of things we like to believe: that life is happy, harmonious and just and that people get what they deserve, which in our case is the best.

The territory staked out by J. Crew in the pages of its catalogue was, until recently, easy to locate—just down the road from where the people in Ralph Lauren's ads lived. The real estate was a little more affordable, the local inhabitants—attractive, unfailingly stylish men and women— weren't quite so stuck-up and self-conscious. Clearly, we were somewhere in America, but in an America that was scenic and vaguely nostalgic, where there were no strip malls or nuclear power plants or fast-food restaurants. In this place, Coca-Cola still came in the old green glass bottles—no garish aluminum cans. The people who lived there drove Land Rovers and convertible two-seaters. They packed their picnics in antique wicker hampers. They painted an old table they bought at a yard sale and got the paint all over themselves. Shucking corn, eating watermelon, drinking iced tea and homemade lemonade, they were caught in the act by the camera, in pictures that could have been snapshots taken by a friend. These people's sailboats and their golden retrievers and their

Alumni Day visit to a university that looked to be either Princeton or Yale situated them squarely in the upper middle class. The men were well groomed, clean shaven, with short hair and high cheekbones. The women wore little or no makeup, and an inordinate number of them were pale and blue-eyed and blond; one, a regular, bore a remarkable resemblance to Glenn Close. (The portfolio of dressier women's clothes modeled by Lauren Hutton, a regular feature every season, has always looked more like a fashion story from Mirabella than a weekday extension of the life depicted in the rest of the catalogue.)

Lately, however, there's been an influx of ethnicity into J. Crew's pages (it's happening in Ralph Lauren's neighborhood, too). This fall, there are not one but four different editions of the J. Crew catalogue—one set in downtown Manhattan, the others in the usual picturesque country retreat, with small inset photographs from the urban version. Our old acquaintances have been moved aside to make room for an aspiring rock band and its assorted hangers-on. The split-rail fences, the stands of trees, the path along the crest of the dunes give way, in the downtown edition, to corrugated fencing, cracked windows held together with duct tape and graffiti. A pick-up basketball game in a city schoolyard includes three blacks, one Asian and a couple of white guys. There are men with long, unruly hair and women who appear to be of Mediterranean extraction, or part-Hispanic, or part-black. Blondes are rare.

But in one sense the demographics are still surprisingly narrow: there are no old people. Here, as in the mythical place where J. Crew's catalogue used to reside, the population ranges in age from late teens to mid-30's, with a handful of children—none of them old enough to wear braces or need advice about birth control.

At first glance, the multiculturalism that has found its way into J. Crew's catalogue looks like an injection of reality into what had been an airtight fantasy, but closer inspection reveals that only the trappings have changed; the fantasy remains the same. This is a world whose affable inhabitants live in harmony. Camaraderie prevails. No one is ever alone, unless it's to read a book, and even then we feel sure that there are friends somewhere close at hand, sleeping late or poring over the Sunday paper or planning dinner. All dark thoughts, all solitary bouts of melancholy and despair, have been banished. On page after page, the good times unfold. Life is a party to which we wish we'd been invited. The only difference is that this season, there are some new people on the guest list.

The voice in the copy that accompanies the photographs remains cordial and sensible-sounding—no flowery odes to a shirt, no wheedling sales pitches about the role it will play in your wardrobe. No full sentences, either. The machine-gun rhythm gets to be a little irritating: "Buttons. Collar. Placket. Seams. A hefty cotton jersey." Every once in a while the polite reserve falls away and then J. Crew gives in to snobbery and name-dropping. "We can't say for sure, but we seem to remember old photos of Jackson Pollock in East Hampton wearing pants like these," one caption claims.

Nearly everything J. Crew sells — new editions of standard sportswear that's in the public domain — seems calculated to be instantly familiar, to take its place beside those favorite items in our wardrobes that have earned the status of old friends. The "barn jackets" are "pre-aged" and appear slightly battered; the twill work shirts are dyed to look as if they've faded over the course of long years. Many of the items are just like something we already own, except for some small detail, some slight improvement that makes us suddenly feel that the version we have is inferior: the phys. ed. shorts are in vivid colors they never came in at school; the rope-soled espadrilles are gingham-checked; the denim jackets have a tartan lining. The appeal of these clothes is based on novelty rather than fashion. . . .

The guys in the J. Crew catalogue are the "new men" we've heard so much about: they throw their arms around each other's shoulders; they know their way around a kitchen; they feed their baby children. Although in the past the men wearing wedding bands outnumbered the women who wore them, there was never the slightest suspicion that the men might be married to somebody else who wasn't pictured — that they'd left their wives at home and run off for an illicit weekend in the catalogue's pages. In fact, it seemed to go without saying that these women *were* the wives and that, while the new men may have relished a wedding ring as a token of commitment, the women were so secure and independent that they didn't need one.

This fall, however, there are fewer men and women wearing wedding bands. What this means for marriage is anybody's guess. Maybe it's still going strong, but the signs of it aren't fashionable anymore. Maybe this crowd is younger and they're still waiting to meet their mates. Or maybe people who live in lofts in New York don't get married as much as people who live in places where Coke still comes in bottles. The old cast of characters had about it an air of satisfaction, of being settled; this new crowd projects a sense of possibilities.

Unlike J. Crew — the name of no one in particular, which conjures up 15 images of oarsmen on the Charles — L. L. Bean was a real person: Leon Leonwood Bean who, as faithful readers of his catalogues have learned over the years, loved to go fishing, hunting and camping, lived to be 94, sent his favorite dog tins of biscuits when he went away on trips and gave each newly married L. L. Bean employee a Hudson's Bay blanket as a wedding present. Though he is no longer the company's animating presence, there's a distinct personality that survives in the tone of the catalogue copy. Plain-spoken, chatty and respectful, the corporate voice of L. L. Bean keeps up a fairly steady monologue in a mature-sounding first-person plural, taking full responsibility for the products for sale, offering bits of arcane information (it takes thirty to fifty gallons of maple-sugar sap to produce a single gallon of syrup), creating the impression that on the other side of the image and the "800" number there's somebody home. "Our product testers found these versatile boots ideal for mountain biking and day hiking," the catalogue announces. At Christmas, L. L. Bean greets its customers with the fond good wishes of an old friend: "We hope to hear from you and hope you have a safe and memorable holiday season."

The people pictured in L. L. Bean's pages look like attractive customers or friends of the employees or teachers at the local elementary school in Freeport, Me., the company's headquarters; they're simply too ordinary to qualify as models. All fantasy, all glamour, all aspirations to a better life than the one in which the readers might find themselves are absent here. The appeal rests entirely on reality—or, rather, on some approximation of reality, since the majority of L. L. Bean's customers probably don't live in log cabins or houses with stone hearths. Where several other, glossier catalogues with pretensions to elegance routinely offer certain items at discreet "marked-down" prices in order to avoid the stigma of discount retailing (in the Victoria's Secret catalogue, the Chancery Lace Bra has been on sale for at least four years now), L. L. Bean makes no bones about appealing to the reader's desire to save a dollar here, a dollar there; thrift is a Yankee virtue. A shirt is advertised as "priced at an exceptional value—$4 less than last year."

The houses are modest. The landscape is strictly local, off the circuit that the power brokers travel. The Christmas trees that appear in the background in the holiday edition are hung not with precious, glittering gold and cut-crystal ornaments, as they are in the Victoria's Secret catalogue, but with pretzels and cranberry strands and strung popcorn. If L. L. Bean is guilty of romanticizing anything, it's the continuous present of the American home, cozy and unbroken, as it exists for most people only in the imagination. Microwave ovens, Nintendo, 12-step programs—the world as we now know it has been held at bay, with no more than a few recent developments like step aerobics selectively admitted. The TV, VCR, stereo and CD player are housed in a cabinet designed to look like an old-fashioned icebox. Though the loving hands that stitch Bean's sampler quilts and crewel-embroidered sweaters are anonymous, their products are suffused with intimations of mythical grandmothers.

The people L. L. Bean depicts, one gathers, are mostly married, with car pools and mortgages and aging parents—the full weight of adult responsibility on their shoulders. They are pictured fetching a few logs from the woodpile, teaching their tow-headed children to read or curled up in their flannel pajamas, book in hand. Personality, 10. Sex appeal, 0. It's not so much the clothes they wear that make them look so dowdy, since many of the items aren't significantly different from their trendier counterparts (J. Crew's Barn Jacket is nearly indistinguishable from Bean's Canvas Field Coat). It's the way the clothes are worn—their tidy fit, their matching colors, their utter lack of any sense of adventure (paradoxical in people who profess to love exploring the outdoors). The cut is prudish at times: the caption for one cotton shirt assures the reader that the V-neck is "not too low." The catalogue repeatedly draws the line between "roomy" and "relaxed" (both desirable traits) and "oversized" (taboo in this context). Fashion is suspect, to be avoided at all costs. The people at L. L. Bean refer consistently to their "apparel designers," in a locution as quaint as a Norman Rockwell illustration. The free and loose style that dominates the pages of J. Crew would surely dismay these adherents to the rule book of convention. Shirts and turtleneck jerseys are worn close to the body and tucked in. Sweaters are ribbed at the cuffs and at the waistband. The effect is Republican.

In the world evoked by the L. L. Bean catalogue, there is no room for the confusion about sex roles that currently besets the rest of our society. Androgyny is prohibited. Those garments that the Bean people countenance for both men and women are designated outright "For Men and Women," with separate sizes or, in a few cases, men's sizes followed by a list of women's equivalents; the word "unisex" is never spoken. Likewise, the people at L. L. Bean have their minds made up on the subject of color palettes and gender. Mock turtlenecks are available in, among other colors: "Maroon (Men's only). Honey (Women's only). Blue (Men's only)." When it comes to the Blanket Plaid Flannel Shirts, the men get brown; the women, red. There is, of course, nothing to prevent a woman from ordering the same shirt in brown, in a men's size, for a fit that's slightly funkier, but the distinctions here are so firmly drawn that so brash an act would be tantamount to cross-dressing.

This catalogue sure is talkative, with a lengthy caption for every item, 20 listing its attributes in scrupulous detail. "Buttons along left side for easy on/off," the catalogue says of a jumper. A jersey dress is "fun to wear— needs no special care." The longstanding Yankee suspicion of fashion is coupled here with the conviction that clothes are a lot of bother.

Ironically, plaid flannel shirts, along with Birkenstocks and several other items L. L. Bean sells, are "hot" right now—a fact of which the Bean people seem oblivious. Where J. Crew takes essentially standard items and presents them in a manner that's glamorous and up to the minute—shirts tied around the waist, shorts two sizes too big, worn low on the hips of young models—L. L. Bean's approach is stolid and plain. The appeal of this is probably lost on people who buy into the heat of the moment, but for those who have opted out of the rat race, including (paradoxically) many full-time fashion types, L. L. Bean is a relief, a refuge from the onslaughts of trendiness.

Bean's style might be called New England provincial, and like all provincial esthetics, it is ultimately corrupted by sentimentality. Ankle socks "patterned with cows and pigs grazing amid tulip rows." The "Warm Feelings Blanket." J. Crew has found a harmless enough outlet for its elegiac impulses in the names of colors, which ramble from the botanical (weed, thistle, yucca, aloe, glade, balsam) to the oceano- graphic (Pacific, surf, kelp, lake, lagoon) to the culinary (Dijon, cola, chili). But L. L. Bean refuses to get carried away in this respect: "yellow, orange, magenta, dark purple, white, turquoise, royal, navy," the cata- logue states flatly. This penchant for simplicity is every so often over- come by some lyric impulse and then the hardheaded Yankee is revealed to be a sap, particularly when it comes to the local landscape: a sweater captures "the soft tones of a Maine seaside garden muted by fog" or a quilt evokes a wave of memories, including "the cry of loons in early morning." But these outbursts, rare and always brief, were outdone in the catalogue this spring by the emotionalism of one C. H. Gray, a cus- tomer from Hillsboro, Ore. His paean to his Maine Hunting Shoes, received in 1945 as a gift from his father, is written in iambic septameter, and the penultimate couplet reads: "These boots have kept my feet warm, comfortable and dry,/or And the thought of simply discarding them can almost make me cry."

In the end, what saves L. L. Bean from bathos is the sense that the people behind the catalogue actually live the life depicted in its pages. The outdoorsy, sports-loving attitude is not a pose. Though L. L. Bean's fishing vest may be worn by photographers and other people in need of lots of pockets, it is designed for someone who actually fishes. The context in which the clothes are presented confirms their authenticity. The Fly Fish- ing catalogue (a separate edition) is packed with fascinating lore, as well as flies called "Mickey Finn," "Fruit Cocktail" and—wonderful finds for the collector of affectionate nicknames—"Rat Face Irresistible" and "Gerbubble Bug." J. Crew may sell all the makings of an outfit that one could wear to go kayaking, but L. L. Bean sells the outfit *and* the kayak.

It is not at all clear whether the Victoria's Secret catalogue is intended for the women who would wear the clothes featured in it or for the men who would like the women in their lives to wear the clothes featured in it—particularly the lingerie. In what is tantamount to an admission that the catalogue has acquired a considerable following among the kind of guys who maintain a small archive of *Sports Illustrated*'s swimsuit issues, the copy goes back and forth, addressing first the women, who are buying for themselves ("a great choice when dinner's at 8 and you're leaving straight from the office") and then the men, who are buying for the women ("a sumptuous gift so wonderful, you might let her have it just a little bit early"). The tone Victoria's Secret takes with men is hushed and conspiratorial, as if this were their girlfriend's best friend talking— steering them clear of all the pitfalls they would otherwise encounter in their search for the perfect gift. Even so, this catalogue is unquestionably a female enclave, like a beauty salon or a harem—a place to which women retreat to make themselves more attractive. And though men are seldom admitted, their presence and power in the world beyond its confines are implied in the women's diligent efforts to please them.

The Victoria's Secret cast revolves around a handful of recognizable 25 stars—"supermodels" who inhabit the pages of *Vogue,* ads for designer clothes and the runways of Europe. Linda Evangelista, Stephanie Seymour and Karen Mulder bring to the catalogue an aura of international glamour, or anyway that seems to be the intent. The truth is that it's always something of a shock to come upon them here, like finding movie stars playing the dinner theater on a cruise ship. Nearly all the women have long hair (long hair and sexy lingerie evidently go together). When it comes to clothing, models always wear the smallest size; when it comes to bras, the women in the Victoria's Secret catalogue look as if they take a medium at the very least.

To my mind, the better part of this catalogue's entertainment value resides in watching the Victoria's Secret people walk the fine line between sexy and trashy. The trappings are endlessly amusing, intended to set a tone of thoroughbred elegance and high propriety by evoking the life of the English aristocracy. But a bona fide Mayfair drawing room would run the risk of being too subtle and musty to trigger in American readers the desired intimidation at the thought of a nation full of people supposedly more civilized than we are. Instead, the Victoria's Secret masterminds have constructed what is essentially a cartoon furnished with hoity-toity, English clichés: silver salvers, Battersea boxes, leather library sofas, paintings of horses. The models—clad in scant, lace-trimmed underwear, their bra straps slipping off their shoulders—look soulfully into the eye of the camera while lying on an Oriental rug or posing next to a tea table.

The catalogue copy is likewise strewn with Britishisms: "centre," "jewellery," "colour," "favourite," "splendour." . . . An ongoing series of bathrobes has identified itself with a distinguished university (the Cambridge Robe), a country house open to tourists (the Chatsworth Robe), a legendary heroine harking back to the days of chivalry (the Guinevere Robe).

214

The merchandise itself, ranging from suits and dresses to sports clothes and what the English call "frocks" for evening, isn't bad, despite a propensity for shiny synthetic fibers that give an impression of simulated satin with an almost adhesive cling. There's a good selection of bras and underpants: demi-cup underwires, halter-neck bras, strapless bustiers, merry widows, garter belts, flutter bikinis, high-cut briefs, G-strings. But over all, the clothing is strictly middle of the road—mall fashion that steers a safe and steady course, with an occasional detour to take in some recent trend. The catalogue would have us believe that its constituency is made up mostly of successful career women; an outfit is touted for its "executive finesse." But the only executives who dress like this are the ones in television miniseries. The colors are a little too bright for the corporate life; the cut calls too much attention to the shape of the body. Five years after fashion designers finally succeeded in abolishing shoulder pads, the people at Victoria's Secret seem either not to know or not to care; nor have they heard about the demotion of the "power suit," which has been discarded by the women it was intended for and taken up by the women who work for them. In fact, the likeliest candidate for the Victoria's Secret customer would appear to be not the *Business Week* subscriber but That Cosmopolitan Girl.

The catalogue speaks the language of romance novels, fraught with histrionic verbs and overwrought adjectives. Bikinis "sizzle," skirts "sweep" and "cascade," necklines "plunge," dresses "bedazzle." The clothes are routinely described as "opulent," "lavish," "sophisticated." Why use a plain word when a fancy one will do? Some of the fabrics are "launderable."

Significantly, the famous models who might have been the obvious 30 choices—buxom blondes like Claudia Schiffer and Anna Nicole Smith, the Brigitte Bardot and Marilyn Monroe look-alikes—are absent here. Victoria's Secret features good girls, well brought up, slightly nymphomaniacal, but only behind closed doors and only when they're in love. Seymour—head back, back arched—writhes with longing. Mulder projects a certain reserve, even when she's reclining on a chaise longue, wearing a push-up bra and bikini briefs. The sex appeal is of the smoldering, read-my-mind variety, not kittenish or playful. Page after page, these contemporary odalisques offer themselves, like Manet's "Olympia," in repose: passive women, waiting for a man to come along and fulfill them—not just any man but the man of their dreams.

A generation that gleaned some of its earliest information about sex by scrutinizing the pages of prosthetic-looking bras and briefs in the Sears catalogue (straightforward, almost clinical—like looking up dirty words in the dictionary) has finally come of age and now studies Victoria's Secret instead. The pleasure this experience holds for men is obvious. But what women get out of it—apart from the convenience of mail-order shopping—has been largely overlooked. There is perhaps an unspoken consensus that the subject is too loaded, that the less said these days about the pleasure women may take in projecting themselves into the role of a sex object, the better. But the fact remains that for many women, looking at pictures of other women is an incitement to fantasy—not because they want to know those women but because they want in some vague way to *be* those women, to evoke in men the feelings they imagine the women in the pictures do.

Lust, however, is only part of the equation. The eroticism is always subordinate to a higher goal: romance. Readers of novels about American girls adrift in international society or about 18th-century virgins ravished by pirates or about small-town daughters who conquer the hearts of lonesome millionaires will recognize in Victoria's Secret's lingerie pages a kindred sensibility. The hot-blooded lover rips the heroine's bodice and discovers . . . the lace-edged, demi-cup, underwire bra on page 14. I have an idea for a new marketing venture: a made-for-television movie subtitled with information about the clothes the characters are wearing (fabric content, sizes, price), along with a toll-free number the viewer can call to order them.

Year in and year out, this hunger for romance and passion—the sight of all these women in heat—is like an obsessive drone so that, finally, what seems most remarkable about Victoria's Secret is a certain self-referential monotony. . . . Victoria's Secret recommends its Tapestry Keepsake Box as the perfect place to store love letters.

The heroine of the Victoria's Secret catalogue is, in many respects, the ideal mail-order customer. House-bound in her lace-trimmed satin teddy, she lounges decoratively, leafing through the catalogues that get delivered to her door while she awaits the man who will transform her life. Every day brings a new harvest of things she never knew she needed: reproduction gargoyles (Design Toscano); copies of baseball uniforms from such historic teams as the Mexican Southwest League Tabasco Bananas and the Toledo Mud Hens (Ebbets Field Flannels); a lease on a lobster trap (Rent Mother Nature); and healing crystals and new-age cards dispensing sage advice: "Live Juicy. . . . Marry Yourself. . . . Be who you truly are and the money will follow" (Red Rose Collection). From "The Best Catalogues in the World" she orders other catalogues. In her Tapestry Keepsake Box she stashes a snack—a chocolate bar in the shape of a topographical map of Israel (The Source for Everything Jewish). . . .

The truth might ruin her illusion. She switches on the television, but 35 the Home Shopping Club, a cross between an auction and a telethon, strikes her as raucous and intrusive, to say nothing of the clinical way the merchandise is displayed, as if it were on exhibit in a courtroom.

216

When information about . . . J. Crew's expanding retail empire makes its way into the papers, she instinctively avoids it. Too many facts would expose the stagecraft.

This is an alternative world she's living in, in which every catalogue seizes on some facet of life and celebrates the hell out of it. J. Crew would have us believe that belonging to a community would fill the empty spaces in our souls. The people at L. L. Bean would turn our enthusiasm for the outdoors into a religion. . . . In Victoria's Secret, it's love. These are not misrepresentations, only exaggerations, and in many respects they are more comfortable than the ambiguities and compromises that permeate our everyday lives. If mail-order shopping is sweeping America, perhaps it's because we're such a willing audience for the fantasies that catalogues present: we've been led to believe that our circumstances can change overnight, that any day now we can get discovered, find true love, hit the jackpot.

So the woman reads the catalogues in solitude, in silence or while listening to "Classics by Request," Victoria's Secret's two-volume tape collection of classical music by Mozart, Vivaldi, Handel and others. In page after page, the catalogues lay out their merchandise for her perusal. They speak to her directly, flattering her vanity, courting her interest. "This is all for you," they say. "You are the only customer in the world."

BILL MCKIBBEN   [b. 1960]

Pie in the Sky

A graduate of Harvard University, environmental writer **Bill McKibben** got his start as a staff writer for the *New Yorker*. He is the author of numerous books on environmental consciousness-raising in our urbanized, consumer culture, including *The End of Nature* (1989), *Maybe One: An Environmental and Personal Argument for Single-Child Homes* (1998), *Hundred Dollar Holiday: The Case for a More Joyful Christmas* (1998), *The Age of Missing Information* (1992), and *Enough: Staying Human in an Engineered Age* (2004). A former fellow at the Harvard University Center for the Study of Values in Public Life, McKibben is currently a scholar-in-residence in environmental studies at Middlebury College. His articles appear frequently in the *New York Review of Books*, *Outside*, and the *New York Times*, and he is a contributing writer to *Mother Jones*. He has been a recipient of both the Guggenheim and Lyndhurst fellowships. In 2000, he was honored with the Lannan Prize in Nonfiction Writing.

In his essay "Pie in the Sky," McKibben highlights America's consumer craze and satirizes contemporary American culture by making fun of several of the ridiculous objects that are available for purchase—items like grilled cheese makers and remote control locator devices.

Question: should anyone who requires a "revolutionary new laser technology system" in order to figure out if they're parking in the right spot inside their own garage really be allowed behind the wheel in the first place? Compared with the other tasks of a driver—making right-hand turns, making left-hand turns, deciphering the red-amber-green vernacular of a stoplight—safely positioning your auto within the confines of your own garage seems like a fairly straightforward task, the kind of thing that might not require a laser.

But you'd be surprised how useful lasers can be. The Hairmax Laser Comb, for instance, used only fifteen minutes a day, three times a week, results in noticeably thicker locks and tresses. And not just lasers. Ions are also surprisingly useful—confusingly, negative ions. A lamp made of salt crystal mined from the Himalayas emits them, aiding you in the fight

Bill McKibben, "Pie in the Sky" from *Orion*, March/April 2006. Reprinted by permission of the author.

against "dust mites" and also "depression."

If there's any piece of writing that defines our culture, I submit it's the SkyMall catalogue, available in the seatback pocket of every airplane in North America. To browse its pages is to understand the essential secret of American consumer life: We've officially run out not only of things that we need, but even of things that we might plausibly desire.

But we in the airline traveling class still have a few problems to solve in our lives. Judging from the joys on offer, our particular worries at the moment might be categorized as follows:

I'm overworked and overtired. In which case, I need a $4,000 massaging recliner with voice control, synthetic leather ("softer, more plush than leather"), and thirty-three airbags—a machine that "pampers your body and soothes your soul." And if perchance I drift off to sleep, "the peaceful progression wake-up clock" will rouse me with infinite care. "Thirty minutes before wake-up time, the light glows softly, brightening over the next half hour, while faint aromatherapy scents release into the air. Fifteen minutes before wake up, the clock generates one of six soft nature sounds." In case that isn't quite enough, I might want to back it up with the "sensory assault alarm clock," whose large, wired vibrating pad placed under the mattress shakes you awake in time to turn off the clock before it emits a ninety-five-decibel alarm and starts flashing a strobe light.

I have an immense supply of trousers, and hence require the closet organizer trouser rack to keep twenty pairs of slacks neatly hung and readily accessible. The five-eighths-inch-diameter birch dowels "reduce creasing of even fine fabrics," and "nylon washers between the dowels ensure smooth swing motion."

I distrust my neighbors and government, and so would benefit from a giant-capacity mailbox that holds up to two weeks of mail (catalogues, presumably). "Don't bother a neighbor to get your mail, and don't tell the post office you'll be away."

I am extremely, extremely clean. I'm therefore thankful that my toothbrush has been ultravioletly cleansed overnight to remove the "millions of germs" that would otherwise accumulate, and my room is protected against "airborne bacteria, viruses, and germs" by a Germ Guardian machine, "proven by a Harvard researcher," which "takes ultraviolet C energy and multiplies its germ-killing power in our exclusive Intensifier Chamber." Also, I have another very similar-looking machine "now with exclusive Ozoneguard" in case any ozone is nearby. And a soap dispenser with infrared sensor technology for my shower, a "no-touch approach that dramatically reduces the chance of spreading germs."

I have way too many watches, and therefore might benefit from a $300 case that will shake them all with "intermittent timers and directional

5

219

controls" to mimic the action of a human wrist and hence keep them fully wound at all times.

I have plugged in so many things that the planet has warmed consider- 10 *ably, reducing the chances that my children will experience a natural winter.* So I have purchased a "weatherproof light projection box that rests on your front lawn and transforms the entire facade of your house into an illuminated snowscape. The box creates the illusion of gently falling snow flurries by directing a bright white beam onto a rotating mirrorball." Flake size and fall rate are, pleasingly, adjustable. I have opted also to purchase an "exclusive heavy duty vinyl snow castle" that will "set up almost anywhere in just minutes with the included electric pump." A real snow castle would, SkyMall notes, "take hours to build and require lots of snow," but this version "encourages children to use their imaginations while having fun."

I have an enormous number of remote controls, and hence need caddies to store them, small "buddy lights" to illuminate them, and locator devices to find them when I have mislaid them.

I may be devolving. Though for eons my ancestors have grilled meat over flames, I am no longer very clear on the concept and so would like a digital barbecue fork that I can stick into my burger or steak and receive a readout indicating whether it is currently rare, medium, or well done. Also, it would help a lot to have all the lights already strung on my artificial Christmas tree, and the difficult task of marinating would be much easier if I had a $199.95 marinating machine. Frankly, I've lately found grilled cheese sandwiches more trouble than I want, but with my dishwasher-safe Toastabag I can simply place a slice of cheese between two slices of bread and pop it in my toaster. (Depressing the toaster lever still requires my thoughtful attention, as does chewing the resulting treat.)

There are a few problems SkyMall can't solve (the lack of community that comes when you live in a giant stuff-filled house marooned on its half-acre lot, the lack of security that comes when your country is spending its money on remote-control golf balls instead of, say, healthcare and retirement savings). And there's always the vexing question of what the people who are making these items think about the people who will buy them.

(I was in a shower curtain factory in rural China last year where the very nice people sewing the curtains told another visitor that they'd never actually encountered a shower curtain outside the factory. If that's true for a shower curtain, one wonders what their fellow workers make of the traveling wine trolley, the pop-up hot dog cooker, the hand-held paper shredder with wood-grain plastic handle.)

But this kind of talk sounds tired, clichéd, left over from the '60s. Everyone knows that the most important thing we can do is grow the economy. When you buy the Designated Driver, a faux golf club that you store in your bag to dispense forty-eight ounces of cold beverages, then you grow the economy. No doubt about it. Also, the Vintage Express Aging Accelerator that ages your bottle of wine ten years in ten seconds by surrounding it with "extremely powerful Neodymium magnets to replicate the Earth's magnetic field." Only a real jerk or a Christian or something would point out that there might possibly be items in this world that it would make more sense to spend our money on. (Insecticide-impregnated bednets to stop the spread of malaria run about five dollars. If only they came in self-erecting pastel versions that would also rouse you out of bed with gentle nature sounds.)

NAOMI KLEIN   [b. 1970]

No Logo

Naomi Klein is a Canadian journalist, author, and activist. Klein attended the University of Toronto, where she experienced her "wake-up call" to feminism after witnessing the murder of fourteen female engineering students by a misogynistic gunman. Klein began a process of activism directed against multinational corporations, both for their mistreatment of indigent workers and their sale of products emblazoned with corporate labels. Klein describes her campaign in the book *No Logo* (2000), an international best-seller that was translated into twenty-five languages and termed a "movement bible" by the *New York Times*. The book energized thousands of young people who had previously avoided politics; they responded to Klein's accusation that corporations exploited the poor and transformed their own consumers into walking advertisements. Klein's second book is *Fences and Windows: Dispatches from the Front Lines of the Globalization Debate* (2002). For six years she has traveled through North America, Asia, Latin America, and Europe in order to track the rise of anti-globalization. She is also a frequent media commentator, guest lecturer, and a regular contributor to the *Globe and Mail*, Canada's national newspaper.

> *As a private person, I have a passion for landscape, and I have never seen one improved by a billboard. Where every prospect pleases, man is at his vilest when he erects a billboard. When I retire from Madison Avenue, I am going to start a secret society of masked vigilantes who will travel around the world on silent motor bicycles, chopping down posters at the dark of the moon. How many juries will convict us when we are caught in these acts of beneficent citizenship?*
>
> —David Ogilvy, founder of the
> Ogilvy&Mather advertising agency, in
> *Confessions of an Advertising Man*, 1963

The astronomical growth in the wealth and cultural influence of multinational corporations over the last fifteen years can arguably be traced back to a single, seemingly innocuous idea developed by management theorists in the mid-1980s: that successful corporations must primarily produce brands, as opposed to products.

Until that time, although it was understood in the corporate world that bolstering one's brand name was important, the primary concern of every solid manufacturer was the production of goods. This idea was the very gospel of the machine age. An editorial that appeared in *Fortune* magazine in 1938, for instance, argued that the reason the American economy had yet to recover from the Depression was that America had lost sight of the importance of making *things*.

> This is the proposition that the basic and irreversible function of an industrial economy is *the making of things:* that the more things it makes the bigger will be the income, whether dollar or real; and hence that the key to those lost recuperative powers lies . . . in the factory where the lathes and the drills and the fires and the hammers are. It is in the factory and on the land and under the land that purchasing power *originates.* [italics theirs].

And for the longest time, the making of things remained, at least in principle, the heart of all industrialized economies. But by the eighties, pushed along by that decade's recession, some of the most powerful manufacturers in the world had begun to falter. A consensus emerged that corporations were bloated, oversized; they owned too much, employed too many people, and were weighed down with *too many things*. The very process of producing—running one's own factories, being responsible for tens of thousands of full-time permanent employees—began to look less like the route to success and more a clunky liability.

At around this same time a new kind of corporation began to rival the traditional all-American manufacturers for market share; these were Nikes and Microsofts, and later, the Tommy Hilfigers and Intels. These pioneers made the claim that producing goods was only an incidental part of their operations, and that thanks to recent victories in trade liberalization and labor-law reform, they were able to have their products made for them by contractors, many of them overseas. What these companies produced primarily were not things they said, but *images* of their brands. Their real work lay not in manufacturing but in marketing. This formula, needless to say, has proved enormously profitable, and its success has companies competing in a race toward weightlessness: whoever owns the least, has the fewest employees on the payroll and produces the most powerful images, as opposed to products, wins the race.

And so the wave of mergers in the corporate world over the last few years is a deceptive phenomenon: it only *looks* as if the giants, by joining 5 forces, are getting bigger and bigger. The true key to understanding these shifts is to realize that in several crucial ways—not their profits, of course—these merged companies are actually shrinking. Their apparent bigness is simply the most effective route toward their real goal: divestment of the world of things.

Since many of today's best-known manufacturers no longer produce products and advertise them, but rather buy products and "brand" them, these companies are forever on the prowl for creative new ways to build and strengthen their brand images. Manufacturing products may require drills, furnaces, hammers and the like, but creating a brand calls for a completely different set of tools and materials. It requires an endless parade of brand extensions, continuously renewed imagery for marketing and, most of all, fresh new spaces to disseminate the brand's idea of itself. In this section of the book, I'll look at how, in ways both insidious and overt, this corporate obsession with brand identity is waging a war on public and individual space: on public institutions such as schools, on youthful identities, on the concept of nationality and on the possibilities for unmarketed space.

THE BEGINNING OF THE BRAND

It's helpful to go back briefly and look at where the idea of branding first began. Though the words are often used interchangeably, branding and advertising are not the same process. Advertising any given product is only one part of branding's grand plan, as are sponsorship and logo licensing. Think of the brand as the core meaning of the modern corporation, and of the advertisement as one vehicle used to convey that meaning to the world.

The first mass-marketing campaigns, starting in the second half of the nineteenth century, had more to do with advertising than with branding as we understand it today. Faced with a range of recently invented products—the radio, phonograph, car, light bulb and so on—advertisers had more pressing tasks than creating a brand identity for any given corporation; first, they had to change the way people lived their lives. Ads had to inform consumers about the existence of some new invention, then convince them that their lives would be better if they used, for example, cars instead of wagons, telephones instead of mail and electric light instead of oil lamps. Many of these new products bore brand names—some of which are still around today—but these were almost incidental. These products were themselves news; that was almost advertisement enough.

The first brand-based products appeared at around the same time as the invention-based ads, largely because of another relatively recent innovation: the factory. When goods began to be produced in factories, not only were entirely new products being introduced but old products— even basic staples—were appearing in strikingly new forms. What made early branding efforts different from more straightforward salesmanship was that the market was now being flooded with uniform mass-produced products that were virtually indistinguishable from one another. Competitive branding became a necessity of the machine age—within a context of manufactured sameness, image based difference had to be manufactured along with the product.

So the role of advertising changed from delivering product news 10 bulletins to building an image around a particular brand-name version of a product. The first task of branding was to bestow proper names on generic goods such as sugar, flour, soap and cereal, which had previously been scooped out of barrels by local shopkeepers. In the 1880s, corporate logos were introduced to mass-produced products like Campbell's Soup, H.J. Heinz pickles and Quaker Oats cereal. As design historians and theorists Ellen Lupton and J. Abbott Miller note, logos were tailored to evoke familiarity and folksiness, in an effort to counteract the new and unsettling anonymity of packaged goods. "Familiar personalities such as Dr. Brown, Uncle Ben, Aunt Jemima, and Old Grand-Dad came to replace the shopkeeper, who was traditionally responsible for measuring bulk foods for customers and acting as an advocate for products . . . a nationwide vocabulary of brand names replaced the small local shopkeeper as the interface between consumer and product." After the product names and characters had been established, advertising gave them a venue to speak directly to would-be consumers. The corporate "personality," uniquely named, packaged and advertised, had arrived.

For the most part, the ad campaigns at the end of the nineteenth century and the start of the twentieth used a set of rigid, pseudoscientific formulas: rivals were never mentioned, ad copy used declarative statements only and headlines had to be large, with lots of white space— according to one turn-of-the-century adman, "an advertisement should be big enough to make an impression but not any bigger than the thing advertised."

But there were those in the industry who understood that advertising wasn't just scientific; it was also spiritual: Brands could conjure a feeling—think of Aunt Jemima's comforting presence—but not only that, entire corporations could themselves embody a meaning of their own. In the early twenties, legendary adman Bruce Barton turned General Motors into a metaphor for the American family, "something personal, warm and human," while GE was not so much the name of the faceless

General Electric Company as, in Barton's words, "the initials of a friend." In 1923 Barton said that the role of advertising was to help corporations find their soul. The son of a preacher, he drew on his religious upbringing for uplifting messages: "I like to think of advertising as something big, something splendid, something which goes deep down into an institution and gets hold of the soul of it. . . . Institutions have souls just as men and nations have souls," he told GM president Pierre du Pont. General Motors ads began to tell about the people who drove its cars—the preacher, the pharmacist or the country doctor who, thanks to his trusty GM, arrived "at the bedside of a dying child" just in time "to bring it back to life."

By the end of the 1940s, there was a burgeoning awareness that a brand wasn't just a mascot or a catchphrase or a picture printed on the label of a company's product; the company as a whole could have a brand identity or a "corporate consciousness," as this ephemeral quality was termed at the time. As this idea evolved, the adman ceased to see himself as a pitchman and instead saw himself as "the philosopher-king of commercial culture," in the words of ad critic Randall Rothberg. The search for the true meaning of brands—or the "brand essence," as it is often called—gradually took the agencies away from individual products and their attributes and toward a psychological/anthropological examination of what brands mean to the culture and to people's lives. This was seen to be of crucial importance, since corporations may manufacture products, but what consumers buy are brands.

It took several decades for the manufacturing world to adjust to this shift. It clung to the idea that its core business was still production and that branding was an important add-on. Then came the brand equity mania of the eighties, the defining moment of which arrived in 1988 when Philip Morris purchased Kraft for $12.6 billion—six times what the company was worth on paper. The price difference, apparently, was the cost of the word "Kraft." Of course Wall Street was aware that decades of marketing and brand bolstering added value to a company over and above its assets and total annual sales. But with the Kraft purchase, a huge dollar value had been assigned to something that had previously been abstract and unquantifiable—a brand name. This was spectacular news for the ad world, which was now able to make the claim that advertising spending was more than just a sales strategy: it was an investment in cold hard equity. The more you spend, the more your company is worth. Not surprisingly, this led to a considerable increase in spending on advertising. More important, it sparked a renewed interest in puffing up brand identities, a project that involved far more than a few billboards and TV spots. It was about pushing the envelope in sponsorship deals, dreaming up new areas in which to "extend" the brand, as well as perpetually probing the zeitgeist to ensure that the "essence" selected for one's brand would resonate karmically with its target market. For reasons that will be explored in the rest of this chapter, this radical shift in corporate philosophy has sent manufacturers on a cultural feeding frenzy as they seize upon every corner of unmarketed landscape in search of the oxygen needed to inflate their brands. In the process, virtually nothing has been left unbranded. That's quite an impressive feat, considering that as recently as 1993 Wall Street had pronounced the brand dead, or as good as dead.

THE BRAND'S DEATH (RUMORS OF WHICH HAD BEEN GREATLY EXAGGERATED)

On April 2, 1993, advertising itself was called into question by the very brands the industry had been building, in some cases, for over two centuries. That day is known in marketing circles as "Marlboro Friday," and it refers to a sudden announcement from Philip Morris that it would slash the price of Marlboro cigarettes by 20 percent in an attempt to compete with bargain brands that were eating into its market. The pundits went nuts, announcing in frenzied unison that not only was Marlboro dead, all brand names were dead. The reasoning was that if a "prestige" brand like Marlboro, whose image had been carefully groomed, preened and enhanced with more than a billion advertising dollars, was desperate enough to compete with no-names, then clearly the whole concept of branding had lost its currency. The public had seen the advertising, and the public didn't care. The Marlboro Man, after all, was not any old campaign; launched in 1954, it was the longest-running ad campaign in history. It was a legend. If the Marlboro Man had crashed, well, then, brand equity had crashed as well. The implication that Americans were suddenly thinking for themselves en masse reverberated through Wall Street. The same day Philip Morris announced its price cut, stock prices nose-dived for all the household brands: Heinz, Quaker Oats, Coca-Cola, PepsiCo, Procter and Gamble and RJR Nabisco. Philip Morris's own stock took the worst beating.

Bob Stanojev, national director of consumer products marketing for Ernst and Young, explained the logic behind Wall Street's panic: "If one or two powerhouse consumer products companies start to cut prices for good, there's going to be an avalanche. Welcome to the value generation."

Yes, it was one of those moments of overstated instant consensus, but it was not entirely without cause. Marlboro had always sold itself on the strength of its iconic image marketing, not on anything so prosaic as

227

its price. As we now know, the Marlboro Man survived the price wars without sustaining too much damage. At the time, however, Wall Street saw Philip Morris's decision as symbolic of a sea change. The price cut was an admission that Marlboro's name was no longer sufficient to sustain the flagship position, which in a context where image is equity meant that Marlboro had blinked. And when Marlboro—one of the quintessential global brands—blinks, it raises questions about branding that reach beyond Wall Street, and way beyond Philip Morris.

The panic of Marlboro Friday was not a reaction to a single incident. Rather, it was the culmination of years of escalating anxiety in the face of some rather dramatic shifts in consumer habits that were seen to be eroding the market share of household-name brands, from Tide to Kraft. Bargain-conscious shoppers, hit hard by the recession, were starting to pay more attention to price than to the prestige bestowed on their products by the yuppie ad campaigns of the 1980s. The public was suffering from a bad case of what is known in the industry as "brand blindness."

Study after study showed that baby boomers, blind to the alluring images of advertising and deaf to the empty promises of celebrity spokespersons, were breaking their lifelong brand loyalties and choosing to feed their families with private-label brands from the supermarket— claiming, heretically, that they couldn't tell the difference. From the beginning of the recession to 1993, Loblaw's President's Choice line, Wal-Mart's Great Value and Marks and Spencer's St. Michael prepared foods had nearly doubled their market share in North America and Europe. The computer market, meanwhile, was flooded by inexpensive clones, causing IBM to slash its prices and otherwise impale itself. It appeared to be a return to the proverbial shopkeeper dishing out generic goods from the barrel in a prebranded era.

THE BRANDS BOUNCE BACK

There were some brands that were watching from the sidelines as Wall 20
Street declared the death of the brand. Funny, they must have thought, we don't feel dead.

Just as the admen had predicted at the beginning of the recession, the companies that exited the downturn running were the ones who opted for marketing over value every time: Nike, Apple, the Body Shop, Calvin Klein, Disney, Levi's and Starbucks. Not only were these brands doing just fine, thank you very much, but the act of branding was becoming a larger and larger focus of their businesses. For these companies, the ostensible product was mere filler for the real production: the brand.

They integrated the idea of branding into the very fabric of their companies. Their corporate cultures were so tight and cloistered that to outsiders they appeared to be a cross between fraternity house, religious cult and sanitarium. Everything was an ad for the brand: bizarre lexicons for describing employees (partners, baristas, team players, crew members), company chants, superstar CEOs, fanatical attention to design consistency, a propensity for monument-building, and New Age mission statements. Unlike classic household brand names, such as Tide and Marlboro, these logos weren't losing their currency, they were in the midst of breaking every barrier in the marketing world—becoming cultural accessories and lifestyle philosophers. These companies didn't wear this image like a cheap shirt—their image was so integrated with their business that other people wore it as *their* shirt. And when the brands crashed, these companies didn't even notice—they were branded to the bone.

So the real legacy of Marlboro Friday is that it simultaneously brought the two most significant developments in nineties marketing and consumerism into sharp focus: the deeply unhip big-box bargain stores that provide the essentials of life and monopolize a disproportionate share of the market (Wal-Mart *et al.)* and the extra-premium "attitude" brands that provide the essentials of lifestyle and monopolize ever-expanding stretches of cultural space (Nike *et al.).* The way these two tiers of consumerism developed would have a profound impact on the economy in the years to come. When overall ad expenditures took a nosedive in 1991, Nike and Reebok were busy playing advertising chicken, with each company increasing its budget to outspend the other. In 1991 alone, Reebok upped its ad spending by 71.9 percent, while Nike pumped an extra 24.6 percent into its already soaring ad budget, bringing the company's total spending on marketing to a staggering $250 million annually. Far from worrying about competing on price, the sneaker pimps were designing ever more intricate and pseudoscientific air pockets, and driving up prices by signing star athletes to colossal sponsorship deals. The fetish strategy seemed to be working fine: in the six years prior to 1993, Nike had gone from a $750 million company to a $4 billion one and Phil Knight's Beaverton, Oregon, company emerged from the recession with profits 900 percent higher than when it began.

Benetton and Calvin Klein, meanwhile, were also upping their spending on lifestyle marketing, using ads to associate their lines with risque art and progressive politics. Clothes barely appeared in these high-concept advertisements, let alone prices. Even more abstract was Absolut Vodka, which for some years now had been developing a marketing strategy in which its product disappeared and its brand was nothing but a blank bottle-shaped space that could be filled with whatever content a particular audience most wanted from its brands: intellectual in *Harper's,* futuristic in *Wired,* alternative in *Spin,* loud and proud in *Out* and "Absolut Centerfold" in *Playboy.* The brand reinvented itself as a cultural sponge, soaking up and morphing to its surroundings.

Saturn, too, came out of nowhere in October 1990 when GM launched a car built not out of steel and rubber but out of New Age spirituality and seventies feminism. After the car had been on the market a few years, the company held a "homecoming" weekend for Saturn owners, during which they could visit the auto plant and have a cookout with the people who made their cars. As the Saturn ads boasted at the time, "44,000 people spent their vacations with us, at a car plant." It was as if Aunt Jemima had come to life and invited you over to her house for dinner.

In 1993, the year the Marlboro Man was temporarily hobbled by "brand-blind" consumers, Microsoft made its striking debut on *Advertising Age*'s list of the top 200 ad spenders — the very same year that Apple computer increased its marketing budget by 30 percent after already making branding history with its Orwellian takeoff ad launch during the 1984 Super Bowl. Like Saturn, both companies were selling a hip new relationship to the machine that left Big Blue IBM looking as clunky and menacing as the now-dead Cold War. 25

And then there were the companies that had always understood that they were selling brands before product. Coke, Pepsi, McDonald's, Burger King and Disney weren't fazed by the brand crisis, opting instead to escalate the brand war, especially since they had their eyes firmly fixed on global expansion. They were joined in this project by a wave of sophisticated producer/retailers who hit full stride in the late eighties and early nineties. The Gap, Ikea and the Body Shop were spreading like wildfire during this period, masterfully transforming the generic into the brand-specific, largely through bold, carefully branded packaging and the promotion of an "experiential" shopping environment. The Body Shop had been a presence in Britain since the seventies, but it wasn't until 1988 that it began sprouting like a green weed on every street corner in the U.S. Even during the darkest years of the recession, the company opened between forty and fifty American stores a year. Most baffling of all to Wall Street, it pulled off the expansion without spending a dime on advertising. Who needed billboards and magazine ads when retail outlets were three-dimensional advertisements for an ethical and ecological approach to cosmetics? The Body Shop was all brand.

The Starbucks coffee chain, meanwhile, was also expanding during this period without laying out much in advertising; instead, it was spinning off its name into a wide range of branded projects: Starbucks airline coffee, office coffee, coffee ice cream, coffee beer. Starbucks seemed to understand brand names at a level even deeper than Madison Avenue, incorporating marketing into every fiber of its corporate concept — from the chain's strategic association with books, blues and jazz to its Euro-latte lingo. What the success of both the Body Shop and Starbucks showed was how far the branding project had come in moving beyond splashing one's logo on a billboard. Here were two companies that had fostered powerful identities by making their brand concept into a virus and sending it out into the culture via a variety of channels: cultural sponsorship, political controversy, the consumer experience and brand extensions. Direct advertising, in this context, was viewed as a rather clumsy intrusion into a much more organic approach to image building.

Scott Bedbury, Starbucks' vice president of marketing, openly recognized that "consumers don't truly believe there's a huge difference between products," which is why brands must "establish emotional ties" with their customers through "the Starbucks Experience." The people who line up for Starbucks, writes CEO Howard Shultz, aren't just there for the coffee. "It's the romance of the coffee experience, the feeling of warmth and community people get in Starbucks stores."

Interestingly, before moving to Starbucks, Bedbury was head of marketing at Nike, where he oversaw the launch of the "Just Do It!" slogan, among other watershed branding moments. In the following passage, he explains the common techniques used to infuse the two very different brands with meaning:

> Nike, for example, is leveraging the deep emotional connection that people have with sports and fitness. With Starbucks, we see how coffee has woven itself into the fabric of people's lives, and that's our opportunity for emotional leverage. . . . A great brand raises the bar—it adds a greater sense of purpose to the experience, whether it's the challenge to do your best in sports and fitness or the affirmation that the cup of coffee you're drinking really matters.

This was the secret, it seemed, of all the success stories of the late eight-30 ies and early nineties. The lesson of Marlboro Friday was that there never really was a brand crisis—only brands that had crises of confidence. The brands would be okay, Wall Street concluded, so long as they believed fervently in the principles of branding and never, ever blinked. Overnight, "Brands, not products!" became the rallying cry for a marketing renaissance led by a new breed of companies that saw themselves as "meaning brokers" instead of product producers. What was changing was the idea of what—in both advertising and branding—was being sold. The old paradigm had it that all marketing was selling a product. In the new model, however, the product always takes a back seat to the real product, the brand, and the selling of the brand acquired an extra component that can only be described as spiritual. Advertising is about hawking product.

Branding, in its truest and most advanced incarnations, is about corporate transcendence.

It may sound flaky, but that's precisely the point. On Marlboro Friday, a line was drawn in the sand between the lowly price slashers and the high-concept brand builders. The brand builders conquered, and a new consensus was born: the products that will flourish in the future will be the ones presented not as "commodities" but as concepts: the brand as experience, as lifestyle.

Ever since, a select group of corporations has been attempting to free itself from the corporeal world of commodities, manufacturing and products to exist on another plane. Anyone can manufacture a product, they reason (and as the success of private-label brands during the recession proved, anyone did). Such menial tasks, therefore, can and should be farmed out to contractors and subcontractors whose only concern is filling the order on time and under budget (ideally in the Third World, where labor is dirt cheap, laws are lax and tax breaks come by the bushel). Headquarters, meanwhile, is free to focus on the real business at hand—creating a corporate mythology powerful enough to infuse meaning into these raw objects just by signing its name.

The corporate world has always had a deep New Age streak, fed—it has become clear—by a profound need that could not be met simply by trading widgets for cash. But when branding captured the corporate imagination, New Age vision quests took center stage. As Nike CEO Phil Knight explains, "For years we thought of ourselves as a production-oriented company, meaning we put all our emphasis on designing and manufacturing the product. But now we understand that the most important thing we do is market the product. We've come around to saying that Nike is a marketing-oriented company, and the product is our most important marketing tool." This project has since been taken to an even more advanced level with the emergence of on-line corporate giants such as Amazon.com. It is on-line that the purest brands are being built: liberated from the real-world burdens of stores and product manufacturing, these brands are free to soar, less as the disseminators of goods or services than as collective hallucinations.

Tom Peters, who has long coddled the inner flake in many a hard-nosed CEO, latched on to the branding craze as the secret to financial success, separating the transcendental logos and the earthbound products into two distinct categories of companies. "The top half—Coca-Cola, Microsoft, Disney, and so on—are pure 'players' in brainware. The bottom half [Ford and GM] are still lumpy-object purveyors, though automobiles are much 'smarter' than they used to be," Peters writes in *The Circle of Innovation* (1997), an ode to the power of marketing over production.

KLEIN / No Logo

When Levi's began to lose market share in the late nineties, the trend 35
was widely attributed to the company's failure—despite lavish ad
spending—to transcend its products and become a free-standing meaning. "Maybe one of Levi's problems is that it has no Cola," speculated
Jennifer Steinhauer in *The New York Times*. "It has no denim-toned
house paint. Levi makes what is essentially a commodity: blue jeans. Its
ads may evoke rugged outdoorsmanship, but Levi hasn't promoted any
particular life style to sell other products."

In this high-stakes new context, the cutting-edge ad agencies no longer
sold companies on individual campaigns but on their ability to act as
"brand stewards": identifying, articulating and protecting the corporate
soul. Not surprisingly, this spelled good news for the U.S. advertising
industry, which in 1994 saw a spending increase of 8.6 percent over the
previous year. In one year, the ad industry went from a near crisis to
another "best year yet." And that was only the beginning of triumphs to
come. By 1997, corporate advertising, defined as "ads that position a
corporation, its values, its personality and character" were up 18 percent
from the year before.

With this wave of brand mania has come a new breed of businessman,
one who will proudly inform you that Brand X is not a product but
a way of life, an attitude, a set of values, a look, an idea. And it sounds
really great—way better than that Brand X is a screwdriver, or a hamburger chain, or a pair of jeans, or even a very successful line of running
shoes. Nike, Phil Knight announced in the late eighties, is "a sports company"; its mission is not to sell shoes but to "enhance people's lives
through sports and fitness" and to keep "the magic of sports alive." Company president-cum-sneaker-shaman Tom Clark explains that "the inspiration of sports allows us to rebirth ourselves constantly."

Reports of such "brand vision" epiphanies began surfacing from all
corners. "Polaroid's problem," diagnosed the chairman of its advertising
agency, John Hegarty, "was that they kept thinking of themselves as
a camera. But the '[brand] vision' process taught us something: Polaroid
is not a camera—it's a social lubricant." IBM isn't selling computers, it's
selling business "solutions." Swatch is not about watches, it is about the
idea of time. At Diesel Jeans, owner Renzo Rosso told *Paper* magazine,
"We don't sell a product, we sell a style of life. I think we have created a
movement. . . . The Diesel concept is everything. It's the way to live, it's
the way to wear, it's the way to do something." And as Body Shop
founder Anita Roddick explained to me, her stores aren't about what
they sell, they are the conveyers of a grand idea—a political philosophy
about women, the environment and ethical business. "I just use the company that I surprisingly created as a success—it shouldn't have been like

this, it wasn't meant to be like this—to stand on the products to shout out on these issues," Roddick says.

The famous late graphic designer Tibor Kalman summed up the shifting role of the brand this way: "The original notion of the brand was quality, but now brand is a stylistic badge of courage."

The idea of selling the courageous message of a brand, as opposed to a product, intoxicated these CEOs, providing as it did an opportunity for seemingly limitless expansion. After all, if a brand was not a product, it could be anything! And nobody embraced branding theory with more evangelical zeal than Richard Branson, whose Virgin Group has branded joint ventures in everything from music to bridal gowns to airlines to cola to financial services. Branson refers derisively to the "stilted Anglo-Saxon view of consumers," which holds that a name should be associated with a product like sneakers or soft drinks; and opts instead for "the Asian 'trick'" of the *keiretsus* (a Japanese term meaning a network of linked corporations). The idea, he explains, is to "build brands not around products but around reputation. The great Asian names imply quality, price and innovation rather than a specific item. I call these 'attribute' brands: They do not relate directly to one product—such as a Mars bar or a Coca-Cola—but instead to a set of values."

Tommy Hilfiger, meanwhile, is less in the business of manufacturing clothes than he is in the business of signing his name. The company is run entirely through licensing agreements, with Hilfiger commissioning all its products from a group of other companies: Jockey International makes Hilfiger underwear, Pepe Jeans London makes Hilfiger jeans, Oxford Industries make Tommy shirts, the Stride Rite Corporation makes its footwear. What does Tommy Hilfiger manufacture? Nothing at all.

So passé had products become in the age of lifestyle branding that by the late nineties newer companies like Lush cosmetics and Old Navy clothing began playing with the idea of old-style commodities as a source of retro marketing imagery. The Lush chain serves up its face masks and moisturizers out of refrigerated stainless-steel bowls, spooned into plastic containers with grocery-store labels. Old Navy showcases its shrink-wrapped T-shirts and sweatshirts in deli-style chrome refrigerators, as if they were meat or cheese. When you are a pure, concept-driven brand, the aesthetics of raw product can prove as "authentic" as loft living.

And lest the branding business be dismissed as the playground of trendy consumer items such as sneakers, jeans and New Age beverages, think again. Caterpillar, best known for building tractors and busting unions, has barreled into the branding business, launching the Cat accessories line: boots, back-packs, hats and anything else calling out for a postindustrial *je ne sais quoi*. Intel Corp., which makes computer parts

234

no one sees and few understand, transformed its processors into a fetish brand with TV ads featuring line workers in funky metallic space suits dancing to "Shake Your Groove Thing." The Intel mascots proved so popular that the company has sold hundreds of thousands of bean-filled dolls modeled on the shimmery dancing technicians. Little wonder, then, that when asked about the company's decision to diversify its products, the senior vice president for sales and marketing, Paul S. Otellini, replied that Intel is "like Coke. One brand, many different products."

And if Caterpillar and Intel can brand, surely anyone can.

There is, in fact, a new strain in marketing theory that holds that even 45 the lowliest natural resources, barely processed, can develop brand identities, thus giving way to hefty premium-price markups. In an essay appropriately titled "How to Brand Sand," advertising executives Sam Hill, Jack McGrath and Sandeep Dayal team up to tell the corporate world that with the right marketing plan, nobody has to stay stuck in the stuff business. "Based on extensive research, we would argue that you can indeed brand not only sand, but also wheat, beef, brick, metals, concrete, chemicals, corn grits and an endless variety of commodities traditionally considered immune to the process."

Over the past six years, spooked by the near-death experience of Marlboro Friday, global corporations have leaped on the brand-wagon with what can only be described as a religious fervor. Never again would the corporate world stoop to praying at the altar of the commodity market. From now on they would worship only graven media images. Or to quote Tom Peters, the brand man himself: "Brand! Brand!! Brand!!! That's the message . . . for the late '90s and beyond."

RONNIE DUGGER

Corporate
Takeover of the Media

Ronnie Dugger is the founding editor of *The Texas Observer*, a progressive political news magazine founded by Frankie Randolph in 1954. He is also cofounder of The Alliance for Democracy, a grassroots organization which, according to its mission statement, strives to "end corporate domination, to establish true political democracy, and to build a just society with a sustainable, equitable economy." Dugger has written biographies on Lyndon Johnson and Ronald Reagan and has contributed numerous articles to national magazines, including *Harper's*, *The Nation*, *The New Yorker*, *The Atlantic Monthly*, and *The Progressive*.

In his essay, "Corporate Takeover of the Media," Dugger argues that corporate ownership of the media inhibits democracy and that the airwaves should be publicly owned and nonprofit.

No anti-democratic trend in the United States during the past quarter-century is more threatening to freedom than the takeover and control of mainstream journalism by gigantic corporations. Under the Bush administration, the government is preparing a crackdown on the public interest in broadcasting such as we have not seen since the Reagan administration abolished the Fairness Doctrine.

Consider some recent events. The Federal Communications Commission (FCC) voted October 11, 2001, to let public television stations run commercial advertisements on some of the five or six new digital channels that Congress stole from the people and gave, absolutely free, to each of the licensed broadcasters under the 1996 telecommunications law. Public television has already been corrupted by commercials mislabeled as "underwriting announcements." Now the FCC is going all out, and openly, to ruin public broadcasting.

Under the 1996 law, which former Senator Bob Dole labeled a $70-billion giveaway, Congress enabled just one corporation to own every radio station in the United States. Before that law, the largest radio group owned thirty-nine stations; now the largest group owns 1,100 of them.

Ronnie Dugger, "Corporate Takeover of the Media" from *Free Inquiry*, Winter 2001. Copyright © 2001 by Ronnie Dugger. Reprinted by permission of the author.

Big-corporate broadcasting companies are winning federal court rulings that hold, contrary to common sense, that antitrust limits on them violate their rights of free speech. These same corporations are pressuring the FCC to abolish the present rules, already pitiful on their face, which provide that no corporation can beam television programs to more than 35 percent of the American population; no cable corporation can control more than 30 percent of the cable market; and no corporation can own a television station and a newspaper in the same market. The Bush-whacked FCC looks ready to buckle, evidently reasoning that, since CBS / Viacom already reaches 41 percent of U.S. households and Tribune Co., Gannett, and News Corp. already operate television stations and newspapers in the same markets, who needs the old limits?

George W. Bush's new chair of the FCC, Michael Powell, has attacked the federal statute, relied upon and illuminated in seventy years of case law, which requires that the FCC consider "the public interest." Powell told the American Bar Association earlier this year that the public-interest standard "is about as empty a vessel as you can accord a regulatory agency." Evidently Michael Powell is about as empty a vessel as you can find to occupy the chairmanship of an agency established to serve the public good.

The deep root of this trouble for democracy is a long line of Supreme 5 Court decisions, starting in 1886, that have bestowed all of the constitutional rights of persons on corporations except (so far) the right to vote and protection under the Fifth Amendment. By these decisions these nine people in black robes have elevated corporations to the status of Super-Citizens, and reduced us mere people to Sub-Citizens. Work on the production line of a major corporation and you'll find out soon enough what has free speech (the corporation) and who doesn't (you). Freedom of the press, which was meant to protect freedom of speech, instead protects big corporations' selling for profit. Democracy has been turned upside down. In effect and outcome, it's a counterrevolution.

Newspapers and radio and television stations have been bought up and linked together under a few powerful conglomerates. In 1945, about 80 percent of U.S. daily newspapers were independently owned; by 1989, about 80 percent were owned by corporate chains. Huge corporations own the four major television networks and run the networks' news divisions.

On the Sunday morning political talk shows, according to a recent study, topics loosely related to corporate power made up only four percent of the discussion topics. When your employer is owned by a just-indicted worldwide price-fixer, how much airtime do you give the story, if any? When your boss is a weapons merchant, what do you report, if anything, about the case against the war?

"The Founders didn't count on the rise of mega-media," Bill Moyers has written. "They didn't count on huge private corporations that would own not only the means of journalism but also vast swaths of the territory that journalism should be covering." As media philosopher Ben Bagdikian writes, "It is normal for all large businesses to make serious efforts to influence the news. . . . Now they own most of the news media they wish to influence."

The big-corporate domination of the media is a mortal threat to democracy. Without a freely and robustly informed people, democracy is an illusion. Day and night the few men at the top of the giant media corporations control what the people are invited to think about—and more important, what they are not invited to think about. Corporate censorship and self-censorship happen. Around the world, too, the means for the mass dissemination of expression are being gobbled up by media-wielding conglomerates. A few media barons are acquiring what may already be, or on present trends will certainly become, the control of mainstream discourse and expression among most of the people of the world. There's never been anything like it.

The power of the major media to make and un-make the news is manifest in the way it handled the question of the legitimacy of the present Bush presidency. In January a consortium of U.S. news organizations, including the *New York Times*, the *Washington Post*, the *Wall Street Journal*, the Associated Press, *Newsweek*, CNN, and several others hired the University of Chicago's National Opinion Research Center to examine 180,000 uncounted Florida ballots from the presidential election last year. This examination was finished in August and reporters and editors from the sponsoring media prepared to review the survey and attempt to say who won Florida: Bush or Gore. But after the mass murders on September 11, the consortium decided to postpone the study "indefinitely." The major media quietly "spiked" the major story of the legitimacy of the Bush presidency. Astoundingly patriotism trumped the biggest story in American democracy since the impeachment of Richard Nixon. The "war on terrorism" trumped the question of who should be the president. Then, on November 12, the consortium served up a slanted interpretation of the survey. Another column would be needed to deal with it.

Yet the worst is just surfacing. The electromagnetic spectrum, "the airwaves," is public property in every country in the world. It is a global commons. But thirty-seven economists proposed to the FCC last February that the licensed corporate broadcasters, who pay nothing for their billion-dollar licenses, be permitted to lease the airwaves and sell and lease them in secondary markets. As Jeremy Rifkin described in an article in the *Guardian* of London, the plan is now afoot to give ownership and control of the world's airwaves to a few global corporations.

238

Congress and both major U.S. political parties are beholden at the top to the corporations and multi-millionaires who finance their elections. We need people to run for high public office as rebels—whether as Democrats, Republicans, Greens, Independents, who cares—rebels who will make corporate control of the mainstream media a sizzling political issue and who will hold forth the vision of a truly public broadcasting system as the keystone of a nonprofit national and local telecommunications information consortium. This consortium, as former NBC News president Lawrence Grossman conceives it, would "serve all of the people, all of the time."

"The ultimate goal," according to communications professor and writer Robert McChesney, "must be to have the public service sector be the dominant component of the broadcasting and media system. Hence the struggle for public service broadcasting cannot avoid direct confrontation and conflict with the existing corporate media giants."

239

MARK HILLRINGHOUSE

Passaic River Journal

November 22nd, bitter cold, strong winds.

At a municipal park on the Passaic River in Fair Lawn, I find the boat launch and see Thomas's jeep with his 17-foot aluminum canoe tied to the roof. He had volunteered to take me out in his canoe after I got his phone number and called him to make a date. I help him get it down. I am bundled up wearing winter gloves, a hooded sweatshirt and I have trouble getting the life jacket on. It is the coldest day of the year and this is only my second time in a canoe. My first was 40 years ago as a scout in summer camp. Thomas tells me that he has never canoed the Passaic River and never canoed this late in the year.

I lower myself into the bow and he pushes off and hops into the stern. I paddle desperately trying not to spill over. The wind is blowing and icicles are forming from the water dripping off my paddle. Half way across the river, my arms are aching from fighting a headwind and a strong current. I tell Thomas that this is madness, but neither of us wants to admit defeat—me a middle-aged college professor, and him, a recent college graduate. I could see the headlines: "Professor's frozen body found in river."

Since I started writing this article, four bodies have been pulled from the river, and it had me wondering why this river attracts so much of this type of tragedy? It is the only press this river ever gets, either human tragedy or environmental.

I tell Thomas that I am writing about the Passaic River and that I am using William Carlos Williams as a literary reference. Thomas offered to take me in his canoe when I called him after getting his number from Tony DeCondo, who works part time at the Paterson Museum and whose name was recently in the New York Times for the work he does finding Indian artifacts on the Passaic River. I spoke to Tony on the phone and he told me about the Indian weirs and that there are two between Paterson and Fair Lawn and that you can see the V formation of rocks when the river is low. It is how the Indians fished these waters before the Dutch and English arrived. He

Originally published in *The American Poetry Review*, vol. 39/No.1, Jan/Feb 2010 has found several arrow heads. He gave me Thomas's number who is a friend of his son's.

Ever since I had moved to Paterson in 1984, in the newly opened "Artist Housing," in the renovated silk mills by the falls, I have been drawn to this river because it is New Jersey's river, and because I consider it part of the "Weird" New Jersey phenomenon with its spooky looking abandoned buildings and because of strange things, aside from dead bodies, that turn up in its waters. Before moving to Paterson, I had already developed a strong connection to Williams. My first poetry job was poetry coordinator for the newly opened Williams Center in Rutherford. This was 1982. My fascination with the poet/doctor from my home state developed into a life-long study. One of the books that came into my possession back then was Williams's Life along the Passaic River, an out-of-print, 1938, New Directions first edition of 19 stories that Williams wrote during the Great Depression.

The more I read, the more I admired the way Williams was able to recreate what life was like for a small town doctor going out on house calls. What I admired most was how he seemed to describe everything with a heightened sense of awareness. Williams in these stories writes the way Walker Evans composed his photographs.

June 17th, 80 degrees, overcast

I wanted to find the street Williams mentions in one of his stories and the bridge he mentions in another, so I called my friend, Mark Tambone, a new instructor at the college where we teach, and who was teaching a class in the city of Passaic that he had just let out. We get in his car and take off in pursuit of Summer Street where Williams confronts the girl from the story, "The Girl with the Pimply Face." We drive past the Gregory Avenue Bridge where teddy bears and flowers keep piling up in an ever growing memorial for the little girl who was drowned by her uncle a few weeks earlier and who was all over the news. The newspapers reported that man's body had just been pulled out of the river.

Summer Street is not far from the river. The homes are old, two-family houses, near the industrial section of town. The street signs are old; the trees are tall and shady. The red brick factories, a couple of blocks away, look like they haven't been open in years. There are guys sitting in front of doorways. I feel like I am driving through one of Williams's stories, as if nothing's changed in seventy years except the cars.

I tell my friend to stop the car so that I can take a photograph of the street sign. I love the way Williams has his doctor/narrator in a kind of stand off with the girl in this story. It is a scenario that is repeated in his other stories in a battle of wills. The doctor is in love with the girls, their tough, street-wise savvy and determination. It is as if he registers that their reproductive force almost guarantees that the species will survive through the sexual power of these feisty immigrant offspring. The doctor senses this animal power much like D. H. Lawrence does with his female characters in his stories.

Back in November, out in the middle of the river, I tried to aim the canoe for the center of the Maple Avenue Bridge in Paterson. The wind and current blew the canoe sideways and we spun around. I was trying to remember everything I had learned in scouts: how to sit, how to hold the paddle and use it as a rudder. The muscles in my arms were burning. I never thought that we would make it under that bridge.

We hugged the Paterson side in the lee as the river curved upstream away from the headwinds. Thomas pointed out the long, black seed pods hanging down from a catalpa tree. "Kids smoke these," he said. He pointed out two types of willow growing on the banks, black and white. The banks were overgrown with bushes and vines, some bushes called poke weed grew dark indigo berries that were poisonous. People use the banks of the Lower Passaic River, especially on the Paterson side, to dump refrigerators and car tires. I saw many shopping carts, car bumpers, hub caps, front ends, engine blocks, some of it covered over in vines. There were also red tailed hawk, mallards, Canada geese, crows and muskrat that I saw as I paddled.

On the map, the river looks like a noose slung around the neck of the City of Paterson. Some think of it as a moat to keep the inner city walled off. No one looking at the Passaic as it plunges 80 feet in a torrent over the Great Falls can imagine this river at its source some sixty miles away, as just a stream only three-feet wide, flowing out of the Great Swamp in Mendham, that was once a glacial lake ten miles across at the end of the last ice age. Locals call this the Upper Passaic, a spate river that always floods its banks during heavy rains. The Lower Passaic (the river Williams was familiar with), is tidal, all 17 miles of it, until it reaches the Dundee Dam in Garfield.

A couple of months after I moved into my artist loft by the falls it rained non stop for eight days. Downtown Paterson flooded out. All the homes in the flood plain along the upper river had to be evacuated. Several people drowned. The West Broadway Bridge in Paterson was under water. Kansas Fried Chicken was under water.

Cars floated away. I saw the contents of flooded-out houses upriver plunge over the falls: television sets bobbed like corks, sofas twirled in maelstroms. I never saw so much water. There were white caps. They say that the flood of 1984 was a 100-year flood, but floods nearly as bad have happened a couple of times since.

My loft in Paterson was in the back away from the street, and faced the "Valley of the Rocks," or the cliffs that make up the Great Falls. Behind my building was a ten-acre site of ruined mills on the river that the city had fenced off because the homeless would set them on fire to keep warm. One of the foundations and walls still standing was the original 1836 Colt Mill where Samuel Colt produced his first revolver—The Paterson Colt. I kept a camera mounted on a tripod and I would often take photographs of these ruins at different times and in different weather. The homeless made their camp sites along the river and at night, I could see their camp fires burning in the pitch darkness. It was like a scene out of some nuclear holocaust movie. A French friend of mine, when he first visited, and stepped into my loft said, "C'est la vue d'enfer mais a pas s'y etre."—like seeing hell without being there.

June 29th, humid, 80 degrees, overcast

I am waiting to meet Jeff Lahm, founder of the Passaic River Rowing Association, and so I am sitting in the Arlington Diner in North Arlington having coffee and listening to Frank Sinatra sing "Strangers in the Night." The coffee is surprisingly good and I am studying the menu deciding on whether to order their "World Famous Cheesecake" that is advertised on the sign above the diner. The diner sits right on the Passaic River across the bridge from Belleville where I can see an old, Dutch church dating from four centuries ago. The church is obscured by Route 21 which passes in front of it. The bridges this far downriver were designed to be raised, or they could be swung sideways to let boats go by, but that was a long time ago. There are no more commercial boats on the Passaic.

I am between counties, Essex County on the other side of the bridge and Hudson County just south of here. North Arlington is the last town in Bergen County. It started to drizzle before I got inside the diner, so I took my rain cover out of my camera bag and fit it over my Nikon so that I could take a photograph of the diner in the rain. I review my images while I wait for the bill and put the camera back in the bag while removing the rain cover.

I check my cell phone and see that it is time to go, so I leave money on the counter and get back in my car and drive a mile north along River Road to Lyndhurst. It is one of the strange things about the Passaic River that I can drive along much of its length and never see a soul on the water, but sometimes I would look out the window and see rowers, teams of young men or women. The rowing club is in the county park in a cement storage facility that looks like an army Quonset hut and which was once used to store a kid's train ride from back in the 50s or so I would find out. I see dozens of needle-like boats on racks and go in and introduce myself to Jeff, a man with a grey beard and who looks remarkably trim and fit for his age.

Jeff shows me the different boats, boats for two rowers, for four, six and eight, and I keep asking him questions. He said that he formed his club twelve years ago. He used to belong to the Nereid Boat Club in Rutherford, the oldest boating club on the river dating from 1870, but that membership got too expensive and it was too private. He wanted to involve the local high schools and get the kids interested in rowing with free lessons for anyone who wanted to learn. The county leased him the storage facility and he raised funds and collected membership fees to build a dock and purchase boats.

I couldn't believe how light they were as he let me lift a sixty-foot, 8-crew member boat that weighed only slightly more than 100 pounds. "That one cost thirty thousand," he said, "carbon fiber," and then showed me the oars and how they fit into the outriggers. "You don't sit in the boats," he said, "you ride on top and you work the oars on the outriggers to balance yourself." The hull was less than an inch thick and it was no wider than a foot and a half. I saw some girls getting lessons from a young woman down at the dock and I watched them practice.

Williams writes a vivid description of the river in his opening paragraph in his opening title story and writes about how the kids made use of the river:

> About noon of a muggy July day, a spot of a canoe filled by the small boy who no doubt made it, lies west of the new 3rd Street Bridge between Passaic and Wallington, midstream opposite the Manhattan Rubber Co.'s red brick and concrete power plant. There's the sound of work going on there, and a jet of water spouts from a pipe at the foundation level below the factory onto the river's narrow mud bank which it has channeled making a way for itself into the brown water of the two-hundred foot wide stream. The boy is drifting with the current but paddling a little also toward a couple of kids in bathing suits and a young man in his shirt sleeves, lying on what looks like grass but is probably weeds across the river at the edge of an empty lot where they dumped ashes some years ago, watching him. These youngsters who make boats out of barrel

hoops and a piece of old duck, wherever they find it, live by the river these hot summer days. It's a godsend to them.

And it's a godsend to the kids who join Jeff's rowing club because they compete in races and regattas against seven high school rowing teams in the area and many of them get rowing scholarships to good schools. I ask him why the Passaic and he tells me that it is relatively straight and about thirty feet deep in this stretch of water, and there is no commercial boat traffic, and the Passaic Valley Sewerage Commission skimmer boats do a good job of cleaning the litter off the surface. When I ask him how far he can row, he said about four miles up to what he called the "Garfield Bend," where the river loops around Passaic, Wallington and Garfield. He tells me that he can row seven miles south to Newark and Kearny. "It's a good workout," he said. "I do it almost every morning. I used to run to stay in shape, but now I row," he smiled.

Back when my friend Mark drove me around the factories in Passaic, after we left Summer Street, I asked him to drive to the different bridges that connect Passaic to the towns of Wallington and Garfield across the river. I saw a white memorial cross and flowers tied to a fence on one of these bridges for another river drowning victim. The "New 3rd Street Bridge" that Williams mentions was torn down and replaced with a "newer" concrete bridge a few years ago. They kept the original bronze plaque dated 1930 from the old New 3rd Street Bridge which is now the Market Street Bridge. Using a fast shutter and focus tracking on my Nikon, I was able to grab shots from the car as we rode past places Williams would have past on his trips into these neighborhoods. There were a couple of Eastern Orthodox churches and a large Russian Orthodox cathedral with spiraling onion domes. A few people were speaking Russian or Ukrainian. These would have been the immigrants that Williams knew.

Paul Mariani, in his biography on Williams, mentions that Williams had just begun a long prose poem that he had titled "Life along the Passaic River." Mariani makes the case that this was Williams's genesis for his nascent yet unborn book-length poem, Paterson, which had been brewing in the doctor's psyche during the summer of 1933. Mariani writes: "...though it looked like prose—he considered it a poem 'in five line sentences (more or less) about the low-life of these parts.' In mid-July he'd driven over to the new Third Street Bridge between Passaic and Wallington to meditate on the Passaic—his river."

Williams once told an interviewer in speaking on the subject of how these stories came to be written, "I was still obsessed by the plight of the poor...the best stories were written at white heat. I would come home from my practice and sit down and write until the story was finished, ten to twelve pages. I seldom revised at all. Williams went on to say that he wrote these stories at the request of the editor of a new magazine and that he promised to write something for him every week (63 Heal).

In many ways, Williams was always struggling to craft a "beautiful thing" out of his patients' working-class world. The words themselves would later become a key phrase that he would use as a refrain in sections of Paterson. The stories are a reflection of not only the time he lived, and the revulsion he sometimes felt for the brute existence of immigrants who often had no money to pay him for his medical service, but for his hope for the children that he was treating. He saw beauty in them, in their struggle to live and beat the odds. It is what Robert Coles would call in one of his books, "the knack of survival in America." Coles, as a young medical student, writes about going out on a house call with Williams, that Williams would instruct him before entering a patient's house, "Look around, let your eye take in the neighborhood—the homes, the stores, the people and places, there waiting to tell you, show you something" (House Calls 8).

I was trying to take in everything I could see as we piloted downriver on the Hackensack and upriver on the Passaic on Captain Bill Sheehan's pontoon boat. After my friend took me to the bridges in Passaic, we drove over to Secaucus to the marina behind the Red Roof Inn on the Hackensack River to wait for the captain. We jumped on board as he pulled up to the dock and then he hit the throttle of his 115-horse Evinrude and we took off. He idled the boat under all the train trestles and steel bridges, some so low we had to duck our heads. A piece of the Pulaski Skyway fell on my friend's head, a small rusted piece of steel, and I could see the repaired cracks in the concrete piers that hold up the ancient structure. It felt like we were in the movie "Apocalypse Now" and like Captain Willard, we had one mission, to get as far up that river as we could.

I showed Captain Bill where I wanted to go on my map and he jokingly said, "We were thinking of calling that our 'Heart of Darkness Tour.'" Captain Bill runs "eco-tours of the Meadowlands for groups and individuals and he is the founder and executive director of the Hackensack Riverkeeper, a non-profit environmental watchdog group that reports polluters, organizes cleanups, and raises money to purchase wetlands. There are two other environmental groups in the region, the Newark Baykeeper and the Passaic River Coalition. And in addition, "The Passaic River Institute" was formed a couple of years ago as a think tank and conference center for environmental groups at Montclair State University.

The map had a blank area on it, a rare thing anywhere in North Jersey, but there was a single trucking road that dead-ended, and after that there was nothing. It was the place where the Hackensack and the Passaic merge, a spot that always fascinated me, a foreboding industrial no man's land of dead end factory roads and rail lines under the shadows of the New Jersey Turnpike and the Pulaski Skyway. I could see several acres of untouched woodland, this was my blank area at the end of Kearny Peninsula, or "Kearny Point" as the captain called it. He said it was as close as you can get to what it may have looked like before Europeans arrived. His idea is to turn it into a park.

We had to stay well out from shore because of the mud flats of tidal Newark Bay, so we stayed outside the buoys as the boat made a wide turn west, northwest and then north up the Passaic River. No one ever gets to see this part of the river, an area that drivers can only glimpse at 75 mph from the New Jersey Turnpike. It is an impenetrable maze of power line transmission towers, refineries, liquid gas storage tanks, waste incinerators, cargo container yards, and deserted factories, warehouses and auto junkyards where a definite toxic presence lurks.

I was thinking back to my first time on the river last November and about being blown sideways in a canoe, and now here I was on the river again, but this time on an ocean-going pontoon boat heading up the Passaic River's mouth.

A huge plume of black smoke rose to the height of a twenty-story building just north of us and Captain Bill got an immediate cell phone call from one of his watchdogs. It was an auto-truck accident on the Eastern Spur of the Turnpike. Just as we rounded Kearny Point, I saw a huge complex of abandoned factory buildings and smokestacks and what looked like office buildings all connected to each other. "That's the old Western Electric plant," Captain Bill said looking over the beige brick compound. A strange feeling passed over me when I realized that that was where my father used to work when he first got out of the army after World War II—the Kearny WE plant. "It is where they made the old telephones," Captain Bill said, "back when you used to lease your phone from the phone company." We motored by a pair of collapsed railroad bridges that had carried freight trains right up to the back of the plant. The company had its own rail line. It all looked so bombed out.

We passed a waste incinerator plant for the City of Newark rising behind some old, abandoned brick warehouse buildings that were built earlier in the last century. There was graffiti scrawled over the sides. A little ways further upriver I could smell the sewage treatment plant, and after that foul odor there was a sickening sweet smell coming from a plant that makes artificial sweetener, and those two odors combined to make me feel slightly nauseated. This is the part of the Passaic that has earned the distinction of being one of the worst polluted rivers in the country. It is a title well earned, since it was one of the nation's first industrial rivers with a history of pollution dating back to the founding of the Society for Useful Manufacturers in 1792—a society dreamt up by Alexander Hamilton after seeing the Great Falls and envisioning Paterson as the manufacturing center for a new nation.

Mariani captures how Williams felt about the nation's first Secretary of the Treasury, whose financial system Williams saw as part of the country's eventual economic downfall—"Hamilton: Williams' enemy and dark doppelganger, whose statue and presence stood overlooking the polluted falls of his Passaic at Paterson" (382). I had been to the falls recently and stood below on the grass by the power generator at the base of the falls looking up the statue of Hamilton that Mariani mentions. Nowhere in Paterson is there a statue of Williams. There's a statue of Paterson native and comedian Lou Costello holding a baseball bat, but not one for the city's most famous poet.

Hamilton set up the S.U.M. as a corporation that would have jurisdiction over all the Passaic River's watershed, a resource back then equal in value to oil today for its industrial power. It wasn't until the 1930s that the monopoly was broken up under anti-trust laws and in its place the Passaic Valley Water and Sewage Commission was formed. When I started to write this article, I discovered near the falls, the last remaining "S.U.M." cast iron grate and took a photograph. Williams describes the industrial pollution in his title story: "It's only been a few years since the river water was so full of sewage and dye-waste from the mills that you didn't want to go near it, much less swim in it as they do now—or boat on it. It was a good job to build the Passaic Valley Sewer and clean up that stink hole." Williams is referring to the fact that he sees kids playing in the river again and that a clean river is what these people need more than the jobs created by river polluters.

From the pontoon boat we see the Passaic Valley Sewerage Commission boat headed downriver towards us as we cruise by going upriver. Captain Bill pointed out that it was a skimmer, a boat that collects floating litter and debris from the surface of the Passaic. We waved to them and the two crew members waved back. Straight ahead I could see the downtown skyline of Newark looming up over a bend in the river. People in Newark don't even realize that they are living in a maritime city because they are cut off from the water because of the freight yards and chemical plants.

As we pull up close to this cement bulkhead, I hear the captain's voice getting louder and angry as a few "F" words slip out of his mouth. He is in full diatribe now about the Diamond Alkali Chemical Plant. He throttles the pontoon boat down to idle and we drift a little in the current near what looks like a cement parking lot with potted trees laid out every so many feet. "This is the single greatest point source for pollution for the entire area," Captain Bill fumes. "It is a toxic scar, an environmental disaster caused by corporate negligence and government inaction," he adds. "The chemical plant made 'Agent Orange' on this site for the Vietnam War and the river mud and former grounds are saturated with dioxin one of the most toxic substances known to man," he continues. "The tides carry this dioxin 17 miles up the Passaic, and crabs have been caught in Jamaica Bay Queens over twenty miles away with this same dioxin in them." I look again and it seems almost like a mausoleum and there's an eerie feeling to the place that nothing is able to live here. It is near the "Iron Bound" section of Newark, which reaps the benefits of all this contamination. The captain tells us that this mausoleum or slurry wall was installed in 2001 and it was capped with tons of cement, and that some progress is being made with a recent legal victory against the subsidiary holding company with the slick name of "Tierra Solutions." Cleanup is scheduled to begin in 2010 but the method used to remediate the site is being debated as is the 80 million dollars in cleanup costs.

I ask Captain Bill what he thinks of the Passaic, and he said, "It is a sorrowful river." He mentions that he organizes 14 to 15 cleanups a year and that 150 volunteers show up. I ask him what he hauls out of the water and he reads off a litany of discarded trash—"Tires, lawn furniture, auto parts, plastic bottles, traffic safety cones, shopping carts." The tides he tells me are strong enough to drag a shopping cart from Passaic to Newark over time. He tells me that as a kid growing up in Secaucus he used to play in the meadowlands where the Harz Mountain Corporation built hundreds of condominiums and that he used to lash logs to 50-gallon drums to make a raft. He started his organization in 1995 as a river cruise project to educate people in the ecology of the area because as he says, "No one understood the issues at the time."

July 14th, skies threatening, dark clouds unseasonably mild.

It is no surprise to see that the front page of the Passaic River Coalition's newsletter features the "Diamond Alkali Chemical" waste site in Newark. I hold a copy in my hands as I sit in Ella Filippone's office, the executive director of the coalition, in her temporary lodgings in Warren, New Jersey. "This is stupid," she says, "They want to remove the contaminated soil by pressing the water out and hauling the dried soil away for burial." Her tone, like the captain's, changes when Tierra Solutions and dioxin is brought up. She sat at her desk piled high with several three-foot stacks of papers. Her computer lies buried under a mountain of file folders filled with documents. She reaches to a crowded shelf above her head and pulls down a book and shows me a slim, dark green volume of poetry titled "Song of the Passaic" by J. A. MacNab published in 1890. She reads a few stanzas of rhyming couplets in the style of Longfellow— then she beams a big smile, "I love it," she says. "I know Williams wrote about the Passaic, but he was a modernist. I prefer this."

So the river had its 19th century bard in the age of Whitman and Longfellow who has fallen into obscurity. I tell her that I am glad to learn about this book and that I will try to locate a copy. I tell her that she should mention the book and its author in her next newsletter and she agrees. I ask her how she became the executive director and she tells me that when she retired from her PR firm in 1969 she needed something to keep her engaged and a friend suggested she join a local environmental group. Her skills running a PR agency and her doctorate in business administration led the other members to nominate her to the position she's held ever since.

"And what do you think is going to happen when they press the soil to dry it?" she asks. I give her the correct answer which is that the dioxin contaminated water will drain back into the river.

She tells me that Congressman Bill Pascrell, Jr. has been a friend and active supporter of what her organization is doing, as well as Governor Jon Corzine, and Mayor Jose "joey" Torres of Paterson, and that they all want to bring life back to the Passaic. Pascrell supports creating a 32 mile kayak and canoe trail on the Lower Passaic and Torres wants to create river walks where the abandoned mills now stand, and he wants to hold boat races on the river the way they did back at the turn-of-the last century. Dr. Fillipone wants to get the raceways near the Great Falls back in shape as part of her organization's effort to clean up the river around the Great Falls.

The raceway system was created to power the mills and took water from the river above the falls and sent it to sluices that powered waterwheels. "I want to spruce it up by removing litter and pulling out weeds and replanting the area with colorful ground roses and flowering bushes so that it will look inviting," she said. I asked her about the water and she lamented that the sewage treatment plant doesn't do enough to remove the phosphates because it is expensive to do and that those chemicals are compromising the health of the river.

As I get up to leave and thank her for her time, she mentions that one of her biggest concerns is for the Passaic River watershed. "The ground water levels are going down in the Highlands," she says. "People who live in the area have to drill deeper to find water. In another few years, there won't be any drinking water." I look up and see how serious her expression is. It is something I haven't thought about, but I have read newspaper articles about feeder streams for the Passaic River drying up in the summer and this scares me.

July 17th, clearing, fair weather clouds by afternoon.

I go to meet Joshua Castano, Historic Preservation Specialist, who works for the City of Paterson's Historic Preservation Commission. The office sits in what looks like a one-room brick schoolhouse that overlooks the Great Falls. The Great Falls was in the news; it had just been designated this year as a national park. I park by the statue of Alexander Hamilton in the shade of tree and go to the door and Joshua lets me in. I can see photography equipment lying about, tripods, camera cases, as well as stacks of documents and maps. There's a lot of interest now in shaping up this former city park now that it will be turned over to the feds. I chat with him for a while about photography and somehow we get on the subject of poetry and then Williams and then he tells me that his mother knows a poet friend of mine who taught her when she was a student at Bloomfield College. I ask him for a copy of the "Master Plan" for the Great Falls, and he tells me that he can give me a CD instead and I thank him.

The plan calls for an amphitheater to be constructed for outdoor concerts at the base of the falls facing the power generator and the river, and I wonder how anyone will be able to hear anything with the noise in the background. There's also a plan for a cliff trail adjacent to the falls with places for rock climbing and even a replica Indian village on the riverbank, as well as a paved historic walkway through the ruined mills along the river. My wish is that it be cleaned up and left in its natural state so that visitors can appreciate the river and the falls as nature intended and not as an industrial silk mill theme park. The plan is over two hundred pages long. What would Williams have thought?

I walk down the side access path to the grass field in front of the power generator plant at the base of the falls and notice that the stairs that lead up to the statue of Hamilton are closed. There are weeds everywhere and graffiti and broken bottles. I take some photographs using an infrared filter. Then I pack away my equipment and walk up the path and out to the street and walk up to the intersection with McBride Avenue so I can continue to the pedestrian walkway that crosses the rock chasm directly over the falls. Then I cross over the Passaic on the Wayne Avenue Bridge to the other side of the river by the old football stadium, "Hinchliffe Stadium." The stadium has been closed for over twenty years and it looks like a deserted and ruined Roman coliseum covered over in graffiti and weeds. There's a path that leads to the river behind the stadium. It is shady and cool and overgrown with trees along the steep cliff side. I spot about a dozen homeless men sitting on rocks or on logs under the trees by the water to keep cool.

I am a little nervous down here at the river's edge up against the rock cliff at the base of the falls. I see a kid fishing and I watch a group of kids climb up on a huge chunk of basalt that fell off the face of the cliff and into the water years ago. The kids climb up easily using handholds and footholds to get purchase on the cracks in the basalt and make it over so that they can sit on another boulder under the spray of the waterfalls. I turn back after one unsuccessful try.

It's a clear summer day and I want to take advantage of the weather, so I walk back to my car and drive Route 80 east to the first exit after crossing the Passaic, Exit 61, and take the old county road 507, that Williams would have driven north to get to Paterson from Rutherford in the 1930s. I drive south towards Garfield. I think I see an access road to the river but I end up in the trucking yard for the Sealed Air Corporation and I have to turn around. I get back on the county road and pull into Eric's Auto World used car lot which is right on the river. The sun is still strong at 6 pm and the riverbank is thickly wooded. I spot the dam and the little park by the dam with a bench and a flagpole. There's a man standing in the river fishing. He is casting his line into the foam at the base of the falling water. The dam is ten feet high and three hundred feet across and holds back what they call "Lake Dundee." I ask the fisherman if he caught anything and he holds up his hands because I can't hear him under the roar of water and he indicates that they were too small.

In his title story, Williams writes: "All the streets of the Dundee section of Passaic have men idling in them this summer. Polacks mostly, walking around—collars open, skinny, pot bellied—or sitting on the steps of the old-time wooden houses, looking out of place, fathers of families with their women folk around them."

I cross the county road from the dam to a small convenience strip mall opposite the used car lot, and look in all the shop windows. All the stores are Polish, the signs are in Polish. There's a Polish deli, a Polish meat store, a Polish travel agency. There are Polish kids with skate boards, and mothers shopping for dinner on their way home. I see a couple of long-haired young men smoking leaning up against a wall, and an old man buying a newspaper. The air glistens with water vapor in the sunlight from the spray of the Dundee Dam. A few days earlier, a woman's body was found floating in the river here and there were police divers and helicopters scanning the river. The woman's body was discovered by two homeless fishermen who were questioned and let go. Life goes on along the Passaic River.

NATHAN GLAZER [b. 1923]

Some Very Modest Proposals for the Improvement of American Education

Nathan Glazer was born in New York City and earned degrees from City College, the University of Pennsylvania, and Columbia, where he was awarded a Ph.D. in sociology in 1962. As one of a group of New York intellectuals, he edited the magazine *Commentary* and coedited *The Public Interest*, a quarterly journal. Currently a professor emeritus in Harvard University's Graduate School of Education, Glazer is a leading authority on issues of race, immigration, and urban development and U.S. social policy. He has been awarded two Guggenheim Fellowships and a Fulbright, and has served on a presidential task force on education and urban policy. He is also a contributing editor of *The New Republic*. Considered a highly influential sociologist and educator, Glazer defies political labels and affiliations. His books include *The Lonely Crowd*, authored with David Reisman and Reuel Denney (1950); *Beyond the Melting Pot* (with Daniel Moynihan); and *The Limits of Public Policy* (1988). In "Some Very Modest Proposals for the Improvement of American Education," published originally in 1984, Glazer offers practical suggestions for the support of teachers and the enhancement of conditions in the schools.

That we can do a great deal for the sorry state of American education with more money is generally accepted. Even apparently modest proposals will, however, cost a great deal of money. Consider something as simple as increasing the average compensation of American teachers—who are generally considered underpaid—by $2,000 a year each. The bill would come to five billion dollars a year. A similar figure is reached by the report of the highly qualified Twentieth Century Fund Task Force on Federal, Elementary, and Secondary Educational Policy, which proposes fellowships and additional compensation for master teachers. Reducing class size

Nathan Glazer, "Some Very Modest Proposals for the Improvement of American Education" from *Daedalus*, 113:4 (Fall, 1984), pp. 169–178. © 1984 by the American Academy of Arts and Sciences. Reprinted by permission of MIT Press Journals.

10 percent, or increasing the number of teachers by the same percentage would cost another five billion dollars. With present-day federal deficits, these look like small sums, but since education is paid for almost entirely by states and local government, these modest proposals would lead to substantial and painful tax increases. (I leave aside for the moment the views of skeptics who believe that none of these changes would matter.)

But the occasional visitor to American schools will note some changes that would cost much less, nothing at all, or even save money—and yet would improve at least the educational *environment* in American schools (once again, we ignore those skeptics who would insist that even a better educational environment cannot be guaranteed to improve educational achievement). In the spirit of evoking further cheap proposals, here is a small list of suggestions that, to my mind at least—and the mind I believe of any adult who visits American public schools—would mean a clear plus for American education:

1. *Disconnect all loudspeaker systems in American schools—or at least reserve them, like the hotline between Moscow and Washington, for only the gravest emergencies.* The American classroom—and the American teacher and his or her charges—is continually interrupted by announcements from central headquarters over the loudspeaker system. These remind teachers to bring in some form or other; or students to bring in some form or other; or students engaged in some activity to remember to come to practice or rehearsal; or they announce a change of time for some activity. There is nothing so unnerving to a teacher engaged in trying to explain something, or a student engaged in trying to understand something, as the crackle of the loudspeaker prepared to issue an announcement, and the harsh and gravelly voice (the systems are not obviously of the highest grade) of the announcement itself.

Aside from questions of personal taste, why would this be a good idea? As I have suggested, one reason is that the loudspeaker interrupts efforts to communicate complicated material that requires undivided attention. Second, it demeans the teacher as professional: every announcement tells her whatever she is doing is not very important and can be interrupted at any time. Third, it accentuates the notion of hierarchy in education—the principal and assistant principal are the most important people, and command time and attention even in the midst of instruction. Perhaps I have been softened by too many years as a college teacher, but it would be unimaginable that a loudspeaker, if one existed, would ever interrupt a college class except under conditions of the gravest and most immediate threat to life and limb. One way of showing students that education is important is not to interrupt it for band-rehearsal announcements.

2. *Disarm the school.* One of the most depressing aspects of the urban 5
school in the United States is the degree of security manifest within it, and
that seems to me quite contradictory to what a school should be. Outer
doors are locked. Security guards are present in the corridors. Internal
doors are locked. Passes are necessary to enter the school or move within
it, for outsiders and for students. Students are marched in groups from
classroom to classroom, under the eye of the teachers. It is understandable that given the conditions in lower-class areas in our large cities—and
not only the lower-class areas—some degree of security-mindedness is
necessary. There is valuable equipment—typewriters, computers, audio-
visual equipment—that can be stolen; vandalism is a serious concern;
marauders can enter the school in search for equipment, or teachers'
pocketbooks, or to threaten directly personal safety in search of money or
sex, and so on. School integration and busing, at least in their initial
stages, have contributed to increased interracial tensions in schools and
have in part severed the link between community and school. The difference in ethnic and racial composition of faculty, other staff, administrators, and students contributes to the same end.

Having acknowledged all this, I still believe the school should feel less
like a prison than it does. One should examine to what extent outside
doors must be closed; to what extent the security guard cannot be
replaced by local parents, volunteer or paid; the degree to which the endless bells indicating "stop" and "go" are really necessary. I suspect that
now that the most difficult period of school integration has passed, now
that teachers and administrators and staff more closely parallel in race
and ethnic background students and community owing to the increase
in black and Hispanic teachers and administrators, we may be saddled
with more security than we need. Here we come to the sticky problem of
removing security measures whose need has decreased. What school
board will open itself to suit or to public criticism by deliberately providing *less* security? And yet one must consider the atmosphere of the
school and a school's primary objective as a reaching agent: can this be
reconciled with a condition of maximum security? Perhaps there are lessons to be learned from colleges and community colleges in older urban
areas, which in my experience do seem to manage with less security. One
reason is that there are more adults around in such institutions. Is that a
hint as to how we could manage better in our public schools?

3. *Enlist the children in keeping the school clean.* Occasionally we see a
practice abroad that suggests possible transfer to the American scene. In
Japan, the children clean the school. There is a time of day when mops and
pails and brooms come out, and the children sweep up and wash up. This
does, I am sure, suggest to the children that this is *their* school, that it is not

simply a matter of being forced to go to a foreign institution that imposes alien demands upon them. I can imagine some obstacles in the way of instituting regular student clean-up in American schools—custodians' unions, for example, might object. But they can be reassured that children don't do that good a job, and they will still be needed. Once again, as in the case of the security problem, one wants to create in the school, if at all possible, a common enterprise of teachers and students, without the latter being bored and resistant, the former, in response, becoming equally indifferent. The school should be seen as everyone's workplace—and participation in cleaning the school will help.

4. *Save old schools.* Build fewer new ones. It has often surprised me that while in schools such as Eton and Oxford—and indeed well-known private schools and colleges in the United States—old buildings are prized, in so many communities older public schools are torn down when to the naked eye they have many virtues that would warrant their maintenance and use. Only a few blocks from where I live, an excellent example of late nineteenth-century fine brickwork and carved stonework that served as the Cambridge Latin School came down for a remodeling. The carved elements are still displayed about the remodeled school, but why a building of such character should have deserved demolition escaped my understanding, particularly since one can take it almost as a given that a school building put up before the 1940s will be built of heavier and sturdier materials than one constructed today. Even the inconveniences of the old can possess a charm that makes them worthwhile. And indeed many of the reforms that seemed to require new buildings (for example, classrooms without walls, concentrated around activities centers in large open rooms) have turned out, on use, to be not so desirable. Our aim should be to give each school a history, a character, something that at least some students respond to. The pressures for new buildings are enormous, and sometimes perfectly legitimate (as when communities expand), but often illegitimate, as when builders and building-trades workers and contract-givers seek an opportunity or when state aid makes it appear as if a new building won't cost anything.

5. *Look on new hardware with a skeptical eye.* I think it likely that the passion for the new in the way of teaching-hardware not only does not contribute to higher education achievement but may well serve as a temporary means to evade the real and hard tasks of teaching—which really require almost no hardware at all, besides textbooks, blackboard, and chalk. Admittedly, when one comes to high-school science, something more is called for. And yet our tendency is to always find cover behind new hardware. It's *fun* to get new audio-visual equipment, new rooms

equipped with them in which all kinds of things can be done by flicking a switch or twisting a dial, or, as is now the case, to decide what kind of personal computers and software are necessary for a good educational program. Once again, foreign experience can be enlightening. When Japanese education was already well ahead of American, most Japanese schools were in prewar wooden buildings. (They are now as up-to-date as ours, but neither their age nor up-to-dateness has much to do with their good record of achievement.) Resisting the appeal of new hardware not only saves money, and provides less in the way of saleable goods to burglarize, but it also prevents distraction from the principal tasks of reading, writing, and calculating. When it turns out that computers and new software are shown to do a better job at these key tasks—I am skeptical as to whether this will ever be the case—there will be time enough to splurge on new equipment. The teacher, alone, up front, explaining, encouraging, guiding, is the heart of the matter—the rest is fun, and very helpful to corporate income, and gives an inflated headquarters staff something new to do. But students will have time enough to learn about computers when they get to college, and getting there will depend almost not at all on what they can do with computers, but how well they understand words and sentences, and how well they do at simple mathematics.

There is nothing wrong with old textbooks, too. Recently, reviewing 10 some recent high-school American history texts, I was astonished to discover they came out in new editions every two years or so, and not because the main body of the text is improved, but because the textbook wants to be able to claim it covers the very last presidential campaign, and the events of the last few years. This is a waste of time and energy and money. There is enough to teach in American history up to 1950 or 1960 not to worry about whether the text includes Reagan's tax cuts. I suspect many new texts in other areas also offer little advantage over the older ones. There is also a virtue in a teacher becoming acquainted with a particular textbook. When I read that a school is disadvantaged because its textbooks are old, I am always mystified. Even the newest advances in physics and biology might well be reserved for college.

6. *Expand the pool from which we draw good teachers.* This general heading covers a number of simple and concrete things, such as: if a teacher is considered qualified to teach at a good private school, that teacher should be considered qualified to teach at a public school. It has always seemed to me ridiculous that teachers accepted at the best private schools in New York City or top preparatory schools in the country would not be allowed to teach in the public school system of New York or Boston. Often, they are willing—after all, the pay is better in public schools and there are greater fringe benefits. They might, it is true, be

driven out of these schools by the challenge of lower- and working-class children. But when they are willing, it seems unbelievable that the teacher qualified (or so Brearley thinks) for Brearley will not be allowed to teach at P.S. 122. Greater use of part-time teachers might also be able to draw upon people with qualities that we are told the average teacher unfortunately doesn't possess — such as a higher level of competence in writing and mathematics.

Our recurrent concern with foreign-language teaching should lead us to recruit foreign-born teachers. There are problems in getting teaching jobs today in Germany and France — yet teachers there are typically drawn from pools of students with higher academic skills than is the case in this country. Paradoxically, we make it easy for teachers of Spanish-language background to get jobs owing to the expansion of bilingual programs — but then their teaching is confined to children whose Spanish accent doesn't need improvement. It would make more sense to expose children of foreign-language background more to teachers with native English — and children from English-speaking families to teachers who speak French, German, Spanish, and, why not, Japanese, and Chinese natively. This would mean that rules requiring that a teacher must be a citizen, or must speak English without an accent, should be lifted for special teachers with special tasks. Perhaps we could make the most of the oversupply of teachers in some foreign countries by using them to teach mathematics — a subject where accent doesn't count. The school system in Georgia is already recruiting from Germany. Colleges often use teaching assistants whose English is not native and far from perfect, including Asians from Korea and China, to assist in science and mathematics courses. (There are many state laws which would not permit them to teach in elementary and secondary schools.)

All the suggestions above eschew any involvement with some great issues of education — tradition or reform, the teaching of values, the role of religion in the schools — that have in the past dominated arguments over education and still do today. But I add one more proposal that is still, I am afraid, somewhat controversial:

7. *Let students, within reason, pick their schools, or let parents choose them for them.* All those informed on school issues will sense the heaving depths of controversy under this apparently modest proposal. Does this mean they might choose parochial schools, without being required to pay tuition out of their own pockets? Or does this mean black children would be allowed to attend schools in black areas, and whites in white areas, or the reverse if each is so inclined? As we all know, the two great issues of religion and race stand in the way of any such simple and commonsensical arrangement. Students are regularly bused from one section of a city

to another because of their race, and students cannot without financial penalty attend that substantial sector of schools—30 percent or so in most Northern and Midwestern cities—that are called "private." I ignore the question of whether, holding all factors constant, students do "better" in private or public schools, in racially well-mixed or hardly mixed schools. The evidence will always be uncertain. What is perhaps less arguable is that students will do better in a school that forms a community, in which teachers, parents, and students all agree that *that* is the school they want to teach in, to attend, to send their children to. I would guess that this is the kind of school most of the readers of this article have attended; it is the kind of school, alas, that our complex racial and religious history makes it harder and harder for those of minority race or of lower- and working-class status to attend.

I have eschewed the grand proposals—for curriculum change, for 15 improving the quality of entering teachers, for checking on the competence of teachers in service, for establishing national standards for achievement in different levels of education—all of which now form the agenda for many state commissions of educational reform, and all of which seem reasonable to me. Rather, I have concentrated on a variety of other things that serve to remove distraction, to open the school to those of quality who would be willing to enter it to improve it, to concentrate on the essentials of teaching and learning as I (and many others) have experienced it. It would be possible to propose larger changes in the same direction: for example, reduce the size of the bureaucracies in urban school systems. Some of my modest proposals are insidiously intended to do this—if there were less effort devoted to building new schools, buying new equipment, evaluating new textbooks, or busing children, there would be no need to maintain quite so many people at headquarters. Or so I would hope.

In the meantime, why not disconnect the loudspeakers?

WILLIAM BRANIGIN

Sweatshops Are Back

For more than thirty years, **William Branigin** has been a staff writer and editor at the *Washington Post*. He has served as a foreign correspondent in Asia, Central America, and the Middle East, and much of his reporting has focused on issues of immigration. In 2000, Branigin received the Eugene Katz Award for Excellence in the Coverage of Immigration from the Center for Immigration Studies. During the war in Iraq, Branigin was an embedded reporter with the Third Infantry Division of the U.S. Army.

In "Sweatshops Are Back," originally published in the *Washington Post* in February 1997, Branigin exposes the prevalence of domestic sweatshops, particularly in major cities like New York City and Los Angeles, operating in the garment industry. According to Branigin, these sweatshops, often run by immigrants from Korea and China, exploit the labor of other immigrants in order to remain competitive.

After an arduous trek across the border from her native Mexico, Aurora Blancas made her way to New York City and took the first job she could find: sweeping floors and packaging clothes sewn by other illegal immigrants at a sweatshop in the garment district.

No experience — or documents — necessary.

"I started working the same day I asked for the job," she said. "The boss asked me my name and how old I was. Nothing more."

But unlike her fellow workers, Blancas, 28, did not accept quietly the exploitation and abuse that followed when she was hired last summer to work in the dilapidated Eighth Avenue building.

Although her willingness to speak out makes Blancas unusual, the 5 place that employed her and the conditions she found there are not.

Despite a ledger of laws against them and periodic pledges by government and business leaders to crack down, sweatshops have made a remarkable comeback in America, evolving from a relative anomaly into a commonplace, even indispensable, part of the U.S. garment industry.

They have also evolved almost entirely into a phenomenon of immigrants. According to federal investigators and union officials, most such factories are owned by newcomers from Asia, who often exploit other immigrants, many of them illegal, either from Asia or Latin America. Typically, both the workers and the employers see themselves as victims of a system dominated by increasingly powerful major retailers.

In Blancas's case, the owner of the 14th-floor shop in which she worked is a South Korean immigrant whose clothes were sold to suppliers of such stores as Wal-Mart and Kmart. According to Blancas and another former worker, he refused to pay the minimum wage or overtime to his three dozen, mostly female employees. The workers typically toiled at their sewing machines and presses for up to 60 hours a week in a room with wires hanging from the ceiling, three small fans that served as the only source of ventilation and no fire exits. Wages, usually paid in cash to avoid taxes, often were arbitrarily cut or delayed if the owner ran short of funds. Employees who missed a day would be illegally "fined" $30, on top of losing a day's pay.

When workers made mistakes, the owner's wife would scream at them, throw garments in their faces and sometimes pull their hair or hit them. One newly arrived young woman was summarily fired for yawning on the job.

Last July, after Blancas demanded higher wages and brought the 10 sweatshop to the attention of a garment workers union, she was fired.

Whether operating openly in decrepit buildings in New York or Los Angeles or hidden away illegally in people's homes in Dallas, sweatshops violate labor and tax laws amid cutthroat competition for orders that filter down from the retailers.

UNDERGROUND ECONOMY

The return of the kind of sweatshops that flourished early this century—and were thought to have been largely eliminated—reflects fundamental changes in the garment industry and, more broadly, in American society. The shops have become part of a vast underground economy, shielded by an overlay of laissez-faire practices and tacit accommodations.

Clothing designers and retailers depend on the sweatshops for fast delivery and big profit margins. Unions, hopeful of eventually organizing these workers, appear to be more interested in preserving manufacturing jobs than driving them out of business. Large pools of illegal immigrants are so anxious for work that they accept the shops' meager wages and are often too fearful to complain. Consumers keep gravitating toward the lowest prices they can find. And government agencies do not field enough investigators or cooperate sufficiently with each other to pursue the shops effectively and enforce the laws that would eradicate them.

Helping sweatshops to thrive have been technological advances that allow retailers to determine instantly what is selling and to order more of it. This allows stores to limit inventory and avoid getting stuck with large volumes of unpopular apparel. But it also requires quick turn-around, which favors domestic manufacturers. The pressures on these manufacturers to produce garments quickly and still compete with cheap foreign imports have tended to drive down wages and working conditions among the sewing shops that lie at the bottom of the industry.

Yet, there is no shortage of workers for these jobs because of a broader 15 change in American society: increasing waves of legal and illegal immigration since the 1970s and growing concentrations of immigrants in cities such as Los Angeles and New York.

The sweatshops' revival also reflects a weakening of unions in the garment industry in recent years, in part because of their difficulties in trying to organize workers who are here illegally in the first place. For them, even a sub-minimum wage in the United States generally beats what they could earn in their homelands.

Although the clandestine nature of much of the industry has made it hard to track, recent federal studies point to a rise in the number of U.S. sweatshops and a worsening of their conditions.

Union and Labor Department officials estimate that minimum wage and overtime violations, two of the basic parameters that define a sweatshop, prevail in more than half the 22,000 U.S. sewing businesses. Many also pay their workers "off the books" to avoid various local, state and federal taxes.

The sweatshop conditions described by Blancas are "typical of the bottom of the industry," said Jeff Hermanson, director of the Garment Workers' Justice Center, a branch of the Union of Needletrades, Industrial and Textile Employees.

"Physical abuse is unfortunately quite common, and there's always the 20 yelling," he said. The long hours, low wages and lack of benefits often found in Korean-owned sweatshops are also routine in shops run by Chinese and Latino owners, he said.

In New York, a garment center where much of the industry's changing dynamics play out, Koreans own up to 40 percent of the city's roughly 4,000 contract sewing shops. Chinese immigrants own almost all the rest. Yet, the Korean-owned shops have attracted relatively more attention

263

from labor investigators, mostly because they tend to hire Latino workers, who are less reluctant to complain than Asian employees.

INTIMIDATION

Chinese-owned shops tend to hire only other Chinese, said Maria Echaveste, administrator of the Labor Department's wage and hour division. In some cases, she said, workers have expressed fear for their lives if they reveal labor violations. Many Chinese sweatshop workers are believed to be indentured servants toiling under a form of debt bondage to pay off the heavy cost of being smuggled into the United States.

"The workers lie to us," one investigator said. "In Chinese shops, the falsification of records is absolutely down to a science. It's almost impossible to break unless the shop goes out of business. It's only then that workers tell you those were not the hours and rates they worked."

In the Korean-owned shops, poor working conditions are often exacerbated by the lack of a common language between the Koreans and their mostly young, female Latino employees.

"They [the Korean owners] think they can make themselves under- 25
stood by yelling," said Hermanson of the Garment Workers' Justice Center, which tries to organize workers and defends them in disputes with shop owners. The result, especially when owners hit their workers, is an "atmosphere of terror and intimidation," he said.

The Korean Apparel Manufacturers Association says it has been trying to get its 400 member companies in New York to pay at least the minimum wage. Most now do so, the group says. But these owners are themselves victims of punishing market forces, the group argues.

"The problem for the sewing companies is that the minimum wage goes higher and higher, and the price from manufacturers stays the same or goes down," said a spokeswoman for the association who gave her name only as Hung.

She acknowledged that some owners treat their workers harshly but said most do not. As for the illegal aliens among them, she conceded, "That's a problem."

For Blancas, trouble started almost immediately after she was hired by a shop called New Young Fashions. The owner, Kim Young Han, paid her less than the $160 a week she said she was promised. She worked six days a week, starting at 7:30 a.m. and finishing at 6 p.m. each weekday. Her pay averaged $2.54 an hour, according to figures compiled by the workers' center.

When she found out what the minimum wage was and told her co- 30
workers they should be getting at least $4.25 an hour, "they were aston-
ished," but refused to back her in a confrontation with the owner and his
Korean wife, Blancas said.

"They were robbing us," she said. "I was very angry. . . . I said, 'Talk,
compañeros, talk,' but they were terrified. The [owner's wife] told me to
shut up and leave, and the others just kept quiet."

Her co-workers, most of them fellow Mexicans and Ecuadorans,
feared being deported as illegal aliens if they complained, Blancas
said.

Interviewed at his factory, Kim said he had resolved all of his employees' complaints and that he is now complying with labor laws.

After Blancas was fired from New Young Fashions, the workers' center
helped her recover some of her back wages. She later found work in
another garment shop that pays more, though still not the minimum
wage. She took a second job in a store.

Blancas said she left her home in Mexico City to seek work in the 35
United States because her husband had died in a car accident a year
earlier and she needed to support her young son. She crossed the border with an uncle, who also works in a sweatshop, and trekked all
night over hills to reach a road that would set them on their way to New
York.

Bertha Morales, a 25-year-old Ecuadoran who worked in another
Korean-owned sweatshop, said she was sent by her boss to help out at
New Young Fashions one day and was shocked by what she saw. At one
point, she said in an interview, the owner's wife struck a worker on the
back for sewing buttons incorrectly. Other workers described similar
punishment, and one told of an incident in which the boss grabbed her
hair and pulled on it.

One new employee, a 19-year-old woman from Nicaragua, was summarily fired by the owner's wife for yawning and left the shop in tears,
Morales said.

THE FOOD CHAIN

Sweatshops such as Kim's lie at the bottom of what the Labor Department describes as a garment industry "food chain" beneath layers of
suppliers, designers and middlemen, who compete fiercely for orders
from the big retailers at the top.

It is a system that regulators and union officials say effectively insu-
lates the big-name stores and fashion labels, allowing them to profess

ock and ignorance of sweatshop conditions in which their clothes were sewn.

Major retailers, such as J.C. Penney, Sears and Wal-Mart, have quality- 40 control inspectors who regularly visit work sites, and they know how much it costs to produce a garment at the minimum wage, a Labor Department official said. But under a 60-year-old law, the retailers can be held liable only if they had "direct knowledge" of labor violations involved in producing their goods.

The system also adds markups far in excess of the actual cost of the labor and material that went into the garments.

Retailers say too many variables go into the final price of a garment to generalize about any of them, but Labor Department and union officials estimate that labor typically accounts for less than 3 percent of the U.S. retail price of clothing made in domestic sweatshops and as little as one-half of 1 percent for garments sewn abroad.

Because of the pressures weighing on those at the low end of the industry, shop owners such as Kim Young Han believe that they, too, are victims of the system.

Sitting at his worn desk in a corner of the shop floor, Kim blamed his problems on creditors, saying he was owed thousands of dollars by garment manufacturers who had subcontracted several large jobs to him. He produced letters to them demanding payment and threatening "legal action." All were written in longhand; he does not have a type-writer.

Wearing jeans and a denim shirt, the lean, craggy-faced Kim, 61, said 45 he had been a lecturer at a junior college in Seoul before coming to the United States years ago to study for a doctoral degree in linguistics under Noam Chomsky. Although that alone makes him a rarity among sweatshop owners, union officials said his violations of labor laws were all too familiar.

Asked about the specific allegations against him by the garment work-ers union, Kim became visibly upset and pleaded for understanding.

"Help me, please," he begged. "I'm in trouble."

Seemingly on the verge of tears, Kim complained of having to com-pete with cheap imports and denied making any windfall profits. "I want to close my factory," he lamented over the din of sewing machines and a radio blaring Spanish songs. "The market's no good. . . . No hope at my age."

The National Retail Federation, which represents 2,000 major U.S. retailers, in turn blames sweatshop conditions on subcontractors such as Kim.

"The retailers don't employ these workers," said Pamela Rucker, a 50 spokeswoman for the federation. "The retailers many times are at least two or three steps removed from the problem." She asserted, "It's not the retailers who are reaping the benefits from these criminal activities. It's the greedy subcontractors."

ENFORCEMENT

Shops at the bottom of the industry often go out of business, relocate and open under new names. Some fail altogether, never to reappear. But despite decades of lawmaking against them — and a public campaign by the Clinton administration following the 1995 exposure of a virtual slave-labor garment factory in Los Angeles — the system designed to eradicate the sweatshops has largely failed, union activists say.

Local, state and federal agencies charged with enforcing labor, immigration and tax laws have often failed to work together, allowing shop owners and workers to slip through the cracks of the system. Under a directive renewed by Mayor Rudolph W. Giuliani, a strong supporter of immigration, New York authorities are prohibited from sharing information with the Immigration and Naturalization Service.

At the direction of the administration and Congress, the INS has thrown the bulk of its resources at the southwestern border to prevent illegal immigrants from crossing into the United States from Mexico. Nationwide, only about 1,700 INS investigators are assigned to the interior of the country, and they spend less than 20 percent of their time enforcing immigration law at work sites of all kinds, according to the agency.

In a special effort in New York last year, INS agents arrested 1,824 illegal aliens during inspections of 150 work sites, most of them garment shops. However, because of a lack of detention space, almost all were released on their own recognizance and told to return for court hearings.

"The percentage that shows up is minute," said Russ Bergeron, an INS 55 spokesman. Most simply find another job in the underground economy, and many return to work at the same shops where they were arrested.

Ironically, labor groups such as the Garment Workers' Justice Center also play a part in keeping the sweatshops in business. Among the literature the center distributes, for example, are fliers in English, Spanish and Korean that advise shop owners how to fend off searches by INS and Labor Department agents.

The fliers encourage employers to challenge inspections on grounds of discrimination and use legal stalling tactics that the INS says often enable them to fabricate employment eligibility records. Fliers in

Spanish urge workers to "remain silent" when asked about their nationality, birthplace or entry into the United States.

The union says its main aim is to protect workers and preserve their jobs, regardless of their immigration status. When faced with labor violations, the justice center usually tries to work out a solution with the employer without government involvement.

Critics call the policy misguided. "If you're trying to defend a living standard, the minimum wage and Social Security and deal with legitimate companies," one independent labor activist argued, "helping these sweatshops exist would seem to be counterproductive."

RETRIBUTION

For some garment workers, the punishment for exposing sweatshop conditions comes from their employers. After complaining about what she saw at New Young Fashions while filling in there last year, Bertha Morales was fired by her own Korean boss, who was a friend of Kim's. 60

Others, including two illegal immigrant sisters from Mexico, said workers do not tell authorities about labor violations and physical abuse out of fear that their shops will then be raided by immigration agents.

In the case of another outspoken worker, the consequences of going public—or at least the perception of those effects—became evident after she appeared at a forum on sweatshops in Arlington last summer. The worker, Nancy Penaloza, 29, said she has labored in Korean-owned sweatshops in New York for nine years, working up to 66 hours a week in filthy conditions. In her current job, she said, she sews high-quality women's suits, earning $6 apiece for garments that usually sell for $120 or more at stores such as J.C. Penney and Ann Taylor.

"I get paid off the books," Penaloza told the forum. "Even though I am working legally, my boss doesn't pay any taxes or Social Security. . . . I never get a vacation. I never even get a whole weekend off." She said she works in constant fear, not only of her temperamental boss but of the "big rats and mice" that continually crawl over her feet.

A day after she spoke, INS agents raided her factory and arrested most of her co-workers, who were illegal immigrants, Penaloza said. Three days after that, a Labor Department wage inspector showed up. Although she is sure the INS raid was a coincidence, because she did not name her employer at the forum, her co-workers blamed it on her.

A former secretary in Mexico, she said she originally crossed the border as an illegal alien herself, then "became legal" a couple of years ago. 65

She said her Korean boss routinely smacks his workers in the head when they make mistakes. He also orders them to tell the Labor Department that they are receiving their proper wages and overtime, she said, and that is what they did during the latest inspection.

"The workers are afraid," Penaloza said. "They don't want to lose their jobs."

And so, she said, "they lied to the inspector," thus perpetuating a cycle that helps the industry to survive.

[1997]

AMITAI ETZIONI   [b. 1929]

Working at McDonald's

Born Werner Falk in 1929 in Cologne, Germany, **Amitai Etzioni** fled from Nazi Germany to Palestine in the 1930s, ultimately studying at the Hebrew University in Jerusalem. A prominent sociologist, he received his Ph.D. in 1958 from the University of California, Berkeley, and then taught for two decades at Columbia University. From 1979 to 1980 he served at the White House as a senior adviser on domestic affairs. The author of twenty-four books, including *The Monochrome Society* (2001), *The Limits of Privacy* (1999), and *The New Golden Rule* (1996), Etzioni has taught at George Washington University since 1980. As director of the university's Institute for Communitarian Policy Studies, Etzioni founded the Communitarian Network, a nonprofit, nonpartisan organization that provides a forum for discussing the impact of moral, social, and political issues on society's well being. He is also the founder of the journal *Responsive Community* and has been awarded numerous honors, including the 2001 John P. McGovern Award in Behavioral Sciences and the Seventh James Wilbur Award for Extraordinary Contributions to the Appreciation and Advancement of Human Values by the Conference on Value Inquiry.

Etzioni's "Working at McDonald's," originally published in the *Miami Herald* in 1986, evaluates the educational merits of adolescents' holding down part-time, paying jobs in fast-food restaurants. Critical of the long hours, the managerial role models, the failure of these jobs to foster independent thought and decision making skills, and the enticements of a questionable consumerism, Etzioni insists that teens "go back to school."

McDonald's is bad for your kids. I do not mean the flat patties and the white-flour buns; I refer to the jobs teen-agers undertake, mass-producing these choice items.

As many as two-thirds of America's high school juniors and seniors now hold down part-time paying jobs, according to studies. Many of these are in fast-food chains, of which McDonald's is the pioneer, trend-setter, and symbol.

Amitai Etzioni, "Working at McDonald's" from *The Miami Herald*, August 24, 1986. Reprinted by permission of the author.

At first, such jobs may seem right out of the Founding Fathers' educational manual for how to bring up self-reliant, work-ethic-driven, productive youngsters. But in fact, these jobs undermine school attendance and involvement, impart few skills that will be useful in later life, and simultaneously skew the values of teen-agers—especially their ideas about the worth of a dollar.

It has been a longstanding American tradition that youngsters ought to get paying jobs. In folklore, few pursuits are more deeply revered than the newspaper route and the sidewalk lemonade stand. Here the youngsters are to learn how sweet are the fruits of labor and self-discipline (papers are delivered early in the morning, rain or shine), and the ways of trade (if you price your lemonade too high or too low . . .).

Roy Rogers, Baskin Robbins, Kentucky Fried Chicken, *et al.*, may at 5 first seem nothing but a vast extension of the lemonade stand. They provide very large numbers of teen jobs, provide regular employment, pay quite well compared to many other teen jobs, and, in the modern equivalent of toiling over a hot stove, test one's stamina.

Closer examination, however, finds the McDonald's kind of job highly uneducational in several ways. Far from providing opportunities for entrepreneurship (the lemonade stand) or self- discipline, self-supervision, and self-scheduling (the paper route), most teen jobs these days are highly structured—what social scientists call "highly routinized."

True, you still have to have the gumption to get yourself over to the hamburger stand, but once you don the prescribed uniform, your task is spelled out in minute detail. The franchise prescribes the shape of the coffee cups; the weight, size, shape, and color of the patties; and the texture of the napkins (if any). Fresh coffee is to be made every eight minutes. And so on. There is no room for initiative, creativity, or even elementary rearrangements. These are breeding grounds for robots working for yesterday's assembly lines, not tomorrow's high-tech posts.

There are very few studies of the matter. One of the few is a 1984 study by Ivan Charper and Bryan Shore Fraser. The study relies mainly on what teen-agers write in response to questionnaires rather than actual observations of fast-food jobs. The authors argue that the employees develop many skills such as how to operate a food-preparation machine and a cash register. However, little attention is paid to how long it takes to acquire such a skill, or what its significance is.

What does it matter if you spend 20 minutes to learn to use a cash register, and then—"operate" it? What skill have you acquired? It is a long way from learning to work with a lathe or carpenter tools in the olden days or to program computers in the modern age.

A 1980 study by A. V. Harrell and P. W. Wirtz found that, among those 10 students who worked at least 25 hours per week while in school, their unemployment rate four years later was half of that of seniors who did not work. This is an impressive statistic. It must be seen, though, together with the finding that many who begin as part-time employees in fast-food chains drop out of high school and are gobbled up in the world of low-skill jobs.

Some say that while these jobs are rather unsuited for college-bound, white, middle-class youngsters, they are "ideal" for lower-class, "non-academic," minority youngsters. Indeed, minorities are "over-represented" in these jobs (21 percent of fast-food employees). While it is true that these places provide income, work, and even some training to such youngsters, they also tend to perpetuate their disadvantaged status. They provide no career ladders, few marketable skills, and undermine school attendance and involvement.

The hours are often long. Among those 14 to 17, a third of fast-food employees (including some school dropouts) labor more than 30 hours per week, according to the Charper-Fraser study. Only 20 percent work 15 hours or less. The rest: between 15 to 30 hours.

Often the stores close late, and after closing one must clean up and tally up. In affluent Montgomery County, Md., where child labor would not seem to be a widespread economic necessity, 24 percent of the seniors at one high school in 1985 worked as much as five to seven days a week; 27 percent, three to five. There is just no way such amounts of work will not interfere with school work, especially homework. In an informal survey published in the most recent yearbook of the high school, 58 percent of the seniors acknowledged that their jobs interfere with their school work.

The Charper-Fraser study sees merit in learning teamwork and working under supervision. The authors have a point here. However, it must be noted that such learning is not automatically educational or wholesome. For example, much of the supervision in fast-food places leans toward teaching one the wrong kinds of compliance: blind obedience, or shared alienation with the "boss."

Supervision is often both tight and woefully inappropriate. Today, 15 fast-food chains and other such places of work (record shops, bowling alleys) keep costs down by having teens supervise teens with often no adult on the premises.

There is no father or mother figure with which to identify, to emulate, to provide a role model and guidance. The work-culture varies from one place to another: Sometimes it is a tightly run shop (must keep the cash registers ringing); sometimes a rather loose pot party interrupted by customers. However, only rarely is there a master to learn from, or much worth learning. Indeed, far from being places where solid adult work values are being transmitted, these are places where all too often delinquent teen values dominate. Typically, when my son Oren was dishing out ice cream for Baskin Robbins in upper Manhattan, his fellow teen-workers considered him a sucker for not helping himself to the till. Most youngsters felt they were entitled to $50 severance "pay" on their last day on the job.

The pay, oddly, is the part of the teen work-world that is most difficult to evaluate. The lemonade stand or paper route money was for your allowance. In the old days, apprentices learning a trade from a master contributed most, if not all of their income to their parents' household. Today, the teen pay may be low by adult standards, but it is often, especially in the middle class, spent largely or wholly by the teens. That is, the youngsters live free at home ("after all, they are high school kids") and are left with very substantial sums of money.

Where this money goes is not quite clear. Some use it to support themselves, especially among the poor. More middle-class kids set some money aside to help pay for college, or save it for a major purchase—often a car. But large amounts seem to flow to pay for an early introduction into the most trite aspects of American consumerism: Flimsy punk clothes, trinkets, and whatever else is the last fast-moving teen craze.

One may say that this is only fair and square; they are being good American consumers and spend their money on what turns them on. At least, a cynic might add, these funds do not go into illicit drugs and booze. On the other hand, an educator might bemoan that these young, yet unformed individuals, so early in life are driven to buy objects of no intrinsic educational, cultural, or social merit, learn so quickly the dubious merit of keeping up with the Joneses in ever-changing fads, promoted by mass merchandising.

Many teens find the instant reward of money, and the youth status 20 symbols it buys, much more alluring than credits in calculus courses, European history, or foreign languages. No wonder quite a few would rather skip school—and certainly homework—and instead work longer at a Burger King. Thus, most teen work these days is not providing early lessons in work ethic; it fosters escape from school and responsibilities, quick gratification, and a short cut to the consumeristic aspects of adult life.

Thus, parents should look at teen employment not as automatically educational. It is an activity—like sports—that can be turned into an educational opportunity. But it can also easily be abused. Youngsters must learn to balance the quest for income with the needs to keep growing and pursue other endeavors that do not pay off instantly—above all education.

Go back to school.

BARBARA EHRENREICH [b. 1941]

Serving in Florida

A renowned social critic and prolific essayist, **Barbara Ehrenreich** was
born in Butte, Montana, in 1941. In 1963 she graduated with a B.A. in
physics from Reed College and went on to earn a Ph.D. in cell biology
from Rockefeller University. Initially she had no intention of becoming
a writer, but she found herself attracted to a career in social activism
rather than research science and began writing investigative articles
for small newsletters. Her articles have appeared in the *New York
Times, Ms.,* the *Atlantic Monthly, In These Times,* and *The New Republic,* among others. From 1991 to 1997 Ehrenreich was a regular columnist for *Time* magazine and is currently a regular columnist for *The
Progressive.* Her national best-seller, *Nickel and Dimed* (2001), narrates
her efforts to survive on low-income wages and her follow-up book,
Bait and Switch (2005), recounts her undercover efforts to find a white-
collar job in corporate America.

The 2001 essay "Serving in Florida" is excerpted from *Nickel and
Dimed.* Ehrenreich describes waiting tables in two Florida restaurants.

I could drift along like this, in some dreamy proletarian idyll, except for
two things. One is management. If I have kept this subject to the margins so far it is because I still flinch to think that I spent all those weeks
under the surveillance of men (and later women) whose job it was to
monitor my behavior for signs of sloth, theft, drug abuse, or worse. Not
that managers and especially "assistant managers" in low-wage settings
like this are exactly the class enemy. Mostly, in the restaurant business,
they are former cooks still capable of pinch-hitting in the kitchen, just as
in hotels they are likely to be former clerks, and paid a salary of only
about $400 a week. But everyone knows they have crossed over to the
other side, which is, crudely put, corporate as opposed to human. Cooks
want to prepare tasty meals, servers want to serve them graciously, but
managers are there for only one reason—to make sure that money is
made for some theoretical entity, the corporation, which exists far away
in Chicago or New York, if a corporation can be said to have a physical

existence at all. Reflecting on her career, Gail tells me ruefully that she swore, years ago, never to work for a corporation again. "They don't cut you no slack. You give and you give and they take."

Managers can sit—for hours at a time if they want—but it's their job to see that no one else ever does, even when there's nothing to do, and this is why, for servers, slow times can be as exhausting as rushes. You start dragging out each little chore because if the manager on duty catches you in an idle moment he will give you something far nastier to do. So I wipe, I clean, I consolidate catsup bottles and recheck the cheese-cake supply, even tour the tables to make sure the customer evaluation forms are all standing perkily in their places—wondering all the time how many calories I burn in these strictly theatrical exercises. In desperation, I even take the desserts out of their glass display case and freshen them up with whipped cream and bright new maraschino cherries; anything to look busy. When, on a particularly dead afternoon, Stu finds me glancing at a *USA Today* a customer has left behind, he assigns me to vacuum the entire floor with the broken vacuum cleaner, which has a handle only two feet long, and the only way to do that without incurring orthopedic damage is to proceed from spot to spot on your knees.

On my first Friday at Hearthside there is a "mandatory meeting for all restaurant employees," which I attend, eager for insight into our overall marketing strategy and the niche (your basic Ohio cuisine with a tropical twist?) we aim to inhabit. But there is no "we" at this meeting. Phillip, our top manager except for an occasional "consultant" sent out by corporate headquarters, opens it with a sneer: "The break room—it's disgusting. Butts in the ashtrays, newspapers lying around, crumbs." This windowless little room, which also houses the time clock for the entire hotel, is where we stash our bags and civilian clothes and take our half-hour meal breaks. But a break room is not a right, he tells us, it can be taken away. We should also know that the lockers in the break room and whatever is in them can be searched at any time. Then comes gossip; there has been gossip; gossip (which seems to mean employees talking among themselves) must stop. Off-duty employees are henceforth barred from eating at the restaurant, because "other servers gather around them and gossip." When Phillip has exhausted his agenda of rebukes, Joan complains about the condition of the ladies' room and I throw in my two bits about the vacuum cleaner. But I don't see any backup coming from my fellow servers, each of whom has slipped into her own personal funk; Gail, my role model, stares sorrowfully at a point six inches from her nose. The meeting ends when Andy, one of the cooks, gets up, muttering about breaking up his day off for this almighty bullshit.

Just four days later we are suddenly summoned into the kitchen at 3:30 p.m., even though there are live tables on the floor. We all—about ten of us — stand around Phillip, who announces grimly that there has been a report of some "drug activity" on the night shift and that, as a result, we are now to be a "drug-free" workplace, meaning that all new hires will be tested and possibly also current employees on a random basis. I am glad that this part of the kitchen is so dark because I find myself blushing as hard as if I had been caught toking up in the ladies' room myself: I haven't been treated this way — lined up in the corridor, threatened with locker searches, peppered with carelessly aimed accusations — since at least junior high school. Back on the floor, Joan cracks, "Next they'll be telling us we can't have *sex* on the job." When I ask Stu what happened to inspire the crackdown, he just mutters about "management decisions" and takes the opportunity to upbraid Gail and me for being too generous with the rolls. From now on there's to be only one per customer and it goes out with the dinner, not with the salad. He's also been riding the cooks, prompting Andy to come out of the kitchen and observe — with the serenity of a man whose customary implement is a butcher knife — that "Stu has a death wish today."

Later in the evening, the gossip crystallizes around the theory that Stu   5
is himself the drug culprit, that he uses the restaurant phone to order up marijuana and sends one of the late servers out to fetch it for him. The server was caught and she may have ratted out Stu, at least enough to cast some suspicion on him, thus accounting for his pissy behavior. Who knows? Personally, I'm ready to believe anything bad about Stu, who serves no evident function and presumes too much on our common ethnicity, sidling up to me one night to engage in a little nativism directed at the Haitian immigrants: "I feel like I'm the foreigner here. They're taking over the country." Still later that evening, the drug in question escalates to crack. Lionel, the busboy, entertains us for the rest of the shift standing just behind Stu's back and sucking deliriously on an imaginary joint or maybe a pipe.

The other problem, in addition to the less-than-nurturing management style, is that this job shows no sign of being financially viable. You might imagine, from a comfortable distance, that people who live, year in and year out, on $6 to $10 an hour have discovered some survival stratagems unknown to the middle class. But no. It's not hard to get my coworkers talking about their living situations, because housing, in almost every case, is the principal source of disruption in their lives, the first thing they fill you in on when they arrive for their shifts. After a week, I have compiled the following survey:

Gail is sharing a room in a well-known downtown flophouse for $250 a week. Her roommate, a male friend, has begun hitting on her, driving her nuts, but the rent would be impossible alone.

Claude, the Haitian cook, is desperate to get out of the two-room apartment he shares with his girlfriend and two other, unrelated people. As far as I can determine, the other Haitian men live in similarly crowded situations.

Annette, a twenty-year-old server who is six months pregnant and abandoned by her boyfriend, lives with her mother, a postal clerk.

Marianne, who is a breakfast server, and her boyfriend are paying $170 a week for a one-person trailer.

Billy, who at $10 an hour is the wealthiest of us, lives in the trailer he owns, paying only the $400-a-month lot fee.

The other white cook, Andy, lives on his dry-docked boat, which, as far as I can tell from his loving descriptions, can't be more than twenty feet long. He offers to take me out on it once it's repaired, but the offer comes with inquiries as to my marital status, so I do not follow up on it.

Tina, another server, and her husband are paying $60 a night for a room in the Days Inn. This is because they have no car and the Days Inn is in walking distance of the Hearthside. When Marianne is tossed out of her trailer for subletting (which is against trailer park rules), she leaves her boyfriend and moves in with Tina and her husband.

Joan, who had fooled me with her numerous and tasteful outfits (hostesses wear their own clothes), lives in a van parked behind a shopping center at night and showers in Tina's motel room. The clothes are from thrift shops.[1]

It strikes me, in my middle-class solipsism, that there is gross improvidence in some of these arrangements. When Gail and I are wrapping silverware in napkins — the only task for which we are permitted to sit — she tells me she is thinking of escaping from her roommate by moving into the Days Inn herself. I am astounded: how she can even think of paying $40 to $60 a day? But if I was afraid of sounding like a social worker, I have come out just sounding like a fool. She squints at me in disbelief: "And where am I supposed to get a month's rent and a month's deposit for an apartment?" I'd been feeling pretty smug about my $500 efficiency, but of course it was made possible only by the $1,300 I had allotted myself for start-up costs when I began my low-wage life: $1,000 for the first month's rent and deposit, $100 for initial groceries and cash

---

[1] I could find no statistics on the number of employed people living in cars or vans, but according to a 1997 report of the National Coalition for the Homeless, "Myths and Facts about Homelessness," nearly one-fifth of all homeless people (in twenty-nine cities across the nation) are employed in full- or part-time jobs.

in my pocket, $200 stuffed away for emergencies. In poverty, as in certain propositions in physics, starting conditions are everything.

There are no secret economies that nourish the poor; on the contrary, there are a host of special costs. If you can't put up the two months' rent you need to secure an apartment, you end up paying through the nose for a room by the week. If you have only a room, with a hot plate at best, you can't save by cooking up huge lentil stews that can be frozen for the week ahead. You eat fast food or the hot dogs and Styrofoam cups of soup that can be microwaved in a convenience store. If you have no money for health insurance—and the Hearthside's niggardly plan kicks in only after three months—you go without routine care or prescription drugs and end up paying the price. Gail, for example, was doing fine, healthwise anyway, until she ran out of money for estrogen pills. She is supposed to be on the company health plan by now, but they claim to have lost her application form and to be beginning the paperwork all over again. So she spends $9 a pop for pills to control the migraines she wouldn't have, she insists, if her estrogen supplements were covered. Similarly, Marianne's boyfriend lost his job as a roofer because he missed so much time after getting a cut on his foot for which he couldn't afford the prescribed antibiotic.

My own situation, when I sit down to assess it after two weeks of work, would not be much better if this were my actual life. The seductive thing about waitressing is that you don't have to wait for payday to feel a few bills in your pocket, and my tips usually cover meals and gas, plus something left over to stuff into the kitchen drawer I use as a bank. But as the tourist business slows in the summer heat, I sometimes leave work with only $20 in tips (the gross is higher, but servers share about 15 percent of their tips with the busboys and bartenders). With wages included, this amounts to about the minimum wage of $5.15 an hour. The sum in the drawer is piling up but at the present rate of accumulation will be more than $100 short of my rent when the end of the month comes around. Nor can I see any expenses to cut. True, I haven't gone the lentil stew route yet, but that's because I don't have a large cooking pot, potholders, or a ladle to stir with (which would cost a total of about $30 at Kmart, somewhat less at a thrift store), not to mention onions, carrots, and the indispensable bay leaf. I do make my lunch almost every day—usually some slow-burning, high-protein combo like frozen chicken patties with melted cheese on top and canned pinto beans on the side. Dinner is at the Hearthside, which offers its employees a choice of BLT, fish sandwich, or hamburger for only $2. The burger lasts longest, especially if it's heaped with gutpuckering jalapeños, but by midnight my stomach is growling again.

So unless I want to start using my car as a residence, I have to find a 10

278

second or an alternative job. I call all the hotels I'd filled out housekeeping applications at weeks ago — the Hyatt, Holiday Inn, Econo Lodge, HoJo's, Best Western, plus a half dozen locally run guest houses. Nothing. Then I start making the rounds again, wasting whole mornings waiting for some assistant manager to show up, even dipping into places so creepy that the front-desk clerk greets you from behind bullet-proof glass and sells pints of liquor over the counter. But either someone has exposed my real-life housekeeping habits — which are, shall we say, mellow — or I am at the wrong end of some infallible ethnic equation: most, but by no means all, of the working housekeepers I see on my job searches are African Americans, Spanish speaking, or refugees from the Central European post-Communist world, while servers are almost invariably white and monolingually English speaking. When I finally get a positive response, I have been identified once again as server material. Jerry's — again, not the real name — which is part of a well-known national chain and physically attached here to another budget hotel, is ready to use me at once. The prospect is both exciting and terrifying because, with about the same number of tables and counter seats, Jerry's attracts three or four times the volume of customers as the gloomy old Hearthside.

Picture a fat person's hell, and I don't mean a place with no food. Instead there is everything you might eat if eating had no bodily consequences — the cheese fries, the chicken-fried steaks, the fudge-laden desserts — only here every bite must be paid for, one way or another, in human discomfort. The kitchen is a cavern, a stomach leading to the lower intestine that is the garbage and dishwashing area, from which issue bizarre smells combining the edible and the offal: creamy carrion, pizza barf, and that unique and enigmatic Jerry's scent, citrus fart. The floor is slick with spills, forcing us to walk through the kitchen with tiny steps, like Susan McDougal in leg irons. Sinks everywhere are clogged with scraps of lettuce, decomposing lemon wedges, water-logged toast crusts. Put your hand down on any counter and you risk being stuck to it by the film of ancient syrup spills, and this is unfortunate because hands are utensils here, used for scooping up lettuce onto the salad plates, lifting out pie slices, and even moving hash browns from one plate to another. The regulation poster in the single unisex rest room admonishes us to wash our hands thoroughly, and even offers instructions for doing so, but there is always some vital substance missing — soap, paper towels, toilet paper — and I never found all three at once. You learn to stuff your pockets with napkins before going in there, and too bad about the customers, who must eat, although they don't realize it, almost literally out of our hands.

The break room summarizes the whole situation: there is none, because there are no breaks at Jerry's. For six to eight hours in a row, you never sit except to pee. Actually, there are three folding chairs at a table immediately adjacent to the bathroom, but hardly anyone ever sits in this, the very rectum of the gastroarchitectural system. Rather, the function of the peritoilet area is to house the ashtrays in which servers and dishwashers leave their cigarettes burning at all times, like votive candles, so they don't have to waste time lighting up again when they dash back here for a puff. Almost everyone smokes as if their pulmonary well-being depended on it—the multinational mélange of cooks; the dishwashers, who are all Czechs here; the servers, who are American natives—creating an atmosphere in which oxygen is only an occasional pollutant. My first morning at Jerry's, when the hypoglycemic shakes set in, I complain to one of my fellow servers that I don't understand how she can go so long without food. "Well, I don't understand how *you* can go so long without a cigarette," she responds in a tone of reproach. Because work is what you do for others; smoking is what you do for yourself. I don't know why the anti-smoking crusaders have never grasped the element of defiant self-nurturance that makes the habit so endearing to its victims—as if, in the American workplace, the only thing people have to call their own is the tumors they are nourishing and the spare moments they devote to feeding them.

Now, the Industrial Revolution is not an easy transition, especially, in my experience, when you have to zip through it in just a couple of days. I have gone from craft work straight into the factory, from the air-conditioned morgue of the Hearthside directly into the flames. Customers arrive in human waves, sometimes disgorged fifty at a time from their tour buses, peckish and whiny. Instead of two "girls" on the floor at once, there can be as many as six of us running around in our brilliant pink-and-orange Hawaiian shirts. Conversations, either with customers or with fellow employees, seldom last more than twenty seconds at a time. On my first day, in fact, I am hurt by my sister servers' coldness. My mentor for the day is a supremely competent, emotionally uninflected twenty-three-year-old, and the others, who gossip a little among themselves about the real reason someone is out sick today and the size of the bail bond someone else has had to pay, ignore me completely. On my second day, I find out why. "Well, it's good to see *you* again," one of them says in greeting. "Hardly anyone comes back after the first day." I feel powerfully vindicated—a survivor—but it would take a long time, probably months, before I could hope to be accepted into this sorority.

I start out with the beautiful, heroic idea of handling the two jobs at once, and for two days I almost do it: working the breakfast/lunch shift at Jerry's from 8:00 till 2:00, arriving at the Hearthside a few minutes late, at 2:10, and attempting to hold out until 10:00. In the few minutes I have between jobs, I pick up a spicy chicken sandwich at the Wendy's drive-through window, gobble it down in the car, and change from khaki slacks to black, from Hawaiian to rust-colored polo. There is a problem, though. When, during the 3:00–4:00 o'clock dead time, I finally sit down to wrap silver, my flesh seems to bond to the seat. I try to refuel with a purloined cup of clam chowder, as I've seen Gail and Joan do dozens of times, but Stu catches me and hisses "No *eating*!" although there's not a customer around to be offended by the sight of food making contact with a server's lips. So I tell Gail I'm going to quit, and she hugs me and says she might just follow me to Jerry's herself.

But the chances of this are minuscule. She has left the flophouse and 15 her annoying roommate and is back to living in her truck. But, guess what, she reports to me excitedly later that evening, Phillip has given her permission to park overnight in the hotel parking lot, as long as she keeps out of sight, and the parking lot should be totally safe since it's patrolled by a hotel security guard! With the Hearthside offering benefits like that, how could anyone think of leaving? This must be Phillip's theory, anyway. He accepts my resignation with a shrug, his main concern being that I return my two polo shirts and aprons.

Gail would have triumphed at Jerry's, I'm sure, but for me it's a crash course in exhaustion management. Years ago, the kindly fry cook who trained me to waitress at a Los Angeles truck stop used to say: never make an unnecessary trip; if you don't have to walk fast, walk slow; if you don't have to walk, stand. But at Jerry's the effort of distinguishing necessary from unnecessary and urgent from whenever would itself be too much of an energy drain. The only thing to do is to treat each shift as a one-time-only emergency: you've got fifty starving people out there, lying scattered on the battlefield, so get out there and feed them! Forget that you will have to do this again tomorrow, forget that you will have to be alert enough to dodge the drunks on the drive home tonight—just burn, burn, burn! Ideally, at some point you enter what servers call a "rhythm" and psychologists term a "flow state," where signals pass from the sense organs directly to the muscles, bypassing the cerebral cortex, and a Zen-like emptiness sets in. I'm on a 2:00–10:00 p.m. shift now, and a male server from the morning shift tells me about the time he "pulled a triple"—three shifts in a row, all the way around the clock—and then got off and had a drink and met this girl, and maybe he shouldn't tell me this, but they had sex right then and there and it was like *beautiful*. . . .

DINESH D'SOUZA [b. 1961]

America the Beautiful: What We're Fighting For

Born in India in 1961, conservative author **Dinesh D'Souza** became a citizen of the United States in 1990. A graduate of Dartmouth College and editor of *The Dartmouth Review*, D'Souza is the Robert and Karen Rishwain Fellow at the Hoover Institution, a conservative public policy think tank at Stanford University where he used to be on the editorial staff of the institute's conservative journal *Policy Review*. From 1987 to 1988 he served as senior domestic policy analyst in Ronald Reagan's administration. Widely controversial and much sought after as a lecturer, D'Souza also frequently appears as a respondent on popular news programs such as *Nightline* and *Firing Line*. His articles have appeared in the *Wall Street Journal*, the *New York Times*, the *Washington Post, Vanity Fair, Forbes,* and the *Atlantic Monthly.* Drawing on his research of the economy and society, civil rights, affirmative action, higher education, and politics, his best selling books include *Illiberal Education* (1991) and *The End of Racism* (1995).

This selection, "America the Beautiful: What We're Fighting For," is taken from D'Souza's recent book *What's So Great about America?* (2002). D'Souza defends American liberalism, freedom and secularism, democracy and capitalism, as the natural consequences of historical experience. In comparison, D'Souza traces the cultural decline of the once powerful and inspired Islamic civilization, alleging that Islamic fundamentalists now at work in the Islamic world act out of humiliation and embarrassment, making headlines only with the murder of their perceived adversaries. In his piece, D'Souza aims to strengthen what he fears is the waning moral self-confidence of Americans in the face of attacks by Islamic fundamentalists and U.S. military involvement in the Middle East.

> *We have it in our power to begin the world all over again.*
> —*THOMAS PAINE*

America represents a new way of being human and thus presents a radical challenge to the world. On the one hand, Americans have throughout their history held that they are special: that their country has been blessed by God, that the American system is unique, that Americans are not like people everywhere else. This set of beliefs is called "American exceptionalism." At the same time, Americans have also traditionally insisted that they provide a model for the world, that theirs is a formula that others can follow, and that there is no better life available elsewhere. Paradoxically enough, American exceptionalism leads to American universalism.

Both American exceptionalism and American universalism have come under fierce attack from the enemies of America, both at home and abroad. The critics of America deny that there is anything unique about America, and they ridicule the notion that the American model is one that others should seek to follow. Indeed, by chronicling the past and present crimes of America, they hope to extract apologies and financial reparations out of Americans. Some even seek to justify murderous attacks against America on the grounds that what America does, and what she stands for, invites such attacks.

These critics are aiming their assault on America's greatest weakness: her lack of moral self-confidence. Americans cannot effectively fight a war without believing that it is a just war. That's why America has only lost once, in Vietnam, and that was because most Americans did not know what they were fighting for. The enemies of America understand this vulnerability. At the deepest level their assault is moral: they seek to destroy America's belief in herself, knowing that if this happens, America is finished. By the same token, when Americans rally behind a good cause, as in World War II, they are invincible. The outcome of America's engagements abroad is usually determined by a single factor: America's will to prevail. In order to win, Americans need to believe that they are on the side of the angels. The good news is that they usually are.

The triumph of American ideas and culture in the global marketplace, and the fact that most immigrants from around the world choose to come to the United States, would seem to be sufficient grounds for establishing the superiority of American civilization. But this is not entirely so, because we have not shown that the people of the world are *justified* in preferring the American way of life to any other. We must contend with the Islamic fundamentalists' argument that their societies are based on high principles while America is based on low principles. The Islamic critics are happy to concede the attractions of America, but they insist that these attractions are base. America, they say, appeals to what is most degraded about human nature; by contrast, Islamic societies may be poor and "backward," but they at least aspire to virtue. Even if they fall short, they are trying to live by God's law.

Americans usually have a hard time answering this argument, in part 5 because they are bewildered by its theological cadences. The usual tendency is to lapse into a kind of unwitting relativism. "You are following what you believe is right, and we are living by the values that we think are best." This pious buncombe usually concludes with a Rodney King–style° plea for tolerance, "So why don't we learn to appreciate our differences? Why don't we just get along?" To see why this argument fails completely, imagine that you are living during the time of the Spanish Inquisition.° The Grand Inquisitor is just starting to pull out your fingernails. You make the Rodney King move on him. "Torquemada,° please stop pulling out my fingernails. Why don't we learn to appreciate our differences?" Most of us probably realize that Torquemada would not find this persuasive. But it is less obvious why he would not. Let me paraphrase Torquemada's argument: "You think I am taking away your freedom, but I am concerned with your immortal soul. Ultimately virtue is far more important than freedom. Our lives last for a mere second in the long expanse of eternity. What measure of pleasure or pain we experience in our short life is trivial compared to our fate in the never ending life to come. I am trying to save your soul from damnation. Who cares if you have to let out a few screams in the process? My actions are entirely for your own benefit. You should be *thanking me* for pulling out your fingernails."

I have recalled the Spanish Inquisition to make the point that the Islamic argument is one that we have heard before. We should not find it so strange that people think this way; it is the way that many in our own civilization used to think not so very long ago. The reason that most of us do not think this way now is that Western history has taught us a hard lesson. That lesson is that when the institutions of religion and government are one, and the secular authority is given the power to be the interpreter and enforcer of God's law, then horrible abuses of power are perpetrated in God's name. This is just what we saw in Afghanistan with the Taliban,° and what we see now in places like Iran. This is not to suggest that Islam's historical abuses are worse than those of the West. But

---

Rodney King: Los Angeles resident whose apparently unprovoked beating by police was videotaped and televised, sparking riots across the city in 1992. **Spanish Inquisition:** Tribunal of the Catholic Church in Spain from 1478 until 1510, famous for its cruelty and intolerance. **Torquemada:** Tomás de Torquemada (1420–1498), Spanish churchman who led the Inquisition and earned infamy for his brutal persecution of Spanish Jews. **the Taliban:** Radical Islamic sect that came to power in Afghanistan in 1996.

the West, as a consequence of its experience, learned to disentangle the institutions of religion and government—a separation that was most completely achieved in the United States. As we have seen, the West also devised a new way of organizing society around the institutions of science, democracy, and capitalism. The Renaissance, the Reformation, the Enlightenment, and the Scientific Revolution were some of the major signposts on Western civilization's road to modernity.

By contrast, the Islamic world did not have a Renaissance or a Reformation. No Enlightenment or Scientific Revolution either. Incredible though it may seem to many in the West, Islamic societies today are in some respects not very different from how they were a thousand years ago. Islam has been around for a long time. This brings us to a critical question: why are we seeing this upsurge of Islamic fundamentalism and Islamic fanaticism now?

To answer this question, we should recall that Islam was once one of the greatest and most powerful civilizations in the world. Indeed, there was a time when it seemed as if the whole world would fall under Islamic rule. Within a century of the prophet Muhammad's° death, his converts had overthrown the Sassanid dynasty in Iran and conquered large tracts of territory from the Byzantine dynasty. Soon the Muslims had established an empire greater than that of Rome at its zenith. Over the next several centuries, Islam made deep inroads into Africa, Southeast Asia, and southern Europe. The crusades were launched to repel the forces of Islam, but the crusades ended in failure. By the sixteenth century, there were no fewer than five Islamic empires, unified by political ties, a common religion, and a common culture: the Mamluk sultans in Egypt, the Safavid dynasty in Iran, the Mughal empire in India, the empire of the Great Khans in Russia and Central Asia, and the Ottoman Empire based in Turkey. Of these, the Ottomans were by far the most formidable. They ruled most of North Africa, and threatened Mediterranean Europe and Austria. Europe was terrified that they might take over all the lands of Christendom. In all of history, Islam is the only non-Western civilization to pose a mortal threat to the West.

Then it all went wrong. Starting in the late seventeenth century, when the West was able to repel the Ottoman siege of Vienna, the power of Islam began a slow but steady decline. By the nineteenth century the Ottoman Empire was known as the "sick man of Europe," and it collapsed completely after World War I, when the victorious European powers carved it up and parceled out the pieces. Not only did the Muslims lose most of the territory they had conquered, but they also found themselves being ruled,

Muhammad: The prophet of Islam (570?–632), whose collected visions and revelations compose the Koran.

either directly or indirectly, by the West. Today, even though colonialism has ended, the Islamic world is in a miserable state. Basically all that it has to offer is oil, and as technology opens up alternative sources of energy, even that will not amount to much. Without its oil revenues, the Islamic world will find itself in the position of sub-Saharan Africa: it will cease to matter. Even now it does not matter very much. The only reason it makes the news is by killing people. When is the last time you opened the newspaper to read about a great Islamic discovery or invention? While China and India, two other empires that were eclipsed by the West, have embraced Western technology and even assumed a leadership role in some areas, Islam's contribution to modern science and technology is negligible.

In addition to these embarrassments, the Islamic world faces a formi- 10 dable threat from the United States. This is not the threat of American force or of American support for Israel. Israel is an irritant, but it does not threaten the existence of Islamic society. By contrast, America stands for an idea that is fully capable of transforming the Islamic world by winning the hearts of Muslims. The subversive American idea is one of shaping your own life, of making your own destiny, of following a path illumined not by external authorities but by your inner self. This American idea endangers the sanctity of the Muslim home, as well as the authority of Islamic society. It empowers women and children to assert their prerogatives against the male head of the household. It also undermines political and religious hierarchies. Of all American ideas, the "inner voice" is the most dangerous because it rivals the voice of Allah as a source of moral allegiance. So Islam is indeed, as bin Laden° warned, facing the greatest threat to its survival since the days of Muhammad.

In recent decades, a great debate has broken out in the Muslim world to account for Islamic decline and to formulate a response to it. One response—let us call it the reformist or classical liberal response—is to acknowledge that the Islamic world has been left behind by modernity. The reformers' solution is to embrace science, democracy, and capitalism. This would mean adaptation—at least selective adaptation—to the ways of the West. The liberal reformers have an honorable intellectual tradition, associated with such names as Muhammad Abduh, Jamal al-Afghani, Muhammad Iqbal, and Taha Husayn. This group also enjoys a fairly strong base of support in the Muslim middle class. In the past two decades, however, the reformers have been losing the argument in the Islamic world to their rival group, the fundamentalists.

bin Laden: Osama bin Laden (b. 1957), son of one of Saudi Arabia's wealthiest families and founder of the international terrorist organization al-Qaeda, which has been linked to numerous attacks on U.S. targets around the world, including the assaults on September 11, 2001.

Here, in short, is the fundamentalist argument. The Koran promises that if Muslims are faithful to Allah, they will enjoy prosperity in this life and paradise in the next life. According to the fundamentalists, the Muslims were doing this for centuries, and they were invincible. But now, the fundamentalists point out, Islam is not winning any more; in fact, it is losing. What could be the reason for this? From the fundamentalist point of view, the answer is obvious: Muslims are not following the true teaching of Allah! The fundamentalists allege that Muslims have fallen away from the true faith and are mindlessly pursuing the ways of the infidel. The fundamentalists also charge that Islamic countries are now ruled by self-serving despots who serve as puppets for America and the West. The solution, the fundamentalists say, is to purge American troops and Western influence from the Middle East; to overthrow corrupt, pro-Western regimes like ones in Pakistan, Egypt, and Saudi Arabia; and to return to the pure, original teachings of the Koran. Only then, the fundamentalists insist, can Islam recover its lost glory.

One can see, from this portrait, that the fundamentalists are a humiliated people who are seeking to recover ancestral greatness. They are not complete "losers": they are driven by an awareness of moral superiority, combined with political, economic, and military inferiority. Their argument has a powerful appeal to proud Muslims who find it hard to come to terms with their contemporary irrelevance. And so the desert wind of fundamentalism has spread throughout the Middle East. It has replaced Arab nationalism as the most powerful political force in the region.

The success of the fundamentalists in the Muslim world should not blind us from recognizing that their counterattack against America and the West is fundamentally defensive. The fundamentalists know that their civilization does not have the appeal to expand outside its precinct. It's not as if the Muslims were plotting to take, say, Australia. It is the West that is making incursions into Islamic territory, winning converts, and threatening to subvert ancient loyalties and transform a very old way of life. So the fundamentalists are lashing out against this new, largely secular, Western "crusade." Terrorism, their weapon of counterinsurgency, is the weapon of the weak. Terrorism is the international equivalent of that domestic weapon of discontent: the riot. Political scientist Edward Banfield once observed that a riot is a failed revolution. People who know how to take over the government don't throw stones at a bus. Similarly terrorism of the bin Laden variety is a desperate strike against a civilization that the fundamentalists know they have no power to conquer.

But they do have the power to disrupt and terrify the people of America 15 and the West. This is one of their goals, and their attack on September 11, 2001, was quite successful in this regard. But there is a second goal: to unify the Muslim world behind the fundamentalist banner and to foment uprisings against pro-Western regimes. Thus the bin Ladens of the world are waging a two-front war: against Western influence in the Middle East and against pro-Western governments and liberal influences within the Islamic world. So the West is not faced with a pure "clash of civilizations."° It is not "the West" against "Islam." It is a clash of civilizations within the Muslim world. One side or the other will prevail.

So what should American policy be toward the region? It is a great mistake for Americans to believe that their country is hated because it is misunderstood. It is hated because it is understood only too well. Sometimes people say to me, "But the mullahs have a point about American culture. They are right about Jerry Springer."° Yes, they are right about Springer. If we could get them to agree to stop bombing our facilities in return for us shipping them Jerry Springer to do with as they like, we should make the deal tomorrow, and throw in some of Springer's guests. But the Islamic fundamentalists don't just object to the excesses of American liberty: they object to liberty itself. Nor can we appease them by staying out of their world. We live in an age in which the flow of information is virtually unstoppable. We do not have the power to keep our ideals and our culture out of their lives.

Thus there is no alternative to facing their hostility. First, we need to destroy their terrorist training camps and networks. This is not easy to do, because some of these facilities are in countries like Iraq, Iran, Libya, and the Sudan. The U.S. should demand that those countries dismantle their terror networks and stop being incubators of terrorism. If they do not, we should work to get rid of their governments. How this is done is a matter of prudence. In some cases, such as Iraq, the direct use of force might be the answer. In others, such as Iran, the U.S. can capitalize on widespread popular dissatisfaction with the government.[1] Iran has a large middle class, with strong democratic and pro-American elements. But the dissenters are sorely in need of leadership, resources, and an effective strategy to defeat the ruling theocracy.

The U.S. also has to confront the fact that regimes allied with America, such as Pakistan, Egypt, and Saudi Arabia, are undemocratic, corrupt, and repressive. Indeed, the misdoings and tyranny of these regimes

---

"clash of civilizations": The title of Samuel P. Huntington's controversial 1996 book, based on a 1993 article published in *Foreign Affairs* magazine, which argues that the culture of the Western democracies, founded on "individualism, liberalism, constitutionalism, human rights, equality, liberty, [and] the rule of law," will inevitably come into conflict with the non-Western cultures across the globe. **Jerry Springer:** Talk show host known for featuring sexually explicit and violent themes and for instigating brawls among his guests.

strengthen the cause of the fundamentalists, who are able to tap deep veins of popular discontent. How do the regimes deal with this fundamentalist resistance? They subsidize various religious and educational programs administered by the fundamentalists that teach terrorism and hatred of America. By focusing the people's discontent against a foreign target, the United States, the regimes of Saudi Arabia, Egypt, and Pakistan hope to divert attention from their own failings. The United States must make it clear to its Muslim allies that this "solution" is unacceptable. If they want American aid and American support, they must stop funding mosques and schools that promote terrorism and anti-Americanism. Moreover, they must take steps to reduce corruption, expand civil liberties, and enfranchise their people.

In the long term, America's goal is a large and difficult one: to turn Muslim fundamentalists into classical liberals. This does not mean that we want them to stop being Muslims. It does mean, however, that we want them to practice their religion *in the liberal way*. Go to a Promise Keepers° meeting in Washington, D.C., or another of America's big cities. You will see tens of thousands of men singing, praying, hugging, and pledging chastity to their wives. A remarkable sight. These people are mostly evangelical and fundamentalist Christians. They are apt to approach you with the greeting, "Let me tell you what Jesus Christ has meant to my life." They want you to accept Christ, but their appeal is not to force but to consent. They do not say, "Accept Christ or I am going to plunge a dagger into your chest." Even the fundamentalist Christians in the West are liberals: they are practicing Christianity "in the liberal way."

The task of transforming Muslim fundamentalists into classical liber- 20 als will not be an easy one to perform in the Islamic world, where there is no tradition of separating religion and government. We need not require that Islamic countries adopt America's strict form of separation, which prohibits any government involvement in religion. But it is indispensable that Muslim fundamentalists relinquish the use of force for the purpose of spreading Islam. They, too, should appeal to consent. If this seems like a ridiculous thing to ask of Muslims, let us remember that millions of Muslims are already living this way. These are, of course, the Muslim immigrants to Europe and the United States. They are following the teachings of their faith, but most of them understand that they must respect the equal rights of others. They have renounced the *jihad*° of the sword and confine themselves to the *jihad* of the pen and the *jihad* of the

---

Promise Keepers: Nationwide organization of Christian men. *jihad:* Arabic for "struggle," denoting the kind of spiritual effort required of Muslims by the teachings of the Koran, and today frequently misinterpreted as being synonymous with the notion of holy war.

heart. In general, the immigrants are showing the way for Islam to change in the same way that Christianity changed in order to survive and flourish in the modern world.

Whether America can succeed in the mammoth enterprises of stopping terrorism and liberalizing the Islamic world depends a good deal on the people in the Middle East and a great deal on us. Fundamentalist Islam has now succeeded Soviet communism as the organizing theme of American foreign policy. Thus our newest challenge comes from a very old adversary. The West has been battling Islam for more than a thousand years. It is possible that this great battle has now been resumed, and that over time we will come to see the seventy-year battle against communism as a short detour.

But are we up to the challenge? There are some who think we are not. They believe that Americans are a divided people: not even a nation, but a collection of separate tribes. The multiculturalists actually proclaim this to be a good thing, and they strive to encourage people to affirm their differences. If, however, the multiculturalists are right in saying that "all we have in common is our diversity," then it follows that we have *nothing* in common. This does not bode well for the national unity that is a prerequisite to fighting against a determined foe. If the ethnic group is the primary unit of allegiance, why should we make sacrifices for people who come from ethnic groups other than our own? Doesn't a nation require a loyalty that transcends ethnic particularity?

Of course it does. And fortunately America does command such a loyalty. The multiculturalists are simply wrong about America, and despite their best efforts to promote a politics of difference, Americans remain a united people with shared values and a common way of life. There are numerous surveys of national attitudes that confirm this,[2] but it is most easily seen when Americans are abroad. Hang out at a Parisian café, for instance, and you can easily pick out the Americans: they dress the same way, eat the same food, listen to the same music, and laugh at the same jokes. However different their personalities, Americans who run into each other in remote places always become fast friends. And even the most jaded Americans who spend time in other countries typically return home with an intense feeling of relief and a newfound appreciation for the routine satisfactions of American life.

It is easy to forget the cohesiveness of a free people in times of peace and prosperity. New York is an extreme example of the great pandemonium that results when countless individuals and groups pursue their diverse interests in the normal course of life. In a crisis, however, the national tribe comes together, and this is exactly what happened in New York and the rest of America following the terrorist attack. Suddenly political, regional, and racial differences evaporated; suddenly Americans stood as one. This surprised many people, including many Americans, who did not realize that, despite the centrifugal forces that pull us in different directions, there is a deep national unity that holds us together.

Unity, however, is not sufficient for the challenges ahead. America also needs the moral self-confidence to meet its adversary. This is the true lesson of Vietnam: Americans cannot succeed unless they are convinced that they are fighting on behalf of the good. There are some, as we have seen, who fear that America no longer stands for what is good. They allege that American freedom produces a licentious, degenerate society that is scarcely worth defending. We return, therefore, to the question of what America is all about, and whether this country, in its dedication to the principle of freedom, subverts the higher principle of virtue.

So what about virtue? The fundamental difference between the society that the Islamic fundamentalists want and the society that Americans have is that the Islamic activists seek a country where the life of the citizens is *directed by others*, while Americans live in a nation where the life of the citizens is largely *self-directed*. The central goal of American freedom is self-reliance: the individual is placed in the driver's seat of his own life. The Islamic fundamentalists presume the moral superiority of the externally directed life on the grounds that it is aimed at virtue. The self-directed life, however, also seeks virtue—virtue realized not through external command but, as it were, "from within." The real question is: which type of society is more successful in achieving the goal of virtue?

Let us concede at the outset that, in a free society, freedom will frequently be used badly. Freedom, by definition, includes freedom to do good or evil, to act nobly or basely. Thus we should not be surprised that there is a considerable amount of vice, licentiousness, and vulgarity in a free society. Given the warped timber of humanity, freedom is simply an expression of human flaws and weaknesses. But if freedom brings out the worst in people, it also brings out the best. The millions of Americans who live decent, praiseworthy lives deserve our highest admiration because they have opted for the good when the good is not the only available option. Even amidst the temptations that a rich and free society offers, they have remained on the straight path. Their virtue has special luster because it is freely chosen. The free society does not guarantee virtue any more than it guarantees happiness. But it allows for the pursuit of both, a pursuit rendered all the more meaningful and profound because success is not guaranteed: it has to be won through personal striving.

By contrast, the externally directed life that Islamic fundamentalists seek undermines the possibility of virtue. If the supply of virtue is insufficient in self-directed societies, it is almost nonexistent in externally directed societies because coerced virtues are not virtues at all. Consider

291

the woman who is required to wear a veil. There is no modesty in this, because the woman is being compelled. Compulsion cannot produce virtue: it can only produce the outward semblance of virtue. And once the reins of coercion are released, as they were for the terrorists who lived in the United States, the worst impulses of human nature break loose. Sure enough, the deeply religious terrorists spent their last days in gambling dens, bars, and strip clubs, sampling the licentious lifestyle they were about to strike out against.[3] In this respect they were like the Spartans,° who—Plutarch° tells us—were abstemious in public but privately coveted wealth and luxury. In externally directed societies, the absence of freedom signals the absence of virtue. Thus the free society is not simply richer, more varied, and more fun: it is also morally superior to the externally directed society. There is no reason for anyone, least of all the cultural conservatives, to feel hesitant about rising to the defense of our free society.

Even if Americans possess the necessary unity and self-confidence, there is also the question of nerve. Some people, at home and abroad, are skeptical that America can endure a long war against Islamic fundamentalism because they consider Americans to be, well, a little bit soft. As one of bin Laden's lieutenants put it, "Americans love life, and we love death." His implication was that Americans do not have the stomach for the kind of deadly, drawn-out battle that the militant Muslims are ready to fight. This was also the attitude of the Taliban. "Come and get us," they taunted America. "We are ready for *jihad*. Come on, you bunch of weenies." And then the Taliban was hit by a juggernaut of American firepower that caused their regime to disintegrate within a couple of weeks. Soon the Taliban leadership had headed for the caves, or for Pakistan, leaving their captured soldiers to beg for their lives. Even the call of *jihad* and the promise of martyrdom could not stop these hard men from—in the words of Mullah Omar° himself—"running like chickens with their heads cut off." This is not to say that Americans should expect all its battles against terrorism and Islamic fundamentalism to be so short and so conclusive. But neither should America's enemies expect Americans to show any less firmness or fierceness than they themselves possess.

. . . The firefighters and policemen who raced into the burning towers 30 of the World Trade Center showed that their lives were dedicated to something higher than "self-fulfillment." The same can be said of Todd Beamer and his fellow passengers who forced the terrorists to crash United Airlines Flight 93 in the woods of western Pennsylvania rather

Spartans: In Classical Greece, the nondemocratic adversaries of the Athenians. **Plutarch:** Greek essayist and biographer (46–119). **Mullah Omar:** Leader of the Taliban (b. 1959).

than flying on to Camp David or the White House. . . . The military has its own culture, which is closer to that of the firefighters and policemen, and also bears an affinity with the culture of the "greatest generation."° Only now are those Americans who grew up during the 1960s coming to appreciate the virtues—indeed the indispensability—of this older, sturdier culture of courage, nobility, and sacrifice. It is this culture that will protect the liberties of all Americans. . . .

As the American founders knew, America is a new kind of society that produces a new kind of human being. That human being—confident, self-reliant, tolerant, generous, future oriented—is a vast improvement over the wretched, servile, fatalistic, and intolerant human being that traditional societies have always produced, and that Islamic societies produce now. In America, the life we are given is not as important as the life we make. Ultimately, America is worthy of our love and sacrifice because, more than any other society, it makes possible the good life, and the life that is good.

American is the greatest, freest, and most decent society in existence. It is an oasis of goodness in a desert of cynicism and barbarism. This country, once an experiment unique in the world, is now the last best hope for the world. By making sacrifices for America, and by our willingness to die for her, we bind ourselves by invisible cords to those great patriots who fought at Yorktown, Gettysburg, and Iwo Jima,° and we prove ourselves worthy of the blessings of freedom. By defeating the terrorist threat posed by Islamic fundamentalism, we can protect the American way of life while once again redeeming humanity from a global menace. History will view America as a great gift to the world, a gift that Americans today must preserve and cherish.

Notes

1. See, for example, Amy Waldman, "In Iran, an Angry Generation Longs for Jobs, More Freedom, and Power," *New York Times*, 7 December 2001.

2. See, for example, John Fetto and Rebecca Gardyn, "An All-American Melting Pot," *American Demographics*, July 2001, 8. The survey was conducted by Maritz Marketing Research.

3. Diane McWhorter, "Terrorists Tasted Lusty Lifestyle They So Despised," *USA Today*, 26 September 2001, 11-A.

the "greatest generation": Refers to the generation that fought in World War II, supposedly distinguished from following generations by their spirit of service and self-sacrifice.   **Yorktown, Gettysburg, and Iwo Jima:** Sites of famous American victories during, respectively, the American Revolution, the Civil War, and World War II.

FRANCINE PROSE [b. 1947]

The Wages of Sin

Born in Brooklyn, New York, **Francine Prose** is a 1968 graduate of
Radcliffe College. Prose has authored numerous novels and collections
of short stories including *The Blue Angel* (2001), a finalist for the
National Book Award, and *A Changed Man* (2005), which won the Dayton Literary Peace Prize. Two of her novels—*The Glorious Ones* (1974)
and *Household Saints* (1981)—were adapted for the stage and film,
respectively. While a prolific fiction writer, Prose has also published
several works of nonfiction including *Gluttony* (2003), from which the
following selection is excerpted, and *Reading Like a Writer* (2006), a
New York Times Notable Book of the Year. She has been honored with
numerous awards and grants, including the 2008 Edith Wharton
Achievement Award for Literature, and in 2007, she was elected president of the PEN American Center. Currently a Bard College Distinguished Writer in Residence, Prose lives and writes in New York City.

In "The Wages of Sin," Prose, taking aim at our current fixation on
food, dieting, and body image, contemplates whether ours has become
a culture in which overeating stands as the preeminent sign of our
moral and physical failure.

More and more often, we read articles and hear TV commentators advocating government intervention to protect us from the greed of a corporate culture that profits from our unhealthy attraction to sugary and fatty
foods. Legal experts discuss the feasibility of mounting class action
suits—on the model of the recent and ongoing litigation against so-called
big tobacco companies—against fast-food restaurants, junk-food manufacturers, and advertisers who target children with ads for salty fried
snacks and brightly colored candy masquerading as breakfast cereal.

What's slightly more disturbing is the notion that not only do fat
people need to be monitored, controlled, and saved from their gluttonous impulses, but that we need to be saved from them—that certain
forms of social control might be required to help the overweight resist
temptation. Writing in the *San Francisco Chronicle*, essayist Ruth Rosen

Francine Prose, "The Wages of Sin." From *Gluttony*, pp. 67–75. Copyright © 2003 by
Francine Prose. Reprinted by permission of Oxford University Press, Inc.

has suggested that such actions might be motivated by compassion for such innocent victims as the parents of a child whose overweight helped lead to diabetes, or the child of a parent who died from weight-related causes. Of course the bottom line is concern for our pocketbooks, for the cost—shared by the wider population—of treating those who suffer from obesity-related ailments. As a partial remedy, Rosen proposes that schools and employers might forbid the sale of junk food on campus and in offices. Finally, she suggests that, in a more glorious future, the host who serves his guests greasy potato chips and doughnuts will incur the same horrified disapproval as the smoker who lights up—and blows smoke in our faces.

Rosen is not alone in her belief that legislation may be required to regulate the social costs of overeating. A recent item on CBS worriedly considered the alarming growth in the number of overweight and obese young people—a group that now comprises 14 percent of American children. According to the news clip, overweight was soon expected to surpass cigarette smoking as the major preventable cause of death: each year, 350,000 people die of obesity-related causes. Thirteen billion dollars is spent annually on food ads directed at children, and four out of five ads are for some excessively sugary or fatty product. The problem is undeniable, but once more the projected solution gives one pause; several interviewees raised the possibility of suing the purveyors of potato chips and candy bars. How far we have come from Saint Augustine and John Cassian and Chrysostom, taking it for granted that the struggle against temptation would be waged in the glutton's heart and mind— and not, presumably, in the law courts.

You're so fat when they pierced your ears, they had to use a harpoon.

You're so fat you've got to put on lipstick with a paint roller.

In studies that have examined the causes and motives behind the stigmatization of the overweight, such prejudice has been found to derive from the widely accepted notion that fat people are at fault, responsible for their weight and appearance, that they are self-indulgent, sloppy, lazy, morally lax, lacking in the qualities of self-denial and impulse control that our society (still so heavily influenced by the legacy of Puritanism) values and rewards. In a 1978 book, *The Seven Deadly Sins: Society and Evil,* sociologist Stanford M. Lyman takes a sociocultural approach to the reasons why we are so harsh in our condemnation of the so-called glutton.

The apparently voluntary character of food gluttony serves to point up why it is more likely to seem "criminal" than sick, an act of moral defalcation rather than medical pathology. Although gluttony is not proscribed by the criminal law, it partakes of some of the social sanctions and moral understandings that govern orientations toward those who commit crimes. . . . Gluttony is an excessive *self*-indulgence. Even in its disrespect for the body it overvalues the ego that it slavishly satisfies.[1]

Most of us would no doubt claim that we are too sensible, compassionate, and enlightened to feel prejudice against the obese. We would never tell the sorts of cruel jokes scattered throughout this chapter. But let's consider how we feel when we've taken our already cramped seat in coach class on the airplane and suddenly our seatmate appears—a man or woman whose excessive weight promises to make our journey even more uncomfortable than we'd anticipated. Perhaps, contemplating a trip of this sort, we might find ourselves inclined to support Southwest Airline's discriminatory two-seats-per-large-passenger rule. Meanwhile, as we try not to stare at our sizable traveling companion, we might as well be the medieval monks glaring at the friar who's helped himself to an extra portion. For what's involved in both cases is our notion of one's proper share, of surfeit and shortage—not enough food in one case, not enough space in the other.

"The glutton is also noticeable as a defiler of his own body space. His appetite threatens to engulf the spaces of others as he spreads out to take more than one person's ordinary allotment of territory. If he grows too large, he may no longer fit into ordinary chairs . . . and require special arrangements in advance of his coming."[2] The glutton's "crime" is crossing boundaries that we jealously guard and that are defined by our most primitive instincts: hunger, territoriality—that is to say, survival.

So we come full circle back to the language of crime and innocence, sin and penance, guilt and punishment—a view of overweight frequently adopted and internalized by the obese themselves. "Many groups of dieters whom I studied," writes Natalie Allon, "believed that fatness was the outcome of immoral self-indulgence. Group dieters used much religious language in considering themselves bad or good dieters—words such as sinner, saint, devil, angel, guilt, transgression, confession, absolution, diet Bible—as they partook of the rituals of group dieting."[3] Nor does the association between gluttony and the language of religion exist solely in the minds of dieters, the obese, and the food-obsessed. In fact it's extremely common to speak of having overeaten as having "been bad"; rich, fattening foods are advertised as being "sinfully delicious"; and probably most of us have thought or confessed the fact that we've felt "guilty" for having eaten more than we should have.

Like the members of other Twelve-Step programs, and not unlike the medieval gluttons who must have felt inspired to repent and pray for divine assistance in resisting temptation, the members of Overeaters Anonymous employ the terminology of religion. *Lifeline*, the magazine of Overeaters Anonymous, is filled with stories of healing and recovery, first-person accounts in which God was asked to intercede, to provide a spiritual awakening, and to remove the dangerous and destructive flaws from the recovering overeater's character.

Routinely, the capacity to achieve sobriety and abstinence—which for OA members means the ability to restrict one's self to three healthy and sensible meals a day—is credited to divine mercy and love, and to the good effects of an intimate and sustaining relationship with God. In one testimonial, a woman reports that coming to her first meeting and identifying herself as a recovering compulsive eater was more difficult for her than to say that she was a shoplifter, a serial killer, or a prostitute. Only after admitting that she was powerless over food and asking for the help of a higher power was she at last able to end her unhappy career as a "grazer and a binger."

For perhaps obvious reasons, the term "gluttony" is now rarely used as a synonym for compulsive eating. Yet Stanford Lyman conflates the two to make the point that our culture's attitude toward the obese is not unlike an older society's view of the gluttonous sinner:

> Societal opposition to gluttony manifests itself in a variety of social control devices and institutional arrangements. Although rarely organized as a group, very fat individuals at times seem to form a much beset minority, objects of calculating discrimination and bitter prejudice. Stigmatized because their addiction to food is so visible in its consequences, the obese find themselves ridiculed, rejected, and repulsed by many of those who do not overindulge. Children revile them on the streets, persons of average size refuse to date, dance, or dine with them, and many businesses, government, and professional associations refuse to employ them. So great is the pressure to conform to the dictates of the slimness culture in America that occasionally an overweight person speaks out, pointing to the similarities of his condition to that of racial and national minorities.[4]

Indeed, the overweight have found a forum in which to speak out, at 10 the meetings, conventions, and in the bimonthly newsletter sponsored by NAAFA—the National Association to Advance Fat Acceptance. A recent issue of the newsletter, available on the internet, calls for readers to write to the government to protest the National Institute of Health's ongoing studies of normal-sized children to find out if obesity might have a metabolic basis. There are directions for giving money and establishing a living trust to benefit NAAFA, reviews of relevant new books, a report on the Trunk Sale at a NAAFA gathering in San Francisco, an update on the struggle to force auto manufacturers to provide seat belts that can save the lives of passengers who weigh over 215 pounds, and an article on the problems—the fear of appearing in public in a bathing suit, the narrow ladders that often provide the only access to swimming pools—that make it more difficult for the overweight to get the exercise that they need. There is a brief discussion of how obesity should be defined, and another about the effectiveness of behavioral psychotherapy in helping patients lose weight. Finally, there are grateful letters from readers whose lives have been improved by the support and sustenance they gain from belonging to NAAFA.

Equally fervent—if somewhat less affirmative and forgiving—are the gospel tracts, also available on-line. One of the most heartfelt and persuasive is the work of a preacher identified only as George Clark:

> After conducting healing campaigns and mailing out thousands of anointed handkerchiefs—since 1930—I have learned that the greatest physical cause of sickness among the people of God is coming from this lust for overindulgence in eating. . . . Tens of thousands of truly converted people are sick and are suffering with heart trouble coming from high blood pressure and other ailments which result from overeating. . . . Did you ever wonder why artists have never depicted any of Jesus' disciples as being overweight or of the fleshy type? No one could have followed Jesus very long and remained overweight. . . . If eating too much has brought on high blood pressure, heart trouble, or many of the other diseases which come from being overweight, then God requires a reduction in your eating.

Given our perhaps misguided sense of living in a secular society, it's startling to find that our relationship with food is still so commonly translated directly into the language of God and the devil, of sin and repentance. But why should we be surprised, when we are constantly being reminded that our feelings about our diet and our body can be irrational, passionate, and closer to the province of faith and superstition than that of reason and science?

[2003]

Notes

1. Stanford M. Lyman, *The Seven Deadly Sins: Society and Evil* (New York: St. Martin's Press, 1978), 220.

2. Ibid., 223.

3. Benjamin Wolman, ed., *Psychological Aspects of Obesity: A Handbook* (New York: Van Nostrand Reinhold, 1982), 148.

4. Lyman, *Seven Deadly Sins*, 218.

Bibliography

Albala, Ken. *Eating Right in the Renaissance.* Berkeley: University of California Press, 2002.

Augustine, Saint. *The Confessions of Saint Augustine,* trans. Edward B. Pusey, D. D. New York: The Modern Library, 1949.

Bell, Rudoph M. *Holy Anorexia.* Chicago: University of Chicago Press, 1985.

Chaucer, Geoffrey. *The Works of Geoffrey Chaucer,* ed. F. N. Robinson. Boston: Houghton Mifflin, 1957.

Chernin, Kim. *The Obsession.* New York: Harper Perennial, 1981.

Chesterton, G. K. *Saint Thomas Aquinas.* New York: Image Books, Doubleday, 2001.

Fielding, Henry. *Tom Jones.* New York: The Modern Library, 1994.

Fisher, M. F. K. *The Art of Eating.* New York: Vintage, 1976.

Lyman, Stanford M. *The Seven Deadly Sins: Society and Evil.* New York: St. Martin's Press, 1978.

Petronius. *The Satyricon,* trans. William Arrowsmith. New York: Meridian, 1994.

Pleij, Herman. *Dreaming of Cockaigne,* trans. Diane Webb. New York: Columbia University Press, 2001.

Rabelais, François. *Gargantua and Pantagruel,* trans. Burton Raffel. New York: W. W. Norton, 1991.

Roth, Geneen. *When Food Is Love.* New York: Plume, 1991.

Schwartz, Hillel. *Never Satisfied: A Cultural History of Fantasies and Fat.* New York: The Free Press, 1986.

Shaw, Teresa M. *The Burden of the Flesh: Fasting and Sexuality in Early Christianity.* Minneapolis: Fortress Press, 1996.

Spenser, Edmund. *The Faerie Queene.* New York: E. P. Dutton & Company, 1964.

Wolman, Benjamin, ed., with Stephen DeBerry, editorial associate. *Psychological Aspects of Obesity: A Handbook.* New York: Van Nostrand Reinhold, 1982.

HENRY LOUIS GATES JR.   [b. 1950]

A Richer American Identity

Henry Louis Gates Jr. was born in Keyser, West Virginia. Despite barriers of culture, race, and geography, Gates attended Yale University and Cambridge University, where he became the first black to earn a Ph.D. In reappraising the literature of African American authors in the United States, Gates combined methods of archeology and literary criticism to formulate a new black critical theory. In *Black Literature and Literary Theory*, published in 1984 and coedited by Gates, he rejects the notion of a traditional Eurocentric canon, arguing for an expanded, multicultural vision of art, music, and literature. Gates's attempts to redefine and expand the canon have fueled most of his significant achievements. In 1991, Gates became chair of the Afro-American Studies Department at Harvard University, energizing the department by attracting prominent black intellectuals. He created the television documentary *The Image of the Black in the Western Imagination*. In conjunction with Microsoft, Gates produced a digitalized black encyclopedia, Encarta Africana, along with a Web site designed to provide a black equivalent to the *Encyclopedia Britannica*. Gates's published works include *The Signifying Monkey: Towards a Theory of Afro-American Literary Criticism* (1988), *Loose Canons* (1992), and numerous scholarly and mainstream articles.

Inspired by *Roots*, a 1977 television miniseries, Gates explores how family history is essential to identity in "A Richer American Identity." He researched the genealogies and DNA profiles of eight well-known African Americans, including Oprah Winfrey and Quincy Jones. However, Gate's work is personal as well; he sought to track down both his white and African American ancestors. This material formed the basis for this essay and his four-part television series, *African American Lives* (2006).

Since 1977, when I sat riveted every night for a week in front of my TV, I have had *Roots* envy. Even if scholars remain deeply skeptical about his methodology, Alex Haley went to his grave believing that he had found

Henry Louis Gates Jr., "My Yiddish Mama." Originally published in *Village Voice Literary Supplement*. Copyright © 1988 by Henry Louis Gates Jr. Reprinted by permission of the author.

the ethnic group from which his African ancestors originated before surviving the dreaded Middle Passage.

Two years before, I proudly told a fellow student at Cambridge, an Anglo-Ghanaian, that I could trace my slave ancestors back to 1819, the birth date of Jane Gates, my paternal great-great-grandmother. I wondered if he could do better?

He invited me to accompany him to the University Library, where, buried deep in the stacks, he found a copy of Burke's Peerage, then walked me through his mother's English ancestry with certainty back to one Richard Crispe who died in 1575, and who, the book said "probably" descended from William Crispe, who had died in 1207. His father's side, members of the Asante people in Ghana, he could trace to the 17th century. The roots of my *Roots* envy?

After years of frustration, I determined to do something about it. So I decided to invite eight prominent African Americans to allow their DNA to be tested and their family histories to be researched for a documentary film. When the paper trail would end, inevitably, in the abyss of slavery, we would then try to find their African roots through science.

Having been involved in after-school programs, I was hoping to get   5
inner-city school kids engaged by the wonders of both genetics and archival research.

But I had ulterior motives, too. I wanted to find my white patriarch, the father of Jane Gates's children. Maybe genetics could verify the family legend that the father of Jane's children was an Irish man from Cresaptown, Maryland, a slave-holder named Samuel Brady. Perhaps I could give Jane her Thomas Jefferson-Sally Hemings moment!

I also had hopes for my African origins. Throughout my adult life, I've always been drawn to Nigeria's Yoruba culture — to its cuisine, its legends, its rhythms and its songs. As a Fela Ransome-Kuti album played in my head, I wondered whether geneticists could determine that I had physical, not only spiritual, affinities to the Yoruba.

Our genealogists as well as our geneticists were given a tough assignment. Five generations ago, each of us has 32 ancestors, or two to the fifth power. If we go back 10 generations, or 300 years, each of us has 1,024 theoretical ancestors, or two to the 10th power. Even with genetics, we can only trace two of our family lines. The first African slaves arrived in Virginia in 1619; the slaves were freed in 1865, and appeared with two legal names for the first time in the 1870 census. Penetrating the name barrier of 1870 required detailed and imaginative sleuthing through the records of slave-holders, praying that they somehow mentioned one of their slaves by first name, in wills, tax records or estate division papers.

The stories that we found are not the sort found in textbooks, which tend either to recreate Black History through the narratives of great women and men, or else through broad social movements. We were able to find stirring stories of heretofore anonymous individuals who made heroic contributions against seemingly insurmountable odds. If the promise of America was the right to own land, very few blacks were able to do so before the middle of the 20th century. But some did.

Oprah Winfrey's great-great-grandfather, Constantine Winfrey, a farm 10 worker in Mississippi, had the audacity to approach a white man, John Watson, in 1876, and make a wager: If he picked 10 bales of cotton in one year, Watson would give Winfrey 80 acres of his land in return. (In 1870, a bale of cotton weighed 500 pounds.) On June 21, 1881, a property deed recorded the land exchange between the two. Constantine is listed in the 1870 census as illiterate; 10 years later, he had learned to read and write. And when, in 1906, the local "colored school" was slated for destruction, Constantine arranged to save it by having it moved to this property.

Chris Tucker's great-great-grandfather, Theodore Arthur Bryant Sr., sold off parcels of his land to his black neighbors for below-market prices so that they would not join the Great Migration to the North, thereby saving the black community of Flat Rock, Georgia.

Whoopi Goldberg's great-great-grandparents, William and Elsa Washington, in 1878 received 104.5 acres in Alachua County, Florida, under the Southern Homestead Act of 1866. Less than 10% of black petitioners in Florida received land. "My country 'tis of thee," Whoopi exclaimed, when she received this news. "My country."

In the case of the astronaut Mae Jemison, we were able, incredibly, to trace three of her family lines deep into slavery, including discovering both a fourth great-grandmother and a fourth or fifth great-grandfather. Four of our subjects are descended from people who owned property in the 1800s, two well before the Civil War, and two more by 1881. The latter two, freed in 1865, in effect got their 40 acres, if not the mule.

Our genetic research also yielded a rich panoply of results, and a few surprises. My subjects share common ancestry with, among others, members of the Mbundu of Angola, the Kpelle of Liberia, the Tikar of Cameroon, the Igbo of Nigeria, the Mandinka and the Pepel of Guinea-Bissau, the Makua of Mozambique, and the Bamileke of Cameroon. I had expected the revelation of their African roots to form the dramatic climax of our research. But our subjects' reactions to their putative genetic identities remained somewhat abstract.

What really stirred them was the light shed on their American heritage, 15 their known world, as Edward Jones put it. It was a world they could touch and imagine, through the branches of their family trees. Genealogy trumped genetics. It was as if Africa, as the poet Langston Hughes wrote, was "so long, so far away." Roots, like charity, start at home.

Contrary to conventional wisdom, and contrary to those who worry about "the geneticization of identity," our sense of identity—in this case at least—seems to be more deeply rooted in the histories of family members we can name than in anonymous ancestors emerging out of the dense shadows of an African past, unveiled through a process admittedly still in its infancy. For my subjects, genealogy seems to have been a way of staking a claim on a richer American identity, an identity established through individual triumphs like the attainment of literacy and the purchasing of land.

What of my own case of "Roots" envy? We advertised for, and found, two male descendants of Samuel Brady, and compared their Y-DNA with mine. My haplotype, common in Western Ireland and the Netherlands, has as much in common genetically with Samuel Brady as it does, I suppose, with half of the males in Galway and Amsterdam. So much for that bit of family lore.

On the other hand, our genealogical research uncovered, to my astonishment, one of my fifth great-grandfathers and two fourth great-grandfathers, two born in the middle of the 18th century. I learned that one, John Redman, a Free Negro, even fought in the American Revolution. Despite the fact that we didn't find Jane Gates's children's father, we believe that we have found her mother, a slave, born circa 1799.

As for my mitochondrial DNA, my mother's mother's mother's lineage? Would it be Yoruba, as I fervently hoped? My Fela Ransome-Kuti fantasy was not exactly borne out. A number of exact matches turned up, leading straight back to that African Kingdom called Northern Europe, to the genes of (among others) a female Ashkenazi Jew. Maybe it was time to start listening to "My Yiddishe Mama."

[2006]

303

WILLIAM J. BENNETT [b. 1943]

Should Drugs Be Legalized?

Born in Brooklyn, New York, **William Bennett** has been a prominent
public figure since the early 1980s. Bennett received a B.A. from
Williams College, a Ph.D. from the University of Texas at Austin, and a
law degree from Harvard Law School. After running the National
Humanities Center for five years, Bennett was appointed by President
Ronald Reagan first as Director of the National Endowment for the
Humanities, and later as Secretary of Education. In 1988, President
George H.W. Bush appointed him as Director of the Office of National
Drug Control Policy, a position also known as "drug czar." The author
and editor of numerous books, including *The Book of Virtues: A Treasury of Great Moral Stories* (1996), Bennett has not been without con-
troversy. In 2005, he made a questionable hypothetical link between
aborting black males and a drop in crime. Bennett is currently the
Washington Fellow of the Claremont Institute, a contributor to CNN,
and the host of his own radio show, *Morning in America.*

In his essay "Should Drugs Be Legalized?," Bennett discusses, then
refutes, arguments in favor of the legalization of drugs. He asserts that
drug use has dropped since the 1970s, which proves that anti-drug
programs are working, and that the fight must continue.

Since I took command of the war on drugs, I have learned from former
Secretary of State George Schultz that our concept of fighting drugs is
"flawed." The only thing to do, he says, is to "make it possible for addicts
to buy drugs at some regulated place." Conservative commentator William
F. Buckley, Jr., suggests I should be "fatalistic" about the flood of cocaine
from South America and simply "let it in." Syndicated columnist Mike
Royko contends it would be easier to sweep junkies out of the gutters
"than to fight a hopeless war" against the narcotics that send them there.
Labeling our efforts "bankrupt," federal judge Robert W. Sweet opts for
legalization, saying, "If our society can learn to stop using butter, it should
be able to cut down on cocaine."

Flawed, fatalistic, hopeless, bankrupt! I never realized surrender was
so fashionable until I assumed this post.

William Bennett, "Should Drugs Be Legalized?" from *Reader's Digest*, March 1990.
Reprinted by permission of William Bennett.

Though most Americans are overwhelmingly determined to go toe-to-toe with the foreign drug lords and neighborhood pushers, a small minority believe that enforcing drug laws imposes greater costs on society than do drugs themselves. Like addicts seeking immediate euphoria, the legalizers want peace at any price, even though it means the inevitable proliferation of a practice that degrades, impoverishes and kills.

I am acutely aware of the burdens drug enforcement places upon us. It consumes economic resources we would like to use elsewhere. It is sometimes frustrating, thankless and often dangerous. But the consequences of *not* enforcing drug laws would be far more costly. Those consequences involve the intrinsically destructive nature of drugs and the toll they exact from our society in hundreds of thousands of lost and broken lives...human potential never realized...time stolen from families and jobs...precious spiritual and economic resources squandered.

That is precisely why virtually every civilized society has found it nec- 5
essary to exert some form of control over mind-altering substances and why this war is so important. Americans feel up to their hips in drugs now. They would be up to their necks under legalization.

Even limited experiments in drug legalization have shown that when drugs are more widely available, addiction skyrockets. In 1975 Italy liberalized its drug law and now has one of the highest heroin-related death rates in Western Europe. In Alaska, where marijuana was decriminalized in 1975, the easy atmosphere has increased usage of the drug, particularly among children. Nor does it stop there. Some Alaskan school-children now tout "coca puffs," marijuana cigarettes laced with cocaine.

Many legalizers concede that drug legalization might increase use, but they shrug off the matter. "It may well be that there would be more addicts, and I would regret that result," says Nobel laureate economist Milton Friedman. The late Harvard Medical School psychiatry professor Norman Zinberg, a longtime proponent of "responsible" drug use, admitted that "use of now illicit drugs would certainly increase. Also, casualties probably would increase."

In fact, Dr. Herbert D. Kleber of Yale University, my deputy in charge of demand reduction, predicts legalization might cause "a five-to-sixfold increase" in cocaine use. But legalizers regard this as a necessary price for the "benefits" of legalization. What benefits?

1. *Legalization will take the profit out of drugs.* The result supposedly will be the end of criminal drug pushers and the big foreign drug wholesalers, who will turn to other enterprises because nobody will need to make furtive and dangerous trips to his local pusher.

But what, exactly, would the brave new world of legalized drugs look 10
like? Buckley stresses that "adults get to buy the stuff at carefully regulated

stores." (Would you want one in *your* neighborhood?) Others, like Friedman, suggest we sell the drugs at "ordinary retail outlets."

Former City University of New York sociologist Georgette Bennett assures us that "brand-name competition will be prohibited" and that strict quality control and proper labeling will be overseen by the Food and Drug Administration. In a touching egalitarian note, she adds that "free drugs will be provided at government clinics" for addicts too poor to buy them.

Almost all the legalizers point out that the price of drugs will fall, even though the drugs will be heavily taxed. Buckley, for example, argues that somehow federal drugstores will keep the price "low enough to discourage a black market but high enough to accumulate a surplus to be used for drug education."

Supposedly, drug sales will generate huge amounts of revenue, which will then be used to tell the public not to use drugs and to treat those who don't listen.

In reality, this tax would only allow government to *share* the drug profits now garnered by criminals. Legalizers would have to tax drugs heavily in order to pay for drug education and treatment programs. Criminals could undercut the official price and still make huge profits. What alternative would the government have? Cut the price until it was within the lunch-money budget of the average sixth-grade student?

2. *Legalization will eliminate the black market.* Wrong. And not just 15 because the regulated prices could be undercut. Many legalizers admit that drugs such as crack or PCP are simply too dangerous to allow the shelter of the law. Thus criminals will provide what the government will not. "As long as drugs that people very much want remain illegal, a black market will exist," says legalization advocate David Boaz of the libertarian Cato Institute.

Look at crack. In powdered form, cocaine was an expensive indulgence. But street chemists found that a better and far less expensive — and far more dangerous — high could be achieved by mixing cocaine with baking soda and heating it. Crack was born, and "cheap" coke invaded low-income communities with furious speed.

An ounce of powdered cocaine might sell on the street for $1200. That same ounce can produce 370 vials of crack at $10 each. Ten bucks seems like a cheap hit, but crack's intense ten- to 15-minute high is followed by an unbearable depression. The user wants more crack, thus starting a rapid and costly descent into addiction.

If government drugstores do not stock crack, addicts will find it in the clandestine market or simply bake it themselves from their legally purchased cocaine.

Currently crack is being laced with insecticides and animal tranquilizers to heighten its effect. Emergency rooms are now warned to expect victims of "sandwiches" and "moon rocks," life-threatening smokable mixtures of heroin and crack. Unless the government is prepared to sell these deadly variations of dangerous drugs, it will perpetuate a criminal black market by default.

And what about children and teen-agers? They would obviously be 20 barred from drug purchases, just as they are prohibited from buying beer and liquor. But pushers will continue to cater to these young customers with the old, favorite come-ons—a couple of free fixes to get them hooked. And what good will anti-drug education be when these youngsters observe their older brothers and sisters, parents and friends lighting up and shooting up with government permission?

Legalization will give us the worst of both worlds: millions of *new* drug users and a thriving criminal black market.

3. *Legalization will dramatically reduce crime.* "It is the high price of drugs that leads addicts to robbery, murder and other crimes," says Ira Glasser, executive director of the American Civil Liberties Union. A study by the Cato Institute concludes: "Most, if not all, 'drug-related murders' are the result of drug prohibition."

But researchers tell us that many drug-related felonies are committed by people involved in crime *before* they started taking drugs. The drugs, so routinely available in criminal circles, make the criminals more violent and unpredictable.

Certainly there are some kill-for-a-fix crimes, but does any rational person believe that a cut-rate price for drugs at a government outlet will stop such psychopathic behavior? The fact is that under the influence of drugs, normal people do not act normally, and abnormal people behave in chilling and horrible ways. DEA agents told me about a teen-age addict in Manhattan who was smoking crack when he sexually abused and caused permanent internal injuries to his one-month-old daughter.

Children are among the most frequent victims of violent, drug-related 25 crimes that have nothing to do with the cost of acquiring the drugs. In Philadelphia in 1987 more than half the child-abuse fatalities involved at least one parent who was a heavy drug user. Seventy-three percent of the child-abuse deaths in New York City in 1987 involved parental drug use.

In my travels to the ramparts of the drug war, I have seen nothing to support the legalizers' argument that lower drug prices would reduce crime. Virtually everywhere I have gone, police and DEA agents have told me that crime rates are highest where crack is cheapest.

4. *Drug use should be legal since users only harm themselves.* Those who believe this should stand beside the medical examiner as he counts the 36 bullet wounds in the shattered corpse of a three-year-old who happened to get in the way of his mother's drug-crazed boyfriend. They should visit the babies abandoned by cocaine-addicted mothers—infants

who already carry the ravages of addiction in their own tiny bodies. They should console the devastated relatives of the nun who worked in a homeless shelter and was stabbed to death by a crack addict enraged that she would not stake him to a fix.

Do drug addicts only harm themselves? Here is a former cocaine addict describing the compulsion that quickly draws even the most "responsible" user into irresponsible behavior: "Everything is about getting high, and any means necessary to get there becomes rational. If it means stealing something from somebody close to you, lying to your family, borrowing money from people you know you can't pay back, writing checks you know you can't cover, you do all those things—things that are totally against everything you have ever believed in."

Society pays for this behavior, and not just in bigger insurance premiums, losses from accidents and poor job performance. We pay in the loss of a priceless social currency as families are destroyed, trust between friends is betrayed and promising careers are never fulfilled. I cannot imagine sanctioning behavior that would increase that toll.

I find no merit in the legalizers' case. The simple fact is that drug use is 30 wrong. And the moral argument, in the end, is the most compelling argument. A citizen in a drug-induced haze, whether on his back-yard deck or on a mattress in a ghetto crack house, is not what the founding fathers meant by the "pursuit of happiness." Despite the legalizers' argument that drug use is a matter of "personal freedom," our nation's notion of liberty is rooted in the ideal of a self-reliant citizenry. Helpless wrecks in treatment centers, men chained by their noses to cocaine—these people are slaves.

Imagine if, in the darkest days of 1940, Winston Churchill had rallied the West by saying, "This war looks hopeless, and besides, it will cost too much. Hitler can't be *that* bad. Let's surrender and see what happens." That is essentially what we hear from the legalizers.

This war *can* be won. I am heartened by indications that education and public revulsion are having an effect on drug use. The National Institute on Drug Abuse's latest survey of current users shows a 37-percent *decrease* in drug consumption since 1985. Cocaine is down 50 percent; marijuana use among young people is at its lowest rate since 1972. In my travels I've been encouraged by signs that Americans are fighting back.

I am under no illusion that such developments, however hopeful, mean the war is over. We need to involve more citizens in the fight, increase pressure on drug criminals and build on antidrug programs that have proved to work. This will not be easy. But the moral and social costs of surrender are simply too great to contemplate.

MALCOLM GLADWELL [b. 1963]

The Tipping Point

Born in England in 1963 to an English father and a West Indian
mother, **Malcolm Gladwell** immigrated with his parents to Canada as
a child. Gladwell received his bachelor's degree in history from the
University of Toronto, after which he began his writing career at the
American Spectator. He subsequently served with the *Washington Post*,
first as a business and science reporter and later as chief of the *Post*'s
New York City bureau. While working as a staff writer for the *New
Yorker*, where he has spent more than fifteen years, Gladwell became
known for his highly readable articles that synthesize complex
research in the sciences and social sciences. He has won numerous
awards, including a National Magazine Award for his 1999 profile of
Ron Popeil, and in 2005, he was named among the top one hundred
most influential people in the world by *Time*. His books include *Blink:
The Power of Thinking without Thinking* (2005) and *Outliers: The Story
of Success* (2008). His latest work, *What the Dog Saw: And Other Adventures* (2009), is a compilation of his contributions to the *New Yorker*.

Gladwell's best-selling book *The Tipping Point: How Little Things Can
Make a Big Difference*, an examination of why change occurs, was published in 2000. The title of the book—and of this excerpt—comes
from epidemiology. As Gladwell defined it in an interview, the tipping
point is "the name given to that moment in an epidemic when a virus
reaches critical mass." Here, Gladwell focuses on the dramatic
decrease in New York City's violent crime rate during the 1990s. The
decrease, as he explains, was fueled in large part by strict policing of
more minor crimes.

During the 1990s violent crime declined across the United States for a
number of fairly straightforward reasons. The illegal trade in crack
cocaine, which had spawned a great deal of violence among gangs and
drug dealers, began to decline. The economy's dramatic recovery meant
that many people who might have been lured into crime got legitimate

jobs instead, and the general aging of the population meant that there were fewer people in the age range—males between eighteen and twenty-four—that is responsible for the majority of all violence. The question of why crime declined in New York City, however, is a little more complicated. In the period when the New York epidemic tipped down, the city's economy hadn't improved. It was still stagnant. In fact, the city's poorest neighborhoods had just been hit hard by the welfare cuts of the early 1990s. The waning of the crack cocaine epidemic in New York was clearly a factor, but then again, it had been in steady decline well before crime dipped. As for the aging of the population, because of heavy immigration to New York in the 1980s, the city was getting younger in the 1990s, not older. In any case, all of these trends are long-term changes that one would expect to have gradual effects. In New York the decline was anything but gradual. Something else clearly played a role in reversing New York's crime epidemic.

The most intriguing candidate for that "something else" is called the Broken Windows theory. Broken Windows was the brainchild of the criminologists James Q. Wilson and George Kelling. Wilson and Kelling argued that crime is the inevitable result of disorder. If a window is broken and left unrepaired, people walking by will conclude that no one cares and no one is in charge. Soon, more windows will be broken, and the sense of anarchy will spread from the building to the street on which it faces, sending a signal that anything goes. In a city, relatively minor problems like graffiti, public disorder, and aggressive panhandling, they write, are all the equivalent of broken windows, invitations to more serious crimes:

> Muggers and robbers, whether opportunistic or professional, believe they reduce their chances of being caught or even identified if they operate on streets where potential victims are already intimidated by prevailing conditions. If the neighborhood cannot keep a bothersome panhandler from annoying passersby, the thief may reason, it is even less likely to call the police to identify a potential mugger or to interfere if the mugging actually takes place.

This is an epidemic theory of crime. It says that crime is contagious—just as a fashion trend is contagious—that it can start with a broken window and spread to an entire community. The Tipping Point in this epidemic, though, isn't a particular kind of person—a Connector like Lois Weisberg or a Maven like Mark Alpert.[1] It's something physical like graffiti. The impetus to engage in a certain kind of behavior is not coming from a certain kind of person but from a feature of the environment.

In the mid-1980s Kelling was hired by the New York Transit Authority as a consultant, and he urged them to put the Broken Windows theory into practice. They obliged, bringing in a new subway director by the name of David Gunn to oversee a multibillion-dollar rebuilding of the subway system. Many subway advocates, at the time, told Gunn not to worry about graffiti, to focus on the larger questions of crime and subway reliability, and it seemed like reasonable advice. Worrying about graffiti at a time when the entire system was close to collapse seems as pointless as scrubbing the decks of the *Titanic* as it headed toward the icebergs. But Gunn insisted. "The graffiti was symbolic of the collapse of the system," he says. "When you looked at the process of rebuilding the organization and morale, you had to win the battle against graffiti. Without winning that battle, all the management reforms and physical changes just weren't going to happen. We were about to put out new trains that were worth about ten million bucks apiece, and unless we did something to protect them, we knew just what would happen. They would last one day and then they would be vandalized."

Gunn drew up a new management structure and a precise set of goals and timetables aimed at cleaning the system line by line, train by train. He started with the number seven train that connects Queens to midtown Manhattan, and began experimenting with new techniques to clean off the paint. On stainless-steel cars, solvents were used. On the painted cars, the graffiti were simply painted over. Gunn made it a rule that there should be no retreat, that once a car was "reclaimed" it should never be allowed to be vandalized again. "We were religious about it," Gunn said. At the end of the number one line in the Bronx, where the trains stop before turning around and going back to Manhattan, Gunn set up a cleaning station. If a car came in with graffiti, the graffiti had to be removed during the changeover, or the car was removed from service. "Dirty" cars, which hadn't yet been cleansed of graffiti, were never to be mixed with "clean" cars. The idea was to send an unambiguous message to the vandals themselves.

---

[1]In an earlier chapter of *The Tipping Point*, Gladwell discusses personality types who trigger major changes in society. Connectors have unusually large social circles, and Mavens are particularly knowledgeable about products, services, and prices. Lois Weisberg and Mark Alpert are two typical Americans whom Gladwell interviewed to illustrate these types.

"We had a yard up in Harlem on One hundred thirty-fifth Street where 5 the trains would lay up over night," Gunn said. "The kids would come the first night and paint the side of the train white. Then they would come the next night, after it was dry, and draw the outline. Then they would come the third night and color it in. It was a three-day job. We knew the kids would be working on one of the dirty trains, and what we would do is wait for them to finish their mural. Then we'd walk over with rollers and paint it over. The kids would be in tears, but we'd just be going up and down, up and down. It was a message to them. If you want to spend three nights of your time vandalizing a train, fine. But it's never going to see the light of day."

Gunn's graffiti cleanup took from 1984 to 1990. At that point, the Transit Authority hired William Bratton to head the transit police, and the second stage of the reclamation of the subway system began. Bratton was, like Gunn, a disciple of Broken Windows. He describes Kelling, in fact, as his intellectual mentor, and so his first step as police chief was as seemingly quixotic as Gunn's. With felonies—serious crimes—on the subway system at an all-time high, Bratton decided to crack down on fare-beating. Why? Because he believed that, like graffiti, fare-beating could be a signal, a small expression of disorder that invited much more serious crimes. An estimated 170,000 people a day were entering the system, by one route or another, without paying a token. Some were kids, who simply jumped over the turnstiles. Others would lean backward on the turnstiles and force their way through. And once one or two or three people began cheating the system, other people—who might never otherwise have considered evading the law—would join in, reasoning that if some people weren't going to pay, they shouldn't either, and the problem would snowball. The problem was exacerbated by the fact fare-beating was not easy to fight. Because there was only $1.25 at stake, the transit police didn't feel it was worth their time to pursue it, particularly when there were plenty of more serious crimes happening down on the platform and in the trains.

Bratton is a colorful, charismatic man, a born leader, and he quickly made his presence felt. His wife stayed behind in Boston, so he was free to work long hours, and he would roam the city on the subway at night, getting a sense of what the problems were and how best to fight them. First, he picked stations where fare-beating was the biggest problem, and put as many as ten policemen in plainclothes at the turnstiles. The team would nab fare-beaters one by one, handcuff them, and leave them standing, in a daisy chain, on the platform until they had a "full catch." The idea was to signal, as publicly as possible, that the transit police were now serious about cracking down on fare-beaters. Previously, police officers had been wary of pursuing fare-beaters because the arrest, the trip to the station house, the filling out of necessary forms, and the waiting for those forms to be processed took an entire day — all for a crime that usually merited no more than a slap on the wrist. Bratton retrofitted a city bus and turned it into a rolling station house, with its own fax machines, phones, holding pen, and fingerprinting facilities. Soon the turnaround time on an arrest was down to an hour. Bratton also insisted that a check be run on all those arrested. Sure enough, one out of seven arrestees had an outstanding warrant for a previous crime, and one out of twenty was carrying a weapon of some sort. Suddenly it wasn't hard to convince police officers that tackling fare-beating made sense. "For the cops it was a bonanza," Bratton writes. "Every arrest was like opening a box of Cracker Jack. What kind of toy am I going to get? Got a gun? Got a knife? Got a warrant? Do we have a murderer here? . . . After a while the bad guys wised up and began to leave their weapons home and pay their fares." Under Bratton, the number of ejections from subway stations — for drunkenness, or improper behavior — tripled within his first few months in office. Arrests for misdemeanors, for the kind of minor offenses that had gone unnoticed in the past, went up five-fold between 1990 and 1994. Bratton turned the transit police into an organization focused on the smallest infractions, on the details of life underground.

After the election of Rudolph Giuliani as mayor of New York in 1994, Bratton was appointed head of the New York City Police Department, and he applied the same strategies to the city at large. He instructed his officers to crack down on quality-of-life crimes: on the "squeegee men" who came up to drivers at New York City intersections and demanded money for washing car windows, for example, and on all the other above-ground equivalents of turnstile-jumping and graffiti. "Previous police administration had been handcuffed by restrictions," Bratton says. "We took the handcuffs off. We stepped up enforcement of the laws against public drunkenness and public urination and arrested repeat violators, including those who threw empty bottles on the street or were involved in even relatively minor damage to property. . . . If you peed in the street, you were going to jail." When crime began to fall in the city — as quickly and dramatically as it had in the subways — Bratton and Giuliani pointed to the same cause. Minor, seemingly insignificant quality-of-life crimes, they said, were Tipping Points for violent crime.

[2000]

STEPHANIE ERICSSON [b. 1953]

The Ways We Lie

Screenwriter and advertising copywriter **Stephanie Ericsson** was
born and raised in San Francisco. Ericsson began her career in film,
working first as a story editor for productions including *A Woman
Called Moses* (1978) with award-winning screenwriter Lonne Elder III,
and later as a screenwriter for *Mork & Mindy*, a popular television
sitcom broadcast on ABC between 1978 and 1982. After moving to
Minneapolis–St. Paul, where she worked as an advertising copywriter
for Campbell-Mithun, Ericsson's second husband passed away suddenly, during her pregnancy with their first child. Ericsson's resulting
grief prompted her to write *Companion through the Darkness: Inner
Dialogues on Grief* (1993). Since its publication, Ericsson has continued to write essays and self-help books on the topic of grief management, all while working as an editor for several books by Stephanie
Zuckerman, including *New Clichés for the 21st Century* (1999) and *Doc,
What's Up?* (2001). Her other publications include *ShameFaced* (1986)
and *Companion into Dawn: Inner Dialogues on Loving* (1997), in which
the following essay appears.

   In "The Ways We Lie," originally published in 1992 in the *Utne
Reader*, Ericsson breaks down and categorizes the different types of
lies we tell with a larger interest at heart—examining the role that
lying plays in our lives and our culture.

The bank called today and I told them my deposit was in the mail, even
though I hadn't written a check yet. It'd been a rough day. The baby I'm
pregnant with decided to do aerobics on my lungs for two hours, our
three-year-old daughter painted the living-room couch with lipstick, the
IRS put me on hold for an hour, and I was late to a business meeting
because I was tired.

   I told my client that traffic had been bad. When my partner came
home, his haggard face told me his day hadn't gone any better than
mine, so when he asked, "How was your day?" I said, "Oh, fine," knowing that one more straw might break his back. A friend called and

wanted to take me to lunch. I said I was busy. Four lies in the course of a day, none of which I felt the least bit guilty about.

We lie. We all do. We exaggerate, we minimize, we avoid confrontation, we spare people's feelings, we conveniently forget, we keep secrets, we justify lying to the big-guy institutions. Like most people, I indulge in small falsehoods and still think of myself as an honest person. Sure I lie, but it doesn't hurt anything. Or does it?

I once tried going a whole week without telling a lie, and it was paralyzing. I discovered that telling the truth all the time is nearly impossible. It means living with some serious consequences: The bank charges me $60 in overdraft fees, my partner keels over when I tell him about my travails, my client fires me for telling her I didn't feel like being on time, and my friend takes it personally when I say I'm not hungry. There must be some merit to lying.

But if I justify lying, what makes me any different from slick politicians 5 or the corporate robbers who raided the S&L industry? Saying it's okay to lie one way and not another is hedging. I cannot seem to escape the voice deep inside me that tells me: When someone lies, someone loses.

What far-reaching consequences will I, or others, pay as a result of my lie? Will someone's trust be destroyed? Will someone else pay *my* penance because I ducked out? We must consider the *meaning of our actions*. Deception, lies, capital crimes, and misdemeanors all carry meanings. *Webster's* definition of *lie* is specific:

1. a false statement or action especially made with the intent to deceive;
2. anything that gives or is meant to give a false impression.

A definition like this implies that there are many, many ways to tell a lie. Here are just a few.

THE WHITE LIE

A man who won't lie to a woman has very little consideration for her feelings. — BERGEN EVANS

The white lie assumes that the truth will cause more damage than a simple, harmless untruth. Telling a friend he looks great when he looks like hell can be based on a decision that the friend needs a compliment more than a frank opinion. But, in effect, it is the liar deciding what is best for the lied to. Ultimately, it is a vote of no confidence. It is an act of subtle arrogance for anyone to decide what is best for someone else.

315

Yet not all circumstances are quite so cut-and-dried. Take, for instance, the sergeant in Vietnam who knew one of his men was killed in action but listed him as missing so that the man's family would receive indefinite compensation instead of the lump-sum pittance the military gives widows and children. His intent was honorable. Yet for twenty years this family kept their hopes alive, unable to move on to a new life.

FAÇADES

Et tu, Brute? —CAESAR

We all put up façades to one degree or another. When I put on a suit to   10
go to see a client, I feel as though I am putting on another face, obeying
the expectation that serious businesspeople wear suits rather than
sweatpants. But I'm a writer. Normally, I get up, get the kid off to school,
and sit at my computer in my pajamas until four in the afternoon. When
I answer the phone, the caller thinks I'm wearing a suit (though the UPS
man knows better).

But façades can be destructive because they are used to seduce others
into an illusion. For instance, I recently realized that a former friend was
a liar. He presented himself with all the right looks and the right words
and offered lots of new consciousness theories, fabulous books to read,
and fascinating insights. Then I did some business with him, and the
time came for him to pay me. He turned out to be all talk and no walk. I
heard a plethora of reasonable excuses, including in-depth descriptions
of the big break around the corner. In six months of work, I saw less than
a hundred bucks. When I confronted him, he raised both eyebrows and
tried to convince me that I'd heard him wrong, that he'd made no commitment to me. A simple investigation into his past revealed a crowded
graveyard of disenchanted former friends.

IGNORING THE PLAIN FACTS

Well, you must understand that Father Porter is only human.
—A MASSACHUSETTS PRIEST

In the '60s, the Catholic Church in Massachusetts began hearing complaints that Father James Porter was sexually molesting children. Rather
than relieving him of his duties, the ecclesiastical authorities simply

moved him from one parish to another between 1960 and 1967, actually providing him with a fresh supply of unsuspecting families and innocent children to abuse. After treatment in 1967 for pedophilia, he went back to work, this time in Minnesota. The new diocese was aware of Father Porter's obsession with children, but they needed priests and recklessly believed treatment had cured him. More children were abused until he was relieved of his duties a year later. By his own admission, Porter may have abused as many as a hundred children.

Ignoring the facts may not in and of itself be a form of lying, but consider the context of this situation. If a lie is *a false action done with the intent to deceive*, then the Catholic Church's conscious covering for Porter created irreparable consequences. The church became a co-perpetrator with Porter.

DEFLECTING

When you have no basis for an argument, abuse the plaintiff.
— CICERO

I've discovered that I can keep anyone from seeing the true me by being selectively blatant. I set a precedent of being up-front about intimate issues, but I never bring up the things I truly want to hide; I just let people assume I'm revealing everything. It's an effective way of hiding.

Any good liar knows that the way to perpetuate an untruth is to deflect 15
attention from it. When Clarence Thomas exploded with accusations that the Senate hearings were a "high-tech lynching," he simply switched the focus from a highly charged subject to a radioactive subject. Rather than defending himself, he took the offensive and accused the country of racism. It was a brilliant maneuver. Racism is now politically incorrect in official circles—unlike sexual harassment, which still rewards those who can get away with it.

Some of the most skilled deflectors are passive-aggressive people who, when accused of inappropriate behavior, refuse to respond to the accusations. This you-don't-exist stance infuriates the accuser, who, understandably, screams something obscene out of frustration. The trap is sprung and the act of deflection successful, because now the passive-aggressive person can indignantly say, "Who can talk to someone as unreasonable as you?" The real issue is forgotten and the sins of the original victim become the focus. Feeling guilty of name-calling, the victim is fully tamed and crawls into a hole, ashamed. I have watched this fighting technique work thousands of times in disputes between men

317

and women, and what I've learned is that the real culprit is not necessarily the one who swears the loudest.

OMISSION

The cruelest lies are often told in silence. —R. L. STEVENSON

Omission involves telling most of the truth minus one or two key facts whose absence changes the story completely. You break a pair of glasses that are guaranteed under normal use and get a new pair, without mentioning that the first pair broke during a rowdy game of basketball. Who hasn't tried something like that? But what about omission of information that could make a difference in how a person lives his or her life?

For instance, one day I found out that rabbinical legends tell of another woman in the Garden of Eden before Eve. I was stunned. The omission of the Sumerian goddess Lilith from Genesis—as well as her demonization by ancient misogynists as an embodiment of female evil—felt like spiritual robbery. I felt like I'd just found out my mother was really my stepmother. To take seriously the tradition that Adam was created out of the same mud as his equal counterpart, Lilith, redefines all of Judeo-Christian history.

Some renegade Catholic feminists introduced me to a view of Lilith that had been suppressed during the many centuries when this strong goddess was seen only as a spirit of evil. Lilith was a proud goddess who defied Adam's need to control her, attempted negotiations, and when this failed, said adios and left the Garden of Eden.

This omission of Lilith from the Bible was a patriarchal strategy to 20 keep women weak. Omitting the strong-woman archetype of Lilith from Western religions and starting the story with Eve the Rib has helped keep Christian and Jewish women believing they were the lesser sex for thousands of years.

STEREOTYPES AND CLICHÉS

Where opinion does not exist, the status quo becomes stereotyped and all originality is discouraged. —BERTRAND RUSSELL

Stereotype and cliché serve a purpose as a form of shorthand. Our need for vast amounts of information in nanoseconds has made the stereotype vital to modern communication. Unfortunately, it often shuts down original thinking, giving those hungry for the truth a candy bar of misinformation instead of a balanced meal. The stereotype explains a situation with just enough truth to seem unquestionable.

All the "isms"—racism, sexism, ageism, et al.—are founded on and fueled by the stereotype and the cliché, which are lies of exaggeration, omission, and ignorance. They are always dangerous. They take a single tree and make it a landscape. They destroy curiosity. They close minds and separate people. The single mother on welfare is assumed to be cheating. Any black male could tell you how much of his identity is obliterated daily by stereotypes. Fat people, ugly people, beautiful people, old people, large-breasted women, short men, the mentally ill, and the homeless all could tell you how much more they are like us than we want to think. I once admitted to a group of people that I had a mouth like a truck driver. Much to my surprise, a man stood up and said, "I'm a truck driver, and I never cuss." Needless to say, I was humbled.

GROUPTHINK

Who is more foolish, the child afraid of the dark, or the man afraid of the light? — MAURICE FREEHILL

Irving Janis, in *Victims of Group Think*, defines this sort of lie as a psychological phenomenon within decision-making groups in which loyalty to the group has become more important than any other value, with the result that dissent and the appraisal of alternatives are suppressed. If you've ever worked on a committee or in a corporation, you've encountered groupthink. It requires a combination of other forms of lying— ignoring facts, selective memory, omission, and denial, to name a few.

The textbook example of groupthink came on December 7, 1941. From as early as the fall of 1941, the warnings came in, one after another, that Japan was preparing for a massive military operation. The navy command in Hawaii assumed Pearl Harbor was invulnerable—the Japanese weren't stupid enough to attack the United States' most important base. On the other hand, racist stereotypes said the Japanese weren't smart enough to invent a torpedo effective in less than 60 feet of water (the fleet was docked in 30 feet); after all, US technology hadn't been able to do it.

On Friday, December 5, normal weekend leave was granted to all the 25 commanders at Pearl Harbor, even though the Japanese consulate in Hawaii was busy burning papers. Within the tight, good-ole-boy cohesiveness of the US command in Hawaii, the myth of invulnerability

319

stayed well entrenched. No one in the group considered the alternatives. The rest is history.

OUT-AND-OUT LIES

The only form of lying that is beyond reproach is lying for its own sake. — OSCAR WILDE

Of all the ways to lie, I like this one the best, probably because I get tired of trying to figure out the real meanings behind things. At least I can trust the bald-faced lie. I once asked my five-year-old nephew, "Who broke the fence?" (I had seen him do it.) He answered, "The murderers." Who could argue?

At least when this sort of lie is told it can be easily confronted. As the person who is lied to, I know where I stand. The bald-faced lie doesn't toy with my perceptions—it argues with them. It doesn't try to refashion reality, it tries to refute it. *Read my lips.* . . . No sleight of hand. No guessing. If this were the only form of lying, there would be no such things as floating anxiety or the adult-children-of-alcoholics movement.

DISMISSAL

Pay no attention to that man behind the curtain!
I am the Great Oz! — THE WIZARD OF OZ

Dismissal is perhaps the slipperiest of all lies. Dismissing feelings, perceptions, or even the raw facts of a situation ranks as a kind of lie that can do as much damage to a person as any other kind of lie.

The roots of many mental disorders can be traced back to the dismissal of reality. Imagine that a person is told from the time she is a tot that her perceptions are inaccurate. *"Mommy, I'm scared."* "No you're not, darling." *"I don't like that man next door, he makes me feel icky."* "Johnny, that's a terrible thing to say, of course you like him. You go over there right now and be nice to him."

I've often mused over the idea that madness is actually a sane reaction 30 to an insane world. Psychologist R. D. Laing supports this hypothesis in *Sanity, Madness and the Family,* an account of his investigation into the families of schizophrenics. The common thread that ran through all of the families he studied was a deliberate, staunch dismissal of the

320

patient's perceptions from a very early age. Each of the patients started out with an accurate grasp of reality, which, through meticulous and methodical dismissal, was demolished until the only reality the patient could trust was catatonia.

Dismissal runs the gamut. Mild dismissal can be quite handy for forgiving the foibles of others in our day-to-day lives. Toddlers who have just learned to manipulate their parents' attention sometimes are dismissed out of necessity. Absolute attention from the parents would require so much energy that no one would get to eat dinner. But we must be careful and attentive about how far we take our "necessary" dismissals. Dismissal is a dangerous tool, because it's nothing less than a lie.

DELUSION

We lie loudest when we lie to ourselves. — ERIC HOFFER

I could write the book on this one. Delusion, a cousin of dismissal, is the tendency to see excuses as facts. It's a powerful lying tool because it filters out information that contradicts what we want to believe. Alcoholics who believe that the problems in their lives are legitimate reasons for drinking rather than results of the drinking offer the classic example of deluded thinking. Delusion uses the mind's ability to see things in myriad ways to support what it wants to be the truth.

But delusion is also a survival mechanism we all use. If we were to fully contemplate the consequences of our stockpiles of nuclear weapons or global warming, we could hardly function on a day-to-day level. We don't want to incorporate that much reality into our lives because to do so would be paralyzing.

Delusion acts as an adhesive to keep the status quo intact. It shamelessly employs dismissal, omission, and amnesia, among other sorts of lies. Its most cunning defense is that it cannot see itself.

The liar's punishment [. . .] is that he cannot believe anyone else. — GEORGE BERNARD SHAW

These are only a few of the ways we lie. Or are lied to. As I said earlier, 35 it's not easy to entirely eliminate lies from our lives. No matter how pious we may try to be, we will still embellish, hedge, and omit to lubricate the daily machinery of living. But there is a world of difference

321

between telling functional lies and living a lie. Martin Buber once said, "The lie is the spirit committing treason against itself." Our acceptance of lies becomes a cultural cancer that eventually shrouds and reorders reality until moral garbage becomes as invisible to us as water is to a fish.

How much do we tolerate before we become sick and tired of being sick and tired? When will we stand up and declare our *right* to trust? When do we stop accepting that the real truth is in the fine print? Whose lips do we read this year when we vote for president? When will we stop being so reticent about making judgments? When do we stop turning over our personal power and responsibility to liars?

Maybe if I don't tell the bank the check's in the mail I'll be less tolerant of the lies told me every day. A country song I once heard said it all for me: "You've got to stand for something or you'll fall for anything."

[1992]

STEPHEN CARTER   [b. 1954]

The Insufficiency of Honesty

Law professor and writer **Stephen Carter** was born in Ithaca, New York. He received his B.A. from Stanford University in 1976 and his J.D. from Yale University in 1979. Currently serving as the William Nelson Cromwell Professor of Law at Yale, Carter began his teaching career after clerking for Supreme Court Justice Thurgood Marshall. He has written several books on legal and social policy, including *Reflections of an Affirmative Action Baby* (1991), *The Culture of Disbelief* (1994), and *God's Name in Vain: The Wrongs and Rights of Religion in Politics* (2001). Carter also contributes a feature column to *Christianity Today* magazine. His most recent book, *The Emperor of Ocean Park* (2002), is a novel whose plot mirrors the Clarence Thomas confirmation hearings.

In "The Insufficiency of Honesty," Carter argues that honesty without integrity can be morally vacuous, claiming we often use honesty as an excuse for not acting with integrity. If, however, we act with integrity, we will act responsibly toward each other, fulfilling our obligations because it is the right thing to do.

A couple of years ago I began a university commencement address by telling the audience that I was going to talk about integrity. The crowd broke into applause. Applause! Just because they had heard the word "integrity": that's how starved for it they were. They had no idea how I was using the word, or what I was going to say about integrity, or, indeed, whether I was for it or against it. But they knew they liked the idea of talking about it.

Very well, let us consider this word "integrity." Integrity is like the weather: everybody talks about it but nobody knows what to do about it. Integrity is that stuff that we always want more of. Some say that we need to return to the good old days when we had a lot more of it. Others say that we as a nation have never really had enough of it. Hardly anybody stops to explain exactly what we mean by it, or how we know it is a good thing, or why everybody needs to have the same amount of it. Indeed, the only trouble with integrity is that everybody who uses the word seems to mean something slightly different.

For instance, when I refer to integrity, do I mean simply "honesty"? The answer is no; although honesty is a virtue of importance, it is a different virtue from integrity. Let us, for simplicity, think of honesty as not lying; and let us further accept Sissela Bok's definition of a lie: "any intentionally deceptive message which is *stated*." Plainly, one cannot have integrity without being honest (although, as we shall see, the matter gets complicated), but one can certainly be honest and yet have little integrity.

When I refer to integrity, I have something very specific in mind. Integrity, as I will use the term, requires three steps: discerning what is right and what is wrong; acting on what you have discerned, even at personal cost; and saying openly that you are acting on your understanding of right and wrong. The first criterion captures the idea that integrity requires a degree of moral reflectiveness. The second brings in the ideal of a person of integrity as steadfast, a quality that includes keeping one's commitments. The third reminds us that a person of integrity can be trusted.

The first point to understand about the difference between honesty 5 and integrity is that a person may be entirely honest without ever engaging in the hard work of discernment that integrity requires: she may tell us quite truthfully what she believes without ever taking the time to figure out whether what she believes is good and right and true. The problem may be as simple as someone's foolishly saying something that hurts a friend's feelings; a few moments of thought would have revealed the likelihood of the hurt and the lack of necessity for the comment. Or the problem may be more complex, as when a man who was raised from birth in a society that preaches racism states his belief in one race's inferiority as a fact, without ever really considering that perhaps this deeply held view is wrong. Certainly the racist is being honest—he is telling us what he actually thinks—but his honesty does not add up to integrity.

TELLING EVERYTHING YOU KNOW

A wonderful epigram sometimes attributed to the filmmaker Sam Goldwyn goes like this: "The most important thing in acting is honesty; once you learn to fake that, you're in." The point is that honesty can be something one *seems* to have. Without integrity, what passes for honesty often is nothing of the kind; it is fake honesty—or it is honest but irrelevant and perhaps even immoral.

Consider an example. A man who has been married for fifty years confesses to his wife on his deathbed that he was unfaithful thirty-five years earlier. The dishonesty was killing his spirit, he says. Now he has cleared his conscience and is able to die in peace.

The husband has been honest—sort of. He has certainly unburdened himself. And he has probably made his wife (soon to be his widow) quite miserable in the process, because even if she forgives him, she will not be able to remember him with quite the vivid image of love and loyalty that she had hoped for. Arranging his own emotional affairs to ease his transition to death, he has shifted to his wife the burden of confusion and pain, perhaps for the rest of her life. Moreover, he has attempted his honesty at the one time in his life when it carries no risk; acting in accordance with what you think is right and risking no loss in the process is a rather thin and unadmirable form of honesty.

Besides, even though the husband has been honest in a sense, he has now twice been unfaithful to his wife: once thirty-five years ago, when he had his affair, and again when, nearing death, he decided that his own peace of mind was more important than hers. In trying to be honest he has violated his marriage vow by acting toward his wife not with love but with naked and perhaps even cruel self-interest.

As my mother used to say, you don't have to tell people everything you 10 know. Lying and nondisclosure, as the law often recognizes, are not the same thing. Sometimes it is actually illegal to tell what you know, as, for example, in the disclosure of certain financial information by market insiders. Or it may be unethical, as when a lawyer reveals a confidence entrusted to her by a client. It may be simple bad manners, as in the case of a gratuitous comment to a colleague on his or her attire. And it may be subject to religious punishment, as when a Roman Catholic priest breaks the seal of the confessional—an offense that carries automatic excommunication.

In all the cases just mentioned, the problem with telling everything you know is that somebody else is harmed. Harm may not be the intention, but it is certainly the effect. Honesty is most laudable when we risk harm to ourselves; it becomes a good deal less so if we instead risk harm to others when there is no gain to anyone other than ourselves. Integrity may counsel keeping our secrets in order to spare the feelings of others. Sometimes, as in the example of the wayward husband, the reason we want to tell what we know is precisely to shift our pain onto somebody else—a course of action dictated less by integrity than by self-interest. Fortunately, integrity and self-interest often coincide, as when a politician of integrity is rewarded with our votes. But often they do not, and it is at those moments that our integrity is truly tested.

ERROR

Another reason that honesty alone is no substitute for integrity is that if forthrightness is not preceded by discernment, it may result in the expression of an incorrect moral judgment. In other words, I may be honest about what I believe, but if I have never tested my beliefs, I may be wrong. And here I mean "wrong" in a particular sense: the proposition in question is wrong if I would change my mind about it after hard moral reflection.

Consider this example. Having been taught all his life that women are not as smart as men, a manager gives the women on his staff less-challenging assignments than he gives the men. He does this, he believes, for their own benefit: he does not want them to fail, and he believes that they will if he gives them tougher assignments. Moreover, when one of the women on his staff does poor work, he does not berate her as harshly as he would a man, because he expects nothing more. And he claims to be acting with integrity because he is acting according to his own deepest beliefs.

The manager fails the most basic test of integrity. The question is not whether his actions are consistent with what he most deeply believes but whether he has done the hard work of discerning whether what he most deeply believes is right. The manager has not taken this harder step.

Moreover, even within the universe that the manager has constructed 15 for himself, he is not acting with integrity. Although he is obviously wrong to think that the women on his staff are not as good as the men, even were he right, that would not justify applying different standards to their work. By so doing he betrays both his obligation to the institution that employs him and his duty as a manager to evaluate his employees.

The problem that the manager faces is an enormous one in our practical politics, where having the dialogue that makes democracy work can seem impossible because of our tendency to cling to our views even when we have not examined them. As Jean Bethke Elshtain has said, borrowing from John Courtney Murray, our politics are so fractured and contentious that we often cannot even reach *disagreement*. Our refusal to look closely at our own most cherished principles is surely a large part of the reason. Socrates thought the unexamined life not worth living. But the unhappy truth is that few of us actually have the time for constant reflection on our views—on public or private morality. Examine them we must, however, or we will never know whether we might be wrong.

None of this should be taken to mean that integrity as I have described it presupposes a single correct truth. If, for example, your integrity-guided search tells you that affirmative action is wrong, and my integrity-guided search tells me that affirmative action is right, we need not conclude that

326

one of us lacks integrity. As it happens, I believe—both as a Christian and as a secular citizen who struggles toward moral understanding—that we *can* find true and sound answers to our moral questions. But I do not pretend to have found very many of them, nor is an exposition of them my purpose here.

It is the case not that there aren't any right answers but that, given human fallibility, we need to be careful in assuming that we have found them. However, today's political talk about how it is wrong for the government to impose one person's morality on somebody else is just mindless chatter. *Every* law imposes one person's morality on somebody else, because law has only two functions: to tell people to do what they would rather not or to forbid them to do what they would.

And if the surveys can be believed, there is far more moral agreement in America than we sometimes allow ourselves to think. One of the reasons that character education for young people makes so much sense to so many people is precisely that there seems to be a core set of moral understandings—we might call them the American Core—that most of us accept. Some of the virtues in this American Core are, one hopes, relatively noncontroversial. About five hundred American communities have signed on to Michael Josephson's program to emphasize the "six pillars" of good character: trustworthiness, respect, responsibility, caring, fairness, and citizenship. These virtues might lead to a similarly noncontroversial set of political values: having an honest regard for ourselves and others, protecting freedom of thought and religious belief, and refusing to steal or murder.

HONESTY AND COMPETING RESPONSIBILITIES

A further problem with too great an exaltation of honesty is that it may 20 allow us to escape responsibilities that morality bids us bear. If honesty is substituted for integrity, one might think that if I say I am not planning to fulfill a duty, I need not fulfill it. But it would be a peculiar morality indeed that granted us the right to avoid our moral responsibilities simply by stating our intention to ignore them. Integrity does not permit such an easy escape.

Consider an example. Before engaging in sex with a woman, her lover tells her that if she gets pregnant, it is her problem, not his. She says that she understands. In due course she does wind up pregnant. If we believe, as I hope we do, that the man would ordinarily have a moral responsibility toward both the child he will have helped to bring into the world and the child's mother, then his honest statement of what he intends does not spare him that responsibility.

This vision of responsibility assumes that not all moral obligations stem from consent or from a stated intention. The linking of obligations to promises is a rather modern and perhaps uniquely Western way of looking at life, and perhaps a luxury that only the well-to-do can afford. As Fred and Shulamit Korn (a philosopher and an anthropologist) have pointed out, "If one looks at ethnographic accounts of other societies, one finds that, while obligations everywhere play a crucial role in social life, promising is not preeminent among the sources of obligation and is not even mentioned by most anthropologists." The Korns have made a study of Tonga, where promises are virtually unknown but the social order is remarkably stable. If life without any promises seems extreme, we Americans sometimes go too far the other way, parsing not only our contracts but even our marriage vows in order to discover the absolute minimum obligation that we have to others as a result of our promises.

That some societies in the world have worked out evidently functional structures of obligation without the need for promise or consent does not tell us what *we* should do. But it serves as a reminder of the basic proposition that our existence in civil society creates a set of mutual responsibilities that philosophers used to capture in the fiction of the social contract. Nowadays, here in America, people seem to spend their time thinking of even cleverer ways to avoid their obligations, instead of doing what integrity commands and fulfilling them. And all too often honesty is their excuse.

LUC SANTE [b. 1954]

What Secrets Tell

Born in Belgium, **Luc Sante** immigrated to the United States with his family at the age of five, a journey that he explores in his memoir *The Factory of Facts* (1988). A writer and critic of popular culture, Sante was raised in New Jersey; from that vantage point, he became enamored of nearby New York City, where he attended Columbia University and about which he wrote *Low Life: Lures and Snares of Old New York* (1991). Sante's reviews and essays have been published in the *New York Review of Books* and the *New Republic*. He has also won several prestigious awards, including a Whiting Writer's Award in 1989, a Guggenheim fellowship in 1992, and a Grammy for his work on the album notes for the *Anthology of American Folk Music* in 1998. Among his most recent books, published in 2007 and 2009 respectively, are *Kill All Your Darlings: Pieces 1990–2005* and *Folk Photography: The American Real-Photo Postcard 1905–1930*. Sante has also taught writing and the history of photography at Bard College and served as a historical consultant for Martin Scorsese's *Gangs of New York*.

In "What Secrets Tell," excerpted from a longer essay that appeared in the *New York Times Magazine*, Sante explores the kinds of secrets people keep, some age-old, some more recent. As Sante sees it, secrets are paradoxical, or self-contradictory: They are hidden, of course, but at the same time they enlarge our sense of the world. This second function makes secrets indispensable, a "motor of life." They offer the enticement of discovery and are an essential ingredient for a life filled with childlike mystery and promise.

Secrets are a permanent feature of the human condition. We need secrets the way we need black holes, for their mystery; the way we need land-speed records, for their enlargement of scale; the way we need sexy models in advertisements, for their seductively false promises; the way we need lotteries, for their vague possibility. We also need them the way we need bank vaults and sock drawers and glove compartments. Anybody who doesn't carry around one or two secrets probably has all the depth of a place mat.

But then the word *secret* conceals under its mantle a teeming and motley population of types. Secrets cater to the entire range of human susceptibilities, from the laughably trivial to the terrifyingly fundamental. Principal landmarks along the way include:

Personal Secrets In other words, those secrets that are chiefly of interest to the persons who carry them around. You know the sort: You pick your nose when no one's looking; your real first name is Eustace; you wear a truss for nonmedical reasons. If such things were revealed, your ego might take a beating and your intimates could gain a weapon for use in squabbles or extortions, but the foundations of your house would not be shaken.

Romantic Secrets They run the gamut. That interval of passion you once shared with your dentist when the two of you were stuck in an elevator with a bottle of Cherry Kijafa may remain swathed in gauze for all eternity, although your partner might eventually demand to know the identity of this "Shirley" whose name you utter in your sleep. That you enjoy above all the erotic sensation of being pinched with tweezers until you bleed might not matter a whole lot to anyone, unless you decide to run for office, and then you will find yourself sending discreet sums of money to people you haven't thought of in years. Couples often tacitly erect a whole edifice of secrets, based on real or imagined causes for jealousy. This can be relatively harmless, or it can be a symptom of the relationship's becoming a regime.

Secrets in Gossip That is, the wheat left over when gossip's chaff is 5 sifted out. Secrets that surface as gossip are usually of the mildest sort, personal eccentricities and romantic peccadilloes not of much interest outside a closed circle. (It is understood that there is a direct correlation between the degree of triviality of the secret transmitted as gossip and the rank of the gossip's subject within that circle.) Gossip, though, demonstrates how secrets can become currency, as the teller invests the hearer with power in exchange for esteem. The possession of a secret concerning another is, like all forms of power, something of a burden, a weight pressing one's lips together, which can be relieved only by telling someone else. This, added to a hunger for knowledge on the part of all within the gossip circle, keeps the wheel of the secret-fueled gossip economy turning.

Trade Secrets The monetary economy, meanwhile, revolves around a wide and diverse range of secrets. A business strategy is a secret until it becomes a fait accompli.[1] The details of the financial health of a company are kept as secret as the law allows. Anyone with a degree of power in the market is continually keeping secrets—from competitors, from the press, from anyone who is an outsider, including friends and family, but sometimes from colleagues and office mates. The reasons are obvious: Everyone is naked in a cutthroat world, and secrets are clothing. It goes without saying that secrets protect innovations and that they also hide various extralegal undertakings—the ostensibly respectable bank that takes in laundry[2] on the side, for example. Business also employs secrets strategically, as secrets qua[3] secrets, usually painting the word *secret* in letters ten stories tall. Naturally the new car model will differ little from the previous year's, but a bit of cloak-and-dagger about it will increase public interest. The "secret recipe" is on a par with "new and improved" as a carny barker's hook. The cake mix or soft drink or laundry soap may, of course, actually include a secret ingredient, known only to staff chemists and highly placed executives, but very often a "secret ingredient" is rumored or bruited about primarily as a lure to the gulls of the public.

Secret Formulas The public hunger for secrets is primordial. It is first and foremost a matter of curiosity, but it also springs from a painful awareness of rank and a belief that things are different upstairs, with a more or less fanciful idea of the specifics. These days, with fortune-building running at a pitch not seen since the 1920s, there is widespread demand for financial folklore. You can make a lot of money catering to the suspicion that there exist shortcuts known only to a few. That some people are richer, thinner, more charismatic or whiter of teeth may be a result of a variety of imponderable factors, but for everyone who in moments of desperation has imagined that there must be some simple trick, some formula or high sign or investment routine or hidden spa, there is an author with a book aimed at the exact combination of vulnerability and prurient imagination. Such publications run along the entire span of implied legitimacy based upon demographics, from the crudities aimed at the supermarket-tabloid constituency (diets centered on junk food named in the Bible, for instance) to the overpriced hardcover pamphlets catering to the anxieties of the managerial class by dressing up received ideas with slogans and numbered lists. For centuries, the secret

---

[1]From French, "a completed act."
[2]Money being channeled illegally.
[3]From Latin, "as" or "in the character of."

has been a sure-fire sales gimmick. All you have to do is combine the banal and the esoteric.

Secret Societies There are probably a lot fewer than there once were, but somewhere in America, no doubt, insurance adjusters and trophy engravers still gather once a month in acrylic gowns and button-flap underwear to exchange phrases in pseudobiblical double Dutch and then get down to the business of drinking beer. It helps them feel special to be the only ones in town who know the three-finger handshake. The setup descends from the heresies of the Middle Ages by the way of the pecking order of the playground. We can laugh at them, now that they are so enfeebled, but there was a time not long ago when they dominated the social life of male middle-class America, and in many ways their pretensions are not so far removed from those of the Mafia or the CIA.

Mystical Secrets The secret is bait. The secret leads votaries by the nose through a maze of connected chambers, in each of which they must ante up. Only when they have finally tumbled to there being no secret (and they have run through the better part of their inheritances) can they truly be counted as initiates. But few have the stamina to get that far, and most instead spend their spare afternoons consuming one tome after another promoting the secrets of, variously, the pyramids, the Templars, the ascended masters, the elders of Mu, the Essene scrolls, and so on through greater and lesser degrees of perceived legitimacy, all of which flutter around the edges of the secret, none of which make so bold as to suggest what it might consist of.

State Secrets "Our laws are not generally known; they are kept secret by   10
the small group of nobles who rule us," wrote Kafka[4] in one of his miniature stories. "We are convinced that these ancient laws are scrupulously administered; nevertheless it is an extremely painful thing to be ruled by laws that one does not know." This is the essence of state secrets. A government does not have to be totalitarian, particularly, to possess a stratum of laws whose existence cannot be generally known because they describe the limits of the knowable. It is forbidden for unauthorized persons to possess certain kinds of information. What kinds of information? Well, that's the trouble; if you knew that, you would already know too much. State secrets range all the way from banal prohibitions on photographing customs booths and power plants to the highest levels of technical esoterica.

[4]Franz Kafka (1883–1924) was a Czech poet and fiction writer.

332

Atomic Secrets "Stop me if you've heard this atomic secret," cracked William Burroughs in *Naked Lunch*.[5] Atomic secrets may be the world's most famous class of secret, an oxymoron, surely, but for the fact that few enough people would recognize or understand an atomic secret if it landed in their mailboxes. The workaday state secret may be a matter of mere protocol or protection of resources, not unlike industries safeguarding the peculiarities of their production methods. The atomic secret, however, ascends to the level of the sacred because it manifests in concrete form the terror that mystics can only suggest: the end of the world. The secret of life may be an empty proposition, but the secret of death is actually legible to those who possess the language and the tools. . . .

People need secrets because they need the assurance that there is something left to discover, that they have not exhausted the limits of their environment, that a prize might lie in wait like money in the pocket of an old jacket, that the existence of things beyond their ken might propose as a corollary that their own minds contain unsuspected corridors. People need uncertainty and destabilization the way they need comfort and security. It's not that secrets make them feel small but that they make the world seem bigger—a major necessity these days, when sensations need to be extreme to register at all. Secrets reawaken that feeling from childhood that the ways of the world were infinitely mysterious, unpredictable and densely packed, and that someday you might come to know and master them. Secrets purvey affordable glamour, suggest danger without presenting an actual threat. If there were no more secrets, an important motor of life would be stopped, and the days would merge into a continuous blur. Secrets hold out the promise, false but necessary, that death will be deferred until their unveiling.

[2000]

---

[5]Burroughs (1914–1997), an American writer, published the controversial novel *Naked Lunch* in 1962.

H. L. MENCKEN   [1880–1956]

The Penalty of Death

H.L. Mencken, one of America's most original journalists, commentators, and critics, was born in Baltimore, Maryland, and educated at the Baltimore Polytechnic. At age eighteen, Mencken became a reporter for the *Baltimore Morning Herald*, and at twenty-five, he became an editor, columnist, and feature writer for the *Baltimore Daily Sun*. Mencken was a cofounder of the *Smart Set* magazine and cofounder and editor of the *American Mercury*. As a writer, thinker and humorist, Mencken was influenced by Frederick Nietzsche and Mark Twain. With a prose style characterized by clear, sweeping sentences and a witty, often ironic tone, Mencken satirized authority figures and the American middle class—what he termed the "Booboisee." For his coverage of the 1925 Scopes ("Monkey") trial, Mencken developed a national reputation. In over 3,000 newspaper columns, Mencken critiqued all elements of society, from the presidential politics of Franklin D. Roosevelt and the New Deal to the hypocrisies of everyday life. His published works include *Newspaper Days* (1899–06), *In Defense of Woman* (1917), and *The American Language* (1919).

Of the arguments against capital punishment that issue from uplifters, two are commonly heard most often, to wit:

1. That hanging a man (or frying him or gassing him) is a dreadful business, degrading to those who have to do it and revolting to those who have to witness it.
2. That it is useless, for it does not deter others from the same crime.

The first of these arguments, it seems to me, is plainly too weak to need serious refutation. All it says, in brief, is that the work of the hangman is unpleasant. Granted. But suppose it is? It may be quite necessary to society for all that. There are, indeed, many other jobs that are unpleasant, and yet no one thinks of abolishing them—that of the plumber, that of the soldier, that of the garbageman, that of the priest hearing confessions, that of the sandhog, and so on. Moreover, what evidence is there that any actual hangman complains of his work? I have heard none. On the contrary, I have known many who delighted in their ancient art, and practiced it proudly.

In the second argument of the abolitionists there is rather more force, but even here, I believe, the ground under them is shaky. Their fundamental error consists in assuming that the whole aim of punishing criminals is to deter other (potential) criminals—that we hang or electrocute A simply in order to so alarm B that he will not kill C. This, I believe, is an assumption which confuses a part with the whole. Deterrence, obviously, is *one* of the aims of punishment, but it is surely not the only one. On the contrary, there are at least a half dozen, and some are probably quite as important. At least one of them, practically considered, is *more* important. Commonly, it is described as revenge, but revenge is really not the word for it. I borrow a better term from the late Aristotle: *katharsis*. *Katharsis*, so used, means a salubrious discharge of emotions, a healthy letting off of steam. A schoolboy, disliking his teacher, deposits a tack upon the pedagogical chair; the teacher jumps and the boy laughs. This is *katharsis*. What I contend is that one of the prime objects of all judicial punishments is to afford the same grateful relief *(a)* to the immediate victims of the criminal punished, and *(b)* to the general body of moral and timorous men.

These persons, and particularly the first group, are concerned only indirectly with deterring other criminals. The thing they crave primarily is the satisfaction of seeing the criminal actually before them suffer as he made them suffer. What they want is the peace of mind that goes with the feeling that accounts are squared. Until they get that satisfaction they are in a state of emotional tension, and hence unhappy. The instant they get it they are comfortable. I do not argue that this yearning is noble; I simply argue that it is almost universal among human beings. In the face of injuries that are unimportant and can be borne without damage it may yield to higher impulses; that is to say, it may yield to what is called Christian charity. But when the injury is serious Christianity is adjourned, and even saints reach for their sidearms. It is plainly asking too much of human nature to expect it to conquer so natural an impulse. A keeps a store and has a bookkeeper, B. B steals $700, employs it in playing at dice or bingo, and is cleaned out. What is A to do? Let B go? If he does so he will be unable to sleep at night. The sense of injury, of injustice, of frustration will haunt him like pruritus. So he turns B over to the police, and they hustle B to prison. Thereafter A can sleep. More, he has pleasant dreams. He pictures B chained to the wall of a dungeon a hundred feet underground, devoured by rats and scorpions. It is so agreeable that it makes him forget his $700. He has got his *katharsis*.

The same thing precisely takes place on a larger scale when there is 5
a crime which destroys a whole community's sense of security. Every
law-abiding citizen feels menaced and frustrated until the criminals
have been struck down—until the communal capacity to get even with
them, and more than even, has been dramatically demonstrated. Here,
manifestly, the business of deterring others is no more than an after-
thought. The main thing is to destroy the concrete scoundrels whose
act has alarmed everyone, and thus made everyone unhappy. Until they
are brought to book that unhappiness continues; when the law has
been executed upon them there is a sigh of relief. In other words, there
is *katharsis*.

I know of no public demand for the death penalty for ordinary crimes,
even for ordinary homicides. Its infliction would shock all men of normal decency of feeling. But for crimes involving the deliberate and inex-
cusable taking of human life, by men openly defiant of all civilized
order—for such crimes it seems, to nine men out of ten, a just and
proper punishment. Any lesser penalty leaves them feeling that the
criminal has got the better of society—that he is free to add insult to
injury by laughing. That feeling can be dissipated only by a recourse to
katharsis, the invention of the aforesaid Aristotle. It is more effectively
and economically achieved, as human nature now is, by wafting the
criminal to realms of bliss.

The real objection to capital punishment doesn't lie against the actual
extermination of the condemned, but against our brutal American habit
of putting it off so long. After all, every one of us must die soon or late,
and a murderer, it must be assumed, is one who makes that sad fact the
cornerstone of his metaphysic. But it is one thing to die, and quite
another thing to lie for long months and even years under the shadow of
death. No sane man would choose such a finish. All of us, despite the
Prayer Book, long for a swift and unexpected end. Unhappily, a murderer, under the irrational American system, is tortured for what, to him,
must seem a whole series of eternities. For months on end he sits in
prison while his lawyers carry on their idiotic buffoonery with writs,
injunctions, mandamuses, and appeals. In order to get his money (or
that of his friends) they have to feed him with hope. Now and then, by
the imbecility of a judge or some trick of juridic science, they actually
justify it. But let us say that, his money all gone, they finally throw up
their hands. Their client is now ready for the rope or the chair. But he
must still wait for months before it fetches him.

That wait, I believe, is horribly cruel. I have seen more than one man
sitting in the death-house, and I don't want to see any more. Worse, it is
wholly useless. Why should he wait at all? Why not hang him the day
after the last court dissipates his last hope? Why torture him as not even

cannibals would torture their victims? The common answer is that he must have time to make his peace with God. But how long does that take? It may be accomplished, I believe, in two hours quite as comfortably as in two years. There are, indeed, no temporal limitations upon God. He could forgive a whole herd of murderers in a millionth of a second. More, it has been done.

Is Google Making Us Stupid?

Nicholas Carr writes on the social, economic, and business implications of technology. Early in his career, he was executive editor of the *Harvard Business Review* and a principal at Mercer Management Consulting. He is the author of *Does IT Matter?* (2004), on the economics of information technology; *The Big Switch: Rewiring the World, from Edison to Google* (2008), on cloud computing; and *The Shallows: What the Internet is Doing to Our Brains* (2010). Carr has also written for many periodical, including the *Atlantic Montly*, the *New York Times Magazine*, *Wired*, the *Financial Times*, the *Futurist*, and *Advertising Age*, and has been a columnist for the *Guardian* and the *Industry Standard*. Carr has also been a speaker at many academic, corporate, governmental, and professional events throughout the world. He is a member of the Encyclopedia Britannica's editorial board of advisers and is on the steering board of the World Economic Forum's cloud computing project.

The essay below was the cover story of the *Atlantic Monthly*'s Ideas issue in 2008. In it, Carr argues that the Internet is having a disturbing effect on our cognitive activities—the work of our brains. As you read, think about your own habits of concentration and focus, considering whether you are able to focus deeply for long periods of time or whether you move from one idea to another fairly swiftly. Also, think about whether concentration has to be sacrificed for the sake of acquiring more information.

"Dave, stop. Stop, will you? Stop, Dave. Will you stop, Dave?" So the supercomputer HAL pleads with the implacable astronaut Dave Bowman in a famous and weirdly poignant scene toward the end of Stanley Kubrick's *2001: A Space Odyssey*. Bowman, having nearly been sent to a deep-space death by the malfunctioning machine, is calmly, coldly disconnecting the memory circuits that control its artificial "brain." "Dave, my mind is going," HAL says, forlornly. "I can feel it. I can feel it."

I can feel it, too. Over the past few years I've had an uncomfortable sense that someone, or something, has been tinkering with my brain, remapping the neural circuitry, reprogramming the memory. My mind isn't going—so far as I can tell—but it's changing. I'm not thinking the way I used to think. I can feel it most strongly when I'm reading. Immersing myself in a book or a lengthy article used to be easy. My mind would get caught up in the narrative or the turns of the argument, and I'd spend hours strolling through long stretches of prose. That's rarely the case anymore. Now my concentration often starts to drift after two or three pages. I get fidgety, lose the thread, begin looking for something else to do. I feel as if I'm always dragging my wayward brain back to the text. The deep reading that used to come naturally has become a struggle.

I think I know what's going on. For more than a decade now, I've been spending a lot of time online, searching and surfing and sometimes adding to the great databases of the Internet. The Web has been a godsend to me as a writer. Research that once required days in the stacks or periodical rooms of libraries can now be done in minutes. A few Google searches, some quick clicks on hyperlinks, and I've got the telltale fact or pithy quote I was after. Even when I'm not working, I'm as likely as not to be foraging in the Web's info-thickets, reading and writing e-mails, scanning headlines and blog posts, watching videos and listening to podcasts, or just tripping from link to link to link. (Unlike footnotes, to which they're sometimes likened, hyperlinks don't merely point to related works; they propel you toward them.)

For me, as for others, the Net is becoming a universal medium, the conduit for most of the information that flows through my eyes and ears and into my mind. The advantages of having immediate access to such an incredibly rich store of information are many, and they've been widely described and duly applauded. "The perfect recall of silicon memory," *Wired*'s Clive Thompson has written, "can be an enormous boon to thinking." But that boon comes at a price. As the media theorist Marshall McLuhan pointed out in the 1960s, media are not just passive channels of information. They supply the stuff of thought, but they also shape the process of thought. And what the Net seems to be doing is chipping away my capacity for concentration and contemplation. My mind now expects to take in information the way the Net distributes it: in a swiftly moving stream of particles. Once I was a scuba diver in the sea of words. Now I zip along the surface like a guy on a Jet Ski.

I'm not the only one. When I mention my troubles with reading to friends and acquaintances—literary types, most of them—many say they're having similar experiences. The more they use the Web, the more they have to fight to stay focused on long pieces of writing.

Some of the bloggers I follow have also begun mentioning the phenomenon. Scott Karp, who writes a blog about online media, recently confessed that he has stopped reading books altogether. "I was a lit major in college, and used to be [a] voracious book reader," he wrote. "What happened?" He speculates on the answer: "What if I do all my reading on the web not so much because the way I read has changed, i.e. I'm just seeking convenience, but because the way I THINK has changed?"

Bruce Friedman, who blogs regularly about the use of computers in medicine, also has described how the Internet has altered his mental habits. "I now have almost totally lost the ability to read and absorb a longish article on the web or in print," he wrote earlier this year. A pathologist who has long been on the faculty of the University of Michigan Medical School, Friedman elaborated on his comment in a telephone conversation with me. His thinking, he said, has taken on a "staccato" quality, reflecting the way he quickly scans short passages of text from many sources online. "I can't read *War and Peace* anymore," he admitted. "I've lost the ability to do that. Even a blog post of more than three or four paragraphs is too much to absorb. I skim it."

Anecdotes alone don't prove much. And we still await the long-term neurological and psychological experiments that will provide a definitive picture of how Internet use affects cognition. But a recently published study of online research habits, conducted by scholars from University College London, suggests that we may well be in the midst of a sea change in the way we read and think. As part of the five-year research program, the scholars examined computer logs documenting the behavior of visitors to two popular research sites, one operated by the British Library and one by a U.K. educational consortium, that provide access to journal articles, e-books, and other sources of written information. They found that people using the sites exhibited "a form of skimming activity," hopping from one source to another and rarely returning to any source they'd already visited. They typically read no more than one or two pages of an article or book before they would "bounce" out to another site. Sometimes they'd save a long article, but there's no evidence that they ever went back and actually read it. The authors of the study report:

> It is clear that users are not reading online in the traditional sense; indeed there are signs that new forms of "reading" are emerging as users "power browse" horizontally through titles, contents pages and abstracts going for quick wins. It almost

seems that they go online to avoid reading in the traditional sense.

Thanks to the ubiquity of text on the Internet, not to mention the popularity of text-messaging on cell phones, we may well be reading more today than we did in the 1970s or 1980s, when television was our medium of choice. But it's a different kind of reading, and behind it lies a different kind of thinking—perhaps even a new sense of the self. "We are not only *what* we read," says Maryanne Wolf, a developmental psychologist at Tufts University and the author of *Proust and the Squid: The Story and Science of the Reading Brain.* "We are *how* we read." Wolf worries that the style of reading promoted by the Net, a style that puts "efficiency" and "immediacy" above all else, may be weakening our capacity for the kind of deep reading that emerged when an earlier technology, the printing press, made long and complex works of prose commonplace. When we read online, she says, we tend to become "mere decoders of information." Our ability to interpret text, to make the rich mental connections that form when we read deeply and without distraction, remains largely disengaged.

Reading, explains Wolf, is not an instinctive skill for human beings. It's not etched into our genes the way speech is. We have to teach our minds how to translate the symbolic characters we see into the language we understand. And the media or other technologies we use in learning and practicing the craft of reading play an important part in shaping the neural circuits inside our brains. Experiments demonstrate that readers of ideograms, such as the Chinese, develop a mental circuitry for reading that is very different from the circuitry found in those of us whose written language employs an alphabet. The variations extend across many regions of the brain, including those that govern such essential cognitive functions as memory and the interpretation of visual and auditory stimuli. We can expect as well that the circuits woven by our use of the Net will be different from those woven by our reading of books and other printed works.

Sometime in 1882, Friedrich Nietzsche bought a typewriter—a Malling-Hansen Writing Ball, to be precise. His vision was failing, and keeping his eyes focused on a page had become exhausting and painful, often bringing on crushing headaches. He had been forced to curtail his writing, and he feared that he would soon have to give it up. The typewriter rescued him, at least for a time. Once he had mastered touch-typing, he was able to write with his eyes closed, using only the tips of his fingers. Words could once again flow from his mind to the page.

But the machine had a subtler effect on his work. One of Nietzsche's friends, a composer, noticed a change in the style of his writing. His already terse prose had become even tighter, more telegraphic. "Perhaps you will through this instrument even take to a new idiom," the friend wrote in a letter, noting that, in his own work, his "'thoughts in music and language often depend on the quality of pen and paper."

"The process works this way. When I sit down to write a letter or start the first draft of an article, I simply type on the keyboard and the words appear on the screen..." By James Fallows

"You are right," Nietzsche replied, "our writing equipment takes part in the forming of our thoughts." Under the sway of the machine, writes the German media scholar Friedrich A. Kittler, Nietzsche's prose "changed from arguments to aphorisms, from thoughts to puns, from rhetoric to telegram style."

The human brain is almost infinitely malleable. People used to think that our mental meshwork, the dense connections formed among the 100 billion or so neurons inside our skulls, was largely fixed by the time we reached adulthood. But brain researchers have discovered that that's not the case. James Olds, a professor of neuroscience who directs the Krasnow Institute for Advanced Study at George Mason University, says that even the adult mind "is very plastic." Nerve cells routinely break old connections and form new ones. "The brain," according to Olds, "has the ability to reprogram itself on the fly, altering the way it functions."

As we use what the sociologist Daniel Bell has called our "intellectual technologies"—the tools that extend our mental rather than our physical capacities—we inevitably begin to take on the qualities of those technologies. The mechanical clock, which came into common use in the 14th century, provides a compelling example. In *Technics and Civilization*, the historian and cultural critic Lewis Mumford described how the clock "disassociated time from human events and helped create the belief in an independent world of mathematically measurable sequences." The "abstract framework of divided time" became "the point of reference for both action and thought."

The clock's methodical ticking helped bring into being the scientific mind and the scientific man. But it also took something away. As the late MIT computer scientist Joseph Weizenbaum observed in his 1976 book, *Computer Power and Human Reason: From Judgment to Calculation*, the conception of the world that emerged from the widespread use of timekeeping instruments "remains an impoverished version of the older one, for it rests on a rejection of those direct experiences that formed the basis for, and indeed constituted, the old reality." In deciding when to eat, to work, to sleep, to rise, we stopped listening to our senses and started obeying the clock.

The process of adapting to new intellectual technologies is reflected in the changing metaphors we use to explain ourselves to ourselves. When the mechanical clock arrived, people began thinking of their brains as operating "like clockwork." Today, in the age of software, we have come to think of them as operating "like computers." But the changes, neuroscience tells us, go much deeper than metaphor. Thanks to our brain's plasticity, the adaptation occurs also at a biological level.

The Internet promises to have particularly far-reaching effects on cognition. In a paper published in 1936, the British mathematician Alan Turing proved that a digital computer, which at the time existed only as a theoretical machine, could be programmed to perform the function of any other information-processing device. And that's what we're seeing today. The Internet, an immeasurably powerful computing system, is subsuming most of our other intellectual technologies. It's becoming our map and our clock, our printing press and our typewriter, our calculator and our telephone, and our radio and TV.

When the Net absorbs a medium, that medium is re-created in the Net's image. It injects the medium's content with hyperlinks, blinking ads, and other digital gewgaws, and it surrounds the content with the content of all the other media it has absorbed. A new e-mail message, for instance, may announce its arrival as we're glancing over the latest headlines at a newspaper's site. The result is to scatter our attention and diffuse our concentration.

The Net's influence doesn't end at the edges of a computer screen, either. As people's minds become attuned to the crazy quilt of Internet media, traditional media have to adapt to the audience's new expectations. Television programs add text crawls and pop-up ads, and magazines and newspapers shorten their articles, introduce capsule summaries, and crowd their pages with easy-to-browse info-snippets. When, in March of this year, *The New York Times* decided to devote the second and third pages of every edition to article abstracts, its design director, Tom Bodkin, explained that the "shortcuts" would give harried readers a quick "taste" of the day's news, sparing them the "less efficient" method of actually turning the pages and reading the articles. Old media have little choice but to play by the new-media rules.

Never has a communications system played so many roles in our lives—or exerted such broad influence over our thoughts—as the Internet does today. Yet, for all that's been written about the Net, there's been little consideration of how, exactly, it's reprogramming us. The Net's intellectual ethic remains obscure.

About the same time that Nietzsche started using his typewriter, an earnest young man named Frederick Winslow Taylor carried a stopwatch into the Midvale Steel plant in Philadelphia and began a historic series of experiments aimed at improving the efficiency of the plant's machinists. With the approval of Midvale's owners, he recruited a group of factory hands, set them to work on various metalworking machines, and recorded and timed their every movement as well as the operations of the machines. By breaking down every job into a sequence of small, discrete steps and then testing different ways of performing each one, Taylor created a set of precise instructions—an "algorithm," we might say today—for how each worker should work. Midvale's employees grumbled about the strict new regime, claiming that it turned them into little more than automatons, but the factory's productivity soared.

More than a hundred years after the invention of the steam engine, the Industrial Revolution had at last found its philosophy and its philosopher. Taylor's tight industrial choreography—his "system," as he liked to call it—was embraced by manufacturers throughout the country and, in time, around the world. Seeking maximum speed, maximum efficiency, and maximum output, factory owners used time-and-motion studies to organize their work and configure the jobs of their workers. The goal, as Taylor defined it in his celebrated 1911 treatise, *The Principles of Scientific Management*, was to identify and adopt, for every job, the "one best method" of work and thereby to effect "the gradual substitution of science for rule of thumb throughout the mechanic arts." Once his system was applied to all acts of manual labor, Taylor assured his followers, it would bring about a restructuring not only of industry but of society, creating a utopia of perfect efficiency. "In the past the man has been first," he declared; "in the future the system must be first."

Taylor's system is still very much with us; it remains the ethic of industrial manufacturing. And now, thanks to the growing power that computer engineers and software coders wield over our intellectual lives, Taylor's ethic is beginning to govern the realm of the mind as well. The Internet is a machine designed for the efficient and automated collection, transmission, and manipulation of information, and its legions of programmers are intent on finding the "one best method"—the perfect algorithm—to carry out every mental movement of what we've come to describe as "knowledge work."

Google's headquarters, in Mountain View, California—the Googleplex—is the Internet's high church, and the religion practiced inside its walls is Taylorism. Google, says its chief executive, Eric Schmidt, is "a company that's founded around the science of measurement," and it is striving to "systematize everything" it does. Drawing on the terabytes of behavioral data it collects through its search engine and other sites, it carries out thousands of experiments a day, according to the *Harvard Business Review*, and it uses the results to refine the algorithms that increasingly control how people find information and extract meaning from it. What Taylor did for the work of the hand, Google is doing for the work of the mind.

The company has declared that its mission is "to organize the world's information and make it universally accessible and useful." It seeks to develop "the perfect search engine," which it defines as something that "understands exactly what you mean and gives you back exactly what you want." In Google's view, information is a kind of commodity, a utilitarian resource that can be mined and processed with industrial efficiency. The more pieces of information we can "access" and the faster we can extract their gist, the more productive we become as thinkers.

Where does it end? Sergey Brin and Larry Page, the gifted young men who founded Google while pursuing doctoral degrees in computer science at Stanford, speak frequently of their desire to turn their search engine into an artificial intelligence, a HAL-like machine that might be connected directly to our brains. "The ultimate search engine is something as smart as people—or smarter," Page said in a speech a few years back. "For us, working on search is a way to work on artificial intelligence." In a 2004 interview with *Newsweek*, Brin said, "Certainly if you had all the world's information directly attached to your brain, or an artificial brain that was smarter than your brain, you'd be better off." Last year, Page told a convention of scientists that Google is "really trying to build artificial intelligence and to do it on a large scale."

Such an ambition is a natural one, even an admirable one, for a pair of math whizzes with vast quantities of cash at their disposal and a small army of computer scientists in their employ. A fundamentally scientific enterprise, Google is motivated by a desire to use technology, in Eric Schmidt's words, "to solve problems that have never been solved before," and artificial intelligence is the hardest problem out there. Why wouldn't Brin and Page want to be the ones to crack it?

Still, their easy assumption that we'd all "be better off" if our brains were supplemented, or even replaced, by an artificial

345

intelligence is unsettling. It suggests a belief that intelligence is the output of a mechanical process, a series of discrete steps that can be isolated, measured, and optimized. In Google's world, the world we enter when we go online, there's little place for the fuzziness of contemplation. Ambiguity is not an opening for insight but a bug to be fixed. The human brain is just an outdated computer that needs a faster processor and a bigger hard drive.

The idea that our minds should operate as high-speed data-processing machines is not only built into the workings of the Internet, it is the network's reigning business model as well. The faster we surf across the Web—the more links we click and pages we view—the more opportunities Google and other companies gain to collect information about us and to feed us advertisements. Most of the proprietors of the commercial Internet have a financial stake in collecting the crumbs of data we leave behind as we flit from link to link—the more crumbs, the better. The last thing these companies want is to encourage leisurely reading or slow, concentrated thought. It's in their economic interest to drive us to distraction.

Maybe I'm just a worrywart. Just as there's a tendency to glorify technological progress, there's a countertendency to expect the worst of every new tool or machine. In Plato's *Phaedrus*, Socrates bemoaned the development of writing. He feared that, as people came to rely on the written word as a substitute for the knowledge they used to carry inside their heads, they would, in the words of one of the dialogue's characters, "cease to exercise their memory and become forgetful." And because they would be able to "receive a quantity of information without proper instruction," they would "be thought very knowledgeable when they are for the most part quite ignorant." They would be "filled with the conceit of wisdom instead of real wisdom." Socrates wasn't wrong—the new technology did often have the effects he feared—but he was shortsighted. He couldn't foresee the many ways that writing and reading would serve to spread information, spur fresh ideas, and expand human knowledge (if not wisdom).

The arrival of Gutenberg's printing press, in the 15th century, set off another round of teeth gnashing. The Italian humanist Hieronimo Squarciafico worried that the easy availability of books would lead to intellectual laziness, making men "less studious" and weakening their minds. Others argued that cheaply printed books and broadsheets would undermine religious authority, demean the work of scholars and scribes, and spread sedition and debauchery. As New York University professor Clay Shirky notes, "Most of the arguments made against the printing press were correct, even prescient." But, again, the doomsayers were unable to imagine the myriad blessings that the printed word would deliver.

So, yes, you should be skeptical of my skepticism. Perhaps those who dismiss critics of the Internet as Luddites or nostalgists will be proved correct, and from our hyperactive, data-stoked minds will spring a golden age of intellectual discovery and universal wisdom. Then again, the Net isn't the alphabet, and although it may replace the printing press, it produces something altogether different. The kind of deep reading that a sequence of printed pages promotes is valuable not just for the knowledge we acquire from the author's words but for the intellectual vibrations those words set off within our own minds. In the quiet spaces opened up by the sustained, undistracted reading of a book, or by any other act of contemplation, for that matter, we make our own associations, draw our own inferences and analogies, foster our own ideas. Deep reading, as Maryanne Wolf argues, is indistinguishable from deep thinking.

If we lose those quiet spaces, or fill them up with "content," we will sacrifice something important not only in our selves but in our culture. In a recent essay, the playwright Richard Foreman eloquently described what's at stake:

> I come from a tradition of Western culture, in which the ideal (my ideal) was the complex, dense and "cathedral-like" structure of the highly educated and articulate personality—a man or woman who carried inside themselves a personally constructed and unique version of the entire heritage of the West. [But now] I see within us all (myself included) the replacement of complex inner density with a new kind of self— evolving under the pressure of information overload and the technology of the "instantly available."

As we are drained of our "inner repertory of dense cultural inheritance," Foreman concluded, we risk turning into "'pancake people'—spread wide and thin as we connect with that vast network of information accessed by the mere touch of a button."

I'm haunted by that scene in *2001*. What makes it so poignant, and so weird, is the computer's emotional response to the disassembly of its mind: its despair as one circuit after another goes dark, its childlike pleading with the astronaut—"I can feel it. I can feel it. I'm afraid"—and its final reversion to what can only be called a state of innocence. HAL's outpouring of feeling contrasts with the emotionlessness that characterizes the human figures in the film, who go about their business with an almost robotic efficiency. Their thoughts and actions feel scripted, as if they're following the steps of an algorithm. In the world of *2001*, people have become so machinelike that the most human character turns out to be a machine. That's the essence of Kubrick's dark prophecy: as we come to rely on computers to mediate our understanding of the world, it is our own intelligence that flattens into artificial intelligence.

[2008]

MICHAEL POLLAN [b. 1955]

In Defense of Food

Born on Long Island, New York, **Michael Pollan** studied at Bennington College and Columbia University, where he received his master's degree in English in 1981. He has been a contributing writer for the *New York Times Magazine* for more than fifteen years, as well as a contributing editor for *Harper's* and the Modern Library Garden Series. Pollan's essays have been published widely in periodicals, including the *New York Times*, *National Geographic*, *Newsweek*, the *Smithsonian*, *Time*, and *Orion*, as well as anthologized in *Best American Essays* and *Best American Science Writing*. He has also published several books of nonfiction including *A Place of My Own: The Education of an Amateur Builder* (1997) and *The Omnivore's Dilemma: A Natural History of Four Meals* (2006). In his most recent book, *Food Rules: An Eater's Manual* (2009), Pollan offers up valuable advice, or rules, for wise consumers who are, or who'd like to be, mindful of what they eat. A recipient of innumerable awards and honors, Pollan was named among *Newsweek's* top ten "New Thought Leaders" in 2008 and *Time's* top one hundred most influential people in the world in 2010. Currently living in the San Francisco Bay Area, he teaches in the Knight Program in Science and Environmental Journalism at the University of California, Berkeley.

Pollan's *In Defense of Food: An Eater's Manifesto* (2008), from which the following selection is excerpted, is a commentary on the industrialized diet of a contemporary, Western society. Considering the flurry of "foodlike substitutes" that have begun to dominate supermarket shelves since the 1980s, Pollan presents a set of rules for the wise consumer, acknowledging, as he says, "[o]rdinary food is still out there," though concealed amid packets of Go-Gurt and Twinkies. Ultimately, Pollan advises that our dollars would be better spent on "quality [over the] convenience" of such products.

The first time I heard the advice to "just eat food" it was in a speech by Joan Gussow, and it completely baffled me. Of course you should eat food—what else is there to eat? But Gussow, who grows much of her own food on a flood-prone finger of land jutting into the Hudson River, refuses to dignify most of the products for sale in the supermarket with that title. "In the thirty-four years I've been in the field of nutrition," she said in the same speech, "I have watched real food disappear from large areas of the supermarket and from much of the rest of the eating world." Taking food's place on the shelves has been an unending stream of food-like substitutes, some seventeen thousand new ones every year—"products constructed largely around commerce and hope, supported by frighteningly little actual knowledge." Ordinary food is still out there, however, still being grown and even occasionally sold in the supermarket, and this ordinary food is what we should eat.

But given our current state of confusion and given the thousands of products calling themselves food, this is more easily said than done. So consider these related rules of thumb. Each proposes a different sort of map to the contemporary food landscape, but all should take you to more or less the same place.

Don't eat anything your great grandmother wouldn't recognize as food.
Why your great grandmother? Because at this point your mother and possibly even your grandmother is as confused as the rest of us; to be safe we need to go back at least a couple generations, to a time before the advent of most modern foods. So depending on your age (and your grandmother), you may need to go back to your great- or even great-great grandmother. Some nutritionists recommend going back even further. John Yudkin, a British nutritionist whose early alarms about the dangers of refined carbohydrates were overlooked in the 1960s and 1970s, once advised, "Just don't eat anything your Neolithic ancestors wouldn't have recognized and you'll be ok."

What would shopping this way mean in the supermarket? Well, imagine your great grandmother at your side as you roll down the aisles. You're standing together in front of the dairy case. She picks up a package of Go-Gurt Portable Yogurt tubes—and has no idea what this could possibly be. Is it a food or a toothpaste? And how, exactly, do you introduce it into your body? You could tell her it's just yogurt in a squirtable form, yet if she read the ingredients label she would have every reason to doubt that that was in fact the case. Sure, there's some yogurt in there, but there are also a dozen other things that aren't remotely yogurtlike, ingredients she would probably fail to recognize as foods of any kind, including high-fructose corn syrup, modified corn starch, kosher gelatin, carrageenan, tricalcium phosphate, natural and artificial flavors, vitamins, and so forth. (And there's a whole other list of ingredients for the "berry bubblegum bash" flavoring, containing everything but berries or bubblegum.) How did yogurt, which in your great grandmother's day consisted simply of milk inoculated with a bacterial culture, ever get to be so complicated? Is a product like Go-Gurt Portable Yogurt still a whole food? A food of any kind? Or is it just a food product?

There are in fact hundreds of foodish products in the supermarket 5 that your ancestors simply wouldn't recognize as food: breakfast cereal bars transected by bright white veins representing, but in reality having nothing to do with, milk; "protein waters" and "nondairy creamer"; cheeselike foodstuffs equally innocent of any bovine contribution; cakelike cylinders (with creamlike fillings) called Twinkies that never grow stale. *Don't eat anything incapable of rotting* is another personal policy you might consider adopting.

There are many reasons to avoid eating such complicated food products beyond the various chemical additives and corn and soy derivatives they contain. One of the problems with the products of food science is that, as Joan Gussow has pointed out, they lie to your body; their artificial colors and flavors and synthetic sweeteners and novel fats confound the senses we rely on to assess new foods and prepare our bodies to deal with them. Foods that lie leave us with little choice but to eat by the numbers, consulting labels rather than our senses.

It's true that foods have long been processed in order to preserve them, as when we pickle or ferment or smoke, but industrial processing aims to do much more than extend shelf life. Today foods are processed in ways specifically designed to sell us more food by pushing our evolutionary buttons—our inborn preferences for sweetness and fat and salt. These qualities are difficult to find in nature but cheap and easy for the food scientist to deploy, with the result that processing induces us to consume much more of these ecological rarities than is good for us. "Tastes great, less filling!" could be the motto for most processed foods, which are far more energy dense than most whole foods: They contain much less water, fiber, and micronutrients, and generally much more sugar and fat, making them at the same time, to coin a marketing slogan, "More fattening, less nutritious!"

The great grandma rule will help keep many of these products out of your cart. But not all of them. Because thanks to the FDA's willingness, post-1973, to let food makers freely alter the identity of "traditional foods that everyone knows" without having to call them imitations, your great grandmother could easily be fooled into thinking that that loaf of bread or wedge of cheese is in fact a loaf of bread or a wedge of cheese. This is why we need a slightly more detailed personal policy to capture these imitation foods; to wit:

Avoid food products containing ingredients that are (a) unfamiliar, (b) unpronounceable, (c) more than five in number, or that include

(d) high-fructose corn syrup. None of these characteristics, not even the last one, is necessarily harmful in and of itself, but all of them are reliable markers for foods that have been highly processed to the point where they may no longer be what they purport to be. They have crossed over from foods to food products.

Consider a loaf of bread, one of the "traditional foods that everyone knows" specifically singled out for protection in the 1938 imitation rule. As your grandmother could tell you, bread is traditionally made using a remarkably small number of familiar ingredients: flour, yeast, water, and a pinch of salt will do it. But industrial bread—even industrial whole-grain bread—has become a far more complicated product of modern food science (not to mention commerce and hope). Here's the complete ingredients list for Sara Lee's Soft & Smooth Whole Grain White Bread. (Wait a minute—isn't "Whole Grain White Bread" a contradiction in terms? Evidently not any more.)

> Enriched bleached flour [wheat flour, malted barley flour, niacin, iron, thiamin mononitrate (vitamin B_1), riboflavin (vitamin B_2), folic acid], water, whole grains [whole wheat flour, brown rice flour (rice flour, rice bran)], high fructose corn syrup [hello!], whey, wheat gluten, yeast, cellulose. Contains 2% or less of each of the following: honey, calcium sulfate, vegetable oil (soybean and/or cottonseed oils), salt, butter (cream, salt), dough conditioners (may contain one or more of the following: mono- and diglycerides, ethoxylated mono- and diglycerides, ascorbic acid, enzymes, azodicarbonamide), guar gum, calcium propionate (preservative), distilled vinegar, yeast nutrients (monocalcium phosphate, calcium sulfate, ammonium sulfate), corn starch, natural flavor, betacarotene (color), vitamin D_3, soy lecithin, soy flour.

There are many things you could say about this intricate loaf of "bread," but note first that even if it managed to slip by your great grandmother (because it is a loaf of bread, or at least is called one and strongly resembles one), the product fails every test proposed under rule number two: It's got unfamiliar ingredients (monoglycerides I've heard of before, but ethoxylated monoglycerides?); unpronounceable ingredients (try "azodicarbonamide"); it exceeds the maximum of five ingredients (by roughly thirty-six) ; and it contains high-fructose corn syrup. Sorry, Sara Lee, but your Soft & Smooth Whole Grain White Bread is not food and if not for the indulgence of the FDA could not even be labeled "bread."

Sara Lee's Soft & Smooth Whole Grain White Bread could serve as a monument to the age of nutritionism. It embodies the latest nutritional wisdom from science and government (which in its most recent food pyramid recommends that at least half our consumption of grain come from whole grains) but leavens that wisdom with the commercial recognition that American eaters (and American children in particular) have come to prefer their wheat highly refined—which is to say, cottony soft, snowy white, and exceptionally sweet on the tongue. In its marketing materials, Sara Lee treats this clash of interests as some sort of Gordian knot—it speaks in terms of an ambitious quest to build a "no compromise" loaf—which only the most sophisticated food science could possibly cut.

And so it has, with the invention of whole-grain white bread. Because the small percentage of whole grains in the bread would render it that much less sweet than, say, all-white Wonder Bread—which scarcely waits to be chewed before transforming itself into glucose—the food scientists have added high-fructose corn syrup and honey to make up the difference; to overcome the problematic heft and toothsomeness of a real whole grain bread, they've deployed "dough conditioners," including guar gum and the aforementioned azodicarbonamide, to simulate the texture of supermarket white bread. By incorporating certain varieties of albino wheat, they've managed to maintain that deathly but apparently appealing Wonder Bread pallor.

Who would have thought Wonder Bread would ever become an ideal of aesthetic and gustatory perfection to which bakers would actually aspire—Sara Lee's Mona Lisa?

Very often food science's efforts to make traditional foods more nutritious make them much more complicated, but not necessarily any better for you. To make dairy products low fat, it's not enough to remove the fat. You then have to go to great lengths to preserve the body or creamy texture by working in all kinds of food additives. In the case of low-fat or skim milk, that usually means adding powdered milk. But powdered milk contains oxidized cholesterol, which scientists believe is much worse for your arteries than ordinary cholesterol, so food makers sometimes compensate by adding antioxidants, further complicating what had been a simple one-ingredient whole food. Also, removing the fat makes it that much harder for your body to absorb the fat-soluble vitamins that are one of the reasons to drink milk in the first place.

All this heroic and occasionally counterproductive food science has been undertaken in the name of our health—so that Sara Lee can add to its plastic wrapper the magic words "good source of whole grain" or a food company can ballyhoo the even more magic words "low fat." Which brings us to a related food policy that may at first sound counterintuitive to a health-conscious eater:

Avoid food products that make health claims. For a food product to make health claims on its package it must first have a package, so right off the bat it's more likely to be a processed than a whole food. Generally speaking, it is only the big food companies that have the wherewithal to secure FDA-approved health claims for their products and then trumpet them to the world. Recently, however, some of the tonier fruits and nuts have begun boasting about their health-enhancing properties, and there will surely be more as each crop council scrounges together the money to commission its own scientific study. Because all plants contain anti-oxidants, all these studies are guaranteed to find something on which to base a health oriented marketing campaign.

But for the most part it is the products of food science that make the boldest health claims, and these are often founded on incomplete and often erroneous science—the dubious fruits of nutritionism. Don't forget that trans-fat-rich margarine, one of the first industrial foods to claim it was healthier than the traditional food it replaced, turned out to give people heart attacks. Since that debacle, the FDA, under tremendous pressure from industry, has made it only easier for food companies to make increasingly doubtful health claims, such as the one Frito-Lay now puts on some of its chips—that eating them is somehow good for your heart. If you bother to read the health claims closely (as food marketers make sure consumers seldom do), you will find that there is often considerably less to them than meets the eye.

Consider a recent "qualified" health claim approved by the FDA for (don't laugh) corn oil. ("Qualified" is a whole new category of health claim, introduced in 2002 at the behest of industry.) Corn oil, you may recall, is particularly high in the omega-6 fatty acids we're already consuming far too many of.

> Very limited and preliminary scientific evidence suggests that eating about one tablespoon (16 grams) of corn oil daily may reduce the risk of heart disease due to the unsaturated fat content in corn oil.

The tablespoon is a particularly rich touch, conjuring images of moms 20 administering medicine, or perhaps cod-liver oil, to their children. But what the FDA gives with one hand, it takes away with the other. Here's the small-print "qualification" of this already notably diffident health claim:

> [The] FDA concludes that there is little scientific evidence supporting this claim.

And then to make matters still more perplexing:

> To achieve this possible benefit, corn oil is to replace a similar amount of saturated fat and not increase the total number of calories you eat in a day.

This little masterpiece of pseudoscientific bureaucratese was extracted from the FDA by the manufacturer of Mazola corn oil. It would appear that "qualified" is an official FDA euphemism for "all but meaningless." Though someone might have let the consumer in on this game: The FDA's own research indicates that consumers have no idea what to make of qualified health claims (how would they?), and its rules allow companies to promote the claims pretty much any way they want—they can use really big type for the claim, for example, and then print the disclaimers in teeny-tiny type. No doubt we can look forward to a qualified health claim for high-fructose corn syrup, a tablespoon of which probably does contribute to your health—as long as it replaces a comparable amount of, say, poison in your diet and doesn't increase the total number of calories you eat in a day.

When corn oil and chips and sugary breakfast cereals can all boast being good for your heart, health claims have become hopelessly corrupt. The American Heart Association currently bestows (for a fee) its heart-healthy seal of approval on Lucky Charms, Cocoa Puffs, and Trix cereals, Yoo-hoo lite chocolate drink, and Healthy Choice's Premium Caramel Swirl Ice Cream Sandwich—this at a time when scientists are coming to recognize that dietary sugar probably plays a more important role in heart disease than dietary fat. Meanwhile, the genuinely heart-healthy whole foods in the produce section, lacking the financial and political clout of the packaged goods a few aisles over, are mute. But don't take the silence of the yams as a sign that they have nothing valuable to say about health.

Bogus health claims and food science have made supermarkets particularly treacherous places to shop for real food, which suggests two further rules:

Shop the peripheries of the supermarket and stay out of the middle. 25
Most supermarkets are laid out the same way: Processed food products dominate the center aisles of the store while the cases of ostensibly fresh food—dairy, produce, meat, and fish—line the walls. If you keep to the edges of the store you'll be that much more likely to wind up with real food in your shopping cart. The strategy is not foolproof, however, because things like high-fructose corn syrup have slipped into the dairy case under cover of Go-Gurt and such. So consider a more radical strategy:

Get out of the supermarket whenever possible. You won't find any high-fructose corn syrup at the farmers' market. You also won't find any elaborately processed food products, any packages with long lists of unpronounceable ingredients or dubious health claims, nothing micro-wavable, and, perhaps best of all, no old food from far away. What you will find are fresh whole foods picked at the peak of their taste and nutritional quality—precisely the kind your great grandmother, or even your Neolithic ancestors, would easily have recognized as food.

Indeed, the surest way to escape the Western diet is simply to depart the realms it rules: the supermarket, the convenience store, and the fast-food outlet. It is hard to eat badly from the farmers' market, from a CSA box (community-supported agriculture, an increasingly popular scheme in which you subscribe to a farm and receive a weekly box of produce), or from your garden. The number of farmers' markets has more than doubled in the last ten years, to more than four thousand, making it one of the fastest-growing segments of the food marketplace. It is true that most farmers' markets operate only seasonally, and you won't find everything you need there. But buying as much as you can from the farmers' market, or directly from the farm when that's an option, is a simple act with a host of profound consequences for your health as well as for the health of the food chain you've now joined.

When you eat from the farmers' market, you automatically eat food that is in season, which is usually when it is most nutritious. Eating in season also tends to diversify your diet—because you can't buy strawberries or broccoli or potatoes twelve months of the year, you'll find yourself experimenting with other foods when they come into the market. The CSA box does an even better job of forcing you out of your dietary rut because you'll find things in your weekly allotment that you would never buy on your own. Whether it's a rutabaga or an unfamiliar winter squash, the CSA box's contents invariably send you to your cookbooks to figure out what in the world to do with them. Cooking is one of the most important health consequences of buying food from local farmers; for one thing, when you cook at home you seldom find yourself reaching for the ethoxylated diglycerides or high-fructose corn syrup. . . .

To shop at a farmers' market or sign up with a CSA is to join a short food chain and that has several implications for your health. Local produce is typically picked ripe and is fresher than supermarket produce, and for those reasons it should be tastier and more nutritious. As for supermarket organic produce, it too is likely to have come from far away—from the industrial organic farms of California or, increasingly, China.* And while it's true that the organic label guarantees that no synthetic pesticides or fertilizers have been used to produce the food, many,

---

*One recent study found that the average item of organic produce in the supermarket had actually traveled farther from the farm than the average item of conventional produce.

if not most, of the small farms that supply farmers' markets are organic in everything but name. To survive in the farmers' market or CSA economy, a farm will need to be highly diversified, and a diversified farm usually has little need for pesticides; it's the big monocultures that can't survive without them.[†]

If you're concerned about chemicals in your produce, you can simply   30 ask the farmer at the market how he or she deals with pests and fertility and begin the sort of conversation between producers and consumers that, in the end, is the best guarantee of quality in your food. So many of the problems of the industrial food chain stem from its length and complexity. A wall of ignorance intervenes between consumers and producers, and that wall fosters a certain carelessness on both sides. Farmers can lose sight of the fact that they're growing food for actual eaters rather than for middlemen, and consumers can easily forget that growing good food takes care and hard work. In a long food chain, the story and identity of the food (Who grew it? Where and how was it grown?) disappear into the undifferentiated stream of commodities, so that the only information communicated between consumers and producers is a price. In a short food chain, eaters can make their needs and desires known to the farmer, and farmers can impress on eaters the distinctions between ordinary and exceptional food, and the many reasons why exceptional food is worth what it costs. Food reclaims its story, and some of its nobility, when the person who grew it hands it to you. So here's a subclause to the get-out-of-the-supermarket rule: *Shake the hand that feeds you.*

As soon as you do, accountability becomes once again a matter of relationships instead of regulation or labeling or legal liability. Food safety didn't become a national or global problem until the industrialization of the food chain attenuated the relationships between food producers and eaters. That was the story Upton Sinclair told about the Beef Trust in 1906, and it's the story unfolding in China today, where the rapid industrialization of the food system is leading to alarming breakdowns in food safety and integrity. Regulation is an imperfect substitute for the accountability, and trust, built into a market in which food producers meet the gaze of eaters and vice versa. Only when we participate in a short food chain are we reminded every week that we are indeed part of a food chain and dependent for our health on its peoples and soils and integrity — on its health.

[†]Wendell Berry put the problem of monoculture with admirable brevity and clarity in his essay "The Pleasures of Eating": "But as scale increases, diversity declines; as diversity declines, so does health; as health declines, the dependence on drugs and chemicals necessarily increases."

"Eating is an agricultural act," Wendell Berry famously wrote, by which he meant that we are not just passive consumers of food but cocreators of the systems that feed us. Depending on how we spend them, our food dollars can either go to support a food industry devoted to quantity and convenience and "value" or they can nourish a food chain organized around values—values like quality and health. Yes, shopping this way takes more money and effort, but as soon you begin to treat that expenditure not just as shopping but also as a kind of vote— a vote for health in the largest sense—food no longer seems like the smartest place to economize.

[2008]

ESTHER DYSON   [b. 1951]

Cyberspace for All

Noted economist and digital technology specialist **Esther Dyson** was born in Zurich, Switzerland in 1951, the daughter of renowned physicist Freeman Dyson and mathematician Esther Dyson. She began studies at Harvard University at sixteen and graduated with a degree in economics in 1972, starting her career as a fact-checker and then reporter for *Forbes* magazine. Since 1983 she has been president and owner of EDventure Holdings, a globally diversified information services company that conducts industry events and analyzes industry trends. She published *Release 2.0: A Design for Living in the Digital Age* in 1997 and an updated version of the same book in 1998 called *Release 2.1. Release 3.0* is Dyson's bimonthly column for the *New York Times* and its syndicate. From 1998 to 2000 she served as one of nine directors of ICANN, the Internet Corporation for Assigned Names and Numbers, a governing body for the Internet.

Influenced by the liberating possibilities of the Internet, Dyson advocates user responsibility in her 1995 *New York Times* article "Cyberspace for All." Dyson claims that cyberspace is zoned much like real estate, with sites having family appeal, commercial opportunities, educational, religious, political, or scientific attractions, or the allure of a red-light district. The beauty of cyberspace, for Dyson, is that individuals can freely choose their desired community.

Something in the American psyche loves new frontiers. We hanker after wide-open spaces; we like to explore; we like to make rules instead of follow them. But in this age of political correctness and other intrusions on our national cult of independence, it's hard to find a place where you can go and be yourself without worrying about the neighbors.

There is such a place: cyberspace. Lost in the furor over porn on the Net is the exhilarating sense of freedom that this new frontier once promised—and still does in some quarters. Formerly a playground for computer nerds and techies, cyberspace now embraces every conceivable constituency: schoolchildren, flirtatious singles, Hungarian-Americans, accountants—along with pederasts and porn fans. Can they all get along? Or will our fear of kids surfing for cyberporn behind their bedroom doors provoke a crackdown?

The first order of business is to grasp what cyberspace *is*. It might help to leave behind metaphors of highways and frontiers and to think instead of real estate. Real estate, remember, is an intellectual, legal, artificial environment constructed *on top of* land. Real estate recognizes the difference between parkland and shopping mall, between red light zone and school district, between church, state, and drugstore.

In the same way, you could think of cyberspace as a giant and unbounded world of virtual real estate. Some property is privately owned and rented out; other property is common land; some places are suitable for children, and others are best avoided by all but the kinkiest citizens. Unfortunately, it's those places that are now capturing the popular imagination: places that offer bomb-making instructions, pornography, advice on how to procure stolen credit cards. They make cyberspace sound like a nasty place. Good citizens jump to a conclusion: better regulate it....

Regardless of how many laws or lawsuits are launched, regulation 5 won't work.

Aside from being unconstitutional, using censorship to counter indecency and other troubling "speech" fundamentally misinterprets the nature of cyberspace. Cyberspace isn't a frontier where wicked people can grab unsuspecting children, nor is it a giant television system that can beam offensive messages at unwilling viewers. In this kind of real estate, users have to *choose* where they visit, what they see, what they do. It's optional, and it's much easier to bypass a place on the Net than it is to avoid walking past an unsavory block of stores on the way to your local 7–11.

Put plainly, cyberspace is a voluntary destination — in reality, many destinations. You don't just get "onto the Net"; you have to go someplace in particular. That means that people can choose where to go and what to see. Yes, community standards should be enforced, but those standards should be set by cyberspace communities themselves, not by the courts or by politicians in Washington. What we need isn't Government control over all these electronic communities: We need self-rule.

What makes cyberspace so alluring is precisely the way in which it's *different* from shopping malls, television, highways and other terrestrial jurisdictions. But let's define the territory:

First, there are private e-mail conversations, akin to the conversations you have over the telephone or voice mail. These are private and consensual and require no regulation at all.

Second, there are information and entertainment services, where 10 people can download anything from legal texts and lists of "great new restaurants" to game software or dirty pictures. These places are like bookstores, malls, and movie houses—places where you go to buy something. The customer needs to request an item or sign up for a subscription; stuff (especially pornography) is not sent out to people who don't ask for it. Some of these services are free or included as part of a broad service like Compuserve or America Online; others charge and may bill their customers directly.

Third, there are "real" communities—groups of people who communicate among themselves. In real-estate terms, they're like bars or restaurants or bathhouses. Each active participant contributes to a general conversation, generally through posted messages. Other participants may simply listen or watch. Some are supervised by a moderator; others are more like bulletin boards—anyone is free to post anything. Many of these services started out unmoderated but are now imposing rules to keep out unwanted advertising, extraneous discussions, or increasingly rude participants. Without a moderator, the decibel level often gets too high.

Ultimately, it's the rules that determine the success of such places. Some of the rules are determined by the supplier of content; some of the rules concern prices and membership fees. The rules may be simple: "Only high-quality content about oil-industry liability and pollution legislation: $120 an hour." Or: "This forum is unmoderated, and restricted to information about copyright issues. People who insist on posting advertising or unrelated material will be asked to desist (and may eventually be barred)." Or: "Only children 8 to 12, on school-related topics and only clean words. The moderator will decide what's acceptable."

Cyberspace communities evolve just the way terrestrial communities do: People with like-minded interests band together. Every cyberspace community has its own character. Overall, the communities on Compuserve tend to be more techy or professional; those on America Online, affluent young singles; Prodigy, family oriented. Then there are independents like Echo, a hip, downtown New York service, or Women's Wire, targeted to women who want to avoid the male culture prevalent elsewhere on the Net. There's SurfWatch, a new program allowing access only to locations deemed suitable for children. On the Internet itself, there are lots of passionate noncommercial discussion groups on topics ranging from Hungarian politics (Hungary-Online) to copyright law.

And yes, there are also porn-oriented services, where people share dirty pictures and communicate with one another about all kinds of practices, often anonymously. Whether these services encourage the fantasies they depict is subject to debate—the same debate that has raged about pornography in other media. But the point is that no one is forcing this stuff on anybody.

What's unique about cyberspace is that it liberates us from the tyranny 15 of government, where everyone lives by the rule of the majority. In a democracy, minority groups and minority preferences tend to get squeezed out, whether they are minorities of race and culture or minorities of individual taste. Cyberspace allows communities of any size and kind to flourish; in cyberspace, communities are chosen by the users, not forced on them by accidents of geography. This freedom gives the rules that preside in cyberspace a moral authority that rules in terrestrial environments don't have. Most people are stuck in the country of their birth, but if you don't like the rules of a cyberspace community, you can just sign off. Love it or leave it. Likewise, if parents don't like the rules of a given cyberspace community, they can restrict their children's access to it.

What's likely to happen in cyberspace is the formation of new communities, free of the constraints that cause conflict on earth. Instead of a global village, which is a nice dream but impossible to manage, we'll have invented another world of self-contained communities that cater to their own members' inclinations without interfering with anyone else's. The possibility of a real market-style evolution of governance is at hand. In cyberspace, we'll be able to test and evolve rules governing what needs to be governed — intellectual property, content and access control, rules about privacy and free speech. Some communities will allow anyone in; others will restrict access to members who qualify on one basis or another. Those communities that prove self-sustaining will prosper (and perhaps grow and split into subsets with ever-more-particular interests and identities). Those that can't survive — either because people lose interest or get scared off — will simply wither away.

In the near future, explorers in cyberspace will need to get better at defining and identifying their communities. They will need to put in place — and accept — their own local governments, just as the owners of expensive real estate often prefer to have their own security guards rather than call in the police. But they will rarely need help from any terrestrial government.

Of course, terrestrial governments may not agree. What to do, for instance, about pornography? The answer is labeling — not banning — questionable material. In order to avoid censorship and lower the political temperature, it makes sense for cyberspace participants themselves to agree on a scheme for questionable items, so that people or automatic filters can avoid them. In other words, posting pornography in "alt.sex. bestiality" would be O.K.; it's easy enough for software manufacturers to build an automatic filter that would prevent you — or your child — from ever seeing that item on a menu. (It's as if all the items were wrapped, with labels on the wrapper.) Someone who posted the same material under the title "Kid-Fun" could be sued for mislabeling.

Without a lot of fanfare, private enterprises and local groups are already producing a variety of labeling and ranking services, along with kid-oriented sites like Kidlink, EdWeb and Kids' Space. People differ in their tastes and values and can find services or reviewers on the Net that suit them in the same way they select books and magazines. Or they can wander freely if they prefer, making up their own itinerary.

In the end, our society needs to grow up. Growing up means under- 20 standing that there are no perfect answers, no all-purpose solutions, no government-sanctioned safe havens. We haven't created a perfect society on earth and we won't have one in cyberspace either. But at least we can have individual choice—and individual responsibility.

MICHAEL SNIDER   [b. 1972]

The Intimacy of Blogs

Michael Snider received his formal education—primarily in high technology—while enrolled in the army. Following his discharge, he worked in academic settings, including Rio Grande Community College and the University of Rio Grande, where he has assisted in technological restructuring. Though Snider also authors a column for *Maclean's*, a Canadian (print) magazine, he has achieved greater recognition for his blog—or Weblog—a forum that allows him to share his opinions and insights with a global audience. In his essay "The Intimacy of Blogs," Snider analyzes the paradoxical nature of the blog, its potential for transcending distance within an artificial community that forces us to redefine traditional ideas regarding intimacy.

When Plain Layne suddenly pulled her site down in early June, a little corner of the blogosphere went nuts. Instead of the 26-year-old Minnesotan's poignant daily entries on her Weblog, an on-line journal, a blunt one-line message greeted visitors: "Take very good care of you." No more honestly introspective narratives of her life. No more unbridled entries detailing the search for her birth parents, sessions with her therapist or her disappointing love affair with Violet, the stubby-tongued Dragon Lady. Comments flooded cyberspace. "Her surprising, unannounced departure is sending me and my overactive imagination into a frenzy of worry," wrote Gudy Two Shoes on his own Weblog. "If she's gone then wish her well," posted Intellectual Poison. "She got me started with this whole blogging thing, something that I am truly grateful for." And Daintily Dirty asked, "Are the relationships we create by our blogging of any value?"

That's a good question. It turned out that Plaine Layne, aka Layne Johnson, wasn't gone for good. She'd just had a week during which she moved into a new house and witnessed the birth of her surrogate little sister's baby before getting her site back up *(http://plainlayne. dreamhost.com)*. But the reaction from her readers was genuine. One of the prime reasons people blog is to make connections with others, and

Michael Snider, "The Intimacy of Blogs" from *Maclean's*, September 15, 2003. Reprinted by permission of Maclean's.

when Plain Layne went missing, it was like a neighbour had just up and moved in the middle of the night, with no forwarding address.

Weblogs are independent Web sites usually operated by a single person or by a small group of people. They serve as frequently updated forums to discuss whatever the blogger wants to discuss. Unmonitored, each blogger is author, editor and publisher, beholden solely to his or her own whims and desires. There are political blogs, media blogs, gay blogs, sports blogs, war blogs, antiwar blogs, tech blogs, photo blogs—hundreds of thousands of blogs, actually (estimates are as high as two million). "Blogging is not people wasting other people's time talking about the minutiae of their lives," says Joe Clark, 38, a Toronto author who operates several blogs. "The thing that's attractive about reading Weblogs is that you know there is one human being or a group of human beings behind them."

Free and easy-to-use publishing programs with names like Blogger, Movable Type and Live Journal spurred the phenomenon. Now, anyone with a computer and an Internet connection can set up their own blog with relative ease. Paul Martin blogs, journalists blog, pundits, critics and social misfits blog. And what can you find there? Well, imagine standing in front of a library of gargantuan magazine racks loaded with glossy covers with everything from newsweeklies to girlie mags.

Blogs break down into two very general groups: linking blogs and personal online journals. Political blogs like Glenn Reynolds' *Instapundit.com,* media blogs like Jim Romenesko's Poynter Online *(www.poynter.org/media news),* or tech blogs like *slashdot.com* are of the former kind. They're link-driven sites that connect readers to theme-related news stories and sometimes add a little commentary along with it. A personal blog is more like a diary entry or column in a daily newspaper, *a la* Rebecca Eckler of the *National Post* or Leah McLaren of the *Globe and Mail*—all about "me and what I think." Writers recount events in their lives—sometimes very private ones—and air their thoughts to a public audience.

Reasons vary. Sometimes, the practice is therapeutic. For some, like Ryan Rhodes, who runs Rambling Rhodes *(http://ramblingrhodes. blogspot.com),* blogging has some functional purposes. Rhodes, from Rochester, Minn., is news editor for an IBM publication called *eServer Magazine* but also writes humour columns for some local newspapers. He figured blogging would be a good writing exercise that might offer him instant feedback from readers. "I like knowing the stuff I write is being read," says Rhodes, "and I like it when it hits someone in a positive way and they tell me, so I can use it later for my column."

Personal blogs are famous for breaking usual standards of disclosure, revealing details considered by some to be very private. Dan Gudy, a 29-year-old Berliner, kept a diary when he was a teenager but gave it up, unhappy with the results. "My first experience was a total failure," says Gudy. "It was only myself talking about myself and I do that enough." But last year, when he created his site, Gudy Two Shoes *(http://gudy. blogspot.com)*, the self-described introvert discovered that blogging opened a release valve. "I had to deal with some problems at the time and somehow needed to let it out. Part of me asked, why not use a blog for that?" Now, Gudy blogs about the books he reads and bike-riding through the German countryside. He also blogs about his sex life with his wife. "People can talk about what a nice bike ride they had or what a nice meal they had, but why can't they talk about what a nice f— they had last night?"

For many, that very willingness to discuss intimate details is one of the most alluring facets of blogging. "Your Weblog becomes an exterior part of you," says Clark, "so you can have some distance from your feelings, even though you're putting them out for everyone to read. But then all your readers are right up close and they know you because you're writing directly to them." In turn, readers can offer their own feedback: personal blogs frequently allow them to comment after each post, with something as easy as clicking a link that opens a pop-up box where they can add their own two cents' worth. "When I first started blogging," writes Daintily Dirty *(http://www.blogdreams.blogspot.com)*, an anonymous 32-year-old blogger who chatted with *Maclean's* via instant messenger, "I had no idea what I was getting into with the personal nature of the interactions. But the connections you find are what keep you coming back."

Layne Johnson's readers can attest to that. An excellent narrative writer who opens her soul to her readers, Plain Layne's daily entries regularly receive dozens of comments. "I hopped from one blog to the next and somewhere found Plain Layne," says Gudy. "What made me stay was her brutal honesty and intimacy of sharing, her very beautiful way of writing." Rhodes echoes the sentiment. "Layne is digital crack," he says. "Hands down, as far as I've read, she's got the best personal blog. I have to read her every day."

Johnson politely turned down a request for an interview, explaining   10 her blogging is a personal exercise that's meant to be cathartic. And somehow, that's the way it should be. Plain Layne does her talking, or typing, on her blog. "I think the hardest thing about sharing your life on-line is that at some point you discover people know you," Johnson wrote in a June post. "They know you from the inside out, the way your mind works, what makes you laugh or cry, your hopes and fears." It's clear to see she uses her blog as an outlet, a place to dump her anxiety and frustration in a search for identity and understanding. It's also a place of amusement and mirth, with stories of stupefying office meetings and uproarious golf outings, all told with a flair and talent that would make some "me" columnists envious.

Blogs might seem too revealing for people who prefer their diaries to remain private. But more and more strangers are inviting millions of other strangers into their lives, with a willingness to share just about anything, finding their own shelf space on the world's most accessible magazine rack, open to anyone who cares to pick up a copy. Welcome to the blogosphere.

DAVID GELERNTER   [b. 1955]

Unplugged: The Myth of Computers in the Classroom

David Gelernter is one of the most respected and influential computer scientists of our time. After earning both his B.A. and M.A. in Hebrew literature from Yale University and his Ph.D. in computer science from the State University of New York at Stony Brook, Gelernter accepted a position in Yale's computer science department, where he has taught ever since. He is also chief scientist at Mirror Worlds Technologies and a member of the National Council on the Arts. In 1983, Nicholas Carriero and he introduced the world to their Linda system and "tuple spaces," which form the basis of many computer-communication and distributed programming systems. Gerlenter's articles, essays, and short fiction have appeared in such publications as the *New York Times, Wall Street Journal, Washington Post, ArtNews,* and the *National Review.* The author of several books, including *Mirror Worlds* (1991) and *Machine Beauty* (1998), Gelernter was a victim of Theodore Kaczynski, the Unabomber, from whom he suffered permanent injury. Gelernter documented the experience in his book *Drawing Life* (1997).

Gelernter's essay, "Unplugged: The Myth of Computers in the Classroom," which first appeared in the *New Republic* in 1994, discusses the pros and cons of technology in the classroom. In the end, the author argues that computers should supplement, not replace, traditional book learning.

Over the last decade an estimated $2 billion has been spent on more than 2 million computers for America's classrooms. That's not surprising. We constantly hear from Washington that the schools are in trouble and that computers are a godsend. Within the education establishment, in poor as well as rich schools, the machines are awaited with nearly religious awe. An inner-city principal bragged to a teacher friend of mine recently that his school "has a computer in every classroom...despite being in a bad neighborhood!"

Computers should be in the schools. They have the potential to accomplish great things. With the right software, they could help make science tangible or teach neglected topics like art and music. They help students form a concrete idea of society by displaying onscreen a version of the city in which they live—a picture that tracks real life moment by moment.

In practice, however, computers make our worst educational nightmares come true. While we bemoan the decline of literacy, computers discount words in favor of pictures and pictures in favor of video. While we fret about the decreasing cogency of public debate, computers dismiss linear argument and promote fast, shallow romps across the information landscape. While we worry about basic skills, we allow into the classroom software that will do a student's arithmetic or correct his spelling.

Take multimedia. The idea of multimedia is to combine text, sound and pictures in a single package that you browse on screen. You don't just *read* Shakespeare; you watch actors performing, listen to songs, view Elizabethan buildings. What's wrong with that? By offering children candy-coated books, multimedia is guaranteed to sour them on unsweetened reading. It makes the printed page look even more boring than it used to look. Sure, books will be available in the classroom, too—but they'll have all the appeal of a dusty piano to a teen who has a Walkman handy.

So what if the little nippers don't read? If they're watching Olivier 5 instead, what do they lose? The text, the written word along with all of its attendant pleasures. Besides, a book is more portable than a computer, has a higher-resolution display, can be written on and dog-eared and is comparatively dirt cheap.

Hypermedia, multimedia's comrade in the struggle for a brave new classroom, is just as troubling. It's a way of presenting documents on screen without imposing a linear start-to-finish order. Disembodied paragraphs are linked by theme; after reading one about the First World War, for example, you might be able to choose another about the technology of battleships, or the life of Woodrow Wilson, or hemlines in the '20s. This is another cute idea that is good in minor ways and terrible in major ones. Teaching children to understand the orderly unfolding of a plot or a logical argument is a crucial part of education. Authors don't merely agglomerate paragraphs; they work hard to make the narrative read a certain way, prove a particular point. To turn a book or a document into hypertext is to invite readers to ignore exactly what counts—the story.

The real problem, again, is the accentuation of already bad habits. Dynamiting documents into disjointed paragraphs is one more expression of the sorry fact that sustained argument is not our style. If you're a newspaper or magazine editor and your readership is dwindling, what's the solution? Shorter pieces. If you're a politician and you want to get elected, what do you need? Tasty sound bites. Logical presentation be damned.

Another software species, "allow me" programs, is not much better. These programs correct spelling and, by applying canned grammatical and stylistic rules, fix prose. In terms of promoting basic skills, though, they have all the virtues of a pocket calculator.

In Kentucky, as *The Wall Street Journal* recently reported, students in grades K–3 are mixed together regardless of age in a relaxed environment. It works great, the *Journal* says. Yes, scores on computation tests have dropped 10 percent at one school, but not to worry: "Drilling addition and subtraction in an age of calculators is a waste of time," the principal reassures us. Meanwhile, a Japanese educator informs University of Wisconsin mathematician Richard Akey that in his country, "calculators are not used in elementary or junior high school because the primary emphasis is on helping students develop their mental abilities." No wonder Japanese kids blow the pants off American kids in math. Do we really think "drilling addition and subtraction in an age of calculators is a waste of time"? If we do, then "drilling reading in an age of multimedia is a waste of time" can't be far behind.

Prose-correcting programs are also a little ghoulish, like asking a computer for tips on improving your personality. On the other hand, I ran this article through a spell-checker, so how can I ban the use of such programs in schools? Because to misspell is human; to have no idea of correct spelling is to be semi-literate. 10

There's no denying that computers have the potential to perform inspiring feats in the classroom. If we are ever to see that potential realized, however, we ought to agree on three conditions. First, there should be a completely new crop of children's software. Most of today's offerings show no imagination. There are hundreds of similar reading and geography and arithmetic programs, but almost nothing on electricity or physics or architecture. Also, they abuse the technical capacities of new media to glitz up old forms instead of creating new ones. Why not build a time-travel program that gives kids a feel for how history is structured by zooming you backward? A spectrum program that lets users twirl a frequency knob to see what happens?

Second, computers should be used only during recess or relaxation periods. Treat them as fillips, not as surrogate teachers. When I was in school in the '60s, we all loved educational films. When we saw a movie in class, everybody won: teachers didn't have to teach, and pupils didn't have to learn. I suspect that classroom computers are popular today for the same reasons.

Most important, educators should learn what parents and most teachers already know: you cannot teach a child anything unless you look him in the face. We should not forget what computers are. Like books—better in some ways, worse in others—they are devices that help children mobilize their own resources and learn for themselves. The computer's potential to do good is modestly greater than a book's in some areas. Its potential to do harm is vastly greater, across the board.

JENNIFER LEE

I Think, Therefore IM

Jennifer Lee is a freelance writer whose nonfiction writing has appeared in the *New York Times* and other publications. In her essay "I Think, Therefore IM," she explores the current phenomenon of instant messaging among young people. In addressing this issue, Lee documents student use of "the conversational style of the Internet" to condense language into a shorthand that eliminates capitalization, punctuation, and formal syntax. The result is a blurring of students' social and academic worlds in a lingua franca that subverts traditional classroom English. Lee's article shows two sides: a belief that this new language undermines formal written English as well as a more accommodating response that views this tendency a "part of a larger arc of language evolution." Lee's article appeared in the September 19, 2002, issue of the *New York Times*.

Each September Jacqueline Harding prepares a classroom presentation on the common writing mistakes she sees in her students' work.

Ms. Harding, an eighth-grade English teacher at Viking Middle School in Guernee, Ill., scribbles the words that have plagued generations of schoolchildren across her whiteboard:

There. Their. They're.

Your. You're.

To. Too. Two.

Its. It's.

This September, she has added a new list: u, r, ur, b4, wuz, cuz, 2.

When she asked her students how many of them used shortcuts like these in their writing, Ms. Harding said, she was not surprised when most of them raised their hands. This, after all, is their online lingua franca: English adapted for the spitfire conversational style of Internet instant messaging.

Ms. Harding, who had seen such shortcuts creep into student papers over the last two years, said she gave her students a warning: "If I see this in your assignments, I will take points off."

"Kids should know the difference," said Ms. Harding, who decided to address this issue head-on this year. "They should know where to draw the line between formal writing." 5

As more and more teenagers socialize online, middle school and high school teachers like Ms. Harding are increasingly seeing a breezy form of Internet English jump from e-mail into schoolwork. To their dismay, teachers say that papers are being written with shortened words, improper capitalization and punctuation, and characters like &, $ and @.

Teachers have deducted points, drawn red circles and tsk-tsked at their classes. Yet the errant forms continue. "It stops being funny after you repeat yourself a couple of times," Ms. Harding said.

But teenagers, whose social life can rely as much these days on text communication as the spoken word, say that they use instant-messaging shorthand without thinking about it. They write to one another as much as they write in school, or more.

"You are so used to abbreviating things, you just start doing it unconsciously on schoolwork and reports and other things," said Eve Brecker, 15, a student at Montclair High School in New Jersey.

Ms. Brecker once handed in a midterm exam riddled with instant-messaging shorthand. "I had an hour to write an essay on *Romeo and Juliet*," she said. "I just wanted to finish before my time was up. I was writing fast and carelessly. I spelled 'you' 'u.'" She got a C. 10

Even terms that cannot be expressed verbally are making their way into papers. Melanie Weaver was stunned by some of the term papers she received from a 10th-grade class she recently taught as part of an internship. "They would be trying to make a point in a paper, they would put a smiley face in the end," said Ms. Weaver, who teaches at Alvernia College in Reading, PA. "If they were presenting an argument and they needed to present an opposite view, they would put a frown."

As Trisha Fogarty, a sixth-grade teacher at Houlton Southside School in Houlton, Maine, puts it, today's students are "Generation Text."

Almost 60 percent of the online population under age 17 uses instant messaging, according to Nielsen/NetRatings. In addition to cellphone text messaging, Weblogs and e-mail, it has become a popular means of flirting, setting up dates, asking for help with homework and keeping in contact with distant friends. The abbreviations are a natural outgrowth of this rapid-fire style of communication.

"They have a social life that centers around typed communication," said Judith S. Donath, a professor at the Massachusetts Institute of Technology's Media Lab who has studied electronic communication. "They have a writing style that has been nurtured in a teenage social milieu."

Some teachers see the creeping abbreviations as part of a continuing 15 assault of technology on formal written English. Others take it more lightly, saying that it is just part of the larger arc of language evolution.

"To them it's not wrong," said Ms. Harding, who is 28. "It's acceptable because it's in their culture. It's hard enough to teach them the art of formal writing. Now we've got to overcome this new instant-messaging language."

Ms. Harding noted that in some cases the shorthand isn't even shorter. "I understand 'cuz,' but what's with the 'wuz'? It's the same amount of letters as 'was,' so what's the point?" she said.

Deborah Bova, who teaches eighth-grade English at Raymond Park Middle School in Indianapolis, thought her eyesight was failing several years ago when she saw the sentence "B4 we perform, ppl have 2 practice" on a student assignment.

"I thought, 'My God, what is this?'" Ms. Bova said. "Have they lost their minds?"

The student was summoned to the board to translate the sentence into 20 standard English: "Before we perform, people have to practice." She realized that the students thought she was out of touch. "It was like 'Get with it, Bova,'" she said. Ms. Bova had a student type up a reference list of translations for common instant-messaging expressions. She posted a copy on the bulletin board by her desk and took another one home to use while grading.

Students are sometimes unrepentant.

"They were astonished when I began to point these things out to them," said Henry Assetto, a social studies teacher at Twin Valley High School in Elverson, Pa. "Because I am a history teacher, they did not think a history teacher would be checking up on their grammar or their spelling," said Mr. Assetto, who has been teaching for 34 years.

But Montana Hodgen, 16, another Montclair student, said she was so accustomed to instant-messaging abbreviations that she often read right past them. She proofread a paper last year only to get it returned with the messaging abbreviations circled in red.

"I was so used to reading what my friends wrote to me on Instant Messenger that I didn't even realize that there was something wrong," she said. She said her ability to separate formal and informal English declined the more she used instant messages. "Three years ago, if I had seen that, I would have been 'What is that?'"

The spelling checker doesn't always help either, students say. For one, 25 Microsoft Word's squiggly red spell-check lines don't appear beneath single letters and numbers such as u, r, c, 2 and 4. Nor do they catch words which have numbers in them such as "l8r" and "b4" by default.

Teenagers have essentially developed an unconscious "accent" in their typing, Professor Donath said. "They have gotten facile at typing and they are not paying attention."

Teenagers have long pushed the boundaries of spoken language, introducing words that then become passe with adult adoption. Now teenagers are taking charge and pushing the boundaries of written language. For them, expressions like "oic" (oh I see), "nm" (not much), "jk" (just kidding) and "lol" (laughing out loud), "brb" (be right back), "ttyl" (talk to you later) are as standard as conventional English.

"There is no official English language," said Jesse Sheidlower, the North American editor of the *Oxford English Dictionary*. "Language is spread not because anyone dictates any one thing to happen. The decisions are made by the language and the people who use the language."

Some teachers find the new writing style alarming. "First of all, it's very rude, and it's very careless," said Lois Moran, a middle school English teacher at St. Nicholas school in Jersey City.

"They should be careful to write properly and not to put these little 30 codes in that they are in such a habit of writing to each other," said Ms. Moran, who has lectured her eighth-grade class on such mistakes.

Others say that the instant-messaging style might simply be a fad, something that students will grow out of. Or they see it as an opportunity to teach students about the evolution of language.

"I turn it into a very positive teachable moment for kids in the class," said Erika V. Karres, an assistant professor at the University of North Carolina at Chapel Hill who trains student teachers. She shows students how English has evolved since Shakespeare's time. Imagine Langston Hughes's writing in quick texting instead of 'Langston writing,'" she said. "It makes teaching and learning so exciting."

Other teachers encourage students to use messaging shorthand to spark their thinking processes. "When my children are writing first drafts, I don't care how they spell anything, as long as they are writing," said Ms. Fogarty, the sixth-grade teacher from Houlton, Maine. "If this lingo gets their thoughts and ideas onto paper quicker, the more power to them." But during editing and revising, she expects her students to switch to standard English.

Ms. Bova shares the view that instant-messaging language can help free up their creativity. With the help of students, she does not even need the cheat sheet to read the shorthand anymore.

"I think it's a plus," she said. "And I would say that with a + sign." 35

BERNARD COOPER   [b. 1951]

A Clack of Tiny Sparks:
Remembrances of a
Gay Boyhood

Novelist, essayist, and short-story writer **Bernard Cooper** was born in
Los Angeles and earned his B.F.A. and M.F.A. at the California Institute of the Arts. He is the winner of the PEN/Ernest Hemingway
Award, an O. Henry Prize, a Guggenheim Fellowship, and a Getty Center for the Arts and Humanities Fellowship. Cooper's publications
include two essay collections—*Maps to Anywhere* (1990) and *Truth
Serum* (1996), the novel *A Year of Rhymes* (1993), a collection of short
stories called *Guess Again* (2000), and *The Bill from My Father: A Memoir* (2006). Cooper's writing has appeared in *Ploughshares*, *Harper's*, the
Paris Review, and the *New York Times Magazine*. He has taught at the
Otis/Parsons Institute of Art and Design, the Southern California Institute of Architecture, and the UCLA Writer's Program, and is currently
employed as an art critic for *Los Angeles Magazine*.

Cooper's "A Clack of Tiny Sparks: Remembrances of a Gay Boyhood" (1991), which first appeared in *Harper's*, is an autobiographical
coming-of-age story recounting Cooper's dawning awareness of his
homosexuality. Anxious and struggling with his sense of self-denial,
Cooper applies oft-heard maxims to his own scenario in an effort to
appear straight, feel straight, be straight.

Theresa Sanchez sat behind me in ninth-grade algebra. When Mr.
Hubbley faced the blackboard, I'd turn around to see what she was reading; each week a new book was wedged inside her copy of *Today's Equa-
tions*. The deception worked; from Mr. Hubbley's point of view, Theresa
was engrossed in the value of X, but I knew otherwise. One week she
perused *The Wisdom of the Orient*, and I could tell from Theresa's con-
templative expression that the book contained exotic thoughts, guidelines handed down from high. Another week it was a paperback novel
whose title, *Let Me Live My Life*, appeared in bold print atop every page,

Bernard Cooper, "A Clack of Tiny Sparks: Remembrances of a Gay Boyhood" from
Harper's Magazine, January 1991. Reprinted with special permission.

and whose cover, a gauzy photograph of a woman biting a strand of pearls, head thrown back in an attitude of ecstasy, confirmed my suspicion that Theresa Sanchez was mature beyond her years. She was the tallest girl in school. Her bouffant hairdo, streaked with blond, was higher than the flaccid bouffants of other girls. Her smooth skin, plucked eyebrows, and painted fingernails suggested hours of pampering, a worldly and sensual vanity that placed her within the domain of adults. Smiling dimly, steeped in daydreams, Theresa moved through the crowded halls with a languid, self-satisfied indifference to those around her. "You are merely children," her posture seemed to say. "I can't be bothered." The week Theresa hid *101 Ways to Cook Hamburger* behind her algebra book, I could stand it no longer and, after the bell rang, ventured a question.

"Because I'm having a dinner party," said Theresa. "Just a couple of intimate friends."

No fourteen-year-old I knew had ever given a dinner party, let alone used the word "intimate" in conversation. "Don't you have a mother?" I asked.

Theresa sighed a weary sigh, suffered my strange inquiry. "Don't be so naive," she said. "Everyone has a mother." She waved her hand to indicate the brick school buildings outside the window. "A higher education should have taught you that." Theresa draped an angora sweater over her shoulders, scooped her books from the graffiti-covered desk, and just as she was about to walk away, she turned and asked me, "Are you a fag?"

There wasn't the slightest hint of rancor or condescension in her voice.   5 The tone was direct, casual. Still I was stunned, giving a sidelong glance to make sure no one had heard. "No," I said. Blurted really, with too much defensiveness, too much transparent fear in my response. Octaves lower than usual, I tried a "Why?"

Theresa shrugged. "Oh, I don't know. I have lots of friends who are fags. You remind me of them." Seeing me bristle, Theresa added, "It was just a guess." I watched her erect, angora back as she sauntered out the classroom door.

She had made an incisive and timely guess. Only days before, I'd invited Grady Rogers to my house after school to go swimming. The instant Grady shot from the pool, shaking water from his orange hair, freckled shoulders shining, my attraction to members of my own sex became a matter I could no longer suppress or rationalize. Sturdy and boisterous and gap-toothed, Grady was an inveterate backslapper, a formidable arm wrestler, a wizard at basketball. Grady was a body at home in his body.

My body was a marvel I hadn't gotten used to; my arms and legs would sometimes act of their own accord, knocking over a glass at dinner or flinching at an oncoming pitch. I was never singled out as a sissy, but I could have been just as easily as Bobby Keagan, a gentle, intelligent, and introverted boy reviled by my classmates. And although I had always been aware of a tacit rapport with Bobby, a suspicion that I might find with him a rich friendship, I stayed away. Instead, I emulated Grady in the belief that being seen with him, being like him, would somehow vanquish my self-doubt, would make me normal by association.

Apart from his athletic prowess, Grady had been gifted with all the trappings of what I imagined to be a charmed life: a fastidious, aproned mother who radiated calm, maternal concern; a ruddy, stoic father with a knack for home repairs. Even the Rogerses' small suburban house in Hollywood, with its spindly Colonial furniture and chintz curtains, was a testament to normalcy.

Grady and his family bore little resemblance to my clan of Eastern 10 European Jews, a dark and vociferous people who ate with abandon— matzo and halvah and gefilte fish; foods the goyim couldn't pronounce— who cajoled one another during endless games of canasta, making the simplest remark about the weather into a lengthy philosophical discourse on the sun and the seasons and the passage of time. My mother was a chain-smoker, a dervish in a frowsy housedress. She showed her love in the most peculiar and obsessive ways, like spending hours extracting every seed from a watermelon before she served it in perfectly bite-sized geometric pieces. Preoccupied and perpetually frantic, my mother succumbed to bouts of absentmindedness so profound she'd forget what she was saying midsentence, smile and blush and walk away. A divorce attorney, my father wore roomy, iridescent suits, and the intricacies, the deceits inherent in his profession, had the effect of making him forever tense and vigilant. He was "all wound up," as my mother put it. But when he relaxed, his laughter was explosive, his disposition prankish: "Walk this way," a waitress would say, leading us to our table, and my father would mimic the way she walked, arms akimbo, hips liquid, while my mother and I were wracked with laughter. Buoyant or brooding, my parents' moods were unpredictable, and in a household fraught with extravagant emotion it was odd and awful to keep my longing secret.

One day I made the mistake of asking my mother what a "fag" was. I knew exactly what Theresa had meant but hoped against hope it was not what I thought; maybe "fag" was some French word, a harmless term like "naive." My mother turned from the stove, flew at me, and grabbed me by the shoulders. "Did someone call you that?" she cried.

"Not me," I said. "Bobby Keagan."

"Oh," she said, loosening her grip. She was visibly relieved. And didn't answer. The answer was unthinkable.

* * *

For weeks after, I shook with the reverberations from that afternoon in the kitchen with my mother, pained by the memory of her shocked expression and, most of all, her silence. My longing was wrong in the eyes of my mother, whose hazel eyes were the eyes of the world, and if that longing continued unchecked, the unwieldy shape of my fate would be cast, and I'd be subjected to a lifetime of scorn.

During the remainder of the semester, I became the scientist of my own desire, plotting ways to change my yearning for boys into a yearning for girls. I had enough evidence to believe that any habit, regardless of how compulsive, how deeply ingrained, could be broken once and for all: The plastic cigarette my mother purchased at the Thrifty pharmacy—one end was red to approximate an ember, the other tan like a filtered tip—was designed to wean her from the real thing. To change a behavior required self-analysis, cold resolve, and the substitution of one thing for another: plastic, say, for tobacco. Could I also find a substitute for Grady? What I needed to do, I figured, was kiss a girl and learn to like it.

This conclusion was affirmed one Sunday morning when my father, seeing me wrinkle my nose at the pink slabs of lox he layered on a bagel, tried to convince me of its salty appeal. "You should try some," he said. "You don't know what you're missing."

"It's loaded with protein," added my mother, slapping a platter of sliced onions onto the dinette table. She hovered above us, cinching her housedress, eyes wet from onion fumes, the mock cigarette dangling from her lips.

My father sat there chomping with gusto, emitting a couple of hearty grunts to dramatize his satisfaction. And still I was not convinced. After a loud and labored swallow, he told me I may not be fond of lox today, but sooner or later I'd learn to like it. One's tastes, he assured me, are destined to change.

"Live," shouted my mother over the rumble of the Mixmaster. "Expand your horizons. Try new things." And the room grew fragrant with the batter of a spice cake.

The opportunity to put their advice into practice, and try out my plan to adapt to girls, came the following week when Debbie Coburn, a member of Mr. Hubbley's algebra class, invited me to a party. She cornered me in the hall, furtive as a spy, telling me her parents would be gone for the evening and slipping into my palm a wrinkled sheet of notebook paper. On it were her address and telephone number, the lavender ink in a tidy cursive. "Wear cologne," she advised, wary eyes darting back and forth. "It's a make-out party. Anything can happen."

The Santa Ana wind blew relentlessly the night of Debbie's party,

15

20

careening down the slopes of the Hollywood hills, shaking the road signs and stoplights in its path. As I walked down Beachwood Avenue, trees thrashed, surrendered their leaves, and carob pods bombarded the pavement. The sky was a deep but luminous blue, the air hot, abrasive, electric. I had to squint in order to check the number of the Coburns' apartment, a three-story building with glitter embedded in its stucco walls. Above the honeycombed balconies was a sign that read BEACHWOOD TERRACE in lavender script resembling Debbie's.

From down the hall, I could hear the plaintive strains of Little Anthony's "I Think I'm Going Out of My Head." Debbie answered the door bedecked in an Empire dress, the bodice blue and orange polka dots, the rest a sheath of black and white stripes. "Op art," proclaimed Debbie. She turned in a circle, then proudly announced that she'd rolled her hair in orange juice cans. She patted the huge unmoving curls and dragged me inside. Reflections from the swimming pool in the courtyard, its surface ruffled by wind, shuddered over the ceiling and walls. A dozen of my classmates were seated on the sofa or huddled together in corners, their whispers full of excited imminence, their bodies barely discernible in the dim light. Drapes flanking the sliding glass doors bowed out with every gust of wind, and it seemed that the room might lurch from its foundations and sail with its cargo of silhouettes into the hot October night.

Grady was the last to arrive. He tossed a six-pack of beer into Debbie's arms, barreled toward me, and slapped my back. His hair was slicked back with Vitalis, lacquered furrows left by the comb. The wind hadn't shifted a single hair. "Ya ready?" he asked, flashing the gap between his front teeth and leering into the darkened room. "You bet," I lied.

Once the beers had been passed around, Debbie provoked everyone's attention by flicking on the overhead light. "Okay," she called. "Find a partner." This was the blunt command of a hostess determined to have her guests aroused in an orderly fashion. Everyone blinked, shuffled about, and grabbed a member of the opposite sex. Sheila Garabedian landed beside me—entirely at random, though I want to believe she was driven by passion—her timid smile giving way to plain fear as the light went out. Nothing for a moment but the heave of the wind and the distant banter of dogs. I caught a whiff of Sheila's perfume, tangy and sweet as Hawaiian Punch. I probed her face with my own, grazing the small scallop of an ear, a velvety temple, and though Sheila's trembling made me want to stop, I persisted with my mission until I found her lips, tightly sealed as a private letter. I held my mouth over hers and gathered her shoulders closer, resigned to the possibility that, no matter how long we stood there, Sheila would be too scared to kiss me back. Still, she exhaled through her nose, and I listened to the squeak of every breath as though it were a sigh of inordinate pleasure. Diving within myself, I monitored my heartbeat and respiration, trying to will stimulation into being, and all the while an image intruded, an image of Grady erupting from our pool, rivulets of water sliding down his chest. "Change," shouted Debbie, switching on the light. Sheila thanked me, pulled away, and continued her routine of gracious terror with every boy throughout the evening. It didn't matter whom I held—Margaret Sims, Betty Vernon, Elizabeth Lee—my experiment was a failure; I continued to picture Grady's wet chest, and Debbie would bellow "change" with such fervor, it could have been my own voice, my own incessant reprimand.

Our hostess commandeered the light switch for nearly half an hour. 25 Whenever the light came on, I watched Grady pivot his head toward the newest prospect, his eyebrows arched in expectation, his neck blooming with hickeys, his hair, at last, in disarray. All that shuffling across the carpet charged everyone's arms and lips with static, and eventually, between low moans and soft osculations, I could hear the clack of my tiny sparks and see them flare here and there in the dark like meager, short-lived stars.

I saw Theresa, sultry and aloof as ever, read three more books—*North American Reptiles*, *Bonjour Tristesse*, and *MGM: A Pictorial History*—before she vanished early in December. Rumors of her fate abounded. Debbie Coburn swore that Theresa had been "knocked up" by an older man, a traffic cop, she thought, or a grocer. Nearly quivering with relish, Debbie told me and Grady about the home for unwed mothers in the San Fernando Valley, a compound teeming with pregnant girls who had nothing to do but touch their stomachs and contemplate their mistake. Even Bobby Keagan, who took Theresa's place behind me in algebra, had a theory regarding her disappearance colored by his own wish for escape; he imagined that Theresa, disillusioned with society, booked passage to a tropical island, there to live out the rest of her days without restrictions or ridicule. "No wonder she flunked out of school," I overheard Mr. Hubbley tell a fellow teacher one afternoon. "Her head was always in a book."

Along with Theresa went my secret, or at least the dread that she might divulge it, and I felt, for a while, exempt from suspicion. I was, however, to run across Theresa one last time. It happened during a period of torrential rain that, according to reports on the six o'clock news, washed houses from the hillsides and flooded the downtown streets. The halls of Joseph Le Conte Junior High were festooned with Christmas decorations: crepe-paper garlands, wreaths studded with plastic berries, and one requisite Star of David twirling above the attendance desk. In Arts and Crafts, our teacher, Gerald (he was the only teacher who allowed us—*required* us—to call him by his first name), handed out blocks of balsa wood and instructed us to carve them into bugs. We would paint eyes and antennae with tempera and hang them on a Christmas tree he'd made the previous night. "Voilà," he crooned, unveiling his creation from a burlap sack. Before us sat a tortured scrub, a wardrobe-worth of wire hangers that were bent like branches and soldered together. Gerald credited his inspiration to a Charles Addams cartoon he's seen in which Morticia, grimly preparing for the holidays, hangs vampire bats on a withered pine. "All that red and green," said Gerald. "So predictable. So *boring*."

As I chiseled a beetle and listened to rain pummel the earth, Gerald handed me an envelope and asked me to take it to Mr. Kendrick, the drama teacher. I would have thought nothing of his request if I hadn't seen Theresa on my way down the hall. She was cleaning out her locker, blithely dropping the sum of its contents—pens and textbooks and mimeographs—into a trash can. "Have a nice life," she sang as I passed. I mustered the courage to ask her what had happened. We stood alone in the silent hall, the reflections of wreaths and garlands submerged in brown linoleum.

"I transferred to another school. They don't have grades or bells, and you get to study whatever you want." Theresa was quick to sense my incredulity. "Honest," she said. "The school is progressive." She gazed into a glass cabinet that held the trophies of track meets and intramural spelling bees. "God," she sighed, "this place is so...barbaric." I was still trying to decide whether or not to believe her story when she asked me where I was headed. "Dear," she said, her exclamation pooling in the silence, "that's no ordinary note, if you catch my drift." The envelope was blank and white; I looked up at Theresa, baffled. "Don't be so naive," she muttered, tossing an empty bottle of nail polish into the trash can. It struck bottom with a resolute thud. "Well," she said, closing her locker and breathing deeply, "bon voyage." Theresa swept through the double doors and in seconds her figure was obscured by rain.

As I walked toward Mr. Kendrick's room, I could feel Theresa's insinuation burrow in. I stood for a moment and watched Mr. Kendrick through the pane in the door. He paced intently in front of the class, handsome in his shirt and tie, reading from a thick book. Chalked on the blackboard behind him was THE ODYSSEY BY HOMER. I have no recollection of how Mr. Kendrick reacted to the note, whether he accepted it with pleasure or embarrassment, slipped it into his desk drawer or the pocket of his shirt. I have scavenged that day in retrospect, trying to see Mr. Kendrick's expression, wondering if he acknowledged me in any way as his liaison. All I recall is the sight of his mime through a pane of glass, a lone man mouthing an epic, his gestures ardent in empty air.

Had I delivered a declaration of love? I was haunted by the need to

382

know. In fantasy, a kettle shot steam, the glue released its grip, and I read the letter with impunity. But how would such a letter begin? Did the common endearments apply? This was a message between two men, a message for which I had no precedent, and when I tried to envision the contents, apart from a hasty, impassioned scrawl, my imagination faltered.

Once or twice I witnessed Gerald and Mr. Kendrick walk together into the faculty lounge or say hello at the water fountain, but there was nothing especially clandestine or flirtatious in their manner. Besides, no matter how acute my scrutiny, I wasn't sure, short of a kiss, exactly what to look for — what semaphore of gesture, what encoded word. I suspected there were signs, covert signs that would give them away, just as I'd unwittingly given myself away to Theresa.

In the school library, a *Webster's* unabridged dictionary lay on a wooden podium, and I padded toward it with apprehension; along with clues to the bond between my teachers, I risked discovering information that might incriminate me as well. I had decided to consult the dictionary during lunch period, when most of the students would be on the playground. I clutched my notebook, moving in such a way as to appear both studious and nonchalant, actually believing that, unless I took precautions, someone would see me and guess what I was up to. The closer I came to the podium, the more obvious, I thought, was my endeavor; I felt like the model of The Visible Man in our science class, my heart's undulations, my overwrought nerves legible through transparent skin. A couple of kids riffled through the card catalogue. The librarian, a skinny woman whose perpetual whisper and rubber-soled shoes caused her to drift through the room like a phantom, didn't seem to register my presence. Though I'd looked up dozens of words before, the pages felt strange beneath my fingers. *Homer* was the first word I saw. *Hominid. Homogenize.* I feigned interest and skirted other words before I found the word I was after. Under the heading HO•MO•SEX•U•AL was the terse definition: *adj. Pertaining to, characteristic of, or exhibiting homosexuality. —n. A homosexual person.* I read the definition again and again, hoping the words would yield more than they could. I shut the dictionary, swallowed hard, and, none the wiser, hurried away.

As for Gerald and Mr. Kendrick, I never discovered evidence to prove or dispute Theresa's claim. By the following summer, however, I had overhead from my peers a confounding amount about homosexuals: They wore green on Thursday, couldn't whistle, hypnotized boys with a piercing glance. To this lore, Grady added a surefire test to ferret them out.

"A test?" I said.

"You ask a guy to look at his fingernails, and if he looks at them like

35

this"—Grady closed his fingers into a fist and examined his nails with manly detachment—"then he's okay. But if he does this"—he held out his hands at arm's length, splayed his fingers, and coyly cocked his head—"you'd better watch out." Once he'd completed his demonstration, Grady peeled off his shirt and plunged into our pool. I dove in after. It was early June, the sky immense, glassy, placid. My father was cooking spareribs on the barbecue, an artist with a basting brush. His apron bore the caricature of a frazzled French chef. Mother curled on a chaise lounge, plumes of smoke wafting from her nostrils. In a stupor of contentment she took another drag, closed her eyes, and arched her face toward the sun.

Grady dog-paddled through the deep end, spouting a fountain of chlorinated water. Despite shame and confusion, my longing for him hadn't diminished; it continued to thrive without air and light, like a luminous fish in the dregs of the sea. In the name of play, I swam up behind him, encircled his shoulders, astonished by his taut flesh. The two of us flailed, pretended to drown. Beneath the heavy press of water, Grady's orange hair wavered, a flame that couldn't be doused.

I've lived with a man for seven years. Some nights, when I'm half-asleep and the room is suffused with blue light, I reach out to touch the expanse of his back, and it seems as if my fingers sink into his skin, and I feel the pleasure a diver feels the instant he enters a body of water.

I have few regrets. But one is that I hadn't said to Theresa, "Of course I'm a fag." Maybe I'd have met her friends. Or become friends with her. Imagine the meals we might have concocted: hamburger Stroganoff, Swedish meatballs in a sweet translucent sauce, steaming slabs of Salisbury steak.

BARBARA LAWRENCE

Four-Letter Words
Can Hurt You

Barbara Lawrence was born in New Hampshire and graduated from Connecticut College with a B.A. in French and from New York University with an M.A. in philosophy. She has served as an editor for numerous periodicals including *McCall's*, *Redbook*, *Harper's Bazaar*, and *The New Yorker*, and her editorials, fiction, and poetry have been published widely. She is a professor of humanities at the State University of New York at Old Westbury.

In "Four-Letter Words Can Hurt You," originally published in the *New York Times*, Barbara Lawrence analyzes the etymology of certain sexually explicit though oft-used words deemed obscene by some and earthy-raw by others. She contends that the specific origins of these terms and the violence implied in their varied roots denigrates women, and she wonders why pejorative language is considered more taboo against ethnic minorities than it is against the female gender.

Why should any words be called obscene? Don't they all describe natural human functions? Am I trying to tell them, my students demand, that the "strong, earthy, gut-honest" — or, if they are fans of Norman Mailer, the "rich, liberating, existential" — language they use to describe sexual activity isn't preferable to "phoney-sounding, middle-class words like 'intercourse' and 'copulate'?" "Cop You Late!" they say with fancy inflections and gagging grimaces, "Now what is *that* supposed to mean?"

Well, what is it supposed to mean? And why indeed should one group of words describing human functions and human organs be acceptable in ordinary conversation, and another, describing presumably the same organs and functions, be tabooed — so much so, in fact, that some of these words still cannot appear in print in many parts of the English-speaking world?

The argument that these taboos exist only because of "sexual hang-ups" (middle-class, middle-age, feminist), or even that they are a result of class oppression — the contempt of the Norman conquerors for the language of their Anglo-Saxon serfs—ignores a much more likely explanation, it seems to me, and that is the sources and functions of the words themselves.

The best known of the tabooed sexual verbs, for example, comes from the German word *ficken*, meaning "to strike"; combined, according to Partridge's etymological dictionary *Origins*, with the Latin sexual verb *futuere*; associated in turn with the Latin *fustis*, "a staff or cudgel"; the Celtic *buc*, "a point, hence to pierce"; the Irish *bot*, "the male member"; the Latin *battuere*, "to beat"; the Gaelic *batair*, "a cudgeller"; the Early Irish *bualaim*, "I strike"; and so forth. It is one of what etymologists sometimes call "the sadistic group of words for the man's part on copulation."

The brutality of this word, then, and its equivalents, is not an illusion of 5 the middle class or a crotchet of Women's Liberation. In their origins and imagery these words carry undeniably painful, if not sadistic, implications, the object of which is almost always female. Consider, for example, what a "screw" actually does to the wood it penetrates: what a painful, even mutilating activity this kind of analogy suggests. "Screw" is particularly interesting in this context since the noun, according to Partridge, comes from words meaning "groove," "nut," "ditch," "breeding sow," "scrofula," and "swelling," while the verb, besides its explicit imagery, has antecedent associations to: "write on," "scratch," "scarify," and so forth; a revealing fusion of a mechanical or painful action with an obviously denigrated object.

Not all obscene words, of course, are as implicitly sadistic or denigrating to women as these, but all that I know do seem to serve a similar purpose: to reduce the human organism (especially the female organism) and human functions (especially sexual and procreative) to their least organic, most mechanical dimension; to substitute a trivializing or deforming resemblance for the complex human reality of what is being described.

Tabooed male descriptives, when they are not openly denigrating to women, often serve to divorce a male organ or function from any significant interaction with the female. Take the word "testes," for example, suggesting "witnesses" (from the Latin *testis*) to the sexual and procreative strengths of the male organ; and the obscene equivalent of this word which suggests little more than a mechanical shape. Or compare almost any of the "rich," "liberating" sexual verbs, so fashionable today among male writers, with that much-derided Latin word "copulate" ("to bind or join together") or even that Anglo-Saxon phrase (which seems to have had no trouble surviving the Norman Conquest) "make love." How arrogantly self-involved the tabooed words seem in comparison with either of the other terms, and how contemptuous of the female partner.

* * *

The more deforming the analogy, incidentally, the stronger the taboo is likely to be. The most severely censored of all the female descriptives are those suggesting (either explicitly or through antecedents) that there is no significant difference between the female channel through which we are all conceived and born, and the anal outlet common to both sexes—a distinction that pornographers have always enjoyed obscuring.

This effort to deny women their biological identity, their individuality, their humanness is such an important aspect of obscene language that one can only marvel at how seldom, in an era preoccupied with definitions of obscenity, this fact is brought to our attention. One problem, of course, is that many of the people in the best position to do this (critics, teachers, writers) are so reluctant today to admit that they are angered or shocked by obscenity. Bored maybe, unimpressed, esthetically displeased, but no matter how brutal or denigrating the material, never angered, never shocked.

And yet how eloquently angered, how piously shocked many of these 10 same people become if denigrating language is used about any other minority group than women; if the obscenities are racial, or ethnic, that is, rather than sexual. Words like "coon," "kike," "spic," "wop," after all, deform identity, deny individuality and humanness in almost exactly the same way that sexual vulgarisms and obscenity do.

No one that I know, least of all my students, would fail to question the values of a society whose literature and entertainment rested heavily on racial or ethnic pejoratives. Are the values of a society whose literature and entertainment rest as heavily as ours on sexual pejoratives any less questionable?

JUDITH ORTIZ COFER   [b. 1952]

The Myth of the Latin Woman: I Just Met a Girl Named Maria

Judith Ortiz Cofer was born in Puerto Rico in 1952 and grew up there
and in New Jersey. She is a poet, fiction writer, and autobiographer,
and teaches literature and writing at the University of Georgia. Much
of her work, such as her novel *The Line of the Sun* (1989) and *The Latin
Deli: Prose and Poetry* (1993), explores her experiences as a Puerto
Rican émigré and a Latina. Her most recent book is *Woman in Front of
the Sun: Becoming a Writer* (2000).

"The Myth of the Latin Woman: I Just Met a Girl Named Maria" considers the stereotypes Americans hold about Latinas, and it does so
through narrative and reflection. At the end of one of the stories she tells
in her essay, dealing with an offensive man, Cofer writes, "My friend
complimented me on my cool handling of the situation" (par. 10), then
notes that what she really wanted to do was push the man into the pool.
Notice, as you read, the ways in which Cofer is able in this essay, as in
that incident, to strike a balance between anger and analysis.

On a bus trip to London from Oxford University where I was earning
some graduate credits one summer, a young man, obviously fresh from a
pub, spotted me and as if struck by inspiration went down on his knees
in the aisle. With both hands over his heart he broke into an Irish tenor's
rendition of "María" from *West Side Story*. My politely amused fellow
passengers gave his lovely voice the round of gentle applause it deserved.
Though I was not quite as amused, I managed my version of an English
smile: no show of teeth, no extreme contortions of the facial muscles—I
was at this time of my life practicing reserve and cool. Oh, that British
control, how I coveted it. But María had followed me to London, re-
minding me of a prime fact of my life: you can leave the Island, master
the English language, and travel as far as you can, but if you are a
Latina, especially one like me who so obviously belongs to Rita Moreno's
gene pool, the Island travels with you.

This is sometimes a very good thing—it may win you that extra minute of someone's attention. But with some people, the same things can make *you* an island—not so much a tropical paradise as an Alcatraz, a place nobody wants to visit. As a Puerto Rican girl growing up in the United States and wanting like most children to "belong," I resented the stereotype that my Hispanic appearance called forth from many people I met.

Our family lived in a large urban center in New Jersey during the sixties, where life was designed as a microcosm of my parents' casas on the island. We spoke in Spanish, we ate Puerto Rican food bought at the bodega, and we practiced strict Catholicism complete with Saturday confession and Sunday mass at a church where our parents were accommodated into a one-hour Spanish mass slot, performed by a Chinese priest trained as a missionary for Latin America.

As a girl I was kept under strict surveillance, since virtue and modesty were, by cultural equation, the same as family honor. As a teenager I was instructed on how to behave as a proper señorita. But it was a conflicting message girls got, since the Puerto Rican mothers also encouraged their daughters to look and act like women and to dress in clothes our Anglo friends and their mothers found too "mature" for our age. It was, and is, cultural, yet I often felt humiliated when I appeared at an American friend's party wearing a dress more suitable to a semiformal than to a playroom birthday celebration. At Puerto Rican festivities, neither the music nor the colors we wore could be too loud. I still experience a vague sense of letdown when I'm invited to a "party" and it turns out to be a marathon conversation in hushed tones rather than a fiesta with salsa, laughter, and dancing—the kind of celebration I remember from my childhood.

I remember Career Day in our high school, when teachers told us to 5 come dressed as if for a job interview. It quickly became obvious that to the barrio girls, "dressing up" sometimes meant wearing ornate jewelry and clothing that would be more appropriate (by mainstream standards) for the company Christmas party than as daily office attire. That morning I had agonized in front of my closet, trying to figure out what a "career girl" would wear because, essentially, except for Marlo Thomas on TV, I had no models on which to base my decision. I knew how to dress for school: at the Catholic school I attended we all wore uniforms; I knew how to dress for Sunday mass, and I knew what dresses to wear for parties at my relatives' homes. Though I do not recall the precise details of my Career Day outfit, it must have been a composite of the above choices. But I remember a comment my friend (an Italian-American) made in later years that coalesced my impressions of that day. She said that at the business school she was attending the Puerto Rican girls always stood out for wearing "everything at once." She meant, of course, too much jewelry, too many accessories. On that day at school, we were simply made the negative models by the nuns who were themselves not credible fashion experts to any of us. But it was painfully obvious to me that to the others, in their tailored skirts and silk blouses, we must have seemed "hopeless" and "vulgar." Though I now know that most adolescents feel out of step much of the time, I also know that for the Puerto Rican girls of my generation that sense was intensified. The way our teachers and classmates looked at us that day in school was just a taste of the culture clash that awaited us in the real world, where prospective employers and men on the street would often misinterpret our tight skirts and jingling bracelets as a come-on.

Mixed cultural signals have perpetuated certain stereotypes—for example, that of the Hispanic woman as the "Hot Tamale" or sexual firebrand. It is a one-dimensional view that the media have found easy to promote. In their special vocabulary, advertisers have designated "sizzling" and "smoldering" as the adjectives of choice for describing not only the foods but also the women of Latin America. From conversations in my house I recall hearing about the harassment that Puerto Rican women endured in factories where the "boss men" talked to them as if sexual innuendo was all they understood and, worse, often gave them the choice of submitting to advances or being fired.

It is custom, however, not chromosomes, that leads us to choose scarlet over pale pink. As young girls, we were influenced in our decisions about clothes and colors by the women—older sisters and mothers who had grown up on a tropical island where the natural environment was a riot of primary colors, where showing your skin was one way to keep cool as well as to look sexy. Most important of all, on the island, women perhaps felt freer to dress and move more provocatively, since, in most cases, they were protected by the traditions, mores, and laws of a Spanish/Catholic system of morality and machismo whose main rule was: *You may look at my sister, but if you touch her I will kill you.* The extended family and church structure could provide a young woman with a circle of safety in her small pueblo on the island; if a man "wronged" a girl, everyone would close in to save her family honor.

This is what I have gleaned from my discussions as an adult with older Puerto Rican women. They have told me about dressing in their best party clothes on Saturday nights and going to the town's plaza to promenade with their girlfriends in front of the boys they liked. The males were thus given an opportunity to admire the women and to express their admiration in the form of *piropos*: erotically charged street poems they composed on the spot. I have been subjected to a few piropos while visiting the Island, and they can be outrageous, although custom dictates that they must never cross into obscenity. This ritual, as I understand it, also entails a show of studied indifference on the woman's part; if she is "decent," she must not acknowledge the man's impassioned words. So I do understand how things can be lost in translation. When a Puerto Rican girl dressed in her idea of what is attractive meets a man from the mainstream culture who has been trained to react to certain types of clothing as a sexual signal, a clash is likely to take place. The line I first heard based on this aspect of the myth happened when the boy who took me to my first formal dance leaned over to plant a sloppy overeager kiss painfully on my mouth, and when I didn't respond with sufficient passion said in a resentful tone: "I thought you Latin girls were supposed to mature early"—my first instance of being thought of as a fruit or vegetable—I was supposed to *ripen*, not just grow into womanhood like other girls.

It is surprising to some of my professional friends that some people, including those who should know better, still put others "in their place." Though rarer, these incidents are still commonplace in my life. It happened to me most recently during a stay at a very classy metropolitan hotel favored by young professional couples for their weddings. Late one evening after the theater, as I walked toward my room with my new colleague (a woman with whom I was coordinating an arts program), a middle-aged man in a tuxedo, a young girl in satin and lace on his arm, stepped directly into our path. With his champagne glass extended toward me, he exclaimed, "Evita!"

Our way blocked, my companion and I listened as the man half- 10 recited, half-bellowed "Don't Cry for Me, Argentina." When he finished, the young girl said: "How about a round of applause for my daddy?" We complied, hoping this would bring the silly spectacle to a close. I was becoming aware that our little group was attracting the attention of the other guests. "Daddy" must have perceived this too, and he once more barred the way as we tried to walk past him. He began to shout-sing a ditty to the tune of "La Bamba"—except the lyrics were about a girl named María whose exploits all rhymed with her name and gonorrhea. The girl kept saying "Oh, Daddy" and looking at me with pleading eyes. She wanted me to laugh along with the others. My companion and I stood silently waiting for the man to end his offensive song. When he finished, I looked not at him but at his daughter. I advised her calmly never to ask her father what he had done in the army. Then I walked between them and to my room. My friend complimented me on my cool handling of the situation. I confessed to her that I really had wanted to push the jerk into the swimming pool. I knew that this same man—probably a corporate executive, well educated, even worldly by most standards— would not have been likely to regale a white woman with a dirty song in

391

public. He would perhaps have checked his impulse by assuming that she could be somebody's wife or mother, or at least *somebody* who might take offense. But to him, I was just an Evita or a María: merely a character in his cartoon-populated universe.

Because of my education and my proficiency with the English language, I have acquired many mechanisms for dealing with the anger I experience. This was not true for my parents, nor is it true for the many Latin women working at menial jobs who must put up with stereotypes about our ethnic group such as: "They make good domestics." This is another facet of the myth of the Latin woman in the United States. Its origin is simple to deduce. Work as domestics, waitressing, and factory jobs are all that's available to women with little English and few skills. The myth of the Hispanic menial has been sustained by the same media phenomenon that made "Mammy" from *Gone with the Wind* America's idea of the black woman for generations: María, the housemaid or counter girl, is now indelibly etched into the national psyche. The big and the little screens have presented us with the picture of the funny Hispanic maid, mispronouncing words and cooking up a spicy storm in a shiny California kitchen.

This media-engendered image of the Latina in the United States has been documented by feminist Hispanic scholars, who claim that such portrayals are partially responsible for the denial of opportunities for upward mobility among Latinas in the professions. I have a Chicana friend working on a Ph.D. in philosophy at a major university. She says her doctor still shakes his head in puzzled amazement at all the "big words" she uses. Since I do not wear my diplomas around my neck for all to see, I too have on occasion been sent to that "kitchen," where some think I obviously belong.

One such incident that has stayed with me, though I recognize it as a minor offense, happened on the day of my first public poetry reading. It took place in Miami in a boat-restaurant where we were having lunch before the event. I was nervous and excited as I walked in with my notebook in my hand. An older woman motioned me to her table. Thinking (foolish me) that she wanted me to autograph a copy of my brand-new slender volume of verse, I went over. She ordered a cup of coffee from me, assuming that I was the waitress. Easy enough to mistake my poems for menus, I suppose. I know that it wasn't an intentional act of cruelty, yet of all the good things that happened that day, I remember that scene most clearly, because it reminded me of what I had to overcome before anyone would take me seriously. In retrospect I understand that my anger gave my reading fire, that I have almost always taken doubts in my abilities as a challenge—and that the result is, most times, a feeling of satisfaction at having won a convert when I see the cold, appraising eyes warm to my words, the body language change, the smile that indicates that I have opened some avenue for communication. That day I read to that woman and her lowered eyes told me that she was embarrassed at her little faux pas, and when I willed her to look up at me, it was my victory, and she graciously allowed me to punish her with my full attention. We shook hands at the end of the reading, and I never saw her again. She has probably forgotten the whole thing but maybe not.

Yet I am one of the lucky ones. My parents made it possible for me to acquire a stronger footing in the mainstream culture by giving me the chance at an education. And books and art have saved me from the harsher forms of ethnic and racial prejudice that many of my Hispanic *compañeras* have had to endure. I travel a lot around the United States, reading from my books of poetry and my novel, and the reception I most often receive is one of positive interest by people who want to know more about my culture. There are, however, thousands of Latinas without the privilege of an education or the entrée into society that I have. For them life is a struggle against the misconceptions perpetuated by the myth of the Latina as whore, domestic or criminal. We cannot change this by legislating the way people look at us. The transformation, as I see it, has to occur at a much more individual level. My personal goal in my public life is to try to replace the old pervasive stereotypes and myths about Latinas with a much more interesting set of realities. Every time I give a reading, I hope the stories I tell, the dreams and fears I examine in my work, can achieve some universal truth which will get my audience past the particulars of my skin color, my accent, or my clothes.

I once wrote a poem in which I called us Latinas "God's brown daugh- 15 ters." This poem is really a prayer of sorts, offered upward, but also, through the human-to-human channel of art, outward. It is a prayer for communication, and for respect. In it, Latin women pray "in Spanish to an Anglo God/with a Jewish heritage," and they are "fervently hoping/ that if not omnipotent,/at least He be bilingual."

[1992]

JUDY BRADY   [b. 1937]

Why I Want a Wife

Judy Brady was born in San Francisco in 1937 and earned a bachelor's degree in painting from the University of Iowa in 1967. Married and divorced, Brady raised two daughters while attending evening classes and working as an administrative assistant. As a freelance writer, she published articles on abortion, education, labor, and the women's movement. Her involvement with the women's movement led to a period of activism in which she visited Cuba to study the influence of class and social change. After surviving breast cancer, Brady edited books that include *Women and Cancer* (1980) and *One in Three: Women with Cancer Confront An Epidemic* (1987). Brady's most frequently reprinted essay, "Why I Want a Wife," initially appeared in the inaugural issue of *Ms.* magazine (1972) and continues to generate debate. Today, Brady remains active in feminist and progressive causes.

I belong to that classification of people known as wives. I am a Wife. And, not altogether incidentally, I am a mother.

Not too long ago a male friend of mine appeared on the scene fresh from a recent divorce. He had one child, who is, of course, with his ex-wife. He is obviously looking for another wife. As I thought about him while I was ironing one evening, it suddenly occurred to me that I, too, would like to have a wife. Why do I want a wife?

I would like to go back to school so that I can become economically independent, support myself, and, if need be, support those dependent upon me. I want a wife who will work and send me to school. And while I am going to school I want a wife to take care of my children. I want a wife to keep track of the children's doctor and dentist appointments. And to keep track of mine, too. I want a wife to make sure my children eat properly and are kept clean. I want a wife who will wash the children's clothes and keep them mended. I want a wife who is a good nurturant attendant to my children, who arranges for their schooling, makes sure that they have an adequate social life with their peers, takes them to the park, the zoo, etc. I want a wife who takes care of the children when they are sick,

Judy Brady, "Why I Want a Wife" from *Ms.*, Volume 1, Number 1, December 31, 1971.
Copyright © 1970 by Judy Brady. Reprinted by permission of the author.

a wife who arranges to be around when the children need special care, because, of course, I cannot miss classes at school. My wife must arrange to lose time at work and not lose the job. It may mean a small cut in my wife's income from time to time, but I guess I can tolerate that. Needless to say, my wife will arrange and pay for the care of the children while my wife is working.

I want a wife who will take care of *my* physical needs. I want a wife who will keep my house clean. A wife who will pick up after me. I want a wife who will keep my clothes clean, ironed, mended, replaced when need be, and who will see to it that my personal things are kept in their proper place so that I can find what I need the minute I need it. I want a wife who cooks the meals, a wife who is a *good* cook. I want a wife who will plan the menus, do the necessary grocery shopping, prepare the meals, serve them pleasantly, and then do the cleaning up while I do my studying. I want a wife who will care for me when I am sick and sympathize with my pain and loss of time from school. I want a wife to go along when our family takes a vacation so that someone can continue to care for me and my children when I need a rest and change of scene.

I want a wife who will not bother me with rambling complaints about 5 a wife's duties. But I want a wife who will listen to me when I feel the need to explain a rather difficult point I have come across in my course of studies. And I want a wife who will type my papers for me when I have written them.

I want a wife who will take care of the details of my social life. When my wife and I are invited out by my friends, I want a wife who will take care of the babysitting arrangements. When I meet people at school that I like and want to entertain, I want a wife who will have the house clean, will prepare a special meal, serve it to me and my friends, and not interrupt when I talk about the things that interest me and my friends. I want a wife who will have arranged that the children are fed and ready for bed before my guests arrive so that the children do not bother us. I want a wife who takes care of the needs of my guests so that they feel comfortable, who makes sure that they have an ashtray, that they are passed the hors d'oeuvres, that they are offered a second helping of the food, that their wine glasses are replenished when necessary, that their coffee is served to them as they like it. And I want a wife who knows that sometimes I need a night out by myself.

I want a wife who is sensitive to my sexual needs, a wife who makes love passionately and eagerly when I feel like it, a wife who makes sure that I am satisfied. And, of course, I want a wife who will not demand sexual attention when I am not in the mood for it. I want a wife who assumes the complete responsibility for birth control, because I do not want more children. I want a wife who will remain sexually faithful to me so that I do not have to clutter up my intellectual life with jealousies. And I want a wife who understands that *my* sexual needs may entail more than strict adherence to monogamy. I must, after all, be able to relate to people as fully as possible.

If, by chance, I find another person more suitable as a wife than the wife I already have, I want the liberty to replace my present wife with another one. Naturally, I will expect a fresh, new life; my wife will take the children and be solely responsible for them so that I am left free.

When I am through with school and have a job, I want my wife to quit working and remain at home so that my wife can more fully and completely take care of a wife's duties.

My God, who *wouldn't* want a wife? 10

PAUL THEROUX [b. 1941]

Being a Man

Paul Theroux was born in Medford, Massachusetts, one of seven children. He graduated from the University of Massachusetts in 1963 and published his first novel, *Waldo*, in 1967. He has written more than two dozen works of fiction, and several of his books, including *The Mosquito Coast* (1982), have been made into movies. He is best known for his travel writing, and his first travel book, *The Great Railway Bazaar: By Train Through Asia* (1975) was a best-seller. His other travel titles include *The Old Patagonian Express* (1979); *Sunrise with Seamonsters: Travels and Discoveries* (1985), a collection of Theroux's articles and essays between 1964 and 1984; *Riding the Iron Rooster: By Train through China* (1988); and *Dark Star Safari: Overland from Cairo to Cape Town* (2003). *Sir Vidia's Shadow* (1998) is an autobiographical portrayal of Theroux's thirty-year friendship and literary relationship with V. S. Naipaul, which ultimately came to an unhappy end. Theroux frequently publishes articles in magazines such as *Esquire, Atlantic Monthly,* and *Men's Journal.* He now divides his time between Hawaii, where he is a beekeeper, and Cape Cod.

"Being a Man" was first published in the *New York Times Magazine* in 1983. In an uncharacteristically serious and straightforward style, Theroux bemoans the choices that society allows a "manly" man to make.

There is a pathetic sentence in the chapter "Fetishism" in Dr. Norman Cameron's book *Personality Development and Psychopathology.* It goes, "Fetishists are nearly always men; and their commonest fetish is a woman's shoe." I cannot read that sentence without thinking that it is just one more awful thing about being a man — and perhaps it is an important thing to know about us.

I have always disliked being a man. The whole idea of manhood in America is pitiful, in my opinion. This version of masculinity is a little like having to wear an ill-fitting coat for one's entire life (by contrast, I imagine femininity to be an oppressive sense of nakedness). Even the expression "Be a man!" strikes me as insulting and abusive. It means: Be stupid, be unfeeling, obedient, soldierly, and stop thinking. Man means "manly"—how can one think about men without considering the terrible ambition of manliness? And yet it is part of every man's life. It is a hideous and crippling lie; it not only insists on difference and connives at superiority, it is also by its very nature destructive—emotionally damaging and socially harmful.

The youth who is subverted, as most are, into believing in the masculine ideal is effectively separated from women and he spends the rest of his life finding women a riddle and a nuisance. Of course, there is a female version of this male affliction. It begins with mothers encouraging little girls to say (to other adults) "Do you like my new dress?" In a sense, little girls are traditionally urged to please adults with a kind of coquettishness, while boys are enjoined to behave like monkeys towards each other. The nine-year-old coquette proceeds to become womanish in a subtle power game in which she learns to be sexually indispensable, socially decorative, and always alert to a man's sense of inadequacy.

Femininity—being lady-like—implies needing a man as witness and seducer; but masculinity celebrates the exclusive company of men. That is why it is so grotesque; and that is also why there is no manliness without inadequacy—because it denies men the natural friendship of women.

It is very hard to imagine any concept of manliness that does not belittle 5 women, and it begins very early. At an age when I wanted to meet girls—let's say the treacherous years of thirteen to sixteen—I was told to take up a sport, get more fresh air, join the Boy Scouts, and I was urged not to read so much. It was the 1950s and if you asked too many questions about sex you were sent to camp—boy's camp, of course: the nightmare. Nothing is more unnatural or prison-like than a boy's camp, but if it were not for them we would have no Elks' Lodges, no pool rooms, no boxing matches, no Marines.

And perhaps no sports as we know them. Everyone is aware of how few in number are the athletes who behave like gentlemen. Just as high school basketball teaches you how to be a poor loser, the manly attitude towards sports seems to be little more than a recipe for creating bad marriages, social misfits, moral degenerates, sadists, latent rapists, and just plain louts. I regard high school sports as a drug far worse than marijuana, and it is the reason that the average tennis champion, say, is a pathetic oaf.

Any objective study would find the quest for manliness essentially right-wing, puritanical, cowardly, neurotic, and fueled largely by a fear of women. It is also certainly philistine. There is no book-hater like a Little League coach. But indeed all the creative arts are obnoxious to the manly ideal, because at their best the arts are pursued by uncompetitive and essentially solitary people. It makes it very hard for a creative youngster, for any boy who expresses the desire to be alone seems to be saying that there is something wrong with him.

It ought to be clear by now that I have something of an objection to the way we turn boys into men. It does not surprise me that when the President of the United States has his customary weekend off he dresses like a cowboy—it is both a measure of his insecurity and his willingness to please. In many ways, American culture does little more for a man than prepare him for modeling clothes in the L. L. Bean catalogue. I take this as a personal insult because for many years I found it impossible to admit to myself that I wanted to be a writer. It was my guilty secret, because being a writer was incompatible with being a man.

There are people who might deny this, but that is because the American writer, typically, has been so at pains to prove his manliness that we have come to see literariness and manliness as mingled qualities. But first there was a fear that writing was not a manly profession—indeed, not a profession at all. (The paradox in American letters is that it has always been easier for a woman to write and for a man to be published.) Growing up, I had thought of sports as wasteful and humiliating, and the idea of manliness was a bore. My wanting to become a writer was not a flight from that oppressive role-playing, but I quickly saw that it was at odds with it. Everything in stereotyped manliness goes against the life of the mind. The Hemingway personality is too tedious to go into here, and in any case his exertions are well known, but certainly it was not until this aberrant behavior was examined by feminists in the 1960s that any male writer dared question the pugnacity in Hemingway's fiction. All the bullfighting and arm wrestling and elephant shooting diminished Hemingway as a writer, but it is consistent with a prevailing attitude in American writing: One cannot be a male writer without first proving that one is a man.

It is normal in America for a man to be dismissive or even somewhat 10 apologetic about being a writer. Various factors make it easier. There is a heartiness about journalism that makes it acceptable—journalism is the manliest form of American writing and, therefore, the profession the most independent-minded women seek (yes, it is an illusion, but that is my point). Fiction-writing is equated with a kind of dispirited failure and is only manly when it produces wealth—money is masculinity. So is drinking. Being a drunkard is another assertion, if misplaced, of manliness. The American male writer is traditionally proud of his heavy drinking. But we are also a very literal-minded people. A man proves his manhood in America in old-fashioned ways. He kills lions, like Hemingway; or he hunts ducks, like Nathanael West; or he makes pronouncements like, "A man should carry enough knife to defend himself with," as James Jones once said to a *Life* interviewer. Or he says he can drink you under the table. But even tiny drunken William Faulkner loved to mount a horse and go fox hunting, and Jack Kerouac roistered up and down Manhattan in a lumberjack shirt (and spent every night of *The Subterraneans* with his mother in Queens). And we are familiar with the lengths to which Norman Mailer is prepared, in his endearing way, to prove that he is just as much a monster as the next man.

When the novelist John Irving was revealed as a wrestler, people took him to be a very serious writer; and even a bubble reputation like Eric (*Love Story*) Segal's was enhanced by the news that he ran the marathon in a respectable time. How surprised we would be if Joyce Carol Oates were revealed as a sumo wrestler or Joan Didion active in pumping iron. "Lives in New York City with her three children" is the typical woman writer's biographical note, for just as the male writer must prove he has achieved a sort of muscular manhood, the woman writer—or rather her publicists—must prove her motherhood.

There would be no point in saying any of this if it were not generally accepted that to be a man is somehow—even now in feminist-influenced America—a privilege. It is on the contrary an unmerciful and punishing burden. Being a man is bad enough; being manly is appalling (in this sense, women's lib has done much more for men than for women). It is the sinister silliness of men's fashions, and a clubby attitude in the arts. It is the subversion of good students. It is the so-called "Dress Code" of the Ritz-Carlton Hotel in Boston, and it is the institutionalized cheating in college sports. It is the most primitive insecurity.

And this is also why men often object to feminism but are afraid to explain why: Of course women have a justified grievance, but most men believe—and with reason—that their lives are just as bad.

MARGARET ATWOOD   [b. 1939]

The Female Body

Born in the city of Ottawa, in Ontario, Canada, **Margaret Atwood** studied at the University of Toronto, Radcliffe College, and Harvard University. A predominant figure in Canadian letters who has written more than thirty books, Atwood is widely known for her concern for human awareness and vitality in a dangerous and exploitive world. Her poetry collections include *The Circle Game* (1964; rev. ed. 1966), which won the 1966 Governor-General's Award in Canada; *The Animals in That Country* (1968); *Procedures for Underground* (1970); *Two-Headed Poems* (1981); *Interlunar* (1984); and the two-volume *Selected Poems* (1976, 1988). Her novels include *The Edible Woman* (1969); *Surfacing* (1972); *Lady Oracle* (1976); *Life Before Man* (1979); *Bodily Harm* (1981); *The Handmaid's Tale* (1985), also made into a film, *Cat's Eye* (1988); *The Robber Bride* (1993); and *Alias Grace* (1996). Among her story collections are *Dancing Girls* (1977), *Bluebeard's Egg* (1983), *Murder in the Dark* (1983), and *Wilderness Tips* (1991).

The essay "The Female Body" first appeared in her collection *Good Bones*. Atwood discusses the physical and symbolic nature of the female body—as well as the ways in which it represents a prison.

1

I agree, it's a hot topic. But only one? Look around, there's a wide range. Take my own, for instance.

I get up in the morning. My topic feels like hell. I sprinkle it with water, brush parts of it, rub it with towels, powder it, add lubricant. I dump in the fuel and away goes my topic, my topical topic, my controversial topic, my capacious topic, my limping topic, my nearsighted topic, my topic with back problems, my badly behaved topic, my vulgar topic, my outrageous topic, my aging topic, my topic that is out of the question and anyway still can't spell, in its oversized coat and worn winter boots, scuttling along the sidewalk as if it were flesh and blood, hunting for what's out there, an avocado, an alderman, an adjective, hungry as ever.

401

2

The basic Female Body comes with the following accessories: garter belt, panti-girdle, crinoline, camisole, bustle, brassiere, stomacher, chemise, virgin zone, spike heels, nose ring, veil, kid gloves, fishnet stockings, fichu, bandeau, Merry Widow, weepers, chokers, barrettes, bangles, beads, lorgnette, feather boa, basic black, compact, Lycra stretch one-piece with modesty panel, designer peignoir, flannel nightie, lace teddy, bed, head.

3

The Female Body is made of transparent plastic and lights up when you plug it in. You press a button to illuminate the different systems. The circulatory system is red, for the heart and arteries, purple for the veins; the respiratory system is blue; the lymphatic system is yellow; the digestive system is green, with liver and kidneys in aqua. The nerves are done in orange and the brain is pink. The skeleton, as you might expect, is white.

The reproductive system is optional, and can be removed. It comes 5 with or without a miniature embryo. Parental judgment can thereby be exercised. We do not wish to frighten or offend.

4

He said, I won't have one of those things in the house. It gives a young girl a false notion of beauty, not to mention anatomy. If a real woman was built like that she'd fall on her face.

She said, If we don't let her have one like all the other girls she'll feel singled out. It'll become an issue. She'll long for one and she'll long to turn into one. Repression breeds sublimation. You know that.

He said, It's not just the pointy plastic tits, it's the wardrobes. The wardrobes and that stupid male doll, what's his name, the one with the underwear glued on.

She said, Better to get it over with when she's young. He said, All right, but don't let me see it.

She came whizzing down the stairs, thrown like a dart. She was stark 10 naked. Her hair had been chopped off, her head was turned back to front, she was missing some toes and she'd been tattooed all over her body with purple ink in a scrollwork design. She hit the potted azalea, trembled there for a moment like a botched angel, and fell.

He said, I guess we're safe.

402

5

The Female Body has many uses. It's been used as a door knocker, a bottle opener, as a clock with a ticking belly, as something to hold up lampshades, as a nutcracker, just squeeze the brass legs together and out comes your nut. It bears torches, lifts victorious wreaths, grows copper wings and raises aloft a ring of neon stars; whole buildings rest on its marble heads.

It sells cars, beer, shaving lotion, cigarettes, hard liquor; it sells diet plans and diamonds, and desire in tiny crystal bottles. Is this the face that launched a thousand products? You bet it is, but don't get any funny big ideas, honey, that smile is a dime a dozen.

It does not merely sell, it is sold. Money flows into this country or that country, flies in, practically crawls in, suitful after suitful, lured by all those hairless pre-teen legs. Listen, you want to reduce the national debt, don't you? Aren't you patriotic? That's the spirit. That's my girl.

She's a natural resource, a renewable one luckily, because those things wear out so quickly. They don't make 'em like they used to. Shoddy goods. 15

6

One and one equals another one. Pleasure in the female is not a requirement. Pair-bonding is stronger in geese. We're not talking about love, we're talking about biology. That's how we all got here, daughter.

Snails do it differently. They're hermaphrodites, and work in threes.

7

Each Female Body contains a female brain. Handy. Makes things work. Stick pins in it and you get amazing results. Old popular songs. Short circuits. Bad dreams.

Anyway: each of these brains has two halves. They're joined together by a thick cord; neural pathways flow from one to the other, sparkles of electric information washing to and fro. Like light on waves. Like a conversation. How does a woman know? She listens. She listens in.

The male brain, now, that's a different matter. Only a thin connection. 20 Space over here, time over there, music and arithmetic in their own sealed compartments. The right brain doesn't know what the left brain is doing. Good for aiming through, for hitting the target when you pull the trigger. What's the target? Who's the target? Who cares? What matters is hitting it. That's the male brain for you. Objective.

This is why men are so sad, why they feel so cut off, why they think of themselves as orphans cast adrift, footloose and stringless in the deep void. What void? she asks. What are you talking about? The void of the universe, he says, and she says Oh and looks out the window and tries to get a handle on it, but it's no use, there's too much going on, too many rustlings in the leaves, too many voices, so she says, Would you like a cheese sandwich, a piece of cake, a cup of tea? And he grinds his teeth because she doesn't understand, and wanders off, not just alone but Alone, lost in the dark, lost in the skull, searching for the other half, the twin who could complete him.

Then it comes to him: he's lost the Female Body! Look, it shines in the gloom, far ahead, a vision of wholeness, ripeness, like a giant melon, like an apple, like a metaphor for "breast" in a bad sex novel; it shines like a balloon, like a foggy noon, a watery moon, shimmering in its egg of light.

Catch it. Put it in a pumpkin, in a high tower, in a compound, in a chamber, in a house, in a room. Quick, stick a leash on it, a lock, a chain, some pain, settle it down, so it can never get away from you again.

[1992]

NOEL PERRIN   [1927–2004]

The Androgynous Man

Noel Perrin was an educator and writer whose subjects included feudal Japanese history, life in rural New England, and his adventures with an electric car. He was educated at Williams College, Duke University, and Cambridge University, England. For nearly forty years, Perrin taught literature at Dartmouth College, where he was considered an authority on the poetry of Robert Frost. Later in his career, Perrin expanded his focus to include environmental studies, a choice made after living for much of his life in a New England farmhouse. Perrin's essays appeared in many publications, including *The Washington Post*. In his "Rediscoveries" column, written monthly for many years, Perrin examined writers whom he believed had been neglected and warranted new attention. Perrin's essays depicting rural life were collected in several books, including *Vermont in All Weathers* (1973), *First Person Rural* (1978), *Second Person Rural* (1980), and *Third Person Rural* (1982). In "The Androgynous Man," which appeared in the *New York Times* in 1984, Perrin examines the restrictive nature of sexual stereotyping.

The summer I was 16, I took a train from New York to Steamboat Springs, Colo., where I was going to be assistant wrangler at a camp. The trip took three days, and since I was much too shy to talk to strangers, I had quite a lot of time for reading. I read all of *Gone With the Wind*. I read all of the interesting articles in a couple of magazines I had, and then I went back and read all the dull stuff. I also took all the quizzes, a thing of which magazines were fuller then than now.

The one that held my undivided attention was called "How Masculine/Feminine Are You?" It consisted of a large number of inkblots. The reader was supposed to decide which of four objects each blot most resembled. The choices might be a cloud, a steam-engine, a caterpillar and a sofa.

When I finished the test, I was shocked to find that I was barely masculine at all. On a scale of 1 to 10, I was about 1.2. Me, the horse wrangler? (And not just wrangler, either. That summer, I had to skin a couple of horses that died—the camp owner wanted the hides.)

The results of that test were so terrifying to me that for the first time in my life I did a piece of original analysis. Having unlimited time on the train, I looked at the "masculine" answers over and over, trying to find what it was that distinguished real men from people like me—and eventually I discovered two very simple patterns. It was "masculine" to think the blots looked like man-made objects, and "feminine" to think they looked like natural objects. It was masculine to think they looked like things capable of causing harm, and feminine to think of innocent things.

Even at 16, I had the sense to see that the compilers of the test were 5 using rather limited criteria—maleness and femaleness are both more complicated than that—and I breathed a hugh sigh of relief. I wasn't necessarily a wimp, after all.

That the test did reveal something other than the superficiality of its makers I realized only many years later. What it revealed was that there is a large class of men and women both, to which I belong, who are essentially androgynous. That doesn't mean we're gay, or low in the appropriate hormones, or uncomfortable performing the jobs traditionally assigned our sexes. (A few years after that summer, I was leading troops in combat and, unfashionable as it now is to admit this, having a very good time. War is exciting. What a pity the 20th century went and spoiled it with high-tech weapons.)

What it does mean to be spiritually androgynous is a kind of freedom. Men who are all-male, or he-man, or 100% red-blooded Americans, have a little biological set that causes them to be attracted to physical power, and probably also to dominance. Maybe even to watching football. I don't say this to criticize them. Completely masculine men are quite often wonderful people: good husbands, good (though sometimes overwhelming) fathers, good members of society. Furthermore, they are often so unself-consciously at ease in the world that other men seem to imitate them. They just aren't as free as androgynes. They pretty nearly have to be what they are; we have a range of choices open.

The sad part is that many of us never discover that. Men who are not 100% red-blooded Americans—say those who are only 75% red-blooded—often fail to notice their freedom. They are too busy trying to copy the he-men ever to realize that men, like women, come in a wide variety of acceptable types. Why this frantic imitation? My answer is mere speculation, but not casual. I have speculated on this for a long time.

Partly they're just envious of the he-man's unconscious ease. Mostly they're terrified of finding that there may be something wrong with them deep down, some weakness at the heart. To avoid discovering that, they spend their lives acting out the role that the he-man naturally lives. Sad.

One thing that men owe to the women's movement is that this kind of 10 failure is less common than it used to be. In releasing themselves from the single ideal of the dependent woman, women have more or less incidentally released a lot of men from the single ideal of the dominant male. The one mistake the feminists have made, I think, is in supposing that all men need this release, or that the world would be a better place if all men achieved it. It wouldn't. It would just be duller.

So far I have been pretty vague about just what the freedom of the androgynous man is. Obviously it varies with the case. In the case I know best, my own, I can be quite specific. It has freed me most as a parent. I am, among other things, a fairly good natural mother. I like the nurturing role. It makes me feel good to see a child eat—and it turns me to mush to see a 4-year-old holding a glass with both small hands, in order to drink. I even enjoyed sewing patches on the knees of my daughter Amy's Dr. Dentons when she was at the crawling stage. All that pleasure I would have lost if I had made myself stick to the notion of the paternal role that I started with.

Or take a smaller and rather ridiculous example. I feel free to kiss cats. Until recently it never occurred to me that I would want to, though my daughters have been doing it all their lives. But my elder daughter is now 22, and in London. Of course, I get to look after her cat while she is gone. He's a big, handsome farm cat named Petrushka, very unsentimental though used from kittenhood to being kissed on the top of the head by Elizabeth. I've gotten very fond of him (he's the adventurous kind of cat who likes to climb hills with you), and one night I simply felt like kissing him on the top of the head, and did. Why did no one tell me sooner how silky cat fur is?

Then there's my relation to cars. I am completely unembarrassed by my inability to diagnose even minor problems in whatever object I happen to be driving, and don't have to make some insider's remark to mechanics to try to establish that I, too, am a "Man With His Machine."

The same ease extends to household maintenance. I do it, of course. Service people are expensive. But for the last decade my house has functioned better than it used to because I have had the aid of a volume called "Home Repairs Any Woman Can Do," which is pitched just right for people at my technical level. As a youth, I'd as soon have touched such a book as I would have become a transvestite. Even though common sense says there is really nothing sexual whatsoever about fixing sinks.

Or take public emotion. All my life I have easily been moved by certain 15 kinds of voices. The actress Siobhan McKenna's, to take a notable case. Give her an emotional scene in a play, and within ten words my eyes are full of tears. In boyhood, my great dread was that someone might notice. I struggled manfully, you might say, to suppress this weakness. Now, of course, I don't see it as a weakness at all, but as a kind of fulfillment. I even suspect that the true he-men feel the same way, or one kind of them does, at least, and it's only the poor imitators who have to struggle to repress themselves.

Let me come back to the inkblots, with their assumption that masculine equates with machinery and science, and feminine with art and nature. I have no idea whether the right pronoun for God is He, She, or It. But this I'm pretty sure of. If God could somehow be induced to take that test, God would not come out macho and not feminismo, either, but right in the middle. Fellow androgynes, it's a nice thought.

KATHA POLLITT   [b. 1949]

Why Boys Don't Play With Dolls

Katha Pollitt is an American feminist author. Educated at Harvard and the Columbia School for the Arts, Pollitt has achieved a national reputation for her poetry and essays. Though she has written nonfiction for a variety of publications, she is best known for her "Subject to Debate" column, which appears regularly in *The Nation* and the *Washington Post*. A suberb stylist, Pollitt is known for her sharp, provocative analyses of popular culture and politics. In 1992, her essay on the culture wars, "Why We Read," won the National Magazine Award for essays and criticism. Pollitt has received a National Endowment for the Arts grant for her poetry, as well as a Guggenheim Fellowship. Pollitt's 1998 book, *The Antarctic Traveller*, received the National Book Critics Circle Award. Pollitt's poems have appeared in the *New Yorker, Atlantic Monthly, New Republic, Yale Review*, and other publications. She has been a guest on National Public Radio's *Fresh Air* and *All Things Considered*, and on several television shows, including *The McLaughlin Group* and *Dateline NBC*.

It's twenty-eight years since the founding of NOW, and boys still like trucks and girls still like dolls. Increasingly, we are told that the source of these robust preferences must lie outside society—in prenatal hormonal influences, brain chemistry, genes—and that feminism has reached its natural limits. What else could possibly explain the love of preschool girls for party dresses or the desire of toddler boys to own more guns than Mark from Michigan.°

True, recent studies claim to show small cognitive differences between the sexes: he gets around by orienting himself in space, she does it by remembering landmarks. Time will tell if any deserve the hoopla with

Mark from Michigan: Mark Koernke, a former right-wing talk-show host who supports the militia movement's resistance to federal government.

Katha Pollitt, "Why Boys Don't Play with Dolls" from *The New York Times Magazine*, October 8, 1995. Copyright © 1995 by Katha Pollitt. Reprinted by permission of The New York Times.

which each is invariably greeted, over the protests of the researchers themselves. But even if the results hold up (and the history of such research is not encouraging), we don't need studies of sex-differentiated brain activity in reading, say, to understand why boys and girls still seem so unalike.

The feminist movement has done much for some women, and something for every woman, but it has hardly turned America into a playground free of sex roles. It hasn't even got women to stop dieting or men to stop interrupting them.

Instead of looking at kids to "prove" that differences in behavior by sex are innate, we can look at the ways we raise kids as an index to how unfinished the feminist revolution really is, and how tentatively it is embraced even by adults who fully expect their daughters to enter previously male-dominated professions and their sons to change diapers.

I'm at a children's birthday party. "I'm sorry," one mom silently mouths   5 to the mother of the birthday girl, who has just torn open her present — Tropical Splash Barbie. Now, you can love Barbie or you can hate Barbie, and there are feminists in both camps. But *apologize* for Barbie? Inflict Barbie, against your own convictions, on the child of a friend you know will be none too pleased?

Every mother in that room had spent years becoming a person who had to be taken seriously, not least by herself. Even the most attractive, I'm willing to bet, had suffered over her body's failure to fit the impossible American ideal. Given all that, it seems crazy to transmit Barbie to the next generation. Yet to reject her is to say that what Barbie represents — being sexy, thin, stylish — is unimportant, which is obviously not true, and children know it's not true.

Women's looks matter terribly in this society, and so Barbie, however ambivalently, must be passed along. After all, there are worse toys. The Cut and Style Barbie styling head, for example, a grotesque object intended to encourage "hair play." The grown-ups who give that probably apologize, too.

How happy would most parents be to have a child who flouted sex conventions? I know a lot of women, feminists, who complain in a comical, eyeball-rolling way about their sons' passion for sports: the ruined weekends, obnoxious coaches, macho values. But they would not think of discouraging their sons from participating in this activity they find so foolish. Or do they? Their husbands are sports fans, too, and they like their husbands a lot.

Could it be that even sports-resistant moms see athletics as part of manliness? That if their sons wanted to spend the weekend writing up their diaries, or reading, or baking, they'd find it disturbing? Too antisocial? Too lonely? Too gay?

410

Theories of innate differences in behavior are appealing. They let parents 10 off the hook—no small recommendation in a culture that holds moms, and sometimes even dads, responsible for their children's every misstep on the road to bliss and success.

They allow grown-ups to take the path of least resistance to the dominant culture, which always requires less psychic effort, even if it means more actual work: just ask the working mother who comes home exhausted and nonetheless finds it easier to pick up her son's socks than make him do it himself. They let families buy for their children, without *too* much guilt, the unbelievably sexist junk that the kids, who have been watching commercials since birth, understandably crave.

But the thing that theories do most of all is tell adults that the *adult* world—in which moms and dads still play by many of the old rules even as they question and fidget and chafe against them—is the way it's supposed to be. A girl with a doll and a boy with a truck "explain" why men are from Mars and women are from Venus, why wives do housework and husbands just don't understand.

The paradox is that the world of rigid and hierarchical sex roles evoked by determinist theories is already passing away. Three-year-olds may indeed insist that doctors are male and nurses female, even if their own mother is a physician. Six-year-olds know better. These days, something like half of all medical students are female, and male applications to nursing school are inching upward. When tomorrow's three-year-olds play doctor, who's to say how they'll assign the roles?

With sex roles, as in every area of life, people aspire to what is possible, and conform to what is necessary. But these are not fixed, especially today. Biological determinism may reassure some adults about their present, but it is feminism, the ideology of flexible and converging sex roles, that fits our children's future. And the kids, somehow, know this.

That's why, if you look carefully, you'll find that for every kid who fits 15 a stereotype, there's another who's breaking one down. Sometimes it's the same kid—the boy who skateboards *and* takes cooking in his afterschool program; the girl who collects stuffed animals *and* A-pluses in science.

Feminists are often accused of imposing their "agenda" on children. Isn't that what adults always do, consciously and unconsciously? Kids aren't born religious, or polite, or kind, or able to remember where they put their sneakers. Inculcating these behaviors, and the values behind them, is a tremendous amount of work, involving many adults. We don't have a choice, really, about *whether* we should give our children messages about what it means to be male and female—they're bombarded with them from morning till night.

The question, as always, is what do we want those messages to be?

411

K. C. COLE   [b. 1946]

Women in Science

Born in Detroit in 1946, **K. C. Cole** spent her childhood in Rio de
Janeiro; Port Washington, New York; and Shaker Heights, Ohio. After
graduating from Barnard College with a degree in political science,
she worked as an editor for Radio Free Europe and covered events in
Eastern Europe and the Soviet Union. She became a writer, almost by
chance, when her story on the consequences of the Soviet invasion
of Czechoslovakia appeared in the *New York Times Magazine*. While
working as a writer and editor of the *Saturday Review*, she developed a
love of science, which become the primary focus of most of her subsequent writing. Today Cole is distinguished by her ability to write
about complex scientific issues in a clear, accessible manner. Since
1994, she has written a science column, "Mind over Matter," for the
Los Angeles Times. Cole is the recipient of several awards, including
the American Institute of Physics Science Writing Award (1995). The
author of seven works of popular nonfiction, including, *Mind Over
Matter: Conversations with the Cosmos* (2003), in 2006 Cole joined the
faculty of the University of Southern California's Annenberg School
for Communication.

I know few other women who do what I do. What I do is write about
science, mainly physics. And to do that, I spend a lot of time reading about
science, talking to scientists, and struggling to understand physics. In
fact, most of the women (and men) I know think me quite queer for
actually liking physics. "How can you write about that stuff?" they ask,
always somewhat askance. "I could never understand that in a million
years." Or more simply, "I hate science."

I didn't realize what an odd creature a woman interested in physics
was until a few years ago when a science magazine sent me to Johns
Hopkins University in Baltimore for a conference on an electrical phenomenon known as the Hall effect. We sat in a huge lecture hall and listened as physicists talked about things engineers didn't understand, and
engineers talked about things physicists didn't understand. What *I* didn't

understand was why, out of several hundred young students of physics and engineering in the room, less than a handful were women.

Some time later, I found myself at the California Institute of Technology reporting on the search for the origins of the universe. I interviewed physicist after physicist, man after man. I asked one young administrator why none of the physicists were women. And he answered: "I don't know, but I suppose it must be something innate. My seven-year-old daughter doesn't seem to be much interested in science."

It was with that experience fresh in my mind that I attended a conference in Cambridge, Massachusetts, on science literacy, or rather the worrisome lack of it in this country today. We three women—a science teacher, a young chemist, and myself—sat surrounded by a company of august men. The chemist, I think, first tentatively raised the issue of science illiteracy in women. It seemed like an obvious point. After all, everyone had agreed over and over again that scientific knowledge these days was a key factor in economic power. But as soon as she made the point, it became clear that we women had committed a grievous social error. Our genders were suddenly showing; we had interrupted the serious talk with a subject unforgivably silly.

For the first time, I stopped being puzzled about why there weren't any women in science and began to be angry. Because if science is a search for answers to fundamental questions then it hardly seems frivolous to find out why women are excluded. Never mind the economic consequences. 5

A lot of the reasons why women are excluded are spelled out by the Massachusetts Institute of Technology experimental physicist Vera Kistiakowsky in a recent article in *Physics Today* called "Women in Physics: Unnecessary, Injurious and Out of Place?" The title was taken from a nineteenth-century essay written in opposition to the appointment of a female mathematician to a professorship at the University of Stockholm. "As decidedly as two and two make four," a woman in mathematics is a "monstrosity," concluded the writer of the essay.

Dr. Kistiakowsky went on to discuss the factors that make women in science today, if not monstrosities, at least oddities. Contrary to much popular opinion, one of those is *not* an innate difference in the scientific ability of boys and girls. But early conditioning does play a stubborn and subtle role. A recent *Nova* program, "The Pinks and the Blues," documented how girls and boys are treated differently from birth—the boys always encouraged in more physical kinds of play, more active explorations of their environments. Sheila Tobias, in her book, *Math Anxiety*, showed how the games boys play help them to develop an intuitive understanding of speed, motion, and mass. The main sorting out of the girls from the boys in science seems to happen in junior high school. As a friend who teaches in a science museum said, "By the time we get to

413

electricity, the boys already have had some experience with it. But it's unfamiliar to the girls." Science books draw on boys' experiences. "The examples are all about throwing a baseball at such and such a speed," said my stepdaughter, who barely escaped being a science drop-out.

The most obvious reason there are not many more women in science is that women are discriminated against as a class, in promotions, salaries, and hirings, a conclusion reached by a recent analysis by the National Academy of Sciences.

Finally, said Dr. Kistiakowsky, women are simply made to feel out of place in science. Her conclusion was supported by a Ford Foundation study by Lynn H. Fox on the problems of women in mathematics. When students were asked to choose among six reasons accounting for girls' lack of interest in math, the girls rated this statement second: "Men do not want girls in the mathematical occupations."

A friend of mine remembers winning a Bronxwide mathematics com- 10 petition in the second grade. Her friends — both boys and girls — warned her that she shouldn't be good at math: "You'll never find a boy who likes you." My friend continued nevertheless to excel in math and science, won many awards during her years at the Bronx High School of Science, and then earned a full scholarship to Harvard. After one year of Harvard science, she decided to major in English.

When I asked her why, she mentioned what she called the "macho mores" of science. "It would have been O.K. if I'd had someone to talk to," she said. "But the rules of comportment were such that you never admitted you didn't understand. I later realized that even the boys didn't get everything clearly right away. You had to stick with it until it had time to sink in. But for the boys, there was a payoff in suffering through the hard times, and a kind of punishment — a shame — if they didn't. For the girls it was O.K. not to get it, and the only payoff for sticking it out was that you'd be considered a freak."

Science is undeniably hard. Often, it can seem quite boring. It is unfortunately too often presented as laws to be memorized instead of mysteries to be explored. It is too often kept a secret that science, like art, takes a well developed esthetic sense. Women aren't the only ones who say, "I hate science." That's why everyone who goes into science needs a little help from friends. For the past ten years, I have been getting more than a little help from a friend who is a physicist. But my stepdaughter — who earned the highest grades ever recorded in her California high school on the math Scholastic Aptitude Test — flunked calculus in her first year at Harvard. When my friend the physicist heard about it, he said, "Harvard should be ashamed of itself."

What he meant was that she needed that little extra encouragement that makes all the difference. Instead, she got that little extra discouragement that makes all the difference. "In the first place, all the math teachers are men," she explained. "In the second place, when I met a boy I liked and told him I was taking chemistry, he immediately said: 'Oh, you're one of those science types.' In the third place, it's just a kind of social thing. The math clubs are full of boys and you don't feel comfortable joining."

In other words, she was made to feel unnecessary, and out of place.

A few months ago, I accompanied a male colleague from the science   15
museum where I sometimes work to a lunch of the history of science faculty at the University of California. I was the only woman there, and my presence for the most part was obviously and rudely ignored. I was so surprised and hurt by this that I made an extra effort to speak knowledgeably and well. At the end of the lunch, one of the professors turned to me in all seriousness and said: "Well, K. C., what do the women think of Carl Sagan?" I replied that I had no idea what "the women" thought about anything. But now I know what I should have said: I should have told him that his comment was unnecessary, injurious, and out of place.

JOYCE CAROL OATES   [b. 1938]

Where Are You Going, Where Have You Been?

For Bob Dylan

Born in Lockport, New York, **Joyce Carol Oates** (b. 1938) is a graduate of Syracuse University and the University of Wisconsin. Astoundingly prolific, she is the author of numerous novels, volumes of poetry, and collections of short stories, many of which deal with destructive forces and sudden violence. She is also a literary theorist. Among her many novels are the trilogy *A Garden of Earthly Delights* (1967); *Expensive People* (1968); and *them* (1969), which won a National Book Award; *Son of the Morning* (1978); *Bellefleur* (1980); *Angel of Light* (1981); *Mysteries of Winterthurn* (1984); *Solstice* (1985); *Marya: A Life* (1986); *American Appetites* (1989); *Black Water* (1992); *First Love: A Gothic Tale* (1996); *Man Crazy* (1997); *My Heart Laid Bare* (1998); *Broke Heart Blues* (1999); and *Blonde* (2000). Her many story collections include *The Wheel of Love* (1970), *Marriages and Infidelities* (1972), *Crossing the Border* (1976), *Night-Side* (1977), *A Sentimental Education* (1981), *Last Days* (1984), *The Assignation* (1989), and *The Collector of Hearts: New Tales of the Grotesque* (1998).

Her name was Connie. She was fifteen and she had a quick nervous giggling habit of craning her neck to glance into mirrors, or checking other people's faces to make sure her own was all right. Her mother, who noticed everything and knew everything and who hadn't much reason any longer to look at her own face, always scolded Connie about it. "Stop gawking at yourself, who are you? You think you're so pretty?" she would say. Connie would raise her eyebrows at these familiar complaints and look right through her mother, into a shadowy vision of herself as she was right at that moment: she knew she was pretty and that was everything. Her mother had been pretty once too, if you could believe those old snapshots in the album, but now her looks were gone and that was why she was always after Connie.

"Why don't you keep your room clean like your sister? How've you got your hair fixed—what the hell stinks? Hair spray? You don't see your sister using that junk."

Her sister June was twenty-four and still lived at home. She was a secretary in the high school Connie attended, and if that wasn't bad enough—with her in the same building—she was so plain and chunky and steady that Connie had to hear her praised all the time by her mother and her mother's sisters. June did this, June did that, she saved money and helped clean the house and cooked and Connie couldn't do a thing, her mind was all filled with trashy daydreams. Their father was away at work most of the time and when he came home he wanted supper and he read the newspaper at supper and after supper he went to bed. He didn't bother talking much to them, but around his bent head Connie's mother kept picking at her until Connie wished her mother was dead and she herself was dead and it was all over. "She makes me want to throw up sometimes," she complained to her friends. She had a high, breathless, amused voice which made everything she said a little forced, whether it was sincere or not.

There was one good thing: June went places with girl friends of hers, girls who were just as plain and steady as she, and so when Connie wanted to do that her mother had no objections. The father of Connie's best girl friend drove the girls the three miles to town and left them off at a shopping plaza, so that they could walk through the stores or go to a movie, and when he came to pick them up again at eleven he never bothered to ask what they had done.

They must have been familiar sights, walking around that shopping plaza in their shorts and flat ballerina slippers that always scuffed the sidewalk, with charm bracelets jingling on their thin wrists; they would lean together to whisper and laugh secretly if someone passed by who amused or interested them. Connie had long dark blond hair that drew anyone's eye to it, and she wore part of it pulled up on her head and puffed out and the rest of it she let fall down her back. She wore a pullover jersey blouse that looked one way when she was at home and another way when she was away from home. Everything about her had two sides to it, one for home and one for anywhere that was not home: her walk that could be childlike and bobbing, or languid enough to make anyone think she was hearing music in her head, her mouth which was pale and smirking most of the time, but bright and pink on these evenings out, her laugh which was cynical and drawling at home—"Ha, ha, very funny"—but high-pitched and nervous anywhere else, like the jingling of the charms on her bracelet.

Sometimes they did go shopping or to a movie, but sometimes they went across the highway, ducking fast across the busy road, to a drive-in restaurant where older kids hung out. The restaurant was shaped like a big bottle, though squatter than a real bottle, and on its cap was a revolving figure of a grinning boy who held a hamburger aloft. One night in midsummer they ran across, breathless with daring, and right away someone leaned out a car window and invited them over, but it was just a boy from high school they didn't like. It made them feel good to be able to ignore him. They went up through the maze of parked and cruising cars to the bright-lit, fly-infested restaurant, their faces pleased and expectant as if they were entering a sacred building that loomed out of the night to give them what haven and what blessing they yearned for. They sat at the counter and crossed their legs at the ankles, their thin shoulders rigid with excitement and listened to the music that made everything so good: the music was always in the background like music at a church service, it was something to depend upon.

A boy named Eddie came in to talk with them. He sat backwards on his stool, turning himself jerkily around in semi-circles and then stopping and turning again, and after a while he asked Connie if she would like something to eat. She said she did and so she tapped her friend's arm on her way out—her friend pulled her face up into a brave droll look—and Connie said she would meet her at eleven, across the way. "I just hate to leave her like that," Connie said earnestly, but the boy said that she wouldn't be alone for long. So they went out to his car and on the way Connie couldn't help but let her eyes wander over the windshields and faces all around her, her face gleaming with the joy that had nothing to do with Eddie or even this place; it might have been the music. She drew her shoulders up and sucked in her breath with the pure pleasure of being alive, and just at that moment she happened to glance at a face just a few feet from hers. It was a boy with shaggy black hair, in a convertible jalopy painted gold. He stared at her and then his lips widened into a grin. Connie slit her eyes at him and turned away, but she couldn't help glancing back and there he was still watching her. He wagged a finger and laughed and said, "Gonna get you, baby," and Connie turned away again without Eddie noticing anything.

She spent three hours with him, at the restaurant where they ate hamburgers and drank Cokes in wax cups that were always sweating, and then down an alley a mile or so away, and when he left her off at five to eleven only the movie house was still open at the plaza. Her girl friend was there, talking with a boy. When Connie came up the two girls smiled at each other and Connie said, "How was the movie?" and the girl said, "You should know." They rode off with the girl's father, sleepy and pleased, and Connie couldn't help but look at the darkened shopping plaza with its big empty parking lot and its signs that were faded and ghostly now, and over at the drive-in restaurant where cars were still circling tirelessly. She couldn't hear the music at this distance.

Next morning June asked her how the movie was and Connie said, "So-so."

She and that girl and occasionally another girl went out several times a week that way, and the rest of the time Connie spent around the house—it was summer vacation—getting in her mother's way and thinking, dreaming, about the boys she met. But all the boys fell back and dissolved into a single face that was not even a face, but an idea, a feeling, mixed up with the urgent insistent pounding of the music and the humid night air of July. Connie's mother kept dragging her back to the daylight by finding things for her to do or saying suddenly, "What's this about the Pettinger girl?"

And Connie would say nervously, "Oh, her. That dope." She always drew thick clear lines between herself and such girls, and her mother was simple and kindly enough to believe her. Her mother was so simple, Connie thought, that it was maybe cruel to fool her so much. Her mother went scuffling around the house in old bedroom slippers and complained over the telephone to one sister about the other, then the other called up and the two of them complained about the third one. If June's name was mentioned her mother's tone was approving, and if Connie's name was mentioned it was disapproving. This did not really mean she disliked Connie and actually Connie thought that her mother preferred her to June because she was prettier, but the two of them kept up a pretense of exasperation, a sense that they were tugging and struggling over something of little value to either of them. Sometimes, over coffee, they were almost friends, but something would come up—some vexation that was like a fly buzzing suddenly around their heads—and their faces went hard with contempt.

One Sunday Connie got up at eleven—none of them bothered with church—and washed her hair so that it could dry all day long, in the sun. Her parents and sister were going to a barbecue at an aunt's house and Connie said no, she wasn't interested, rolling her eyes, to let mother know just what she thought of it. "Stay home alone then," her mother said sharply. Connie sat out back in a lawn chair and watched them drive away, her father quiet and bald, hunched around so that he could back the car out, her mother with a look that was still angry and not at all softened through the windshield, and in the back seat poor old June all dressed up as if she didn't know what a barbecue was, with all the running yelling kids and the flies. Connie sat with her eyes closed in the sun, dreaming and dazed with the warmth about her as if this were a kind of love, the caresses of love, and her mind slipped over onto thoughts of the boy she had been with the night before and how nice he had been, how sweet it always was, not the way someone like June would suppose but sweet, gentle, the way it was in movies and promised in songs; and when she opened her eyes she hardly knew where she was, the back yard ran off into weeds and a fenceline of trees and behind it the sky was perfectly blue and still. The asbestos "ranch house" that was now three years old startled her—it looked small. She shook her head as if to get awake.

It was too hot. She went inside the house and turned on the radio to drown out the quiet. She sat on the edge of her bed, barefoot, and listened for an hour and a half to a program called XYZ Sunday Jamboree, record after record of hard, fast, shrieking songs she sang along with, interspersed by exclamations from "Bobby King": "An' look here you girls at Napoleon's—Son and Charley want you to pay real close attention to this song coming up!"

And Connie paid close attention herself, bathed in a glow of slow-pulsed joy that seemed to rise mysteriously out of the music itself and lay languidly about the airless little room, breathed in and breathed out with each gentle rise and fall of her chest.

After a while she heard a car coming up the drive. She sat up at once, startled, because it couldn't be her father so soon. The gravel kept crunching all the way in from the road—the driveway was long—and Connie ran to the window. It was a car she didn't know. It was an open jalopy, painted a bright gold that caught the sun opaquely. Her heart began to pound and her fingers snatched at her hair, checking it, and she whispered "Christ. Christ," wondering how bad she looked. The car came to a stop at the side door and the horn sounded four short taps as if this were a signal Connie knew.

She went into the kitchen and approached the door slowly, then hung out the screen door, her bare toes curling down off the step. There were two boys in the car and now she recognized the driver: he had shaggy, shabby black hair that looked crazy as a wig and he was grinning at her.

"I ain't late, am I?" he said.

"Who the hell do you think you are?" Connie said.

"Toldja I'd be out, didn't I?"

"I don't even know who you are."

She spoke sullenly, careful to show no interest or pleasure, and he spoke in a fast bright monotone. Connie looked past him to the other boy, taking her time. He had fair brown hair, with a lock that fell onto his forehead. His sideburns gave him a fierce, embarrassed look, but so far he hadn't even bothered to glance at her. Both boys wore sunglasses. The driver's glasses were metallic and mirrored everything in miniature.

"You wanta come for a ride?" he said.

420

Connie smirked and let her hair fall loose over one shoulder.

"Don'tcha like my car? New paint job," he said. "Hey."

"What?"

"You're cute."

She pretended to fidget, chasing flies away from the door.

"Don'tcha believe me, or what?" he said.

"Look, I don't even know who you are," Connie said in disgust.

"Hey, Ellie's got a radio, see. Mine's broke down." He lifted his friend's arm and showed her the little transistor the boy was holding, and now Connie began to hear the music. It was the same program that was playing inside the house.

"Bobby King?" she said.

"I listen to him all the time. I think he's great."

"He's kind of great," Connie said reluctantly.

"Listen, that guy's *great*. He knows where the action is."

Connie blushed a little, because the glasses made it impossible for her to see just what this boy was looking at. She couldn't decide if she liked him or if he was just a jerk, and so she dawdled in the doorway and wouldn't come down or go back inside. She said, "What's all that stuff painted on your car?"

"Can'tcha read it?" He opened the door very carefully, as if he was afraid it might fall off. He slid out just as carefully, planting his feet firmly on the ground, the tiny metallic world in his glasses slowing down like gelatine hardening and in the midst of it Connie's bright green blouse. "This here is my name, to begin with," he said. ARNOLD FRIEND was written in tar-like black letters on the side, with a drawing of a round grinning face that reminded Connie of a pumpkin, except it wore sunglasses. "I wanta introduce myself, I'm Arnold Friend and that's my real name and I'm gonna be your friend, honey, and inside the car's Ellie Oscar, he's kinda shy." Ellie brought his transistor up to his shoulder and balanced it there. "Now these numbers are a secret code, honey," Arnold Friend explained. He read off the numbers 33, 19, 17 and raised his eyebrows at her to see what she thought of that, but she didn't think much of it. The left rear fender had been smashed and around it was written, on the gleaming gold background: DONE BY CRAZY WOMAN DRIVER. Connie had to laugh at that. Arnold Friend was pleased at her laughter and looked up at her. "Around the other side's a lot more—you wanta come and see them?"

"No."

"Why not?"

"Why should I?"

"Don'tcha wanta see what's on the car? Don'tcha wanta go for a ride?"

"I don't know."

"Why not?"

"I got things to do."

"Like what?"

"Things."

He laughed as if she had said something funny. He slapped his thighs. He was standing in a strange way, leaning back against the car as if he were balancing himself. He wasn't tall, only an inch or so taller than she would be if she came down to him. Connie liked the way he was dressed, which was the way all of them dressed: tight faded jeans stuffed into black, scuffed boots, a belt that pulled his waist in and showed how lean he was, and a white pull-over shirt that was a little soiled and showed the hard small muscles of his arms and shoulders. He looked as if he probably did hard work, lifting and carrying things. Even his neck looked muscular. And his face was a familiar face, somehow: the jaw and chin and cheeks slightly darkened, because he hadn't shaved for a day or two, and the nose long and hawk-like, sniffing as if she were a treat he was going to gobble up and it was all a joke.

"Connie, you ain't telling the truth. This is your day set aside for a ride with me and you know it," he said, still laughing. The way he straightened and recovered from his fit of laughing showed that it had been all fake.

"How do you know what my name is?" she said suspiciously.

"It's Connie."

"Maybe and maybe not."

"I know my Connie," he said, wagging his finger. Now she remembered him even better, back at the restaurant, and her cheeks warmed at the thought of how she sucked in her breath just at the moment she passed him—how she must have looked to him. And he had remembered her. "Ellie and I come out here especially for you," he said. "Ellie can sit in back. How about it?"

"Where?"

"Where what?"

"Where're we going?"

He looked at her. He took off the sunglasses and she saw how pale the skin around his eyes was, like holes that were not in shadow but instead in light. His eyes were like chips of broken glass that catch the light in an amiable way. He smiled. It was as if the idea of going for a ride somewhere, to some place, was a new idea to him.

"Just for a ride, Connie sweetheart."

"I never said my name was Connie," she said.

"But I know what it is. I know your name and all about you, lots of things," Arnold Friend said. He had not moved yet but stood still leaning back against the side of his jalopy. "I took a special interest in you, such

422

a pretty girl, and found out all about you like I know your parents and sister are gone somewheres and I know where and how long they're going to be gone, and I know who you were with last night, and your best friend's name is Betty. Right?"

He spoke in a simple lilting voice, exactly as if he were reciting the words to a song. His smile assured her that everything was fine. In the car Ellie turned up the volume on his radio and did not bother to look around at them.

"Ellie can sit in the back seat," Arnold Friend said. He indicated his friend with a casual jerk of his chin, as if Ellie did not count and she could not bother with him.

"How'd you find out all that stuff?" Connie said.

"Listen: Betty Schultz and Tony Fitch and Jimmy Pettinger and Nancy Pettinger," he said, in a chant. "Raymond Stanley and Bob Hutter—"

"Do you know all those kids?"

"I know everybody."

"Look, you're kidding. You're not from around here."

"Sure."

"But—how come we never saw you before?"

"Sure you saw me before," he said. He looked down at his boots, as if he were a little offended. "You just don't remember."

"I guess I'd remember you," Connie said.

"Yeah?" He looked up at this, beaming. He was pleased. He began to mark time with the music from Ellie's radio, tapping his fists lightly together. Connie looked away from his smile to the car, which was painted so bright it almost hurt her eyes to look at it. She looked at that name, ARNOLD FRIEND. And up at the front fender was an expression that was familiar—MAN THE FLYING SAUCERS. It was an expression kids had used the year before, but didn't use this year. She looked at it for a while as if the words meant something to her that she did not yet know.

"What're you thinking about? Huh?" Arnold Friend demanded. "Not worried about your hair blowing around in the car, are you?"

"No."

"Think I maybe can't drive good?"

"How do I know?"

"You're a hard girl to handle. How come?" he said. "Don't you know I'm your friend? Didn't you see me put my sign in the air when you walked by?"

"What sign?"

"My sign." And he drew an X in the air, leaning out toward her. They were maybe ten feet apart. After his hand fell back to his side the X was still in the air, almost visible. Connie let the screen door close and stood perfectly still inside it, listening to the music from her radio and the boy's blend together. She stared at Arnold Friend. He stood there so stiffly relaxed, pretending to be relaxed, with one hand idly on the door handle as if he were keeping himself up that way and had no intention of ever moving again. She recognized most things about him, the tight jeans that showed his thighs and buttocks and the greasy leather boots and the tight shirt, and even that slippery friendly smile of his, that sleepy dreamy smile that all the boys used to get across ideas they didn't want to put into words. She recognized all this and also the singsong way he talked, slightly mocking, kidding, but serious and a little melancholy, and she recognized the way he tapped one fist against the other in homage to the perpetual music behind him. But all these things did not come together.

She said suddenly, "Hey, how old are you?"

His smile faded. She could see then that he wasn't a kid, he was much older—thirty, maybe more. At this knowledge her heart began to pound faster.

"That's a crazy thing to ask. Can'tcha see I'm your own age?"

"Like hell you are."

"Or maybe a coupla years older, I'm eighteen."

"Eighteen?" she said doubtfully.

He grinned to reassure her and lines appeared at the corners of his mouth. His teeth were big and white. He grinned so broadly his eyes became slits and she saw how thick the lashes were, thick and black as if painted with a black tar-like material. Then he seemed to become embarrassed, abruptly, and looked over his shoulder at Ellie. "*Him*, he's crazy," he said. "Ain't he a riot, he's a nut, a real character." Ellie was still listening to the music. His sunglasses told nothing about what he was thinking. He wore a bright orange shirt unbuttoned halfway to show his chest, which was a pale, bluish chest and not muscular like Arnold Friend's. His shirt collar was turned up all around and the very tips of the collar pointed out past his chin as if they were protecting him. He was pressing the transistor radio up against his ear and sat there in a kind of daze, right in the sun.

"He's kinda strange," Connie said.

"Hey, she says you're kinda strange! Kinda strange!" Arnold Friend cried. He pounded on the car to get Ellie's attention. Ellie turned for the first time and Connie saw with shock that he wasn't a kid either—he had a fair, hairless face, cheeks reddened slightly as if the veins grew too close to the surface of his skin, the face of a forty-year-old baby. Connie felt a wave of dizziness rise in her at this sight and she stared at him as if waiting for something to change the shock of the moment, make it all right again. Ellie's lips kept shaping words, mumbling along with the words blasting his ear.

424

"Maybe you two better go away," Connie said faintly.

"What? How come?" Arnold Friend cried. "We come out here to take you for a ride. It's Sunday." He had the voice of the man on the radio now. It was the same voice, Connie thought. "Don'tcha know it's Sunday all day and honey, no matter who you were with last night today you're with Arnold Friend and don't you forget it!—Maybe you better step out here," he said, and this last was in a different voice. It was a little flatter, as if the heat was finally getting to him.

"No. I got things to do."

"Hey."

"You two better leave."

"We ain't leaving until you come with us."

"Like hell I am—"

"Connie, don't fool around with me. I mean—I mean, don't fool *around*," he said, shaking his head. He laughed incredulously. He placed his sunglasses on top of his head, carefully, as if he were indeed wearing a wig, and brought the stems down behind his ears. Connie stared at him, another wave of dizziness and fear rising in her so that for a moment he wasn't even in focus but was just a blur, standing there against his gold car, and she had the idea that he had driven up the drive-way all right but had come from nowhere before that and belonged nowhere and that everything about him and even the music that was so familiar to her was only half real.

"If my father comes and sees you—"

"He ain't coming. He's at a barbecue."

"How do you know that?"

"Aunt Tillie's. Right now they're—uh—they're drinking. Sitting around," he said vaguely, squinting as if he were staring all the way to town and over to Aunt Tillie's back yard. Then the vision seemed to clear and he nodded energetically. "Yeah. Sitting around. There's your sister in a blue dress, huh? And high heels, the poor sad bitch—nothing like you, sweetheart! And your mother's helping some fat woman with the corn, they're cleaning the corn—husking the corn—"

"What fat woman?" Connie cried.

"How do I know what fat woman. I don't know every goddamn fat woman in the world!" Arnold Friend laughed.

"Oh, that's Mrs. Hornby. . . . Who invited her?" Connie said. She felt a little light-headed. Her breath was coming quickly.

"She's too fat. I don't like them fat. I like them the way you are, honey," he said, smiling sleepily at her. They stared at each other for a while, through the screen door. He said softly, "Now what you're going to do is this: you're going to come out that door. You're going to sit up front with me and Ellie's going to sit in the back, the hell with Ellie, right? This isn't Ellie's date. You're my date. I'm your lover, honey."

"What? You're crazy—"

"Yes, I'm your lover. You don't know what that is but you will," he said. "I know that too. I know all about you. But look: it's real nice and you couldn't ask for nobody better than me, or more polite. I always keep my word. I'll tell you how it is, I'm always nice at first, the first time. I'll hold you so tight you won't think you have to try to get away or pretend anything because you'll know you can't. And I'll come inside you where it's all secret and you'll give in to me and you'll love me—"

"Shut up! You're crazy!" Connie said. She backed away from the door. She put her hands against her ears as if she'd heard something terrible, something not meant for her. "People don't talk like that, you're crazy," she muttered. Her heart was almost too big now for her chest and its pumping made sweat break out all over her. She looked out to see Arnold Friend pause and then take a step toward the porch lurching. He almost fell. But, like a clever drunken man, he managed to catch his balance. He wobbled in his high boots and grabbed hold of one of the porch posts.

"Honey?" he said. "You still listening?"

"Get the hell out of here!"

"Be nice, honey. Listen."

"I'm going to call the police—"

He wobbled again and out of the side of his mouth came a fast spat curse, an aside not meant for her to hear. But even this "Christ!" sounded forced. Then he began to smile again. She watched this smile come, awkward as if he were smiling from inside a mask. His whole face was a mask, she thought wildly, tanned down onto his throat but then running out as if he had plastered make-up on his face but had forgotten about his throat.

"Honey—? Listen, here's how it is. I always tell the truth and I promise you this: I ain't coming in that house after you."

"You better not! I'm going to call the police if you—if you don't—"

"Honey," he said, talking right through her voice, "honey, I'm not coming in there but you are coming out here. You know why?"

She was panting. The kitchen looked like a place she had never seen before, some room she had run inside but which wasn't good enough, wasn't going to help her. The kitchen window had never had a curtain, after three years, and there were dishes in the sink for her to do—probably—and if you ran your hand across the table you'd probably feel something sticky there.

"You listening, honey? Hey?"

426

"—going to call the police—"

"Soon as you touch the phone I don't need to keep my promise and can come inside. You won't want that."

She rushed forward and tried to lock the door. Her fingers were shaking. "But why lock it," Arnold Friend said gently, talking right into her face. "It's just a screen door. It's just nothing." One of his boots was at a strange angle, as if his foot wasn't in it. It pointed out to the left, bent at the ankle. "I mean, anybody can break through a screen door and glass and wood and iron or anything else if he needs to, anybody at all and specially Arnold Friend. If the place got lit up with a fire, honey, you'd come runnin' out into my arms, right into my arms an' safe at home— like you knew I was your lover and'd stopped fooling around, I don't mind a nice shy girl but I don't like no fooling around." Part of those words were spoken with a slight rhythmic lilt, and Connie somehow recognized them—the echo of a song from last year, about a girl rushing into her boy friend's arms and coming home again—

Connie stood barefoot on the linoleum floor, staring at him. "What do you want?" she whispered.

"I want you," he said.

"What?"

"Seen you that night and thought, that's the one, yes sir. I never needed to look any more."

"But my father's coming back. He's coming to get me. I had to wash my hair first—" She spoke in a dry, rapid voice, hardly raising it for him to hear.

"No, your daddy is not coming and yes, you had to wash your hair and you washed it for me. It's nice and shining and all for me. I thank you, sweetheart," he said, with a mock bow, but again he almost lost his balance. He had to bend and adjust his boots. Evidently his feet did not go all the way down; the boots must have been stuffed with something so that he would seem taller. Connie stared out at him and behind him at Ellie in the car, who seemed to be looking off toward Connie's right, into nothing. Then Ellie said, pulling the words out of the air one after another as if he were just discovering them, "You want me to pull out the phone?"

"Shut your mouth and keep it shut," Arnold Friend said, his face red from bending over or maybe from embarrassment because Connie had seen his boots. "This ain't none of your business."

"What—what are you doing? What do you want?" Connie said. "If I call the police they'll get you, they'll arrest you—"

"Promise was not to come in unless you touch that phone, and I'll keep that promise," he said. He resumed his erect position and tried to force his shoulders back. He sounded like a hero in a movie, declaring something important. He spoke too loudly and it was as if he were

427

speaking to someone behind Connie. "I ain't made plans for coming in that house where I don't belong but just for you to come out to me, the way you should. Don't you know who I am?"

"You're crazy," she whispered. She backed away from the door but did not want to go into another part of the house, as if this would give him permission to come through the door. "What do you . . . You're crazy, you. . . ."

"Huh? What're you saying, honey?"

Her eyes darted everywhere in the kitchen. She could not remember what it was, this room.

"This is how it is, honey: you come out and we'll drive away, have a nice ride. But if you don't come out we're gonna wait till your people come home and then they're all going to get it."

"You want that telephone pulled out?" Ellie said. He held the radio away from his ear and grimaced, as if without the radio the air was too much for him.

"I toldja shut up, Ellie," Arnold Friend said, "you're deaf, get a hearing aid, right? Fix yourself up. This little girl's no trouble and's gonna be nice to me, so Ellie keep to yourself, this ain't your date—right? Don't hem in on me, don't hog, don't crush, don't bird dog, don't trail me," he said in a rapid, meaningless voice, as if he were running through all the expressions he'd learned but was no longer sure which one of them was in style, then rushing on to new ones, making them up with his eyes closed. "Don't crawl under my fence, don't squeeze in my chipmunk hole, don't sniff my glue, suck my popsicle, keep your own greasy fingers on yourself!" He shaded his eyes and peered in at Connie, who was backed against the kitchen table. "Don't mind him, honey, he's just a creep. He's a dope. Right? I'm the boy for you and like I said, you come out here nice like a lady and give me your hand, and nobody else gets hurt, I mean, your nice old bald-headed daddy and your mummy and your sister in her high heels. Because listen: why bring them in this?"

"Leave me alone," Connie whispered.

"Hey, you know that old woman down the road, the one with the chickens and stuff—you know her?"

"She's dead!"

"Dead? What? You know her?" Arnold Friend said.

"She's dead—"

"Don't you like her?"

"She's dead—she's—she isn't here any more—"

"But don't you like her, I mean, you got something against her? Some grudge or something?" Then his voice dipped as if he were conscious of rudeness. He touched the sunglasses on top of his head as if to make sure they were still there. "Now you be a good girl."

"What are you going to do?"

"Just two things, or maybe three," Arnold Friend said. "But I promise it won't last long and you'll like me that way you get to like people you're close to. You will. It's all over for you here, so come on out. You don't want your people in any trouble, do you?"

She turned and bumped against a chair or something, hurting her leg, but she ran into the back room and picked up the telephone. Something roared in her ear, a tiny roaring, and she was so sick with fear that she could do nothing but listen to it—the telephone was clammy and very heavy and her fingers groped down to the dial but were too weak to touch it. She began to scream into the phone, into the roaring. She cried out, she cried for her mother, she felt her breath start jerking back and forth in her lungs as if it were something Arnold Friend was stabbing her with again and again with no tenderness. A noisy sorrowful wailing rose all about her and she was locked inside it the way she was locked inside this house.

After a while she could hear again. She was sitting on the floor, with her wet back against the wall.

Arnold Friend was saying from the door, "That's a good girl. Put the phone back."

She kicked the phone away from her.

"No, honey. Pick it up. Put it back right."

She picked it up and put it back. The dial tone stopped.

"That's a good girl. Now you come outside."

She was hollow with what had been fear but what was now just an emptiness. All that screaming had blasted it out of her. She sat, one leg cramped under her, and deep inside her brain was something like a pinpoint of light that kept going and would not let her relax. She thought, I'm not going to see my mother again. She thought, I'm not going to sleep in my bed again. Her bright green blouse was all wet.

Arnold Friend said, in a gentle-loud voice that was like a stage voice, "The place where you came from ain't there any more, and where you had in mind to go is cancelled out. This place you are now—inside your daddy's house—is nothing but a cardboard box I can knock down any time. You know that and always did know it. You hear me?"

She thought, I have got to think. I have got to know what to do.

"We'll go out to a nice field, out in the country here where it smells so nice and it's sunny," Arnold Friend said. "I'll have my arms tight around you so you won't need to try to get away and I'll show you what love is like, what it does. The hell with this house! It looks solid all right," he said. He ran a fingernail down the screen and the noise did not make Connie shiver, as it would have the day before. "Now put your hand on your heart, honey. Feel that? That feels solid too but we know better. Be nice to me, be sweet like you can because what else is there for a girl like you but to be sweet and pretty and give in?—and get away before her people get back?"

She felt her pounding heart. Her hand seemed to enclose it. She thought for the first time in her life that it was nothing that was hers, that belonged to her, but just a pounding, living thing inside this body that wasn't really hers either.

"You don't want them to get hurt," Arnold Friend went on. "Now get up, honey. Get up all by yourself."

She stood.

"Now turn this way. That's right. Come over to me—Ellie, put that away, didn't I tell you? You dope. You miserable creepy dope," Arnold Friend said. His words were not angry but only part of an incantation. The incantation was kindly. "Now come out through the kitchen to me honey and let's see a smile, try it, you're a brave sweet little girl and now they're eating corn and hotdogs cooked to bursting over an outdoor fire, and they don't know one thing about you and never did and honey you're better than them because not a one of them would have done this for you."

Connie felt the linoleum under her feet; it was cool. She brushed her hair back out of her eyes. Arnold Friend let go of the post tentatively and opened his arms for her, his elbows pointing in toward each other and his wrists limp, to show that this was an embarrassed embrace and a little mocking, he didn't want to make her self-conscious.

She put out her hand against the screen. She watched herself push the door slowly open as if she were back safe somewhere in the other door-way, watching this body and this head of long hair moving out into the sunlight where Arnold Friend waited.

"My sweet little blue-eyed girl," he said in a half-sung sigh that had nothing to do with her brown eyes but was taken up just the same by the vast sunlit reaches of the land behind him and on all sides of him—so much land that Connie had never seen before and did not recognize except to know that she was going to it.

[1966]

ERNEST HEMINGWAY   [1899–1961]

A Clean, Well-Lighted Place

Born in Oak Park, Illinois, **Ernest Hemingway** (1899–1961) led an active, vigorous life from childhood, summering in the wilds of northern Michigan with his physician father and boxing and playing football at school. His first job as a writer was as a reporter for the Kansas City *Star.* During World War I he served as an ambulance driver in Italy; severely wounded before he had turned nineteen, he was decorated by the Italian government. Later, while working in Paris as a correspondent for the Toronto *Star,* he met Gertrude Stein, Ezra Pound, F. Scott Fitzgerald, and other artists and writers who had a significant influence on his work. Hemingway's first book, *Three Stories and Ten Poems* (1923), was followed by the well-known story collection *In Our Time* (1924; rev. and enl. ed., 1925). His novel *The Sun Also Rises* (1926) brought acclaim as well as recognition of Hemingway as the spokesman for the "lost generation." *A Farewell to Arms* (1929), based on his wartime experiences in Italy, and *For Whom the Bell Tolls* (1940), drawn from his time as a correspondent during the civil war in Spain, established his enduring reputation. In World War II he served as a correspondent and received a Bronze Star. His frequent travels took him to Spain for the bullfights, on fishing trips to the Caribbean, and on big-game expeditions to the American West and to Africa. In his later years he suffered from declining physical health and severe depression, which led to his suicide at his home in Ketcham, Idaho. The fullest collection of his short stories, the Finca-Vigia edition, came out in 1991. Hemingway was awarded the Nobel Prize in literature in 1954.

It was late and everyone had left the café except an old man who sat in the shadow the leaves of the tree made against the electric light. In the day time the street was dusty, but at night the dew settled the dust and the old man liked to sit late because he was deaf and now at night it was quiet and he felt the difference. The two waiters inside the café knew that the old man was a little drunk, and while he was a good client they knew that if he became too drunk he would leave without paying, so they kept watch on him.

"Last week he tried to commit suicide," one waiter said.

"Why?"

"He was in despair."

"What about?"

"Nothing."

"How do you know it was nothing?"

"He has plenty of money."

They sat together at a table that was close against the wall near the door of the café and looked at the terrace where the tables were all empty except where the old man sat in the shadow of the leaves of the tree that moved slightly in the wind. A girl and a soldier went by in the street. The street light shone on the brass number on his collar. The girl wore no head covering and hurried beside him.

"The guard will pick him up," one waiter said.

"What does it matter if he gets what he's after?"

"He had better get off the street now. The guard will get him. They went by five minutes ago."

The old man sitting in the shadow rapped on his saucer with his glass. The younger waiter went over to him.

"What do you want?"

The old man looked at him. "Another brandy," he said.

"You'll be drunk," the waiter said. The old man looked at him. The waiter went away.

"He'll stay all night," he said to his colleague. "I'm sleepy now. I never get into bed before three o'clock. He should have killed himself last week."

The waiter took the brandy bottle and another saucer from the counter inside the café and marched out to the old man's table. He put down the saucer and poured the glass full of brandy.

"You should have killed yourself last week," he said to the deaf man. The old man motioned with his finger. "A little more," he said. The waiter poured on into the glass so that the brandy slopped over and ran down the stem into the top saucer of the pile. "Thank you," the old man said. The waiter took the bottle back inside the café. He sat down at the table with his colleague again.

"He's drunk now," he said.

"He's drunk every night."

"What did he want to kill himself for?"

"How should I know."

"How did he do it?"

"He hung himself with a rope."

"Who cut him down?"

"His niece."

"Why did they do it?"

"Fear for his soul."

"How much money has he got?"

"He's got plenty."

"He must be eighty years old."

"Anyway I should say he was eighty."

"I wish he would go home. I never get to bed before three o'clock. What kind of hour is that to go to bed?"

"He stays up because he likes it."

"He's lonely. I'm not lonely. I have a wife waiting in bed for me."

"He had a wife once too."

"A wife would be no good to him now."

"You can't tell. He might be better with a wife."

"His niece looks after him. You said she cut him down."

"I know."

"I wouldn't want to be that old. An old man is a nasty thing."

"Not always. This old man is clean. He drinks without spilling. Even now, drunk. Look at him."

"I don't want to look at him. I wish he would go home. He has no regard for those who must work."

The old man looked from his glass across the square, then over at the waiters.

"Another brandy," he said, pointing to his glass. The waiter who was in a hurry came over.

"Finished," he said, speaking with that omission of syntax stupid people employ when talking to drunken people or foreigners. "No more tonight. Close now."

"Another," said the old man.

"No. Finished." The waiter wiped the edge of the table with a towel and shook his head.

The old man stood up, slowly counted the saucers, took a leather coin purse from his pocket and paid for the drinks, leaving half a peseta tip.

The waiter watched him go down the street, a very old man walking unsteadily but with dignity.

"Why didn't you let him stay and drink?" the unhurried waiter asked. They were putting up the shutters. "It is not half-past two."

"I want to go home to bed."

"What is an hour?"

"More to me than to him."

"An hour is the same."

"You talk like an old man yourself. He can buy a bottle and drink at home."

"It's not the same."

"No, it is not," agreed the waiter with a wife. He did not wish to be unjust. He was only in a hurry.

"And you? You have no fear of going home before your usual hour?"

"Are you trying to insult me?"

"No, hombre, only to make a joke."

"No," the waiter who was in a hurry said, rising from pulling down the metal shutters. "I have confidence. I am all confidence."

"You have youth, confidence, and a job," the older waiter said. "You have everything."

"And what do you lack?"

"Everything but work."

"You have everything I have."

"No. I have never had confidence and I am not young."

"Come on. Stop talking nonsense and lock up."

"I am of those who like to stay late at the café," the older waiter said. "With all those who do not want to go to bed. With all those who need a light for the night."

"I want to go home and into bed."

"We are of two different kinds," the older waiter said. He was now dressed to go home. "It is not only a question of youth and confidence although those things are very beautiful. Each night I am reluctant to close up because there may be some one who needs the café."

"Hombre, there are bodegas open all night long."

"You do not understand. This is a clean and pleasant café. It is well lighted. The light is very good and also, now, there are shadows of the leaves."

"Good night," said the younger waiter.

"Good night," the other said. Turning off the electric light he continued the conversation with himself. It is the light of course but it is necessary that the place be clean and pleasant. You do not want music. Certainly you do not want music. Nor can you stand before a bar with dignity although that is all that is provided for these hours. What did he fear? It was not fear or dread. It was a nothing that he knew too well. It was all a nothing and a man was nothing too. It was only that and light was all it needed and a certain cleanness and order. Some lived in it and never felt it but he knew it was nada y pues nada y pues nada. Our nada who art in nada, nada be thy name thy kingdom nada thy will be nada in nada as it is in nada. Give us this nada our daily nada and nada us our nada as we nada our nadas and nada us not into nada but deliver us from nada; pues nada. Hail nothing full of nothing, nothing is with thee. He smiled and stood before a bar with a shining steam pressure coffee machine.

"What's yours?" asked the barman.

"Nada."

"Otro loco mas," said the barman and turned away.

"A little cup," said the waiter.

The barman poured it for him.

"The light is very bright and pleasant but the bar is unpolished," the waiter said.

The barman looked at him but did not answer. It was too late at night for conversation.

"You want another copita?" the barman asked.

"No, thank you," said the waiter and went out. He disliked bars and bodegas. A clean, well-lighted café was a very different thing. Now, without thinking further, he would go home to his room. He would lie in the bed and finally, with daylight, he would go to sleep. After all, he said to himself, it is probably only insomnia. Many must have it.

[1933]

MAYA ANGELOU   [b. 1928]

Champion of the World

Born Marguerite Johnson in St. Louis, Missouri, in 1928, **Maya
Angelou** has been a successful dancer, actor, poet, playwright, fiction
writer, producer, director, newspaper editor, civil rights leader, and
academic, among other accomplishments. Her autobiographical book
I Know Why the Caged Bird Sings (1969) was nominated for a National
Book Award. In 1993 she delivered her poem, "On the Pulse of Morning," at the inauguration of President Clinton.

In "Champion of the World," from *I Know Why the Caged Bird Sings*,
Angelou describes the camaraderie of her townfolk as they listen,
crowded and apprehensive, to a radio broadcast playing a fight between heavyweight boxing champion Joe Louis and a white contender.
United in the hope for the Brown Bomber's victory, the spirits among
listeners soar and plummet as the fight progresses. Angelou's narration
draws the reader into the story, to share in the anxiety of the fight, to
burn with anguish at the possibility of defeat, and to burst with pride
in the resounding victory, a victory that reaffirms the self-worth and
humanity of all black Americans.

The last inch of space was filled, yet people continued to wedge themselves along the walls of the Store. Uncle Willie had turned the radio up
to its last notch so that youngsters on the porch wouldn't miss a word.
Women sat on kitchen chairs, dining-room chairs, stools and upturned
wooden boxes. Small children and babies perched on every lap available
and men leaned on the shelves or on each other.

The apprehensive mood was shot through with shafts of gaiety, as a
black sky is streaked with lightning.

"I ain't worried 'bout this fight. Joe's gonna whip that cracker like it's
open season."

"He gone whip him till that white boy call him Momma."

At last the talking finished and the string-along songs about razor   5
blades were over and the fight began.

"A quick jab to the head." In the Store the crowd grunted. "A left to the head and a right and another left." One of the listeners cackled like a hen and was quieted.

"They're in a clinch, Louis is trying to fight his way out."

Some bitter comedian on the porch said, "That white man don't mind hugging that niggah now, I betcha."

"The referee is moving in to break them up, but Louis finally pushed the contender away and it's an uppercut to the chin. The contender is hanging on, now he's backing away. Louis catches him with a short left to the jaw."

A tide of murmuring assent poured out the door and into the yard.   10

"Another left and another left. Louis is saving that mighty right..." The mutter in the Store had grown into a baby roar and it was pierced by the clang of a bell and the announcer's "That's the bell for round three, ladies and gentlemen."

As I pushed my way into the Store I wondered if the announcer gave any thought to the fact that he was addressing as "ladies and gentlemen" all the Negroes around the world who sat sweating and praying, glued to their "master's voice."

There were only a few calls for R. C. Colas, Dr. Peppers, and Hires root beer. The real festivities would begin after the fight. Then even the old Christian ladies who taught their children and tried themselves to practice turning the other check would buy soft drinks, and if the Brown Bomber's victory was a particularly bloody one they would order peanut patties and Baby Ruths also.

Bailey and I laid the coins on top of the cash register. Uncle Willie didn't allow us to ring up sales during a fight. It was too noisy and might shake up the atmosphere. When the gong rang for the next round we pushed through the near-sacred quiet to the herd of children outside.

"He's got Louis against the ropes and now it's a left to the body and a   15
right to the ribs. Another right to the body, it looks like it was low... Yes, ladies and gentlemen, the referee is signaling but the contender keeps raining the blows on Louis. It's another to the body, and it looks like Louis is going down."

My race groaned. It was our people falling. It was another lynching, yet another Black man hanging on a tree. One more woman ambushed and raped. A Black boy whipped and maimed. It was hounds on the trail of a man running through slimy swamps. It was a white woman slapping her maid for being forgetful.

The men in the Store stood away from the walls and at attention. Women greedily clutched the babes on their laps while on the porch the shufflings and smiles, flirtings and pinching of a few minutes before were gone. This might be the end of the world. If Joe lost we were back in slavery and beyond help. It would all be true, the accusations that we were lower types of human beings. Only a little higher than apes. True that we were stupid and ugly and lazy and dirty and, unlucky and worst of all, that God Himself hated us and ordained us to be hewers of wood and drawers of water, forever and ever, world without end.

We didn't breathe. We didn't hope. We waited.

"He's off the ropes, ladies and gentlemen. He's moving towards the center of the ring." There was no time to be relieved. The worst might still happen.

"And now it looks like Joe is mad. He's caught Carnera with a left hook 20
to the head and a right to the head. It's a left jab to the body and another left to the head. There's a left cross and a right to the head. The contender's right eye is bleeding and he can't seem to keep his block up. Louis is penetrating every block. The referee is moving in, but Louis sends a left to the body and it's an uppercut to the chin and the contender is dropping. He's on the canvas, ladies and gentlemen."

Babies slid to the floor as women stood up and men leaned toward the radio.

"Here's the referee. He's young. One, two, three, four, five, six, seven... Is the contender trying to get up again?"

All the men in the store shouted, "NO."

"—eight, nine, ten." There were a few sounds from the audience, but they seemed to be holding themselves in against tremendous pressure.

"The fight is all over, ladies and gentlemen. Let's get the microphone 25
over to the referee... Here he is. He's got the Brown Bomber's hand, he's holding it up... Here he is..."

Then the voice, husky and familiar, came to wash over us — "The winnah, and still heavyweight champeen of the world... Joe Louis."

Champion of the world. A Black boy. Some Black mother's son. He was the strongest man in the world. People drank Coca-Colas like ambrosia and ate candy bars like Christmas. Some of the men went behind the Store and poured white lightning in their soft-drink bottles, and a few of the bigger boys followed them. Those who were not chased away came back blowing their breath in front of themselves like proud smokers.

It would take an hour or more before the people would leave the Store and head for home. Those who lived too far had made arrangements to stay in town. It wouldn't do for a Black man and his family to be caught on a lonely country road on a night when Joe Louis had proved that we were the strongest people in the world.

SANDRA CISNEROS   [b. 1954]

The House on Mango Street

Born in a Hispanic neighborhood in Chicago, **Sandra Cisneros** (b. 1954) spoke Spanish at home with her Mexican father, Chicana mother, and six brothers. At ten she began writing poetry, and soon experimented with other forms. In 1977, when she was studying in the M.F.A. program at the University of Iowa Writers' Workshop, she came to see herself as a Chicana writer. Cisneros has published three books of poems; a book of interrelated narratives, *The House on Mango Street* (1983); and a fiction collection, *Woman Hollering Creek and Other Stories* (1991).

We didn't always live on Mango Street. Before that we lived on Loomis on the third floor, and before that we lived on Keeler. Before Keeler it was Paulina, and before that I can't remember. But what I remember most is moving a lot. Each time it seemed there'd be one more of us. By the time we got to Mango Street we were six—Mama, Papa, Carlos, Kiki, my sister Nenny, and me.

The house on Mango Street is ours, and we don't have to pay rent to anybody, or share the yard with the people downstairs, or be careful not to make too much noise, and there isn't a landlord banging on the ceiling with a broom. But even so, it's not the house we'd thought we'd get.

We had to leave the flat on Loomis quick. The water pipes broke and the landlord wouldn't fix them because the house was too old. We had to leave fast. We were using the washroom next door and carrying water over in empty milk gallons. That's why Mama and Papa looked for a house, and that's why we moved into the house on Mango Street, far away, on the other side of town.

They always told us that one day we would move into a house, a real house that would be ours for always so we wouldn't have to move each year. And our house would have running water and pipes that worked. And inside it would have real stairs, not hallway stairs, but stairs inside like the houses on T.V. And we'd have a basement and at least three washrooms so when we took a bath we wouldn't have to tell everybody. Our house would be white with trees around it, a great big yard and grass growing without a fence. This was the house Papa talked about when he held a lottery ticket and this was the house Mama dreamed up in the stories she told us before we went to bed.

But the house on Mango Street is not the way they told it at all. It's small and red with tight steps in front and windows so small you'd think they were holding their breath. Bricks are crumbling in places, and the front door is so swollen you have to push hard to get in. There is no front yard, only four little elms the city planted by the curb. Out back is a small garage for the car we don't own yet and a small yard that looks smaller between the two buildings on either side. There are stairs in our house, but they're ordinary hallway stairs, and the house has only one washroom. Everybody has to share a bedroom—Mama and Papa, Carlos and Kiki, me and Nenny.

Once when we were living on Loomis, a nun from my school passed by and saw me playing out front. The laundromat downstairs had been boarded up because it had been robbed two days before and the owner had painted on the wood YES WE'RE OPEN so as not to lose business.

Where do you live? she asked.

There, I said pointing up to the third floor.

You live *there?*

There. I had to look to where she pointed—the third floor, the paint peeling, wooden bars Papa had nailed on the windows so we wouldn't fall out. You live *there?* The way she said it made me feel like nothing. *There.* I lived *there.* I nodded.

I knew then I had to have a house. A real house. One I could point to. But this isn't it. The house on Mango Street isn't it. For the time being, Mama says. Temporary, says Papa. But I know how those things go.

[1983]

440

TONI CADE BAMBARA   [1939–1995]

The Lesson

Born in New York City and raised in Harlem, **Toni Cade Bambara**
(1939–1995) attended Queens College, where she wrote stories, poems,
scripts, and other works and was part of the staff of the literary magazine. She continued writing stories as she studied for an M.A. at City
College. After her story collection *Gorilla, My Love* (1972) was published, her sense of herself as a black writer gradually clarified and
deepened. Her other story collections include *The Black Woman*
(1970), *Tales and Stories for Black Folks* (1971), and *The Sea Birds Are
Still Alive* (1977). Her two novels are *The Salt Eaters* (1980) and *If
Blessing Comes* (1987). *Deep Sightings and Rescue Missions*, a collection of fiction and nonfiction, appeared posthumously, in 1996.

Back in the days when everyone was old and stupid or young and foolish and me and Sugar were the only ones just right, this lady moved on
our block with nappy hair and proper speech and no makeup. And quite
naturally we laughed at her, laughed the way we did at the junk man
who went about his business like he was some big-time president and
his sorry-ass horse his secretary. And we kinda hated her too, hated the
way we did the winos who cluttered up our parks and pissed on our
handball walls and stank up our hallways and stairs so you couldn't
halfway play hide-and-seek without a goddamn gas mask. Miss Moore
was her name. The only woman on the block with no first name. And
she was black as hell, cept for her feet, which were fish-white and
spooky. And she was always planning these boring-ass things for us to
do, us being my cousin, mostly, who lived on the block cause we all
moved North the same time and to the same apartment then spread out
gradual to breathe. And our parents would yank our heads into some
kinda shape and crisp up our clothes so we'd be presentable for travel
with Miss Moore, who always looked like she was going to church,
though she never did. Which is just one of the things the grownups
talked about when they talked behind her back like a dog. But when she
came calling with some sachet she'd sewed up or some gingerbread
she'd made or some book, why then they'd all be too embarrassed to

turn her down and we'd get handed over all spruced up. She'd been to college and said it was only right that she should take responsibility for the young ones' education, and she not even related by marriage or blood. So they'd go for it. Specially Aunt Gretchen. She was the main gofer in the family. You got some ole dumb shit foolishness you want somebody to go for, you send for Aunt Gretchen. She been screwed into the go-along for so long, it's a blood-deep natural thing with her. Which is how she got saddled with me and Sugar and Junior in the first place while our mothers were in a la-de-da apartment up the block having a good ole time.

So this one day, Miss Moore rounds us all up at the mailbox and it's puredee hot and she's knockin herself out about arithmetic. And school suppose to let up in summer I heard, but she don't never let up. And the starch in my pinafore scratching the shit outta me and I'm really hating this nappy-head bitch and her goddamn college degree. I'd much rather go to the pool or to the show where it's cool. So me and Sugar leaning on the mailbox being surly, which is a Miss Moore word. And Flyboy checking out what everybody brought for lunch. And Fat Butt already wasting his peanut-butter-and-jelly sandwich like the pig he is. And Junebug punchin on Q.T.'s arm for potato chips. And Rosie Giraffe shifting from one hip to the other waiting for somebody to step on her foot or ask her if she from Georgia so she can kick ass, preferably Mercedes'. And Miss Moore asking us do we know what money is, like we a bunch of retards. I mean real money, she say, like it's only poker chips or monopoly papers we lay on the grocer. So right away I'm tired of this and say so. And would much rather snatch Sugar and go to the Sunset and terrorize the West Indian kids and take their hair ribbons and their money too. And Miss Moore files that remark away for next week's lesson on brotherhood, I can tell. And finally I say we oughta get to the subway cause it's cooler and besides we might meet some cute boys. Sugar done swiped her mama's lipstick, so we ready.

So we heading down the street and she's boring us silly about what things cost and what our parents make and how much goes for rent and how money ain't divided up right in this country. And then she gets to the part about we all poor and live in the slums, which I don't feature. And I'm ready to speak on that, but she steps out in the street and hails two cabs just like that. Then she hustles half the crew in with her and hands me a five-dollar bill and tells me to calculate 10 percent tip for the driver. And we're off. Me and Sugar and Junebug and Flyboy hangin out the window and hollering to everybody, putting lipstick on each other cause Flyboy a faggot anyway, and making farts with our sweaty armpits. But I'm mostly trying to figure how to spend this money. But

they all fascinated with the meter ticking and Junebug starts laying bets
as to how much it'll read when Flyboy can't hold his breath no more.
Then Sugar lays bets as to how much it'll be when we get there. So I'm
stuck. Don't nobody want to go for my plan, which is to jump out at the
next light and run off to the first bar-b-que we can find. Then the driver
tells us to get the hell out cause we there already. And the meter reads
eighty-five cents. And I'm stalling to figure out the tip and Sugar say give
him a dime. And I decide he don't need it bad as I do, so later for him.
But then he tries to take off with Junebug foot still in the door so we talk
about his mama something ferocious. Then we check out that we on
Fifth Avenue and everybody dressed up in stockings. One lady in a fur
coat, hot as it is. White folks crazy.

"This is the place," Miss Moore say, presenting it to us in the voice she
uses at the museum. "Let's look in the windows before we go in."

"Can we steal?" Sugar asks very serious like she's getting the ground
rules squared away before she plays. "I beg your pardon," say Miss
Moore, and we fall out. So she leads us around the windows of the toy
store and me and Sugar screamin, "This is mine, that's mine, I gotta have
that, that was made for me, I was born for that," till Big Butt drowns
us out.

"Hey, I'm going to buy that there."

"That there? You don't even know what it is, stupid."

"I do so," he say punchin on Rosie Giraffe. "It's a microscope."

"Whatcha gonna do with a microscope, fool?"

"Look at things."

"Like what, Ronald?" ask Miss Moore. And Big Butt ain't got the first
notion. So here go Miss Moore gabbing about the thousands of bacteria
in a drop of water and the somethinorother in a speck of blood and the
million and one living things in the air around us is invisible to the
naked eye. And what she say that for? Junebug go to town on that
"naked" and we rolling. Then Miss Moore ask what it cost. So we all jam
into the window smudgin it up and the price tag say $300. So then she
ask how long'd take for Big Butt and Junebug to save up their allow-
ances. "Too long," I say. "Yeh," adds Sugar, "outgrown it by that time."
And Miss Moore say no, you never outgrow learning instruments. "Why,
even medical students and interns and," blah, blah, blah. And we ready
to choke Big Butt for bringing it up in the first damn place.

"This here costs four hundred eighty dollars," say Rosie Giraffe. So we
pile up all over her to see what she pointin out. My eyes tell me it's a
chunk of glass cracked with something heavy, and different-color inks
dripped into the splits, then the whole thing put into a oven or something. But for $480 it don't make sense.

"That's a paperweight made of semi-precious stones fused together under tremendous pressure," she explains slowly, with her hands doing the mining and all the factory work.

"So what's a paperweight?" ask Rosie Giraffe.

"To weigh paper with, dumbbell," say Flyboy, the wise man from the East.

"Not exactly," say Miss Moore, which is what she say when you warm or way off too. "It's to weigh paper down so it won't scatter and make your desk untidy." So right away me and Sugar curtsy to each other and then to Mercedes who is more the tidy type.

"We don't keep paper on top of the desk in my class," say Junebug, figuring Miss Moore crazy or lyin one.

"At home, then," she say. "Don't you have a calendar and a pencil case and a blotter and a letter-opener on your desk at home where you do your homework?" And she know damn well what our homes look like cause she nosys around in them every chance she gets.

"I don't even have a desk," say Junebug. "Do we?"

"No. And I don't get no homework neither," say Big Butt.

"And I don't even have a home," say Flyboy like he do at school to keep the white folks off his back and sorry for him. Send this poor kid to camp posters, is his specialty.

"I do," says Mercedes. "I have a box of stationery on my desk and a picture of my cat. My godmother bought the stationery and the desk. There's a big rose on each sheet and the envelopes smell like roses."

"Who wants to know about your smelly-ass stationery," say Rosie Giraffe fore I can get my two cents in.

"It's important to have a work area all your own so that . . ."

"Will you look at this sailboat, please," say Flyboy, cutting her off and pointin to the thing like it was his. So once again we tumble all over each other to gaze at this magnificent thing in the toy store which is just big enough to maybe sail two kittens across the pond if you strap them to the posts tight. We all start reciting the price tag like we in assembly. "Handcrafted sailboat of fiberglass at one thousand one hundred ninety-five dollars."

"Unbelievable," I hear myself say and am really stunned. I read it again for myself just in case the group recitation put me in a trance. Same thing. For some reason this pisses me off. We look at Miss Moore and she lookin at us, waiting for I dunno what.

"Who'd pay all that when you can buy a sailboat set for a quarter at Pop's, a tube of glue for a dime, and a ball of string for eight cents? It must have a motor and a whole lot else besides," I say. "My sailboat cost me about fifty cents."

"But will it take water?" say Mercedes with her smart ass.

"Took mine to Alley Pond Park once," say Flyboy. "String broke. Lost it. Pity."

"Sailed mine in Central Park and it keeled over and sank. Had to ask my father for another dollar."

"And you got the strap," laugh Big Butt. "The jerk didn't even have a string on it. My old man wailed on his behind."

Little Q.T. was staring hard at the sailboat and you could see he wanted it bad. But he too little and somebody'd just take it from him. So what the hell. "This boat for kids, Miss Moore?"

"Parents silly to buy something like that just to get all broke up," say Rosie Giraffe.

"That much money it should last forever," I figure.

"My father'd buy it for me if I wanted it."

"Your father, my ass," say Rosie Giraffe getting a chance to finally push Mercedes.

"Must be rich people shop here," say Q.T.

"You are a very bright boy," say Flyboy. "What was your first clue?" And he rap him on the head with the back of his knuckles, since Q.T. the only one he could get away with. Though Q.T. liable to come up behind you years later and get his licks in when you half expect it.

"What I want to know is," I says to Miss Moore though I never talk to her, I wouldn't give the bitch that satisfaction, "is how much a real boat costs? I figure a thousand'd get you a yacht any day."

"Why don't you check that out," she says, "and report back to the group?" Which really pains my ass. If you gonna mess up a perfectly good swim day least you could do is have some answers. "Let's go in," she say like she got something up her sleeve. Only she don't lead the way. So me and Sugar turn the corner to where the entrance is, but when we get there I kinda hang back. Not that I'm scared, what's there to be afraid of, just a toy store. But I feel funny, shame. But what I got to be shamed about? Got as much right to go in as anybody. But somehow I can't seem to get hold of the door, so I step away from Sugar to lead. But she hangs back too. And I look at her and she looks at me and this is ridiculous. I mean, damn, I have never been shy about doing nothing or going nowhere. But then Mercedes steps up and then Rosie Giraffe and Big Butt crowd in behind and shove, and next thing we all stuffed into the doorway with only Mercedes squeezing past us, smoothing out her jumper and walking right down the aisle. Then the rest of us tumble in like a glued-together jigsaw done all wrong. And people lookin at us. And it's like the time me and Sugar crashed into the Catholic church on a dare. But once we got in there and everything so hushed and holy and the candles and the bowin and the handkerchiefs on all the drooping heads, I just couldn't go through with the plan. Which was for me to run up to the altar and do a tap dance while Sugar played the nose flute and messed around in the holy water. And Sugar kept given me the elbow. Then later teased me so bad I tied her up in the shower and turned it on and locked her in. And she'd be there till this day if Aunt Gretchen hadn't finally figured I was lying about the boarder takin a shower.

Same thing in the store. We all walkin on tiptoe and hardly touchin the games and puzzles and things. And I watched Miss Moore who is steady watchin us like she waitin for a sign. Like Mama Drewery watches the sky and sniffs the air and takes note of just how much slant is in the bird formation. Then me and Sugar bump smack into each other, so busy gazing at the toys, 'specially the sailboat. But we don't laugh and go into our fat-lady bump-stomach routine. We just stare at that price tag. Then Sugar run a finger over the whole boat. And I'm jealous and want to hit her. Maybe not her, but I sure want to punch somebody in the mouth.

"Watcha bring us here for, Miss Moore?"

"You sound angry, Sylvia. Are you mad about something?" Givin me one of them grins like she tellin a grown-up joke that never turns out to be funny. And she's lookin very closely at me like maybe she plannin to do my portrait from memory. I'm mad, but I won't give her that satisfaction. So I slouch around the store being very bored and say, "Let's go."

Me and Sugar at the back of the train watchin the tracks whizzin by large then small then getting gobbled up in the dark. I'm thinkin about this tricky toy I saw in the store. A clown that somersaults on a bar then does chin-ups just cause you yank lightly at his leg. Cost $35. I could see me askin my mother for a $35 birthday clown. "You wanna who that costs what?" she'd say, cocking her head to the side to get a better view of the hole in my head. Thirty-five dollars could buy new bunk beds for Junior and Gretchen's boy. Thirty-five dollars and the whole household could go visit Grand-daddy Nelson in the country. Thirty-five dollars would pay for the rent and the piano bill too. Who are these people that spend that much for performing clowns and $1000 for toy sailboats? What kinda work they do and how they live and how come we ain't in on it? Where we are is who we are, Miss Moore always pointin out. But it don't necessarily have to be that way, she always adds then waits for somebody to say that poor people have to wake up and demand their share of the pie and don't none of us know what kind of pie she talking about in the first damn place. But she ain't so smart cause I still got her four dollars from the taxi and she sure ain't gettin it. Messin up my day with this shit. Sugar nudges me in my pocket and winks.

Miss Moore lines us up in front of the mailbox where we started from, seem like years ago, and I got a headache for thinkin so hard. And we lean all over each other so we can hold up under the draggy-ass lecture

she always finishes us off with at the end before we thank her for borin
us to tears. But she just looks at us like she readin tea leaves. Finally she
say, "Well, what did you think of F.A.O. Schwarz?"

Rosie Giraffe mumbles, "White folks crazy."

"I'd like to go there again when I get my birthday money," says Mercedes, and we shove her out the pack so she has to lean on the mailbox
by herself.

"I'd like a shower. Tiring day," say Flyboy.

Then Sugar surprises me by sayin, "You know, Miss Moore, I don't
think all of us here put together eat in a year what that sailboat costs."
And Miss Moore lights up like somebody goosed her. "And?" she say, urging Sugar on. Only I'm standin on her foot so she don't continue.

"Imagine for a minute what kind of society it is in which some people
can spend on a toy what it would cost to feed a family of six or seven.
What do you think?"

"I think," say Sugar pushing me off her feet like she never done before,
cause I whip her ass in a minute, "that this is not much of a democracy if
you ask me. Equal chance to pursue happiness means an equal crack at
the dough, don't it?" Miss Moore is besides herself and I am disgusted
with Sugar's treachery. So I stand on her foot one more time to see if
she'll shove me. She shuts up, and Miss Moore looks at me, sorrowfully
I'm thinkin. And somethin weird is goin on, I can feel it in my chest.

"Anybody else learn anything today?" lookin dead at me. I walk away
and Sugar has to run to catch up and don't even seem to notice when I
shrug her arm off my shoulder.

"Well, we got four dollars anyway," she says.

"Uh, hunh."

"We could go to Hascombs and get half a chocolate layer and then go
to the Sunset and still have plenty money for potato chips and ice cream
sodas."

"Uh, hunh."

"Race you to Hascombs," she say.

We start down the block and she gets ahead which is O.K. by me cause
I'm going to the West End and then over to the Drive to think this day
through. She can run if she want to and even run faster. But ain't nobody
gonna beat me at nuthin.

[1972]

447

NAGUIB MAHFOUZ [1911–2006]

Zaabalawi

TRANSLATED BY DENYS JOHNSON-DAVIES, 1967

Born and raised in the al-Jamaliyya district of Cairo, Egypt, **Naguib Mahfouz** began writing at seventeen and studied philosophy at the University of Cairo. For most of his working years, he was a civil servant in ministry offices. Since 1966, when his novel *Midaq Alley* (1947) was translated into English, he has continued to hold a leading position in the Arab literary world while gaining a vast international readership. He was awarded a Nobel Prize in 1988. Among other honors, he has received two Egyptian state prizes and the Presidential Medal of American University in Cairo. In 1992 he was named an honorary member of the American Academy and Institute of Arts and Letters, and in 1995 was awarded an honorary degree from American University in Cairo. By now he has written almost forty novels and fourteen collections of stories. Among his best-known novels in translation are *Midaq Alley* and the three novels of the Cairo trilogy: *Palace Walk, Palace of Desire,* and *Sugar Street* (1956–1957).

Finally I became convinced that I had to find Sheikh Zaabalawi.

The first time I had heard his name had been in a song:

Oh what's become of the world, Zaabalawi?
They've turned it upside down and taken away its taste.

It had been a popular song in my childhood, and one day it had occurred to me to demand of my father, in the way children have of asking endless questions:

"Who is Zaabalawi?"

He had looked at me hesitantly as though doubting my ability to understand the answer. However, he had replied, "May his blessing descend upon you, he's a true saint of God, a remover of worries and troubles. Were it not for him I would have died miserably—"

"Zaabalawi" from *Modern Arabic Short Stories*, edited and translated by Denys Johnson-Davies. Reprinted with permission of Oxford University Press (UK).

In the years that followed, I heard my father many a time sing the praises of this good saint and speak of the miracles he performed. The days passed and brought with them many illnesses, for each one of which I was able, without too much trouble and at a cost I could afford, to find a cure, until I became afflicted with that illness for which no one possesses a remedy. When I had tried everything in vain and was overcome by despair, I remembered by chance what I had heard in my childhood: Why, I asked myself, should I not seek out Sheikh Zaabalawi? I recollected my father saying that he had made his acquaintance in Khan Gaafar at the house of Sheikh Qamar, one of those sheikhs who practiced law in the religious courts, and so I took myself off to his house. Wishing to make sure that he was still living there, I made inquiries of a vendor of beans whom I found in the lower part of the house.

"Sheikh Qamar!" he said, looking at me in amazement. "He left the quarter ages ago. They say he's now living in Garden City and has his office in al-Azhar Square."

I looked up the office address in the telephone book and immediately set off to the Chamber of Commerce Building, where it was located. On asking to see Sheikh Qamar, I was ushered into a room just as a beautiful woman with a most intoxicating perfume was leaving it. The man received me with a smile and motioned me toward a fine leather-upholstered chair. Despite the thick soles of my shoes, my feet were conscious of the lushness of the costly carpet. The man wore a lounge suit and was smoking a cigar; his manner of sitting was that of someone well satisfied both with himself and with his worldly possessions. The look of warm welcome he gave me left no doubt in my mind that he thought me a prospective client, and I felt acutely embarrassed at encroaching upon his valuable time.

"Welcome!" he said, prompting me to speak.

"I am the son of your old friend Sheikh Ali al-Tatawi," I answered so as to put an end to my equivocal position.

A certain languor was apparent in the glance he cast at me; the languor was not total in that he had not as yet lost all hope in me.

"God rest his soul," he said. "He was a fine man."

The very pain that had driven me to go there now prevailed upon me to stay.

"He told me," I continued, "of a devout saint named Zaabalawi whom he met at Your Honor's. I am in need of him, sir, if he be still in the land of the living."

The languor became firmly entrenched in his eyes, and it would have come as no surprise if he had shown the door to both me and my father's memory.

"That," he said in the tone of one who has made up his mind to terminate the conversation, "was a very long time ago and I scarcely recall him now."

Rising to my feet so as to put his mind at rest regarding my intention of going, I asked, "Was he really a saint?"

"We used to regard him as a man of miracles."

"And where could I find him today?" I asked, making another move toward the door.

"To the best of my knowledge he was living in the Birgawi Residence in al-Azhar," and he applied himself to some papers on his desk with a resolute movement that indicated he would not open his mouth again. I bowed my head in thanks, apologized several times for disturbing him, and left the office, my head so buzzing with embarrassment that I was oblivious to all sounds around me.

I went to the Birgawi Residence, which was situated in a thickly populated quarter. I found that time had so eaten away at the building that nothing was left of it save an antiquated façade and a courtyard that, despite being supposedly in the charge of a caretaker, was being used as a rubbish dump. A small, insignificant fellow, a mere prologue to a man, was using the covered entrance as a place for the sale of old books on theology and mysticism.

When I asked him about Zaabalawi, he peered at me through narrow, inflamed eyes and said in amazement, "Zaabalawi! Good heavens, what a time ago that was! Certainly he used to live in this house when it was habitable. Many were the times he would sit with me talking of bygone days, and I would be blessed by his holy presence. Where, though, is Zaabalawi today?"

He shrugged his shoulders sorrowfully and soon left me, to attend to an approaching customer. I proceeded to make inquiries of many shopkeepers in the district. While I found that a large number of them had never even heard of Zaabalawi, some, though recalling nostalgically the pleasant times they had spent with him, were ignorant of his present whereabouts, while others openly made fun of him, labeled him a charlatan, and advised me to put myself in the hands of a doctor—as though I had not already done so. I therefore had no alternative but to return disconsolately home.

With the passing of days like motes in the air, my pains grew so severe that I was sure I would not be able to hold out much longer. Once again I fell to wondering about Zaabalawi and clutching at the hope his venerable name stirred within me. Then it occurred to me to seek the help of the local sheikh of the district; in fact, I was surprised I had not thought of this to begin with. His office was in the nature of a small shop, except that it contained a desk and a telephone, and I found him sitting at his desk, wearing a jacket over his striped galabeya. As he did not interrupt his conversation with a man sitting beside him, I stood waiting till the man had gone. The sheikh then looked up at me coldly. I told myself that I should win him over by the usual methods, and it was not long before I had him cheerfully inviting me to sit down.

"I'm in need of Sheikh Zaabalawi," I answered his inquiry as to the purpose of my visit.

He gazed at me with the same astonishment as that shown by those I had previously encountered.

"At least," he said, giving me a smile that revealed his gold teeth, "he is still alive. The devil of it is, though, he has no fixed abode. You might well bump into him as you go out of here, on the other hand you might spend days and months in fruitless searching."

"Even you can't find him!"

"Even I! He's a baffling man, but I thank the Lord that he's still alive!"

He gazed at me intently, and murmured, "It seems your condition is serious."

"Very."

"May God come to your aid! But why don't you go about it systematically?" He spread out a sheet of paper on the desk and drew on it with unexpected speed and skill until he had made a full plan of the district, showing all the various quarters, lanes, alleyways, and squares. He looked at it admiringly and said, "These are dwelling-houses, here is the Quarter of the Perfumers, here the Quarter of the Coppersmiths, the Mouski, the police and fire stations. The drawing is your best guide. Look carefully in the cafés, the places where the dervishes perform their rites, the mosques and prayer-rooms, and the Green Gate, for he may well be concealed among the beggars and be indistinguishable from them. Actually, I myself haven't seen him for years, having been somewhat preoccupied with the cares of the world, and was only brought back by your inquiry to those most exquisite times of my youth."

I gazed at the map in bewilderment. The telephone rang, and he took up the receiver.

"Take it," he told me, generously. "We're at your service."

Folding up the map, I left and wandered off through the quarter, from square to street to alleyway, making inquiries of everyone I felt was familiar with the place. At last the owner of a small establishment for ironing clothes told me, "Go to the calligrapher Hassanein in Umm al-Ghulam — they were friends."

I went to Umm al-Ghulam, where I found old Hassanein working in a deep, narrow shop full of signboards and jars of color. A strange smell, a mixture of glue and perfume, permeated its every corner. Old Hassanein was squatting on a sheepskin rug in front of a board propped against the

wall; in the middle of it he had inscribed the word "Allah" in silver letter-
ing. He was engrossed in embellishing the letters with prodigious care. I
stood behind him, fearful of disturbing him or breaking the inspiration
that flowed to his masterly hand. When my concern at not interrupting
him had lasted some time, he suddenly inquired with unaffected gentleness, "Yes?"

Realizing that he was aware of my presence, I introduced myself. "I've
been told that Sheikh Zaabalawi is your friend; I'm looking for him," I
said.

His hand came to a stop. He scrutinized me in astonishment.
"Zaabalawi! God be praised!" he said with a sigh.

"He *is* a friend of yours, isn't he?" I asked eagerly.

"He was, once upon a time. A real man of mystery: he'd visit you so
often that people would imagine he was your nearest and dearest, then
would disappear as though he'd never existed. Yet saints are not to be
blamed."

The spark of hope went out with the suddenness of a lamp snuffed by
a power-cut.

"He was so constantly with me," said the man, "that I felt him to be a
part of everything I drew. But where is he today?"

"Perhaps he is still alive?"

"He's alive, without a doubt. . . . He had impeccable taste, and it was
due to him that I made my most beautiful drawings."

"God knows," I said, in a voice almost stifled by the dead ashes of
hope, "how dire my need for him is, and no one knows better than you of
the ailments in respect to which he is sought."

"Yes, yes. May God restore you to health. He is in truth, as is said of
him, a man, and more. . . ."

Smiling broadly, he added, "And his face possesses an unforgettable
beauty. But where is he?"

Reluctantly I rose to my feet, shook hands, and left. I continued wandering eastward and westward through the quarter, inquiring about
Zaabalawi from everyone who, by reason of age or experience, I felt might
be likely to help me. Eventually I was informed by a vendor of lupine
that he had met him a short while ago at the house of Sheikh Gad, the
well-known composer. I went to the musician's house in Tabakshiyya,
where I found him in a room tastefully furnished in the old style, its
walls redolent with history. He was seated on a divan, his famous lute
beside him, concealing within itself the most beautiful melodies of our
age, while somewhere from within the house came the sound of pestle
and mortar and the clamor of children. I immediately greeted him and
introduced myself, and was put at my ease by the unaffected way in
which he received me. He did not ask, either in words or gesture, what

had brought me, and I did not feel that he even harbored any such curiosity. Amazed at his understanding and kindness, which boded well, I said, "O Sheikh Gad, I am an admirer of yours, having long been enchanted by the renderings of your songs."

"Thank you," he said with a smile.

"Please excuse my disturbing you," I continued timidly, "but I was told that Zaabalawi was your friend, and I am in urgent need of him."

"Zaabalawi!" he said, frowning in concentration. "You need him? God be with you, for who knows, O Zaabalawi, where you are."

"Doesn't he visit you?" I asked eagerly.

"He visited me some time ago. He might well come right now; on the other hand I mightn't see him till death!"

I gave an audible sigh and asked, "What made him like that?"

The musician took up his lute. "Such are saints or they would not be saints," he said, laughing.

"Do those who need him suffer as I do?"

"Such suffering is part of the cure!"

He took up the plectrum and began plucking soft strains from the strings. Lost in thought, I followed his movements. Then, as though addressing myself, I said, "So my visit has been in vain."

He smiled, laying his cheek against the side of the lute. "God forgive you," he said, "for saying such a thing of a visit that has caused me to know you and you me!"

I was much embarrassed and said apologetically, "Please forgive me; my feelings of defeat made me forget my manners."

"Do not give in to defeat. This extraordinary man brings fatigue to all who seek him. It was easy enough with him in the old days, when his place of abode was known. Today, though, the world has changed, and after having enjoyed a position attained only by potentates, he is now pursued by the police on a charge of false pretenses. It is therefore no longer an easy matter to reach him, but have patience and be sure that you will do so."

He raised his head from the lute and skillfully fingered the opening bars of a melody. Then he sang:

"I make lavish mention, even though I blame myself,
   of those I love,
For the stories of the beloved are my wine."

With a heart that was weary and listless, I followed the beauty of the melody and the singing.

"I composed the music to this poem in a single night," he told me when he had finished. "I remember that it was the eve of the Lesser

Bairam. Zaabalawi was my guest for the whole of that night, and the poem was of his choosing. He would sit for a while just where you are, then would get up and play with my children as though he were one of them. Whenever I was overcome by weariness or my inspiration failed me, he would punch me playfully in the chest and joke with me, and I would bubble over with melodies, and thus I continued working till I finished the most beautiful piece I have ever composed."

"Does he know anything about music?"

"He is the epitome of things musical. He has an extremely beautiful speaking voice, and you have only to hear him to want to burst into song and to be inspired to creativity. . . ."

"How was it that he cured those diseases before which men are powerless?"

"That is his secret. Maybe you will learn it when you meet him."

But when would that meeting occur? We relapsed into silence, and the hubbub of children once more filled the room.

Again the sheikh began to sing. He went on repeating the words "and I have a memory of her" in different and beautiful variations until the very walls danced in ecstasy. I expressed my wholehearted admiration, and he gave me a smile of thanks. I then got up and asked permission to leave, and he accompanied me to the front door. As I shook him by the hand, he said, "I hear that nowadays he frequents the house of Hagg Wanas al-Damanhouri. Do you know him?"

I shook my head, though a modicum of renewed hope crept into my heart.

"He is a man of private means," the sheikh told me, "who from time to time visits Cairo, putting up at some hotel or other. Every evening, though, he spends at the Negma Bar in Alfi Street."

I waited for nightfall and went to the Negma Bar. I asked a waiter about Hagg Wanas, and he pointed to a corner that was semisecluded because of its position behind a large pillar with mirrors on all four sides. There I saw a man seated alone at a table with two bottles in front of him, one empty, the other two-thirds empty. There were no snacks or food to be seen, and I was sure that I was in the presence of a hardened drinker. He was wearing a loosely flowing silk galabeya and a carefully wound turban; his legs were stretched out toward the base of the pillar, and as he gazed into the mirror in rapt contentment, the sides of his face, rounded and handsome despite the fact that he was approaching old age, were flushed with wine. I approached quietly till I stood but a few feet away from him. He did not turn toward me or give any indication that he was aware of my presence.

"Good evening, Mr. Wanas," I greeted him cordially.

He turned toward me abruptly, as though my voice had roused him from slumber, and glared at me in disapproval. I was about to explain what had brought me when he interrupted in an almost imperative tone of voice that was nonetheless not devoid of an extraordinary gentleness, "First, please sit down, and second, please get drunk!"

I opened my mouth to make my excuses, but, stopping up his ears with his fingers, he said, "Not a word till you do what I say."

I realized I was in the presence of a capricious drunkard and told myself that I should at least humor him a bit. "Would you permit me to ask one question?" I said with a smile, sitting down.

Without removing his hands from his ears he indicated the bottle. "When engaged in a drinking bout like this, I do not allow any conversation between myself and another unless, like me, he is drunk, otherwise all propriety is lost and mutual comprehension is rendered impossible."

I made a sign indicating that I did not drink.

"That's your lookout," he said offhandedly. "And that's my condition!"

He filled me a glass, which I meekly took and drank. No sooner had the wine settled in my stomach than it seemed to ignite. I waited patiently till I had grown used to its ferocity, and said, "It's very strong, and I think the time has come for me to ask you about—"

Once again, however, he put his fingers in his ears. "I shan't listen to you until you're drunk!"

He filled up my glass for the second time. I glanced at it in trepidation; then, overcoming my inherent objection, I drank it down at a gulp. No sooner had the wine come to rest inside me than I lost all willpower. With the third glass, I lost my memory, and with the fourth the future vanished. The world turned round about me, and I forgot why I had gone there. The man leaned toward me attentively, but I saw him—saw everything—as a mere meaningless series of colored planes. I don't know how long it was before my head sank down onto the arm of the chair and I plunged into deep sleep. During it, I had a beautiful dream the like of which I had never experienced. I dreamed that I was in an immense garden surrounded on all sides by luxuriant trees, and the sky was nothing but stars seen between the entwined branches, all enfolded in an atmosphere like that of sunset or a sky overcast with cloud. I was lying on a small hummock of jasmine petals, more of which fell upon me like rain, while the lucent spray of a fountain unceasingly sprinkled the crown of my head and my temples. I was in a state of deep contentedness, of ecstatic serenity. An orchestra of warbling and cooing played in my ear. There was an extraordinary sense of harmony between me and my inner self, and between the two of us and the world, everything being in its rightful place, without discord or distortion. In the whole world there was no single reason for speech or movement, for the universe moved in a rapture of ecstasy. This lasted but a short while. When I opened my eyes, consciousness struck at me like a policeman's fist, and I saw Wanas al-Damanhouri peering at me with concern. Only a few drowsy customers were left in the bar.

"You have slept deeply," said my companion. "You were obviously hungry for sleep."

I rested my heavy head in the palms of my hands. When I took them away in astonishment and looked down at them, I found that they glistened with drops of water.

"My head's wet," I protested.

"Yes, my friend tried to rouse you," he answered quietly.

"Somebody saw me in this state?"

"Don't worry, he is a good man. Have you not heard of Sheikh Zaabalawi?"

"Zaabalawi!" I exclaimed, jumping to my feet.

"Yes," he answered in surprise. "What's wrong?"

"Where is he?"

"I don't know where he is now. He was here and then he left."

I was about to run off in pursuit but found I was more exhausted than I had imagined. Collapsed over the table, I cried out in despair, "My sole reason for coming to you was to meet him! Help me to catch up with him or send someone after him."

The man called a vendor of prawns and asked him to seek out the sheikh and bring him back. Then he turned to me. "I didn't realize you were afflicted. I'm very sorry. . . ."

"You wouldn't let me speak," I said irritably.

"What a pity! He was sitting on this chair beside you the whole time. He was playing with a string of jasmine petals he had around his neck, a gift from one of his admirers, then, taking pity on you, he began to sprinkle some water on your head to bring you around."

"Does he meet you here every night?" I asked, my eyes not leaving the doorway through which the vendor of prawns had left.

"He was with me tonight, last night, and the night before that, but before that I hadn't seen him for a month."

"Perhaps he will come tomorrow," I answered with a sigh.

"Perhaps."

"I am willing to give him any money he wants."

Wanas answered sympathetically, "The strange thing is that he is not open to such temptations, yet he will cure you if you meet him."

"Without charge?"

"Merely on sensing that you love him."

The vendor of prawns returned, having failed in his mission.

I recovered some of my energy and left the bar, albeit unsteadily.

At every street corner I called out "Zaabalawi!" in the vague hope that I would be rewarded with an answering shout. The street boys turned contemptuous eyes on me till I sought refuge in the first available taxi.

The following evening I stayed up with Wanas al-Damanhouri till dawn, but the sheikh did not put in an appearance. Wanas informed me that he would be going away to the country and would not be returning to Cairo until he had sold the cotton crop.

I must wait, I told myself; I must train myself to be patient. Let me content myself with having made certain of the existence of Zaabalawi, and even of his affection for me, which encourages me to think that he will be prepared to cure me if a meeting takes place between us.

Sometimes, however, the long delay wearied me. I would become beset by despair and would try to persuade myself to dismiss him from my mind completely. How many weary people in this life know him not or regard him as a mere myth! Why, then, should I torture myself about him in this way?

No sooner, however, did my pains force themselves upon me than I would again begin to think about him, asking myself when I would be fortunate enough to meet him. The fact that I ceased to have any news of Wanas and was told he had gone to live abroad did not deflect me from my purpose; the truth of the matter was that I had become fully convinced that I had to find Zaabalawi.

Yes, I have to find Zaabalawi.

[1962]

RICHARD MARRANCA

Dragon Sutra, Chapter 15

"It's always been a dream to go to Angkor, but not like this," she said.

Our plan was to take a boat from Phnom Penh to Angkor Wat, the ancient capital of the great empire, one of the world navels.

We traveled many hours on the bloated river. Rachany carried sadness like a bag of rice. Sometimes birds flew overhead and children ran alongside us. It was an elemental and ancient panorama.

I felt sad that one of her great desires was tainted, though she seemed pleased to take a boat. We needed time to be together, to rid ourselves of the volcanic spill of events. It would give me time to think. In contrast, she could not be consoled. She had ripened too fast and had dark rings around her mordant eyes.

I sat next to her, sometimes pointing out the sights. A village appeared. Each view was a treasure house, a gift of the river. A long boat shaped like a canoe floated alongside our boat, its deck filled with overflowing baskets of fruit. The family looked like people from hill tribes. Someone said they were the Hmong – I remembered they had fought for America during the Vietnam War. Afterwards, they were persecuted and scattered, some ending up on house boats or in jungles or anywhere they could, like Texas or LA, and a few ended up in a recent Clint Eastwood movie, *Gran Torino*.

We saw makeshift homes on stilts and rows of floating homes. People had been living this way for centuries, but were the vanguard of what would arrive everywhere, as the glaciers melted.

Finally, our boat stopped at a floating store. It had a thatched roof and an awning over the entrance, earth hued with blue etched around one window and clothes hanging from the edges. Next to it was a boat with blue paint rubbed to invisibility. This society used everything until it sank. Fish lines searched for anything that could be hooked in the depths of the mocha water.

The river had traveled a long distance, through countryside, villages and cities. Cambodia got what was left. People lived in water world, ate and slept on it, made babies on it, laughed on it, got drunk on it, died on it – everything but drown. If they lived a life of meditation, it was that of water. Thales, the great philosopher who inaugurated the West's scientific quest, said that life came from water. In Cambodia you didn't need a philosopher. You needed a boat.

"What would you like?" I said to her.

"Only sleep."

"You can't just--"

"Life is nothing."

I gasped. When a traditional person says that, it means something. It's not like an existentialist mouthing off at a café, coffee and cigarette in hand. Usually, she was immersed in life's bounty, not in abstraction and depression. She hid her face in her hands, looking defeated. In contrast, I was used to dark thoughts whose authenticity I found comforting. I accepted reality and got on with it, like a fish accepts the immensity of the water, no matter how fetid.

For hours she didn't have water or food. She appeared catatonic. I asked her to look at children sitting in a hammock, all bunched up with puppies. Rachany loved all of life equally and embodied the notion of interdependence, but it was the crazy, bouncing puppy that elicited a smile.

A woman with dark feet hanging over the house boat cooked food. I eyed the vegetables and she fried it all up with sauces and spices and placed it next to a mound of rice on a plastic container, and her daughter handed us miniature chopsticks.

I passed a room with an old woman sleeping with her mouth open, a cat beside her. For a moment I wanted to change places with this family, to live in old patterns. I'm sure they wanted my life even more.

The children were drawn like magnets to my movie camera. I showed them how to use it and they pointed it at everything, including their grandmother sleeping. They laughed until realizing they better not and aimed it at the foreigners, the ones wearing shorts and running shoes.

A few minutes later, a young man came over and bowed. "Chum reeup sooa. Hello, I can speak English," he said. "I go to university. Would you like to stay the night? I'm getting married soon. It would be an honor. This is very propitious. I think that is the word."

"That's the best offer I've had in a while, but I have to ask my friend," I replied.

Fortunately, Rachany saw us and walked over. They spoke while I looked at the river. A few heron sailed along the water.

Afterwards, she told me that the party would begin soon, that we could sleep on the house boat, and that in the morning another boat would stop by to pick us up.

"You will meet the village," the young guy said.

Rachany and I walked around for a few hours and then took a nap in separate rooms. I gave pens and a notebook to the children, one of whom drew pictures of a boat.

As twilight settled, the party began. It stretched out on the house boat/store, with rows of lanterns and lollypop-colored lights glowing at the roof's edge. The family set up tables filled with plates of meat and rice and Coke bottles filled with rice wine. A band (guitarist, organist, singer) stood on one end of the boat with a squeezed area for dance. The locals drifted in, about thirty people.

"We're all lit up," said Rachany. "We could be shot."

I looked at her, chagrined. "They could have got us a dozen times. Enjoy the music then. It might be our last."

Rachany vanished into the sleeping area, returning in a few minutes with a change of clothes – all black -- and her hair spread over her face.

The groom to be and his fiancé dragged us to the dance floor, but once there I was amused. Like demons rushing through the night, the music thundered in our ears. Luckily, the rice wine numbed my senses, for people kept filling my glass and I kept drinking, and everything felt lurid and warm, and we could forget the backdrop of our escape.

My head spun and I viewed stars and big teeth in laughing mouths. Rachany drank water and looked at me with ambiguity and fear. I realized the groom had an endearing gap between his front teeth.

The men were "characters" in their dancing, with one of them using fast motions and rap-like hand movements, while another did a mix of moves, even the twist and the bump and another thing that looked like a crab. The women did variations of Apsara with elegant hand gestures harkening back to early temples, harking back to the original, heavenly Apsaras who are the consorts of Indra's servants and caretakers of heroes, intermediaries between heaven and earth.

The women seemed like animated dolls. While I stared gleefully, they moved in slow motion.

They were compact, gentle people whose joy and power was the community.

"I am so so so glad you came to my wedding. But you are a week early," said the groom, wobbling toward me. He had meaty alcoholic breath and put his arms around our shoulders, and continued: "This is Cambodia. Here, each marriage – I can't explain it – is like the marriage of Preah Thong and the dragon princess, Neang Nieak."

"It recreates an early marriage?" I asked, filming with my camera. "We're glad to be with you."

The groom, swaying a few times, held up the peace sign and sang *I am the Walrus*.

He drank more wine, filled the glass again and handed it to me. His fiancé, appearing even younger, had long black hair with a wave and wore a silk aquamarine sarong. She was jejune and could not fathom her own elegance, her perfection.

The groom spoke to Rachany and afterwards stomped over to me. "You are being chased by men with guns?"

I nodded. "And one of them is a lady boy in clown makeup."

"Make big joke?"

"I never joke about such things."

Rachany cried with her mouth stuck open. I felt like clamping her mouth down, to snap the whole enterprise shut. I had had enough. I wanted to have some joy fall upon us.

The groom spoke to the others, who made guttural sounds and huddled around him. In fury, one guy slapped his knees – he turned out to be the astrologer who had sanctioned their wedding. Two of the older men said they had guns; they went into the storeroom and returned with an AK-47s and two fancy pistols. Another guy brought out a machete and a belt with rusty grenades.

In amazement I shook my head, saying "We must save Morpheus."

I was drunk and oblivious, and everything rushed at me like famished monkeys. I tilted my head to the sky, looking for evidence of god but finding a furious silence. We danced and cavorted with the Milky Way, which sparkled across the sky's black skull. I had a wow experience – yes, the stars were billions of miles away, some dead & others sized beyond imagination, perhaps sucking in matter on its giant black tongue, to cast time backward to the empire.

The groom gave me more rice wine, standing over me as it went down heavy like a clunky elevator.

"Watch this," he said, extinguishing the candle with his tongue, which made a hissing sound.

After swallowing, I said, "I can catch bullets in my teeth. Ask Rachany."

"You couldn't catch an idiot," she said.

I didn't know what she meant, but I knew it wasn't good. The groom played with that for a few seconds, humming behind his smile and burst out laughing. He opened another bottle, took a long swig from the greenish-white throat.

The groom said, "We want you on our honeymoon."

Through glazed eyes, I looked at the uneaten rice and odd shapes of meat orbited by flies. (I hadn't eaten meat since childhood and had grown too peaceful to deal with the underworld.)

"You are kind," I finally said. "But I have to be fitted for a new suit in a few days."

He exhaled, out of breath, shivering in the night air with alcoholic blood discombobulating his mind-body. "Americans are crazy. We'll make you clothes, two suits. Okay, forget it. But you have to come and teach English."

I agreed and emptied another glass of rice wine. It was going down easy now, and I heard the mechanical gulp and got a warm feeling in the belly that spread over my skin like a massage. I felt like a sacrifice for the god of rice wine. My head throbbed, my body drooped.

I lurched over the rail and fell into the dismal dark river -- crash, silence, surface, ha. In a flash I imagined snakes and giant fish and alligators and cutting rocks.

The groom jumped in and we returned to the boat arm and arm. We'd float or drown together. I loved these people. Again, I felt like they were the dead generations of my family I had never met. They were real. They weren't atomized units separated by money and education. They felt real feelings.

As I dried off, an old man set up the Karaoke contraption. Rachany gave me a weird look, and reminded me that her parents never drank alcohol or smoked cigarettes. In one night, I broke centuries-old rules going back to Confucius, the old fortune cookie maker. She wore a cold mask. I had lost face, a serious transgression.

They held onto me while they conveyed Rachany to the matt next to the chatty grandmother.

Later, during the silent part of night when the stars furnished answers that are really feelings, I lost my thoughts. This twinkling of consciousness, of aloneness, began with early humans looking up at the stars – no, with chimpanzees looking up – pondering the big questions.

The boat was still, the moon the color of tofu. The water licked and gurgled like lovers, as granny recited her dream, the song of the 20th century. She was nearly 100. She babbled and moaned, fluttering her eyes: births and deaths, TV and wars, celebrations and cataclysms, came and went. Maybe she was a child running along the river.

At dawn, I surveyed the glistening water and jungle backdrop. Only a single boat drifted on the brown river. Butterflies – ambassadors from far away whose wings can set in motion events on the other side of the world – fluttered in auras. It was misty, impossible to see anything until it broke through. I looked at the parallel dirt road and the man bouncing on mist, and seconds later witnessed another. These mist-shrouded men were mahouts on elephants. After a few seconds another emerged, until there were eight, one behind the other, giants led by the trumpeting matriarch.

CHRISTINE REDMAN-WALDEYER

Abraham

His voice coming through like some Wizard
of Oz over a loudspeaker at the grocery store
announcing sales in one aisle,
free taste samples in another, closing time.

"Find another plot of land
that will bear fruit, use it
until rain comes over your own land."
You can never forget Hagar

but she is not Sarah, you cannot love Ishmael
more than Isaac but you can visit that place,
spend time with it as you would with a lover.
Kiss her all over until she moans,
breathe heavily into her ear, rise above her,
below her, press her heart into yours,
receive, reseed, recede.

Originally published in SVJ, Schulylkill Valley Journal, Spring 2010 print and online edition

WILLIAM BLAKE   [1757–1827]

The Sick Rose

William Blake (1757–1827) was born and raised in London. His only formal schooling was in art — he studied for a year at the Royal Academy and was apprenticed to an engraver. He later worked as a professional engraver, doing commissions and illustrations, assisted by his wife, Catherine Boucher. Blake, who had started writing poetry at the age of eleven, later engraved and handprinted his own poems, in very small batches, with his own illustrations. His early work was possessed of a strong social conscience, and his mature work turned increasingly mythic and prophetic.

O Rose, thou art sick.
The invisible worm
That flies in the night
In the howling storm

Has found out thy bed   5
Of crimson joy,
And his dark secret love
Does thy life destroy.

[1794]

JUDITH ORTIZ COFER   [b. 1952]

Latin Women Pray

Judith Ortiz Cofer was born and raised in Puerto Rico, but moved to New Jersey in her childhood. She is a poet, fiction writer, and auto-biographer, and teaches literature and writing at the University of Georgia. Much of her work, such as her novel *The Line of the Sun* (1989) and *The Latin Deli: Prose and Poetry* (1993), explores her experiences as a Puerto Rican émigré and a Latina. Her most recent book is *Woman in Front of the Sun: Becoming a Writer* (2000). "Latin Women Pray" was the title poem of Cofer's original poetry collection.

Latin women pray
in incense-sweet churches;
they pray in Spanish to an Anglo God
with a Jewish heritage.

And this Great White Father,   5
imperturbable in His marble pedestal
looks down upon His brown daughters,
votive candles shining like lust
in His all-seeing eyes,
unmoved by their persistent prayers.   10

Yet year after year,
before his image they kneel,
Margarita, Josefina, María and Isabel,
all fervently hoping
that if not omnipotent,   15
at least He be bilingual.

[1981]

GWENDOLYN BROOKS [1917–2000]

The Mother

Born in Topeka, Kansas, **Gwendolyn Brooks** (1917–2000) was raised in Chicago and wrote her first poems at age seven. She began studying poetry at the Southside Community Art Center. Her second collection of poems, *Annie Allen* (1949), earned the first Pulitzer Prize given to an African American poet. She served as Consultant in Poetry at the Library of Congress from 1985 to 1986 and worked in community programs and poetry workshops in Chicago to encourage young African American writers.

Abortions will not let you forget.
You remember the children you got that you did not get,
The damp small pulps with a little or with no hair,
The singers and workers that never handled the air.
You will never neglect or beat   5
Them, or silence or buy with a sweet.
You will never wind up the sucking-thumb
Or scuttle off ghosts that come.
You will never leave them, controlling your luscious sigh,
Return for a snack of them, with gobbling mother-eye.   10

I have heard in the voices of the wind the voices of my dim killed children
I have contracted. I have eased
My dim dears at the breasts they could never suck.
I have said, Sweets, if I sinned, if I seized
Your luck   15
And your lives from your unfinished reach,
If I stole your births and your names,
Your straight baby tears and your games,
Your stilted or lovely loves, your tumults, your marriages, aches, and
    your deaths,
If I poisoned the beginnings of your breaths,   20
Believe that even in my deliberateness I was not deliberate.

Though why should I whine,
Whine that the crime was other than mine? —
Since anyhow you are dead.
Or rather, or instead,   25
You were never made.
But that too, I am afraid,
Is faulty: oh, what shall I say, how is the truth to be said?
You were born, you had body, you died.
It is just that you never giggled or planned or cried.   30

Believe me, I loved you all.
Believe me, I knew you, though faintly, and I loved, I loved you
All.

[1945]

MARTÍN ESPADA   [b. 1957]

The Saint Vincent de Paul
Food Pantry Stomp

Madison, Wisconsin, 1980

Born in Brooklyn, New York, **Martín Espada** (b. 1957) has an eclectic
résumé: radio journalist in Nicaragua, welfare-rights paralegal, advocate for the mentally ill, night desk clerk in a transient hotel, attendant in a primate nursery, groundskeeper at a minor league ballpark,
bindery worker in a printing plant, bouncer in a bar, and practicing
lawyer in Chelsea, Massachusetts. Author of five books of poetry, he is
regarded as one of the leading poets of Puerto Rican heritage in the
United States. He presently teaches at the University of Massachusetts,
Amherst.

Waiting for the carton of food
given with Christian suspicion
even to agency-certified charity cases
like me,
thin and brittle   5
as uncooked linguini,
anticipating the factory-damaged cans
of tomato soup, beets, three-bean salad
in a welfare cornucopia,
I spotted a squashed dollar bill   10
on the floor, and with
a Saint Vincent de Paul food pantry stomp
pinned it under my sneaker,
tied my laces meticulously,
and stuffed the bill in my sock   15
like a smuggler of diamonds,
all beneath the plaster statue wingspan
of Saint Vinnie,

"The Saint Vincent de Paul Food Pantry Stomp" from *Rebellion in the Circle of a Lover's
Hands,* Curbstone Press, 1990. Reprinted with permission of Curbstone Press. Distributed by Consortium.

who was unaware
of the dance
named in his honor   20
by a maraca shaker
in the salsa band
of the unemployed.

[1990]

MARGE PIERCY   [b. 1936]

Barbie Doll

Born in working-class Detroit, **Marge Piercy** (b. 1936) studied at the University of Michigan and Northwestern University. She has published fourteen books of poetry, fifteen novels, and a collection of essays on poetry, *Parti-Colored Blocks for a Quilt* (1982). Much of her work deals with both the subtle and the blatant forms of oppression of women.

This girlchild was born as usual
and presented dolls that did pee-pee
and miniature GE stoves and irons
and wee lipsticks the color of cherry candy.
Then in the magic of puberty, a classmate said: 5
You have a great big nose and fat legs.

She was healthy, tested intelligent,
possessed strong arms and back,
abundant sexual drive and manual dexterity.
She went to and fro apologizing.   10
Everyone saw a fat nose on thick legs.

She was advised to play coy,
exhorted to come on hearty,
exercise, diet, smile and wheedle.
Her good nature wore out   15
like a fan belt.
So she cut off her nose and her legs
and offered them up.

In the casket displayed on satin she lay
with the undertaker's cosmetics painted on,   20
a turned-up putty nose,
dressed in a pink and white nightie.
Doesn't she look pretty? everyone said.
Consummation at last.
To every woman a happy ending.   25

[1973]

THEODORE ROETHKE   [1908–1963]

My Papa's Waltz

Theodore Roethke (1908–1963) was the son of a commercial green-house operator in Saginaw, Michigan. As a child he spent much time in greenhouses, and the impressions of nature he formed there later influenced the subjects and imagery of his verse. Roethke graduated from the University of Michigan and studied at Harvard University. His eight books of poetry were held in high regard by critics, some of whom considered Roethke among the best poets of his generation. *The Waking* was awarded the Pulitzer Prize in 1954; *Words for the Wind* (1958) received the Bollingen Prize and the National Book Award. He taught at many colleges and universities, his career interrupted several times by serious mental breakdowns, and gained a reputation as an exceptional teacher of poetry writing.

The whiskey on your breath
Could make a small boy dizzy;
But I hung on like death:
Such waltzing was not easy.

We romped until the pans   5
Slid from the kitchen shelf;
My mother's countenance
Could not unfrown itself.

The hand that held my wrist
Was battered on one knuckle;   10
At every step you missed
My right ear scraped a buckle.

You beat time on my head
With a palm caked hard by dirt,
Then waltzed me off to bed   15
Still clinging to your shirt.

[1948]

PAUL LAURENCE DUNBAR [1872–1906]

We Wear the Mask

Paul Laurence Dunbar (1872–1906) was the first African American to gain national eminence as a poet. Born and raised in Dayton, Ohio, the son of former slaves, he was an outstanding student. The only African American in his class, he was both class president and class poet. Although he lived to be only thirty-three years old, Dunbar was prolific, writing short stories, novels, librettos, plays, songs, and essays as well as the poetry for which he became well-known. Popular with both black and white readers of his day, Dunbar's style encompasses two distinct voices—the standard English of the classical poet and the evocative dialect of the turn-of-the-century black community in America.

We wear the mask that grins and lies,
It hides our cheeks and shades our eyes,—
This debt we pay to human guile;
With torn and bleeding hearts we smile,
And mouth with myriad subtleties.   5

Why should the world be over-wise,
In counting all our tears and sighs?
Nay, let them only see us, while
   We wear the mask.

We smile, but, O great Christ, our cries   10
To thee from tortured souls arise.
We sing, but oh the clay is vile
Beneath our feet, and long the mile;
But let the world dream otherwise,
   We wear the mask!   15

[1896]

ALLISON JOSEPH [b. 1967]

On Being Told I Don't Speak
Like a Black Person

Born in London to Caribbean parents, **Allison Joseph** (b. 1967) grew up in Toronto and the Bronx. She earned her B.A. from Kenyon College and her M.F.A. from Indiana University. She is the author of three collections of poetry: *What Keeps Us Here* (winner of Ampersand Press's 1992 Women Poets Series Competition and the John C. Zacharis First Book Award), *Soul Train* (1997), and *In Every Seam* (1997). Her poems are often attuned to the experiences of women and minorities. She formerly taught at the University of Arkansas and currently is an associate professor at Southern Illinois University, Carbondale, where she is editor of the *Crab Orchard Review*.

Emphasize the "h," you hignorant ass,
was what my mother was told
when colonial-minded teachers
slapped her open palm with a ruler
in that Jamaican schoolroom.   5
Trained in England, they tried
to force their pupils to speak
like Eliza Doolittle after
her transformation, fancying themselves
British as Henry Higgins,   10
despite dark, sun-ripened skin.
Mother never lost her accent,
though, the music of her voice
charming everyone, an infectious lilt
I can imitate, not duplicate.   15
No one in the States told her
to eliminate the accent,
my high school friends adoring
the way her voice would lift

when she called me to the phone,   20
A-ll-i-son, it's friend Cathy.
Why don't you sound like her?,
they'd ask. I didn't sound
like anyone or anything,
no grating New Yorker nasality,   25
no fastidious British mannerisms
like the ones my father affected
when he wanted to sell someone
something. And I didn't sound
like a Black American,   30
college acquaintances observed,
sure they knew what a black person
was supposed to sound like.
Was I supposed to sound lazy,
dropping syllables here, there,   35
not finishing words but
slurring the final letter so that
each sentence joined the next,
sliding past the listener?
Were certain words off limits,   40
too erudite, too scholarly
for someone with a natural tan?
I asked what they meant,
and they stuttered, blushed,
said you know, Black English,   45
applying what they'd learned
from that semester's text.
Does everyone in your family
speak alike?, I'd question,
and they'd say don't take this the   50
wrong way, nothing personal.

Now I realize there's nothing
more personal than speech,
that I don't have to defend
how I speak, how any person,   55
black, white, chooses to speak.
Let us speak. Let us talk
with the sounds of our mothers
and fathers still reverberating
in our minds, wherever our mothers   60
or fathers come from:

Arkansas, Belize, Alabama,
Brazil, Aruba, Arizona.
Let us simply speak
to one another,   65
listen and prize the inflections,
differences, never assuming
how any person will sound
until her mouth opens,
until his mouth opens,   70
greetings familiar
in any language.

[1999]

ANNE SEXTON [1928–1974]

Cinderella

Born in Newton, Massachusetts, **Anne Sexton** (1928–1974) dropped out of Garland Junior College to get married. After suffering nervous breakdowns following the births of her two children, she was encouraged to enroll in a writing program. Studying under Robert Lowell at Boston University, she was a fellow student with Sylvia Plath. Like the work of other "confessional" poets, Sexton's poetry is an intimate view of her life and emotions. She made the experience of being a woman a central issue in her poetry, bringing to it such subjects as menstruation and abortion as well as drug addiction. She published at least a dozen books of poetry—*Live or Die* was awarded the Pulitzer Prize for poetry in 1966—as well as four children's books co-authored with Maxine Kumin. Sexton's emotional problems continued, along with a growing addiction to alcohol and sedatives, and she committed suicide in 1974.

You always read about it:
the plumber with twelve children
who wins the Irish Sweepstakes.
From toilets to riches.
That story.   5

Or the nursemaid,
some luscious sweet from Denmark
who captures the oldest son's heart.
From diapers to Dior.°
That story.   10

Or a milkman who serves the wealthy,
eggs, cream, butter, yogurt, milk,
the white truck like an ambulance
who goes into real estate
and makes a pile.   15
From homogenized to martinis at lunch.

---

9. Dior: Fashions designed by the French house of Dior, established by Christian Dior (1905–1957).

Or the charwoman
who is on the bus when it cracks up
and collects enough from the insurance.
    From mops to Bonwit Teller.°   20
    That story.

Once
the wife of a rich man was on her deathbed
and she said to her daughter Cinderella:
Be devout. Be good. Then I will smile   25
down from heaven in the seam of a cloud.
The man took another wife who had
two daughters, pretty enough
but with hearts like blackjacks.
Cinderella was their maid.   30
She slept on the sooty hearth each night
and walked around looking like Al Jolson.°
Her father brought presents home from town,
jewels and gowns for the other women
but the twig of a tree for Cinderella.   35
She planted that twig on her mother's grave
and it grew to a tree where a white dove sat.
Whenever she wished for anything the dove
would drop it like an egg upon the ground.
The bird is important, my dears, so heed him.   40

Next came the ball, as you all know.
It was a marriage market.
The prince was looking for a wife.
All but Cinderella were preparing
and gussying up for the big event.   45
Cinderella begged to go too.
Her stepmother threw a dish of lentils
into the cinders and said: Pick them
up in an hour and you shall go.
The white dove brought all his friends;   50
all the warm wings of the fatherland came,
and picked up the lentils in a jiffy.
No, Cinderella, said the stepmother,

---

20. Bonwit Teller: A fashionable and expensive department store.
32. Al Jolson: American entertainer (1888–1950), known particularly for singing in blackface.

you have no clothes and cannot dance.
That's the way with stepmothers.   55

Cinderella went to the tree at the grave
and cried forth like a gospel singer:
Mama! Mama! My turtledove,
send me to the prince's ball!
The bird dropped down a golden dress   60
and delicate little gold slippers.
Rather a large package for a simple bird.
So she went. Which is no surprise.
Her stepmother and sisters didn't
recognize her without her cinder face   65
and the prince took her hand on the spot
and danced with no other the whole day.

As nightfall came she thought she'd better
get home. The prince walked her home
and she disappeared into the pigeon house   70
and although the prince took an axe and broke
it open she was gone. Back to her cinders.
These events repeated themselves for three days.
However on the third day the prince
covered the palace steps with cobbler's wax   75
and Cinderella's gold shoe stuck upon it.

Now he would find whom the shoe fit
and find his strange dancing girl for keeps.
He went to their house and the two sisters
were delighted because they had lovely feet.   80
The eldest went into a room to try the slipper on
but her big toe got in the way so she simply
sliced it off and put on the slipper.
The prince rode away with her until the white dove
told him to look at the blood pouring forth.   85
That is the way with amputations.
They don't just heal up like a wish.
The other sister cut off her heel
but the blood told as blood will.
The prince was getting tired.   90
He began to feel like a shoe salesman.
But he gave it one last try.
This time Cinderella fit into the shoe
like a love letter into its envelope.

At the wedding ceremony
the two sisters came to curry favor
and the white dove pecked their eyes out.
Two hollow spots were left
like soup spoons.

Cinderella and the prince
lived, they say, happily ever after,
like two dolls in a museum case
never bothered by diapers or dust,
never arguing over the timing of an egg,
never telling the same story twice,
never getting a middle-aged spread,
their darling smiles pasted on for eternity.
Regular Bobbsey Twins.
That story.

[1971]

Quick Editing Guide

A. Editing for Common Grammar Problems
B. Editing to Ensure Effective Sentences
C. Editing for Common Punctuation Problems
D. Editing for Common Mechanics and Format Problems

Editing and proofreading are needed at the end of the writing process because writers—*all* writers—find it difficult to write error-free sentences the very first time they try. Sometimes as a writer you pay more attention to what you want to say than to how you say it. Sometimes you inaccurately remember spelling or grammar or punctuation. At other times you are distracted or simply make keyboarding errors. Once you are satisfied that you have expressed your ideas, you should make sure that each sentence and word is concise, clear, and correct.

This Quick Editing Guide provides an overview of grammar, style, punctuation, and mechanics problems typical of college writing. Certain common errors in Standard Written English are like red flags to careful readers: they signal that the writer is either ignorant or careless. Use the editing checklist below to check your paper for these problems; then use the editing checklists in each section to help you correct specific errors. Concentrate on any problems likely to reappear in your writing. [For brief definitions of grammatical terms, turn to the glossary at the end of this guide.]

EDITING CHECKLIST

Common and Serious Problems in College Writing

Grammar Problems

☐ Have you avoided writing sentence fragments?   A1

☐ Have you avoided writing comma splices or fused sentences?   A2

☐ Have you used the correct form for all verbs in the past tense?   A3

☐ Do all verbs agree with their subjects?   A4

(continued)

X. J. Kennedy, Dorothy M. Kennedy, and Marcia F. Muth, *The Bedford Guide for College Writers*, Eighth Edition. Copyright © 2008 by Bedford/St. Martin's.

481

☐ Have you used the correct case for all pronouns?   A5
☐ Do all pronouns agree with their antecedents?   A6
☐ Have you used adjectives and adverbs correctly?   A7

Sentence Problems

☐ Does each modifier clearly modify the appropriate sentence element?   B1
☐ Have you used parallel structure where needed?   B2

Punctuation Problems

☐ Have you used commas correctly?   C1
☐ Have you used apostrophes correctly?   C2
☐ Have you punctuated quotations correctly?   C3

Mechanics and Format Problems

☐ Have you used capital letters correctly?   D1
☐ Have you spelled all words correctly?   D2
☐ Have you used correct manuscript form?   D3

A   EDITING FOR COMMON GRAMMAR PROBLEMS

A1   Check for any sentence fragments.

A complete sentence is one that has a subject, has a predicate, and can stand on its own. A *sentence fragment* lacks a subject, a predicate, or both, or for some other reason fails to convey a complete thought. It cannot stand on its own as a sentence.

Although they are common in advertising and fiction, fragments are usually ineffective in college writing because they do not communicate coherent thoughts. To edit for fragments, examine each sentence carefully to make sure that it has a subject and a verb and that it expresses a complete thought. To correct a fragment, you can make it into a complete sentence by adding a missing part, dropping an unnecessary subordinating conjunction, or joining it to a complete sentence nearby, if that would make more sense.

FRAGMENT	Roberto has two sisters. Maya and Leeza.
CORRECT	Roberto has two sisters, Maya and Leeza.
FRAGMENT	The children going to the zoo.
CORRECT	The children were going to the zoo.
CORRECT	The children going to the zoo were caught in a traffic jam.

FRAGMENT	Last night when we saw Cameron Diaz's most recent movie.
CORRECT	Last night we saw Cameron Diaz's most recent movie.

EDITING CHECKLIST

Fragments

☐ Does the sentence have a subject?

☐ Does the sentence have a complete verb?

☐ If the sentence contains a subordinate clause, does it contain a clause that is a complete sentence too?

☐ If you find a fragment, can you link it to an adjoining sentence, eliminate its subordinating conjunction, or add any missing element?

A2 Check for any comma splices or fused sentences.

A complete sentence has a subject and a predicate and can stand on its own. When two sentences are joined together to form one sentence, each sentence within the larger one is called a *main clause*. However, there are rules for joining main clauses, and when writers fail to follow these rules, they create serious sentence errors — comma splices or fused sentences, also called run-on sentences. A *comma splice* is two main clauses joined with only a comma. A *fused sentence* is two main clauses joined with no punctuation at all.

COMMA SPLICE	I went to the mall, I bought a new coat.
FUSED SENTENCE	I went to the mall I bought a new coat.

To find comma splices and fused sentences, examine each sentence to be sure it is complete. If it has two main clauses, make sure they are joined correctly. If you find a comma splice or fused sentence, correct it in one of these four ways, depending on which makes the best sense:

ADD A PERIOD	I went to the mall. I bought a new coat.
ADD A COMMA AND A COORDINATING CONJUNCTION	I went to the mall, and I bought a new coat.
ADD A SEMICOLON	I went to the mall; I bought a new coat.
ADD A SUBORDINATING CONJUNCTION	I went to the mall where I bought a new coat.

483

EDITING CHECKLIST

Comma Splices and Fused Sentences

☐ Can you make each main clause a separate sentence?

☐ Can you link the two main clauses with a comma and a coordinating conjunction?

☐ Can you link the two main clauses with a semicolon or, if appropriate, a colon?

☐ Can you subordinate one clause to the other?

A3   Check for correct past tense verb forms.

The *form* of a verb, the way it is spelled and pronounced, can change to show its *tense*—the time when its action did, does, or will occur (in the past, present, or future). A verb about something in the present will often be spelled and pronounced differently than a verb about something in the past.

PRESENT   Right now, I *watch* only a few minutes of television each day.

PAST   Last month, I *watched* television shows every evening.

Many writers fail to use the correct form for past tense verbs for two different reasons, depending on whether the verb is regular or irregular.

Regular verbs are verbs whose forms follow standard rules; they form the past tense by adding *-ed* or *-d* to the end of the present tense form: *watch/watched*, *look/looked*, *hope/hoped*. Check all regular verbs in the past tense to be sure you have used one of these endings.

FAULTY   I *ask* my brother for a loan yesterday.

CORRECT   I *asked* my brother for a loan yesterday.

FAULTY   Nicole *race* in the track meet last week.

CORRECT   Nicole *raced* in the track meet last week.

TIP: If you say the final *-d* sound when you talk, you may find it easier to add the final *-d* or *-ed* when you write past tense regular verbs.

Irregular verbs do not follow standard rules to make their forms. Their unpredictable past tense forms have to be memorized: *eat/ate*, *see/saw*, *get/got*. In addition, the past tense form may differ from the past participle: "She *ate* the whole pie; she *has eaten* two pies this week." The most troublesome irregular verbs are actually very common, so if you make the effort to learn the correct forms, you will quickly improve your writing.

FAULTY	My cat *laid* on the tile floor to take her nap.
CORRECT	My cat *lay* on the tile floor to take her nap.
FAULTY	I *have swam* twenty laps every day this month.
CORRECT	I *have swum* twenty laps every day this month.

TIP: In college papers, follow convention by using the present tense, not the past, to describe the work of an author or the events in a literary work.

FAULTY	In "The Lottery," Shirley Jackson *revealed* the power of tradition. As the story *opened*, the villagers *gathered* in the square.
CORRECT	In "The Lottery," Shirley Jackson *reveals* the power of tradition. As the story *opens*, the villagers *gather* in the square.

EDITING CHECKLIST
Past Tense Verb Forms

☐ Have you identified the main verb in the sentence?

☐ Is the sentence about the past, the present, or the future? Does the verb reflect this sense of time?

☐ Is the verb regular or irregular?

☐ Have you used the correct form to express your meaning?

Principal Parts of Common Irregular Verbs

INFINITIVE (BASE)	PAST TENSE	PAST PARTICIPLE
be	was	been
become	became	become
begin	began	begun
blow	blew	blown
break	broke	broken
bring	brought	brought
burst	burst	burst
catch	caught	caught
choose	chose	chosen
come	came	come
do	did	done

(continued)

INFINITIVE (BASE)	PAST TENSE	PAST PARTICIPLE
draw	drew	drawn
drink	drank	drunk
drive	drove	driven
eat	ate	eaten
fall	fell	fallen
fight	fought	fought
freeze	froze	frozen
get	got	got, gotten
give	gave	given
go	went	gone
grow	grew	grown
have	had	had
hear	heard	heard
hide	hid	hidden
know	knew	known
lay	laid	laid
lead	led	led
let	let	let
lie	lay	lain
make	made	made
raise	raised	raised
ride	rode	ridden
ring	rang	rung
rise	rose	risen
run	ran	run
say	said	said
see	saw	seen
set	set	set
sing	sang	sung
sit	sat	sat
slay	slew	slain
slide	slid	slid
speak	spoke	spoken
spin	spun	spun
stand	stood	stood
steal	stole	stolen
swim	swam	swum
swing	swung	swung
teach	taught	taught

(*continued*)

INFINITIVE (BASE)	PAST TENSE	PAST PARTICIPLE
tear	tore	torn
think	thought	thought
throw	threw	thrown
wake	woke, waked	woken, waked
write	wrote	written

For the forms of irregular verbs not on this list, consult your dictionary. (Some dictionaries list principal parts for all verbs, some just for irregular verbs.)

A4 Check for correct subject-verb agreement.

The *form* of a verb, the way it is spelled and pronounced, can change to show *number*—whether the subject is singular (one) or plural (more than one). It can also show *person*—whether the subject is *you* or *she*, for example.

SINGULAR	Our instructor *grades* every paper carefully.
PLURAL	Most instructors *grade* tests using a standard scale.
SECOND PERSON	You *write* well-documented research papers.
THIRD PERSON	She *writes* good research papers, too.

A verb must match (or *agree with*) its subject in terms of number and person. Regular verbs (those that follow a standard rule to make the different forms) are problems only in the present tense, where they have two forms: one that ends in *-s* or *-es* and one that does not. Only the subjects *he, she, it,* and singular nouns use the verb form that ends in *-s* or *-es.*

I like	we like	Dan likes
you like	you like	the child likes
he/she/it likes	they like	the children like

The verbs *be* and *have* do not follow the *-s/no -s* pattern to form the present tense; they are irregular verbs, so their forms must be memorized. The verb *be* is also irregular in the past tense.

Problems in agreement often occur when the subject is difficult to find, is an indefinite pronoun, or is confusing for some other reason. In particular, make sure that you have not left off any *-s* or *-es* endings and that you have used the correct form for irregular verbs.

Forms of *Be* and *Have* at a Glance

THE PRESENT TENSE OF *BE*		THE PAST TENSE OF *BE*	
I am	we are	I was	we were
you are	you are	you were	you were
he/she/it is	they are	he/she/it was	they were

THE PRESENT TENSE OF *HAVE*		THE PAST TENSE OF *HAVE*	
I have	we have	I had	we had
you have	you have	you had	you had
he/she/it has	they have	he/she/it had	they had

FAULTY	Jim *write* at least fifty e-mails a day.
CORRECT	Jim *writes* at least fifty e-mails a day.
FAULTY	The students *has* difficulty with the assignment.
CORRECT	The students *have* difficulty with the assignment.
FAULTY	Every one of the cakes *were* sold at the fundraiser.
CORRECT	Every one of the cakes *was* sold at the fundraiser.

EDITING CHECKLIST
Subject-Verb Agreement

☐ Have you correctly identified the subject and the verb in the sentence?

☐ Is the subject singular or plural? Does the verb match?

☐ Have you used the correct form of the verb?

A5 Check for correct pronoun case.

Depending on the role a pronoun plays in a sentence, it is said to be in the *subjective case*, *objective case*, or *possessive case*. Use the subjective case if the pronoun is the subject of a sentence, the subject of a subordinate clause, or a subject complement (after a linking verb). Use the objective case if the pronoun is a direct or indirect object of a verb or the object of a preposition. Use the possessive case to show possession.

SUBJECTIVE	*I* will argue that our campus needs more parking.
OBJECTIVE	This issue is important to *me*.
POSSESSIVE	*My* argument will be quite persuasive.

There are many types of pronouns, but only some change form to show case. The personal pronouns *I*, *you*, *he*, *she*, *it*, *we*, and *they* and the relative pronoun *who* each have at least two forms.

Pronoun Cases at a Glance

SUBJECTIVE	OBJECTIVE	POSSESSIVE
I	me	my, mine
you	you	your, yours
he	him	his
she	her	hers
it	it	its
we	us	our, ours
they	them	their, theirs
who	whom	whose

There are two common errors in pronoun case. First, writers often use the subjective case when they should use the objective case—sometimes because they are trying to sound formal and correct. Instead, choose the correct form for a personal pronoun based on its function in the sentence. If the sentence pairs a noun and a pronoun, try the sentence with the pronoun alone.

FAULTY	My company gave my husband and *I* a trip to Hawaii.
PRONOUN ONLY	My company gave *I* a trip?
CORRECT	My company gave my husband and *me* a trip to Hawaii.
FAULTY	The argument occurred because my uncle and *me* had different expectations.
PRONOUN ONLY	*Me* had different expectations?
CORRECT	The argument occurred because my uncle and *I* had different expectations.
FAULTY	Jack ran faster than *me*.
PRONOUN ONLY	Jack ran faster than *me* ran?
CORRECT	Jack ran faster than *I*.

A second common error with pronoun case involves gerunds. Whenever you need a pronoun to modify a gerund, use the possessive case.

FAULTY   Our supervisor disapproves of *us* talking in the hallway.

CORRECT   Our supervisor disapproves of *our* talking in the hallway.

EDITING CHECKLIST
Pronoun Case

☐ Have you identified all the pronouns in the sentence?

☐ Does each one function as a subject, an object, or a possessive?

☐ Given the function of each, have you used the correct form?

A6   **Check for correct pronoun-antecedent agreement.**

The *form* of a pronoun, the way it is spelled and pronounced, changes depending on its use in a particular sentence. The form can change to show *number*—whether the subject is singular (one) or plural (more than one). It can change to show *gender*—masculine or feminine, for example—or *person:* first (*I, we*), second (*you*), or third (*he, she, it, they*).

SINGULAR   My brother took *his* coat and left.

PLURAL   My brothers took *their* coats and left.

MASCULINE   I talked to Steven before *he* had a chance to leave.

FEMININE   I talked to Stephanie before *she* had a chance to leave.

In most cases, a pronoun refers to a specific noun or pronoun mentioned nearby; that word is called the pronoun's *antecedent*. The connection between the pronoun and the antecedent must be clear so that readers know what the pronoun means in the sentence. One way to make this connection clear is to ensure that the pronoun and the antecedent match (or *agree*) in number and gender.

A common error in pronoun agreement is using a plural pronoun to refer to a singular antecedent. This error often crops up when the antecedent is difficult to find, when the antecedent is an indefinite pronoun, or when the antecedent is confusing for some other reason. When editing

490

for pronoun-antecedent agreement, look carefully to find the correct antecedent, and make sure you know whether it is singular or plural. Then make the pronoun match its antecedent.

FAULTY   Each of the boys in the Classic Club has *their* own rebuilt car.

CORRECT   Each of the boys in the Classic Club has *his* own rebuilt car.

[The word *each*, not *boys*, is the antecedent. *Each* is an indefinite pronoun and is always singular, so any pronoun referring to it must be singular as well.]

FAULTY   Everyone in the meeting had *their* own cell phone.

CORRECT   Everyone in the meeting had *his or her* own cell phone.

[*Everyone* is an indefinite pronoun that is always singular, so any pronoun referring to it must be singular as well.]

Indefinite Pronouns at a Glance

ALWAYS SINGULAR

			ALWAYS PLURAL
anybody	everyone	nothing	both
anyone	everything	one (of)	few
anything	much	somebody	many
each (of)	neither (of)	someone	several
either (of)	nobody	something	
everybody	no one		

FAULTY   Neither Luz nor Pam has received approval of *their* financial aid yet.

CORRECT   Neither Luz nor Pam has received approval of *her* financial aid yet.

[*Neither Luz nor Pam* is a compound subject joined by *nor*. Any pronoun referring to it must agree with only the nearer part of the compound. In other words, *her* needs to agree with *Pam*, which is singular.]

Indefinite pronouns as antecedents are troublesome when they are grammatically singular but create a plural image in the writer's mind. Fortunately, most indefinite pronouns are either always singular or always plural.

EDITING CHECKLIST

Pronoun-Antecedent Agreement

☐ Have you identified the antecedent for each pronoun?

☐ Is the antecedent singular or plural? Does the pronoun match?

☐ Is the antecedent masculine, feminine, or neuter? Does the pronoun match?

☐ Is the antecedent first, second, or third person? Does the pronoun match?

A7 Check for correct adjectives and adverbs.

Adjectives and *adverbs* describe or give more information about (*modify*) other words in a sentence. Many adverbs are formed by adding *-ly* to adjectives: *simple, simply; quiet, quietly.* Because adjectives and adverbs resemble one another, writers sometimes mistakenly use one instead of the other. To edit, find the word that the adjective or adverb modifies. If that word is a noun or pronoun, use an adjective. (An adjective typically describes which or what kind.) If that word is a verb, adjective, or another adverb, use an adverb. (An adverb typically describes how, when, where, or why.)

FAULTY Kelly ran into the house *quick*.

CORRECT Kelly ran into the house *quickly*.

Comparison of Irregular Adjectives and Adverbs

	POSITIVE	COMPARATIVE	SUPERLATIVE
ADJECTIVES	good	better	best
	bad	worse	worst
	little	less, littler	least, littlest
	many, some, much	more	most
ADVERBS	well	better	best
	badly	worse	worst
	little	less	least

FAULTY Gabriela looked *terribly* after her bout with the flu.

CORRECT Gabriela looked *terrible* after her bout with the flu.

492

Adjectives and adverbs that have similar comparative and superlative forms can also cause trouble. Always ask whether you need an adjective or an adverb in the sentence, and then use the correct word.

FAULTY His scar healed so *good* that it was barely visible.

CORRECT His scar healed so *well* that it was barely visible.

Good is an adjective; it describes a noun or pronoun. *Well* is an adverb; it modifies or adds to a verb (*heal*, in this case) or an adjective.

EDITING CHECKLIST
Adjectives and Adverbs

☐ Have you identified which word the adjective or adverb modifies?

☐ If the word modified is a noun or pronoun, have you used an adjective?

☐ If the word modified is a verb, adjective, or adverb, have you used an adverb?

☐ Have you used the correct comparative or superlative form?

B   EDITING TO ENSURE EFFECTIVE SENTENCES

B1   Check for any misplaced or dangling modifiers.

For a sentence to be clear, the connection between a modifier and the thing it modifies must be obvious. Usually, a modifier should be placed right before or right after the sentence element it modifies. If the modifier is placed too close to some other sentence element, it is a *misplaced modifier*. If there is nothing in the sentence that the modifier can logically modify, it is a *dangling modifier*. Both of these errors cause confusion for readers — and they sometimes create unintentionally humorous images. As you edit, be sure that a modifier is placed directly before or after the word modified and that the connection between the two is clear.

MISPLACED George found the leftovers when he visited in the refrigerator.

CORRECT George found the leftovers in the refrigerator when he visited.

[In the faulty sentence, *in the refrigerator* seems to modify George's visit. Obviously the leftovers are in the refrigerator, not George.]

493

DANGLING	Looking out the window, the clouds were beautiful.
CORRECT	Looking out the window, I saw that the clouds were beautiful.
CORRECT	When I looked out the window, the clouds were beautiful.

[In the faulty sentence, *looking out the window* should modify *I*, but *I* is not in the sentence. The modifier is left without anything logical to modify — a dangling modifier. To correct this, the writer has to edit so that *I* is in the sentence.]

EDITING CHECKLIST

Misplaced and Dangling Modifiers

☐ What is each modifier meant to modify? Is the modifier as close as possible to that sentence element? Is any misreading possible?

☐ If a modifier is misplaced, can you move it to clarify the meaning?

☐ What noun or pronoun is a dangling modifier meant to modify? Can you make that word or phrase the subject of the main clause? Or can you turn the dangling modifier into a clause that includes the missing noun or pronoun?

B2 Check for parallel structure.

A series of words, phrases, clauses, or sentences with the same grammatical form is said to be *parallel*. Using parallel form for elements that are parallel in meaning or function helps readers grasp the meaning of a sentence more easily. A lack of parallelism can distract, annoy, or even confuse readers.

To use parallelism, put nouns with nouns, verbs with verbs, and phrases with phrases. Parallelism is particularly important in a series, with correlative conjunctions, and in comparisons using *than* or *as*.

FAULTY	I like to go to Estes Park for skiing, ice skating, and to meet interesting people.
CORRECT	I like to go to Estes Park to ski, to ice skate, and to meet interesting people.
FAULTY	The proposal is neither practical, nor is it innovative.
CORRECT	The proposal is neither practical nor innovative.

FAULTY   A parent should have a few firm rules rather than having many flimsy ones.

CORRECT   A parent should have a few firm rules rather than many flimsy ones.

Take special care to reinforce parallel structures by repeating articles, conjunctions, prepositions, or lead-in words as needed.

AWKWARD   His dream was that he would never have to give up his routine but he would still find time to explore new frontiers.

PARALLEL   His dream was that he would never have to give up his routine but *that* he would still find time to explore new frontiers.

EDITING CHECKLIST

Parallel Structure

☐ Are all the elements in a series in the same grammatical form?

☐ Are the elements in a comparison parallel in form?

☐ Are the articles, conjunctions, or prepositions between elements repeated rather than mixed or omitted?

☐ Are lead-in words repeated as needed?

C EDITING FOR COMMON PUNCTUATION PROBLEMS

C1 Check for correct use of commas.

The *comma* is a punctuation mark indicating a pause. By setting some words apart from others, commas help clarify relationships; they prevent the words on a page and the ideas they represent from becoming a jumble. Here are some of the most important conventional uses of commas.

1. Use a comma before a coordinating conjunction (*and, but, for, or, so, yet, nor*) joining two main clauses in a compound sentence.

   The discussion was brief, *so* the meeting was adjourned early.

2. Use a comma after an introductory word or word group unless it is short and cannot be misread.

   After the war, the North's economy developed rapidly.

3. Use commas to separate the items in a series of three or more items.

   The chief advantages will be *speed*, *durability*, and *longevity*.

4. Use commas to set off a modifying clause or phrase if it is non-restrictive—that is, if it can be taken out of the sentence without significantly changing the essential meaning of the sentence.

   Good childcare, *which is difficult to find*, should be provided by the employer.

   Good childcare *that is reliable and inexpensive* is the right of every employee.

5. Use commas to set off a nonrestrictive appositive, an expression that comes directly after a noun or pronoun and renames it.

   Sheri, my sister, has a new job as an events coordinator.

6. Use commas to set off parenthetical expressions, conjunctive adverbs, and other interrupters.

   The proposal from the mayor's commission, however, is not feasible.

EDITING CHECKLIST
Commas

☐ Have you added a comma between two main clauses joined by a coordinating conjunction?

☐ Have you added commas needed after introductory words or word groups?

☐ Have you separated items in a series with commas?

☐ Have you avoided putting commas before the first item in a series or after the last?

☐ Have you used commas before and after each nonrestrictive word, phrase, or clause?

☐ Have you avoided using commas around a restrictive word, phrase, or clause?

☐ Have you used commas to set off appositives, parenthetical expressions, conjunctive adverbs, and other interrupters?

C2 Check for correct use of apostrophes.

An *apostrophe* is a punctuation mark that either shows possession (*Sylvia's*) or indicates that one or more letters have intentionally been left out to form a contraction (*didn't*). Because apostrophes are easy to overlook, writers often omit a necessary apostrophe, use one where it is not needed, or put one in the wrong place. An apostrophe is never used

496

to create the possessive form of a pronoun; use the possessive pronoun form instead.

FAULTY	*Mikes* car was totaled in the accident.
CORRECT	*Mike's* car was totaled in the accident.
FAULTY	*Womens'* pay is often less than *mens'*.
CORRECT	*Women's* pay is often less than *men's*.

Possessive Personal Pronouns at a Glance

PERSONAL PRONOUN	POSSESSIVE CASE
I	my, mine
you	your, yours (*not* your's)
he	his
she	her, hers (*not* her's)
it	its (*not* it's)
we	our, ours (*not* our's)
they	their, theirs (*not* their's)
who	whose (*not* who's)

FAULTY	Che *did'nt* want to stay at home and study.
CORRECT	Che *didn't* want to stay at home and study.
FAULTY	The dog wagged *it's* tail happily.
CORRECT	The dog wagged *its* tail happily.
FAULTY	*Its* raining.
CORRECT	*It's* raining. [it's = it is]

EDITING CHECKLIST
Apostrophes

☐ Have you used an apostrophe when letters are left out in a contraction?

☐ Have you used an apostrophe to create the possessive form of a noun?

☐ Have you used the possessive case — rather than an apostrophe — to show that a pronoun is possessive?

☐ Have you used *it's* correctly (to mean *it is*)?

C3 Check for correct punctuation of quotations.

When you quote the exact words of a person you have interviewed or a source you have read, be sure to enclose those words in quotation marks. Notice how student Betsy Buffo presents the words of her subject in this passage from her essay "Interview with an Artist":

> Derek is straightforward when asked about how his work is received in the local community: "My work is outside the mainstream. Because it's controversial, it's not easy for me to get exposure."

She might have expressed and punctuated this passage in other ways:

> Derek says that "it's not easy" for him to find an audience.
>
> Derek struggles for recognition because his art falls "outside the mainstream."

If your source is quoting someone else (a quotation within a quotation), put your subject's words in quotation marks and the words he or she is quoting in single quotation marks. Always put commas and periods inside the quotation marks; put semicolons and colons outside.

> As Betsy Buffo explains, "Derek struggles for recognition because his art falls 'outside the mainstream.'"

Substitute an ellipsis mark (. . .)—three spaced dots—for any words you have omitted from the middle of a direct quotation. If you are following MLA style, you may place the ellipses inside brackets ([. . .]) when necessary to avoid confusing your ellipsis marks with those of the original writer. If the ellipses come at the end of a sentence, add another period to conclude the sentence. You don't need an ellipsis mark to show the beginning or ending of a quotation that is clearly incomplete.

In this selection from "Playing Games with Women's Sports," student Kelly Grecian identifies both quotations and an omission:

"The importance of what women athletes wear can't be underestimated," Rounds claims. "Beach volleyball, which is played . . . by bikini-clad women, rates network coverage" (44).

Common errors in punctuating quotations include leaving out necessary punctuation marks or putting them in the incorrect place or sequence.

EDITING CHECKLIST

Punctuation with Quotations

☐ Are the exact words quoted from your source enclosed in quotation marks?

☐ Are commas and periods placed inside closing quotation marks?

☐ Are colons and semicolons placed outside closing quotation marks?

☐ Have you used ellipses to show where any words are omitted from the middle of a quotation?

D EDITING FOR COMMON MECHANICS AND FORMAT PROBLEMS

D1 Check for correct use of capital letters.

Capital letters are used in three general situations: to begin a new sentence; to begin names of specific people, nationalities, places, dates, and things (proper nouns); and to begin main words in titles. Writers sometimes use capital letters where they are not needed, such as for emphasis, or fail to use them where they are needed.

FAULTY   During my Sophomore year in College, I took World Literature, Biology, History, Psychology, and French—courses required for a Humanities Major.

CORRECT   During my sophomore year in college, I took world literature, biology, history, psychology, and French—courses required for a humanities major.

EDITING CHECKLIST

Capitalization

☐ Have you used a capital letter at the beginning of each complete sentence, including sentences that are quoted?

☐ Have you used capital letters for proper nouns and pronouns?

(continued)

499

☐ Have you avoided using capital letters for emphasis?

☐ Have you used a capital letter for each main word in a title, including the first word and the last word? (Prepositions, coordinating conjunctions, and articles are not considered main words.)

Capitalization at a Glance

Capitalize the following:

THE FIRST LETTER OF A SENTENCE, INCLUDING A QUOTED SENTENCE
She called out, "Come in! The water's warm."

PROPER NAMES AND ADJECTIVES MADE FROM THEM
Cranberry Island   Marie Curie
a Freudian reading   Smithsonian Institution

RANK OR TITLE BEFORE A PROPER NAME
Ms. Olson   Professor Santocolon

FAMILY RELATIONSHIP ONLY WHEN IT SUBSTITUTES FOR OR IS PART OF A PROPER NAME
Grandma Jones   Father Time

RELIGIONS, THEIR FOLLOWERS, AND DEITIES
Islam   Orthodox Jew   Buddha

PLACES, REGIONS, GEOGRAPHIC FEATURES, AND NATIONALITIES
Palo Alto   the Berkshire Mountains   Egyptians

DAYS OF THE WEEK, MONTHS, AND HOLIDAYS
Wednesday   July   Labor Day

HISTORICAL EVENTS, PERIODS, AND DOCUMENTS
the Boston Tea Party   the Middle Ages   the Constitution

SCHOOLS, COLLEGES, UNIVERSITIES, AND SPECIFIC COURSES
Temple University   Introduction to Clinical Psychology

FIRST, LAST, AND MAIN WORDS IN TITLES OF PAPERS, BOOKS, ARTICLES, WORKS OF ART, TELEVISION SHOWS, POEMS, AND PERFORMANCES

The Decline and Fall of the Roman Empire   "The Lottery"

D2 Check spelling.

Misspelled words are difficult to spot in your own writing. You usually see what you think you wrote, and often pronunciation or faulty memory may interfere with correct spelling. When you proofread for spelling, check for words that sound alike but are spelled differently (*accept* and *except,* for example), words that are spelled differently than they are pronounced, words that do not follow the basic rules for spelling English words (*judgment,* for example), and words that you habitually confuse and misspell.

EDITING CHECKLIST
Spelling

☐ Have you checked for the words you habitually misspell?

☐ Have you checked for commonly confused or misspelled words?

☐ Have you applied the standard spelling rules, including their exceptions?

☐ Have you checked a dictionary for any words you are unsure about?

☐ Have you run your spell checker? Have you read your paper carefully for errors that it would miss?

COMMONLY CONFUSED HOMONYMS

accept (v., receive willingly); **except** (prep., other than)
Mimi could *accept* all of Lefty's gifts *except* his ring.

affect (v., influence); **effect** (n., result)
If the new rules *affect* us, what will be their *effect*?

allusion (n., reference); **illusion** (n., fantasy)
Any *allusion* to Norman's mother may revive his *illusion* that she is upstairs, alive, in her rocking chair.

capital (adj., uppercase; n., seat of government); **capitol** (n., government building)
The *Capitol* building in our nation's *capital* is spelled with a *capital* C.

cite (v., refer to); **sight** (n., vision or tourist attraction); **site** (n., place)

Did you *cite* Aunt Peg as your authority on which *sites* feature the most interesting *sights*?

complement (v., complete; n., counterpart); **compliment** (v. or n., praise)

For Lee to say that Sheila's beauty *complements* her intelligence may or may not be a *compliment*.

desert (v., abandon; n., hot, dry region); **dessert** (n., end-of-meal sweet)

Don't *desert* us by leaving for the *desert* before *dessert*.

elicit (v., bring out); **illicit** (adj., illegal)

By going undercover, Sonny should *elicit* some offers of *illicit* drugs.

formally (adv., officially); **formerly** (adv., in the past)

Jane and John Doe-Smith, *formerly* Jane Doe and John Smith, sent cards *formally* announcing their marriage.

led (v., past tense of *lead*); **lead** (n., a metal)

Gil's heart was heavy as *lead* when he *led* the mourners to the grave.

principal (n. or adj., chief); **principle** (n., rule or standard)

The *principal* problem is convincing the media that our school *principal* is a person of high *principles*.

stationary (adj., motionless); **stationery** (n., writing paper)

Hubert's *stationery* shop stood *stationary* until a flood swept it away.

their (pron., belonging to them); **there** (adv., in that place); **they're** (contraction of *they are*)

Sue said *they're* going over *there* to visit *their* aunt.

to (prep., toward); **too** (adv, also or excessively); **two** (n. or adj., numeral: one more than one)

Let's not take *two* cars *to* town—that's *too* many unless Hal comes *too*.

who's (contraction of *who is*); **whose** (pron., belonging to whom)

Who's going to tell me *whose* dog this is?

your (pron., belonging to you); **you're** (contraction of *you are*)

You're not getting *your* own way this time!

COMMONLY MISSPELLED WORDS

absence
academic
acceptable
accessible
accidentally
accommodate
achievement
acknowledgment
acquaintance
acquire
address
advertisement
advice
advise
aggravate
aggressive
aging
allege
all right
all together (all in
 one group)
a lot
already
although
altogether (entirely)
amateur
analysis
analyze
answer
anxiety
appearance
appetite
appreciate
appropriate
arctic
argument
ascent
assassinate
assistance
association

athlete
athletics
attendance
audience
average
awkward
basically
beginning
believe
beneficial
benefited
breath (noun)
breathe (verb)
bureaucracy
business
calendar
careful
casualties
category
cemetery
certain
changeable
changing
characteristic
chief
choose (present
 tense)
chose (past tense)
climbed
column
coming
commitment
committed
comparative
competition
conceive
condemn
congratulate
conscience
conscientious

conscious
consistent
controlled
criticism
criticize
curiosity
curious
deceive
decision
defendant
deficient
definite
dependent
descendant
describe
description
desirable
despair
desperate
develop
development
device (noun)
devise (verb)
diary
difference
dilemma
dining
disappear
disappoint
disastrous
discipline
discussion
disease
dissatisfied
divide
doesn't
dominant
don't
drunkenness
efficiency

(continued)

503

COMMONLY MISSPELLED WORDS (*continued*)

eighth
either
embarrass
entirety
environment
equipped
especially
exaggerate
exceed
excel
excellence
exercise
exhaust
existence
experience
explanation
extremely
familiar
fascinate
February
fiery
financial
foreign
foresee
forth
forty
forward
fourth (number four)
frantically
fraternities
friend
fulfill
gaiety
genealogy
generally
genuine
government
grammar
grief
guarantee

guard
guidance
harass
height
heroes
herring
humorous
illiterate
illogical
imitation
immediately
incredible
indefinite
independence
indispensable
infinite
influential
intelligence
intentionally
interest
interpret
interrupt
irrelevant
irresistible
irritable
island
its (possessive)
it's (it is, it has)
jealousy
judgment
knowledge
laboratory
led (past tense of
    lead)
library
license
lightning
literature
loneliness
loose (adjective)

lose (verb)
lying
magazine
maintenance
marriage
mathematics
medicine
miniature
mischievous
misspell
muscle
mysterious
necessary
neither
niece
ninety
ninth
noticeable
notorious
nuclear
nucleus
numerous
obstacle
occasionally
occur
occurrence
official
omission
omitted
opinion
opportunity
originally
outrageous
paid
pamphlet
panicky
parallel
particularly
pastime
peaceable

(*continued*)

COMMONLY MISSPELLED WORDS *(continued)*

perceive
performance
permanent
permissible
persistence
personnel
persuade
physical
playwright
possession
possibly
practically
precede
predominant
preferred
prejudice
prevalent
privilege
probably
procedure
proceed
professor
prominent
pronounce
pronunciation
pursue
quantity
quiet
quite
quizzes
realize
rebelled
recede
receipt
receive
recipe
recommend
reference
referring

regrettable
relevance
relief
relieve
religious
remembrance
reminisce
reminiscence
repetition
representative
resistance
restaurant
review
rhythm
ridiculous
roommate
sacrifice
safety
scarcely
schedule
secretary
seize
separate
siege
similar
sincerely
sophomore
source
specifically
sponsor
strategy
strength
stretch
succeed
successful
suddenness
supersede
suppress
surprise

suspicious
technical
technique
temperature
tendency
therefore
thorough
thoroughbred
though
thought
throughout
tragedy
transferred
traveling
truly
twelfth
tyranny
unanimous
unnecessary
unnoticed
until
useful
usually
valuable
vengeance
vicious
view
villain
warrant
weather
Wednesday
weird
whether
who's (who is)
whose (possessive of
  who)
withhold
woman
women

D3   Check for correct manuscript form.

In case you have received no particular instructions for the form of your paper, here are some general, all-purpose specifications.

GENERAL MANUSCRIPT STYLE FOR COLLEGE ESSAYS, ARTICLES, AND REPORTS

1. Pick a conventional, easy-to-read typeface such as Courier, Times New Roman, or Palatino. Make sure you have a fresh cartridge in your printer. If you handwrite your paper, keep your handwriting legible.

2. Print in black ink. Use dark blue or black ink if you write by hand.

3. Write or print on just one side of standard letter-size bond paper (8½ inches by 11 inches). If you handwrite your paper, use 8½-by-11-inch paper with smooth edges (not torn from a spiral-bound notebook).

4. For a paper without a separate title page, place your name, your instructor's name, the number and section of the course, and the date in the upper left or right corner of the first page, each item on a new line. (Ask whether your instructor has a preference for which side.) Double-space and center your title. Don't underline the title, don't put it in quotation marks or use all capital letters, and don't put a period after it. Capitalize the first and last words, the first word after a colon or semicolon, and all other words except prepositions, coordinating conjunctions, and articles. Double-space between the title and the first line of your text. (Most instructors do not require a title page for short college papers. If your instructor requests one but doesn't give you any guidelines, see number 1 under Additional Suggestions for Research Papers, below.)

5. Number your pages consecutively, including the first. For a paper of two or more pages, use a running header to put your last name in the upper right corner of each sheet along with the page number. (Use the heading option under View or Edit.) Do not type the word *page* or the letter *p* before the number and do not follow it with a period or parenthesis.

6. Leave ample margins—at least an inch—left, right, top, and bottom.

7. If you use a word processor, double-space your manuscript; if you handwrite, use wide-ruled paper or skip every other line.

8. Indent each new paragraph five spaces or one-half inch.

9. Long quotations should be double-spaced like the rest of your paper but indented from the left margin—ten spaces (one inch) if you're

following MLA (Modern Language Association) guidelines, five spaces (one-half inch) if you're using APA (American Psychological Association) guidelines. Put the source citation in parentheses immediately after the final punctuation mark of the block quotation.

10. Label all illustrations. Make sure any insertions are bound securely to the paper.

11. Staple the paper in the top left corner, or use a paper clip as MLA advises. Don't use any other method to secure the pages unless one is recommended by your instructor.

12. For safety's sake and peace of mind, make a copy of your paper, and back up your file.

ADDITIONAL SUGGESTIONS FOR RESEARCH PAPERS

For research papers, the format is the same as recommended in the previous section, with the following additional specifications.

1. The MLA guidelines do not recommend a title page. If your instructor wants one, type the title of your paper, centered and double-spaced, about a third of the way down the page. Go down two to four more lines and type your name, the instructor's name, the number and section of the course, and the date, each on a separate line and double-spaced.

2. Do not number your title page; number your outline, if you submit one with your paper, with small roman numerals (i, ii, iii, and so on). Number consecutively all subsequent pages in the essay, including your "Works Cited" or "References" pages, using arabic numerals (1, 2, 3, and so on) in the upper right corner of the page.

3. Double-space your list of works cited or references.

HOW TO MAKE A CORRECTION

Before you produce your final copy, make any large changes in your draft, edit and proofread carefully, and run your spell checker. When you give your paper a last once-over, however, don't be afraid to make small corrections in pen. In making such corrections, you may find it handy to use certain symbols used by printers and proofreaders.

A transposition mark (∩∪) reverses two words or two letters:

The nearby star Tau Ceti closely resembles our sun.

Close-up marks ⊂⊃ bring together the parts of a word accidentally split. A separation mark (|) inserts a space where one is needed:

The nearby star Tau Ceti closely re͡sembles our|sun.

To delete a letter or punctuation mark, draw a line with a curlicue through it:

The nearby star Tau Ceti closely res̸embles our sun.

Use a caret (∧) to indicate where to insert a word or letter:

The nearby star Tau Ceti closely re^sembles our sun.
                                   ∧

The symbol ¶ before a word or a line means "start a new paragraph":

Recently, astronomers have reduced their efforts to study dark nebulae. ¶ That other solar systems may also support life makes for another fascinating speculation.

To make a letter lowercase, draw a slanted line through it. To make a letter uppercase, put three short lines under it:

i̲ read it for my ⫽history class.

You can always cross out a word neatly, with a single horizontal line, and write a better one over it.

closely
The nearby star Tau Ceti ~~somewhat~~ resembles our sun.

Finally, if a page has many corrections on it, print or write it over again.

GLOSSARY OF GRAMMATICAL TERMS

appositive: A word or group of words that adds information about a subject or object by identifying it in a different way: my dog *Rover*, Hal's brother *Fred*.

article: The words *a, an,* or *the*.

conjunctive adverb: A linking word that can connect independent clauses and show a relationship between two ideas: Armando is a serious student; *therefore*, he studies every day.

coordinating conjunction: A one-syllable linking word (*and, but, for, or, nor, so, yet*) that joins elements with equal or near-equal importance: Jack *and* Jill, sink *or* swim.

508

correlative conjunction: A pair of linking words (such as *either/or, not only/but also*) that appear separately but work together to join elements of a sentence: *Neither* his friends *nor* hers like pizza.

gerund: A form of a verb, ending in *–ing*, that functions like a noun: Lacey likes *playing* in the steel band.

indefinite pronoun: A pronoun standing for an unspecified person or thing, including singular forms (*each, everyone, no one*) and plural forms (*both, few*): *Everyone* is soaking wet.

main clause: A group of words that has both a subject and a verb and can stand alone as a complete sentence: *My sister has a friend.*

modifier: A word (such as an adjective or adverb), phrase, or clause that provides more information about other parts of a sentence: Plays *staged by the drama class* are *always successful.*

object: The target or recipient of the action of the verb: Some geese bite *people.*

parenthetical expression: An aside to readers or a transitional expression such as *for example* or *in contrast.*

participle: A form of a verb that cannot function alone as a main verb, including present participles ending in *–ing* (*dancing*) and past participles often ending in *–ed* or *–d* (*danced*).

predicate: The part of a sentence that makes an assertion about the subject involving an action (Birds *fly*), a relationship (Birds *have feathers*), or a state of being (Birds *are warm-blooded*).

preposition: A transitional word (such as *in, on, at, of, from*) that leads into a phrase.

pronoun: A word that stands in place of a noun (*he, him,* or *his* for *Nate*).

subject: The part of a sentence that names something — a person, an object, an idea, a situation — about which the predicate makes an assertion: The *king* lives.

subject complement: A noun, an adjective, or a group of words that follows a linking verb (*is, become, feel, seem,* or another verb that shows a state of being) and that renames or describes the subject: This plum tastes *ripe.*

subordinating conjunction: A word (such as *because, although, if, when*) used to make one clause dependent on, or subordinate to, another: *Unless* you have a key, we are locked out.

verb: A word that shows action (The cow *jumped* over the moon) or a state of being (The cow *is* brown).

BARBARA FISTER

Working with Sources: Using MLA, Seventh Edition Style

A. A Checklist for Working with Sources

B. For MLA-Style In-Text Citations

C. For an MLA-Style Works Cited List

Sources not only provide information and ideas but can help establish your credibility and strengthen your argument when used as "expert witnesses." You should cite your sources to allow readers to track down your sources easily and to avoid plagiarizing words and ideas, a serious academic offense. Consult the *MLA Handbook for Writers of Research Papers*, Seventh Edition, for additional examples and advice.

A. A CHECKLIST FOR WORKING WITH SOURCES

Did I Use the Best Possible Evidence for My Assertions?

- **Are all of my claims supported by evidence?** If a section of your paper needs stronger support or if you need to verify a fact, consult with a reference librarian for suggestions.

- **Do my sources present balanced perspectives?** If a source you rely on promotes an agenda and ignores alternative viewpoints, you may want to substitute one that is more balanced and less likely to be dismissed by your readers as unreliable. Make sure to address alternate perspectives.

- **Will my readers consider my sources persuasive evidence for my assertions?** A medical research report on a treatment for cancer is more impressive as a source than a magazine article that describes the treatment. If you need scholarly sources, look for ones written by researchers that include documented references to other sources.

510

- **If writing about literature, have I chosen effective illustrations to support my thesis?** Choose quotations from the text or summarize passages that illustrate your main points. Be sure to explain how each quotation or summary relates to your thesis.

Are My Sources Integrated into My Writing Smoothly and Correctly?

- **Have I used more sources than necessary?** Use sources to support your ideas, not replace them. If two sources provide similar information, use the one that carries the most clout.

- **Do my sources back up what I say—or do they speak for me?** When possible, convey information in your own words. Don't quote a source when paraphrase or summary will do.

- **Have I used my sources ethically?** Provide a reference for anything from a source that isn't common knowledge, even if you have put it in your own words. Facts available in multiple sources—such as dates and well-known historical events—are considered common knowledge and do not need to be cited.

- **Are quotations presented correctly?** If quoting four lines or more from a source, set it off as a block quote by indenting the entire passage an inch from the left margin; do not put quotation marks around a block quote. If quoting two lines from a poem, separate the lines with a slash. If quoting three or more lines, set them off as a block quote.

- **Have I introduced each source effectively?** Never drop in a quote without introducing it. Use signal phrases such as "according to..." or "...Smith argues." If possible, include the author's credentials: "Poet Seamus Heaney has noted...."

Are My Sources Cited Clearly and Completely?

- **Did I provide a reference for every idea that came from a source?** Indicate the original source by naming the author and page.

- **Do all of my in-text references have a complete citation in my bibliography or works cited list?** Double-check to make sure every source referred to in the text can be found easily in your bibliography or works cited list.

- **Did I provide all the information necessary for my readers to locate my sources?** Make sure you include all required information, specified on the following pages, including information about electronic versions of print sources.

B. FOR MLA-STYLE IN-TEXT CITATIONS

In-text citations point your readers toward the full citations for sources that you provide in the works cited list at the end of your paper. Provide author and page numbers for in-text citations. Readers can look up the author's name in the alphabetized list of works cited at the end of the paper. The page number will lead them directly to the portion of the work that you are citing.

- Use the author's name to introduce the quote in your text and put page numbers in parentheses after the material you are citing. Or you can include the author's name with the page number in parentheses: Jones asserts...(15) or (Jones 15).
- If there is no author, use a shortened version of the title: ("Mind" 69).
- If there are multiple works by one author, include a short title: (Markoff, "Attack" A1); if there are multiple authors with the same last name, include the first initial (J. Markoff A1).
- Leave out page numbers if the source doesn't have them. Use a PDF version of an online source if it is an option; it will usually include original page numbers.
- When quoting from a Shakespeare play, use act, scene, and line numbers instead of page numbers. For quotations from the Bible, use chapter and verse.
- When quoting from a source found in another source, indicate the original author and the page of the source you found it in: According to philosopher Michael Oakeshott...(qtd. in Smith 22).

C. FOR AN MLA-STYLE WORKS CITED LIST

At the end of your paper, provide all the details readers need to find the sources you used in your text. Arrange the entries alphabetically by authors' last names (or, if a source has no author, by the title). Some of the information may be hard to find, especially in online sources. The sponsor of a Web site, for instance, may appear at the bottom of an internal page, on the home page, or on an information page ("Contact Us," "About Us"). Don't give up too easily; do your best to uncover all the information about the sources you are citing.

If a source has no author, begin with the title. For sources without other required information, use the following abbreviations: "n.d." (no date), "n. pag." (no page numbers), and "n.p." (no publisher; no sponsor for an online source). Include the medium of publication or delivery for all sources (for example, "Print," "Web," "Television," "Film," "DVD," "Photograph"). Do not include a URL for online sources (except for a source that would be difficult for readers to find in a search).

An alternative to a works cited list is a bibliography that includes sources consulted but not necessarily cited. The examples that follow are based on the *MLA Handbook for Writers of Research Papers*, Seventh Edition. For more examples and for explanations, see the *MLA Handbook*.

Articles

Journal Article

Last name, First name. "Title of Article." *Title of Journal* volume.issue (year): page number(s). Medium.

Moore, Peter. "The Nature of *King Lear*." *English Studies* 87.2 (2006): 169-90. Print.

O'Connor, Stephen. "Words and the World at a New York Public School: Can Writing Really Matter to Inner City Children?" *Teachers and Writers* 32.2 (Nov.-Dec. 2000): 1-8. Print.

Journal Article from an Electronic Database

Last name, First name. "Title of Article." *Title of Journal* volume.issue (year): page number(s) [n. pag. if no page numbers in database]. *Name of Database*. Medium. Date accessed.

Dougherty, James. "Presence, Silence, and the Holy in Denise Levertov's Poems." *Renascence* 58.4 (2006): 305-26. *Academic Search Premier*. Web. 12 May 2007.

Magazine Article

Last name, First name. "Title of Article." *Title of Magazine* date: page number(s). Medium.

Gladwell, Malcolm. "Open Secrets." *New Yorker*. 8 Jan. 2007: 44-53. Print.

Magazine Article from an Electronic Database

Last name, First name. "Title of Article." *Title of Magazine* date: page number(s) [n. pag. if no page numbers in database]. *Name of Database*. Medium. Date accessed.

Graeber, David. "Army of Altruists: On the Alienated Right to Do Good." *Harper's* Jan. 2007: 31-38. *Expanded Academic*. Web. 15 Feb. 2007.

Online Magazine Article

Last name, First name. "Title of Article." *Title of Online Magazine*. Sponsor of Web Site, date. Medium. Date accessed.

Burton, Robert. "The Certainty Epidemic." *Salon.com*. Salon Media Group, 29 Feb. 2008. Web. 18 Jan. 2009.

Newspaper Article

Last name, First name. "Title of Article." *Title of Newspaper* date, edition [if any], section title, number, or letter [if not part of page number(s)]: page number(s). Medium.

Markoff, John. "Attack of the Zombie Computers Is a Growing Threat, Experts Say." *New York Times* 7 Jan. 2007: A1+. Print.

Newspaper Article from an Electronic Database

Last name, First name. "Title of Article." *Title of Newspaper* date, edition [if any], section title, number, or letter [if not part of page number(s)]: page number(s) [n. pag. if no page numbers in database]. Medium. Date accessed.

Eberstadt, Nicholas. "Why Poverty Doesn't Rate." *Washington Post* 3 Sept. 2006: B1. *Newspaper Source*. Web. 12 Feb. 2007.

Online Newspaper Article

Last name, First name. "Title of Article." *Title of Online Newspaper*. Sponsor of Web Site, date. Medium. Date accessed.

Choi, Candice. "Modest Earners to Get Relief for Student Loans." *Boston Globe*. NY Times, 29 June 2009. Web. 6 Jul. 2009.

Books

Book by One Author

Last name, First name. *Title of Book*. City: Publisher, year. Medium.

Updike, John. *Terrorist*. New York: Knopf, 2006. Print.

Book by Multiple Authors

Last name, First name, First name Last name, and First name Last name. *Title of Book*. City: Publisher, year. Medium.

Singer, Peter, and Jim Mason. *The Way We Eat: Why Our Food Choices Matter*. Emmaus, PA: Rodale, 2006. Print.

Book with an Editor

Last name of editor, First name, ed. *Title of Book*. City: Publisher, year. Medium.

Lerer, Seth, ed. *The Yale Companion to Chaucer*. New Haven: Yale UP, 2006. Print.

Book with an Author and an Editor

Last name of author, First name. *Title of Book*. Ed. Editor's First name Last name. City: Publisher, year. Medium.

Plath, Sylvia. *The Unabridged Journals of Sylvia Plath*. Ed. Karen V. Kukil. New York: Anchor-Doubleday, 2000. Print.

Book in an Edition Other than First

Last name, First name. *Title of Book*. Number of edition. City: Publisher, year. Medium.

Smith, Steven S., Jason M. Roberts, and Ryan J. Vander Weilen. *The American Congress*. 4th ed. Cambridge: Cambridge UP, 2006. Print.

Work in an Anthology or Collection of Essays

Last name, First name. "Title of Essay." *Title of Anthology*. Ed. Editor's First name Last name [if different from essay author]. City: Publisher, year. Page number(s) of essay. Medium.

Dvorak, Marta. "Margaret Atwood's Humor." *The Cambridge Companion to Margaret Atwood*. Ed. Coral Ann Howells. Cambridge: Cambridge UP, 2006. 114-29. Print.

Short Story in a Collection

Last name, First name. "Title of Short Story." *Title of Collection*. Ed. Editor's First name Last name [if different from short story author]. City: Publisher, year. Page number(s) of short story. Medium.

Braverman, Kate. "Cocktail Hour." *Pushcart Prize XXXI: Best of the Small Presses*. Ed. Bill Henderson. Wainscott: Pushcart Press, 2007. 52-68. Print.

Poem in a Collection

Last name, First name. "Title of Poem." *Title of Collection*. Ed. Editor's First name Last name [if different from author of poem]. City: Publisher, year. Page number(s) of poem. Medium.

Reed, Ishmael. "Poison Light." *New and Collected Poems, 1964-2006*. New York: Carroll & Graf, 2006. 123-24. Print.

Play

Last name, First name. *Title of Play*. City: Publisher, year. Medium.

Wilson, August. *Seven Guitars*. New York: Dutton, 1996. Print.

Encyclopedia or Dictionary Entry

Last name, First name [if given]. "Title of Entry." *Title of Encyclopedia or Dictionary*. Number of edition. City: Publisher, year. Medium.

516

Frakes, Jerold C. "Literature, Jewish." *Encyclopaedia Judaica*. 2nd ed. Detroit: Macmillan Reference, 2007. Print.

Online Book

Last name, First name. *Title of Book [or Book-Length Work]*. City: Publisher, year. *Title of Web Site or Scholarly Project*. Medium. Date accessed.

Tienda, Marta, and Faith Mitchell, eds. *Hispanics and the Future of America*. Washington, DC: National Academies Press, 2006. *National Academies Press*. Web. 10 Feb. 2007.

Web Pages

Entire Web Site

Last name, First name [if given]. *Title of Web Site*. Sponsor of Web Site, update date. Medium. Date accessed.

Nobelprize.org. Nobel Foundation Rights Association, 2009. Web. 12 Feb. 2009.

Short Work from a Web Site

Last name, First name [if given]. "Title of Short Work." *Title of Web Site*. Sponsor of Web Site, date. Medium. Date accessed.

Pamuk, Orhan. "My Father's Suitcase." *Nobelprize.org*. Nobel Foundation Rights Association, 7 Dec. 2006. Web. 15 Jan. 2007.

Entry in a Weblog (Blog)

Last name, First name. "Title of Blog Entry." *Title of Blog*. Sponsor of Blog, date of entry. Medium. Date accessed.

Mayer, Caroline. "Some Surprising Findings about Identity Theft." *The Checkout*. Washington Post, 28 Feb. 2006. Web. 19 Jan. 2009.

Entry in a Wiki

"Title of Wiki Entry." *Title of Wiki*. Sponsor of Wiki, date of entry. Medium. Date accessed.

"Negation in Languages." *UniLang Wiki*. UniLang, 25 Oct. 2004. Web. 9 Dec. 2008.

Other Sources (Print and Online Versions)

Work of Art

Last name of artist, First name. *Title of Work*. Date of composition. Medium of composition. Institution, City.

Cézanne, Paul. *Postman Joseph Roulin*. 1888. Oil on canvas. Museum of Fine Arts, Boston.

Work of Art (Online)

Last name of artist, First name. *Title of Work*. Date of composition. Institution, City. *Title of Web Site*. Medium. Date accessed.

Cézanne, Paul. *Postman Joseph Roulin*. 1888. Museum of Fine Arts, Boston. *Museum of Fine Arts, Boston*. Web. 23 Feb. 2009.

Government Document

Government [Country]. Department. Agency [if any]. *Title of Document*. Place: Publisher, year. Medium.

United States. Dept. of Justice. Federal Bureau of Investigation. *Crime in the United States, 2005*. Washington, DC: GPO, 2006. Print.

Government Document (Online)

Government [Country]. Department. Agency [if any]. *Title of Document*. Place: Publisher, year. *Title of Web Site* [if different from document]. Sponsor of Web Site, date. Medium. Date accessed.

United States. Dept. of Justice. Bureau of Justice Statistics. *Homicide Trends in the United States*. Washington, DC: GPO, 2006. *Office of Justice Programs*. OJP, 2009. Web. 17 Feb. 2009.

Personal Interview

Last name of person interviewed, First name. Personal interview. Date of interview.

Charlier, Terry. Personal interview. 10 Feb. 2007.

Radio or Television Program

"Title of Segment or Episode." *Title of Program* [*or Series*]. Host, By, Narr., Dir., or Perf. First name Last name. Network. Local station, City, date of broadcast. Medium.

"The Super." *This American Life*. Host Ira Glass. Public Radio International. WBEZ, Chicago, 5 Jan. 2007. Radio.

Radio or Television Program (Online)

"Title of Segment or Episode." *Title of Program* [*or Series*]. Host, By, Narr., Dir., or Perf. First name Last name. Network, date of broadcast. *Title of Web Site*. Medium. Date accessed.

"Elif Shafak: Writing under a Watchful Eye." *Fresh Air*. Host Terry Gross. Natl. Public Radio, 6 Feb. 2007. *NPR.org*. Web. 22 Feb. 2009.

Film or Video

Title. Dir. Director's First name Last name. Perf. First and Last name(s) [of lead actor(s)]. Distributor, year of release. Medium.

Crash. Dir. Paul Haggis. Perf. Sandra Bullock, Don Cheadle, and Matt Dillon. Lion's Gate, 2004. DVD.

Online Video Clip

Last name of creator, First name [if any]. "Title of Video Clip." *Title of Web Site*. Sponsor of Web Site, date. Medium. Date accessed.

Murphy, Beth. "Tips for a Good Profile Piece." *YouTube*. YouTube, 7 Sept. 2008. Web. 19 Mar. 2009.

Podcast

Last name, First name [if any]. "Title of Podcast." Host, By, Narr., Dir., or Perf. First name Last name. *Title of Web Site*. Sponsor of Web Site, date. Medium. Date accessed.

"Calculating the Demand for Charter Schools." Host David Guenthner. *Texas PolicyCast*. Texas Public Policy Foundation, 28 Aug. 2008. Web. 10 Jan. 2009.

Advertisement

Name of product or company. Advertisement. Print or online publication information. [See previous relevant models.]

Symantec. Advertisement. *Newsweek* 12 Feb. 2006: 62. Print.

Sound Recording

Last name, First name of the composer, performer, or conductor. "Title of Recording" [if a short work or song]. *Title of Recording* [if a long work or CD]. Perf. First name Last name of performers or musicians. Orchestra [if relevant]. Cond. First name Last name [if relevant]. Manufacturer, year of release. Medium.

Fleck, Bela. *The Hidden Land*. Perf. Bela Fleck and the Flecktones. Sony, 2006. CD.

E-mail Message

Last name of writer, First name. "Subject Line." Message to the author. Date of message. Medium.

Barnes, Phil. "Finding Information." Message to the author. 25 Feb. 2007.
    E-mail.

Posting to an E-mail Discussion List (LISTSERV) or Newsgroup Forum

Last name of writer, First name. "Title of Posting." *Listserv, Forum,* or *Group
    Name.* Sponsor of the Web Site, date. Medium. Date accessed.

Smith, Kevin. "Style." *DorothyL.* Diane K. Kovacs, 3 Jan. 2007. Web. 25 Feb.
    2007.

Real-time Communication

Last name of writer, First name. Description of event. *Forum name.* Sponsor of
    Forum, date of event. Medium. Date accessed.

Martin, Lawrence B. Rank Beginner. *Chronicle Live Discussions.* The Chronicle
    of Higher Education, 10 Jan. 2007. Web. 25 Feb. 2007.

Map or Chart

Last name, First name [if given]. *Title of Map or Chart.* Medium of presenta-
    tion [map or chart]. Print or online publication information. [See pre-
    vious, relevant models.]

National Parks System. Map. Washington, DC: US Dept. of the Interior, 2007.
    Print.